Multiliteracies and Technology Enhanced Education:
Social Practice and the Global Classroom

Darren L. Pullen
University of Tasmania, Australia

David R. Cole
University of Technology, Sydney, Australia

Information Science REFERENCE

INFORMATION SCIENCE REFERENCE
Hershey · New York

Director of Editorial Content: Kristin Klinger
Senior Managing Editor: Jamie Snavely
Assistant Managing Editor: Michael Brehm
Publishing Assistant: Sean Woznicki
Typesetter: Michael Brehm
Cover Design: Lisa Tosheff
Printed at: Yurchak Printing Inc.

Published in the United States of America by
Information Science Reference (an imprint of IGI Global)
701 E. Chocolate Avenue
Hershey PA 17033
Tel: 717-533-8845
Fax: 717-533-8661
E-mail: cust@igi-global.com
Web site: http://www.igi-global.com/reference

Library of Congress Cataloging-in-Publication Data

Multiliteracies and technology enhanced education : social practice and the global classroom / Darren L. Pullen and David R. Cole, editors.
p. cm.
Includes bibliographical references and index.
Summary: "This book will help readers understand the ways in which literacy is changing around the world, and to keep up to date with literacy research and reporting techniques"--Provided by publisher.
ISBN 978-1-60566-673-0 (hardcover) -- ISBN 978-1-60566-674-7 (ebook) 1. Literacy. 2. Educational technology. 3. Education--Effect of technological innovations on. I. Pullen, Darren L. II. Cole, David R.
LC149.M86 2009
302.2'244--dc22
2009010454

British Cataloguing in Publication Data
A Cataloguing in Publication record for this book is available from the British Library.

Editorial Advisory Board

List of Reviewers

Molly Dugan, *Boston College, USA*
P.G. Schrader, *UNLV–Las Vegas, USA*
Pam Wright , *Latrobe University, Melbourne, Australia*
Radha Iyer, *Queensland University of Technology, Australia*
Robyn Henderson , *University of Southern Queensland, Australia*
Rosary Lalik, *Virginia Tech, USA*
Ryan Schowen, *University of Alaska Anchorage, USA*
Scott Cebulski, *Mahomet-Seymour High School, USA*
Sezgin Vuran, *Anadolu University College of Open Education, Turkey*
Theresa Rogers , *University of British Columbia, Canada*
Vikashni Moyle, *University of Tasmania, Australia*
Elena Railean, *State University of Moldova, Republic of Moldova*
Matthew Kearney, *Kuring-gai Campus University of Technology, Australia*
Sandy Schuck, *Kuring-gai Campus University of Technology, Australia*
Jonathan Binns, *Australian Maritime College, Australia*
Gulsun Kurubacak, *Anadolu University College of Open Education, Turkey*
Karen Martin, *Queensland University of Technology, Australia*
Ross Harley, *University of New South Wales, Australia*
Scott Cebulski, *University of Illinois, USA*
Pam Wright, *Latrobe University, Melbourne, Australia*
P.G. Schrader, *UNLV–Las Vegas, USA*

Table of Contents

Section 2
Sociocultural Aspects of Technology Through a Multiliteracies Perspective

Section 3
Multiliteracies in Practice

Detailed Table of Contents

This first chapter in the book provides a general overview of literacy, technology and the notion of multilitearcies. As such its purpose is to help orientate the reader and contextualise the concept of literacy and its evolution into multiliteracies through a chronological review of literacy, and specifically literacy pedagogy, over the last quarter of a century. Following this journey the concept of literacy combined with technology is expanded on. This chapter therefore provides the reader with an overview and understanding of the field of literacy and how technology has resulted in a range of multi-modal forms of communication known as multiliteracies.

This chapter examines how knowledge processes of the different types of text are central to the notion of multiliteracies. The authors argue that new textual types that ICT gives rise to have a direct impact on the literacy creativity of students. This creativity is figured as the process of connecting existing literacies to new literacies through design. The authors demonstrate their concept through the use of a vignette.

The authors of this chapter use Jenkins' theory of convergence to analyse students' online participation in recreational websites. The chapter shows how multiliteracies may be built upon through criticality and convergence in order to explain important cultural processes that have an impact on school life as well as the lifestyle choices of children.

This chapter explores notions taken from complexity theory to conceptualise the dynamic nature of multimodal texts in an educational setting. The authors include two case studies in their work that exemplifies this problem and points to possible solutions. The chapter closes with an informative discussion about how the application of enabling constraints often works to simultaneously reveal institutional practices of power, and these can be explained with reference to the habitus.

The authors of this chapter describe a cross cultural study between the US and Australia, that examines graduate student participation in watching 'foreign' TV sitcoms and commenting on the corresponding cultural norms and resultant multiliterate practices.

This chapter explores the differences in literacy practice between Indigenous and non Indigenous students in Australia. These differences are explored through a mixture of narrative excerpts from the lives of two indigenous students and theorisation about the types of literacy practice that their stories exhibit.

The authors have investigated the concept of spatial literacy in an Australian boys' boarding school. The authors highlight the inherent tensions that the school community encounters between the design of building structures, which cater for a traditional form of teaching instruction, and a more contemporary curriculum which requires a less rigid learning and teaching environment. The chapter discuss the history and tradition of the college whilst simultaneously critically examining issues through the use of spatial literacy with the students.

The authors of this chapter have expanded the multiliteracies framework to include cam-capture literacy, which may be defined as the social practice of using small cameras attached to computers for communicative purposes. Cam-capture literacy consists of visual literacy, information literacy and personal literacy. The authors conclude that cam-capture zones are useful markers for literacy teachers in order to reengage their students in their designated activities. Cam-capture literacy can be deployed by teachers for self-reflection and as a purposeful link between traditional print literacies and the new literacies that are becoming apparent due to digital technology.

The author of this chapter has taken data from two major research projects in British Columbia and applied it to understanding complex identity construction in a multimodal context. The chapter illustrates how the creativity and messages that media production may unlock in youth, and the ways in which making videos, songs and art may be deployed to extract important self-reflective moments.

This chapter describes how a Hong Kong teacher education degree has implemented a 12-hour new literacies course in their teacher-training programme. The chapter describes how the new course had been designed and the ways in which the students have approached its completion. The authors finish their investigation with an earnest reflection on the power related issues that their new course has highlighted, and they describe possible ways forward for teacher education.

The authors of this chapter present an interpretive case study of two Singaporean secondary schools. In this context, the pedagogic value of ICT has been investigated, and in particular the ways in which computer use has impacted (or otherwise) on the Malay language curriculum.

In this chapter the authors have used multiliteracies as a means to scaffold development in chemistry literacy, and as a manner of gauging representational competence with respect to multimodal texts and chemistry. The chapter includes a detailed description of a chemistry unit of work and the ways in which applying the multiliteracies framework works in this context.

This chapter describes how a practicing primary school teacher has used robotics in the curriculum as a way of expanding literacies and engaging students in multimodal problems. The chapter concludes with a number of suggestions for others to think about if they want to incorporate robotics in their own school curriculum.

Section 4
Selected Readings

Foreword

When we got together in 1994, the members of what was to become known as the New London Group could barely have imagined how far and wide the ideas we explored and fashioned in that week might travel over the ensuing fifteen years. This is all the more surprising in a context where the world of meaning-making and representation a decade and a half later have been radically transformed, and in ways that could hardly be imagined back then. Today's world, saturated as it is with websites, wikis, blogs, digital images, MP3s and digital video, was barely conceivable then. And perhaps soon we face the imminent demise or at least radical recasting of the newspaper, network television, bookstores and maybe even books, the music industry, cinema—some of the most familiar and foundational sites for the creation of meaning in the modern era. Nobody could have envisioned the proportions of these changes.

Yet somehow the ideas that emerged from our conversations have proven conceptually apt, and it seems from the growing use of these concepts, practically useful as well.

We wanted to say that the emerging world of meaning making would be more multimodal—the first of two facets of 'multi'-ness—in which written, oral, visual, spatial, gestural and tactile modes of representation would be more closely intertwined. An alphabetical definition and pedagogical practice of literacy not only restricted literacy teaching to an artificially narrow spectrum within the range of human meaning-making; that narrowing, we felt, was becoming increasingly anachronistic. We could not have imagined the scale and speed of the drift towards multimodal communications that has subsequently occurred.

We also wanted to say that, despite its imperiousness, global English was becoming more and more internally differentiated and the range of its social languages was burgeoning—a marker of diverging and proliferating cultural identities, technical domains, professional practices, personal interests, affinity group sensibilities, peer group dispositions, and sites of formal or informal community. This was the other side of our two-faceted 'multi'-ness. Here too, heritage English teaching was missing the mark, teaching exclusively to a single 'standard' form and singular literary canon. It was time to recognise, we claimed, that the main name of the representational game was to cross boundaries between the discourse communities in our everyday working, public and personal lives, rather than to teach to a ostensibly singular standard. Here too, nobody could have envisaged the pace of subsequent development of a deep civic pluralism and radical globalisation.

To address these profound transformations, we suggested that as literacy educators, we need to re-orient our pedagogical practices in some fundamental ways. These we captured in an overarching vision of meaning-making as design, and translated this into a pragmatic pedagogy of Multiliteracies: situated practice, overt instruction, critical framing and transformed practice.

The design idea brings agency back into the meaning making process. A meaning maker has a range of available representational resources at their disposal (contextually variable grammars of the linguistic, the visual etc.). These we called 'available designs'. They draw on these meanings to make meaning, always remaking the world as they go and always in ways never quite heard or seen before, expressing the timbre of their voice, the uniqueness of their life experience, the depth of their identity, all in the most subtle but nevertheless important ways. This we called 'designing'. Meaning-makers also transform themselves, building their identities through the act of meaning. These then become residues in the world of meaning. These are 'the redesigned'. In turn, the redesigned becomes available designs for others, found representational objects for a new cycle of meaning making.

Moving away from the legacy didactic pedagogies of modern institutionalised schooling, where learners were to imbibe the disciplines of correct form, we suggested a pedagogy which recognised agency, difference and transformation, and which used these as resources for learning. Once again, we could never have envisaged the scale of the subsequent transformations in meaning making and the breadth of the participatory cultures of the new media which have blurred the once clearly defined social roles of writer and reader, creator and consumer, artist and audience, professional and amateur.

We have come to call this a shift in the balance of agency (Kalantzis & Cope, 2008). Video games are now a bigger business than Hollywood, and instead of a vicarious involvement in the narrative, a player assumes a role and the outcomes of the narrative contingent. Generic, mass produced products are being displaced by customised and customisable products. Top 40 playlists on broadcast radio are being displaced by personally constructed and infinitely varied iPod playlists. A handful of broadcast television stations are being replaced by a myriad of cable channel choices, interactive TV in which viewing options are customisable, and tens of millions of YouTube videos where amateur and professional stand undifferentiated. Everywhere, the balance of agency is shifting from a society of a few creators and many consumers, to a society of users, a more participatory culture, a culture of vibrant and by and large respectful difference.

This is a book which captures the spirit of our times. One cannot but be struck by the vivid stories of learners and their schools, and the astounding variety of their concerns and practices: the grade one students and their teacher working on digital storybooks; children's interactions with *Barbie*, *American Girl*, *Transformers* and *Hot Wheels*, simultaneously on websites, with objects and in social relationships; Beatrice, Will and Dana, three students in a hallway discussing how they are going with their digital videos; students comparing Australian to American television humor; an Indigenous Australian boy whose mother's art narrates their country; a school doing spatial literacy as it adds a gallery, a designated environmental space, and a walking tour to its physical setting; students working in computer cam-capture literacy zones; the video two young women made on the subject of peer pressure; a new literacies course in Hong Kong centred around a model of collaborative and dispersed ownership in a wiki; ICT used to support second language learning of Malay in Singapore classrooms; using the Multiliteracies pedagogy to teach chemistry; the multimodality of robotics in the curriculum. It would have been hard to imagine any of these vignettes of life in school even a decade ago.

This book brings a kaleidoscope of new learning practices to the light of day. Together, these tell of innovative uses of new media in learning, deep sensitivity to learner difference and the application of pedagogies of engagement and transformation. It is a powerful evidence base exemplifying new learning experiences and supporting new teaching practices.

It is also a book full of big ideas, difficult ideas, challenging ideas. Too often, educational research that is evidence rich is theoretically poor. This book represents big thinking and hard conceptual work at the same time as it is grounded in a powerful evidence base. It is a milestone in the evolution of ideas that began on the cusp of a new era, some fifteen years ago. It adds significant clarity to new pedagogies and new sociabilites which are yet still emergent and whose shape is sometimes blurred by the pace of contemporary transformations.

— *Mary Kalantzis and Bill Cope*
June, 2009

REFERENCES

Kalantzis, M. & Cope, B. (2008). *New Learning: Elements of a Science of Education*. Cambridge UK: Cambridge University Press.

Mary Kalantzis *is Dean of the College of Education at the University of Illinois at Urbana-Champaign, USA, and formerly Dean of the Faculty of Education, Language and Community Services at RMIT University, Melbourne, Australia, and President of the Australian Council of Deans of Education.*

Bill Cope *is a research professor in the Department of Educational Policy Studies at the University of Illinois at Urbana-Champaign, USA, and an adjunct professor in the Globalism Institute at RMIT University, Melbourne, Australia. Together with Mary, Bill was one of the founding members of the New London Group.*

Preface

WHAT IS THE GLOBAL CLASSROOM?

This handbook represents a collaboration of researchers from the US, Canada, Singapore, Australia and Hong Kong. These theorists and teachers are unified in the use of technology to transform education. At the beginning of the 21st century, technological transformations are not a periphery concern for educational practice, but organising factors that involve government, democracy and the ways in which pedagogy and educational power are being redistributed in contexts of high technology. In the 1990s, the development of the Internet gave rise to conceptions such as the global village, and new ways of teaching and learning involving hypertext, multimodality and virtual classrooms. In this handbook, these conceptions of education are being redrawn to take into account the actual working practices of classrooms that may or may not been hardwired into the *global classroom*.

One could therefore say that the global classroom is a place where the educational uses of technology are coming together in terms of development and application and new ways of teaching and learning are becoming apparent. At the cutting edge of this plane of change is the relationship between tacit and designated learning opportunities that new technologies give rise to. For example, the learning communities that one finds online or in social networking software programmes are at the same time part of the complex identity units and distribution facilities for ideas about current culture. Teachers in these situations need to be aware how new forms of language, values, group dynamics and shifts in behaviour will change the learning requirements of their cohorts. This does not mean that one should become immediately conversant in SMS (short message service) messaging to be a teacher - but that understanding about how cultural homogeny mediated through technology determines the ways in which students may take a stance or hold attitudes that have previously been part of face-to-face performances (Pullen, Baguley & Marsden, 2009). Dialogic pedagogies such as debating or asking leading questions to get at the truth are transformed in an online environment into straw poles and contributions to discussion groups. The global classroom is the place where the transformation and translation from old ways of working into the new are taking place, and includes regressions, misunderstandings and retardation as well as fast-paced and irreversible change.

The global classroom is consequently not an ideal space. The parallel development of communication technology with liberal democracy, has given rise to the ways in which these two practices cross over and project each other's virtues. Communication may be seen as 'perfectable' in this context, and this conception is enhanced by the unreal clarity that digital technology may afford, especially with respect to the reproduction and malleability of images. Likewise, democracy has entered another phase, contained within the context of digital networks and media distribution that blurs the boundaries between the active choice-making of citizens and the manipulation of issues by interested parties. The global classroom is contained within this conjunction as a means to consolidating democratic rights and active participation in the processes of government that are increasingly involved with global capital flows, and the ways in which civil society is under pressure from the forces contained within global capitalism (Cole, 2007). Every classroom now has the global classroom running through it, not as an ideal way in which technology may join the learning space to every other classroom in the world, but as a flow of matter and ideas that takes students, teacher and administrators further into a technological mediated world where values may be conjoined through "affinity spaces" (Gee, 2005).

Decisions about the make-up and uses of the global classroom are therefore vital to the future of liberal democratic society. Research into its functioning is the only way in which coherent educational policy and knowledge frameworks may be developed in order to prepare populations for new curricula. This research may take the form of qualitative studies, charting insider-knowledges and user-end stories. Investigating the global classroom may also produce factual evidence of a statistical nature that helps one to appreciate the ways in which this space is full of diverse elements that are competing for access and resources to augment fluid capital exchange. The research nexus is the point at which this handbook plugs into the global classroom. The coverage of three continents that this volume achieves, and by using a variety of educational methodologies, both gives the reader an expansive view of the changes that are apparent due to the global classroom. The global classroom may be characterised in this context as a plane of transformation involving personal and group identities learning through technological mediation.

One could counter that there are still places in the world where the notion of a global classroom is irrelevant. Serious conflicts, poverty and remote rural communities may still interrupt the idea that technology is producing a new space for learning that joins the behaviours of populations. Yet within these potential social barriers to technological access are the ideas and links to becoming involved with the global classroom. For example, serious conflicts may eventually lead to peace or a social equilibrium where access to new learning behaviours becomes all the more important in an effort to avoid future conflicts. The world's poor are joined by the struggle to overcome their material conditions, and research has shown that the most significant factor in order to achieve this is education. The global classroom is therefore present in the lives of the poor as an escape route from their circumstances, perhaps in the absence of organised educational facilities. Remote rural communities have potential access to new technology as it becomes more mobile and affordable. Hand-held computers and satellite communication may beam in the ways in which learning is changing to rural areas - as access is driven by the search for new markets. The global classroom is therefore ubiquitous, though fluid and resistant to characterisation as an ideal outcome of localised educational practice.

HOW DO MULTILITERACIES AND TECHNOLOGY ENHANCE EDUCATION?

Since the characterisation of multiliteracies in (1996) by the New London Group, much has changed in the field of literacy studies. The landmark aspect of the article in the *Harvard Educational Review* was to make a connection between the multiplicity of literacies that are present in learning contexts, and the wider plane of social change, so that teachers may make sense of this multiplicity of literacies and utilise it in the form of new pedagogies that correspond to diverse learning options – and with special reference to evolving technological applications. At the end of the article, the authors voice the hope that their article would be a beginning of changing educational conditions - so that the ideas contained within it could be distributed and used by teachers to improve educational outcomes through multiple literate opportunities in real classrooms. Has this hope materialised? How successful was their vision of new realms of literate and educational behaviours?

Opinion in the field of literacy studies about these questions remains divided. There is a large and powerful body of evidence, which states that direct intervention in the literate behaviours of children, is the best way in order to initiate change. The many studies that have explored this phenomena use investigations into the application of synthetic phonics, to show how direct intervention has resulted in improved literacy results. Recent reports in the US (NICHHD, 2000), UK (Rose, 2006) and Australia (NITL, 2005) also criticise literacy ideologies that are based on constructivism or whole language ideology, and that may lead away from the direct intervention in the literate progress of children. The framework of multiliteracies stands on both sides of this fence, as it advocates switching between pedagogic modes, and utilising both direct instruction and situated practice that may be derived from progressive approaches to teaching wherever necessary. It is therefore unclear from the perspective of mainstream literacy research as to how successful or otherwise the multiliteracies framework has been in shaping real change in literacy classrooms.

In Australia, multiliteracies has been incorporated into curriculum statements and state funded literacy projects. Educational research has however shown that the penetration of these ideas is limited. Even though teacher training in Australia has taken up the ideas contained in multiliteracies and shared them with their pre-service students, evidence shows that once the students get out into the workplace and practise teaching - the theoretical and practical aspects of multiliteracies seem to separate. Teachers readily identify with the use of critical literacy in the field, in that students should be taught how to critically analyse text, and teachers often combine critical literacy with Multiple Intelligences - so that their pedagogy does not always employ language, but also includes images, music, synaesthetics, numbers and spatiality. Multiliteracies is therefore transformed into multiple opportunities to critically analyse differing text styles and forms. The framework of multiliteracies is more pertinently identified by teachers in the long run with the use of technology in education, and the fact that software applications simultaneously require linguistic, visual, mathematic and logical skills. The practice of multiliteracies is therefore qualified and delimited by the technical confidence of the teachers, the technological facilities of the school and the ways in which technology has been integrated into the curriculum and how the teachers follow such mandates.

The identification of multiliteracies with the use of educational technology has perhaps been its most abiding relationship in practice. In the UK, the term technological literacy is more readily employed to explain this situation. In the US digital literacies are more frequently referred to. The field of educational practice and research has also seen a mushrooming of new literacies, which sit between multiliteracies and actual technological applications as a type of map that shows how the field of ICT (information and communications technology) innovation and capital flow are forming new ways to communicate and build relationships. The questions about how technology changes and potentially enhances education and where multiliteracies fits into this are therefore complex. Some argue that the introduction of ICT into the curriculum heralds a new dawn of educational practice as any knowledge field can be uploaded and transmitted through digital media. Educational technologists might advocate desktop computers in every classroom, where students can access their files, work though the curriculum in an electronic form, and make their designs, calculations and explanations given available knowledge on the subject focus and any corresponding syllabus outcomes. Traditional 'face-to-face' apologists in education might throw up their arms at this suggestion and point to the lack of social and communal contact that this situation would encourage. It could also be argued that the wide-scale introduction of this kind of individualised computer technology might also be a ploy on the part of computer and software companies to shift product.

The truth of the matter lies somewhere in between these two scenarios. Education has been enhanced and is still being enhanced through new developments in ICT. Yet there are still many areas of education that do not and should not use ICT as a form of mediation. For example, physical drama may be put forward as an important part of education that embodies narrative, ideas and concepts without recourse to digital technology. Students should have access and training in the most relevant and useful ICT applications, as the contemporary workplace increasingly requires such entry skills – yet educators should also be wary of the tendency to overload the curriculum with computer mediated activities that might take away from the students' abilities in physical forms of learning and performance. Educational enhancement could therefore be sketched out as a balance between digital mediation and the physical embodiment of ideas (Cole & Throssell, 2008). Students involved with a balanced curriculum will become competent in working with new digital environments and be able to actively embody these ideas through their actions. Multiliteracies has this perspective written into its programme through the desire to create social futures. These futures are not dominated by ICT provision in education, but point to the ways in which technology may be deployed purposely in order to make life better…

THE CHAPTERS OF THE HANDBOOK

This Handbook commences with an introductory overview of literacy, technology and introduces the concept of multiliteracies. The purpose of this first chapter is to orientate the reader, both new and familiar, to the notion of what is multiliteracies. Following this orientation the authors demonstrate how multiliteracies is shaping our understanding and practice of what it means to be a literate person in the digital age.

Chapter Two is *Multimodal, Multiliteracies: Texts and Literacies for the 21st Century*. Radha Iyer and Carmen Luke have brought together the knowledge processes of different text types with the central multiliteracies notion of Design. The authors argue that new textual types that ICT gives rise to and allows for have a direct impact on the literacy creativity of students. This creativity is figured as the process of connecting existing literacies to new literacies through design. The chapter incorporates a vignette of grade one students creating a digital storybook to illustrate this theory. The theory evident in this chapter draws heavily on the multiliteracies framework, and steers a path around print based definitions of literacy practice. The authors argue that the New London Group's definition of multiliteracies has become more relevant since its inception due to an increasing number of ICT applications that are now part of everyday life. Furthermore, the importance of social justice as a transformative force in education, and the ambiguous notion of Design as a central pillar of multiliteracies, both add to the flexibility and applicability of the framework in changing learning conditions. The authors finish their overview of relevant multiliteracies ideas by describing its pedagogy, which they argue enhances the creativity of classroom practice and focuses on knowledge processes in multimodal texts. The vignette that is provided in this chapter shows how students in one particular grade one class produced a digital narrative. The teacher employed PowerPoint, Microsoft Paint software and audio recording so that the students could place story frames in sequence. This vignette demonstrates the principles of multiliteracies in action, and points to the knowledge processes of multimodality and the ways in which they may transform student creativity through learning.

Chapter Three is named, *Convergence: A Framework for a "New" Critical Literacy*. Working in Alaska, Jennifer C Stone & Ryan A Schowen have recognised the significance of critical literacy to multiliteracies. Their chapter uses Jenkins' theory of convergence to analyse students' online participation in recreational websites. This participation has been shown to be an important activity in young people's lives and a subsequent factor in their development that deserves critical attention. The authors firstly contrast the ways in which critical literacy has been used to examine online web sites in the research literature. On one side, critical literacy has been deemed to be an extension of reading practices and the cognitive elements that accompany such activities. Web sites incorporate new ways to represent information and therefore new ways to read, and critical literacy is considered by some to be part of this changing practice. On the other side, and in line with the multiliteracies frame, critical literacy pedagogy importantly uncovers the political and ideological nature of text. The authors side with the second definition of critical literacy, that they propose is a preparation for real life encounters with text and any possible manipulations of meaning that are especially relevant in online environments. This is where the authors deploy the notion of convergence as a means to critically explaining the processes of meaning integration in web sites. The authors focus on the convergent aspects of textual practices, relationships of consumption and social relationships to critically analyse online texts. They analyse four web sites for aspects of ideological gender manipulation, and find that their critically convergent frame is a useful way of understanding how these web sites engage and keep young participants as users. This chapter shows how multiliteracies may be built upon through criticality and convergence in order to explain important cultural processes that have an impact on school life as well as the lifestyle choices of children.

Chapter Four has the title, *The Dynamic Design of Learning with Text: The Grammar of Multiliteracies*. Lisa Patel Stevens & Molly Dugan deploy notions taken from complexity theory to conceptualise the dynamic nature of multimodal texts in an educational setting. The fundamental problem that permeates their chapter is to achieve a coherent theorisation of learning spaces that parallels multiliteracies. The authors include two case studies in their work that exemplifies this problem and points to possible solutions. It is noted that educational spaces are not necessarily set up for learning, and that they are "traditionally marked by relatively inflexible patterns of interactions". This inflexibility can lead to a reversion in linear pedagogic modes of transmission when exploring multimodal text types, and that is clearly a hindrance with respect to following the divergent options that multimodality can lead to. To explain a means to circumventing this blockage, the authors suggest that one looks at the underlying grammar of multimodal texts, and henceforth fit this grammar into 'schooling'. Grammar in this context is defined as sets of parameters and constraints, which show how different modes of multimodality function. This grammar is at odds with educational practice as defined by linear and normalising processes such as lesson plans and rigid curricula maps. This is the pivot at which complexity theory can lend a hand to educationalists in that the notion of enabling constraints is a basis for learning design that allows diversity to flourish. The authors describe two case studies to show how complexity theory works in this context, the first being teacher education, the second is a high school classroom. Both studies show how enabling constraints work to free up the relevant notion of text and help to fit corresponding pedagogies to this emerging textual dynamics. The chapter closes with an informative discussion about how the application of enabling constraints often works to simultaneously reveal institutional practices of power, and these can be explained with reference to the *habitus*.

Chapter Five is called, *Riding Critical and Cultural Boundaries: A Multiliteracies Approach to Reading Television Sitcoms.* Julie Faulkner & Bronwyn T Williams describe a cross cultural study between the US and Australia, that examines graduate student participation in watching 'foreign' TV sitcoms and commenting on the corresponding cultural norms and resultant multiliterate practices. The American students watched *Kath and Kim*, whilst the Australians viewed *Arrested Development.* The author's position multiliteracies as a manner of understanding the multiple ways in which young people now become literate through exposure to the media and computer mediated texts. Furthermore, the cultural differences and consequent literate identities of individuals and groups are now caught up in the ways in which texts interrelate across cultural borders, and form new ways of understanding communication and society. This chapter uses these changing cultural conditions to investigate the ways in which audience behaviour in relation to popular cultural is also caught up in multiliterate mores. In the past, audiences of cultural events were perhaps considered as passive receivers of information and values, which could only be discussed with immediate contacts. Now, online forums and email give audiences instantaneous ways in which to communicate their reactions to cultural artefacts. In fact, audience participation through electronic communication could now be figured as a critical factor in cultural growth. The study of this chapter places humour as a bridge between the societies the US and Australia, as the two TV shows that were chosen for the study have humorous affects in their respective host cultures. The authors analyse the two audience reactions to the shows and deconstruct the responses in terms of the cultural, linguistic and social parts. These parts are important elements in order to understand how multiliteracies relates to global cultural convergence and any consequent social practice.

Chapter Six is about *Rethinking Literacy in Culturally Diverse Classrooms*. Jennifer Rennie writes about the differences in literacy practice between Indigenous and non Indigenous students in Australia. These differences are explored through a mixture of narrative excerpts from the lives of Kelly and Arnie and theorisation about the types of literacy practice that their stories exhibit. The author takes the position that literacy is a social practice, so one must describe the social life of the two boys in order to understand their respective literacy. Kelly, who lives in an urban context, has access to technology and does well at English even though he does not enjoy the books that he is asked to read. Arnie struggles with his English studies - he comes from a remote Aboriginal community, and does not have easy access to the latest technology, even though he likes to play computer games. Rennie uses ideas from the multiliteracies framework to help explain the differences in literacy practice between Kelly and Arnie - as literacy may be seen as a function of design, learning and place. Kelly has access to many learning opportunities in his place, whilst Arnie is dislocated from his community as he moves from his rural setting to an urban high school. Arnie's school needs to design literacy practices that take account of his lifeworld, whereas Kelly is empowered at his school and in the design of his literacy activities due to his lifestyle, social position and place of residence. The author latterly concentrates on the situation of Arnie because the questions of literacy that his case raises are of particular importance and interest. There has been a lot of research into indigenous literacies in Australia, and the disparities in achievement that has often been noted. In the particular case of Arnie, designing literacy activities that positively includes his social background could mitigate the move to a highly organised high school and help him to explore the new institutional ways of learning with reference to his place of origin.

Chapter Seven is *Pragmatism and Philosophy: Enriching Students' Lives through a Critical Investigation of Spatial Literacy in Shared Spaces*. Margaret Baguley, Toni Riordan and Martin Kerby have investigated the concept of spatial literacy in an Australian boys' boarding school established since 1891. The inherent tensions they encountered were between the design of building structures which catered for a traditional form of teaching instruction and a contemporary curriculum which required less rigid learning and teaching spaces. A substantial building program, in conjunction with a whole school curriculum plan, sought to challenge preconceived notions of what the college represented. The investigation of spatial literacy was contextualised through this curriculum plan which seeks to educate students through a student-centred curriculum that aims to develop critically aware and culturally sensitive world citizens. The increasing use of school spaces in order to address political, philosophical and environmental issues supports the multiliteracies approach and has worked effectively with the students who appear to learn more effectively through physical encounter. The history of the college is also physically evidenced in a range of monuments scattered around the campus which students pass as they move between buildings. The monuments, buildings, and environmental areas have subsequently been utilised as valuable ways to discuss the history and tradition of the college whilst simultaneously critically examining issues through the use of spatial literacy with the students.

Chapter Eight has the title, *Cam-Capture Literacy and Its Incorporation into Multiliteracies.* David R Cole and Vikashni Moyle have expanded the multiliteracies framework to include cam-capture literacy, which may be defined as the social practice of using small cameras attached to computers for communicative purposes. Cam-capture literacy consists of visual literacy, information literacy and personal literacy. The students learn about visual aspects of representation through their self-recorded videos, they also have to make decisions about the information they wish to represent, and explore personal aspects of representation, especially as they are able to view and share their videos amongst themselves and with the teacher. The research context for this chapter is a middle school environment in a lower social economic area of Tasmania. In this context, cam-capture literacy is positioned as an easy and relatively cheap way to empower the students with a technologically mediated practice. The participants in the study spoke about their mainstream school literacy studies, their hopes and methods for improving their literacy, as well as taking standard spelling, reading and writing tests at the beginning and end of the research. The authors perform a social qualitative analysis of the self-recorded video data, to produce what they terms as the, 'cam-capture zones'. The quantitative results of the research reveal significant improvements in the print literacy skills of the students who took part in the project. The cam-capture zones are useful markers for literacy teachers in order to reengage their students in their designated activities. Cam-capture literacy can be deployed by teachers for self-reflection and as a purposeful link between traditional print literacies and the new literacies that are becoming apparent due to digital technology.

Chapter Nine is named, *Theorizing Media Productions as Complex Literacy Performances Among Youth In and Out of Schools.* Theresa Rogers has taken data from two major research projects in British Columbia and applied it to understanding complex identity construction in a multimodal context. The individuals involved with the research have shown a reluctance to engage with mainstream print literacy exercises, but become fully involved with the processes and potential messages that media production presents. The author argues that this change in agency that is brought about by media production; shows how education may be reorganised to include such processes in the learning cycle. The chapter includes a theoretical background in imagining, designing and communicating, whereby the 'youth' involved in the project may explore their identities. Furthermore, the social and cultural stereotypes of youth, boys and girls, are put into erasure through this research as the author has encouraged the participants to explore these questions of identity and labelling. The case studies have been taken from an alternative secondary school and an anti-violence project. They illustrate the creativity and messages that media production may unlock in youth, and the ways in which making videos and songs and art may be deployed to extract important self-reflective moments. One of the many impressive aspects of the case studies is the deep analysis and cultural significance that may be attached to the products. For example, the use of discursive play and cultural critique are both important teaching and learning themes that should be incorporated into pre-service training.

Chapter Ten is about teacher training and has the title, *Practicing or Preaching? Teacher Educators and Student Teachers Appropriating New Literacies.* Margaret Lo & Matthew Clarke in Hong Kong have implemented a 12-hour new literacies course in their teacher-training programme. The chapter describes how the new course had been designed and the ways in which the students have approached its completion. The context of research that is learning English in Hong Kong means that the pre-service teachers following the course are playing a 'high-stakes' game in terms of their qualifications and future job prospects. The investigators of this project are therefore faced with a potential contradiction between the theoretical background to understanding how new technology may be employed in literacy learning and the institutional reality of pre-service teachers in Hong Kong. For example, many of the teacher trainees were familiar and competent with respect to the social networking aspects of digital technology such as *Facebook*. Yet the trainees would not always make a connection between this behaviour and the types of online communities that the lecturers and researchers were trying to encourage. The theoretical background that the authors draw upon includes the ideas of a 'community of practice', 'affinity spaces' and 'the new literacies'. These theoretical strands mark important parts of the multiliteracies framework that also includes the pedagogy of transformed practice and critical literacy. The Hong Kong new literacies course was based around a shared wiki, webblogging, fanfiction and producing a multimedia unit of work for a secondary school. The chapter includes fascinating data from the pre-service teachers who have taken part in the course and their reactions to the openness and the 'freedom' of the new pedagogic structure. The authors finish their investigation with an earnest reflection on the power related issues that their new course has highlighted, and they describe possible ways forward for teacher education.

Chapter Eleven is *ICT Integration in Second Language Writing: A Malay Language Case Study.* Christina Gitsaki, Abduyah Ya'akub & Eileen Honan present an interpretive case study of two Singaporean secondary schools. In this context, the pedagogic value of ICT has been investigated, and in particular the ways in which computer use has impacted (or otherwise) on the Malay language curriculum. The authors argue that even though Singapore is an extremely technologically advanced society with appropriate and extensive educational technology policy and provision, the use of computer technology in the classroom is still a 'work-in-progress'. The particular focus of second language writing makes the point that more thinking around how to encourage students to write with ICT is needed to fully utilise this technology in education. The case study is broken down into process, contextualisation and learner-centredness, and includes details about teaching styles and classroom action in the two schools involved with the case study. These details are in line with the multiliteracies framework that encourages a critical investigation of pedagogic roles and the ways in which these roles are changing or under pressure due to new technologies. The authors conclude that the under utilisation of computer technology in second language writing is due to the socialisation of teachers, and the ways in which knowledge and practice have come together in education. In effect, ICT represents a new mode of writing that requires new pedagogy and a new way of conceptualising educative writing.

Chapter Twelve is about *Multiliteracies in Secondary Chemistry: A Model for Using Digital Technologies to Scaffold the Development of Students' Chemical Literacy.* This study takes place in the Australian state of Queensland, where perhaps the multiliteracies framework has been most widely applied in Australian schools. The researchers have used multiliteracies as a means to scaffold development in chemistry literacy, and as a manner of gauging representational competence with respect to multimodal texts and chemistry. The chapter begins with a discussion about the complicated ways in which students are challenged to represent data in chemistry. Digital technology has increased the complexity of representation in chemistry, as students now have a fleet of software packages that enable formulas, equations, diagrams, tables and description to be represented. The authors draw on multiliteracies research that has investigated ways in which students represent ideas, and applies these findings to chemistry. In particular, 'writing-to-learn' research is referred to as a useful means to scaffold chemical understanding. Furthermore, the central multiliteracies concept of Design, and the combinational pedagogic approach contained in the multiliteracies manifesto, are also explored by the writers as positive ways of scaffolding chemistry literacy. The chapter includes a detailed description of a chemistry unit of work and the ways in which applying the multiliteracies framework works in this context. The students were involved with conducting experiments and using their results to build data with respect to various biomaterials. The results of the study are presented in terms of quantitative and qualitative data, which show how the students have improved in their chemistry literacy by using computer technology. The chapter ends with recommendations for teachers, students and schools for using multiliteracies in education.

Chapter Thirteen in the volume is called, *Robotics as a Vehicle for Multiliteracies.* Classroom teacher Marissa J Saville has described the use of robotics in the curriculum as a way of expanding literacies and engaging students in multimodal problems. The students may assemble and programme robots, and in so doing have to function multimodally in terms of understanding visual, mathematical and print text and transferring this knowledge into the kinetics and interactivity of the robots. The author supplements the theory of robots with multiliteracies in terms of explaining classroom and recess action and the ways in which the robotics club has enthused and excited her students. The action of 'playing' with robots could be considered to be a multiliterate educative act, in that it opens up lateral paths and communicative powers. The robots are in a sense proxy communication devices that may embody the ideas of the users. This is in line with the multiliteracies notion of designing social futures, that may be mediated through technological innovation and the cultural paths to the future opened up via robotic play – for example, the software/hardware interface that computer operated robots display.

CONCLUSION

The collection of chapters in this handbook demonstrates the diverse range of interests and educational locations that multiliteracies may encompass. It is therefore impossible to delimit the scope of the project - and to position in it terms of political intent or technological development. The multiliteracies framework is crucially where the two worlds of educational technology and the need for social justice in education collide. This is a dynamic place - that is figured by users in real time - as much as theorists or academics trying to explain the ways in which this dynamic is reshaping learning, society and culture. For example, a youth alienated from mainstream education in British Columbia may post their self-reflective video film on *YouTube,* and it is latterly watched and the ideas picked up by a dejected school student in Singapore, who uses it as inspiration for a piece of multimodal writing! All this happens due to the conduits and interfaces now available through digital technology, and the flexible ways in which these pieces of the multiliteracies puzzle may synchronously fit together. In contrast to the new literacies movement, that could be limited and explained as a mapping of the ways in which digital technology is opening up new cultural, social and educative forms; the multiliteracies framework more readily accepts the dynamic interface between technology and justice that gives rise to new ways to interpret diversity. This gives educators a greater freedom and more precise way of integrating the potential otherness of contemporary culture into their everyday lesson and curriculum planning (Cole & Burke, 2008).

REFERENCES

Cole, D. R. (2007). Virtual Terrorism and the Internet E-Learning Options. *E-Learning*, 4 (2): 116-127.

Cole, D. R., & Burke, L. B., (2008). Curriculum design at a crossroads: A comparative approach to re-evaluating knowledge frameworks. *Curriculum Perspectives,* Volume 28, Number 3: 27-37.

Cole, D. R., & Throssell, P. (2008). Epiphanies in action: Teaching and learning in synchronous harmony. *The International Journal of Learning*, Volume 15, Issue 7: 175-184.

Gee, J. P. (2005). Semiotic social spaces and affinity spaces: From the age of mythology to today's schools. In D. Barton & K. Tusting (Eds.), *Beyond communities of practice: Language, power, and social context* (pp. 214-232). Cambridge: Cambridge University Press.

National Institute of Child Health and Human Development - NICHHD (2000). Report of the National Reading Panel. *Teaching Children to Read: An evidence-based assessment of the scientific research literature on reading and its implications for reading instruction.* (NIH Publication No. 00-4769). Washington, DC: U.S. Government Printing Office. Retrieved September, 29, 2008, from http://www.nationalreadingpanel.org/Publications/summary.htm.

National Inquiry into the Teaching of Literacy - NITL (Australia), Chair: K. Rowe, (2005). *Teaching Reading.* Canberra: Department of Education, Science and Training.

Pullen, D., Baguley, M. & Marsden, A. (2009). Communitive collaboration in schools. Salmons, J. &. Wilson, L. (Eds).*The Handbook of Research on Electronic Collaboration and Organizational Synergy* (pp. 205-222). Hershey: Idea Science Reference.

Rose, J. (2006). *Independent Report of the Teaching of Early Reading: Final report.* UK Department of Education and Skills. Retrieved October, 10, 2008, from http://www.standards.dfes.gov.uk/phonics/report.pdf.

The New London Group. (1996). A pedagogy of multiliteracies: Designing social futures. *Harvard Educational Review,* 66: 60-93.

Acknowledgment

Deep gratitude goes to the contributing authors who generously shared their work in this handbook. Their response to our call for chapters demonstrates the willingness of educators to share and 'tell their stories'.

We are grateful to the many peer reviewers, whose careful reading and constructive comments enabled the authors to improve and develop their chapters. Nonetheless, the co-editors take full responsibility for any errors, omissions, or weaknesses in this work.

We also acknowledge that without the continual support of IGI Global, *Multiliteracies and Technology Enhanced Education: Social Practice and the Global Classroom* would not have been possible. In particular we would like to acknowledge the important contributions given to us by the IGI editorial team. To Tyler Heath, Heather Probst and Kristin Roth we thank you for your continued support and encouragement.

Finally, we thank you, the reader, for giving this book your attention. We hope that after reading this handbook you will be motivated and inspired to use a multiliteracies approach to your own teaching. We hope that when a future call for chapters goes out, you will be ready to share your discoveries by contributing a chapter.

Sincerely,

Darren L. Pullen
University of Tasmania, Australia

David R. Cole
University of Technology, Sydney, Australia

Section 1
Theoretical Frameworks for Technology and Multiliteracies

Chapter 1
Multiliteracies and the New World Order

Margaret Baguley
University of Southern Queensland, Australia

Darren L. Pullen
University of Tasmania, Australia

Megan Short
University of Tasmania, Australia

ABSTRACT

Due to the importance of literacy as a key component in many education programs it appears that more than any other curriculum area its history has been marked by continual change in terms of theoretical positioning, shifts in definition and pedagogical practice. Whilst change is often viewed as a positive occurrence, recently teachers of literacy have experienced a rapid period of change in both their practice and the theoretical and research based beliefs that underpin it. This chapter will provide a brief overview of some of the ways in which literacy pedagogy has encompassed a diverse range of forms of communication and meaning making commonly referred to as 'multiliteracies'.

INTRODUCTION

The purpose of this introductory chapter is to help orientate the reader and contextualise the concept of literacy and its evolution into multiliteracies through a chronological review of literacy, and specifically literacy pedagogy, over the last quarter of a century. This necessarily brief overview is important in providing the reader with an evolutionary understanding of the term 'multiliteracies'. Following this journey the concept of literacy is expanded on together with the impact of technology on this area. This chapter therefore provides the reader with an overview and understanding of the field of literacy and how technology has resulted in a range of multi-modal forms of communication known as multiliteracies.

The History of Literacy

The history of literacy is a vast and complex subject and involves consideration of human development in terms of political, social, technological, linguistic, religious, institutional and ideological events,

DOI: 10.4018/978-1-60566-673-0.ch001

the explication of which will not be attempted in this chapter. Rather, attention will be directed toward a brief consideration of some of the ways in which literacy has been conceptualised since the latter part of the twentieth century in English language literacy teaching. The issue of definition is significant in discussions of literacy – what literacy "is" and "is not" is just one of the many definitional impasses and binaries that require deliberation and consideration. As the conception of what literacy is has changed, so too has pedagogical responses, strategies and philosophies. The journey from a hegemonic discourse of literacy to the possibilities encapsulated by mulitiliteracies is, in some sense, one that is signposted by key historical and culturally contingent beliefs about what literacy is.

Part of any discussion of a history of literacy subsequently also includes a history of education. The connections between literacy and education are often complex and intractable (Kellner, 2001; Larson & Marsh, 2005). Any discussion of one is necessarily a discussion of the other. Traditionally, literacy in English speaking contexts has been conceived of in relatively narrow terms with prominence accorded to writing as the dominant mode through which meaning is constructed and received. A simplified, uncomplicated and traditional notion of literacy is that it consists of textual practices in which the text is an alphabetic script written on a page able to be read for meaning by a reader. Being literate is commonly described as having the skills and ability to read and write. In a traditional classroom context, the skills associated with reading and writing were a major preoccupation for both the teacher and the learner and achievement of these skills was considered attainment of a literate state. In some ways, this has not changed as reading and writing skills are still a significant aspect of the needs of readers and writers, although it could be argued the form and presentation of the text is different.

A traditional approach to the teaching of literacy was characterised by a unitary approach to the teaching of skills requisite for reading and writing (Graff, 1987; Kalantzis, Cope & Fehring, 2002). Such an approach involved assumptions about the learner, which was for the most part narrowly defined in terms of their linguistic, socioeconomic and cultural background. In Australia, for example, the student was conceived of as being from an Anglo-Saxon heritage, had English as a first language, was from a two parent wage earning household and could reasonably be expected to gain employment upon leaving school. The world of work, at least until the 1980s, that the school leaving population would enter was dominated by opportunities in manufacturing and service provision and it was expected that the young person would most likely stay employed in the same area for their productive working life. Schooling prepared the young person for their life in the workforce by providing them with skills in reading, writing and numeracy in addition to broad, culturally heterogeneous understandings about their social, natural and political environment. The discourse of schooling in Australia up until the 1960s was one of a dominant 'top down' curriculum that took very little notice of the larger social, linguistic, political and ideological changes that were occurring. The interplay between technology and pedagogical practice was restricted to aids for instruction such as film projectors, slide projectors and typewriters. Literacy education in this context was predominantly based on written and oral instruction. Teachers of literacy were therefore seen as teachers of reading and writing who used predominately written texts to "deliver" their teaching.

The texts used by literacy teachers in the past were restricted to those that were comprised mostly of alphabetic print and were easily portable. They included such items as books, comics, newspapers, magazines, pamphlets, atlases, maps and charts. The operational pedagogic definition of literacy as comprised of reading and writing was supported by a widely held view of text as being print-based (Lankshear, Snyder & Green, 2000; Larson & Marsh, 2005). The widening of the concept of text in the last twenty years has offered a challenge to educators and students. The certainty of a text as a print-based artefact has therefore been disrupted by a broadening of this concept. As Fairclough (1995, p. 3) states, "Texts are social spaces in which two fundamental social processes simultaneously occur: cognition and representation of the world, and social interaction ... texts in their ideational form constitute systems of knowledge and belief". If the work of literacy education is possible only through interaction with text, the subsequent expansion of the definition of text which occurred in the later twentieth century must in a significant way alter the way in which literacy education is conceptualised and performed. What a text "is" and what it "means" is essential to the purpose of education.

A traditional approach to literacy education positioned the teacher and the student in a stable, largely pre-determined relationship to one another. The teacher was invested with the bulk of the decision making in terms of, for example, curriculum content, pedagogical approach, time spent on tasks and assessment; essentially what "knowledge" and "learning" consisted of was determined by the teacher. The classroom was viewed as an easily identified site in which certain activities occurred, for the most part in a similar fashion in a suburb, a city, or a nation. It was taken for granted that the classroom was an uncomplicated social environment with a clear and unambiguous set of purposes that could remain largely unquestioned and unexamined.

The function of schooling, and in particular literacy education, as an important indicator of success both within and outside the school environment, can perhaps account for the intensity of the debate that continues to be generated around it. Green, Hodgen and Luke (1997) identified four "central visions of a literate subject" which are connected to particular historical and social periods in Australia. The 1950s was concerned with the development of "the moral subject" whose schooling involved engagement with traditional texts valued for their moral tenor. The "technical/skilled subject" was identified as an ideal literate subject in the 1960s with an emphasis on skill development in order to join in a global era of prosperity and progress. In the 1970s social upheavals such as the Vietnam War and rapid changes in public awareness and attitudes towards disadvantage and inequality, such as the Feminist movement and considerations of Indigenous access to education reconfigured attitudes towards the value of literacy as a means of social access and created a "deficit/disadvantaged subject". Concerns about social justice that were present but largely ignored in the curriculum of the 1960s were included in educational policy in the 1970s. Advances in cognitive science and pedagogical applications stemming from disciplines such as linguistics, psychology and sociology also provided educators with tools for remediation. A period of rapid economic change for the Australian economy in the 1980s and a need for a workforce able to adapt to emerging new technologies produced conditions for "the economic subject" a context in which one who could participate fully in an uncertain but vigorous economic environment (Green, Hodgen & Luke, 1997, pp. 20-21; Lankshear, Snyder & Green, 2000).

A praxis between schooling and social change results in the formation of socially constructed subjects according to dominant discourses of schooling. One of the demands of literacy education is a utilitarian one, to provide access to valued competencies, skills, social and cognitive resources to enable full participation in meaningful and socially determined activities such as work, relationships and creative endeavours. The rapid social changes that have occurred in the last two decades have altered the way the world "works" in terms of the way we represent the world to ourselves and to others, the ways in which we communicate, construct knowledge and how we make and ascribe meaning using a variety of semiotic tools (Anstey & Bull, 2006; Cope & Kalantzis, 2000; Kalantzis, 2001).

The emergence of new ways of communicating, making meaning, being understood, expressing a sense of self and connection to others through a continually growing range of technologies provides each of us with choices that allow for sophisticated visual, auditory, graphic and digital representation which require new understandings of how messages are sent, received, stored, replicated and reshaped. Some of the skills that are needed to negotiate an increasingly multi-modal communicative environment have not changed – we need to be able to decode alphabetic print, know how to make grammatical choices in order to construct meaningful written and visual texts for particular audiences and generally have access to a range of linguistic resources (Kress, 2003; Larson & Marsh, 2005; Unsworth, 2001). The social conditions and expectations for becoming literate have changed, as they always have throughout the history of literacy and education.

LITERACY AND THE ROLE OF TECHNOLOGY IN EDUCATION

Literacy in its various guises has assumed prominence in most compulsory education sectors (Davis, 2008; Lankshear & Knobel, 2003). Over time various forms or models of literacy and literate practices have been advocated. For example, during the 1980s theorists such as Hirsch (1987) proposed cultural literacy, and more recently the concepts of critical literacy (Freebody & Luke, 1990) and technoliteracy (Lankshear, Snyder & Green, 2000) have been advocated and supported. However, advances in technology, specifically multimedia capable computers and the World Wide Web, together with workplace and educational reforms have meant a reconceptualising of what literacy is and what literate skills are required for the twenty-first century. Given the aforementioned changes a group of literacy academics proposed the concept of "multiliteracies" in 1996 (New London Group, 1996). Multiliteracies is a way to comprehend the literacy curriculum as extending beyond formal school learning and as being supportive of productive participation in the community.

Multiliteracies as a Concept

The advent of technology, in particular such digital technologies as personal computers, mobile phones and the internet, has enabled communication to rapidly spread from the local context to an international level. This rapid and global proliferation of technologies and communication mediums has not only increased the multiplicity of communication channels but has led to an increasing awareness of, and exposure to, cultural and linguistic diversity. The proliferation of technology and communication has in turn moved the notion of literacy from being a singular concept which has tended to relate to written and oral language through to the notion of literacy practices which encapsulates a broader notion of literacy inherently related to specific cultural contexts.

During this period of change the notion of what is considered to be a *text* has evolved. To a layperson a text is anything that is written using the symbols of their language. For instance, a layperson may describe a text as a book, newspaper and/or a magazine which is identifiable by the use of the written word and/or segmented written text in columns using a small font (Kress, 2003). However, if the same person was asked to describe the internet they would probably describe an environment that utilises written text, sound, still and moving images and which supports user interactivity via hyperlinks. In effect they have described a text which is multimodal (Anstey & Bull, 2004; Kress & van Leeuwen, 2001). This multimodal nature has been enhanced during the latter part of the last century due to advances in technology. From radio through to television the Internet and interactive TV (e.g. TiVo) the presentation of information, or text, in a variety of modes such as audio, visual, video, text and spatial has been made possible.

All of these advances have challenged the nature of literacy and what it means to be literate in the twenty-first century (Davis, 2008; Goldman, 2004; New London Group, 1996).

The broadening of the concept of literacy has required educators, whether from the schooling or training sectors, to re-encapsulate "what is literacy" and "what literacy" skills are required for students and workers in a global economy - often referred to as the "knowledge" or "innovation" economy. In response to the demands confronting educating students and workers in an ever increasing digitally complex world, the New London Group published the article *A Pedagogy of Multiliteracies* (1996) in the Harvard Educational Review. The writers of this article formulated the notion of multiliteracies as a way of addressing the changes facing society resulting from digitalisation and globalisation. In providing justification for the formulation of multiliteracies two members of the New London Group, Bill Cope and Mary Kalantzis (2000, p. 19) outlined a rationale for multiliteracies: "... our personal, public and working lives are changing in some dramatic ways, and these changes are transforming our cultures and the ways we communicate. This means that the way we have taught literacy, and what counts for literacy, will also have to change".

In providing a rationale for multiliteracies the New London Group (1996) based their work on two propositions. The first concerns the multiplicity of communication channels, their associated media and their implications for teaching practices. In formulating the first proposition the notion of literacy was expanded from written, oral and aural to encompass other forms which have been made available by increasing digitalisation. Digitalisation has meant that communication has moved away from being primarily linguistic to multimodal. Digital technology such as websites, video, podcasts and electronic games, for example "Guitar Hero" and the "Wii board", are able to incorporate other literacy modes such as linguistic, visual, audio, gestural and spatial.

Digitalisation has enabled the globalisation of communication thereby increasing cultural and linguistic diversity which is the second proposition of the New London Group. Associated with both propositions is *identity*. "Literacy is ...a set of discourse practices, that is, as ways of using language and making sense both in speech and writing. These discourse practices are tied to the particular world views (beliefs and values) of a particular social or cultural group ... a change of discourses is a change of identity" (Gee, 1994, pp.168-169). As such learning "requires taking on a new identity" (Gee, 2003, p. 51) which is where the multimodal nature of multiliteracies comes to the fore.

The concept of multiliteracies builds on the multimodal cross-cultural nature offered by digital communication media. This cross-cultural aspect in turn causes an ongoing change and reconstruction of meaning being offered by this form of communication. This continual process of transformation brings with it uncertainty and a major cultural shift that is contributing to changing identities and a change in literary practices from print to visual (Green & Bigum, 1993) to multimodal (New London Group, 1996; 2000). These changes are also influenced by the proliferation of multimodal environments and technologies which cross social and cultural boundaries (Cope & Kalantzis, 1997; New London Group, 1996, 2000).

The concept of multiliteracies is an attempt to understand and bring together the multiple text forms that have resulted from new technologies and subsequent media forms, such as blogs and wikis, through a pedagogy that gives teachers the opportunity to present information to students using multiple text and media forms (See Appadurai, 1990). The utilisation of multiple text and media forms provides students with the opportunity to comprehend and relate to the "increasing complexity and interrelationship of different modes of meaning" (New London Group, 2000, p. 25). Multimodal texts also allow students to interpret and experience the presented information in both a global as well as a local context (Kalantzis, Cope & Harvey, 2003; The New London Group, 1996). As such a multiliteracies perspective is concerned about using various mediums, such as print, audio or spatial. Within an education context "the role of pedagogy is to develop an epistemology of pluralism that provides access without people having to erase or leave behind different subjectivities" (New London Group, 2000, p. 18). Therefore the pedagogy of multiliteracies is concerned with using the multimodal layers of the learners' world in the classroom to engage students with the tools and technology that they are already familiar with.

EMERGING TRENDS

As noted earlier in the chapter, literacy has undergone many significant changes due to the advent of technologies and their subsequent effect on how people relate to one another in a range of contexts. The rapid increase and proliferation of communication technologies, and the integration of these technologies in the workplace, have resulted in a disjuncture between the *actual* skills and knowledge which people possess as opposed to what knowledge they are *presumed* to have. The next section will discuss how changes in society, which have occurred through technological advances, have impacted upon the concept of literacy.

Literacy and Sociocultural Perspectives

A sociocultural approach to literacy includes three equally integrated dimensions of learning and practice: operational, cultural and critical (Green, 1988; Larson & Marsh, 2005; Street, 1984). Lankshear, Snyder and Green (2000) describe these aspects as follows. The operational aspect focuses on the language aspect of literacy, the ability to read and write appropriately within a range of contexts. The cultural aspect is concerned with the ability to make and comprehend the meaning of the text in relation to other contexts. The critical aspect involves an awareness that one can participate in an existing literacy but is also able to transform and actively produce it. These aspects are important considerations in teaching multiliteracies in a relevant and meaningful way. However, participating in a range of literacies still requires the ability to read and write. The ability to compare and contrast texts and make meaning from them is essential. The critical dimension enables the learner to critique the information they are presented with and evaluate it in relation to, for example, its moral and social implications.

At the beginning of this decade Gee (2000) described the term 'new literacy studies', which emphasise that literacy is a social practice. This term has evolved from the recognition that literacy is a part of, and subsequently shapes, social relations and structures (Barton, Hamilton & Ivanic, 2000; Larson & Marsh, 2005). This emphasis on the social context of literacy appears to correspond with the increasing effects of globalisation described by Bruffee (1993, p. 21) as being an era of 'necessary interdependence'. As traditional concepts and roles are overturned at a progressively faster rate, societies are seemingly becoming more reliant on one another. This has resulted in a greater willingness by communities to accommodate difference and to work in cooperative and collaborative ways.

The increase in cooperative and collaborative approaches is evidenced in global efforts to control pollution, population, and more recently the threat of terrorism. This contradicts the traditional Western approach which has emphasised competitiveness and self-promotion (Barrentine, 1993; Burns, 1978; Clark, 1996; Hellriegel, Slocum & Woodman, 1992; Rogoff, 2003; Sharpnack, 2005; Sowers, 1983). Additionally, technological advances in communication have resulted in a greater awareness of the global community in which we live and interact. New communication technologies have resulted in meaning being made in increasingly multimodal ways (Anstey & Bull, 2004; Cope & Kalantzis, 2000; Kalantzis, Cope & Fehring, 2002). Therefore, literacy is evident in many different formats many of which encourage multiple authorship through sites such as blogs and wikis. The social context of literacy has evolved from the lone author/reader with a portable print based text to multi-modal sites which can be created, constructed and shared with large numbers of people. The ability to discover and use sites based on personal interest enables people to create electronic social groups who may never meet one another but who are connected daily.

Literacy and the Education Context

The development of new technologies has implications for the way literacy is taught. As Durrant and Green (1998, p. 3) state "the creation of new technologies continues to change society's concept of literacy, just as it has always done". Although there are a number of important benefits to supporting technological literacy, significant concerns are being raised regarding the importance of maintaining a sound theoretical understanding of technology in combination with maintaining high quality literacy practices across a range of educational contexts (Lankshear, Snyder & Green, 2000; Scanlon, 2009; Solvie, 2008). The importance of this approach is described by Lankshear, Snyder and Green (2000, p. 133) who state: " ... educational work is high-level work, not amenable to easy solutions and quick fixes, electronic or otherwise ... enhanced practice at the literacy-technology-learning interface calls for a good deal of reflective, interpretive thinking work, together with a strong foundation of personal experience of social practices involving new technologies".

It appears that one of the primary social practices which need to be considered before meaningful teaching and learning can occur is the belief that young people are technologically literate. The term "digital native" describes anyone born after 1980 that has grown up in a world saturated with digital technology (Palfrey & Gasser, 2008; Prensky, 2001). "Digital Natives" is also the name of the interdisciplinary research collaboration between the Berkman Center for Internet & Society at Harvard University and the Research Centre for Information Law at the University of St Gallen (www.digitalnative.org/#about). The aim of the project is to understand and support young people as they grow up in a digital age. However, as the website notes, those who were not "born digital" can be just as connected, if not more so, than their younger counterparts. Therefore, not everyone born since 1981 is a "digital native". Prensky (2001) also highlights a distinction between the "natives" (students) and the "immigrants" (teachers). He describes teachers as "immigrants" because of the perception that they are struggling to teach a group of people a new language using the outdated language they already use.

With an awareness of these issues and a mandate to engage students from this technologically literate context, university administrators are creating courses which they believe will cater for students' alleged affinity with technology. Some academics such as Scanlon (2009) however, have found that a majority of his 'digital natives' approach computers cautiously and in fact find them just as frustrating as many older students. This observation coupled with a substantial review undertaken by Kuiper, Volman and Terwel (2005) of the ability of students to research on the Internet found that they often had difficulty locating and finding relevant and reliable information and were unable to effectively evaluate and compare data with other sources; an indication of issues pertaining to technological illiteracy. Scanlon (2009) contends that the divergence between claims about 'digital natives' and the reality of the classroom is related to class, commercial interest and confusion. For example, students from less privileged backgrounds do not have the same access to, or affinity with, computers. This situation creates an equity issue amongst students who are unable to afford computers at home and have limited access to computers at their educational institution.

Commercial interest has been generated in the technological literacy area evidenced in the creation of numerous game-based programs. Education providers seek to remain current with, and provide the most effective and recent innovations in teaching and learning in order to attract and engage students. These game-based programs ostensibly seek to attract the technologically literate skills of 'digital natives' yet also are cleverly marketed to appeal to a perceived need in the educational context. Lankshear, Snyder and Green (2000, p. 132) note that this trend is especially apparent in literacy education "where commercial developers, freelancers and university 'researcher-consultants' fight it out for the chance to 'deliver' off-the-shelf, packaged approaches to literacy, remedial intervention programs, diagnostic kits, together with training in their use".

The increased use of technology in educational settings has also been observed by Freebody (2007) who notes that attached to these programs are also expectations about more sophisticated and efficient learning. However, Scanlon (2009) proposes that the ability of 'digital natives' to navigate around and download material from ready-made online environments such as Facebook or Google does not necessarily reveal a general ease with technology. As he states: "From my experiences in the computer lab, once students stray outside of the safe confines of pre-built, pre-configured online environments provided by the likes of Hotmail or Facebook, they often turn out to be just as confused as the rest of us" (Scanlon, 2009, p. 33). Scanlon contends that it is important that educators assess students' individual strengths and weaknesses, such as determining their affinity with computer technology, in order to equip students to operate effectively in a digital world.

This view is supported by Solvie (2008) who examined the use of computer technology through utilising Wikis in teaching preservice teachers how to teach reading. She found that the collaborative writing encouraged by Wikis did not ensure that all participants were equally represented in the process, although all were given the opportunity. Therefore the technology employed in this teaching and learning process resulted in some students either not being able to use, or resisting the opportunity to demonstrate, their technological literacy. Solvie (2008) proposes that although current technologies should be used to teach literacy, reflective and interpretive consideration should also be given to what constitutes literacy, how it is used in daily life and evaluating effective practices for literacy instruction. Lankshear, Snyder and Green (2000) agree that the education sector is a complex field and does not benefit from ill-considered 'solutions' to perceived problems in the sector.

In Australia, the Prime Minister Kevin Rudd proposed the institution of a one billion dollar "education revolution", in a policy paper during his term as Opposition Leader in 2007. This proposal, which is currently in the process of being instituted, aims to provide access to a computer for every secondary school student from year's nine to 12 (Archer, 2007; Australian Labor Party, 2007; Coorey, 2007). Rudd based this decision on recent data from the Organisation for Economic Co-operation and Development (OECD) which indicated that Australia spends well below the average on early childhood education and has one of the lowest retention records for secondary school students. Rudd contends that Australia's prosperity will decline unless the quality and funding of education from early childhood through to adulthood is raised substantially. He states that "there is now incontrovertible evidence that education should be understood as an economic investment" (Coorey, 2007). The "education revolution" appears to support his understanding that technological literacy is essential to enable students to function effectively in society.

Research undertaken by Papert (1998) and Dickinson and Tabors (2001) indicates that the majority of classroom literacy practices are still grounded in traditional reading and writing literacy models. They contend that students who are technologically literate are being denied access to multiple modes of literacy and therefore are disadvantaged. Although Luke (2003) recognises that there are inequities to students' access to various form of technology, and consequently multiple forms of literacy, he believes that without support, the socio-economic gap between the advantaged and the disadvantaged will become wider and eventually affect developed countries' social and economic successes. Gee (2003) argues that technologically literate students perceive text heavy learning environments as being irrelevant in preparing them for life outside of their educational institution.

"Reverse mentoring" is seen by many educational institutions as an important collaborative approach in overcoming some of the obstacles mentioned in the previous section. Reverse mentoring has been used in the business sector to help support older personnel in learning about, and becoming comfortable with, digital environments. The skills and knowledge of technologically savvy, and often younger, employees is utilised (Hendricks, 2002; Miller, 2001). This strategy has been co-opted by the education sector through projects such as GenYES, originally known as GenWHY, which has spread to hundreds of schools throughout the world. Originally created in 1996 in the United States, it is one of the largest of several global curriculum projects which supports technologically literate school students to teach their teachers about using technology (www.genyes.org). This approach subverts the traditional teacher/student relationship by replacing it with an approach that is more collaborative and one in which the participants are learning together. The website states that the resulting collaboration provides the students with project-based learning and teachers with on-site sustainable technology integration and support. Although many schools currently rely on the goodwill of technologically savvy students to assist their peers, and in some cases their teachers, this program actually formalises the relationship through a curriculum initiative. As Lankshear, Snyder and Green (2000) note, an enormous amount of pressure is placed on teachers who are often underprepared for the task of integrating new technologies and therefore another form of literacy into the classroom context. This observation is also supported by Mantei and Kervin (2007) who reveal that many teachers feel ill-equipped to use technology to support learning even when they are provided with in-service opportunities.

This brief overview has described a number of issues which educators are dealing with in the context of literacy. As in any learning context there are learners with a wide range of skills and expertise. Technological literacy is a skill which needs to be learned in order to interact with a range of digital environments. The rapid increase of technology however has, in many cases, required a collaborative approach to learning which has subverted the traditional teacher/student relationship.

The Twenty-First Century and Multiliteracies

In the twenty-first century a broader view of literacy has emerged which is part of a larger discussion regarding educational global reform. Van Heertum and Shane (2006) propose that providing students with skills in technological literacy fosters creativity and motivates young people whilst improving their economic opportunities. Creativity is also seen to be the new economic driver for international competitiveness in the new economy known variously as the "knowledge" or "innovation" economy (Davis, 2008; Robinson, 2001; Sawyer, 2006, Wind, 2006). The value of arts-based pedagogies, multiple ways of knowing and multiple intelligences (Bamford, 2006; Eisner, 2002; Gardner, 1993; Wright, 2003) have been advocated by educators in enhancing the effectiveness of learning environments for students. In addition to fostering opportunities to engage students in multiliteracies, these contexts also support the contention of Davis (2008) that high-level creativity is increasingly becoming an essential skill for students.

Chiapello (2004) notes that the business sector is also realising the value of innovation and creativity, even likening business attributes to artistic ones: "Management literature has gone out of its way to explain that while wage labourers may have lost job security in the latest transformation of the world of work, they have gained more creative, more varied, more autonomous labour, closer to an artistic lifestyle" (p. 593). Conversely, ostensibly creative areas such as the arts have been urged towards business models, evident in the rise of the "creative industries", and a call for art to be made comprehensible to the public. As Van Heertum and Shane (2006) note, the contradictory nature of multiple literacies sits within the broader critique of these changes described by Robins and Webster in *Times of the Technoculture* (1999). The authors propose that educational progressivism characterised by flexibility, adaptability, cooperation, creativity and relevant student autonomy may paradoxically prove disempowering to students and inevitably empower corporations "to dictate the content and nature of education towards their needs and ends, eliding the more holistic approach progressive educators once stressed" (Van Heertum & Shane, 2006, p. 253).

This approach has been recently evidenced in the arts, often the visual barometer for issues in society, in Australia. Perkin (2006) contends that although the Government remains the chief provider of funding for the arts, increasingly cultural organisations are being encouraged to develop and sustain relationships with the corporate sector. Chiapello (2004) believes that the effectiveness of the arts, which have traditionally provided an active critique of society, is slowly being lessened due to their gradual commodification by the business sector. Shillito, Beswick and Baguley (2008) argue that the arts build capacity for creativity and innovation within students; however they cannot effectively operate against a corporate agenda. Multiple literacy education therefore provides a necessary focus on the needs of twenty-first century students by acknowledging socio-cultural differences and the importance of developing and sustaining skills in a range of communication technologies. This ability to interpret and use a range of texts that employ linguistic, visual, audio, gestural and spatial modes of meaning for social, cultural, political, civic and economic purposes in various contexts identifies a person who is multiliterate (Anstey & Bull, 2006; Kalantzis, 2001; Kalantzis, Cope & Fehring, 2002). This approach also prepares students to not only meet the needs of the new economy, but to actively critique issues of gender, race and class and in the process create an authentic and equitable democracy (Cobb, 1992; Davis, 2008; Heertum & Share, 2006). Lankshear, Snyder and Green (2000) believe that this approach can be achieved if learners are involved in a coherent social practice in which they are able to make genuine connections with what they know, which in turn will assist them in evaluating and engaging with different social and cultural contexts. This is particularly important if teachers lack knowledge and experience in current communication technologies and are consequently unable to accommodate the "language" of their students.

Competency in a range of literacies in the twenty-first century is considered essential in effectively engaging with and operating in a society which has seen a rapid increase in a range of communication technologies and various modes of communication. Although there has traditionally been a disjuncture between the knowledge of teachers and their students due to a range of factors such as cognitive development, it has become apparent that "digital natives" possess high level of skills and expertise in digital environments which may far exceed that of their teachers.

Leadership and Multiliteracies

Recent conferences such as the Australian *Future Directions in Literacy: International Conversations 2007* provide an important indicator and forum regarding future international developments in literacy pedagogy and practice. The keynote address from the conference emphasised that literacy is a collective responsibility throughout the school and wider community (Freebody, 2007). It is evident that cooperative and collaborative leaders in education are becoming increasingly important in engaging with the complex area of multiliteracies and specifically communication technologies. Mattessich, Murray-Close and Monsey (2004) reveal that this form of leadership relies on a mutually beneficial relationship which suggests that educators, students and the wider community need to feel a sense of ownership for both the teaching and learning process. For some educators this requires a shift in their thinking from the traditional role of the educator as the ultimate authority to someone who recognises the skills and expertise students already have and a preparedness to work with them during the learning process. It also requires educators to recognise limitations they may have in specific areas, such as accessing and navigating digital environments, and a willingness to further their knowledge and skills.

Mantei and Kervin (2007) have found, through their research on a teachers from Kindergarten to Year 6, that those who used technology in their daily lives, such as paying bills on the internet, downloading music and movies or searching for information to enhance their pedagogical practice, were more likely to incorporate technology into their teaching and learning. Abas and Khalid (2007) note that even though educational institutions may be able to afford the latest technology it will be to no avail without appropriate inservice opportunities and willingness by educators to engage with technology and more importantly with the pedagogical issues to effect purposeful learning. As Roblyer (2006) notes, technology is an opportunity to help teachers communicate more effectively with their students, and although it can make good teaching better, it cannot improve poor teaching performances. Essentially, technology is not a substitute for sound pedagogical practice.

However, the use of technology in an educational setting does not translate to instant engagement with learning by students. This finding supports that of Lankshear, Snyder and Green (2000) who contend that effective learning results in the creation of socially meaningful places which occurs when learning is linked to authentic social practices. Drath and Paulus (1994) propose that making meaning collectively creates leaders through such processes as framing problems, setting goals, engaging in dialogue and building and testing theories. Technology can therefore be used to enhance the learning experience of students from a range of social and cultural backgrounds by enhancing their skills in multiliteracies by enabling them to find relevant information in a global context. This in turn will assist them in constructing their opinions and hypotheses about the world in a supportive environment which encourages and values cooperative and collaborative learning.

The collaborative leadership style of the educator combined with highly developed pedagogical skills are important attributes for the twenty-first century learning context. The current proliferation of communication technologies and globalisation has resulted in a rapidly changing educational landscape. Shriberg, Lloyd, Shriberg & Williamson (1997, p. v) propose that easier access to information has resulted in a re-evaluation of the leader as "omnipotent hero." Bensimon and Neumann (1993, p. 12) believe that collaborative leadership is necessary to respond to the saturation of information and complexity of the twenty-first century and describe the ideal leader in this context as:

... someone who knows how to find and bring together diverse minds – minds that reflect variety

in their points of view, in their thinking processes and in their unique capacities as well as unique limitations ... Moreover as the world grows more complex ... it is likely that we will stop thinking of leadership as the property or quality of just one person. We will begin to think of it in its collective form: leadership as occurring among and through a group of people who think and act together.

This relational form of leadership necessarily involves the wider community and thereby allows everyone, even those who have traditionally been marginalised, to make important contributions. Lankshear, Snyder and Green (2000) propose the leadership required to enhance classroom practice at the literacy-technology-learning interface is instigated through a whole school approach. This approach would include regular all-staff activities to evaluate the school's current situation and would be supported by school based policy, planning and development. In addition they believe it is powerfully educative for schools to seek outside expertise from people with relevant experience in various forms of technology which could be utilised in the classroom. Through this process equity issues such as lack of professional development opportunities, the ability to provide current and relevant information to students, resourcing and time could be addressed by the collaborative leaders of individual schools with the support of the wider community.

CONCLUSION

"Old" and "new" are problematic constructs in that they are largely relativistic and situated in specific historical, political and ideological contexts. To talk of "old" and "new" conceptions of literacy and literacy pedagogy is to reduce the complexity of the issues and to invoke absolutist overtones. It is possible, however, to map out changes, shifts and activities and attempt to describe them in terms of a larger narrative of education. Such narratives are important as they seek to remind us that literacy, as a socially constructed practice, has always been shaped by the social conditions in which it is created.

This chapter has provided an overview of literacy and the general changes that have occurred as the concept of literacy has evolved into the multi-modal form of multiliteracies. The history of literacy is complex and has been affected by human development and a range of innovations such as developments in communication technology. The incorporation of communication technologies in the workplace and home environment, resulting in rapid social change, has necessarily affected the education sector. Therefore it is evident that the traditional approach to literacy, based solely on reading and writing, is not appropriate for effective engagement in a twenty-first century context. Additionally, the traditional positioning of the teacher as the sole source of information did not allow for meaningful and effective engagement with students.

The growing range of technologies has resulted in a diverse range of modes and discourses to occur resulting in a global context in which to search for and present information. Educators have necessarily re-evaluated what literacy skills students require in order to function effectively as members of society. A number of assumptions about learners have been made in this process including that young people are necessarily technologically literate. However, it appears that this cannot always be assumed and that a cooperative, collaborative approach is required throughout society to enable its participants to understand and communicate using the various modes related to a range of electronic texts.

Educators have to be willing to learn about and engage with new technologies so that, as with any discipline area, they are aware of new developments and how these can be used to inform the learning environment. The complex role of the educator has been made more difficult by pressures which can occur both within and outside an educational community. This can result from externally imposed expectations on teaching and learning, for example through the benchmarking of results; issues of equity and access in relation to funding between schools; commercial gain related to technological innovations and the pressure to use particular programs; and the disparity between students of particular competencies related to their learning.

Strategies such as providing computers to every secondary student in Australia are only beneficial if supported by the whole school, adopted into policy and practice with significant professional development given where it is needed. The recognition that some students are a vital resource in terms of technological literacy and may be able to provide mentoring within the school, both for their peers and teachers, is a significant development within education global reform. Technological literacy has been found to foster creativity and the ability innovate and create is valued as an important commodity in the current "knowledge" or "innovation" economy. A multiliterate person will, for example, be able to analyse and evaluate how the commercial sector uses various modes of meaning-making to promote particular products and brands. This ability to interpret and also use a range of texts prepares students to live and work effectively in the new economy but also to be critical and active agents of change in a variety of social and cultural contexts.

REFERENCES

Abas, Z., & Khalid, H. (2007). Achieving pedagogical richness to meet the needs of ODL learners. In P. Tsang, R. Kwang & R. Fox (Eds.). *Enhancing learning through technology*, (pp. 161 – 170). London: World Scientific Publishing.

Anstey, M., & Bull, G. (2004). *The literacy labyrinth* (2nd ed.). Sydney: Pearson Education Australia.

Anstey, M., & Bull, G. (2006). *Teaching and learning multiliteracies: Changing Times, Changing Literacies*. South Australia: Australian Literacy Educators' Association: International Reading Association.

Appadurai, A. (1990). Disjuncture and difference in the global cultural economy. *Theory, Culture & Society*, *7*, 295–310. doi:10.1177/026327690007002017

Archer, L. (2007). Kevin Rudd promises computers for every student. *news.com.au*. Retrieved January 20, 2009, from www.news.com.au/story/0,23599,22754187-2,00.html?from=public_rss

Australian Labor Party. (2007). *The Australian economy needs an education revolution* [policy paper]. Retrieved January 20, 2009, from www.alp.org.au/download/now/education-revolution.pdf

Bamford, A. (2006). *The Wow Factor: Global research compendium of the arts in education*. New York: Waxmann.

Barrentine, P. (Ed.). (1993). *When The Canary Stops Singing*. San Francisco: Berrett-Koehler Publishers.

Barton, D., Hamilton, M., & Ivanic, R. (Eds.). (2000). *Situated literacies: Reading and writing in context*. New York: Routledge.

Bensimon, E. M., & Neumann, A. (1993). *Redesigning Collegiate Leadership*. Baltimore: The Johns Hopkins University Press.

Bruffee, K. A. (1993). *Collaborative learning: Higher education, interdependence, and the authority of knowledge*. Baltimore: Johns Hopkins University Press.

Burns, J. (1978). *Leadership*. New York: Harper & Row.

Chiapello, E. (2004). Evolution and Co-optation. *Third Text, 18*(6), 585–594. doi:10.1080/0952882042000284998

Clark, J. (1996). Reflections on Lichtenstein. *Artonview, 5*, 34–36.

Cobb, N. (1992). *Adolescence: Continuity, change and diversity*. London: Mayfield Publishing Company.

Coorey, P. (2007). Rudd vows education revolution. *The Sydney Morning Herald*, January 23, 2007. Retrieved January 20, 2009, from www.smh.com.au/news/national/rudd-vows-education-revolution/2007/01/22/1169330827940.html?page=fullpage

Cope, B., & Kalantzis, M. (1997). *Productive diversity: A new Australian model for work and management*. Annandale, Australia: Pluto Press.

Cope, B., & Kalantzis, M. (Eds.). (2000). *Multiliteracies: literacy learning and the design of social futures*. New York: Routledge.

Davis, D. (2008). *First we see: The national review of visual education*. Australian Government.

Dickinson, D., & Tabors, P. (Eds.). (2001). *Beginning literacy with language: Young children learning at home and at school*. Baltimore: Paul Brookes.

Digital Natives. Retrieved January 20, 2009, from http://www.digitalnative.org/#about

Drath, W. H., & Paulus, C. J. (1994). *Making Common Sense: Leadership as Meaning Making in a Community of Practice*. Greensboro, NC: Centre for Creative Leadership.

Durrant, C., & Green, B. (1998). *Literacy and the New Technologies in School Education: Meeting the L(IT)erarcy Challenge?"* Presented Paper. Sydney, NSW: NSW Department of Education and Training.

Eisner, E. (2002). *Arts and the creation of mind*. New Haven, CT: Yale University Press.

Fairclough, N. (1995). *Critical discourse analysis: The critical study of language*. London: Longman.

Freebody, P. (2007). Building literacy education: pasts, futures, and "the sum of effort." In A. Simpson (Ed.). *Future Directions in Literacy: International Conversations conference 2007*, (pp. 96 – 114). Sydney: Sydney University Press.

Freebody, P. (2007). *Literacy Education in School: Research perspectives from the past, for the future*. Camberwell, Australia: Australian Council for Educational Research.

Freebody, P., & Luke, A. (1990). Literacies programs: Debates and demands in cultural context. *Prospect: Australian Journal of TESOL, 5*(3), 7–16.

Gardner, H. (1993). *Frames of mind: the theory of multiple intelligences*. New York: Basic Books.

Gee, J. (1994). Orality and literacy: from the savage mind to ways with words. In J., Maybin & J. Clevedon (Eds), *Language and literacy in social practice*. Buckingham, UK: Multilingual Matters Ltd & The Open University.

Gee, J. (2000). The new literacy studies: From 'socially situated' to the work of the social. In Barton, D., Hamilton, M. & Ivanic, R. (Eds.), *Situated literacies: Reading and writing in context*. New York: Routledge.

Gee, J. (2003). *What video games have to teach us about learning and literacy*. New York: Palgrave Macmillan.

GenYes. Retrieved January 20, 2009, from www.genyes.org

Goldman, S. R. (2004). Cognitive aspects of constructing meaning through and across multiple texts. In N. Shuart-Ferris & D. M. Bloome (Eds.), *Uses of intertextuality in classroom and educational research* (pp. 313-347). Greenwich, CT: Information Age Publishing.

Graff, H. (1987). *The legacies of literacy: Continuities and contradictions in western culture and society.* Bloomington and Indianapolis: Indiana University Press.

Green, B. (1988). Subject-specific literacy and school learning: a focus on writing. *Australian Journal of Education, 32*(2), 156–179.

Green, B., & Bigum, C. (1993). Aliens in the classroom. *Australian Journal of Education, 37*(2), 119–141.

Green, B., Hodgen, J., & Luke, A. (1997). Debating literacy in Australia: History lessons and popular f(r)ictions. *Australian Journal of Language and Literacy, 20*(1), 6–24.

Hellriegel, D., Slocum, J., & Woodman, R. (1992). *Organizational Behaviour* (6th Ed.). St Paul, MN: West Publishing Company.

Hendricks, M. (2002). Kids These Days. *Entrepreneur Magazine*, May. Retrieved January 20, 2009, from www.entrepeneur.com/magazine/entrepreneur/2002/may/51084.html

Hirsch, E. D. (1987). *Cultural literacy: What every American needs to know.* Boston: Houghton Mifflin.

Kalantzis, M. (Ed.). (2001). *Transformations in language and learning: Perspectives on multiliteracies.* Melbourne, Australia: Common Ground Publishing.

Kalantzis, M., Cope, B., & Fehring, H. (2002). Multiliteracies: Teaching and learning in the new communications environment. *Primary English Teaching Association, 133*, 1–8.

Kalantzis, M., Cope, B., & Harvey, A. (2003). Assessing multiliteracies and the new basics. *Assessment in Education: Principles . Policy & Practice, 10*(1), 15–26.

Kellner, D. (2001). New technologies/new literacies: Reconstructing education for the new millennium. *International Journal of Technology and Design Education, 11*, 67–81. doi:10.1023/A:1011270402858

Kress, G. (2003). *Literacy in the new media age.* London: Routledge.

Kress, G., & van Leeuwen, T. (2001). *Multimodal discourse: The modes and media of contemporary communication.* London: Arnold.

Kuiper, E., Volman, M., & Terwel, J. (2005). The web as an information resource in K-12 education: strategies for supporting students in searching and processing information. *Review of Educational Research, 75*(3), 285–328. doi:10.3102/00346543075003285

Lankshear, C., & Knobel, M. (2003). *New literacies: Changing knowledge and classroom learning*. Buckingham, UK; Philadelphia: Open University Press.

Lankshear, C., Snyder, I., & Green, B. (2000). *Teachers and Technoliteracy: Managing literacy, technology and learning in schools*. St Leonards, Australia: Allen & Unwin.

Larson, J., & Marsh, J. (2005). *Making Literacy Real: Theories and Practices for Learning and Teaching.* London: Sage Publications.

Luke, A. (2003). Literacy and the Other: A sociological approach to literacy research and policy in multilingual societies. *Reading Research Quarterly, 38*(1), 138–141.

Mantei, J., & Kervin, L. (2007). Looking for clarity amongst the challenges faced by teachers as they consider the role of ICT in classroom literacy learning experiences. In A. Simpson (Ed.), *Future Directions in Literacy: International Conversations conference 2007,* (pp. 170 – 189). Sydney, Australia: Sydney University Press.

Mattessich, P., Murray-Close, M., & Monsey, B. (2004). *Collaboration: What Makes It Work* (2nd Ed.). Saint Paul, MN: Amherst H. Wilder Foundation.

Miller, M. (2001). Out of the Minds of Babes: In school and the workplace the young are guiding their older colleagues through the technical landscape. *Los Angeles Times*. Retrieved January 20, 2009, from: www.genyes.org/news/mindsofbabes

New London Group. (1996). A pedagogy of multiliteracies: Designing social futures. *Harvard Educational Review, 66*(1), 60–92.

New London Group. (2000). A pedagogy of multiliteracies: Designing social futures. In B. Cope & M. Kalantzis (Eds), *Multiliteracies: Literacy learning and the design of social futures* (pp. 9-38). South Yarra, Australia: Macmillan.

Palfrey, J., & Gasser, U. (2008). *Born Digital: Understanding the First Generation of Digital Natives*. New York: Basic Books.

Papert, S. (1998). *Technology in schools, to support the system or to render it obsolete: Thinking about the "impossible."* Miliken Family Foundation. Retrieved January 20, 2009, from www.mff.org/edtech/article.taf?_function=detial&content_uid1=106

Perkin, C. (2006, September 2 - 3). No friend of the big ego. *The Weekend Australian,* p. 19.

Prensky, M. (2001). Digital Natives, Digital Immigrants. *On the Horizon, 9*(5), October 2001. Retrieved January 20, 2009, from http://www.marcprensky.com/writing/Prensky%20-%20Digital%20Natives,%20Digital%20Immigrants%20-%20Part1.pdf

Robinson, K. (2001). *Out of our minds: Learning to be creative*. Chichester, UK: Capstone.

Roblyer, M. (2006). *Integrating Educational Technology into Teaching,* (4th Ed.). Upper Saddle River, NJ: Pearson/Merrill Prentice Hall/International Society for Technology in Education.

Rogoff, B. (2003). *The Cultural Nature of Human Development*. New York: Oxford University Press.

Sawyer, R. K. (2006). *Explaining Creativity*. New York: Oxford University Press.

Scanlon, C. (2009). The natives aren't quite so restless. *The Australian,* p. 33.

Sharpnack, R. (2005). The Power of Shifting Context. In L. Coughlin, E. Wingard & K. Hollihan (Eds.), *Enlightened Power* (pp. 39 - 52). San Francisco, CA: Jossey-Bass.

Shillito, S., Beswick, K., & Baguley, M. (2008). The aims of art education: An analysis of visual art in Tasmania's Essential Learnings Curriculum. *Australian Online Journal of Arts Education, 4*(1), 1–16.

Shriberg, A., Lloyd, C., Shriberg, D., & Williamson, M. (1997). *Practicing Leadership: Principles and Applications*. New York: John Wiley & Sons, Inc.

Solvie, P. (2008). Use of the Wiki: Encouraging preservice teachers' construction of knowledge in reading methods courses. *The Journal of Literacy and Technology, 9*(2), 58–87.

Sowers, R. (1983). The Myth of Collaboration. *American Craft, Dec/Jan, 44 – 45,* 96.

Street, B. (1984). *Literacy in Theory and Practice.* Cambridge, UK: Cambridge University Press.

Unsworth, L. (2001). *Teaching multiliteracies across the curriculum: Changing contexts of text and image in classroom practice*. Buckingham, U.K: Open University Press.

Van Heertum, R., & Shane, J. (2006). A new direction for multiliteracy education. *McGill Journal of Education, 41*(3), 249–265.

Wind, Y. (2006). Managing creativity. *Rotman Magazine,* Spring/Summer, 20 – 23.

Wright, S. (2003). *The Arts, Young Children, and Learning*. Boston: Allyn & Bacon.

Chapter 2
Multimodal, Multiliteracies: Texts and Literacies for the 21st Century

Radha Iyer
Queensland University of Technology, Australia

Carmen Luke
Queensland University of Technology, Australia

ABSTRACT

The shift from traditional definitions of literacy focused upon print, primarily reading and writing, to multiple literacies has highlighted the significance of attending to different modes of text design and multiple forms of knowledge processes. Today's students engage with complex semiotic systems; therefore, while teaching and learning attends principally to print media, multimodality and multiliteracies have become central to effective pedagogical practice. Some teachers have moved away from a singular focus on print texts to incorporating multiple design modes that are linguistic, spatial, visual, gestural and aural – to enable valuable, comprehensive learning for today's multiliterate, multiskilled students. In this chapter, the authors discuss the Design modes proposed by the New London Group (1996; 2000), and the Learning by Design pedagogy advocated by Kalantzis and Cope (2005) to highlight effective learning based on multimodal, multiliteracies. The chapter provides a vignette of a multimodal activity in a primary class and argues for the extension of such learning through the incorporation of multiliteracies. They conclude the chapter by providing a framework for a possible multiliteracies project incorporating multiliteracies pedagogies and learning from the classroom vignette.

INTRODUCTION

The literacy landscape in the 21st century has shifted from a print saturated system to a multimodal semiotic system (Kress, 2003; A. Luke, 1996). While schools celebrate print literacy practices, young children increasingly engage with multimodal, multimedia practices along with print based literacy practices in informal settings. Therefore, as critics (Boulter, 1999; Durrant & Green, 2000; C. Luke, 1997; Lankshear & Knobel, 2003; Mackey, 1994; Unsworth, 2001) observe, changes to literacy practices as increasingly multimodal, plural practice needs to be taken into account.

DOI: 10.4018/978-1-60566-673-0.ch002

In this chapter, we discuss a digital text produced by a primary class using western fairy tales as an illustrative exercise in multimodal activity. Further, the chapter examines the possibility of extending narratives such as personal narratives, fairy tales, myths and legends through a multiliteracies project demonstrating Learning by Design proposed by Kalantzis and Cope (2005). In order to achieve this aim, the chapter examines the theoretical framework and various Designs for learning proposed by the pedagogical approaches of multiliteracies (Kalantzis & Cope 2004; The New London Group, 1996; 2000). In doing so, we recognise the importance of Learning by Design and explore how a shift from a print based to a techno-oriented philosophy of teaching aims at an inclusive, holistic focus on literacy.

The chapter first examines the theoretical framework of pedagogies of multiliteracies and the four knowledge processes. Secondly, the chapter describes the pedagogical actions of a teacher in producing a digital text with her Grade One class as a multimodal activity developed from the four knowledge processes. Drawing on these theoretical and lived understandings, the chapter then proposes a schema for using narratives as a basis for real life projects utilising various Designs and knowledge processes. More generally, the chapter suggests ways that can extend classroom activities to incorporate multicultural knowledges, thereby producing deeper insights in understanding and gaining from social and cultural differences and, in turn, what this implies for literacy. We conclude by discussing how a multiliteracies framework helps to develop a local/global interface and reinforces the social and cultural context of literacy.

One Literacy Leads to Another

The arrival of ICTs in classrooms has meant that reading, writing, visual, spatial and aural literacies have changed considerably (C.Luke, 2000; C. Luke, 2003; Jewitt, 2005a; Jewitt, 2005b; Kenner, 2004; Kress, 2003; Kress & van Leeuwen, 2001; Nixon, 2003). There has been a substantial dissolving of the linear, rigidly compartmentalised literacies of earlier times and recognition of multicultural, multimodal, multiliteracies as necessary to a relevant pedagogy. Building on concepts proposed by Kalantzis and Cope (2000a, 2000b, 2004, 2005), in this chapter we explore the powerful intermix of print and visual literacies through the representational means of ICTs. In the process, it is discovered that an engagement with these Designs calls almost instinctively for the incorporation of other Designs such as gestural and aural, illustrating the multifaceted, complex literacies children engage with every day.

We present here the digital storybook project undertaken by a group of twenty-eight Grade One students as an exercise in multimodal literacy activities: the teacher and children imagined a project that was inclusive of speech, gestures, images and text. In creating the digital storybook, a popular children's narrative was modified through the superimposition of western fairy tale characters. In the process of re-writing the text, the popular fairy tales were also modified to suit the narrative and visuals, thereby successfully re-creating a new, imaginative version of both the fairy tales and the original text of the narrative. More importantly, the intermix of the different Designs and student creativity within the narrative and visuals shifted the entire process from a literacy activity using ICTs to an imaginative and original exercise invested with an engagement with different knowledge processes. This process served to foreground complex understandings of different literacies by primary level students. Building on a rather serendipitous exercise by an enterprising teacher, this chapter suggests ways that can extend literacy engagements into a multiliteracies project. Thus, one of the significant questions posed in this chapter is: given the multimodal knowledges students bring to school, how might a teacher extend these knowledges through multiliteracies pedagogic practices to illustrate literacy as an inclusive, fluid practice?

Table 1. The four knowledge processes and their equivalent curriculum orientations (adapted from Kalantzis & Cope, 2005, p. 73)

Situated learning ↔ Experiencing the known and the new	Overt instruction ↔ Conceptualising by naming and theorising
Critical framing ↔ Analysing functionally and critically	Transformative or transformed practice ↔ Applying knowledge correctly and creatively

BACKGROUND

Teachers today are faced with the challenge of using multimedia techniques and multimodal literacies to provide a holistic learning experience. As Cope and Kalantzis (2000) reaffirm, "literacy is in its nature multimodal – a matter of visual as well as linguistic design" (p. 234). Teachers have to re-envision their teaching to include the diversity of their students in situated contexts. The shift from print based literacy practices to multimodal, multiliteracies has demanded a change in the manner in which teachers approach curriculum, planning and teaching. Moving away from the transmission mode has meant an insightful engagement at the curriculum orientation level with the four knowledge processes (Kalantzis & Cope 2004, p. 64) in a conscious and critical manner. Briefly, as explained by Kalantzis and Cope (2005, p.73), these four knowledge processes are: experiencing the known and the new, conceptualising through naming and theorising, analysing functionally and critically, applying appropriately and creatively. In Table 1 we represent the four knowledge processes and the curriculum orientations. In Table 1 we represent the four knowledge processes and the curriculum orientations.

Multiliteracies: The Concept

Since literacy assumed a central role in education, various conceptions of literacy have had historical prominence (Lankshear & Knobel, 2003, p.10). Various forms and models of literacy and literate practices were advocated since the 1980s with theorists such as Hirsch (1987) proposing cultural literacy, and the concepts of 'critical literacy', techno literacy becoming popular in 1990s. Prominent models of critical literacy have been developed such as the four resource model (Freebody & A. Luke, 1990), and the three- dimension model (Green, 1988).

More recently, advances in ICTs, workplace and educational requirements have revamped the notions of multimodal and multimedia literacy as originally proposed by the New London Group (1996; 2000). Through informed debates on the changing demands of literacy, the authors contend that today's students have complex requirements of literacy beyond the skills of reading and writing. Learners are faced with a challenging environment of local and global changes compounded by a complex amalgam of technological innovations from the cell phone, Wi-Fi, PDAs (personal digital assistant) to communicative exchange on email, FaceBook, You Tube or MySpace. Thus, the first challenge signifies social, cultural and linguistic diversity and acknowledgement of difference, while the second proposes the intrusion and inclusion of various digital technologies in learning. Multimodality, or the application of various Designs such as linguistic, visual, audio, spatial and gestural are perceived as integral to contemporary learning. Making meaning of texts which immerse students has, thus, become a complex process of engaging with new knowledges and new forms of learning.

For the New London Group (2000) that initiated the notion of multiliteracies, the concept has a holistic and inclusive meaning. It is a means to comprehend literacy curriculum as extending beyond formal school learning and as inclusive of productive participation in the community. Multiliteracies is, moreover, dedicated to coming to terms with the post-Fordist society that is invested in mobility, fluidity and a knowledge society that promotes multiple forms of semiotic systems (see Kalantzis & Cope, 2005). Multiliteracies is an attempt to comprehend and target the multiple text forms that have resulted from new technologies and new media forms, through a pedagogy that allows students to comprehend and deal with the "increasing complexity and interrelationship of different modes of meaning" (The New London Group, 2000, p. 25). Going beyond print based technologies, the New London Group considers all forms of semiotic systems as texts – from digital modes to music and inclusive of formal and informal texts.

Multiliteracies and multimodal literacies are a comprehensive response to the mobile semiotics of contemporary society. Flows of people, images and ideas (see Appadurai, 1990), have meant the impact is experienced globally as well as locally and contextually (Kalantzis, Cope & Harvey, 2003; The New London Group, 1996). Along with New Literacy Studies (Street, 1998; 2003), multiliteracies framework has as its central focus a socially just and culturally inclusive curriculum. Further, informed by critical pedagogy and critical literacy, multiliteracies has, at its conceptual centre, a transformative pedagogy aimed at effective learning across social and cultural differences, and across different learning styles. To attend to the change in social futures, multiliteracies has, at its nexus, student knowledges, lived experiences and student centred resources. A significant step undertaken by multiliteracies advocates and practitioners is both the inclusion of students' life worlds and a serious consideration of informal literacies alongside formal school based literacies. Subsequently, students' social and cultural life world experiences are considered central and intrinsic for text production. Thus, studies by Labbo (2000), Labbo, Sprague, Montero and Font (2000), Marsh (2006), Millard (2005), and Pahl (2003), illustrate how print and multimodal texts are produced from students' prior knowledge acquisition. Newfield et al., (2003), illustrate a successful integration of linguistic, social and cultural diversity in their project that resulted in student agency and a transformative pedagogy. Multiliteracies and multimodal literacies more than traditional literacy provide a space for cultural diversity to be reaffirmed within formal learning while providing a site for an interlinked, intertextual transfer of knowledges through different meaning making modes (C. Luke, 2000, p. 73).

Central to multiliteracies is the concept of Design. The New London Group indicates the numerous ways by which signification occurs. More recently, as Kalantzis and Cope (2005) describe it, "there is a nice ambiguity in the word 'design'… Design can denote morphology or the sense of invisible inner structures or inherent relationships of cause and effect" (p. 41). Kalantzis and Cope (2005) use Design in a comprehensive manner to denote "agency" as the "stuff of the characteristically self-conscious pedagogical moves, teaching frameworks and organisational forms of education as we currently understand it" (p. 41). In brief, as Falk (2001) observes, for the New London Group, Design expresses "the active role of the literacy learner in constructing new meaning from existing resources" (p. 314). Because Design rejects isolated, abstract and decentralised learning, it demands "production of the new rather than replication of the old" (Kress, 2000, p. 141). In Design, the learner is actively creating and re-creating while having choices in learning that did not exist in traditional print based models of literacy.

The modes or Design concepts are: linguistic, visual, audio, spatial and gestural; however, the New London Group do not perceive each of these literacies as singular and isolated from other literacies. Rather, they advance the concept of an integrated learning experience that is particular to the social and cultural context of the learner. In this framework, multimodality is of particular relevance as it "represents the patterns of interconnection among the other modes" (The New London Group, 2000, p. 25). Multiliteracies aims to target literacy practices currently favoured in schools as well as literacy practices children acquire at home, and in other informal settings. In this sense, multiliteracies approaches are mindful and inclusive of the diverse and complex cultural perspectives of learners and their diverse learning styles.

The pedagogy of multiliteracies, as discussed by the New London Group (2000), is constituted of four components, or knowledge processes: situated practice, overt instruction, critical framing and transformed practice. Kalantzis and Cope (2000a) argue that, when all four aspects are combined, these are "enhanced and transformed by the others" (p. 240). Situated practice enables teachers to draw on the socio-cultural practices of learners, providing crucial learning sequences that are important to learner identities. Overt instruction from the teacher is explicit modelling and explanation, or theorisation, provided to help students develop deep insights and comprehensive understanding. Adopting a critical framing lens to analyse helps to produce innovative work by developing the critical and creative capabilities of students. Transformed practices are the demonstrable ways by which performatives of the task are determined. Transformed practice provides critical feedback both to the teacher and to the students about applicability and creativity invested in the task. As Kalantzis and Cope advocate (2000a, p. 240), the interlinking between these four pedagogical processes is significant and must be kept in mind. Situated practice when linked with and scaffolded by overt instruction becomes a mode for analytic and reflective thinking. Overt instruction – because it works on the lived and situated experiences of the learner and operates as teacher scaffolding and mediation – is far removed from linear teacher directed learning. Similarly, when critical framing is linked with transformative practice, it is grounded in reflective practice and becomes critique that is defended by praxis rather than an abstract critique of ideology. However, Kalantzis and Cope (2000a) warn that there is a danger in perceiving these in "lock-step learning progression" (p. 242); crucially, the pedagogy of multiliteracies proposes that one can lead into the other in ways that continually refresh the learning experience (see Kalantzis & Cope, 2000a).

For students who engage with the four knowledge processes there is deep understanding and proactive learning:

- **Experiencing**: through the known and the new, where the evidence data from the prior knowledge and life experience of the learner is combined with immersion in new knowledge and new experience in meaningful settings.
- **Conceptualising**: abstract concepts and theoretical synthesis by the process of naming and theorising. This enables the learner to define, apply concepts and comprehend the abstract generalised meanings in concepts and visual representations.
- **Analysing**: analysing, interpreting functions capably, through the comprehension of the role of knowledge and critically by analysing purpose and intentions.
- **Applying**: knowledge appropriately and creatively by understanding suitable situations to apply knowledge and extending it to create new knowledges.

Teachers in the primary grades often use narratives and fairy tales as a means to enable students to engage in various knowledge processes and to achieve literacy. Envision a group of lower primary students who are from diverse backgrounds. Imagine some students from backgrounds such as China, Bangladesh, India, Hong Kong and Japan; as a teacher you are invariably confronted with complex social, cultural, and linguistic diversity. To involve them in literacy lessons, you may read well known western fairy stories. This approach would reflect a teacher who is fairly confident of the need to expose children from middle class families to get familiar with the highly popular Disney world. Then you would want them to extend the learning by assisting them to add their own knowledge of narratives and Designs. You develop a unit of work where you explore a digital story book. However, you realise it will be a brief project. Moreover, it is a multimodal unit of learning. How can you extend it further to become a multiliteracies project? Thus, a crucial question would be: how can a multimodal project on myths and legends be extended into a real life project; a topic that is meaningful to the lives and lived experiences of students in terms of the four knowledge processes, its curriculum orientations and Design modes?

In the following section, we provide an actual scenario where the teacher engaged in a multimodal project with her Grade One class to produce a PowerPoint project that was presented to the parents at the end of term (Iyer, 2007). While outlining the project we would like to emphasise that the vignette was not a multiliteracies project. We present the vignette as a means to discuss how a multimodal project can be developed into a multiliteracies project.

MULTIMODAL EXPERIENCE: VIGNETTE

In a study that was conducted in a primary school in Australia, Julie[1], a primary grade teacher was observed over a term conducting literacy sessions with a Grade One class (Iyer, 2007). Julie had daily reading aloud sessions and used these to discuss themes from stories and to draw on the knowledges students brought to school – in a way inviting them to share their 'virtual school bag' (Thomson, 2002). This was followed by students sometimes reading aloud and by writing activities, with the teacher often focusing on the narrative text type, inviting the students to write about their weekend or any such similar non-school activity. Although trained in the traditional mode of teaching, Julie was interested in moving beyond teaching sound–symbol and simple narrative text types to students. While classes were incorporating computers or ICT based learning, it was more as 'edutainment' (Underwood, 2000), while Julie was interested in integrating learning through computers. Therefore, she engaged in developing a digital story book, inviting the students to re-write a text by drawing on fairy tale characters. The story taken for this purpose was Alexei Tolstoy's *The Great Big Enormous Turnip*.

Digital storybooks are understood as narratives written and produced through the medium of ICT such as PowerPoint, often integrating Paint software to produce hand drawn images to complement the stories. The students were familiar to a certain degree with the use of computers and technology as the teacher often used Inspiration software to demonstrate concepts. However, the experience of writing and producing a digital story book with the freedom to use and employ fairy tale characters was, indeed, a novel one. Moreover, using technology with Grade One students who were only just beginning to read and write, and employing different groups to do sets of activities that could be combined later to become the digital storybook, was a daunting task.

In the following sections, we discuss how the unit of work became a multimodal digital story production drawing comprehensively on the four knowledge processes. The four knowledge processes were fully ingrained in the entire unit. A detailed discussion follows on how these knowledge processes were integrated throughout each stage of the unit plan that was taught over the second semester of the calendar year. First, a sample road map for the unit is outlined in Table 2.

Table 2. Sample plan for a digital narrative

Rationale	• Language learners require creative means to share their known knowledges of language, vocabulary writing skills and narratives. Such knowledges can be further developed through scaffolded discussion, and activities that draw on multimodal, multiliteracies.
Stage One	• Read the original story of *The Great Big Enormous Turnip.* • Examine aspects of the story book, such as the vocabulary, visuals and paralinguistic cues. • Discuss the narrative aspects: beginning, middle and end. Discuss characters, role, and story progression.
Stage Two	• Discuss characters, progression of theme and conclusion through the question – what if the story had different characters? Elicit from students the characters they would prefer. List characters on white board. • Display student responses on a concept map. Map the sequence of the story on the white board. List sentences required for the introduction, transitions and the conclusion. • List any term or phrase students decide to include.
Stage Three	• Investigate student preparedness, interest and knowledge of ICT. Discuss key board skills and computer use to establish knowledge base in technology. • Invite parents and senior students to promote preparedness. • Show and discuss examples of digitally produced stories and allow students to explore PowerPoint and Paint software. • Provide worksheets to train students in basic techniques of Power Point, Word and Paint software.
Stage Four	• Form groups to work on one aspect of the story and its visual features. Negotiate student preferences. • Invite groups to choose one sentence from the shared narrative produced and displayed in class. • Hand a copy of the jointly produced narrative to each group and ask groups to choose the sentence they want to focus for the text and visuals. • Ask groups to draw and colour on paper the image to be drawn on Paint initially and then transferred to PowerPoint slide. • Make arrangements to save work on Word file.
Stage Five	• Scaffold groups one at a time to ensure they are on task; applaud efforts. • Rectify any writing errors by asking students to read and spell. • Scaffold group's effort to draw using Paint software. • Once all students produce their slide, collate into one Power Point file.
Stage Six	• Print slides to be handed to students to read and practice. • Conduct individual reading practice and training in tone, style, and gestures. • Conduct group practice: Group students in pairs and scaffold each group for practice in tone, style and gesture. • Mock presentation in class. • Final presentation to parents.

Experiencing the Known and the New

At the outset, Julie engaged in situated practice to bridge the known and the new, getting students to share their knowledges. There was active discussion around fairy tales with which the class was familiar, and characters were closely examined to check their suitability to the task. The teacher engaged in a number of critical questions to ascertain that they knew what a narrative text type consists of, and although the class consisted of different ethnicities, she also found the children were familiar with different western fairy tales.

As new ideas stemmed from experiencing the known, the production of the digital story book became a multimodal project. The discourses of fantasy and myth creation alternated with curriculum discourses of narrative as a text type. Creating a digital story book provided greater flexibility in the choice of characters; thus Julie used the framework of the story to create the order of the characters, and a suitable ending that the class wanted which, of course, was different to the original.[2] Thus, while the digital story was being mapped on a well known story, it was being modified through a list of innovative characters and a completely new ending. Through a concept map, Julie also had to introduce the idea of a cohesive story with an explicit discussion of introduction, body, and conclusion. The entire process of creating a narrative was grounded in the lived experience of students telling stories and narratives, rather than through teacher dominated overt instruction.

In experiencing the new, moreover, the students had to decide what software to use and how to use it. For example, the class had to decide whether to use Paint software to draw images or to use images from books and scan them for the PowerPoint presentation. In order to succeed in this highly complex task, the students had to develop new skills and gain confidence with unfamiliar software and technology. Using technology for the purpose of creating images enabled students to focus on the symbolism of including images, rather than understanding them simply as decorative embellishments to the story.

Conceptualising by Naming and Theorising

In engaging with conceptualising by naming, the students attended to the concepts of theme, story line, narrative, genre, and coherent text. Linguistic concepts discussed were: orientation, complication and re-orientation. Conventions of vocabulary, sentence structure, transitions, and structural cohesion were discussed. In visual Design, concepts of colour, framing, slide background, colour contrasts, font size, and paralinguistic cues were discussed. Julie showed the class a number of ways to use Paint software by modelling different font sizes, and different shapes for the face and body, thereby providing students with imaginative examples to help complete the task. The explicit, overt instruction in PowerPoint and Paint software through exemplars and teacher modelling resulted in higher order thinking and deep understanding of the group activities students were meant to do.

Further, in conceptualising by theorising, students discussed the importance of the narrative for the digital story book. Julie used interactive CD ROMs to outline the importance of narrative progression, and her introduction of the concept map of a narrative structure enabled students to learn specific aspects of narrative continuity. Finally, students theorised the importance of a contextual ending, thereby interweaving the traditional fairy tales and the mythic past with present practical situations. Theorisation also involved students trading off the past for the practicality of the task, creatively deciding on the selection and mix of characters and discussing the significance of each character in specific fairy tales. We reproduce two of the slides (Figure 1) prepared by students using Microsoft Paint technology:

Analysing Functionally and Critically

The scaffolded learning provided students with adequate conceptual knowledge to begin developing deep understanding of the story line and proceed toward judicious editing of the story to suit their purpose. Students chose certain characters over others, and there was joyful intermix of various characters regardless of the actual role these occupied in the original tale. Cinderella, Sleeping Beauty, the Big Bad Wolf, the Woodcutter, the Three Little Pigs and Rapunzel were picked, while charming princes and witches were left out. Significantly, the framework of a narrative was understood accurately to begin with an appropriate protagonist, in this case, Pinocchio.

Analysing functionally and critically meant students had to comprehend the metalanguage of various Designs such as linguistic, visual, spatial, gestural, and audio. The students were not only able to articulate the new, or use characters in a creative manner. They were able to discuss frames and background for images, and appropriate voice over for audio; in short, developing a language to describe the processes of meaning making (Kalantzis & Cope, 2000a, p. 246). Similarly,

Figure 1. Student work samples

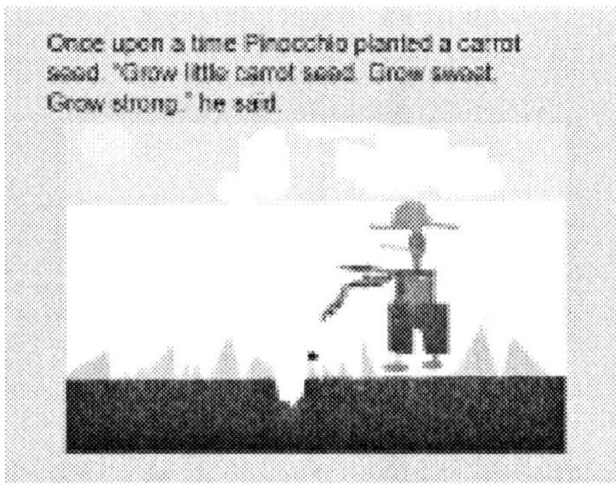

the tools of PowerPoint, and Paint software were conceptualised and theorised before being applied. Thus, font size, background colour, colour combinations, slide transitions and Designs were comprehended and discussed before being creatively applied.

Applying Appropriately and Creatively

The scaffolding over, Julie asked students to create their own Designs, practice the audio presentation in pairs (which required developing correct tone, pitch, and pace) and, in terms of ICT, collate slides done by different groups into one appropriate PowerPoint presentation. This required students to collaborate and decide the sequence of the slides, providing a creative order of the characters engaged in retrieving the carrot. Appropriate critical questions and scaffolding by peers and teacher enabled students to move beyond the given framework and to be creative in deciding the framework of the story and its ending. The transformative practice occurred with the students reading the digital story aloud in pairs to their parents. Thus, with its text, visual and sound units, the project had elements of hypermodality that Lemke (2002), describes as "semiotic artifacts in which signifiers on different scales of syntagmatic organization are linked in complex networks or webs" (p. 300).

Julie acknowledged that this was not conceived of as a multiliteracies project; it was a digital story writing task, using multimodal techniques of various texts to engage in literacy practices. Julie reflected that it had been conceived only as an extension to the daily literacy practice of reading stories, with an emphasis on comprehension; a project that accidentally evolved through student discussion and critical understanding into a digital story book. Julie conceded that if it had been a multiliteracies project it would have been much more complex, devised as episodic, cyclic learning through extensive engagement with a number of Design repertoires and through a number of different outcomes.

Yet, it was an important pedagogical investment. In all this extended activity, the teacher was shifting her practice from a transmission model of teaching to a constructivist model or, as Kalantzis and Cope (2005) term it, an "epistemologically grounded theory of pedagogy", where the focus is on understanding "how knowing happens" (p. 70). The teacher as facilitator and co-collaborator enabled the children to be creators of text and to have as much priority and input as the teacher herself. Appreciably, through play and instruction, Julie built on the knowledges the students brought to school; thus, the extended exercise in multimodal literacies was an attempt to recognise and value the potential of students, and to consider them capable of creatively engaging in a problem based task.

The project outlined above as a multimodal activity was not without its problems. Julie had to accommodate students who were on either end of the continuum with regards to literacy and ICT knowledges. Some students had adequate literacy skills and were proficient in the use of technology while others were at the beginning stages of reading and writing. While Julie overcame the difference in skills by pairing students to work collaboratively, there were multiple tasks that required careful planning. In conducting the project, Julie acknowledged that teachers desiring to conduct multimodal projects should acquire knowledge of multiliteracies.

Although a complex project for the primary level, multimodal exercises such as the one described here reaffirm student knowledges and highlight the value of formal learning. The multimodal approach demonstrates how cultural and knowledge boundaries can be blurred, re- mixed and re-texted. The new relationships demonstrated by the new images and the new text also demanded new, critical and creative knowledges from students. Their choice of Design modes, images and text demonstrated different knowledges and different learning styles.

Furthermore, literacy knowledges were demonstrated by the manner in which the modes were chosen, the pedagogic approaches of the teacher, teacher and student facilitation and the final artefact. Multimodal approaches, as studies have shown (Kress, 2000; Kress, Jewitt, Ogborn & Tsatsarelis, 2001; see also Kress et al., 2005; Lemke, 1998), use multiple Design modes, illustrating the diverse ways in which students make meaning. The conceptual change in knowledges that were utilized and produced indicated a shift from "collection to connection" (C. Luke, 2003, p. 400) whereby semiotic systems enabled students to re- write traditional print based texts with a semiotically enriched multimodal production.

Learning from the Vignette

The question that arises from this vignette is: how can a multiliteracies project evolve in a primary class with a diverse group of students? We now turn to developing a sample project, building on the knowledge gained from Julie's practice and from multiliteracies pedagogy. A project directed by the following question could be suitable for a diverse group of learners: What stories do people have to share?

The knowledge domains targeted would be as much literacy as Arts, Studies of Society, and Science. The project is aimed at applying productive pedagogies (Education Queensland, 2006) and literacy models developed in Australia. Productive pedagogies emphasises intellectual quality and connectedness to the world. This project highlights deep understanding of narrative histories and cultural knowledges. When students are asked to share stories, there is connectedness of formal learning with informal lived experiences. Diversity becomes central when the teacher encourages students to bring in artefacts or stories from their own cultures. The teacher could begin by familiarising students with fairy tales and narratives from different countries such as Chinese fairy tale *Mulan*, Papuan fairy tale, *The Cassowary* and *The Magic Almonds,* Samoan legend, *The Legend of Lea and Lea* and from India, *Tales from the Panchatantra.*

The project could also involve inviting a number of community members from various cultural communities – including Indigenous elders – to work with students; ICT experts and parents who are scientists or artists could help students or provide advisory sessions. The project could target the following texts as outcomes that could be provided to each group created in the class:

- **Puppet Theatre or Claymation**: storyboard 'My Myth/ My Fairy Tale'.
- **Radio talk**: Sharing cultural histories, myths and narrations about self which

involve linguistic, aural and spatial Design aspects.

- **Collage:** pictures and images of various lands, peoples, monuments and flora and fauna with brief notes. Images of cultural artefacts, mythical characters and heroes with brief descriptions.
- **Process drama:** enacting a short snippet from a legend or folk tale; dress ups and voice overs to accompany the drama.
- **ICT and webpage**: Webpage of different racial or ethnic groups, cultures ancient and present.
- **Booklet of cultures**: stories from different lands; scientific or geographic trail of different racial groups.

The project is situated in literacy as a social and cultural practice and draws on productive pedagogies (Education Queensland, 2006), to propose a close examination of the shared histories that students bring to learning. This is linked to their life worlds, to various Key Learning Area (KLAs) or subjects at school and, importantly, emphasises attention to cultural diversity and history as a positive difference. Greater awareness of the self and appreciation of difference could occur when members of the community are invited to talk on different racial and ethnic groups, and different myths, folk tales and legends from different parts of the world. This is particularly important in a media saturated world of western fairy tales and a Disney-fied world of popular culture.

In this project, learning will be based on realistic awareness-raising among young learners on issues of links between different cultures and peoples. During the project, a number of learning episodes would be scheduled with the entire class participating in learning, and the final text outcomes could be produced by individual groups in the class. Teacher, community member mentors and senior students of the school could be facilitators rather than knowledge experts as a multiliteracies project envisions on-going and collaborative learning. The four knowledge processes (Kalantzis & Cope, 2005) at work in this project are set out in Table 3, below:

Throughout the multiliteracies project different Design modes can be applied. Drawing on the New London Group's (2000, p. 26) Design elements, the following are proposed (Table 4).

Texts can be designed using the vast range of choices that are available, and as the New London Group (2000, p. 29) state, the concept of Design indicates not just a use of the modes of meaning available but also transformation and the end product which is the 're-Designed' meaning making mode. Pedagogy therefore is conceptualised as a complex site where situated practice draws on the learner's modes and experiences; overt instruction redefines the known modes of Design into novel forms through explicit instruction in metalanguage; critical framing provides opportunities for learners to analyse and question purposes of different modes; and transformative practice assists in applying the Designs and meaning making modes in a critical and creative manner (The New London Group, 2000).

FUTURE TRENDS

The chapter outlined how multimodality and multiliteracies are significant to the literacy practices of today's students. In so doing, it illustrated the constructive use of multimodality by a teacher in the primary grades and the digital text that was the productive outcome from student engagement with different Design modes. The chapter also reiterated the pressing need to move beyond multimodal productions to real life multiliteracies projects that interweave knowledges across the curriculum. Central to the multiliteracies project is the aim of enabling students transit from passive bodies to proactive, dialogic beings making meaning and changing the practices of reading and writing across the curriculum. The vignette studied here is a micro study with one teacher and

Table 3. The project and the four knowledge processes

Experiencing the Known	Experiencing the New
• Share knowledge of stories from different countries. • Narration about the cultural self/ stories about childhood: Where do I come from? • Share cultural artefacts: Show and Tell and collage. • Concept mapping with teacher- a story on the cultural self.	• Learn new information about countries and peers. • Learn about cultures and artefacts. • Invite Indigenous elders and other community members from different countries to share stories, myths and folk tales. • Visit by scientist to talk about different races. • Explore ICTs: websites on different cultures.
Conceptualising by Naming • Learn schema of narrative genre; fairy tales, myths, folk tales. Apply schema to mind mapping. • Apply schema to writing stories about self. • Discuss indigenous community values of respect for Dreamtime stories.	**Conceptualising by Theorising** • Identify origins of different races. • Theorise how themes of legends are tied to nature/environment/ creation. • Identify similar/dissimilar themes in folk/fairytales. • Identify Design aspects of webpage.
Analysing Functionally • The use of oral tradition in story telling. • The importance of gender; the use of magic, animals in fairytales and legends. • Identify the various aspects of a website and the combination of elements to create an impact. • Analyse characters in myths/legends for example, qualities of a hero. • Draw images of fairy tale creatures, heroes and yourself for collage. **Applying Appropriately** • Create your own story and text with members of the class for radio talk. • Produce collage with depictions of different mythical characters, images of heroes, mythical animals, and self as narratives for presentation. • Produce the text for the puppet theatre on 'My myth'.	**Analysing Critically** • How people of diverse race differ in terms of colour of skin and features (physically, socially). • How are people similar in terms of living, celebrating, socialising. • Attempt different narrative endings to fairy tales, myths/ your own story. • Survey peers on food, customs, festivals, myths and creation stories. • Research the similarities between myths and folk tales from different lands. • Critically analyse myths on the environment and elements. • Discuss why it is important to share and live together. **Analysing Creatively** • Write a report on similarities and difference between people of different races, lands. • Manipulate gender relationships in fairy tales; myths. • Present process drama to convey message of shared history of people on themes of good and evil. • Produce a webpage that can be loaded on intranet site.

it is, in this sense, partial; however, the proposal for a multiliteracies project is based on theories that are still being expanded and extended but also in various stages of application to classroom practices. In Australia, the multiliteracies approach has been significantly adopted (see Kalantzis & Cope, 2005), yet the global uptake and impact of multiliteracies and multimodal approaches

Table 4. Design modes and elements

Linguistic Mode	Audio Mode	Visual Mode
Narrative text type Report writing Script writing for role play Radio talk script Notes for class presentation and PowerPoint	Voice control Intonation Tone Pauses; speed of speech Voice projection, volume and pitch	Props Vector, size, shape of images Colour and white space; borders Costumes Perspective Concept maps
Gestural Mode Behaviour (group/ individual) Posture Sensually/tactilely handling clay, collage items, artefacts Kinesics in role play	**Spatial Mode** Performer positions in role play Movement Proxemics Layout of collage Layout of Power Point	

requires deeper study. Further, multiliteracies projects require deeper integration into subject specific learning so that every discipline is oriented toward incorporating Learning Designs and applying knowledge processes. While multiliteracies approaches have been widely incorporated by Australian teachers, there remains an urgent need to recognise the value of multiple semiotic modes and students as active creators of meaning making. Further, instead of singular classes doing multiliteracies projects, we urge a broader across the curriculum integration of multiliteracy approaches, and sustained efforts through multiple projects that consider flexible time periods for the fruitful completion of a project. As was demonstrated in the vignette and cued in the multiliteracies project outlined above, acknowledging a productive integration of diversity and cultural context must be central to achieve maximum learning. As Kalantzis and Cope (2005) indicate, schools that adopt the multiliteracies and multimodal approach will, among other commitments, "be more transparent and accountable"; "foster lateral communications between learners" and "foster digital literacy" (p. 154).

CONCLUSION

To reiterate, in a post-Fordist society that is fragmented and fluid, multiple forms of semiotic systems, social and cultural diversity are evident. Teaching and learning occurs within a multilingual, multicultural context, and teachers require a deep understanding of the pluralistic composition of their classes. As Fairclough (2000, p. 171) observes, multiliteracies encompasses the twin notions of cultural hybridity and multimodality. These two aspects denote attention to the multicultural nature of many societies, communities and neighbourhoods, and thus the importance of multiple text Designs. Attention to the four knowledge processes enables teachers to address and incorporate both cultural hybridity and multimodality in their pedagogical practice and engage with learners and learning. In a multiliteracies context such as outlined above, experiencing the known and the new provides opportunities for students to showcase lived experience and establish relatedness to learning. In conceptualising, students learn the metalanguage of the discipline and move toward higher order skills of problem solving and deductive reasoning. With a diverse group of learners, conceptualising by naming and theorising provides an opportunity to express, recognise and accept diverse cultural knowledges. In analysing functionally, students come to understand the structures and processes of the real world, locating knowledge in cultural settings, and moving on to critically framing, "comparative and cross-cultural analysis" (Kalantzis & Cope, 2005, p. 86-87). In the vignette and the sample project described above, applying exemplifies knowing the world deeply and extending relationships between cultures. The multimodal activity practised by Julie and the multiliteracies project outlined above encompass the Design elements or meaning making modes – linguistic, visual, spatial, gestural and audio. The difference lies in multiliteracies providing a site for student engagement with real life problems and learning, along with an integrated curriculum and active implementation of productive pedagogies.

The above is, indeed, only a sketch of the complex project of multiliteracies. The multiliteracies approach is invested in productive pedagogies and ensure best practice, high quality teaching by promoting metalanguage awareness, higher order thinking, analysis, synthesis, and evaluation. Multiliteracies promotes deep understanding of various interrelated yet diverse concepts and Designs; furthermore it presents knowledge as problematic by allowing students to manipulate and challenge, in this case, stories that people share, in order to create and be innovative.

Multiliteracies is in its formative years and has, as any major pedagogical shift, challenges that include teachers being mindful of an on-going focus on problem solving, critical thinking and higher order thinking; targeting key concepts so that there is adequate knowledge being developed. At the level of achievement it would involve a high degree of coordination of community members and teachers, joint collaborative work across key learning areas, and positioning students as knowledge producers.

The value of gaining deep knowledge of different Designs and thereby a holistic learning experience through multiliteracies projects cannot be discounted. The concept of multiliteracies underpins literacy as a social and cultural practice and takes into account the cultural, social, and linguistic diversity in contemporary classrooms. Through a pedagogy based on multiliteracies, teachers become critical facilitators of learning by acknowledging the potential of providing agency to students and by helping students develop critical awareness through on-going critical framing. Teachers take serious account of the complex and intersecting diversity of gender, class, ethnic, religious, regional and sexual cultures present in their classes. Moreover, they become aware of difference between dominant/ non-dominant, margin/ centre, self/other perspectives and attempt to mediate these through collaborative, shared, deep knowledges.

As Kalantzis and Cope (2005) emphasise, schools that adopt learning by Design, an essential component of multiliteracies, will "harness and build upon the energies of learners", "blur the physical and institutional boundaries between school and the wider world of family, community and workplace", and promote "learner diversity" which ensures acknowledgement of difference and a cohesive learning environment (pp. 154-155). In terms of students as cultural beings, multiliteracies provide a platform for exploring the complexities of diverse cultures, and collaborative work. Following Vygotsky, Kalantzis and Cope (2005), view multiliteracies as a"social [rather] than a individual psychological construct," with learning by Design as "acts of knowing" and learners as agents of knowing (p. 30). Multiliteracies promotes reflective learning, and a classroom where learning occurs at alternative starting points, learning styles and patterns of engagement (Kalantzis & Cope, 2005, p. 32). As Cazden (2000) affirms, "the Multiliteracies framework stresses the importance of opportunities for learning new discourse skills, oral and written, through a lifetime of changing social and employment contexts" (p. 261). In classrooms composed of multiple forms of diversity, schools must attempt to develop, as Kalantzis and Cope (2000b) advocate, "an ability to engage in the difficult dialogues that are an inevitable part of negotiating diversity" (p. 139). Sharing stories of the cultural self and of different cultures, ethnic and racial group through the learning by Design mode and knowledge processes develops multiple forms of identity, a shared membership of the local and global contexts and, importantly, "extension of cultural repertoires appropriate to the range of contexts where difference has to be negotiated" (Kalantzis & Cope, 2000b, p. 139).

Significantly, as A. Luke(2003) points out, "teachers [are] struggling with recognition of difference…have difficulty dealing with linguistic and cultural diversity, with issues of gendered equity of participation in classrooms, with the inclusion of kids with learning difficulties"(p. 74). To overcome such difficulties, as Allan Luke (2003), Cazden (2000) and Kalantzis and Cope (2000b) indicate, schools need to focus on intellectual connectedness, pluralism and diversity that complements rather than opposes, and productive learning that can occur when difference is recognised and interwoven in learning, in brief, a global classroom that attends to the social and cultural contexts of its students.

REFERENCES

Appadurai, A. (1990). Disjuncture and difference in the global cultural economy. *Theory, Culture and Society, 7*, 295-310. Falk, I. (2001). Literacy by Design, not default: Social capital's role in literacy learning. *Journal of Research in Reading, 24*(3), 313–323.

Boulter, J. D. (1999). *Writing space: The computer, hypertext, and the history of writing.* Hillsdale, NJ: Lawrence Erlbaum.

Cazden, C. (2000). Taking cultural differences into account. In B. Cope & M. Kalantzis (Eds.), *Multiliteracies: Literacy learning and the design of social futures* (pp. 249-266). London: Routledge.

Cope, B., & Kalantzis, M. (2000). Design for social futures. In B. Cope & M. Kalantzis (Eds.), *Multiliteracies: Literacy learning and the design of social futures* (pp. 203- 234). London: Routledge.

Durrant, C., & Green, B. (2000). Literacy and the new technologies in school education: Meeting the l(IT)eracy challenge? *The Australian Journal of Language and Literacy, 23*(2), 89–107.

Education Queensland. (2006). *Productive Pedagogies*. Retrieved June 29, 2008, from http://education.qld.gov.au/public_media/reports/curriculum-framework/productive-pedagogies/html/manual.html

Fairclough, N. (2000). Multiliteracies and language: Orders of discourse and intertextuality. In B. Cope & M. Kalantzis (Eds.), *Multiliteracies: Literacy learning and the design of social futures* (pp.162- 181). London: Routledge.

Falk, I. (2001). Literacy by Design, not default: Social capital's role in literacy learning. *Journal of Research in Reading, 24*(3), 313–323. doi:10.1111/1467-9817.00152

Freebody, P., & Luke, A. (1990). Literacies programs: Debates and demands in cultural context. *Prospect: Australian Journal of TESOL*, 5.3, 7-16.

Green, B. (1988). Subject specific school learning: A focus on writing. *Australian Journal of Education, 32*(2), 156–179.

Hirsch, E. D. (1987). *Cultural literacy: What every American needs to know* Boston : Houghton Mifflin.

Iyer, R. (2007). Pedagogies of design and multiliterate learner identities. *International Journal of Learning, 13*(11), 25–34.

Jewitt, C. (2005a). Multimodality, "reading," and "writing" for the 21st century. *Discourse: Studies in the Cultural Politics of Education, 26*(3), 315–331. doi:. doi:10.1080/01596300500200011

Jewitt, C. (2005b). *Technology, literacy, learning.* London: RoutledgeFalmer.

Kalantzis, M., & Cope, B and the Learning by Design Group (2005). *Learning by Design*. Melbourne, Australia: Victorian Schools Innovation Commission.

Kalantzis, M., & Cope, B. (2000a). A multiliteracies pedagogy: A pedagogical supplement. In B. Cope & M. Kalantzis (eds.) for the New London Group, *Multiliteracies: Literacy learning and the design of social futures* (pp. 239-248). London: Routledge.

Kalantzis, M., & Cope, B. (2000b). Changing the role in schools. In B. Cope & M. Kalantzis (Eds.), for the New London Group, *Multiliteracies: Literacy learning and the design of social futures* (pp. 121-148). London: Routledge.

Kalantzis, M., & Cope, B. (2004). Designs for learning. *E-Learning, 1*(1), 38–93. doi:. doi:10.2304/elea.2004.1.1.7

Kalantzis, M., Cope, B., & Harvey, A. (2003). Assessing multiliteracies and the new basics. *Assessment in Education: Principles . Policy & Practice*, *10*(1), 15–26.

Kenner, C. (2004). *Becoming biliterate: Young children learning different writing systems*. Stoke-on-Trent, UK: Trentham Books.

Kress, G. (2000). A curriculum for the future. *Cambridge Journal of Education*, *30*(1), 133–145. doi:. doi:10.1080/03057640050005825

Kress, G. (2003). *Literacy in the new media age*. London: Routledge.

Kress, G., Jewitt, C., Bourne, J., Franks, A., Hardcastle, J., Jones, K., & Reid, E. (2005). *English in urban classrooms: A multimodal perspective on teaching and learning*. London: Routledge-Falmer.

Kress, G., Jewitt, C., Ogborn, J., & Tsatsarelis, C. (2001). *Multimodal teaching and learning: the rhetoric of the science classroom*. London: Continuum.

Kress, G., & van Leeuwen, T. (2001). *Multimodal discourse: The modes and media of contemporary communication*. London: Arnold.

Labbo, L. D. (2000). 12 things young children can do with a talking book in a classroom computer center. *The Reading Teacher*, *53*(7), 542–546.

Labbo, L. D., Sprague, L., Montero, M. K., & Font, G. (2000, July). Connecting a computer center to themes, literature, and kindergartners' literacy needs. *Reading Online, 4*(1). Retrieved May 25, 2008, from http://www.readingonline.org/electronic/labbo/

Lankshear, C., & Knobel, M. (2003). *New literacies: Changing knowledge and classroom learning*. Buckingham, UK: Open University Press.

Lemke, J. (1998). Multiplying meaning: Visual and verbal semiotics in scientific text. In J. R. Martin & R. Veel (Eds.), *Reading science* (pp. 87-113). London: Routledge.

Lemke, J. (2002). Travels in hypermodality. *Visual Communication*, *1*(3), 299–325. doi:. doi:10.1177/147035720200100303

Luke, A. (1996). Text and discourse in education: An introduction to critical discourse analysis. *Review of Research in Education*, *21*(3), 3–48.

Luke, A. (2003). Making literacy policy and practice with a difference. *Australian Journal of Language and Literacy*, *26*(3), 58–82.

Luke, C. (1997). Technological literacy. *Adult Literacy Research Network, 4*. CAN: Language Australia.

Luke, C. (2000). Cyber-schooling and technological change: Multiliteracies for new times. In B. Cope & M. Kalantzis (Eds.), *Multiliteracies: Literacy learning and the design of social futures* (pp. 69-91). South Yarra, Australia: Macmillan.

Luke, C. (2003). Pedagogy, connectivity, multimodality, and interdisciplinarity. *Reading Research Quarterly*, *38*(3), 397–403.

Mackey, M. (1994). The new basics: Learning to read in a multimedia world. *English Education*, *28*(1), 9–19. doi:. doi:10.1111/j.1754-8845.1994.tb00697.x

Marsh, K. (2006). Global, local/public, private: Young children's engagement in digital literacy practices in the home. In K. Pahl & J. Rowsell (Eds.), *Travel notes from the New Literacy Studies: Instances of practice* (pp.19-38). Clevedon, UK: Multilingual Matters.

Millard, (2005). To enter the castle of fear: Engendering children's story writing from home to school at KS2. *Gender and Education*, *17*(1), 57-63.

Newfield, D., Andrew, D., Stein, P., & Maungedzo, R. (2003). No number can describe how good it was: Assessment issues in the multimodal classroom. *Assessment in Education: Principles . Policy & Practice*, *10*(1), 61–81.

The New London Group. (1996). A pedagogy of multiliteracies: Designing social futures. *Harvard Educational Review*, *66*(1), 60–92.

The New London Group. (2000). A pedagogy of multiliteracies: Designing social futures. In B. Cope & M. Kalantzis (Eds.), *Multiliteracies: Literacy learning and the design of social futures* (pp. 9-37). South Yarra, Australia: Macmillan.

Nixon, H. (2003). New research literacies for contemporary research into literacy and new media? *Reading Research Quarterly*, *38*(3), 407–413.

Pahl, (2003). Children's text-making at home: Transforming meaning across modes. In C. Jewitt & G. Kress (Eds.), *Multimodal literacy* (pp.139-154). New York: Peter Lang.

Street, B. (1998). New literacies in theory and practice: what are the implications for language in education? *Linguistics and Education*, *10*(1), 1–24. doi:10.1016/S0898-5898(99)80103-X

Street, B. (2003). What's "new" in New Literacy Studies? Critical approaches to literacy in theory and practice. *Current Issues in Comparative Education*, *5*(2), 77–91.

Thomson, P. (2002). *Schooling the rustbelt kids: Making the difference in changing times.* Crows Nest, Australia: Allen & Unwin.

Tolstoy, A. (1968). *The great big enormous turnip.* New York: F. Watts.

Underwood, J. (2000). A comparison of two types of computer support for reading development. *Journal of Research in Reading*, *23*(2), 136–148. doi:. doi:10.1111/1467-9817.00110

Unsworth, L. (2001). *Teaching multiliteracies across the curriculum: Changing contexts of text and image in classroom practice*. Buckingham, UK: Open University Press.

ENDNOTES

1 Pseudonym

2 We reproduce the story titled *The Great Big Enormous Carrot* here: Once upon a time Pinocchio planted a carrot seed. "Grow little carrot seed. Grow sweet. Grow strong," he said. The carrot grew big and sweet and strong. "I'm going to pull up this great big enormous carrot," he said. BUT he could not pull it up. Pinocchio called Rapunzel to help. Rapunzel called the Three Little Pigs to help. The Three Little Pigs called the Big Bad Wolf to help. The Big Bad Wolf called Cinderella to help. Cinderella called The Ugly Duckling to help. The Ugly Duckling called Sleeping Beauty to help. Sleeping Beauty called Jack and the Beanstalk to help. Jack and the Beanstalk called the Woodcutter to help. They pulled and **pulled and pulled**. Up came the carrot at last! They took the carrot home and made a great big carrot cake for dessert.

Chapter 3
Convergence:
A Framework for a "New" Critical Literacy

Jennifer C. Stone
University of Alaska Anchorage, USA

Ryan A. Schowen
University of Alaska Anchorage, USA

ABSTRACT

Online participation is becoming a significant part of many young people's recreational literate lives. Nonetheless, the range of online literacies available in children's out-of-school lives is rarely addressed in school-based literacy curricula and instruction. To address this gap, this chapter develops and illustrates a critical literacy framework based on Jenkins' (2006) concept of "convergence." Building on Jenkins' theory of convergence, the authors pull together ideas from media studies, multiliteracies, and semiotics to develop a cohesive framework for unpacking the textual practices, practices of consumption, and social networks common in new media. The authors then illustrate this framework through an analysis of ideologies of gender in popular websites among elementary-age children, including Barbie, American Girl, Transformers, and Hot Wheels.

INTRODUCTION

For contemporary youth living in developed countries, computer and Internet access have risen significantly in recent years. Roberts, Foehr, and Rideout (2005), in a large-scale survey of children living in the United States, found that 96% of youth ages 8-18 have Internet access in home, school, and/or community settings. Of the young people surveyed, 74% now have Internet connections in their homes. Additionally, the survey found that children spend an average of 48 minutes per day using the Internet for recreational purposes, including visiting websites, playing games, instant messaging, chatting, e-mailing, and creating websites.

Without a doubt, online participation is becoming a significant part of many young people's literate lives. Nonetheless, the range of online literacies available in children's out-of-school lives is ill-addressed in school-based curricula. Similarly, as Roberts, Foehr, and Rideout (2005) found, children's online literacy practices largely are unmediated at

DOI: 10.4018/978-1-60566-673-0.ch003

home, as well. At best, schools address these new literacies in terms of evaluating information and safety; at worst, schools fail to address critical online literacies and focus solely on old literacies that do not adequately prepare young people for their present and future educational, civic, personal, and work lives. While, of course, evaluating information and safety are central concerns for addressing digital literacies, such curricula do not address the need for a critical literacy framework that can account for new media technologies and literacies connected with online participation.

This chapter develops a critical literacy framework based on Jenkins' (2006) concept of "convergence." Building on Jenkins' theory of convergence, we pull together ideas from media studies, multiliteracies, and semiotics to develop a cohesive framework for unpacking the textual practices, practices of consumption, and social networks common in new media. We illustrate this framework through an analysis of ideologies of gender in popular websites among elementary-age children. Although a focus on critical literacy has been central to work on multiliteracies from its inception (Cope & Kalantzis, 2000; A. Luke, 2000; New London Group, 1996), when enacted in classroom spaces, critical literacy tends to focus on older media—such as magazine ads, books, television, and newspapers—leaving teachers and their students hard-pressed to find ways to talk about online texts and literacy practices in productively critical ways beyond evaluating information and safety.

The authors (henceforth referred to as we) argue that understanding young people's unofficial uses of digital literacies can open essential pathways for designing literacy curricula that are simultaneously relevant to their out-of-school lives and that prepare them for the complex, technologically-mediated literacy activities that are becoming central to our culture. We do not argue that such forms of popular media necessarily should be incorporated into school curricula or that we should encourage youth to participate in these websites; rather, our concern here is to illustrate the sorts of websites that attract youth and to unpack how we might use such sites to develop a "new" critical literacy.

BACKGROUND

Critical Literacy and Popular Websites

There is wide variation in how critical literacy has developed in educational contexts around the world. Critical literacy, as it has been taken up in many North American contexts, is akin to higher order thinking. Developing skills such as inference, metacognition, response to literature, and analysis of authorial positions are the primary foci of this approach to critical literacy (see Alvermann, Moon & Hagood, 1999; Myers & Beach, 2004; Vasquez, 2004 for examples of notable exceptions). As Allan Luke (2000) argues, such interpretations of critical literacy focus on the development of skills and strategies in individuals rather than on the relationship between texts and the broader social, cultural, economic, and political contexts in which they are used. In other words, this version of critical literacy is remarkably uncritical in both its focus on individual development and its failure to address the situated nature of literacy.

It makes sense, then, that the majority of curricular trends and common classroom practices surrounding online textual practices in North America tend to focus on depoliticized versions of "critical" media literacy or un-critical concerns involved in online reading. Much of the work that could fall under the umbrella of "critical" media literacy tends to address narrow aspects of online reading, such as evaluating information (Eisenberg & Berkowitz, 2003; Leu, 2005) and maintaining safety online (Goodstein, 2007; Willard, 2007). Indeed, the majority of research on websites in education focuses on how websites support and extend existing developmental and cognitive aspects of literacy curricula. These include identifying new reading practices in hyperlinked environments (Coiro, 2003; Schmar-Dobler, 2003), employing hypertext to support struggling readers (Coiro, 2003; Johnson & Hegarty, 2003), and developing cognitive reading strategies (Horning, 2004; Schmar-Dobler, 2003).

Although we agree that it is important for children to learn how to evaluate information, engage safely in online communication, and use online texts to develop and support their ability to read, these perspectives do not account for the broader array of literacy practices available online. Outside of evaluating the truthfulness of information or the safety of Internet users, critical literacy's adaptation to new literacy practices has been given little weight. Additionally, this body of work supports traditional understandings of literacy rather than examining literacy's evolution, and thus how literacy education must adapt. Finally, the implications of addressing popular websites for literacy education, particularly sites that provide opportunities for social interaction and entertainment, are not examined in this body of work.

In contrast to psychological and personal growth models of literacy education, the New Literacy Studies or multiliteracies framework (Cope & Kalantzis, 2000; Gee, 1996; Street, 1995) has impacted on curricula and classroom practice significantly in Australia, and takes a very different perspective on critical literacy. Building on critical theory and media studies (e.g. Fairclough, 1995; Freire, 2000; Hall, 1980) functional linguistics (Halliday, 1994; Martin, Matthiessen & Painter, 1997), and semiotics (Kress & van Leeuwen, 1996, 2001), the New Literacy Studies frame critical literacy in terms of the social and political nature of texts and textual practices. Although there is not total agreement about what critical literacy is or how it should be used, many of the researchers and theorists in this tradition focus on the following key areas: 1) the relationship between texts and social contexts, 2) the relationship between authors and audiences, 3) the analysis of how texts work, and 4) the importance of multiple interpretations and opportunities for redesign.

One of the focal points of literacy study and writings is the relationship between texts and the social contexts in which they are created, understood, and used. From this point of view, texts and textual practices are inseparable from broader social, cultural, economic, historical, and material contexts (Green, 2001). Rather than framing reading and writing as neutral acts, literacy is framed as ideological (Evans, 2005; Muspratt, A. Luke & Freebody, 1997; Street, 1995). One of the primary goals of critical literacy, then, is to render the implicit explicit, thereby disrupting the commonplace and exposing the hidden agendas and ideologies of texts (Stevens & Bean, 2007; Warnick, 2002).

Building on the connection between text and context, a second concern of critical literacy is the relationship between authors and audiences. This perspective is concerned with identifying who authors are and how they anticipate their audiences. It examines how authors position and influence their audiences and how they, in so doing, both include and exclude audience members (Evans, 2005). It also examines the author's standpoint and purpose, highlighting the persuasive role of texts (Stevens & Bean, 2007; Warnick, 2002). Conversely, this aspect of critical literacy examines the role of audience members in making meaning, often beyond the intentions of authors, as well.

To address the relationships between text and context as well as author and audience, another key dimension of critical literacy is the analysis of how texts work. Taking a broad definition of "text" to include non-print media, multimodal texts, and traditional print texts (Evans, 2005; McDaniel, 2006), this aspect of critical literacy seeks to engage young people as textual analysts and researchers of language and other forms of representation (Comber, 2001; McLaughlin &

DeVoogd, 2004). In addition to becoming code breakers, meaning makers, and text users (A. Luke, 2000), this element of critical literacy argues that one of the major goals of literacy education should be to focus on the analysis of how texts construct knowledge of the world and possible positions in it (Alvermann, Moon, & Hagood, 1999). As Carmen Luke (1997) points out, sustained and serious study of media affects how young people read, view, and interpret texts in their everyday lives.

The goals of such analyses raise a final aspect of critical literacy: the importance of multiple interpretations and opportunities for redesign. As a number of scholars have argued, the rise of consumerism, fast capitalism, and the abundance of media outside of school makes it imperative that young people are equipped with the ability to critically analyze the textual world around them (Alvermann, Moon & Hagood, 1999; Stevens & Bean, 2007). This dimension of critical literacy focuses on the need for bringing multiple perspectives and interpretations to bear on texts, addressing key social issues, and promoting reflection, transformation, and action (Dozier, Johnston & Rogers, 2006; Fehring & Green, 2001; Heffernan, 2004; McDaniel, 2006; McLaughlin & DeVoogd, 2004). This perspective argues that not only should educators guide young people in textual critique, but that they must also provide opportunities for redesigning texts and creating counternarratives (C. Luke, 1997; Heffernan, 2004; Vasquez, 2005; Warnick, 2002). Ultimately, this aspect of critical literacy is concerned with the agency of readers and writers as they participate in a textual world that is designed to dissuade such agency (Alvermann, Moon & Hagood, 1999; Dozier, Johnston & Rogers, 2006).

Although most contemporary writings on literacy learning and education provide a strong foundation from which to engage young people in critical readings of popular texts such as advertisements, television shows, and the like, we have found that it is not well-equipped to deal with complex, interactive texts like popular websites. Few scholars of critical literacy specifically address online literacies (see Evans, 2005; Warnick, 2002 for notable exceptions). For this reason, we draw upon and develop Jenkins' (2006) theory of "convergence" to account for the types of texts and textual practices that now dominate a significant part of many young peoples' literate lives. Even though Jenkins uses the concept of convergence descriptively to understand fan participation in a range of media, we believe that its potential lies as a basis for an analytic framework that can account for contemporary texts and textual practices. Building on Jenkins' theory of convergence, we pull together concepts from media studies, multiliteracies, and semiotics to construct a framework for analyzing the textual practices, practices of consumption, and social networks that commonly ground new media. In so doing, we propose convergence as a framework for a "new" critical literacy and an important addition to the multiliteracies framework.

Convergence as a Framework for a "New" Critical Literacy

Within the media industry, convergence is typically talked about as the bundling of multiple applications into a single technological tool. However, recent work in literacy and media studies has broadened the scope and focus of this concept. For example, Leu & Kinzer (2000) discuss convergence as the coming together of literacy and computer technology in classrooms. Leander & Lovvorn (2006) employ convergence to examine the range of configurations between space and time available to people online. Jenkins (2006) uses convergence to describe the cultural shift brought about by networked technologies where consumers actively participate in building connections between media content. Also, Peppler & Kafai (2007) apply convergence to the potential of digital media production for supporting critical understandings of new media. Each of these perspectives on convergence points to a number of fundamental shifts in the way we engage with media. Here, we focus on three of these, including textual practices, relationships of consumption and social relationships. In so doing, we construct a framework for analyzing online texts and textual practices.

One dimension of convergence includes the emergence of new textual practices. Drawing on work in semiotics and media studies, our understanding of convergence includes several important concepts for understanding how websites engage children in textual practices. First, multimodality examines the use of a range of systems of representation including images, print, movement, sound, etc. (Evans, 2005; Kress & van Leeuwen, 1996, 2001; Lemke, 1998).

Second, intertextuality describes the connections made between texts, including hyperlinks and references (Warnick, 2002). Finally, because of the more active role of consumers in new media, consumers are often encouraged to take on the role of producer, remixing existing media to suit their own purposes and sharing this remixed media with others (Lankshear & Knobel, 2006). These practices form the basis for realizing new relationships of production and social relationships.

In addition to emerging textual practices, popular websites also allow for new configurations between consumers, producers and media. One key concept in this changing relationship is that of "brand extension" or the flow of content across media, creating multiple points of contact between consumers and products. A second aspect of these new configurations is what we call "cross-affinity extension" where fans of one brand are presented with multiple opportunities to cross over to similar products, brands, affinity groups, and activities. Along with this, consumers are no longer spectators of media, but are active participants. As Jenkins (2006) describes, consumers must make connections among media and actively piece together information and experiences from multiple sources. Indeed, users of online media must make sense of a seemingly endless array of media, including toys, movies, cartoons, commercials, demonstrations, games, and fan creations.

Finally, convergence provides a lens for understanding a reformulation of social relationships. Although many popular websites support traditional relationships, such as those between young people and their families and local friends, they also engage young people in affinity groups. Affinity groups, according to Gee (2000/2001), are globally distributed groups who connect around a central topic or cause, creating affiliations between individuals who may share little else. Such groups are enabled and sustained through media participation and networked technologies. By using popular websites, young people are joining other fans across the world with similar interests. Many of these sites give children the opportunity to interact with other fans through sharing fan creations, forums and chat platforms. Likewise, these sites encourage parallel play among users in their respective affinity groups.

CONVERGENCE IN POPULAR WEBSITES

To illustrate this framework of analysis, we apply it to a sample of websites that are popular among elementary-age children. These websites have been collected over the past several years from children representing a range of socioeconomic backgrounds. The sites were recommended by young people because they frequently use them outside of school. We identify these websites as "popular" not because of the number of young users they attract (although many of the sites we discuss have millions of fans), but because of how young people use these sites in unofficial spaces for unofficial purposes (Alvermann, 2003).

For this analysis, we selected four of these websites, two that target girls and two that target boys. In contrast to much of the research conducted on popular websites, which tends to look at primarily interactive, participant-driven sites such as chat rooms (Lam, 2000) and fan fiction (Black, 2005), we emphasize websites where content is mediated primarily by a single entity, although many of these sites incorporate interactive characteristics as well. We chose to analyze this type of website because they represent the interests and online literacy practices described most by elementary-aged children.

The websites targeted at girls that we examine included:

- **Barbie®** (http://barbie.everythinggirl.com/), the official Mattel, Inc. website for its line of Barbie® toys and products. This site includes a range of activities including online messaging and games, as well as advertisements for associated media and products.
- **American Girl ™** (http://www.americangirl.com/), the official website for the American Girl™ line of dolls, magazine subscriptions, stores, and other products. This site focuses on the "Historical Characters" and "Girl of the Year" lines of dolls and offers users many games, on- and offline activities, background information about each doll, and a variety of purchasing opportunities.

The websites targeted at boys that we discuss include:

- **Transformers©** (http://www.hasbro.com/transformers/), the official Hasbro, Inc. website for the Transformers© line of toys and products. It offers games, activities, comics, videos, downloads, and information about other Hasbro products, as well as access to information and products related to the recent popular film *Transformers.*
- **Hot Wheels®** (http://www.hotwheels.com/index_hwkids.aspx), the official website for Mattel's line of Hot Wheels® toys and products. Product information, games, downloads, videos, and information for collectors are available on the site.

We chose to concentrate on these websites for many reasons. Primarily, these websites require relatively little investment and offer easy access—they are free for users, require no special equipment (other than a computer with Internet access), and can be used in one short sitting. Additionally, these websites and games are connected both directly and indirectly to other representational systems, communities, and practices. These sites are embedded in media networks that include movies, toys, and television shows, as well as ideologies. Finally, these sites demonstrate the interests of young children who remain underrepresented in research regarding young people's online literate lives outside of school.

Two levels of analysis were conducted on each of the four websites. Broad analyses focused on the sites themselves as media artifacts, including audits of design features, images, and the activities and games available to users. Closer analyses focused on several games and activities from each site, specifically those described by children as the most fun, engaging, and/or interesting on each site. We also emphasized the more complex exercises in terms of problem solving and literacy activities required by users. The content of these sites is constantly changed and updated—for example, at one point Barbie suddenly had two friends with her in her bedroom and games were added or deleted from several of the sites. The ever-changing nature of these sites provides a moving target for analysis. To account for this, we limited our data collection to a two-month period from March to May 2008.

In particular, we use the three aspects of convergence—textual practices, relationships of consumption, and social relationships—to understand how these websites engage young people in ideologies of gender. Although we could use this framework to discuss a range of ideologies—such as those surrounding social class, diversity, and technology to name a few—we chose to examine ideologies of gender because they are so salient in sites for this age group.

Convergence of Textual Practices

Although the textual practices embedded in many popular websites overlap significantly with those valued in schools (Stone, 2007), they include a number of textual practices that are often unaddressed in educational contexts. While there are a number of changes to textual practices in online literacies, here we focus on several of these practices that are most evident in the websites, and that are most significant for communicating ideologies of gender. Each of the websites discussed in this analysis engages young people in literacy practices involving multiple modes of representation, building extensive connections to other texts, remixing existing media for new purposes, and opportunities for sharing commercial and fan-created media.

Multimodality

First, the convergence of multiple modes represents a major change in new media texts. Like all texts, websites are multimodal in that they draw upon multiple systems of representation, including but exceeding print. However, in new media texts, other modes of representation, such as visual, auditory, and spatial, play more dominant roles (Evans, 2005; Kress & van Leeuwen, 2001). All of the websites require users to "read" and even "write" using a number of representational systems. Users know what to do and where to go based on the convergence of these systems, rather than any single system of representation. For example, the game "Transformers Video Mash-Up" enables young people to make a Transformers-themed music video. To play this game users must read print-based instructions, use visual and spatial cues to navigate through the activity, select video clips and transitions from a range of choices, select audio tracks and sound effects, organize audio portions using visual representations of sound, write print-based credits, and coordinate across visual, auditory, and textual resources to create a final product.

The sites also draw on multiple modes of representation to target specific genders. Through print, color choices, images, and sounds, each site situates its audience as male or female. Each of the sites identifies its audience as boys or girls through print. For instance, the Barbie website greets visitors with the statement "Hi, Barbie Girl" and the American Girl site is titled "Fun for Girls." The Transformers and Hot Wheels sites are less explicit about their audiences in terms of print. Rather than addressing or labeling their audiences as boys explicitly in the main pages of the sites, they only name their audiences as boys in parent pages. For example, the parents' page for Hot Wheels describes the site as "The ultimate online destination for boys…" and the Transformers site includes access to "Parenting Tips for Parents of Boys." Child-users, however, must rely mainly on visual and auditory cues to identify the sites' intended audiences.

In terms of visual references, the sites use color and images to further identify their audiences. The sites targeted at girls use pastel color palates with pinks and purples as the dominant colors, whereas the sites targeted at boys use primary colors, with blues and black as the dominant colors. Very few images of the opposite sex are found on any of the sites; indeed the Transformers and Hot Wheels sites contain no images of females. The Barbie and American Girls site each contain a few images of males, usually in supporting roles as in the "Historical Characters" section of the American Girl site where they show each character's network of family and friends. The Barbie site also includes a game called "Give Ken a New Look" where users can dress up Ken and select his ideal interests and future goals.

Finally, the sites utilize sound and music in different ways. Users of Barbie are greeted by pop-music and Barbie orally introducing herself and her friends. The American Girl site is the most limited in terms of auditory resources, only including music and sound effects in games. The music used in these games matches the character, time period, and activity it's tied to—for instance the game "A Life in Freedom" for Addy, a newly freed slave after the Civil War, has a ragtime soundtrack, whereas "Samantha's Scavenger Hunt" which accompanies the Victorian era doll has a classical soundtrack. In contrast, the sites targeted at boys greet users with mechanical sounds, heavy metal music, and deep male voices.

Through the convergence of multiple modes, including print, visual, and auditory, each site clearly identifies its audience as either male or female. This provides the basis for an ideology of gender where boys and girls rarely interact and where males and females are largely excluded from each other's worlds.

Intertextuality

In addition to the convergence of modes, each of the sites engages young people in the convergence of texts—or intertextuality—as well. While multimodality emphasizes the relationships between representational systems, intertextuality highlights the interrelatedness of texts (Kristeva, 2001; Warnick, 2002). The importance of intertextuality, although present in all texts, is more complex in online texts. Indeed, users of popular websites must navigate a seemingly endless, interconnected web of media, products, characters, storylines, and fan activity associated with each site.

Hyperlinks are a major vehicle for building intertextual connections for each of the sites. Indeed, each of the sites' homepages offer users an approximately 30-50 direct links to games, activities, information about products, opportunities to purchase products, other media, and related websites. Each of these links leads to another web page with a number of links, creating networks of hundreds of related pages. For example, the Barbie home page includes links to various "rooms" in Barbie's house such as her bedroom, game room, garden, and closet, each of which is filled with related activities. Users have the option to decorate the page and make it their home page. They can also access shopping opportunities as well as commercials for Barbie dolls and the movie *Mariposa*. There are also links to websites based on other products and media for girls, such as Polly Pocket and High School Musical 2. There is some redundancy in these links, as well, offering multiple pathways for navigating through the site. For instance, users can get to Barbie's bedroom through an image of a stuffed teddy bear, a blueprint of Barbie's house, or advice from one of Barbie's friends who depicted on the homepage with her. Finally, surrounding the central part of the site are small links for adult users, covering such topics as information for parents, collectors, and legal statements.

In addition to hyperlinks, there are a range of print, visual, and auditory references to other media. For example, the American girl site provides extensive background information through print and images for each doll. The Transformers site greets visitors with the statement "Autobots, transform and roll out!" which is a key phrase from the Transformers cartoons and movie. And Barbie's bedroom has a CD player that allows users to listen to clips of popular music and potentially purchase CDs of the full songs. Simply put, users of all of these sites must negotiate a complex network of hyperlinks in addition to a seemingly endless stream of references to characters, storylines, and products.

Overall, the links and references channel users through gender-specific opportunities. The Barbie site, for instance, is part of a network of websites called Everything Girl, which is owned by Mattel, Inc. Within this network, users can easily access four similar websites base on other Mattel products. Each of these sites is similar to Barbie in that they specifically target girls. Likewise, the Hot Wheels site provides links to Tyco R/C and Matchbox, both of which are websites for other lines of car toys and, like Hot Wheels, specifically address boys. In contrast, the American Girl site only includes internal links to the site. The Transformers site is the only website from this sample that offers the potential to cross gender audiences. Through several of the activities on the site, users are channeled to Monkey Bar TV, which provides crossover opportunities with other media for both girls and boys. However, even though these crossover opportunities exist, they are often buried deep within the link structure of the site.

Remixing and Sharing

Another type of textual convergence that each of the websites supports is remixing. According to Lankshear and Knobel (2006), remixing involves taking preexisting representational resources and rearranging them into new texts. For example, "Transformers Video Mash-Up" lets young people engage in editing a short music video. Players piece together video clips, transitions, sound effects, and music to create an original Transformers video, using a similar interface to common video editing software like iMovie. Similarly, in "Fashion Fever: Styled by Me" on the Barbie website, children select one of four styles ("Preppy & Pretty" or "Funky & Fab," for example). Then they put together an outfit with choices of colors, fabrics, and cuts for items like Barbie's jacket, shirt, purse and shoes. By participating in these activities, users take existing media and rearrange them to create original texts, or what Ito (2006) calls a "media mix."

Sharing is another important textual practice available on these websites. After completing these remixing activities, and many others on all of the sites, users get to see their creations, and if they want, they can e-mail them to friends, save them electronically, and/or print them out to share with others. In the "Transformers Video Mash-Up" game, users can even submit their videos to be posted on the site and view other fans' submissions. Several of the sites also allow users to share specific activities with others via e-mail. For instance, each game on the Hot Wheels site offers users the option to "Send to a Friend." This allows the use of games and activities to spread through informal peer networks.

Through remixing and sharing, users not only consume products from each of these sites, but they can also participate in creating new media or sharing existing media that can become the textual focus for other fans. In so doing, they are "writers" of new media texts, in addition to "readers." They also engage in multimodality by coordinating multiple modes of representation, including print, images, and/or sound. Additionally, they insert themselves and their textual creations into the burgeoning array of intertextual references available from each site.

Like the opportunities for intertextual links and use of multimodal resources, the materials for remixing tend to be gender-specific. For example, in the game "Fashion Fever: Styled by Me" described above, users choose clothing to dress up Barbie from a range of pre-set styles. In a similar game, "Give Ken a New Look" users create their ideal Ken by dressing him in various male styles, selecting his hair, and choosing his interests and career goals. While these games offer an array of clothing and accessory choices to players, they still offer a relatively narrow spectrum of possible archetypes of maleness and femaleness from which to choose. Players cannot mix Ken's and Barbie's clothes; nor can users extend beyond the prescribed categories of the activity—there are no choices such as "Geeky and Gaudy" or "Flamboyant and Feminine" that extend beyond mainstream ideals of girlhood and boyhood.

One exception to gender-specific remixing opportunities is available on the Transformers site. The game "Transformers Print Shop" takes users to "Monkey Bar TV" which ties together a range of media from Hasbro, Inc. for both boys and girls. In this game, users can create a number of remixed products—such as bookmarks, posters, or cards—that be printed or e-mailed. When users first enter the game, they are presented with several images of Transformers characters that can be dragged and dropped onto a changeable background. However, with some work, users can rotate through dozens of images from Hasbro products. So, conceivably, a user could create posters or bookmarks that include an image of Optimus Prime next to an Easy-Bake Oven on a lavender background, thus creating cross-gendered representations. However, such opportunities are rare and, when available, difficult to access on the websites.

Overall, through textual convergence, the websites we analyzed lay the foundation for an ideology of gender where boys and girls are largely segregated from each other. Although both boys and girls must negotiate a textual world where multiple modes are needed to make meaning, texts are deeply interrelated, and media can be remixed and shared with others, boys and girls are encouraged to play in parallel but largely separate media landscapes. Also, the sites provide narrow representations of ideals of maleness and femaleness. These textual elements of convergence lay the groundwork for convergence of consumption and convergence of social relationships.

Convergence in Relationships between Consumers, Producers, and Media

Building on the elements of textual convergence described above, each of the sites also provides a number of opportunities for young people to participate in convergence of relationships of consumption. Unlike traditional theories of communication (and literacy, for that matter), where producers are viewed as the active creators of meaning and consumers are framed as passive receivers of meaning (e.g. Horkheimer & Adorno, 1972), convergence accounts for the active role that both consumers and producers play in meaning making. This reformulation of the relationship between consumers, producers, and media is evident in several phenomena associated with new media, including brand extension, cross-affinity extension, and participation in media.

In terms of brand extension, each of the sites provides only one of many points of contact between the consumer, media, and other products. Each of the sites offers entry into vast media networks that tie together websites, games, movies, books, magazines, music, virtual and physical stores, dolls, action figures, toys, and accessories. For example, the American Girl website is based on two lines of dolls including "Historical Characters," representing different cultures and historical periods, and "Girl of the Year," based on modern, culturally diverse models of girlhood. For each of these dolls, which can also be purchased along with accessories, users can play games, find out more about the dolls' friends and families, read book excerpts, and create media such as cards and computer wallpapers. They can also take a virtual adventure around the world with their doll, through the activity "A Doll's Journey" where users can learn about various locations such as Tanzania, Singapore, and Belize. During their journey, users find out "fun facts" about the culture, language, and food of each location, play cultural games, create a travel diary for a doll, and design other media. Also, on the site, users can view trailers for American Girl movies, give and get advice, take quizzes, shop for dolls, purchase a magazine subscription, and find out about events at American girl store. In other words, users of this site, and all of the sites for that matter, are immersed in a vast network of opportunities to engage in activities that cross a range of media.

Not only do these websites provide within-brand opportunities to connect media, many also provide opportunities for cross-affinity extension, as well. Three of the four websites include multiple links to other websites with related content.

Directly from the homepages, users of the Barbie site are encouraged to peruse other sites such as Polly Pocket, users of Hot Wheels can easily access other car toy sites, and users of Transformers can "Explore Hasbro" and access any of the other Hasbro sites. The only exception is American Girl, which provides no external links, likely because it is not connected to a larger brand label. Through this cross-affinity extension, many of the sites enable young people not only to engage in brand-extension, but also expand and/or transfer their attention to other brands, as well.

In addition to brand-extension and cross-affinity extension, each of the sites also hails young people into actively participating in the production of and making connections among media. In each of the sites, young people can extend their experiences with other media by participating in a range of games and other activities, through what Jenkins (2006) calls participatory culture. Since the textual networks of new media are so widespread and complex, it stands to follow that users must piece together information from multiple sources to make meaning. Users of the Transformers site, for instance, must negotiate multiple texts, including the movie, cartoon show, games, commercials, and embodied play experiences to learn about key characters, storylines, and developments associated with Transformers. Also, as described above in regard to remixing, users on all of these sites have multiple opportunities to become producers of media, as well. Whether playing "Transformers Video Mash-Up" or "Fashion Fever: Styled by Me," users of these sites can build on and extend existing media to create their own original media. In so doing, users are not only the receivers of meaning, but active producers as well.

Undoubtedly, these elaborate media networks, both within brand and across affinities, in addition to opportunities to participate in production, are attempts by commercial entities to encourage high levels of consumption. However, these new media phenomena also give consumers a great deal of control and, indeed, reconfigure the relationship between consumers, producers, and media. Users, not commercial entities, decide which aspects of media they want to explore—they can choose which links to follow within and outside of specific sites, which activities and games to play, and whether or not they wish to engage with particular media. They can also design their own ideal media within certain activities.

Nonetheless, it is important to note that these activities are controlled to some extent. Most of the opportunities for brand extension and cross-affinity extension channel users through gender-specific experiences and media. Likewise, many of the materials available for participation provide carefully controlled arrays of media resources from which to draw, limited by gender, brands, and/or commercial networks.

Convergence of Social Relationships

Not only do the sites engage in textual convergence and convergence of consumption, but they also provide opportunities for convergence between both "new" and "old" social relationships.

Each of the four sites is tied to a particular affinity group, including affinities around lines of toys, movies, and other media. By using these websites and embedded games, young people are joining other fans across the world with similar interests. However, it is likely because of the young age of their audiences, these sites are not solely focused on affinity group participation alone. Alongside these affinity groups, young people are also encouraged to participate in more traditional social relationships, including those surrounding family and real life friends. Through the convergence of social relationships, each of the sites encourages children to take on particular gendered identities.

Each of the sites is one of many opportunities for young people to engage in affinity groups. These affinity groups, based on fandoms surrounding toys and media, allow children to play with, talk to, create media for, and engage in parallel play with other fans. The Hot Wheels website, for instance, includes many games where children can race or play against each other or compare their scores on games to those of others. In the game "Rebellion Race," players participate in a car race against up to four other players. Each player is assigned a preset name and can choose from a list of taunts to say to opponents at the start of the race, such as "Pedal to the metal" or "Eat my dust." At the end of the race, players see each other's race times and can also view high scores in the game. By winning races, players unlock faster and fancier cars that make it more likely that they will be able to win races. Although these activities do not allow for free dialogue between players, they can still communicate and compete against players from all over the world. The Barbie website includes a virtual world, called "Barbie Girls" where users can create an avatar, decorate a room, chat with friends through drop down menus, and play games alone or with other players. Several activities on the Transformers site, such as "Transformers Video Mash-Up" allow players to share fan-created media with other fans. Also, on the American Girl site, users can share stories, experiences, and give and get advice about topics like school, family, and friends in "Girls Speak Out." They can also share their thoughts about a weekly question posed by Kit Kittredge, who is the main character in an American Girl movie. All of the sites include a range of individual activities, as well, where children can engage in parallel play with other members of each affinity group.

Each of the sites also addresses social relationships with real life friends. In many of the activities and games available on the sites, children can e-mail their fan creations to friends, as in "Transformers Video Mash-Up." Also, some of the sites allow children to e-mail links to games to friends, thus advertising these activities through informal peer networks, as with all of the games on the Hot Wheels site. Additionally, both the Barbie and American girl sites provide tools for coordinating social interactions with friends. For instance, the Barbie site shopping area provides sets of party planning materials for purchase. Also, the American Girl site offers a "Book Club Kit," which provides all the materials necessary (printable invitations, bookmarks, calendars, and pledge promises) to set up a book club for reading and discussing American Girl books.

In addition to affinity groups and real life friends, the sites also attend to the participation of family in young people's use of the sites. All of the sites provide access to special pages for parents, which recommend related family activities, discuss the educational value of each activity, give parenting tips, provide links to parenting advice sites, and offer information about shows, movies, and broadcast schedules. These pages tend to focus on products, services, and lifestyle advice related to the sites—after all, parents are the ones holding the credit cards. For example, on the Barbie sites parents' page, parents can have Barbie call their daughter and buy the newest Barbie toys and accessories. It also includes activities and advice for what parents can do with their daughters, focusing on topics such as diet, fitness, crafts, and Internet safety. Several of the sites also enable children to create wish lists of toys and accessories they like for family and friends.

Across each of these social relationships addressed by the sites, girls and boys are encouraged to engage in very different sets of activities and take on different identities. Through providing separate, but parallel mediascapes for girls and boys, the sites support ideologies for activities and related identities that are appropriate for girls and boys. The sites for girls tend to provide activities for girls that focus on activities in social and domestic domains. In contrast, the activities supported by Transformers and Hot Wheels sites focus on competition and technical know-how.

Many of the activities on the sites targeted at girls focus on activities surrounding the domestic sphere such as gardening, cooking, cleaning, dressing up, and care giving. The Barbie site, for instance, includes a game called "Shoe Hunt" where players assist Barbie's friend Kayla with cleaning up several sets of matching shoes hidden throughout her bedroom. Also, in the game "Let's Take Care of Baby" players babysit for baby Krissy by taking her grocery shopping, as well as dressing, feeding, and cleaning her. The Barbie site also includes a number of dress-up games such as "Fashion Fever: Styled by Me" and "Superstar Makeovers." The Barbie site is also organized by the "rooms" of Barbie's house, where each room, which is accessible via image links and a blueprint of the house, provides a set of activities, thus, further locating the Barbie activities in the domestic sphere. Similarly, on the American Girl site, girls are encouraged to engage in activities such as growing a garden as in "Molly's Victory Garden," taking care of animals as in "Net Pet," baking and crafts as described in the "Magazine Activities" section of the site, and a number of scrapbooking opportunities as on "Doll Scrapbook Online" and "A Doll's Journey."

In addition to domestic activities, the Barbie and American Girl sites also focus on socializing with friends. Both of the sites provide a number of opportunities for and images of social interaction. For instance, images of Barbie on her homepage, in her garden, and in her game room show Barbie hanging out with friends. Also, from the home page, there is an image of a laptop that links to "Barbie Girls" where fans can chat, party, and play with each other online. Additionally, as described above, many of the activities allow girls to share their creations by email with friends. The American Girl site also includes a number of images of friendship, both through pictures of groups of girls and girls holding their doll "friends." The site includes an advice column "Girls Speak Out" where girls can get and give advice. Also, the American Girl website provides materials for several social activities, including starting a book club and building a small business.

In contrast, the sites targeted at boys encourage activities and identities related to competition and technical know-how. The Transformers site, for instance, encourages boys to engage in activities that revolve around strategic competition. Competition in this site primarily centers on good versus evil. Indeed, all of the games focus on the conflict between the evil Decepticons and the Transformers. Many of the games involve embarking on essential missions to defeat the Decepticons. One example is the game "Key Recovery" where players search several planets to recover a key. In so doing, they are expected to understand how to use a radar screen in the upper left-hand corner to navigate across a grid. Also, boys playing the game "Energon Within" must launch missiles while digitally controlling the velocity of missiles being launched while managing a reserve of missiles. In these games, users must manipulate technology (the robots and items they transform into) and rely on technical know-how, such as using radar and understanding of velocity, to successfully wage strategic competition on their enemies.

Similarly, the Hot Wheels site encourages boys to engage in activities that revolve around competition and building. Many of the games on the website focus on competing with real and virtual others, either in battles or races. For instance, in "Rebellion Race" users compete against other players online. They race against four other cars on 12 tracks and unlock new cars as they win events. Other games include users in battles against their environments or enemies, as in "Aerial Attack Robot Swarm." In this game, players control aerial attack vehicles, which are responsible for shooting and attacking flying bugs that are trying to destroy them. A number of activities also ask users to build cars or race tracks. For example, "The Factory: Tag Rides" players choose a car and use various machines in a factory setting to modify and decorate their car with decals, wheels, paint, and suspension.

Simply put, each of the sites engages young people in ideologies of which activities are appropriate for girls or boys, along with related identities. Whereas boys are encouraged to engage in activities and identities surrounding competition and technical know-how, girls are being recruited into activities and identities focused on domestic duties and socializing with others. Although all of the sites provide opportunities to engage in important aspects of multiliteracies, the gendered ideologies put forth by the websites, as well as the lack of opportunities to expand beyond these ideologies, are problematic if treated uncritically (for a more detailed analysis of gendered activities on popular websites, see Stone & Veth, 2008).

DISCUSSION & CONCLUSION

Users of popular websites are being introduced into literacies that are multimodal, rather than print-based; intertextual, rather than monotextual; and that expect children to actively (re)produce media themselves. To participate, users must engage not just as consumers of media from single sources, but must manage, consume, and produce media from multiple sources. Users can create new potential connections between themselves and others interested in similar topics, both in "real" life and online.

In so doing, however, popular websites use a range of convergence strategies, including social convergence, convergence of consumption, and textual convergence to engage young people in the consumption not only of products and media, but also of ideologies. As we have illustrated, sites such as Barbie, American Girl, Transformers, and Hot Wheels recruit children into potentially problematic ideologies surrounding gender. As discussed above, the websites frame girls' and boys' worlds as parallel, but primarily separate. Indeed, little significant mention of the opposite sex is made on any of the sites. Media materials for remixing and links to related media, with the exception of a few activities on the Transformers site, are primarily focused on one gender to the exclusion of the other gender. Likewise, each of the sites upholds problematic views of appropriate activities and identities for girls and boys.

We agree with Butler (2004) that the gendered categories of "boy" and "girl" are historical and cultural concepts, not natural ones. According to Butler, gender is a "performative act" that is often not voluntary. Rather, gender is realized over time and across situations, through the regular replication of gendered actions. Overall, in the websites discussed here, boys are being targeted to engage in competitive, technologically-oriented activities, whereas girls are being groomed for lives in social and domestic spheres. Through repeated play with these websites, girls and boys are learning to perform gendered identities. Even though there are numerous websites for this age group, such as Disney and Nickelodeon that do not segregate genders quite as noticeably as these sites, it is useful to critique the gendered ideologies supported by websites specifically targeted at boys or girls, since these encompass some of the most extensively used websites by this age group and therefore set gendered agendas.

Although we illustrate that these sites engage children in problematic representations of gender through a range of convergence strategies, we are not arguing for a response of censorship. Indeed, all of the popular websites discussed in this analysis engage children in many of the new literacies that are valued in today's world and therefore benefit children in fundamental ways we are only now beginning to understand. Rather, we argue that such analyses have the potential to provide students with the capacity to development counternarratives as literate agents. In other words, the pedagogical goal of engaging in critical analyses of websites through the lens of convergence should not just be to critique such texts, but to actively engage in their redesign.

Within critical literacy scholarship, two major concerns have been raised about practices of textual analysis and social action. The first argues that critical literacy practices must, like the texts they analyze, be situated in local instructional contexts (McDaniel, 2006; Muspratt, A. Luke & Freebody, 1997). For this reason, we stress that the framework of convergence we develop here is not a prescriptive method; rather it is suggestive of key starting points for educators to consider and adapt to their instructional contexts. Nonetheless, it captures several key dimensions of the contemporary, online literacy practices that dominate many young people's out-of-school lives. A second concern is the infringement on students' pleasurable uses of literacy. Whereas most critical literacy scholars would agree that it is important to use real and relevant texts (Gilbert, 2001), several have raised concerns about co-opting fandoms, neutralizing school-based texts, and destroying the pleasures of children's out-of-school literate lives (Alvermann, Moon & Hagood, 1999; Christian-Smith, 1997; Stevens & Bean, 2007). Convergence as an analytic framework of media participation maintains students' active roles in participatory culture, thereby simultaneously allowing both pleasurable and critical stances toward new media texts.

It is also important to mention that, as Dyson (1997) and Newkirk (2002) have discussed, children often use texts like popular websites and other media in critical and unintended ways. Therefore, a textual analysis, as we have conducted here, can only provide a partial picture of the gendered ideologies and identities in which children engage in practice. However, children's gendered practices and understandings of literacy are shaped by the texts, textual practices, and ideologies they are granted access to across domains of their lives. As Brandt (2001) demonstrates, individuals' opportunities for literacy learning (and we would extend this to the ideologies embedded in literacy contexts), are shaped by their contact with "sponsors" or individuals and institutions that enable or deny access to particular literacies and life pathways. If we view popular websites as one of many sets of sponsors in young people's live, we can see the value of critically engaging children with such texts.

Meanwhile, school-based literacy curricula have little to do with engaging in such literacy practices; nor do many children have the opportunity to step back and unpack how convergence shapes their lives, literacies, and world views. This is not to say that young people are not capable of being critically literate outside of school (Lankshear & Knobel, 2006), but that school could and should be taking a more active stance toward such literacies.

One place where schools can have an impact on children's understandings of popular websites and other media is by introducing young people to alternate interpretations and ideologies related to the online texts that now play such significant roles in their recreational lives. This extends far beyond the present focus in many educational contexts that frame online texts in terms of finding information and safety issues. Rather, we need to broaden the focus of literacy education to account for multiliteracies, like popular websites, that are now taking center stage in many children's lives. This does not imply necessarily that we should bring websites like Barbie or Transformers into classroom settings, but it does indicate that it is our responsibility as educators to equip children with ability to critically analyze such sites. Through engaging children in analyses of the convergence strategies used by websites and other contemporary media—including textual convergence, convergence of consumption, and convergence of social relationships—we can engage children in more nuanced and less limiting views of gender and other ideologies of childhood.

REFERENCES

Alvermann, D. (2003). Children's everyday literacies: Intersections of popular culture and language arts. *Language Arts*, *81*(2), 145–154.

Alvermann, D., Moon, J. S., & Hagood, M. C. (1999). *Popular culture in the classroom: teaching and researching critical media literacy.* Newark, DE: International Reading Association; Chicago: National Reading Conference.

Black, R. W. (2005). Access and affiliation: The literacy and composition practices of English-Language Learners in and online fanfiction community. *Journal of Adolescent & Adult Literacy, 49*(2), 118–128. doi:10.1598/JAAL.49.2.4

Brandt, D. (2001). *Literacy in American lives.* New York: Cambridge University Press.

Butler, J. (2004). Performative acts and gender constitution. In J. Rivkin & M. Ryan (Eds.), *Literary Theory: An Anthology* (2nd ed., pp. 900–11). Malden, MA: Blackwell.

Christian-Smith, L. (1997). Pleasure and danger: Children, media, and cultural systems. In S. Muspratt, A. Luke, & P. Freebody (Eds.), *Constructing critical literacies: Teaching and learning textual practice* (pp. 51-58). St. Leonards, Australia: Allen & Unwin.

Coiro, J. (2003). Reading comprehension on the internet: Expanding our understanding of reading comprehension to encompass new literacies. *The Reading Teacher, 56*(5), 458–464.

Comber, B. (2001). Classroom explorations in critical literacy. In H. Fehring & P. Green (Eds.), *Critical literacy: A collection of articles from the Australian Literacy Educators' Association* (pp. 75-83). Newark, DE & Norwood, South Australia: International Reading Association and Australian Literacy Educators' Association.

Cope, B., & Kalantzis, M. (Eds.). (2000). *Multiliteracies: Literacy learning and the design of social futures.* London: Routledge.

Dozier, C., Johnston, P., & Rogers, R. (2006). *Critical literacy/critical teaching: Tools for preparing responsive teachers.* New York: Teachers College Press.

Dyson, A. (1997). *Writing superheroes: Contemporary childhood, popular culture, and classroom literacy.* New York: Teachers College Press.

Eisenberg, M., & Berkowitz, R. (2003). *The definitive Big6 workshop handbook.* Worthington, OH: Linworth.

Evans, J. (Ed.). (2005). *Literacy moves on: Popular culture, new technologies, and critical literacy in the elementary classroom.* Portsmouth, NH: Heinemann.

Fairclough, N. (1995). *Media discourse.* London: Arnold.

Fehring, H., & Green, P. (Eds.). (2001). *Critical literacy: A collection of articles from the Australian Literacy Educators' Association.* Newark, DE & Norwood, South Australia: International Reading Association and Australian Literacy Educators' Association.

Freire, P. (2000). *Pedagogy of the oppressed* (30th Anniversary Ed.). (M.B. Ramos, Trans.). New York: Continuum.

Gee, J. (1996). *Social linguistics and literacies: Ideology in discourses* (2nd Ed.). Philadelphia: Falmer Press.

Gee, J. (2000/2001). Identity as an analytic lens for research in education. *Review of Research in Education, 25*, 99–125.

Gilbert, P. (2001). (Sub)versions: Using sexist language practices to explore critical literacy. In H. Fehring & P. Green (Eds.), *Critical literacy: A collection of articles from the Australian Literacy Educators' Association* (pp. 75-83). Newark, DE & Norwood, Australia: International Reading Association and Australian Literacy Educators' Association.

Goodstein, A. (2007). *Totally wired: What teens and tweens are really doing online.* New York: Saint Martin's Griffin.

Green, P. (2001). Critical literacy revisited. In H. Fehring & P. Green (Eds.), *Critical literacy: A collection of articles from the Australian Literacy Educators' Association.* Newark, DE & Norwood, Australia: International Reading Association and Australian Literacy Educators' Association.

Hall, S. (1980). Encoding/decoding. In *Culture, Media, Language: Working Papers in Cultural Studies,* 1972-79 (pp. 128-138). London: Hutchinson.

Halliday, M. A. K. (1994). *An introduction to functional grammar* (2nd Ed.). London: Arnold.

Heffernan, L. (2004). *Critical literacy and writer's workshop: Bringing purpose and passion to student writing.* Newark, DE: International Reading Association.

Horkheimer, M., & Adorno, T. W. (1972). *Dialectic of enlightenment.* (J. Cumming, Trans.). New York: Continuum.

Horning, A. S. (2004). Digital critical literacy for generation 1.5 and everyone else. *The Reading Matrix, 4*(3), 134–144.

Ito, M. (2006). Japanese media mixes and amateur cultural exchange. In D. Buckingham & R. Willet (Eds.) *Digital Generations* (pp. 49-66). Mahwah, NJ: Lawrence Erlbaum.

Jenkins, H. (2006). *Convergence culture: Where old and new media collide.* New York: New York University Press.

Johnson, R., & Hegarty, J. (2003). Websites as education motivators for adults with learning disability. *British Journal of Educational Technology, 34*(4), 479–486. doi:10.1111/1467-8535.00344

Kress, G., & van Leeuwen, T. (1996). *Reading images: The grammar of visual design.* New York: Routledge.

Kress, G., & van Leeuwen, T. (2001). *Multimodal discourse: The modes and media of contemporary communication.* London: Arnold.

Kristeva, J. (2001). Revolution in poetic language. In V. Leitch (Ed.), *The Norton anthology of theory and criticism* (pp. 2156-2179). New York: Norton.

Lam, E. (2000). Literacy and the design of the self: A case study of a teenager writing on the internet. *TESOL Quarterly, 34*(3), 457–482. doi:10.2307/3587739

Lankshear, C., & Knobel, M. (2006). *New literacies: Everyday practice & classroom learning.* Buckingham, UK: Open University Press.

Leander, K. M., & Lovvorn, J. F. (2006). Literacy networks: Following the circulation of texts, bodies, and objects in the schooling and online gaming of one youth. *Cognition and Instruction, 24*(3), 291–340. doi:10.1207/s1532690xci2403_1

Lemke, J. (1998). Metamedia literacy: Transforming meanings and media. In D. Reinking, M. C. McKenna & L. Labbo (Eds.), *Handbook of Literacy and Technology: Transformation in a Post-Typographic World* (pp. 283-302). Mahwah, NJ: Lawrence Erlbaum Associates.

Leu, D. (2005). *New literacies, reading research, and the challenges of change: A deictic perspective of our research worlds.* Paper presented at the National Reading Conference, Miami, FL.

Leu, D. J., & Kinzer, C. K. (2000). The convergence of literacy instruction with networked technologies for information and communication. *Reading Research Quarterly, 35*(1), 108–127. doi:10.1598/RRQ.35.1.8

Luke, A. (2000). Critical literacy in Australia: A matter of context and standpoint. *Journal of Adolescent & Adult Literacy, 43*(5), 448–461.

Luke, C. (1997). Media literacy and cultural studies. In S. Muspratt, A. Luke, & P. Freebody (Eds.), *Constructing critical literacies: Teaching and learning textual practice* (pp. 19-49). St. Leonards, Australia: Allen & Unwin.

Martin, J. R., Matthiessen, C., & Painter, C. (1997). *Working with functional grammar.* London: Arnold.

McDaniel, C. A. (2006). *Critical literacy: A way of thinking, a way of life.* New York: P. Lang.

McLaughlin, M., & DeVoogd, G. L. (2004). *Critical literacy: Enhancing students' comprehension of text.* New York: Scholastic.

Muspratt, S., Luke, A., & Freebody, P. (Eds.). (1997). *Constructing critical literacies: Teaching and learning textual practice.* St. Leonards, Australia: Allen & Unwin.

Myers, J., & Beach, R. (2004). Hypermedia authoring as critical literacy. *Journal of Adolescent & Adult Literacy, 44*(6), 538–547.

New London Group. (1996). A pedagogy of multiliteracies: Designing social futures. *Harvard Educational Review, 66*(1), 60–92.

Newkirk, T. (2002). *Misreading masculinity: Boys, literacy, and popular culture*. Portsmouth, NH: Heinemann.

Peppler, K. A., & Kafai, Y. B. (2007). From SuperGoo to Scratch: Exploring creative digital media production in informal learning. *Learning, Media and Technology, 32*(2), 149–166. doi:10.1080/17439880701343337

Roberts, D. F., Foehr, U. G., & Rideout, V. (2005). *Generation M: Media in the lives of 8-18 year-olds.* Menlo Park, CA: Kaiser Family Foundation.

Schmar-Dobler, E. (2003). Reading on the internet: The link between literacy and technology. *Journal of Adolescent & Adult Literacy, 47*(1), 80–85.

Stevens, L. P., & Bean, T. W. (2007). *Critical literacy: Context, research, and practice in the K-12 classroom.* Thousand Oaks, CA: SAGE Publications.

Stone, J. C. (2007). Popular websites in adolescents' out-of-school lives: Critical lessons on literacy. In M. Knobel & C. Lankshear (Eds.), *A new literacies sampler* (pp. 49-66). New York: P. Lang.

Stone, J. C., & Veth, E. S. (2008). Rethinking the new literatures of childhood: Cultural models of gender in popular websites. *Journal of Language and Literacy Education, 4*(2), 21–39.

Street, B. (1995). *Social literacies*. New York: Longman.

Vasquez, V. M. (2004). *Negotiating critical literacies with young children*. Mahwah, NJ: L. Erlbaum Associates.

Vasquez, V. M. (2005). Creating opportunities for critical literacy with young children: Using everyday issues and everyday text. In J. Evans (Ed.), *Literacy moves on: Popular culture, new technologies, and critical literacy in the elementary classroom* (pp. 83-105). Portsmouth, NH: Heinemann.

Warnick, B. (2002). *Critical literacy in a digital era: Technology, rhetoric, and the public interest.* Mahwah, NJ: Lawrence Erlbaum Associates.

Willard, N. E. (2007). *Cyber-safe kids, cyber-savvy teens: Helping young people learn to use the Internet safely and responsibly.* San Francisco: Jossey-Bass.

Chapter 4
The Dynamic Design of Learning with Text:
The Grammar of Multiliteracies

Lisa Patel Stevens
Boston College, USA

Molly Dugan
Boston College, USA

ABSTRACT

In this chapter, the authors explore the current challenges facing educational institutions to design learning spaces congruent for learning with and through multimodal textual practices. The chapter reviews the inherent design, or grammar, of multimodal literacy practices and that of learning with these texts. Using examples from secondary and tertiary contexts, constructs from complexity theory offer a theoretical lens that is more generative for conceptualizing and analyzing dynamic literacy practices in educational institutions than multimodal literacy. The chapter concludes with a discussion of the tensions that arise form these examples, using Bourdieu's (1984) habitus to problematize the future of designing dynamic educational spaces.

BACKGROUND

Across various academic fields, the advent of the information age, with its explosion in quantity and format of multimodal texts, has ushered in various reconsiderations and investigations into the nature of textual practices and systems. Within education, the publication of the New London Group's landmark treatise (1996) on literacy, information communication technologies (ICT), and pedagogy initiated myriad inquiries into research and practice, most often within literacy education, information communication technologies, and critical literacy. The New London Group were largely credited with coining the phrase, 'multiliteracies.' The 1996 publication set forth a call and need for educators to address literacy learning which the Group believed were always inextricably connected to available technologies of the time. In this way, the Group emphasized that investigations into literacy and literacy pedagogy must be in concert with new and yet-to-be-seen communications media. Underpinning the work of the New London Group and our work recanted in this chapter, is a view of

DOI: 10.4018/978-1-60566-673-0.ch004

literacy from sociocultural perspectives. As such, our theoretical perspective on literacy positions language and text as always implicated by culturally situated processes of making, conveying and negotiating meaning. People in situated contexts have opportunities to both express themselves and make sense of the world through multiple and multiply designed modes of communication (linguistic/textual, visual/graphical, musical/audio, spatial, gestural).

Throughout these quantitative and qualitative changes in textual practices, the field of literacy research and investigations into literacy pedagogy have been keenly interested in what counts as literacy, literacy competency, and assessment thereof (e.g., Leu, Kinzer, Coiro & Cammack, 2004.

A lesser addressed question, and the focus here, is what parallels can and must be drawn between theories of learning spaces and theories of multiliteracies. A particular focus of this chapter is the exploration of this question, in light of some of the problems schools have encountered as they have worked to educate students in these textual practices. Now that multiliteracies, multimodal texts, and digital literacies are far from 'new,' we extend upon New London Group's initial theorizing about these changes in textual processes to more deeply investigate the complexities involved in planning deliberately for and with multimodality.

To anchor our analyses, the authors (we) present two case studies to explore learning and multiliteracies and examine these case studies and relevant theories through the filter of praxis. Praxis is a key concept outlined by Brazilian educator, Paulo Freire, as part of his mapping of the actions and perspectives central to sincere and purposeful social change. Within this outline, Freire underscored the necessity of praxis, "reflection and action upon the world in order to transform it" (Freire, 1970, p. 36). As we explore the two case studies' uses of dynamic designs of learning with multimodal texts, we employ praxis to note what we can learn from available theories of learning and multimodality and also what educators should pay attention to among the dynamics of texts, space, and participants when hoping for change in practice. To contextualize this work, we first turn to a discussion of the historical problems that have emerged as schools have attempted to adopt a multiliteracies perspective.

ISSUES: HISTORICAL PROBLEMATICS IN SCHOOLING MULTILITERACIES

While multiliteracies offer compelling reasons for consideration and use, their appropriation into institutional spaces of education also demands investigation into the kinds of learning processes and practices that are compatible with these texts. The incorporation of a multiliteracies approach requires a fundamental shift in how teaching and learning spaces are conceptualized, including the particular challenges of reconceptualizing these spaces within the school. Such reconceptualizations of space will be explored in the case studies offered in this chapter. Through the use of selective case studies, it was not assumed that the educational institution contained spaces automatically inclined towards learning, and more so, learning with and about multimodal textual practices. While it is facile and common to conflate learning with education, our inquiry into the intersections of learning spaces and multimodal texts requires an intentional attention to learning, which occurs in all kinds of spaces, public, institutional, and countercultural. While public pedagogies, those that occur outside of the orchestrated contexts of schools, tend to be marked by user-driven inquiries and highly utilitarian teaching/learning exchanges, the roles of learner, teacher, within the spatial boundaries and temporal rhythms of classroom learning have yet to be similarly transformed (Gee, 2003). Institutional spaces of education, however, are traditionally marked by relatively inflexible patterns of interactions (Hargreaves, 1994).

Further complicating the institutional culture of schooling is the generational divide across literacy practices (Hagood, Stevens & Reinking, 2003). For example, in classrooms across post-industrial nations, students use and create multimediated texts, but these texts and their surrounding pedagogical contexts do not necessarily reconstruct the classroom space to be either terribly dynamic or transformative (Rogers & Schofield, 2005). The typical response of schools and education to information age technologies and texts has been a rather arbitrary and successive sampling of various textual practices. From zines to blogs, the appropriation of these practices is often conducted in a desire to be innovative in practices, to take advantage of the 'newness' of various texts and practices found outside of schools. However, these attempts to incorporate practices, without a view of underlying principles, has typically led to an approach that assimilates these textual practices in the traditionally linear processes of classrooms. This process veritably works to flatten dynamic and nonlinear textual practices into the worn patterns of teacher-led, didactic sequences of following step-by-step instructions. The assimilation and subsequent transformation of dynamic literacy practices into hierarchical and linearly ordered classroom exchanges echoes the cliché of the square peg into a round hole. The mismatch is one of grammar, the underlying logic that underpins both various textual practices and learning processes. As used in fields such as systemic functional linguistics, grammar is a term that connotes an attention to both logic and options.

The challenge is then how to reconceptualize not only what counts as literacy, but also what are conceptualizations of learning that are up to the challenge of multimodal and dynamic literacy practices. How can schools and teachers reposition themselves to provide pedagogy that not only makes use of multiliteracies but is in concert with their underlying lines of logic? To do so, we must review the inherent logic systems, or grammar, of both multimodal literacy practices and how learning has been framed in schooling contexts, including those detailed in the chapter's case studies. In the following section, we detail the paradigmatic shifts in text usage that are part and parcel of a reconsideration of the very logic, or grammars (Halliday, 1993) of various textual practices.

GRAMMATICAL CONSIDERATIONS OF MULTIMODAL TEXTUAL PRACTICES

To better understand the grammar of multimodal textual practices, we begin by examining both the logic of multimodal texts and the logic underpinning the literacy practices of users of text. Through both theoretical and practice-based points, we examine the design and structures of text itself and the various roles and cultural significations that are part of the context of the literacy practices.

In digital modes, interactions with texts are changed. Some researchers (Darley, 2000; Gee, 2003; Lankshear & Knobel, 2003; Lemke, 1995; Unsworth, 2001) have discussed the effects on social and semiotic power through new modes of interactivity and hypertextuality. Reading and writing become less about a static finished product and more reflective of a permeable process. An example is the difference between a published, print volume of an encyclopedia and Wikipedia. The former is constructed as a finished product; the latter is constructed as a work in progress.

As roles shift and literacy practices move from a receptive mode of interacting with "finished" texts, the agency to construct meaning is more explicitly felt as distributed among the participants. This enhanced interactivity allows users to write back to producers of texts, thus affecting traditional social power structures and the power dynamic between producers and consumers. This permeability and possibility to destabilize the authorial role is neither exclusive to nor derivative only from multimodal texts, but we are argue that it is more explicitly felt with these texts.

As hypertextuality allows users to link to other texts, users have multiple entryways into texts and multiple exits from produced text through hyperlinks. New semiotic modes (i.e., animation, sound, and video) afford expanded opportunities to produce text that convey meaning in ways unavailable in unitary, linear forms. These non-linear ways of interacting with texts challenge traditionally-oriented temporal and interpretive semiotics and transform the conceptual and structural grammar of schools.

Recognizing the shifting roles among consumers, producers and users of multimodal texts is central to understanding the sea change that is taking place in both textual practices and, more so, how people take up conscious positions within literacy practices. The chapter's case studies will illustrate how the logic of multimodal textual practices may be in (and out) of sync with learning processes in schools.

One way to think about changing engagements with texts (e.g., possibilities offered through hypertextuality and multiple semiotic modes) is to consider how people may engage with multimediated literacy practices in ways more akin to play (Darley, 2000). For example, the ways in which a person might create a pastiche of various video texts into a themed montage and then post this to a networked website, such as youtube.com, is more like play: manipulating, transforming, and co-opting.

In the grammar of multimodal textual practices, play seems organic to the production of text. However, types of play run along a continuum with the parameters set by the architecture of the space. The tension runs between strict regulations to no constraints. In other words, certain types of play are occasioned (Davis & Sumara, 1997) by how tight or how loose the parameters are in the design. Thus, simplistic assumptions about play in the production of text should be tempered by logic of grammar and by asking, "What are the particular attributes and conventions that underpin such practices and the experiences they engender?" (Darley, 2000). This is an important consideration when contemplating the inclusion of multimodal textual practices in schools. An out-of-school literacy practice like playing a networked online game is a different literacy practice with a different purpose and different stakes than an in-school assignment to create a multimodal research project. The parameters and constraints are different thus engendering a different type of play and a different experience. The conventions and attributes of the context are central to the experience.

Engagement with multimodal texts is built on the understanding that the grammar of these texts is different from the grammar of linear texts. The design challenge in curriculum and instruction is to consider the distinct representational and communicational affordances of particular modes and contexts rather than to fit multimodal literacy practices into existing literacy practices in schools. A more nuanced understanding of the grammar of schools and the grammar of multimodal texts may illuminate a more logical course for mapping the necessary actions and perspectives necessary to engage in sincere and purposeful social change or praxis.

GRAMMATICAL CONSIDERATIONS OF LEARNING SPACES

In keeping with our use of the metaphor and heuristic of grammar to forefront the particular designs, features, and contexts of multimodal texts, we now extend this conceptual node in relation to learning spaces and propose an alternative for framing learning with multimodal texts. As mentioned previously, our intention here is to purposefully evade a conflation of learning and education, or more precisely, of learning spaces and educational institutions. To be sure, learning occurs frequently within educational institutions, but the construction of an educational institution, despite its requisite plans for curriculum and pedagogy, does not necessarily guarantee a presence or continuity of learning. In fact, closer inspection of the tradition approaches to the design of learning through curricular mapping and lesson planning shows potential contradictions to the grammars of multimodal texts.

Consider the typical lesson plan format provided in Table 1 which is a commonplace lesson template for preservice, inservice teacher education, and used by classroom teachers on a daily basis. This typical lesson plan template provides a textual tool that captures and reifies the inherent logic, or grammar, of most formal educational spaces, including roles for participants and activities. This grammar first assumes that a learning objective is unilateral for a classroom full of students, then delineates in chronological fashion, the steps and materials that each of those students will follow and use towards the learning objectives, and lastly provides space for consideration of modifications from this sequence. However, these modifications are only to be mapped from a conceptualization of students who are outside of normalized developmental curve, such as those that have been labeled as developmentally delayed or who are operating in the class through a second language. This grammar contains within it an ascription of the variance to the interiority of individuals, rather than also having to do with the context, the task, the materials, or the other participants, to name just a few of the possible factors that can impact any activity. Traditionally, education uses a textual tool whose logic and grammar demands and reflects a linear prediction of activities and pathologizes individual students who do not fit the model. Put simply, the logic is anything but dynamic. In light of the literature on multimodal texts and their affordances, such an approach to learning is without a doubt out of sync with multimodality. Our purpose in criticizing this approach is not simply to deconstruct this text and its logic as undesirable. In fact, depending upon the learning activity and space, such a unilateral, linear logic could well be the best grammatical tool to map the activities, participants, and tools. Therein lies the point: what 'works' is a pliable, moving feast, one that should be considered, reconsidered, and constantly recontextualized given the learning activity at hand. On the whole, we are not arguing for one grammar, or logic, of learning over another, but for a consideration of the learning activity, including the textual practices, to produce more organically design learning spaces. Such a stance affords space to examine productive matches between grammars of learning and text while always keeping the context central.

A GRAMMAR OF LEARNING THAT IS CONSIDERATE OF MULTIMODALITY

In our exploration of and for spaces that are generative for learning with and through multimodal texts, we take strong cues from public pedagogies. Across practices that occur outside of formal educational institutions, working with multimodal texts and their accompanying roles of production, transformation, and alteration often is linked to learning that is more on-demand and user-driven than prescriptively detailed. This learning is more directionally dynamic and circuitous than teleologic in nature. For example, a new user of the afore-mentioned youtube.com website who has a query about how to post a video might email other users, use a link for frequently asked questions, and/or conduct a search through a different search engine with keywords about the issue, to name just a few of the available routes for learning. This kind of dynamic learner-driven interaction is part and parcel of digital textual practices, particularly those that are highly networked. However, the prospect of learning with and through multimodal texts in schools presents a tension between innovation and prescription. Literacy educators are charged with delineating and developing the various skills, process, and practices necessary for success in society. This,

Table 1. Lesson plan template (used with permission from LessonPlansPage.com)

Lesson Plan Title:
Concept / Topic To Teach:
Standards Addressed:
General Goal(s):
Specific Objectives:
Required Materials:
Anticipatory Set (Lead-In):
Step-By-Step Procedures:
Plan For Independent Practice:
Closure (Reflect Anticipatory Set):
Assessment Based On Objectives:
Adaptations (For Students With Learning Disabilities):
Extensions (For Gifted Students):
Possible Connections To Other Subjects:

traditionally, both forefronts the role of the teacher in the learning process and begs a certain amount of prescription for the learning process, as seen in the lesson plan design in Table 1. Culturally speaking, the highly individualized practices of schooling (Lortie, 1974) also are distant from the networked learning found in public pedagogies around multimodal texts. However, as Gee discusses (2003), education would do well to pay closer attention to the ways that learning occurs dynamically in noninstitutional spaces. The tension still exists to find a conceptualization of learning that can be leveraged by educators to serve the grammars of multimodal texts. In fact, from the perspective of a literacy educator, this is the salient demand, to architect learning spaces that are not only considerate of the features of multimodal texts but that allow for the divergent uptakes of learning, authorial stances, and products. Since the traditional discourses of linear lesson planning are inept to deal with this challenge, we propose drawing upon a different conceptualization of science, that of complexity science.

While it is beyond the scope of this chapter to describe well the bodies of knowledge stemming from chaos and complexity theory, in the spirit of

Davis and Sumara's (2006) call for educational research to revisit which sciences inform pursuit of knowledge, we draw upon the complexity theories in search of a conceptual fit between grammars of learning and multimodal texts. In particular, the concept of enabling constraints offers a compelling alternative to linear lesson planning. Simply put, enabling constraints are the necessary conditions of limitation within which diversity flourishes and supports the emergence of complexity. Complexity, in this sense, is the emergence of dynamically rich learning, in which the contributing components of the system work together to produce work, i.e., learning, that comes together under "grander cognitive unities" (Davis & Sumara 2006, p. 316). This perspective, or template, of learning provides a potentially productive fit for the grammatical challenge of this chapter, as it, in part, assumes diversity of participants, processes, and outcomes. Working from this stance, enabling constraints are the necessary parameters of activity, rather than scripts of predicted behaviors. As an explanatory or planning heuristic, they set out the bare minimum of borders within which the salient function of a project is accomplished while allowing for innovation, emergence, and transformation.

For example, the process of photosynthesis, in a very simple rendering, requires a plant organism, light energy, carbon dioxide, and water. However, from that simple set of constraints, myriad versions of this process take place. Science writer Michael Pollan (2001) has explicated the ways in which various plants, such as tulips, apples, and marijuana, and potatoes have engaged in complicated and surprising histories of co-evolution with humans. With innovations in their abilities to intoxicate and satiate at a variety of levels, these plants illustrate variations on photosynthesis that have, interactionally with humans, maximized their abilities to flourish (Pollan, 2001). From a small set of enabling constraints, a general pattern of photosynthesis occurs, but with widely varying consequences impossible to predict. The concept of enabling constraints can aptly contend with framing and explaining this dynamic phenomenon, and it can perform a similar function in discussions of learning.

In educational terms, this concept of enabling constraints means designing pedagogical parameters that create opportunities for and nurture diverse textual engagement and production, rather than producing a linear series of steps to be followed by all learners. To explore the praxis (Freire, 1970) of enabling constraints with multimodal texts, we describe and problematize two classrooms whose activities are characterized more by a grammar of dynamics, difference, and emergence than a predictive process of lesson planning. One context is a graduate literacy pedagogy class taught by Lisa and the other was a high school technology classroom where Molly was a researcher and participant. In both, the pedagogical approach echoes the New London Group's call for a pedagogy of multiliteracies and complexity theory's concepts of enabling constraints. In the next section, we provide a brief description of sample activities from these classes and then move to a discussion that problematizes the manifestation of dynamic activities among context, tools, users, and learning in educational institutions.

INSTITUTIONAL SPACE: TEACHER EDUCATION

In this secondary literacy pedagogy course taught by Lisa, the majority of the students are completing their undergraduate studies with a concentration in a discipline area in combination with courses in pedagogy and assessment from educational perspectives. The goals of the class are to provide these emerging teachers with the conceptual nodes and skills necessary to facilitate their pupils' disciplinary and literacy learning. The course is based on a definition of multiliteracies, one that takes for granted that 1) literacy is at once a sociocultural construct and is experienced socioculturally, and 2) effective literacy pedagogy must consider the skills, practices, and processes demanded and used in spaces well outside of educational institutions. In consideration of secondary schooling as a context, the course also emphasizes that adolescence is an overly clichéd view of young people and must be interrogated by active research into the lived realities and perceptions of secondary students (Stevens, et al., 2007), particularly within times marked by globalization and transnationalism. These three tenets of the class are important in understanding the major assignment of the class and how that assignment makes use of enabling constraints.

The proposal and supposition in using enabling constraints for the major work in the course is a deliberate pedagogical approach, one that is characterized by design rather than prediction. That is pre-service teachers must first experience and 'live' through a non-linear teaching approach if they are to successfully engage in similar pedagogical practices with their own classes. This supposition also rests on the fact that for the vast majority of the students, even those raised in years well after the dawn of the information age, their schooling experiences have been marked by factory models of organization and linear, didactic relationships of textual practices. In his classical work, sociologist Dan Lortie (1974) explained how teachers, when they are students, engage in 12 or more years of apprenticeship of observation, and this apprenticeship offers a compelling explanation as to why so many teachers replicate and reify the methods used with them when they were students. In that sense, beginning teachers must themselves experience participation in dynamic learning spaces with multimodal texts if they are to then leverage these techniques in designing their classrooms as learning spaces.

Consequently, for the major project of the class, which is a qualitative case study of a secondary school pupil and its representation, the university students are issued a 'design challenge.' Within this design challenge, they must gather first-hand information about the lived realities of a secondary school student, relevant research into compelling aspects of the student's life, and convey this information and their learning about multiliteracies, adolescence, and textual design through a text format of their choice. The text format must be in concert with information conveyed and the intended audience and the student must also provide an explanation of the design of the text in relationship to its contents and context. In this sense, the enabling constraints of this design challenge are: 1) investigation of two types, 2) design of a text, and 3) metanarration about the text and its design. An important note here is that these enabling constaints differ strongly from the more traditional concept of assignment requirements. A list of requirements is more predictive of what must be included as items in a text, whereas enabling constraints mark out rough parameters and then participants must engage in interpretation and innovation to create the text.

From this set of constraints, across four instantiations of the course and its project, students produced various types and genres of texts, including informational websites, chronological blogs, podcasts, linear essays, and reproductions of students' Facebook and MySpace websites. To produce these texts, the students engaged in a variety of learning strategies, including, but not limited to asking each other for help, when certain students had more expertise in areas than others, using help/support lines from the university's information communication technologies services, initiating an online suggestion board for the class' use, and eliciting help from other experts located through the Internet, through friends, and through commercial companies.

The assignment and its use of enabling constraints was a successful match between grammars of texts and grammar of learning when viewed from the manifestation of a few enabling constraints through the processes used and products authored by the students. First, there was a wide and continually changing collection of text types and genres that the students produced. Within these texts, students took up various authorial positions of author: sometimes working independently, sometimes co-authoring explicitly with each other, sometimes co-authoring the subject of the case study and other times opening their text for comments, additions and authorship from other students in the class. Second, the students initiated and used a wide variety of techniques and resources to support their mastery and use of a multimodal text. Many students worked with each other to support technical and pragmatic processes of web design, video editing and other processes. This particular tactic eventuated in an online 'help' discussion board exclusively for the class, an example of a textual product that is more implicated in the process of learning than in a predicted list of assignment requirements. In other instances, students pursued tutorials and assistance from contacts outside of the university. From the perspective of multimodalities, the variation of textual type and genre reflected a greater and deeper use of various logographic, visual, and auditory symbols than is typically possible and/or used within essay assignments and submissions. However, the successful match between grammars of text and learning were not without concomitant issues and areas of conceptual tension.

The first issue that arose, in each of the four course sections, was equity in grading across different text types. For example, in an exit interview from one class, a student who produced a technically sophisticated website summarized the tension this way:

"Well, I was confused at first how you were going to grade, like, my website and somebody else's paper. And, you know, I know how to make a website. What if someone didn't know, and they put in all this effort to do it. How does that count next to a paper, that, you know, everyone knows how to do."

The tension here is one of equity, across text types, learning challenges, and learner effort that are not equal. From this student's perspective, the variation in learning and products for this assignment presented a significant break with pedagogy based on fairness manifested through sameness. Of note here is the different location of diversity from the perspective of traditional pedagogy, where diversity presents a problem or complication to the unitary plan for all, and from that of complexity theory, where diversity is not only assumed but integral to the emergency of complexity in the system.

The second issue that arose was, similarly, within the confines of the course, and that was with the mechanical, pragmatic problems that students encountered as they were learning how to design, create, and publish text types that were new to them. This issue took the form in frequent updates from the students to the professor, of various setbacks, challenges, and glitches, for lack of a better word. Typical of these kinds of updates is this email update from a student:

[__________],

I have a minor problem, and I mean this has the potential to be a very big problem. I have re-recorded the important video clips with my case study and have converted them from .mov files to .wmv files. I have created a folder on my desktop and included the converted movie files and incomplete powerpoint presentation. I intend to zip up the folder and send that off. It was once I had gotten about 1/3 of the way through the actual compositon of the presentation that I decided to test the sending of it. In doing so from gmail, the computer sat in an idle state for almost 30 minutes before I called it quits. I tried it again and then discovered (by a phone call to the ex again) that the file was obscenely large. I have done everything I can to make the folder smaller, but with so many video clips, it is difficult. This being said, the submission on WebCT might be my best option for submission; however, I do not know what the size restriction is for uploading a file. If there is in fact a restriction that I can't meet, and because I can not break up the folder (because of the converted files) I would have to find a way to give you a hard copy of the presentation. This presents the greatest problem because after losing hours while my computer practically shut down tonight, I do not think I will be done during work hours tomorrow to get it to you. Even if you say that WebCT should work for my large submission, if it doesn't, there is no way to resubmit and I couldn't try it again. That would leave me to plan B, which I don't really have because of the timing of this due date. So, I welcome your suggestions and thoughts. I apologize that this problem has come up and the timing issue presents itself. I did not anticipate this and really don't think I could have with my knowledge on this subject. I was really pleased with how the presentation was turning out and do not want to resort to just writing a paper to make this all go away. Until I hear from you, I will just continue creating the slides.

Thanks,

Alexandra

In designing and using multimodal texts, problems such as those encountered by Alexandra are commonplace, in fact, they are to be expected. But Alexandra is taking on this task in the context of a graduate course, and as such, these glitches are presented within the specific time constrains of a semester and therefore represent potential damage and violence to her grade in the course. In the example used before, someone posting their video to youtube.com, when encountering problems and issues, can take their time at resolving the issue or even decide to abandon the project altogether. The students in this class are engaging in these learning and designing activities within the institutional space of a university, and that brings with it all of the power differentials, cultural habits, and *studenting* patterns that are entirely logical and also effect the nature of the activity. No longer is this a public pedagogy, in which the latitude to explore different learning pathways is without consequence outside of the manifestation of the text itself. Issues such as these present rich opportunities for analysis of design of learning and space. In the next section, we provide similar examples from a secondary context and use both in the final analysis of the grammars of learning and text.

INSTITUTIONAL SPACE: HIGH SCHOOL CLASSROOM

The context of Molly's study is a media class in an urban high school. The high school was once considered one of the city's best, but today, on standardized measures, is one of the worst-performing high schools in the state. The state board of education has given the high school one year to improve or risk closure.

Molly is a researcher and participant in the class two to three days a week, documenting the intersection of spaces, texts, and participants is a goal of the study. For the purpose of this chapter and the focus on design, the discussion will more closely examine a view of the classroom that is informed by the teacher's description of the plans and processes of the class. These data serve to illuminate the choices the teacher, Mr Smith[1], makes in the design of the assignments and the use of enabling constraints as a pedagogical approach. The enabling constraints include: 1) multimodal text production, 2) collaborative design and execution, 3) individual roles and responsibilities, 4) collective accountability.

From this set of constraints, students are responsible for four genres of film a semester (e.g., commercials, public service announcements, interviews, documentaries). The best films are selected to be on the high school's TV show. Students from several different classes constitute the executive council that produce, direct, and broadcast the show.

Mr Smith organizes the class as a media lab. Depending on the activity, students move around the class (and the school) to write scripts, scout locations, shoot film, digitize, and edit. Based on their production schedule, groups are working on different aspects of the project each day. A group is out filming, another student is at a computer editing film shot the previous day, another student is searching Google images for footage, other students are recruiting actors, and other groups are downloading music and recording voiceovers. Mr Smith describes the design saying:

They (the students) have a finish line/an endgame, but the process to that isn't scripted. There are checks along the way. I try to keep the kids at about the same time line in preproduction, but they are all doing different things and I'm conferencing with them in groups and individually. I have them do the commercials first because they can suck, they're not that important. The projects are designed to increase in technical complexity.

Mr Smith takes many pedagogical cues from his out of school experience as a project manager in a corporation. In designing the concept of the media lab, Mr Smith seeks to mirror the skills and knowledge required to run a production company. In the lab, the interactions between teacher/ student and student/student are highly utilitarian. At the beginning of the year, Mr Smith sets up a "boot camp" to teach the technical skills of filmmaking. He takes several days on cameras and lenses. The class sits in a circle and he shows them how to use the equipment. He sets up time trials that incorporate the different skills he's taught. The students have to work in teams on the time trials. At that point they start to negotiate leadership.

In addition to learning how to use the camera, lights, and audio to shoot film, students learn how to use computer software (e.g., iMovie, Limewire) to edit and to add text and sound to complete the digital productions. Asked about the learning process in the class, Mr Smith explained:

They just figure it out. I also show them www.atomiclearning.com

(X goes to site on his laptop). It's a site that shows little movies to explain how different software works. It was designed for 'Oh, shoot how do you do that thing again? You can get a tutorial on how to do anything with iMovie.

One of the first things I do is demystify the computer. I show them the guts of the computer, the hard drive, the screen. This is a liminal stage. I show them the basics of the computer…that it's a system that all works together. I teach them editing. Show how to cut and paste, set up the desktop, how to save. I get them ramped up on Macs. Kids will say, "I don't know Macs. I don't know computers. We spend about two months of getting to understand the computer. I teach them how to do research. How to do proper, more effective web searches. I teach them how to use keyword in Google. They take ownership. I give assignments/quizzes – a series of checks.

I want them to learn to find things on themselves. This year I decentralized the knowledge. If they want to know how to put their iPod in the computer I show them where they can find the instructions. I teach them the correct terms like 'synching' the iPod. If they don't use the correct terms, I say, "What's the word?" I showed them how to read the instructions online. Taught them how to look through to find want they want-to scan.

I used to just do or ask them to do things, now I take the extra sixty seconds to explain to kids why I'm asking them to do something a certain way (e.g., searching images, the lighting, the camera angles)

Beginning the study midway through the school year, Molly observed a smooth running, user-driven operation. Instead of the usual student to teacher exchange of

"What are we doing today?" Mr Smith would ask the students, "What are you doing today?" Students use their pre-production to-do checklists, script breakdown and storyboard to guide the execution of their projects. Before beginning filming, Mr Smith meets with the crew to "greenlight" their projects. In this exchange, the students walk Mr Smith through all aspects of the film (i.e., concept, locations, actors, camera angles).

As mentioned, differentiated roles and responsibilities are an enabling constraint of the design. Each project consists of teams, or crews, of three students assigned the roles of director, producer, or grip. The assignment of teams and the organization of groups is a source of tension in the class for two reasons. First, Mr Smith wrestles with the tension between "wanting really good production, really good content…Me make the groups and put all the skilled kids together or how I'm doing it by mixing up the groups and giving them all opportunities to be the director, producer, editor." Second, as often is the case in groups, some students contribute more than others and students often prefer one role to another. The result is that students often gravitate to a particular role (i.e., editor, cameraperson, director) even if it's not their assigned role. However, because the students are working toward the collective goal of a winning production (i.e., one selected to be broadcast on the TV show), students also authentically collaborate and use each others' skills and knowledge. The following dialogue is an example of the way students negotiated the process. Beatrice, Will, and Dana are in the hallway discussing how to shoot a scene:

Will: "I've been talking to other people about what might work."

Beatice- "We can have a split screen."

Will- He (X) said it could be done like the last video "The Heist."

Beatrice –"By Monday? I'm panicking hard. We're still going to have to edit it... add music, voiceovers"

W- "I can get it done."

Beatrice to Dana- "What do you think?" (This is the first time that Beatrice has asked Dana an open ended question or asked for his input.)

Dana-"We could have him hiding and come out of there. We could shoot it from this angle."

Will- "I like that idea. You know how in the movies they show the bad guy. They show the beginning and then not till the end."

Beatrice - "OK. Where's the "to do" list?"

This brief exchange offers an example of how the design of Mr Smith's class and the students' uptake of the design is in concert with multimodal literacy practices. Through the enabling constraints of the design, students are aware of the affordances of different modes of communication (e.g., visual, spatial, gestural, musical, linguistic) as well as the affordances (e.g., knowledge and skills) of their fellow students. In this process, the agency to construct meaning is distributed among the participants and across modes in the production of text.

Just as the literacy practices are more emergent and dynamic so is the design of the learning space. Less driven by a predictive process of lesson planning or a goal of unilateral outcomes, the expectation is rather one of rigorous processes and quality products, or as Mr Smith says, "Hope for the best, plan for the worst" and "make it awesome."

In this design, congruity exists between the grammar of multimodality and the grammar of the learning space. The intersection of texts, contexts, and participants construct a dynamic and synchronous learning space. This synchronicity, however, is an anomaly in the school. Everything about what this class does and how they do it is at odds with the way the rest of the system works structurally and culturally.

The mantra of the school is "graduation for all." This slogan is plastered around the school and on the lips of administrators, guidance counselors, and teachers. However, how 'success' is understood in Mr Smith's class and in the larger school context varies greatly from the perspective of the students. Students say that Mr Smith expects and demands quality work. If any aspect of the project falls short, the students know that they'll have to re-shoot, add voiceovers, or re-edit. From the perspective and language of complexity theory, success of the system is dependent upon collective collaboration. In contrast, students share stories about the poor quality of work that they or their peers do in other classes and are passed and even praised. Students recognize that a low bar exists for "achievement" in the school. With graduation as the goal, learning is second to meeting institutional benchmarks. What counts as achievement in Mr Smith's class is in tension with the institutional culture of the school and its understanding of what counts as achievement and learning.

However, the differences between this class and the larger educational system of the school are also felt in both the contrastive identities that Mr Smith and his students construct in relation to the school and how other members of the school community react to this class' activities. First, Mr Smith, like many of his students, in many ways, defies the institutional culture of the school and the institutionalized roles of what it means to be a teacher or a student. Mr Smith's students don't simply follow teacher-led directions, and Mr Smith is iconoclastic in his role as teacher and in his design of assignments and assessments.

Second, other teachers and administrators question the students' movement around the school and the "interruptions" that filming may cause in the course of the school day. Restricted access to the web is a constant source of frustration for Mr Smith and the students because they waste time navigating the firewall. A proxy through Mexico brought them broader access, but once the administration discovered it, it was shut down. Even after countless successes and accomplishments (e.g., winning teacher of the year, the students' win of a state wide high school news competition, applying for and winning grants to enhance the technology in his classroom), Mr Smith is questioned by the administration and some other teachers about whether he's onboard with the rules and if he's member of the team. For example, Mr Smith is reprimanded for not having his room ready for state-wide assessment because he and his students have been building new sets and redesigning the classroom themselves. The class is often criticized for the content of their productions by teachers and administrators who say it's too risqué, not enough about school, takes too much time from academic work and, through the grapevine, too "ghetto." From this view, the innovative design of the class and its success in producing collaborative multimodal texts is in tension with the institution's cultural and structural brick walls.

DISCORD, DISSONANCE, AND DISRUPTION

We used the concept of enabling constraints to draw attention to the emergence of complexity, the emergence of innovation and learning within a system, as a different filter or lens for what counts as learning and what conditions seem to promote that emergence. Through our experiences in these two educational settings, the filter of enabling constraints proves to be a productive conceptual fit with the grammatical challenge currently felt within the architecture of learning institutions when attempting to appropriate multimodal texts. Through this perspective of constraints, we are more easily able to engage in a discussion of the learning and teaching processes, the participants, and the products or texts, and how these components work together dynamically to produce those grander cognitive unities. We are more clearly able to see how the design of the spaces works best with parameters or constraints. However, in both examples, we have also listed some of the tensions that have arisen in these contexts. It would be foolhardy to expect innovation to not instigate such arenas of constentation. Inherent to the definition of innovation is a break with what is known and used. As such, innovation is perhaps not terribly innovative if there are not spaces of discomfort. In this section, still in the spirit, of learning, we want to pay particular attention to the areas, themes, and tones of dischord, to examine what dynamic spaces and practices with multimodal texts might tell us about the structures of educational institutions and practices.

As Davis and Sumara (2006) discussed in their analysis of what complexity theory has to offer educational research and its notions of science, the tensions that arose within and around these examples should be examined, for what they reveal about the underlying systems of logic within educational institutions and their structures:

"Rather than prescriptions, the useful generalizations of complexity-based research comes in the form of, for example, classrooms that meet minimal conditions for student co-participation in the development of interpretive possibilities around key ideas, or resources that are not parsed into disjointed bits of intertwined concepts or vocabularies that reveal the pervasiveness and limitations of linearized structures of modern schools" (p. 318).

In fact, through the description of tensions from the two classes and their projects, the salient location of discord was cultural institution of learning. In the teacher education contexts, the areas of disruption did not occur as the university students grappled with, the challenges and obstacles in authoring their multimodal and interconnected texts. On the contrary, this was the site of the most highly dynamic and interrelated patterns of learning's. Students worked with each other, restitched their own concepts about texts, writing, and publishing. The areas of dissonance occurred as students engaged in these activities but felt pressure from what the particular time/space configurations of a semester-long course and what they had come to know and apprenticed through observation as the normalized practices in these spatial configurations. The configurations of learning within this and most other educational institutions are premised upon individualized processes and assessments, completion of learning and products within a set timeframe, and equity (similarity) in learning processes and products. These configurations are perhaps the polar opposite of the tenets of differentiation, unpredictability, and dynamically cumulative knowledge found in the emergence of complex systems.

Within the high school, though, examples and conversations that display dissonance with dynamism did not involve the students in the classroom but more so the relationship of this classroom with the larger context of the school. From examples of teachers who experienced discomfort with the students' learning practices that broke the time and physical space configurations of the class to the ways in which the school's administration proves to be a constant obstacle requiring wire, rewire, and reroute access to a compatible server and security filter, the discord for this complex learning situation is with the larger, neighboring institutional context. Arguably, it is this type of innovation that complex learning systems display as unscriptable variations in learning, but of note here is the protracted relationship with the larger institution, and this relationship is one of contestation. However, while complexity theory offers rich filters for reconceptualizing learning, it does not have the theoretical tools to articulate the historical complications in innovative schooling practices. To contend with the varied and deeply complicated interactions among individuals, institutions, and society, we turn to the concepts of practice and habitus.

Across these two contextual examples is that the cultural knowledge of what counts as learning with texts, what is appropriate activity for educational institutions, in short, what is 'normal' practice. However, these practices are only partially implicated in the explicit curriculum of schools and colleges of teacher education. Strongly illustrated in these examples of discord and, arguably more salient, are the normalized knowledges and practices that participants bring with them into various learning situations. In this sense, the expectations, practices, and protests lie neither within the social institutions of learning nor in the participants but in the constant, active colocalization between them.

The reproduction and space for agency in maintaining, changing, reformulating and/or coopting the design of learning lies within neither the individual nor the institution but a constant social mediation between conditions and practices, or simply put, habitus. Most widely and significantly attributed to French social theorist and activist, Pierre Bourdieu (1984), this idea of habitus means to collocate the personal, the individual, with the collective, as a social subjectivity[2]. As Holt annotates, "The habitus is an abstracted, transposable system of schema that both classifies the world and structures action. Bourdieu emphasizes that the contents of the habitus are largely presuppositional rather than discursive and that the habitus structures actions through a process of creative typification to particular situations," (Holt, 1998, p. 3).

The concept of habitus is a complicated theory of social practices that resists an oversimplification of locating reproduction and agency within either pole of the individual or the institution. To be sure, the use of such a frame makes it notably more complicated and difficult to engage in a discussion of educational implications for multimodal textual practices within educational institutions. From the theoretical perspective of habitus, it is impossible to jump to a discussion of best practices, as practices as socially mediated and indiscernible from the accumulated sets of knowledges that individuals bring to bear in various institutional spaces. To engage, though, in social scientific research that explores the relationship of individuals within society in relationship to particular practices, such as those involving multimodal texts, we must make use of frames such as these that prevent us from overly simplifying areas of complexity, discord, and innovation to individually exclusive categories of individuals, institutions, or activities.

CONCLUSION

Within the examples provided in this chapter, the 'creative typification' of participants within and beyond the learning contexts brings to bear assumptions and prefabricated notions of learning, student/teacher roles, and products of learning. Perhaps the most productive steps that educational research, teacher education, and educational institutions can take, in concert with the active engagement of complex learning spaces, is to actively trace the ways in which habitus is shaped and manifest normalized notions of learning, text, and educational achievement. Actively tracing the ways that habitus is shaped requires a rigorous awareness and interrogation of the cultural contexts and practices that take on the shape of what is 'normal.' This can provide opportunities for participants to reflect on how their beliefs can be undermined in decision making through these subtle processes. In fact, it may be that the most potent contribution from learning with multimodal texts is not an assemblage of multimodal skills and processes but more what the appropriation of these practices can tell us about the current social practices in education and how they maybe conceptualized and reconstituted by individuals.

REFERENCES

Bourdieu, P. (1984). *Distinction: A social critique of the judgement of good taste*. Trans: R. Nice. Cambridge, MA: Harvard University Press.

Darley, A. (2000). *Visual digital culture: Surface play and spectacle in new media genres*. London: Routledge.

Davis, B., & Sumara, D. (2006). *Complexity and education: Inquiries into learning, teaching, and research*. Mahwah, NJ: Erlbaum.

Davis, B., & Sumara, D. J. (1997). Cognition, complexity, and teacher education. *Harvard Educational Review, 67*(1), 105–125.

Freire, P. (1970). *Pedagogy of the oppressed.* New York: Continuum Publishing Co.

Gee, J. P. (2003). *What video games have to teach us about learning and literacy*. New York: Palgrave Macmillan.

Hagood, M. C., Stevens, L. P., & Reinking, D. (2003). What do THEY have to teach US? Talkin' cross generations! In D. E. Alvermann (Ed.), *Adolescents and literacies in a digital world* (pp. 68-83). New York: Peter Lang.

Halliday, M. A. K. (1993). Some grammatical problems in scientific English. In M.A.K. Halliday & J.R. Martin (Eds.), *Writing science: Literacy and discursive power* (pp. 69-85). Pittsburgh, PA: University of Pittsburgh Press.

Hargreaves, A. (1994). *Changing teachers, changing times*. New York: Teachers College Press.

Holt, D. (1998). Does cultural capital structure American consumption? *The Journal of Consumer Research, 25*(1), 1–25. doi:10.1086/209523

Lankshear, C., & Knobel, M. (2003). *New literacies: changing knowledge and classroom learning.* Philadelphia: Open University Press.

Lemke, J. L. (1995). *Textual politics: discourse and social dynamics*. Bristol, PA: Taylor & Francis Inc.

Lesson Plans Page. (2008). Retrieved December 30, 2008, from http://www.lessonplanspage.com/LessonTemplate.htm

Leu, D., Kinzer, C. K., Coiro, J. L., & Cammack, D. W. (2004). Toward a theory of new literacies emerging from the Internet and other information and communication technologies. In *Theoretical models and processes of reading (5th Ed.)*. Newark, DE: International Reading Association.

Lortie, D. (1974). *Schoolteacher: A sociological study*. Chicago: University of Chicago Press.

Pollan, M. (2001). *The botany of desire: a plant's eye view of the world*. New York: Random House.

Rogers, T., & Schofield, A. (2005). Things thicker than words: Portraits of youth multiple literacies in an alternative secondary program. In J. Anderson, M. Kendrick, T. Rogers, & S. Smythe (Eds). *Portraits of literacy across family, community, and schools: Intersections and tensions* (pp. 205-220). Mahwah, NJ: Erlbaum.

Stevens, L. P., Hunter, L., Carrington, V., Pendergast, D., & Bahr, N. (2007). Reconfiguring "adolescence": Ambiguous bodies in ambivalent settings. *Australian Educational Researcher, 2*(34), 107–128.

The New London Group. (1996). A pedagogy of multiliteracies: Designing social futures. *Harvard Educational Review, 66*(1), 60–92.

Unsworth, L. (2001). *Teaching multiliteracies across the curriculum: changing contexts of text and image in classroom practice*. Philadelphia, PA: Open University Press.

ENDNOTES

1 A pseudonym

2 Bourdieu's theoretical frameworks and concepts of habitus, field, capital, agency, and doxa are profoundly both more complicated and interrelated than can be adequately summarized within the scope of this chapter. For a more developed interaction with his ideas, readers are encouraged to consult his publications, including *Distinction* (1984) and his work with Passeron and Waicquant.

Section 2
Sociocultural Aspects of Technology Through a Multiliteracies Perspective

Chapter 5
Riding Critical and Cultural Boundaries:
A Multiliteracies Approach to Reading Television Sitcoms

Julie Faulkner
RMIT, Australia

Bronwyn T. Williams
University of Louisville, USA

ABSTRACT

This chapter explores the impact of new technologies on young peoples' literacy practices, with a particular focus on humour as text. Acknowledging ways in which rapidly-changing cultural and technological conditions have reshaped how people work and play, the authors work within expanded definitions of literacy, or multiliteracies. Exploring the potential of humour to interrogate cultural assumptions, Australian and American students participated in a cross cultural television study. They viewed a 'foreign' sitcom, asking to what extent knowledge of the sitcom's cultural norms was fundamental to an appreciation of the intended humour of the series. The student cohorts then communicated on line, developing their reading of the sitcoms in a cross cultural forum. The study asks how the students' multiliterate practices, including their critical interpretations of television comedy, hold implications for literacy education.

INTRODUCTION

Popular media texts offer high levels of engagement for viewers, as well as providing generative texts to study concepts connected to multiliteracies. Appreciation of comedy depends to a large extent on levels of cultural understanding – and one could ask how do such elements as accents, issues, stereotypes, class-based references and even local production styles influence the ways we respond to television humour? How might these elements be read by cross cultural audiences?

This study investigates the interaction between graduate students in the US and Australia, exploring the cultural dimensions of humour, as well as political aspects of distribution in a globalised entertainment market. A group of American students viewed a popular Australian sitcom, *Kath and Kim*, while a similar cohort of Australian students

DOI: 10.4018/978-1-60566-673-0.ch005

watched the US series *Arrested Development*, discussing separately, then online together, their responses to the two programs. The extent to which 'local' humour crosses cultural borders was examined by participants in relation to a cultural background, combined with number of different modes of meaning making, specifically cultural stereotypes, language, genre and production elements. This chapter contextualises popular viewing practices in a fast and global world and asks what the implications are for the contemporary literacy classroom. It explores ways that a critical reading of humour might disrupt acceptance of 'natural' cultural practices, and how laughter serves to reinforce or challenge group cultural identities.

MULTILITERACIES AND THE NEW LEARNER

The rapid proliferation of ICT, globalisation, and increasing social and cultural diversity has contributed to the notion of multiliteracies, or multiple modes of communicative competence. Students are able to create and maintain a variety of these texts, and personas, for a variety of different audiences. As Thomas (2007) notes about young people's multiliteracy practices, the "transition between roles is quick and spontaneous, [with] many young people ... able to engage in multiple scripts, playing multiple roles (both online and offline) simultaneously" (p. 168). She suggests that a linear, print-based approach to teaching literacy will no longer meet the needs of what Camille Paglia described as teenagers' 'multilayered, multitrack ability to deal with the world' (Paglia, quoted in Birkerts, 1994, p. 8). Young people growing up with computers and communications technologies – Mark Prensky's (2001) 'digital natives' – process multiple semiotic systems in multiple modes from a very early age. Formal schooling, working from narrow, print-based pedagogies, thus requires learners to 'power down', and consequently constraining student engagement and learning.

Anstey and Bull (2004) point to a second aspect of multiliteracies: the multiplicity of social and cultural influences on ways that literacies are constructed and used. According to Cope and Kalantzis (2000), "Cultural differences and rapidly shifting communications media mean that the very nature of the subject of literacy pedagogy [is] changing rapidly" (p. 5). Words, images and video can now flow across national borders instantaneously. The ease with which texts can be transmitted across borders does not mean reading and writing happen without the influence of culture. Rain falls without noticing borders but the cultures on either side of a border may describe the rain in very different ways. Yet this world of rapid cross-cultural communication is the world in which our students will be reading and writing. In fact many students, through email or instant messaging or online games, are already engaged in reading and writing with young people in other countries. Their literate lives will be increasingly lived in contact with people in countries they may never visit. Their literate identities will be read by people in cultures unfamiliar to them.

How, then, do we teach reading and writing in a digital age of cross-cultural communication? As global connectedness challenges traditional geographic and cultural boundaries, technology has the potential to blur (or support) previously distinct group identities. Severing the link between physical location and physical settings, ICT may also create new ones, for example through online discussion forums and MSN chat rooms.

Meyrowitz (1985) argues that electronic media have the potential to create a feeling of sharing and belonging as well as one of exclusion and isolation. The relationship between group identity and group territory was tied traditionally to the relationship between place and information access. Electronic and now digital media, by severing the link between physical location and physical settings, blur previously distinct boundaries and allow for new ones to form. For first generation computer users, long-established sites of socialisation, such as the school, have shifted to the agencies of digital culture and popular entertainment. The theories of Meyrowitz predate the internet, but the rapidly-expanding sense of context and genuinely connected relationships through email, SMS, chat rooms, MySpace and Facebook attest to his observations.

Jenkins (2006) notes that the conversations about television programs that used to happen face-to-face in living rooms or around water coolers, now can happen the instant the program is over with other audience members across the country or around the world.Jenkins calls this interactive popular culture "convergence culture." For Jenkins, the elements that mark convergence culture are the opportunities for participation by the audience, the creation of a collective intelligence by the public as a result of this participation, and the flow of information across multiple media platforms. These elements combine to encourage an interactive and "migratory behavior of media audiences who will go almost anywhere in search of the kinds of entertainment experiences they want" (p. 2).

One of the most significant developments of convergence culture is the way that online technologies have altered what it means to be a member of a popular culture audience. In the last century, mass popular culture audiences were considered, at best, to be readers and interpreters of popular culture. Millions across a country might be watching a television program, but an individual viewer could only discuss it with the friends and families she or he could see face to face. Only the most devoted fans wrote letters or went to fan conventions. By contrast, a person watching a television program today can immediately go online and discuss the show with others from across the street or around the world. Or the viewer could write a fanfiction or create a webpage about the program characters and get comments from readers thousands of miles away. Convergence culture is not simply about the opportunity for participation by individuals, it is about the expectation that anyone can have a say about a program in an online community of like-minded fans. The role of the audience member has changed toward both producers of popular culture and other members of the audience in active ways, that should forever put to rest the cliché of the passive consumer of popular culture.

What is of particular interest to literacy scholars about the development of participatory popular culture is that the online communication happens through the reading and writing of multimodal texts. Participants in fan forums carry on their discussions through print, fans of shows write multimodal blogs and web pages, often appropriating images, video, and sound from popular culture for their online texts. Fans now have to interpret and compose ideas about popular culture to others who may be across the street or around the world. So as fan forums and fan fictions and websites change the experience of popular culture, the literacy practices happen in cross-cultural settings. Reading the profiles of members of fan forums and fan fictions make it immediately clear that the communities span the world.

Numerous scholars (Buckingham, 1994; 1993; Fiske, 1994; Morely, 1992) have challenged the popular but reductive conception of uncritical audience reception of mass popular culture. Although popular culture certainly reflects and reproduces dominant cultural ideologies, research indicates that this process is not accepted unquestioningly by audience members. Instead popular culture texts are interpreted in the contexts of individuals' life experiences and adapted to ideas that may or may not conform to dominant cultural values. Far from being passive dupes, individuals have always engaged in interactions with mass popular culture, such as discussing television programs with friends. As individuals read and adapt popular culture texts to individual needs such texts influence both identity construction and community building.

When we think about students' multiliterate practices then, we need to consider their active engagement with reading and writing popular culture, an engagement we rarely see in the classroom but which constitutes a vital learning environment in terms of issues of audience and multimodal reading and writing.

A significantly enabling element of multiliterate practice calls for the development of a critical perspective, or an understanding of how practices are valued and shaped through language and other modes of meaning. Critical literacy examines relationships between text and context, constructions of texts, and ways in which readers are positioned by such constructions. Further, readers engaging at this level critically frame whose interests are served through the construction and uses of the text.

BACKGROUND TO THE STUDY

To explore how young people understood texts across cultural borders, two university educators, one from Australia and the other an American, engaged their respective cohorts in the viewing of an Australian and a US sitcom. Kalantzis and Cope (2005) identify the challenge of educating generations of learners who are increasingly engaged in digital and global environments, "from the entertainment sources they choose to the way they work and learn" (p. v). As productive reading strategies, literacies associated with popular texts, we argue, lay claim to a far stronger place in education than currently exists: importantly, they provide an interface between out-of-school and in-school literacy practices. Mobilising learners' cultural expertise to extend their textual practices enhances teachers' capacities to bridge informal and formal literacies. Further access to critical reading approaches would be facilitated through forging connections between readers' uses of popular texts and a broader range of textual understandings.

Popular media texts offer high levels of engagement for young people, who are generally expert readers of their complex semiotic worlds (Hodge & Tripp, 1986; Johnson-Eilola, 1997; Kress & Van Leeuwen, 2001). However, while young people make discriminations about and within their chosen texts, they do not always consciously evaluate or articulate the criteria they use (Buckingham, 1994; Doecke & McCleneghan, 1998).

Again, the development of convergence culture has influenced how many students read and respond to popular culture. On fan forums about television programs, for example, much of the content revolves around interpretive questions about the texts. People post summaries, questions, ideas, suppositions, predictions or spoilers for upcoming episodes, covering the smallest detail to the most sweeping theories and ranging in tone from humour to sober reflection. Unlike the more detached analysis practiced by academic critics on fan forums:

criticism is playful, speculative, subjective. Fans are concerned with the particularity of textual detail...Fan critics work to resolve gaps, to explore excess details and undeveloped potentials" (Jenkins, 1992, p. 278).

This approach to discussing television programs, for example, creates a collaborative ethos in the online community. In research with undergraduate university students (Williams, forthcoming) participants of fan forums demonstrated a willingness to both ask questions and offer interpretations and an expectation that others in the conversation will work toward enriching everyone's knowledge of the program. The confidence of forum participants in ability to read, question, and make meaning from what they see stands in stark contrast to the often much more tentative interpretive moves the same students may make in the classroom.

Students' confidence in discussing popular culture texts arises from their long and varied experiences in interpreting and evaluating movies, television, music and so on. It also helps that authority figures, such as parents and teachers, generally deride popular culture as trivial, allowing students to play with and explore their interpretations of popular culture without worrying about being corrected by adults. Such interpretive play results in the confidence to explore and express more evaluative and analytic ideas. Consequently, research with students at a different age levels (Alvermann, Moon & Hagood, 1999; Buckingham, 1993; Smith & Wilhem, 2002; Williams, 2002) demonstrates that students are much more willing to engage in confident conversations with their peers about television programs than they are with school-sanctioned texts. These conversations have now moved online. Jenkins (2006) speculates that fan forums are particularly popular among university students where they can "exercise their growing competencies in a space where there are not yet prescribed experts and well-mapped disciplines" (p. 52).

As literacy educators, we can use the collaborative ethos of online discussions of popular culture to explore with students' concepts of literacy and context in cross-cultural settings. We felt confident that when given the opportunity to discuss, question, and debate television programs with students in another country, the students in our classes would engage in collaborative meaning making that would help them think about issues of reading texts across cultural boundaries. That our students were older than secondary students actually put them at a disadvantage in this online setting, as younger students are more likely to have spent time in online forums and chat rooms.

Humour, because of its reliance on cultural context, seemed a particularly fruitful choice to challenge students to think about how cultural context influences literacy practices. Although the form of the sitcom might be familiar to both sets of students, the contexts for the humor within the form would require students to work together to make meaning and would highlight for them the situated nature of the text. At the same time, discussing sitcoms would offer a low-stakes conversation embedded in texts and forms with which they could feel confident and comfortable in their interaction. Moreover, appreciation of comedy depends to a large extent on levels of cultural understanding – how do semiotic elements such as language, accents, issues, stereotypes, class-based references and even local production styles influence the ways we respond to comedy particularly that made for television?

WHY DO WE LAUGH?

Kellner (1995) argues that pleasure is learned. We learn what to enjoy and what we should avoid. From a cultural studies perspective, every text grows from, and reflects its own cultural context. Our capacity to respond to the text is dependent upon our existing cultural knowledge, or the social and political reference points in our everyday lives.

Awareness of the elements which constitute the fabric of our lives is necessary if we are to realise the ways that humour plays with our perceptions and sense of dislocation. The inherently ambiguous logic of humour allows for multiple interpretations of social phenomena (Mulkay, 1988). For theorists such as Mulkay, the world is constructed, arbitrary, multiple and tenuous.

The cultural anthropologist, Mary Douglas (1975), in writing about jokes as a form of humour, highlights the disruption to accepted patterns of social order that the play upon form, or joke, delivers. It is the clash of disparate elements, she argues, which questions the dominant ordering of experience and makes the viewer, through laughter, aware that:

the accepted pattern has no necessity. [The joke's] excitement lies in the suggestion that any particular ordering of experience may be arbitrary and subjective. It is frivolous in that it produces no real alternative, only an exhilarating sense of freedom from form in general. (p. 96)

In tension with the potentially subversive function described by Douglas, Misson (1997) asserts that a powerful social purpose of humour is to create solidarity. Collective laughter asserts common values, and humour thus serves as an 'embedded, interactive and referential' process within a group (Fine & de Soucey, 2005, p. 1).

'Natural' practices are thrown into relief through juxtaposition, exaggeration or adopting an unexpected point of view in comedy. Moreover, because so much popular culture circulates on a global scale today, yet humour is so dependent on local cultural contexts, sitcoms provide particularly intriguing texts to examine the ways in which people make meaning of texts that cross, or fail to cross cultural borders.

The culturally-situated nature of humour offers a reminder of the limitations of the concept of "global popular culture". Certainly the technological advances of recent years, the same ones that have given rise to the practices of convergence culture; have allowed movies, television, music and video games to cross cultural boundaries with relative ease. It is also true that young people around the world often draw on popular culture that originates somewhere else in the world in their choices about popular culture and how it allows them to express their identities. Consequently, it is not necessarily surprising to see the same kind of clothing or same song or same catchphrase from a movie popular in countries that are oceans apart. At the same time, however, it is important to remember that texts circulating globally are still read and employed locally. Local uses of any text are always specific to those contexts, and therefore are not always predictable. Hip hop, for example, has as a musical form and a culture spread across the world. Yet hip hop has been adapted by local youth to express ideas about local conditions, and thus often becomes less comprehensible to youth in other cultures. "The creation of new styles may involve elements of imitation, but the imitation acquires a new meaning as a result of the person who appropriates it and the context in which it occurs" (De Block & Rydin, 2006, p. 300). Such local responses to "global" popular culture offer creative opportunities, but also tensions and contested readings. Within our own cultures we often look to popular culture as common cultural touchstones that are understandable to all in the society. When popular culture texts are read in different contexts, however, our expectations of common understanding of the movie or television program can be resisted or denied.

Television sitcoms also often cross cultural borders, but are read in ways specific to local cultural contexts. The form may be familiar, but the common cultural touchstones that provide the context for interpretation are different. Because we draw on different intertextual backgrounds to make meaning of the program, our readings may be very different from those in another culture. When trying to understand a sitcom and humour from another culture, our intextextual connections also invariably include our perceptions of and power relationships with the country in which the program was created. Thus the laughter of the people across the ocean may puzzle, or even offend us.

Using reflexive notions of humour's capacity to build commonalities as well as to disrupt accepted patterns of social order, we designed our cross-cultural study around two 'local' television sitcoms. Both were popular among their target audiences and offered rich material for discovering how far, and in what ways, group references might be shared and reflected upon.

THE STUDY

To explore aspects of humour in a multiliteracy context, Julie Faulkner, as the Australian researcher and Bronwyn Williams, the American counterpart, exchanged recordings of sitcoms which originated in Australia and the US respectively. As far as possible, we chose programs which we assumed the respective overseas cohorts knew little or nothing of. *Kath and Kim* is a satirical view of Australian life in the aspirational suburbs of Melbourne. Originally commissioned by the government broadcaster at prime time, its success gained the show a commercial sale for its fourth season. *Kath and Kim* focuses on a parent-child relationship, a relationship sadly lacking by conventional *Father Knows Best* standards. The central characters verge on the comically grotesque as they strive to be what they are not, falling well below inflated expectations of themselves. The series was extraordinarily successful by Australian television standards, winning many awards and securing a 2008 NBC version in the US.

Arrested Development is a US sitcom about another dysfunctional family. The patriarch, head of an apparently successful business, has been jailed for embezzlement and left his grasping wife, one ambitious and two eccentric sons, materialistic daughter and their various spouses and offspring to fend for themselves. The pace of the series is fast, editing slick and script construction tight. It attracted a strong cult audience but was cancelled after three seasons on the FOX network.

For the study, the viewers of these sitcoms numbered approximately 12-15 students, and were, in Australia, Graduate Diploma of Education English method students. In the United States the students were postgraduate Masters and Doctoral students enrolled in a course on Popular Culture and Literacy. Students were asked to view several episodes of their relevant series and respond to an initial question about what they found, or failed to find funny. Each cohort then met face-to-face to discuss their responses collectively. They then entered an online forum where they joined a threaded discussion with their international partners, which continued over a period of approximately two weeks.

The face to face and digital discussions amongst Julie, Bronwyn and participating students were collected as data. Responses were analysed around themes raised by the discussants themselves. Using MacLachlan and Reid's framing theory (1994); we then explored the extent to which laughter might be related to contextual knowledge based on media representations and further, what this knowledge might hold for literacy learning. Machlachlan and Reid suggest framing curriculum within extratextual, circumtextual, intertextural and intratextural approaches. Extratextual knowledge involves the understandings that the reader brings to the text, circumtextual elements describe what sits around the text to influence the reader, while intertextual framing brings related texts to enhance appreciation of the original. Intratextual framing seeks to identify generic conventions within the text.

WHAT DO WE NEED TO KNOW IN ORDER TO GET THE JOKE?

Early cultural references in a comparison between Australian and American television programs include accent and vocabulary. No Australian student made any comment about these aspects in relation to *Arrested Development*. Kath and Kim's Australian accents are broad ('look at moie') and, for an Australian audience, are locatable within a certain socioeconomic stratum. The characters use many mixed metaphors and malapropisms, usually in their attempts to sound, as one character remarks, more 'effluent'. Like *Arrested Development*, much humour flows from the interplay between the verbal and visual. While some of the humour works broadly within western conventions of farce, other jokes depend on local cultural knowledge. Kim, for example, takes a cantaloupe from the fridge and whines 'Well, Brett and I just can't elope!' The joke depends on reading the fruit in her hand as a 'canteloupe' rather than a 'rockmelon', although this term is not used universally, or even throughout Australia, so the joke is diffused.

The US cohort expressed no difficulty with Kath and Kim's accents. One student asked the meaning of 'a cushman', 'a little b.' and 'trim little p.i's'. Australian students were able to identify a 'cushman' as a 'cushion (soft) man' and explain 'b.' as a 'noice' abbreviation of 'bitch'. However, 'p.i's' remained unexplained until it was realised that it was most likely referred to 'p. a's.' (personal assistants) in a Kath and Kim accent.

Occasional examples of cultural knowledge were referenced. *Kath and Kim* typically ends with a 'mother and daughter' moment sitting in the back yard. In one instance, Kath and Kim are leafing through gossip magazines and it is mentioned by Kim that she wished Nicole Kidman were featured more often on the cover. Rebecca from Australia comments that this postscript is only funny if you have stood in Australian supermarkets and walked past ubiquitous images of Nicole Kidman on magazines. Similarly, Kath and her new husband, Kel, are trapped inside the airport in one episode and spend their time duty-free shopping. A camera shot has them riding up the escalator in matching Coogee jumpers, but again, this is only funny if the viewer is familiar with the range of Australiana in duty free shops, knowing that most Australians would never buy the rather-too-obvious products. Such examples, however, when raised by Australians, received the American response: 'it's hard to know what didn't come through to American viewers because we obviously wouldn't miss what we didn't know we didn't catch, (if that makes sense)' (Cynthia). Cynthia's reflexive stance raises the question of what levels of prior cultural knowledge are necessary to grasp a sense of what someone doesn't know.

American participants reported that the only Australian film and television texts with which they were familiar at the time included *The Crocodile Hunter, Crocodile Dundee* and *Outback Jack*. This access contrasts starkly with the range of programs Australian viewers have grown up with and their familiarity with the American accent and television conventions.

Another view might be that local differences are blurring as the popular culture industry becomes increasingly fast and global, and the industry is largely US controlled. In the light of this, the wider questions of exposure and representation remain open. Bronwyn Williams in the US struggled to find television texts that Australians had never seen. Between the time he suggested *Arrested Development* and the videotape arrived in Melbourne, a number of episodes had already been aired in Australia on a commercial network in the 10pm time slot. The ease of digital downloading further encouraged participants to view episodes, quickly made popular by word-of-mouth. This prompted Bronwyn to add another question to the online discussion: what did Australian students feel about the dominance of US programming on their screens?

(POP)CULTURAL HEGEMONY

On one hand, there was cool appraisal of market realities and the impact on production quality among the students:

I think differences in consistency and script come down to money and [...] the US concept of a team of writers all pooling ideas. (As opposed to Jane Turner and Gina Riley, essentially doing nearly all the work for Kath and Kim). Arrested Development was produced with a potential domestic audience of 280 million and almost a guarantee of overseas syndication. Kath and Kim was made for a potential domestic audience of only 20 million and a touch-and-go chance of export. In the light of that, I find the surprise success of Kath and Kim far more impressive than that of Arrested Development, even if I'm not always laughing at the jokes. (Rebecca)

On the other hand, 'cherry picking' of British texts by American television was commented on ('note the amount of television programming the US routinely adapts from British television, sometimes successfully and sometimes not,' David). While it was recognised that *Kath and Kim* followed a conventional sitcom structure and 'we do absorb the cultural influences of America,' Rebecca further argues that *Kath and Kim* could not be mistaken for an American program. (The forthcoming adaptation of the series to the US market, with Turner and Riley as executive producers, will add a further dimension to conversations about cultural humour). As Willis (1990) argues, popular culture involves not merely reproducing, but appropriating the meanings of commercial culture in new ways. Meanings are 'selected, reselected, highlighted, and recomposed' to make some statement about individuals' views of themselves and their social worlds. (Willis, 1990, p. 21) In this case, Kath and Kim's characters are represented as a broader type of Australian suburban identity.

KATH, KIM, SUBURBS AND CLASS

Misson (1997) asserts that humour can powerfully bind groups through collective laughter. However, an element of unease was identified by both US and Australian viewers while watching the Australian program, *Kath and Kim*. While recognising the stereotypical nature of the characters, the students articulated some disquiet over their amusement. James began to feel ill at ease about the ideological assumptions of the show:

Something about the premise of the show made me think that I was laughing (and I did laugh – it's a funny show) at the expense of the characters' social status.

Several US participants were not clear whether Kath and Kim represented the working or middle class and vacillated between categories. Similarly, a Sydney radio interviewer linked Kath and Kim to 'westies' or western suburbs, blue collar Australians. (In fact, the Melbourne location of *Kath and Kim* is in the more upwardly-mobile south east). Students were similarly unclear where, exactly, the program was positioning them as viewers. Cynthia writes 'I am not sure I can separate my pleasure from my politics' and asks 'are we supposed to feel sympathy for the characters or with the characters or feel derision for them and their urge to be 'effluent'?

An Australian response to the American concern was to assert her own opinion that *Kath and Kim* is not classist in its intent. Rather, it 'challenges the idealised version of suburban bliss that we have been living with for decades through soap operas like *Neighbours*'. (Rebecca) An observation such as Rebecca's comes from an awareness of the traditions and context within which *Kath and Kim* sits. Stripped from its context, *Kath and Kim* might look like a cheap shot, but an argument is made here for a more complex range of responses to the content (and intent?).

Discomfort, however, was not limited to the American audience. Susana, an Australian, was overseas when popularity over *Kath and Kim* reached its height. Urged by friends to view the show, she felt 'embarrassed and surprised that so many people were embracing it'. Susana attempts to articulate her own viewing stance, or the awkward multiple stances which *Kath and Kim* work her into:

Sure we would all agree that Kath and Kim are try hards, but this mocking of people from the 'burbs' and then in the same light almost celebrating them, for me seemed to be ironic and/or contradictory.

Magda Szubanski, who plays Sharon, Kim's friend, in *Kath and Kim,* raises this theme of satire and suburbanity in a recent interview in *Preview,* the weekend magazine of *The Age* Melbourne newspaper (2005). She credits Barry Humphries' character, Edna Everage, as an intertextual reference, one which has paved the way for *Kath and Kim*:

I think he was first to understand how our suburbanity is our single most defining characteristic. The suburbs are our cultural magnetic north. We can never be anywhere but in relation to them; fearing and loving them, running away from them or to them. Kath and Kim follows along the trail he blazed, sitting proudly, if somewhat uncomfortably, smack bang in the fault line of love and hate that generates so much energy. (p. 6)

Interestingly, the 2008 US version of *Kath and Kim* focused on the mother daughter relationship and almost entirely omitted reference to class. Reviews of the US one season series were generally negative (it lasted only two weeks in Australia), adding further to the complexities of 'translating' a local text.

THE CAMERA AS THE EYE

Such observations suggest a context for more nuanced discussion of what we appreciate as humour, and why. However, the focus of the participant conversation moved from what we are seeing to *how* we are seeing it. The American students raised the issue of the production process, as well as the content, adding a further layer of unease to the demographic issues already raised. The home video camera style and use of a real house as opposed to a set invited viewers in to Kath and Kim's home and shared a close up version of their lives. Dan from the US elaborates:

It seems like the Americans had a harder time with Kath and Kim. I know I did. And I think part of it (for me) has to do with the way it was filmed – the jerky, moving camera and the actual house setting. That made the relationship between Kath and Kim even more realistic - and even more uncomfortable with some of the comments they would make to each other [...] I enjoy cruel humour - but it's softened in say Fawlty Towers when the whole thing still looks like it's a play on a proscenium stage.

Aspects of verisimilitude in relationship to film sets seem to be an under-explored element of viewer response, deserving of further attention. Dan's comments echo Stephanie's remarks which speculate whether amusement also depends on 'some sort of distance [being] created between them and us'. We can laugh when we see the characters as 'other', but less readily see the humour of screen entities in ourselves.

If *Arrested Development* promoted what one American student labeled 'colorful and shiny' production values, the relative rawness of *Kath and Kim* led another student to describe the episodes as 'primitive'. She did not elaborate further on her choice of adjective, but the crassness of the characters' language and situations was a thread of the discussion. Although generally agreed that *Arrested Development* was the more sophisticated sitcom, production-wise, one student found the 'tackiness and inappropriateness, the insensitivity and self-absorption of Portia de Rossi's character from *Arrested Development'* as very similar to Kim from *Kath and Kim* (Fiona). Fiona, an Australian, continues to comment that it is the degree to which the characterisations are extended that allows us to accept *Kath and Kim* as satire:

I think the nastiness of the characters and their inability to see their truly appalling behaviour for what it is that has enabled Turner and Riley [the writers] to present Australian audiences with a portrait of our worst characteristics in a way which is palatable. I think no one here would ever admit to being even a little like Kath or Kim, yet I recall after seeing Kim with her tacky acrylic nails, unsightly bulges and pathetic attempts to pursue the latest suburban trends, I stopped going to the nail salon and I swear I never even considered a G-string or Ugg boots!

The extent to which Fiona is parodying herself is not clear in the written conversation, but she points to exaggeration as well as the satirical elements of the familiar, raised earlier in this chapter. The extent to which individual viewers recognise themselves in textual representations directly influences the 'palatability' factor and consequently, the degree of laughter.

CONCLUSION

Educators in the twenty-first century face challenges unknown to previous generations of teachers. Green and Bigum (1993) argue that the contemporary student is one who is subjectively different by virtue of her or his relationship with digital technologies – one with new needs and new capacities. The relations and practices of students to the new technologies are forming different youth and student subjectivities from those we have known before, producing 'aliens in the classroom'.

If educators wish to avoid becoming the 'aliens' themselves, they need to engage with a range of multimodal texts across geographical and political boundaries. Popular media texts offer high levels of engagement for teenagers, and thus rich opportunities to explore deeper reading practices. Levels of participation in online communities across cultural boundaries continue to rise and to powerfully connect young people in ways that conventional schooling does not. Educators need to understand the dimensions of convergence culture literacies and how they might offer stimulating links to more formal learning.

Interpretation of popular texts – in this case, comedy, depends to a large extent on levels of cultural understanding and how humour might work as a culturally-constructed phenomenon. Looking more deeply at responses to an engaging text provides a potentially fresh learning perspective, one which involves more complex understandings of systems of representation and interpretation. Moreover, such a study engages learners in situated practice (New London Group, 1996), exploring the interface between local textual practices and the convergence culture described by Jenkins (2006). Exploring popular television texts with overseas peers offers generative cross-cultural comparisons, but also provides spaces for sophisticated analysis and critical thinking using a multiliteracies approach.

REFERENCES

Alvermann, D. E., Moon, J. S., & Hagood, M. C. (1999). *Popular culture in the classroom: Teaching and researching critical media literacy.* Chicago: National Reading Conference.

Anstey, A., & Bull, G. (2004). *The literacy labyrinth* (2nd Ed.). Frenchs Forest, Australia: Pearson Education Australia.

Buckingham, D. (1993). *Children talking television: The making of television literacy.* London: Falmer Press.

Buckingham, D. (1994). Media education: The limits of a discourse. *Curriculum Studies, 24*(4), 296–313.

Cope, B., & Kalantzis, M. (2000). Multiliteracies: The beginnings of an idea. In B. Cope & M. Kalantzis (Eds.), *Multiliteracies: Literacy learning and the design of social futures* (pp. 3-8). London: Routledge.

De Block, L., & Rydin, I. (2006). Digital rapping in media productions: Intercultural communication through youth culture. In D. Buckingham & R. Willett (Eds.), *Digital generations: Children, young people, and new media* (pp. 295-312). Mahwah, NJ: Lawrence Erlbaum.

Doecke, B., & McCleneghan, D. (1998). Reconceptualising experience: Growth pedagogy and youth culture. In W. Sawyer, K. Watson & E. Gold (Eds.) *Re-viewing English* (pp. 46-57). Sydney: Clair Press.

Douglas, M. (1975). *Implicit meanings: Essays in anthropology.* London: Routledge & Kegan Paul.

Fine, G., & de Soucey, M. (2005). Joking cultures: Humor themes as social regulation in group life. *Humor: International Journal of Humor Research, 18*(1), 1–22. doi:10.1515/humr.2005.18.1.1

Fiske, J. (1994). Moments of television: Neither the text nor the audience. In E. Seiter, H. Borchers, G. Kreutzner & E-M. Warth (Eds.), *Remote control television, audiences and cultural power* (pp. 56-78). London: Routledge.

Green, B., & Bigum, C. (1993). Aliens in the classroom. *Australian Journal of Education, 33*(2), 119–134.

Hodge, B., & Tripp, D. (1986). *Children and television: A semiotic approach.* Cambridge, UK: Polity Press.

Jenkins, H. (1992). *Textual poachers: Television fans and participatory culture.* London: Routledge.

Jenkins, H. (2006). *Convergence culture: Where old and new media collide.* New York: New York University Press.

Johnson-Eilola, J. (1997). Living on the surface: Learning in the age of global communication networks. I. Snyder (Ed.), *Page to screen: Taking literacy into the electronic era* (pp. 185-210). Sydney: Allen & Unwin.

Kalantzis, M., & Cope, B. (2005). *Learning by design.* Melbourne, Australia: Common Ground.

Kellner, D. (1995). *Media culture: Cultural studies, identity and politics between the modern and the postmodern.* London: Taylor & Francis.

Kress, G., & Van Leeuwen, T. (2001). *Multimodal discourse.* London: Edward Arnold.

MacLachlan, G., & Reid, I. (1994). *Framing and interpretation.* Carlton, Australia: Melbourne University Press.

Meyrowitz, J. (1985). *No sense of place: the impact of electronic media on social behaviour.* New York: Oxford University Press

Misson, R. (1997, October). *"Only joking": Being critical and keeping sense of humour.* Paper presented at SAETA Conference, Adelaide.

Morely, D. (1992). *Television, audiences and cultural studies.* London: Routledge.

Mulkay, M. (1988). *On humor: Its nature and its place in modern society.* Oxford: Blackwell.

New London Group. (1996). A pedagogy of multiliteracies: Designing social futures. *Harvard Educational Review, 66*(1), 60–92.

Paglia, C. quoted in Birkets, S. (1994). *The Gutenberg elegies: The fate of reading in an electronic age.* Boston: Faber and Faber.

Prensky, M. (2001). Digital natives, Digital immigrants. *Horizon, 9*(5).

Smith, M. W., & Wilhem, J. D. (2002). *"Reading don't fix no Chevys": Literacy in the lives of young men.* Portsmouth, NH: Heinemann.

Szubanski, M. (2005). 'Fears of a clown' interview by B. Hallett. *The Age, Preview Magazine,* May 8, 4-6.

Thomas, A. (2007). *Youth online: Identity and literacy in the digital age.* New York: Peter Lang.

Williams, B. T. (2002). *Tuned in: Television and the teaching of writing.* Portsmouth, NH: Boynton/Cook.

Williams, B. T. (Forthcoming). *Shimmering literacies: Popular culture and reading and writing online.* London: Peter Lang.

Willis, P. (1990). *Common culture.* Buckingham, UK: Open University

Chapter 6
Rethinking Literacy in Culturally Diverse Classrooms

Jennifer Rennie
Monash University, Australia

ABSTRACT

Literate demands on our youth today have become increasingly more complex due to a technological revolution, increased local diversity and a stronger connectedness with our global neighbours (New London Group, 1996). Contemporary classrooms are characterised by a diverse range of learners that come from different places, with different life world experiences and preferred ways of learning and knowing. Texts are no longer confined to print and comprehending texts involves understanding how different modes such as the audio, visual and spatial integrate to make meaning. Despite this, schools continue to measure and describe student's literacy in relation to their ability to encode and decode print. The recent Program for International Student Assessment results (OECD, 2006) show that Australia has dropped from 5th ranking to 6th in the world in terms of reading literacy. More disturbing is the fact that this assessment showed a continuing widening gap in academic achievement between Australia's Indigenous and non Indigenous students with very little improvement since 2000. Similarly in the United States recent literacy results show that despite some gains in the achievements of minority groups, there has been little narrowing in the gap between white students and minority students (Lee, Grigg et al., 2007). This chapter adopts a socio-cultural view of literacy and calls for a rethinking of what might count as literacy in school. It reports on a study which documented the literacy practices valued in the home community, community school and urban high school of seven Aboriginal students as they moved from Year 7 in their community school to Year 8 in their new urban high school (Rennie, Wallace et al. 2004). It discusses theoretical ideas related to a multiliteracies framework (Cope & Kalantzis, 2000), literacy as an act of translation (Somerville, 2006) and Aboriginal world views and knowledge (Martin, 2008) as a means to explore ways we might rethink the teaching of literacy in diverse and culturally rich classrooms.

DOI: 10.4018/978-1-60566-673-0.ch006

INTRODUCTION

Kelly comes home from school. He drops his bag and makes his way to the kitchen to prepare an afternoon snack. He then goes to his room where he turns on the computer, signs on to MSN and starts chatting with his mates. On a different afternoon Kelly goes down to the local swimming club for training.

Arnie finishes school. He doesn't go home but drops by the local art centre to see his Mum and Dad. He talks to his Mum about the painting she is doing. He then heads up to the sport and recreation centre where he grabs a snack and plays football with his mates. On a different afternoon Arnie stays at school and plays games on the computer.

Kelly and Arnie are both young boys who live in two different places in Australia. Arnie lives on a remote Aboriginal community in the North and Kelly in a large urban centre. The two scenarios described would be common activities that the boys might engage in after school.

A SOCIO-CULTURAL VIEW

Depending on how one defines literacy some might argue that both boys are 'doing' literacy and that literacy is an integral part of their afternoon activities. They might also say that literacy helps to shape these activities and that each activity requires a different set of literacies. Further they might argue that these literacies are better understood through the relationships between the boys and their mates and the individual communities in which they live. This thinking is characteristic of those who espouse socio-cultural views of literacy, literacy teaching and learning where literacy is not simply understood as a discrete set of skills but rather as variable forms of social practice, see for example, "New Literacy studies" (Barton & Hamilton, 1998), "social literacies" (Gee, 1996; Street, 1993), or "situated literacies" (Barton, Hamilton et al., 2000).

Many scholars from different fields have contributed to knowledge about literacy including psychologists, sociologists, linguists, educationalists and policy makers and the way in which it is defined largely depends on their beliefs about how it is learned, how and whether it can be measured, what it does and what it is. Although Kelly and Arnie went to different primary schools they both went to the same high school. This was due to the fact that Arnie's community did not have access to secondary education. Despite the similarities in their afternoon activities during primary school they had very different experiences at high school. Kelly is a day student and Arnie stays at the school as a boarder. Both boys are not that fond of school and would rather be home doing other things. Kelly does well in his English classes and although he enjoys reading does not care much for what he is required to read and write in school. Arnie on the other hand was placed in an Intensive English class and he does not enjoy reading and writing probably because he struggles with the task.

It is not the purpose of this chapter to present, critique or debate different perspectives on what literacy is or how it should be taught. These debates have been well documented elsewhere (see for example Chall, 1967; Christie, Devlin et al., 1991; Flippo, 1999; Louden, Rohl et al., 2005; DEST, 2005). However, it is important to understand that one's beliefs about what literacy 'is' or 'does' directly influences the ways in which it is taught in schools. It is also important to acknowledge that a student's personal experience with and understanding of literacy can affect the ways in which they engage with literacy in school. Recent research that has investigated the literacy practices of homes, schools and communities have found marked differences in the literacy practices and values of schools and their families in the ways they used and defined literacy (Cairney & Ruge, 1997; Fleer & Williams-Kennedy, 2001; Heath, 1986; 1998; Hill, Comber et al., 1998; Hill, Comber et al., 2002; Rennie, Wallace et al., 2004; White-Kaulaity, 2007). Furthermore, school literacy practices served to empower some whilst they disempowered others and the students who were most likely to succeed in school came from home backgrounds where 'family literacy practices' most closely resembled those of school (Cairney & Ruge, 1997; Barton & Hamilton, 1998; Fleer & Williams-Kennedy, 2001; Heath, 1986; Hill, Comber et al., 1998; Hill, Comber et al., 2002).

A socio-cultural view of literacy allows one to talk about school literacy as being distinct from the literacies that are integral to Kelly and Arnie's afternoon activities. It also allows us to talk about Kelly's literacies as distinct from Arnie's literacies.

Over recent decades a number of different approaches to teaching school literacy have been used including holistic approaches (Cambourne, 1988), genre based approaches (Martin, Christie et al., 1987), skills based approaches (Aukerman, 1984) and socio-cultural approaches (Freebody & Luke, 1990). In the classroom many teachers tend to adopt an eclectic position on teaching literacy by combining useful elements from a variety of different approaches. On a state level English curriculum is generally divided into the three broad areas of reading, writing and oral language. Although these curricula include a variety of text types which are commonly used in contemporary society such as multimedia texts, visual texts and print there tends to be a focus on the encoding and decoding of print.

Nationally and internationally students' literacy achievements are measured and described in terms of their ability to read, understand and write print based texts. From 2008 Australian National mandates require all students in Australia in Years 3, 5, 7 and 9 to do the same test in their year level at the same time of the year. Results from these tests will be used to paint a picture of the state of affairs of 'literacy' in relation to our youth. Similar testing regimes occur in other nations such as the United States and the United Kingdom as part of national educational policy such as "No Child Left Behind" in the US and the "National Literacy Strategy" in the UK. These testing regimes are commensurate with behaviourist and cognitivist views of reading and writing that are inherent in many skills based literacy approaches and they tend to ignore the complex social, cultural and technological worlds of our students. These tests in many ways mirror the society that was prevalent in the 1950s and they have failed to keep up with the fast changing nature and pace of contemporary society.

NEW LITERATE DEMANDS

Literate demands on our youth today have become increasingly more complex due to a technological revolution, increased local diversity and a stronger connectedness with our global neighbours. In 1994 a group of national and international scholars met in New London, New Hampshire to discuss what might constitute appropriate literacy teaching now and into the future in light of these three major changes in society (New London Group, 1996). The group acknowledged that meaning making is more complex. Meaning is not just conveyed through linguistic modes but incorporates other modes such as the visual, audio, spatial and behavioural. Furthermore, these different modes are often integrated within the same text each contributing to the overall meaning of the text. A web page is a good example of the complexity of texts today. It often consists of a number of different modes such as the visual, textual and audio. Web pages are also often multi generic in that they might contain combinations of persuasive, report and procedural writing. Finally, web pages are intertextual in the ways they link to other layers within the same text and to texts outside of the text.

In addition to the complexity of meaning making practices the group also acknowledged the diversity in local communities and an ever increasing connectedness to our global neighbours (New London Group, 1996). For example, the time when it took days to communicate to the rest of Australia yet alone the world that Darwin in the Northern Territory had been wiped off the face of the Earth by a cyclone have disappeared. It is common for our youth to take jobs and study in other countries and today's classrooms comprise learners who often have two or three languages, other than English. With the fast pace of technology it is almost certain that ways of making meaning will continue to change and it is almost certain that our student population will become more diverse than it currently is (Au & Raphael, 2000).

Both Kelly and Arnie speak more than one language. Kelly speaks English and Japanese and Arnie English and Tiwi. However Kelly's first language is English and Arnie's first language is Tiwi. The high school they attended uses English for instruction. Kelly is technologically savvy. He began pulling computers apart when he was only eight years old. He enjoys gaming with his friends and attends LAN (Local Area Network) gatherings where large groups of people get together and play games in teams. He uses the computer daily for a number of different activities including shopping, socialising and learning. Arnie does not own a computer but enjoys using the computers both during and after school. In many ways Kelly and Arnie's lives in school reflect the changes described by the New London Group. They both use and embrace technology although Arnie's place is not well served by the communication giants. Furthermore Arnie's parents unlike Kelly's parents have never been in a position to provide Arnie with all the latest technology. Kelly and Arnie both attended a high school that was buzzing with cultural diversity. The school enrols students from over 40 different Aboriginal and Torres Strait Islander communities. In addition to the Aboriginal students in the school there are students from and with connections to places such as Greece, China, Indonesia and East Timor. These kinds of classrooms are common all over the globe. For example, a recent classroom I visited in the US had white, black, Hispanic and Asian students.

MULTILITERACIES: RETHINKING PEDAGOGY

The years following the original discussions of the New London Group led to the development of a new pedagogical framework "Learning by Design" which would facilitate some of the complexities of contemporary society (Kalantzis, Cope et al., 2005).

The pedagogical framework that emerged had four key phases and was based on the concept of 'design'. The idea that teachers become designers of learning and that 'Design' describes the different forms of meaning. They proposed that the production of texts which involves any semiotic activity is a matter of 'Design' and that this involves three elements – Available Design, Designing and the Redesigned. Available Designs are seen as the resources we have for making meaning and include such things as the grammars of languages and other semiotic systems. Designing is seen as the work which occurs with 'Available Designs' and involves knowledge transformation as it represents and constructs 'reality' in different ways. The Redesigned results in new meanings and includes the resources that are produced through the 'Design' process (Cope & Kalantzis, 2000). Situated Practice, Overt Instruction, Critical Framing and Transformed Practice comprise the four phases identified in the pedagogical model. Situated practice involves experiencing the new and the known. Overt Instruction involves conceptualising or 'naming'. Critical Framing involves an understanding of the cultural and social implications of what is learned and Transformed Practice results in new meaning and some kind of application (Kalantzis, Cope et al., 2005).

Difference: Transformative but Risky

Underpinning this framework is the idea that there are two essential conditions for successful learning (Kalantzis, Cope et al., 2005). First, it is important for students to feel they belong to the learning which includes the content being learned, ways of knowing and the learning community itself. This idea shares similarity with those who also highlight the importance of making connections to students' lifeworlds, (see for example Comber & Kamler, 2005; Moll, Amanti et al., 1992).

The need for a 'sense of belonging' acknowledges the fact that every learner's subjectivity is particular. It is argued that differences such as race, gender, socio-economic status and (dis)ability are only a beginning point for thinking about diversity in the classroom. Kalantzis and Cope (2005) suggest a second layer of difference which includes such things as values, social orientations, world experiences, dispositions and ways of learning and knowing. They suggest it is this in conjunction with the broader socially ascribed categories of difference that help us to construct our personal identities (Kalantzis, Cope et al., 2005). They argue it is the second layer of difference that we should be working with in the classroom.

The second condition for effective learning is the idea that learning needs to transform the learner in some way. Learning within a context of 'difference' is seen as a means to enact 'personal and cultural' transformation. It involves taking the learner on a journey and out of the 'comfort zone' of their own lifeworlds. Traditionally, schools have tended to deal with multicultural education in a conservative way which simply recognises and affirms difference (Kalantzis, Cope et al., 2005). This idea suggests that we actually engage with difference and as such the experience may be 'risky' and 'unsettling' but that it will result in some personal and cultural transformation. This notion is similar to those who advocate 'Place' as a productive framework to learn about the local and the global, see for example (Gruenewald, 2003; Read, 2000). According to Gruenewald, place is profoundly pedagogical: "as centres of experience, places teach us about how the world works, and how our lives fit into the spaces we occupy. Further, places make us: As occupants of particular places with particular attributes, our identity and our possibilities are shaped" (Gruenewald, 2003, p. 621). It is suggested that place provides a space where different stories or lifeworlds might meet, intersect and negotiate difference. This is seen as highly significant for the relationship between Indigenous and other marginalised knowledge and Western academic thought. This space has been described as a 'contact zone' (Somerville & Perkins, 2003) which is potentially transformative (Haig-Brown, 2001). Working in the contact zone is also described as being 'risky' whilst at the same time an opportunity for opening up 'new possibilities' (Somerville & Perkins, 2003). A multiliteracies pedagogy and place-pedagogy approaches both suggest that truly engaging with 'difference' is a necessary, dangerous and a transformative business.

Literacy: An Act of Translation

One final theoretical idea worth considering for working with difference in classrooms relates to an idea described by Somerville (2005; 2006). She calls for a redefinition of literacy and discusses body and spatial literacies which evolve from a highly developed learned understanding of our own identities in relation to the places and spaces in which we work and live. According to Somerville (2006) literacy is something which occurs in the translation between these embodied knowledge's and different textual forms. Somerville (2006) argues that literacy is always an act of translation which begins in childhood. She suggests it is something that begins at birth as we move from "inchoate sensory experience to forms of representation, expressed initially in gesture, then sounds, and finally marks on a page later differentiated into drawing and writing."

She further argues that this process should not be viewed as a developmental process where all else is lost on our journey to print literacy but all the different modes of literacy need to be maintained so that we can move freely between these different modalities. In order to understand how we might acquire print literacy we need to understand the "acts of translation" that occur between these various modalities and need to facilitate these translations. Somerville (2006) argues further that the movement from inchoate experience through to marks on a page should not be conceived as a developmental pathway where we lose all that precedes print literacy.

The ideas explored through the work of Kalantzis and Cope (2005) and Somerville (2006) are helpful for thinking about diversity. They both suggest we should be thinking about literacy differently and that it needs to incorporate other modalities other than print such as audio, visual, gestural and body. Somerville (2006) goes further to say that literacy is embodied and that it evolves through our relationships to the places and spaces in which we work and live. Both suggest that different modalities should be acknowledged and explored and that one is not inferior to the other as they are all in isolation or combined essential to making meaning. Kalantzis and Cope (2005) talk about 'Available Designs' and about understanding how different modalities might contribute to the meaning of text. Somerville (2006) discusses the idea that literacy should not be viewed as a developmental pathway and we should not lose what we acquire on our journey towards print literacy. She comments further that if we ignore the embodied nature of literacies we have to ask ourselves what actually gets lost in the process. Both also talk about the need to help learners understand the designs that are available to them and the need to help learners understand and use literacies that are not as familiar to them. Somerville (2006) describes this as understanding the 'acts of translation' and Kalantzis and Cope (2005) take up this idea through the 'Overt Instruction' phase of their pedagogical framework. Finally as stated earlier both acknowledge that diversity is a resource and that engaging with it in genuine ways is both 'risky' but potentially transformative.

A number of the ideas explored in the paper so far are important to Kelly and Arnie. Despite their similarities these two students need to be able to affirm their own identities. The boys differ according to the first layer of difference suggested by Kalantzis and Cope (2005). For example Kelly, a teenage boy comes from a white middle class background. Arnie also a young teenage boy comes from a low socio economic Indigenous background. According to Kalantzis and Cope (2005) it would be unproductive to stop here when thinking about these boys as learners in schools. Instead, they need to be understood in relation to the second layer of difference which includes such things as their social orientations, experiences of the world, dispositions and their preferred ways of knowing and learning. This is important if both boys are going to be able to affirm their own identities and experience a sense of belonging in school in terms of the content being learned, the ways in which they are required to know and learn and the school learning community in general. Further, it is important that both boys experience cultural and social transformation in relation to their learning. In this respect both boys have lifeworld experiences that would contribute to the social and cultural transformation of the other. Similarly, Au (1998) imagines classrooms where students engage with a wide variety of texts created from a range of viewpoints that reflect the diversity of their "racial, social, cultural and linguistic backgrounds" (p. 548).

Despite the similarities shared by the two boys and the potentially rich resources that each had to offer the other they were both described quite differently as literacy learners in the school. Arnie was not described as successful in relation to the ways in which schools measure and report on school literacy outcomes or achievement. He was in an Intensive English class and teachers in his school said that students like Arnie rarely achieved their high school certificate. Kelly on the other hand did well in his English classes and was expected to graduate from high school. The reasons for the discrepancies in their literacy achievement are complex but it is argued here that a rethinking of what might count as literacy and knowledge and a rethinking of how we engage with difference would enhance the school experiences and outcomes for both boys. For the remainder of this chapter the discussion will concentrate on Arnie's experiences both in and out of school since the data discussed originates from the study in which he participated. As such, the decision to concentrate on Arnie's experiences is not meant to devalue what Kelly has to offer or to say that his learning is not important but it is Arnie who would appear most disadvantaged in terms of his learning. Some of the theoretical ideas explored so far will be discussed in relation to how they might help facilitate Arnie's learning in an institution that has a white middle class orientation.

Arnie is of Aboriginal descent and so it is important to also consider some of the research conducted relating to the issues of teaching English literacies for Aboriginal learners.

ENGLISH LITERACIES AND ABORIGINAL LEARNERS

The latest results from the Programme for International Student Assessment (PISA) suggest that Australian Indigenous students are about two and a half years behind non-Indigenous students (Thomson & De Bortoli, 2007). These figures are mirrored in reported literacy outcomes of the various states and territories. For example in the Northern Territory in 2006 only 36.5% of Indigenous Year 7 students met the national literacy reading benchmark compared with 90.2% of non-Indigenous students. In 2006 there were 3,635 Indigenous students and 6073 non-Indigenous students enrolled in high schools across the Northern Territory. In the same year 92 Indigenous students graduated with their high school certificate compared to 632 non-Indigenous students (DEET, 2007). In a country such as Australia that has a highly reputable education system internationally these statistics feel extremely unsettling and as educators we should not be comfortable with them. These statistics are mirrored for other groups of students considered to be 'minority' groups across the globe. For example the results of the 2005 National Assessment of Educational Progress in the US showed that the average reading score for African American eighth grade students was 243 whilst the average for their white counterparts was 271. Similar gaps existed between Hispanic and white students and Native Americans and white students (Perie, Grigg et al., 2005).

Since 1997 it has been a national thrust of the Australian Government's Policy to lift literacy and numeracy standards for all students and to develop a more socially just education system that will facilitate equitable participation and appropriate outcomes for Indigenous students. The Adelaide Declaration of Schooling (MCEETYA, 1999) stated that *"Aboriginal and Torres Strait Islander students have equitable access to, and opportunities in, schooling so that their learning outcomes improve, and over time, match those of other students"*.

Despite this promise almost a decade ago outcomes for Australian Indigenous students remain well short of their non-Indigenous counterparts. The issues related to literacy education for Aboriginal students are complex and varied. There is continuous debate relating to what counts as relevant pedagogy for Aboriginal students. Some take a more culturally inclusive perspective (Nakata, 2000; 2007) whilst there are others who argue for the provision of access to what is seen as the more powerful or dominant forms of literacy (Gray, 1985; 2007).

The body of research which informs those who call for a more culturally inclusive curriculum suggest that an Aboriginal world view differs considerably from a Western world view. This research largely followed the seminal work of Stephen Harris (1984) who described traditional learning styles among Aboriginal communities. Whilst this work heightened educator's awareness of cultural difference the work has also been criticised of representing a particular anthropological model of culture that positions Aboriginal culture as being completely incompatible with and different from Western culture and thus contributing to the ideology of cultural binarism and racism (Mishra, 1996; Nicholls, Crowley et al., 1996). Despite this more recent studies continue to describe and affirm significant differences in Aboriginal worldviews and knowledge.

Martin describes the essence of Aboriginal worldviews as 'relatedness', a complex idea which is defined as "sets of conditions, processes, and practices that occur among and between elements of a particular place, and across contexts that are physical, social, political, and intellectual" (2008, p. 61). Aboriginal worldviews constitute "coming to know the world", understanding "relatedness to the elements in that world" and how one relates to these elements. She highlights the importance for educators to have an understanding of the nature of 'relatedness' (Martin, 2008, p. 62). She goes further to explain how knowledge is contained within Stories and points out that these are not merely for entertainment but a legitimate way through which elements such as the land, skies, animals and people express relatedness and identity (Martin 2008, p. 62). These Stories are deeply connected to the literacies that Aboriginal children acquire and involves knowing who your people are and where you come from. Finally she explains that for Aboriginal people, knowledge involves "knowing your Stories of relatedness (Ways of Knowing) and respecting these Stories (Ways of Being) and the ways this relatedness is then expressed (Ways of Doing)" (Martin, 2008, p. 63). She highlights the importance of maintaining, living and expressing relatedness 'appropriately and respectfully' and that although these Stories might be expressed, translated or represented through such things as gestures, paintings or dance and that these are only artefacts of relatedness (Martin, 2008, p. 65).

Somerville (2006) also highlights the importance of story. She argues that relationships to place are constructed in our stories and representations and that language is the primary medium through which our relationships to place are constructed and that Aboriginal stories can be represented in other artefacts such as dance, painting and song. She also suggests that there can be non-Aboriginal stories or alternative stories connected to place and that when these stories intersect it can create connections between people and places (Somerville, 2005).

Over a period of 12 months I came to know Arnie both in his home community and at school. He told me stories about himself, his family and his place. In his community, Arnie was very knowledgeable about many things. He knew many of his Stories of relatedness. He was an accomplished learner. He could paint, carve and dance. He could speak two languages. He played many sports and he was respectful of those who he considered to be older and wiser. In high school Arnie was not so confident. He struggled with many of his classes. He often got himself into trouble and he missed his family and community.

Getting to Know Arnie

Arnie is one of the children who participated in an extensive study that generated detailed case study information about the transition experiences of seven Aboriginal children as they moved from Year 7 in their community school to Year 8 in their new urban high school (Rennie, Wallace et al., 2004). In particular, the study documented the literacy practices valued in the home community, community school and urban high school and highlighted the continuities and discontinuities between them (Lincoln & Guba, 1985). The study in which Arnie participated used ethnographic techniques of observation, document analysis and interviews during the data collection phases. Qualitative techniques were used to analyse the data. In the initial phase of the analysis, data collected from the home, community school and urban high school was analysed separately and coding of the data sets occurred (Miles & Huberman, 1994).

The second phase of the analysis involved an ethnographically grounded approach to discourse analysis. Gee and Green (1997, p. 139) identified four dimensions of social activity - World building, Activity building, Identity building and Connection building World building referred to how participants assembled "situated meanings about "reality," present and absent, concrete and abstract". Activity building described the construction of situated meanings connected to the activity itself. Identity building concerned the identities that were relevant to the situation and included ways of knowing, believing, acting and interacting. Finally, Connection building related to how interactions connected to past and future interactions (Gee & Green, 1997, p. 139).

The third phase of the analysis involved constant comparative analysis between the data sets to assist in identifying discontinuities between the data (Guba & Lincoln, 1981; Lincoln & Guba, 1985). This assisted in identifying the extent to which school literacy practices reflected those valued by the community.

Discontinuities were found in the ways in which children engaged in the various activities. Further, the data highlighted a lack of understanding, valuing and acknowledgement of the various community literate practices by schools. The results of the study suggested that student identities embodied different forms of knowledge and skills and these qualitatively different identities played key roles in the students' effectiveness as learners in our schools.

Arnie's Place

Arnie's community is in the North of Australia and has a population of approximately four hundred. It is serviced by a local store, bank, primary school, recreation hall, sporting facilities, social club, police, women's and men's centre, library, post-office, art and health centre. The community is very traditional with the children and their families participating in hunting and ceremonial activities regularly. At the time of the study, Arnie's primary school had an enrolment of approximately 80 students and Arnie's class comprised students from Years 5, 6 and seven. The urban high school that Arnie relocated to after competing primary school had a population of about 800 students, the majority of which were day students. The school provided boarding places for Aboriginal children from over forty different remote locations.

The following discusses some of the data specific to Arnie. Arnie and his parents were interviewed a number of times during the last six months of his primary school years and the first six months of his high school years. The following section provides a summary of the data collected from one interview with Arnie and his parents at the local art centre where his parents work as paid artists.

A Learner in his Community

I met Arnie after school and we walked down to the art centre together. His Mum was working on a painting when we arrived and his Dad on a carving. We all sat down together near where his father was carving. He talked about his Mother's painting.

He explained that his Mother's paintings were special and that they were "connected to people dying". Although some of them were just for decoration. He said that after the person has passed away for a couple of years and when it's time for ceremony that his Mother makes a painting for that person. And that the painting was "something you remember that person by". He explained that the design had meaning and contained information about their "skin group, tribe and totem".

Arnie said that he would like to be a painter one day and that he often comes down and sits and watches his Mother paint. His Mother said it was important for the "young ones" to watch and talk to their elders as they had a responsibility to pass it on to them and that one day they would be expected to do the same. Arnie explained how he makes paint from ochre and told me that the "colours were important". He said there were only three colours and that these represented "totem, skin group and dreaming". He also knew about his Dad's carving and how he made totem poles. He told me that this was also connected to people who had passed away. He explained how the totem pole represented the deceased person's family and that the family chose who they wanted to make the totem. I got the impression it was honourable to be chosen to carve a totem. He showed me a carving he had made of a fish and explained that you needed to find "iron wood" or "heavy" wood for carving.

Arnie also talked about his dances and how he learns them the same way by participating in the ceremony and watching the others. Arnie said he liked dancing just like he enjoyed painting and carving.

He talked about his relationships with others in the community. The community taught him about the importance of the "right skin group" and how they are required to marry within a certain group, understanding who his cousins are and how he is not allowed to interact with particular people. Again he was required to learn all of this from his family.

Arnie talked about stories his Mum, Nanna and Dad told him and how he keeps these stories in his mind. He knew he would be expected to retell these stories. He said Nanna tells him the stories of "last years when she was a little girl and they had war".

He also talked about his special place "Taracumbie" which is his country. His father said that when he married this would become his children's country as well and that he would also have connections to his wife's country. He told me stories of when he goes out hunting with his family and explained that his Dad teaches him all the things he needs to know in terms of what to hunt, how to hunt and how to survive when he is out there. He knows how to find water, to follow tracks and use markers to help him find his way back. He spoke of imminent dangers and explained that when you are "catching crabs" you have to be wary of "stingrays". Also when you are walking in the swamp looking for 'goose' you have to have your "gun out in front of you" and look carefully for signs of crocodiles. Again he emphasised the importance of going with someone who is older so they can "show you". He knows all about what foods are good and where to find it. He told me how he makes spears for hunting which he uses to catch crabs and fish. Arnie said that "goose" was his favourite food. The hunting experience was one that Arnie enjoyed. It was a family time and they explained how they always "share equally" their spoils from the day with everyone no matter who catches it or whether they were actually there on the day.

His parents said that education was important and that they wanted Arnie to learn English well at school. His father said Arnie would "always remember Tiwi language" but that English was important for him to be successful. Both his parents also believed that learning is very important both in English and Tiwi culture.

In addition to his embodied knowledge about place and his Stories of relatedness Arnie knew many other things. He was a good AFL footballer, he learned to drive a car when he was ten years old, he helped out in the canteen at the local sport and recreation centre, loved swimming, watching movies, writing letters to his brothers, listening to music and enjoyed playing games such as "Cliff Hanger" and "Predator" in the community with his mates.

I had several other interviews with Arnie individually, with his friends and with his parents. He knew a great deal about his community. He had started to accumulate his Stories of relatedness. He also knew a great deal about many other things. He was comfortable with using story as a means to tell me these things.

KNOWLEDGE LEARNING AND LITERACY: A COMMUNITY PERSPECTIVE

The study found that children and parents interviewed had extensive knowledge about the various activities in which they participated. A great deal of emphasis was placed on the sharing of this knowledge. In fact, parents suggested it was their responsibility to pass this knowledge on to their children and there was a strong expectation that their children would do the same. Cultural knowledge was very important. There was also a feeling that this knowledge was part of who they were. It helped to construct their identity (Rennie, 2006). As Martin (2008) suggests it was important that Aboriginal children knew their Stories of relatedness (Ways of knowing), that they and respected these Stories (Ways of Being) and that they expressed these Stories (Ways of Doing). Knowledge was not written down. Neither was it learned by reading books. The knowledge was part of who they were-it was embodied. It constructed identity and assisted in making connection to places, things and others.

Learning and teaching was highly valued in the community. The children in this study learned about hunting by going out with a skilled other. Parents, grandparents and older siblings used the activity of hunting as a means to teach younger siblings. There was also the sense that everyone could learn and everyone could teach as older children also taught their younger brothers and sisters. The children learned about hunting, ceremony, dance, painting and the like by participating, watching, talking to others, listening and asking questions. Parent and community members expected their children would learn during the various community activities. Children had to learn these things and they needed to be in a position later in life to pass their knowledge on to others.

Story featured as an important aspect of the data. Community activities such as hunting were a means to share Stories. Children talked about listening to stories from older members of their family and parents talked about the sharing of stories with their children. Stories were embodied and they were represented through gestures, and other artefacts such as paintings, carvings and dance. The stories were to entertain, share, maintain cultural knowledge and teach. They were often about previous hunting trips, places of significance and stories of survival. There was also evidence of different reading practices throughout the data. Children not only read traditional print and digital text forms but they also read the land, the water, the mind and body, paintings and dance (Rennie, 2006).

Arnie: A Learner in School

Arnie was not that fond of school but explained there were some things he didn't mind doing. In primary school he said he liked it when he could write about things he did in his community. He particularly enjoyed writing about his weekend hunting experiences and felt good when he did well in his spelling and mental mathematics tests. He liked it when his class went to the local swimming hole on Thursdays and when they had culture lessons. He enjoyed events when important people visited the community such as the AFL footballers, cricketers and famous bands. He seemed generally happy with his primary school experiences. When I visited Arnie over the first six months of his high school years he seemed less happy and told me how he missed his family and community.

When Arnie first came to high school he was required to do a number of literacy and numeracy tests in order to assist the school in placing him in an appropriate class. First he was placed in a supported mainstream environment which has tutors that come in to assist individual students. After a couple of months he was moved to an Intensive English class where the focus was on the improvement of literacy and numeracy skills. School became very difficult for Arnie.

Arnie in Class: An English Lesson

I walked into the classroom and sat with two of the Tiwi children. Other students were busily taking out their English books and writing implements. The teacher supplied Darcy and Arnie with pen and paper. After the normal routine of re-establishing the classroom rules and procedures the teacher wrote "The Purposes of Writing" on the whiteboard. The students were orientated to the lesson and asked to write a list of all the different kinds of writing. Darcy and Arnie began their list which included shopping list, email, timetable, newspaper, books and magazines. Darcy began to write the word 'painting' and looked to me for approval. I told him it was a good thing to include. After all he had told me some of the stories in his Grandmother's paintings. Then Arnie said, "What about dance?" I told him it also was a very good example to include. I had seen their dances and they had told me how they represented their various totems. Both children became excited and started adding other less conventional forms of writing to their list including tracks, songs and the seasons. The teacher asked each group to call out their lists. She began to compile a list of all the students' ideas. Darcy and Arnie were pleased that their ideas were recorded. Following this the teacher chose four of the examples the class had offered and erased the remainder of the students' responses. The final list included novels, dictionary, map legend and email. She continued with the lesson and the groups were asked to think about purpose and audience in relation to the remaining four genres.

Knowledge Learning and Literacy: A School Perspective

In school knowledge was constructed very differently. It included knowledge related to 'doing school' and knowledge related to the 'curriculum'. Students needed to know about the rules, routines, procedures and expectations of being a student in high school, some of which are familiar and others not so familiar. The children had much to learn about 'doing high school' during their first term. They had moved to a highly organised institution with a structured timetable, different classes, subjects and teachers, dress and behaviour codes, homework and assessments. In addition, students had to learn about the boarding side of their new life, as well as the academic and classroom side. Curriculum knowledge was also important in school. Interviews with teachers suggested that there was tension between having to meet requirements connected to the curriculum and meeting individual student's needs. The reported low literacy and numeracy levels of these students posed many problems for these high school teachers as they battled to meet curriculum requirements and design activities that the students could do.

Teachers in the school belonged to different faculties and as much as possible the teachers planned together to ensure consistency across the various grades and testing. This was particularly evident in the mainstream and supported secondary classes in the areas of mathematics and science. Textbooks tended to dominate the content taught in these subjects.

Students learned to varying degrees through listening, copying notes, reading, writing and discussion. In some classes, it appeared to the researchers that teachers used many worksheets and students spent a great deal of time copying notes, questions and problems off the board. It was common for students to have unfinished work. In the classes observed, students learned as a whole group, in small groups and independently, although generally independent learning was favoured over whole class or small group learning. In classes where independent learning was a preferred method, the teacher often discouraged the practice of sharing answers or of students assisting each other. Reading was also a means to learn. Teachers directed students to read particular parts of their notes or textbooks during homework activities so they would be adequately prepared for tests. There was a distinct emphasis on the encoding and decoding of print.

FUTURE POSSIBILITIES: MAKING SCHOOL LESS DIFFICULT FOR ARNIE

The study found that many of the discontinuities for Arnie and others who participated in the study lay in the fact that who the children were and what the children knew, preferred to do and could do was often not valued and acknowledged in the school setting. Despite being a very successful learner in his home community Arnie was not as successful in school. The irony of the latter point was clear in the data: Continuities in knowledge and identity can be seen to provide the bridges and connections (based on what the children can do and who they are) that build learning and new knowledge and identities. Discontinuities in knowledge and identity prohibit effective and engaged learning. Other studies provide support for these ideas. Au and Raphael (2000) report that it is not uncommon for students of diverse backgrounds to appear highly "literate and accomplished when literacies other than those of the school are considered" (p.173). A study on Native American Reading practices found Native Americans have preferred ways of learning and have experiences of literacy events and practices often overlooked in American classrooms (White-Kaulaity, 2007).

Some of the theoretical ideas explored earlier related to multiliteracies and diversity are worth considering in relation to how we might improve Arnie's and others like him, experiences in school. First, the ideas related to a rethinking of what might constitute literacy. If we acknowledge that literacy is a social practice and that it is largely shaped through our participation in various events then it allows us to talk about Arnie's literate competence in much broader terms than the current narrow view which is used to describe Arnie as a literate person in school. Second, the idea that contemporary society is characterised by multiliteracies and as such comprises a range of different modalities and integration of modes to make meaning. If we adopt this idea then it means we acknowledge there is a great deal of 'available designs' out there which can include a range of modes such as gestural, audio, visual, and spatial and body. Arnie's literacies are embodied. Further he is comfortable encoding and decoding a wide array of available designs including painting, dance and story. Finally, the idea that we might consider literacy is an 'act of translation'. Arnie is competent at knowing how various artefacts express his Stories of relatedness but is less competent in using school literacies. If we are going to understand how to assist Arnie in school we first need to understand as Martin (2008) suggests the concept of relatedness and as Somerville (2006) suggests we also need to understand how to help Arnie make the translation to print literacy.

The second set of ideas worth consideration relate to the conditions of learning. In many ways Arnie did not feel a sense of belonging in school. What he knew, what he preferred to do and how he preferred to learn were not acknowledged in the school setting. The literacy example described earlier provides a good example. When asked to give examples of writing the boys offered examples of writing that made sense to them, for example painting and dance. These examples were not explored in any great detail. Writing was discussed and presented as it is described within the school curriculum. If a multiliteracies framework had been adopted then the teacher would have incorporated a wider range of 'Available Designs' which might have included the 'Designs' that Arnie and his friends put forward. In putting these designs forward Arnie and his friends were also trying to establish a sense of identity within the classroom community. Others including the teacher would have had a better understanding of who Arnie was. The second condition of learning relates to personal and social transformation. Earlier in this chapter it was suggested that both Kelly and Arnie had a great deal to offer each other in this regard. The literacy lesson is an example where this could have happened. Putting forward Arnie's designs would have presented different possibilities for other learners like Kelly and an exploration of these designs may have led to redesigning, new possibilities and transformed practice.

CONCLUSION

Whilst this chapter focussed primarily on one Indigenous Australian student the theoretical ideas discussed could be applied across the range of diverse learners in our classrooms through the use of a multiliteracies framework and a rethinking of how we engage with diversity to enact personal and cultural transformation. McCarthey and Dressman (2000) imagine future classrooms as a "multicultural quilt created from the diverse experiences and backgrounds of children and teachers, stitched together by their contacts with one another within the seams of schools" with the image of the quilt breaking down the hierarchy and "the rhizomatic spread of innovative literacy experience" (p. 548).

REFERENCES

Au, K., H., & Raphael, T.E. (2000). Equity and literacy in the next millenium. *Reading Research Quarterly, 35*(1), 170–188. doi:10.1598/RRQ.35.1.12

Au, K. H. (1998). Social constructivism and the school literacy learning of students of diverse cultural backgrounds. *Journal of Literacy Research, 30*(2), 297–319.

Aukerman, R. C. (1984). *Approaches to beginning reading.* New York: Wiley.

Barton, D., & Hamilton, M. (1998). *Local literacies: Reading and writing in one community.* London: Routledge.

Barton, D., Hamilton, M., & Ivanic, R. (Eds.). (2000). *Situated literacies: Reading and writing in context.* New York: Routledge.

Cairney, T. H., & Ruge, J. (1997). *Community literacy practices and schooling: Towards effective support for students.* Canberra, Australia: Department of Employment, Education, Training and Youth Affairs.

Cambourne, B. (1988). *The whole story: Natural learning and the acquisition of literacy in the classroom.* Auckland, New Zealand: Ashton Scholastic.

Chall, J. (1967). *Learning to read: The great debate.* New York: McGraw-Hill.

Christie, F., Devlin, B., Freebody, P., Luke, A., Martin, J. R., & Threadgold, T. (1991). *Teaching English literacy: A project of national significance on the preservice preparation of teachers to teach English literacy.* Darwin, Australia: Centre for Studies of Language in Education, Northern Territory University.

Comber, B., & Kamler, B. (Eds.). (2005). *Turn-around pedagogies: Literacy interventions for at-risk students.* Newtown, Australia: Primary English Teaching Association.

Cope, B., & Kalantzis, M. (Eds.). (2000). *Multiliteracies: Literacy learning and the design of social futures.* South Yarra, Australia: Macmillan.

DEET. (2007). *Annual Report 2006-2007.* Darwin, Australia: Department of Employment Education and Training.

Department of Education Science and Training (DEST) (2005). Teaching reading: Report and recommendations. *National Inquiry into the Teaching of Literacy*. Canberra: Australian Government.

Fleer, M., & Williams-Kennedy, D. (2001). *Building bridges: Literacy development in young indigenous children.* Canberra, Australia: Australian Early Childhood Association Inc.

Flippo, R. F. (1999). Redefining the reading wars: The war against reading researchers. *Educational Leadership*, *57*(2), 38–41.

Freebody, P., & Luke, A. (1990). 'Literacies' programs: Debates and demands in cultural context. *Prospect*, *5*(3), 7–16.

Gee, J. (1996). *Social linguistics and literacies: Ideology in discourses.* London: Taylor and Francis.

Gee, J. P., & Green, J. (1997). Discourse analysis, learning, and social practice: A methodological study. *Review of Research in Education*, *23*, 119–169.

Gray, B. (1985). Helping children to become language learners in the classroom. In M. Christie (Ed.), *Aboriginal perspectives on experience and learning.* Geelong, Australia: Deakin University Press.

Gray, B. (2007). *Accelerating the literacy development of indigenous students.* Darwin, Australia: Charles Darwin University Press.

Gruenewald, D. A. (2003). The best of both worlds: A critical pedagogy of place. *Educational Researcher*, *32*(4), 3–12. doi:doi:10.3102/0013189X032004003

Guba, E., & Lincoln, Y. Y. (1981). *Effective evaluation.* San Francisco: Jossey-Bass.

Haig-Brown, A. (2001). Continuing collaborative knowledge production: Knowing when where why and how. *Journal of Intercultural Studies (Melbourne, Vic.)*, *22*(1), 19–32. doi:10.1080/07256860120037391

Harris, S. (1984). *Culture and Llearning: Tradition and education in northeast Arnhem Land.* Canberra, Australia: Australian Institute of Aboriginal Studies.

Heath, S. (1986). What no bedtime story means: Narrative skills at home and school. In B. Schheifflin & E. Ohs (Eds.), *Language socialisation across cultures* (pp. 97-124). Boston: Cambridge University Press.

Hill, S., Comber, B., Louden, W., Rivalland, J., & Reid, J. (1998). *100 children go to school: Connections and disconnections in literacy development in the year prior to school and the first year of school.* Canberra, Australia: Department of Training, Employment and Youth Affairs.

Hill, S., Comber, B., Louden, W., Rivalland, J., & Reid, J. (2002). *100 children turn 10.* Canberra, Australia: DEET.

Kalantzis, M., & Cope, B. (2005). *Learning by design.* Melbourne, Australia: VSIC, Common Ground.

Lee, J., Grigg, W., & Donahue, P. (2007). *The nation's report card: Reading 2007.* Retrieved May 30, 2008, from http://nces.ed.gov/nationsreportcard/pubs/main2007/2007496.asp.

Lincoln, Y. S., & Guba, E. G. (1985). *Naturalistic inquiry.* Beverly Hills, CA: Sage Publications.

Louden, W., Rohl, M., Barratt-Pugh, C., Brown, C., Cairney, T., & Elderfield, J. (2005). In teachers' hands: Effective literacy pratices in the early years of schooling. *Australian Journal of Language and Literacy, 28*(3).

Martin, J. R., Christie, F., & Rothery, J. (1987). Social processes in education. *The Teaching of English: Journal of the English Teachers' . Association of New South Wales, 53*, 3–22.

Martin, K. (2008). The intersection of aboriginal knowledges, aboriginal literacies and new learning. In Healy, A. (Ed.), *Multlilieracies and diversity in education. New pedagogies for expanding landscapes* (pp. 58-81). South Melbourne, Australia: Oxford University Press.

McCarthey, S. J., & Dressman, M. (2000). How will diversity affect literacy in the next millenium. *Reading Research Quarterly, 35*(4), 548–552. doi:10.1598/RRQ.35.4.6

MCEETYA. (1999). *The Adelaide declaration on national goals for schooling in the twenty-first century.* Retrieved May 30, 2008, from http://www.mceetya.edu.au/mceetya/nationalgoals/natgoals.htm.

Miles, M. B., & Huberman, M. A. (1994). *Qualitative data analysis.* Beverly Hills, CA: Sage.

Mishra, V. (1996). Postmodern racism. *Meanjin, 2*, 346–357.

Moll, L., Amanti, C., Neff, D., & Gonzalez, N. (1992). Funds of knowledge for teaching: Using a qualitative approach to connect homes and classroom. *Theory into Practice, 31*(2), 132–141.

Nakata, M. (2000). History, cultural diversity and English language teaching. In B. Cope & M. Kalantzis (Eds.) *Multiliteracies* (pp. 106-120). London: Macmillan.

Nakata, M. (2007). *Discipling the savages: Savaging the disciplines.* Canberra, Australia: Aboriginal Studies Press.

New London Group. (1996). A Pedagogy of Multiliteracies: Designing Social Futures. *Harvard Educational Review, 66*(1), 60–92.

Nicholls, C., Crowley, V., & Watt, R. (1996). Theorising Aboriginal education: Surely it's time to move on? *Education Australia, 33*(6-9).

Organisation for Economic Co-Operation and Development [OECD]. (2006). *PISA 2006 Science Competencies for Tomorrow's World.* Retrieved January, 5, 2009 from http://www.oecd.org/pages/0,3417,en_32252351_32236191_1_1_1_1_1,00.html

Perie, M., Grigg, W. S., & Donahue, P. (2005). *The nation's report card: Reading 2005.* Retrieved May 20, 2008 from http://nces.ed.gov/pubsearch/pubsinfo.asp?pubid=2006451.

Read, P. (2000). *Belonging: Australians, place and aboriginal ownership.* UK: Cambridge University Press.

Rennie, J. (2006). Meeting kids at the school gate: The literacy and numeracy practices of a remote indigenous community. *Australian Educational Researcher, 33*(3), 123–140.

Rennie, J., Wallace, R., & Falk, I. (2004). *Discontinuities in literacy and numeracy practices between indigenous community schooling and urban high school* (pp. 121). Canberra, Australia: Department Education, Science and Training.

Somerville, M. (2005). Researching place pedagogies. In *Proceedings of the 1st International Conference of Qualitative Inquiry, University of Illinois, USA.*

Somerville, M. (2006). *Literacy as translation.* Australian Council of Adult Literacy: Annual Conference, Adelaide, Australia.

Somerville, M., & Perkins, T. (2003). Border work in the contact zone: Thinking Indigenous/non-Indigenous collaboration spatially . *International Journal of Intercultural Studies*, *24*(3), 253–266. doi:10.1080/0725686032000172597

Street, B. V. (Ed.). (1993). *Cross-cultural approaches to literacy.* UK: Cambridge University Press.

Thomson, S., & De Bortoli, L. (2007). *Exploring scientific literacy: How Australia measures Up*. Retrieved May 27, 2008, from http://www.acer.edu.au/ozpisa/reports.html.

White-Kaulaity, M. (2007). Reflections on Native Amercian reading: A seed, a tool, and a weapon. *Journal of Adolescent & Adult Literacy*, *50*(7), 560–569. doi:10.1598/JAAL.50.7.5

Chapter 7
Pragmatism and Philosophy: Enriching Students' Lives through a Critical Investigation of Spatial Literacy in Shared Spaces

Margaret Baguley
University of Southern Queensland, Australia

Toni Riordan
St Joseph's Nudgee College, Australia

Martin Kerby
St Joseph's Nudgee College, Australia

ABSTRACT

The purpose of this paper was to investigate how a secondary boys' College has sought to create a cultural alliance between a spatial literacy which expresses an officially sanctioned version of the past and a contemporary curriculum that embraces a far broader understanding of this concept. This investigation of spatial literacy was contextualised through the curriculum plan of the College which seeks to educate students through a student-centred curriculum that aims to develop critically aware and culturally sensitive world citizens. The perceptions of key teachers were also examined which revealed their increasing use of school spaces to address political, philosophical and environmental issues in their pedagogical approach.

INTRODUCTION

Within the education sector it is recognised that students need to be aware of and learn a range of skills in order to critically evaluate the multifarious ways they receive and view information (Anstey & Bull, 2006; Davis, 2008; Kalantzis, Cope & Fehring 2002; Unsworth, 2001). As Davis (2008, p. 10) notes, current evidence suggests that "the curriculum stalwarts of literacy and numeracy are no longer sufficient to equip students with the basics they need to operate in the innovation oriented, digitally wired twenty first century". The importance of educating for multiple ways of understanding and relaying information, also known as 'multiliteracies', was formalised by the New London Group[1] The members of this group proposed that an educationally func-

DOI: 10.4018/978-1-60566-673-0.ch007

tional grammar for the future would include "the textual and the visual, as well as the multi-modal relations between the different meaning-making processes that are now so critical in media texts and texts of electronic multimedia" (New London Group, 1996, p. 77).

There is extensive literature regarding the value of the multiliteracies approach (Anstey & Bull, 2004; Cope & Kalantzis, 2000; Kalantzis, 2001; Kress, 2000; Luke & Freebody, 1997; New London Group, 1996; Unsworth, 2002) and how its effective use in the education sector can enable teachers to "equip their students with the knowledge, skills, strategies and attitudes that will enable them to meet new situations and cope with them" (Anstey & Bull, 2006, p. 18). In response to rapid changes in technology and society on a local and global scale, literacy knowledge, skills and processes have also changed. There has been an increased emphasis on placing the student at the centre of learning resulting in greater emphasis on the learner for accepting responsibility for their learning (Betts, 1992; Marsh, 2008; McComb, 1997; Weimer, 2002). A clear link has also been drawn to how developing a range of literacies is particularly important for students from diverse backgrounds in order for them to be able to more effectively negotiate learning in school curriculum areas (Unsworth, 2001). As Anstey and Bull (2006) note in order to be multiliterate a person should be able to "interpret, use and produce a range of electronic, live and paper texts that employ linguistic, visual, auditory, gestural, and spatial semiotic systems for social, cultural, political, civic and economic purposes in socially and cultural diverse contexts" (p. 41).

This chapter will examine the Curriculum Plan of St Joseph's Nudgee College which emphasises the autonomy of the learner through an inclusive educational philosophy utilising a range of literacies. Spatial literacy will be a specific focus of this chapter as the College campus and its history is an intrinsic part of the students' daily lives and, for many, their motivation to attend this particular college. The perceptions of key teachers will be utilised in addition to relevant curriculum documents to gauge the effectiveness of the multiliteracies approach in preparing students to become critically aware and sensitive world citizens.

BACKGROUND

St Joseph's Nudgee College[2] situated in the north of Brisbane in the state of Queensland is an Australian Catholic school for boys whose philosophy is based on the Edmund Rice tradition[3]. The college's current enrolment stands at 1350 boys in Years 5 – 12, including 300 boarders. The demographic breakdown of the student cohort is 1205 Australian, 74 international (majority from Asia), 38 Papua New Guinea and 33 Indigenous students. When the college was established in 1891 it had a distinct Irish identity and catered mostly for 'boys from the bush' with the majority of these leaving home to board at Nudgee.

The campus covering 137 hectares is one of the largest in the state. The architecture of the college is diverse, reflecting a range of buildings and styles which are testament to the pressures – both past and current – to cater for population growth and a major demographic shift in the socio-economic status of the student clientele. Nudgee possesses open, well maintained grounds and renowned sporting facilities, including a golf course, Olympic sized pool and a national standard athletics track. The campus offers a physical reminder of the changing nature of the school; from its traditional past firmly rooted in the Irish/Australian experience and a modern search for identity in a new millennium. In 2008, another chapter of Nudgee commenced with the introduction of three primary year levels 5 to 7 (10 – 12 years of age) in addition to the traditional five secondary year levels of 8 – 12 (13 – 17 years of age).

IDENTITY & PRAGMATISM

Nudgee's Administration is in the process of searching for what McLaughlin describes as "an authentic identity and its accompanying integrity" (2007, p. xviii). For a College whose history predates Federation[4] by a decade, this search becomes a politically charged balancing act between the often competing needs to market a thoroughly modern curriculum, while simultaneously remaining true to a heritage that stretches back to nineteenth-century Ireland. However, in an educational institution such as a boarding school with fifth generation students, it is inevitable that there are myths which compete, and even oppose the officially sanctioned history. Therefore it is not surprising that the two initiatives at the vanguard of this change process at Nudgee are inspired by inherently contradictory impulses. The first is the development of a whole school curriculum plan inspired by the importance of teaching multiliteracies and a range of thinking strategies in a contemporary curriculum. It is at the forefront of a wider College focus on academic results, a focus sometimes obscured by Nudgee's standing as one of the Commonwealth's pre-eminent sporting Colleges. The second initiative is an architectural renewal and environmental programme, which is part of a 20 year strategic plan with a budget allocation of over 15 million Australian dollars.

In another institution this contradiction might well create a dangerous internal tension, with the proponents of either approach locked in an abstract argument for the soul of the College. Yet to this point there has been little, if any internal dissension over the direction or scope of the plan. One of the College's greatest strengths, and at times its greatest weakness is that at its core there is an entrenched pragmatism underpinning any decision making. This pragmatism is both a philosophy as well as a site specific response to the financial pressures of educating the poor which has driven the College to the edge of bankruptcy on numerous occasions. It was present in the work of Edmund Rice, the founder of the Christian Brothers, who never saw schools as "ends in themselves but as a means toward the fulfilment of the mission of the poor and their liberation from the poverty trap" (Cardinal Edward Clancy, quoted in McLaughlin, 2007, p. xv). This characteristic permeated the Brothers' schools, which though imbued with a Christian culture, also "introduced their boys to a pragmatic curriculum that promoted a robust social mobility" (McLaughlin 2007, p. xviii).

The College's strong historical and philosophical traditions have therefore caused the current administration to seek a visual and spatial connection through the current building program, to the mono-cultural, insular environment that spawned the first great phase of College building between 1891 and 1919. In this way it is hoped that Nudgee will project through its built environment a twenty-first century identity which provides its students with a sense of its history, their place within the Nudgee tradition and opportunities to contribute as active citizens imbued with the values of Edmund Rice education.

THE CURRICULUM PLAN

In 2000 Nudgee established a Curriculum Council to develop a 'whole school' approach to the curriculum. The Curriculum Council subsequently developed a Curriculum Framework of whole school learning outcomes informed by the document *Years 1 – 10 Curriculum Framework* (Education Queensland, 2002) which provided guiding values and principles for schools working on issues of boys' education within a gender equity framework. After extensive consultation and discussion Nudgee adopted a whole school curriculum plan which has been implemented during the period 2004 – 2008. The Nudgee College Curriculum Plan describes the curriculum structure that supports overall student learning. It defines the four elements of the Nudgee curriculum as: Core Learnings, Pedagogy, Assessment and Reporting and also outlines the Professional Development processes that are available to assist teacher development. There are eight core learnings which underpin the curriculum, described as the essential understandings and skills identified as: congruence, acknowledgement of core values, inclusivity, flexibility, integration, a developmental approach, collaboration and social responsibility. The plan is congruent with the school's philosophy and aims to instil in students the attributes of a life-long learner. These attributes complement the eight core learnings and are identified as: a knowledgeable person with deep understanding; a complex thinker; a creative person; an active investigator; an effective communicator; a participant in an interdependent world and a reflective and self-directed learner (Defining the Future of the Nudgee College Curriculum, 2004).

In addition to the eight Core Learnings the three elements of the Curriculum Plan encompass pedagogy, assessment and reporting. The pedagogical element of the plan reflects the Nudgee College Curriculum Council's commitment to embracing multiliteracies as a core element in the educational process. The assessment element recognises the active participation of students in their learning in addition to valuing meaningful and relevant connections to the curriculum. The reporting element provides opportunities to assist students in recognising strengths and opportunities to improve in curriculum areas. The following extract (Table 1) from the Curriculum Plan demonstrates how the three interrelated elements of pedagogy, assessment and reporting underpinned by the eight core learnings are being utilised to effectively enhance student learning.

It is evident that approaches to pedagogy, assessment and reporting provide the context for a range of multiliteracies approaches to occur including the provision of authentic and 'real world' experiences, utilising a range of technologies, involving students as active participants in their learning, using complex thinking and examining how curriculum, pedagogy and assessment enable students to develop academic and social skills (Anstey & Bull, 2006; Cope & Kalantzis, 2000; Leander & Sheehy, 2004; Unsworth, 2001; Vadeboncoeur & Stevens, 2005). In addition to the recognition of the importance of incorporating a multiliteracies approach in contemporary curriculum, it is also evident that in recent years there has been a change in how education is viewed. Education is now viewed as social capital in which knowledge is seen as a primary source of economic productivity (Burnheim, 2004; Fine, 2001; Harriss, 2002). This requires educators, as evidenced in the Nudgee curriculum plan, to educate students in a range of skills and approaches which are expected to be transferable beyond the classroom context.

SPATIAL LITERACY AND THE SEARCH FOR IDENTITY

The Nudgee Curriculum Plan is testament to a curriculum approach that recognises the increasing importance of multiliteracies and the invaluable opportunities outside of the classroom to engage students. The incorporation of spatial literacy has been used within the whole school curriculum approach at Nudgee to "help students engage in critical reflections of space and place" and to understand that "particular spaces are a commentary on social structures" (Chacko, 2005, p. 12). The new term 'visuacy' has recently been utilised in the Australian National Review of Visual Education and is defined as "the ability to create, process, critique and appreciate the spectrum of visual phenomena in the individual's external and internal environment" (Davis, 2008, p. 11). The essence of the visual is intimately connected with the spatial and therefore both approaches are essential when used to effectively engage students with a range of environments such as the school environment.

Cotterell (1996) contends that schools are more than a mere backdrop for social interaction

Table 1. Nudgee College Curriculum Plan 2004 – 2008

Pedagogy	• Provide authentic, flexible and innovative learning experiences. • Use information and communication technologies to improve curriculum. • Encourage students to discuss and understand their learning. • Plan collaboratively and share effective teaching strategies. • Consistently review practice. • Implement practices that reflect international best practice.
Assessment	• Use a range of techniques and instruments. • Involve students as active participants in their assessment and learning. • Seek meaningful and relevant connections to the curriculum and "real world" settings. • Utilise complex thinking and problem solving. • Implement social moderation processes when judging standards. • Promote equity and other principles of assessment.
Reporting	• Recognise, acknowledge and give credit for what students have achieved and experienced. • Contribute to students' personal development and progress, improve motivation, provide encouragement and increase their awareness of strengths, weaknesses, and opportunities as a basis for intervening in problems. • Assist the College in identifying how well the curriculum, pedagogy and assessment enable students to develop academic and social skills • Assist students and their parents/carers to determine future pathways. • Provide opportunities for teachers and administrators to talk about individuals' and groups' progress and about possible interventions and curricular approaches.

as their settings, organisational structures and activities affect and influence students' values, attitudes and motivations. Soja (2004) notes putting space first enables a balance of social, historical, and spatial elements, particularly important in a school environment such as Nudgee. Sheehy and Leander (2004) propose that space is a "product and process of socially dynamic relations" and is not static (p. 1). Therefore, a student-centred approach which includes the students' 'lifeworlds' (Cope & Kalantzis, 2000) – the world that exists outside school – enables them to interact with the spaces of Nudgee in a way that is relevant and meaningful for them. There are unofficial spaces around Nudgee which are designated to particular groups, such as the area around 'the Year 12 tree'. However, the College has attempted to absorb this unofficial use of space by creating attractive areas throughout the College by opening up previously closed spaces and allowing longer vistas so that the students see and feel they are part of a community. An examination of such political use of space is encouraged in a curriculum which is both student centred and caters for a range of literate practices and multiple modes (Anstey & Bull, 2006; Cope & Kalantzis, 2000; Leander & Sheehy, 2004).

Although students have seemingly unlimited opportunities to access information they often do not appear to have the same opportunities to 'encounter' (Butcher-Younghans, 1993). It is the student's encounter with the world they inhabit that should be the cornerstone of an effective pedagogy (Anstey & Bull, 2006; Cope & Kalazntzis, 2000; Leander & Sheehy, 2004). Such an encounter is denied when learning is constrained by traditional thinking in relation to literacy. This is particularly relevant to an institution such as Nudgee, which in the past catered almost entirely to the basic reading and writing literacy needs of a poor, rural Irish Catholic demographic. The College is now racially and culturally diverse, with a staff attuned to preparing students to engage in a rapidly changing world. In order to address some of these changes the College has included specific references to the importance of 'space' and its relationship in a range of initiatives designed to both inform and challenge Nudgee students. This form of literacy encompasses the meanings of both environmental and architectural spaces, and creates not just an understanding of the past, but enables students to question 'master narratives', such as the Irish Catholic heritage and patriarchal structures in Nudgee's case, and analyse these same spatial politics in their daily lives. However, in order to effectively utilise these opportunities teachers at Nudgee have had to undergo a paradigm shift in their thinking in which they avoid viewing the College purely as a teaching environment, but rather as a diverse community in which "students will need to acquire the skills, strategies, and practices they need for work and leisure; active citizenship; participation in social, cultural and community activities; and personal growth" (Anstey & Bull, 2006, p. 19). This approach supports students of this age who seek "to construct their identity in relation to their school context and the larger sociolcultural context outside the school" (Vadeboncoeur, 2005, p. 129).

DISCOVERING WHICH SONG

Given the size and diversity of Nudgee's campus, the most effective way of facilitating a student's discovery of the meanings of the architectural and environmental spaces, was to develop three mutually supportive initiatives: establishment of a museum/gallery; an orientation/heritage walking tour and a designated environmental area. Each of these initiatives occurred in 2002 when the first lay Principal of the college was appointed due to the Christian Brothers becoming increasingly removed from the College through age and ill-health. During this year one of the teachers with an extensive history background was also employed as a Curator and Archivist with the mandate to make the College's history more accessible to classroom teachers and students.

Prior to committing resources to these initiatives, the first task facing a teacher who wishes to utilise spatial literacy in their pedagogical practice is to discover "what song the campus sings best" (Lloyd, 2002, p. 219). The song can best be articulated by answering the following questions: What does the campus illustrate best about the past? How can the school's resources amplify and communicate the historical message? How can we link our messages and resources to develop a viable educational resource? How can we present the campus in a way that connects with the contemporary lives and interests of the students? (Adapted from Levy et. al., 2001, p. xii). These questions have been effectively responded to in the way Nudgee has utilised, analysed and communicated its stories using a multi-modal approach and contextualising it in a relevant and meaningful way for its students.

At Nudgee a museum was seen as a mid- to long-term project requiring considerable financial support, although the process of collecting items for display began almost immediately. The Curator/Archivist received an inaugural staff development grant this year to prepare electronic classroom resources so that students would be able to access photographs, sound recordings and textual data housed in the Nudgee College Museum. In conjunction with this resource classroom teachers have devised assignments which encourage students to explore Nudgee's history and to discover the stories of its Old Boys who had fought for their country or excelled in sporting and cultural pursuits. Many of the students are surprised when undertaking their research of the ages of some of the Nudgee Old Boys who had sacrificed their lives in various wars. The importance of this sacrifice is also emphasised by the whole school ANZAC[5] ceremony to which a lesser number of surviving Nudgee Old Boy servicemen are able to attend each year.

A heritage tour of the grounds was also organised by the Curator/Archivist and informed by his knowledge of the College's history. It was seen as an achievable and relatively high profile means of acknowledging the importance of spatial literacy in the curriculum. It also offered a low cost means of providing orientation programs for new students. The thematic tour used the site's most significant resources – its architecture, historical context and the stories of past students.

The Heritage Tour introduces students to the built environment in terms of the historical development of the campus. However, due to financial constraints over the course of a century there have been limited attempts to maintain any sense of architectural integrity. The students are able to view the number of significant visual and spatial changes occurring within the College grounds. During the tour they are informed of the building styles and the reasons for their existence. For example, the Mediterranean style of the campus buildings constructed between 1891 and 1919 clash with the concrete utilitarian buildings from the 1970s, which in turn seem out of place with the demountable classroom hastily erected in the 1990s to cope with the increase in student numbers. An ambitious building program commenced at the end of 2007 and has sought to bring architectural continuity to the Campus. Even the rather eclectic structures from the 1970s are being rendered and painted in a more traditional style. While this is certainly testament to the changing socio/cultural background of the College, spatial literacy is perhaps best demonstrated through an examination of the statues placed around the College and their subsequent political iconography.

IF THESE STONES COULD SPEAK

Located on the right hand side of the main drive into the College stands an imposing granite statue titled 'True Blue'[6] (See Figure 1). It is an inherently flawed and controversial attempt to return the College community to a traditional myth. Like so many traditional statues it commemorates a generic type, not an individual. It is a statue of a stockman, which celebrates the national foundation myth with its roots in the pioneering families who settled remote and regional areas in rural Queensland. A section of the prominent plaque at the base of the statue reads:

This monument honours the founding ideals of the Christian Brothers and the Community of St Joseph's Nudgee College to provide an education for young men from the bush and to engender, in all Nudgee students, the enduring ideals of the outback, mateship and loyalty.

Significantly the text on the plaque is designed to be understood by Australian students, many of whom have never been to 'the bush'. Students from different cultural backgrounds may feel excluded from this quintessential 'Australian' language and therefore the inclusion of 'True Blue' within the heritage tour is part of the complex task of teachers who need to assist students from diverse backgrounds to develop a range of literacies (Bianco, 2000; Cobb, 1992; Unsworth, 2001; Vadebonoceur & Stevens, 2005). Although 'True Blue' was widely perceived by the school community to be anachronistic, it was criticised primarily on aesthetic and budgetary grounds, rather than on its reactionary ideology. Currently there are plans to move the statue to a less prominent spot in the College and replace it with a Celtic cross; however, it might be argued that the celebration of the College's Irish roots merely replaces one anachronistic symbol with an even older one. 'True Blue' also provides a valuable introduction to the manner in which inanimate objects can 'speak,'

Figure 1. True Blue sculpted by Chris McKenzie(©2008, St Joseph's Nudgee College. Used with permission.)

even if their message is a flawed one, or one open to misinterpretation[7].

The Curator/Archivist explained that many of the students arrive at the College aware that it has an important history. However, they do not appear to have a simultaneous knowledge of Australian history. The tour of the campus therefore gives historical reality to a mythological discussion which has occurred due to the stories passed down from previous generations, such as their parents and grandparents, who have attended the College. It also allows the Curator/Archivist opportunity to relate historical events with the texts the students are viewing. Past student stories are also woven into the tour to enrich and enliven the spaces the students are moving through.

The front lawn of Nudgee is an overt political colonisation of space. Staring at each across the well kept lawn are the statues of St Patrick, patron saint of Ireland, and St Francis Xavier, patron saint of Australia, mute observers of the twin calls on the loyalty of Irish Australians (See Fig. 2). They were gifts from the students of 1904, three years after Federation and at a time when the loyalties of Irish Catholic Australians were openly questioned. O'Farrell (1986) in his history of the

Figure 2. Statues of St Patrick and St Francis Xavier(©2008, St Joseph's Nudgee College. Used with permission.)

Irish in Australia described them as "ambivalent, ambiguous people thinking Irish, talking English; hating the tyranny, yet serving the tyrant" (p. 1) This is also evident in the previous College Historian's (Boland, 1991) description of students at the College just prior to the outbreak of World War One as "conventional, patriotic, imperialist, even jingoistic…they accepted the manifest destiny of the British races to hold dominion over palm and pine" (p. 38). Students are given a brief historical background and then asked why the students may have gifted both statues at the same time to the College. They are then asked to consider the year the statues were gifted and to envision what students at that time may have discussed in terms of Federation, their position in Australia as Irish Catholics and their potential involvement in World War I. They are also asked to examine the style of the statues, their size, placement and the symbolic connotations associated with each.

Such a politically laden statement at the very heart of the Campus offers enormous scope for an examination of spatial literacy in a meaningful context, and a sense of encounter with what the College once was, and by implication, what it has become. After preliminary discussions about 'True Blue', students are then often able to make connections with other examples of political iconography which may be easily overlooked. Wide ranging discussions occur concerning subliminal messages such as a good 'Nudgee Man' which is understood as someone who is a good citizen, with loyalties to school, state, and nation. Students are also asked to critically analyse why Nudgee students are referred to generically as 'men' on public occasions which results in a spirited discussion of 'manly' virtues, particularly given the range of cultural backgrounds in the school community. Elements within the spaces such as the flags and the presence of the Union Jack on the Australian and Queensland flags flown at the campus which once housed a belligerently Irish Catholic community are also discussed.

The prominent placement of the war memorials at the door of the Chapel next to the commemorative listing of Christian Brothers who served at the College provides further valuable discussion points. These can range from the legitimacy conferred by such a placement, augmented by the Latin inscriptions and Classical scroll work, to society's changing views of warfare. It can also place the Irish Australian experience as felt at the College into the broader context of the nation's first significant experience of war between 1914 and 1918. The Irish, with suspect loyalties amidst the passions engendered by the Easter Rebellion and the divisive question of conscription[8], eventually supported the war, though not its direction, as much as any other group in Australia at the time. Over 250 Old Boys served in World War One, with 53 killed in action or dying of wounds. This is consistent statistically with the national experience (337,000 served overseas with slightly more than 60,000 deaths, the highest proportion per capita of any of the combatants). Coming from poor backgrounds, all but one of the deaths was of men serving in the artillery and infantry, with only one having reached the rank of officer.

The Second World War Memorial at the College is much less ornate and lists 103 Old Boys killed in action or who died while prisoners of war. Seventy five of those killed served in the Royal Australian Air Force (RAAF), many of them officers, a change indicative of both technological advances and the improving level of education and social mobility offered to the students. That many of these died not in direct defence of Australia, but while serving in Europe and North Africa facilitates a valuable discussion concerning Australia's national links to Imperial policy, even after Pearl Harbour and the fall of Singapore (See Fig. 3). In contrast, the Vietnam Memorial, which was only added in 2002, reflects both a much smaller military commitment and the political controversy it engendered. Each memorial reflects a world view, frozen in time, memorialised in marble and bronze. They each facilitate curriculum links to areas as diverse as foreign policy and race relations. Therefore students who may struggle in submitting formal written responses often enjoy the opportunity to verbally respond to the non-textual messages generated by such monuments. Not only are students thus able to gather, sort and analyse evidence of spatial literacy on campus they can then extrapolate the evidence they have gathered to reach considered opinions. As White and Hunter (1995) note, utilising the site itself is a highly effective way to "evoke a powerful empathetic connection with the people and events that compose that history and culture" (p. 19).

After initial questions regarding preconceptions, expectations and how they first heard about Nudgee students are then asked to critically analyse what they are viewing during the Heritage Tour of the College by considering the following questions:

1. What is the purpose of this text (statue, building, sign etc.)?
2. From whose perspective is this text constructed? How do you know this?
3. Who is excluded or included in this text? Why do you think this is?
4. Are stereotypes represented or challenged in this text? Who or what are they?
5. How do you think the changes you have seen in the built environment at Nudgee been mirrored in wider Australian society?

These questions endeavour to challenge students to examine the images, monuments, buildings and other elements of the spatial environment from a critical literacy perspective in order to interrogate these texts and spaces and to potentially

Figure 3. World War I and World War II Memorials(©2008, St Joseph's Nudgee College. Used with permission.)

transform or influence their lifeworld through their awareness of injustice or inequity (Cotterell, 1996; Leander & Sheehy, 2004; Massey, 1998). Such questions can stimulate discussions about contemporary events such as wars, dislocation, identity, social structures and how the structures being analysed are imparting a particular viewpoint. These skills can be transferred to students' own lives and enable them to challenge the meaning of texts and spaces they encounter.

SPATIAL LITERACY AND THE NATURAL ENVIRONMENT

The grounds of Nudgee College are considered to be one of the largest areas of natural and semi-natural open space in the coastal area of South East Queensland. In conjunction with the adjoining Boondall Wetlands Reserve, the area forms one of the most important remaining areas of Coastal lowlands vegetation in the South East Queensland region. The importance of this area has been recognised by the Federal Government in a grant to Nudgee from its Natural Heritage Trust Funding. As well as being of regional significance, the Wetlands have been recognised internationally as a World Heritage Listed Area under the Ramsar Convention[9].

Nudgee's Wetlands Conservation Plan has investigated strategies that will protect and restore the native vegetation, so that it can conserve the unique biological diversity of the area and contribute to the sustainable management of this natural resource. A recent Fauna and Flora survey included recording, collating and documentation of various species from this area was carried out by students studying Horticulture, Conservation and Land Care in their Vocational Education program. Regeneration work in zoned areas saw the study of and the management of weed species, strategic removal where necessary, collection of seeds for propagation, planting and mulching. The students' endeavours were also supported by expertise from the wider community. Through these studies the College will be able to develop walking trails, interpretive signage and programs for studies in the Environment, Geography, and Science curriculum areas which can be accessed by other schools.

In the future there is a plan to develop a low impact Bush Camp and Interpretive Centre on the Wetlands reserve that will allow students both young and old to appreciate this unique experience. It will provide programs that incorporate Aboriginal and Welfare Heritage Values, will expand biodiversity studies in the educational curricula and promote Wetland Management issues through Community based Education programs. Operating in conjunction with these programs the Year Eight students are introduced to environmental stewardship in their Social Science Course and in their Religious Education classes.

The environmental stewardship project has sought to identify and put in place strategies that will allow the College to continue its commitment to manage and protect this area of land for future generations. This process was commenced by developing a Proposed Environmental Vision that was in line with the College's mission statement. The Environmental Mission Statement reads:

As a sign of faith and a commitment to God's world, we as members of the Nudgee College family who hold stewardship of the grounds of Nudgee College undertake to care for them in such a way that future generations of our family can appreciate their beauty and value as we do and through this stewardship contribute to our development as citizens.

The implication for a multiliteracies pedagogy, as evidenced in the Nudgee curriculum, is to provide authentic opportunities for students to participate so that they can experience the profound impact such knowledge about the environment can have on their lives and those around them. Additionally, as the Mission statement above reveals, Nudgee is inculcating the values of good citizenship and a sense of responsibility by addressing environmental issues which are both relevant and meaningful to students' lives and their futures.

CONCLUSION

There have been substantial changes at Nudgee College since 1891. Now primarily a day school, the College draws its clientele primarily from Brisbane and other major urban centres. Yet there is still a significant minority with links to rural Australia, their numbers augmented by a sizeable group from China, Taiwan, Thailand and Papua New Guinea. Most students are from middle or upper class families, yet there are others from remote indigenous communities on scholarships, indicative that the Christian Brothers' mission and philosophy has survived the passage of the years.

The College has embarked on a continual search for an identity that is mindful of its traditions yet is responsive to changes in Australian culture and local and global society. It has sought to achieve this by ensuring its curriculum is responsive to globalisation and technological advances. As Anstey and Bull (2006, p. 2) state:

Students not only need a broader knowledge base about texts and literacy; they also need the resources, attitudes, and strategies to adjust to and develop responsive and appropriate literate practices when necessary. They need to be able to cope with changing times and changing literacies.

Therefore, a school, which can be likened to a 'second home' for many students, is imbued with its own values, attitudes and beliefs much like a family home. These values, attitudes and beliefs which have been constructed by others can then be critiqued by students through guided learning approaches. In this way the students develop the confidence and competence to actively construct and analyse meaning from a range of texts as they move beyond the home/school context.

Simple changes in the traditional school structures at Nudgee, along with research, professional development and recruitment of enthusiastic and dynamic staff, are resulting in improved student achievement and engagement. Although the outer skin of the school - the buildings and associated symbols - remains firmly rooted in an often overt celebration of the past, the curriculum is anything but traditional. The inclusion of a multiliteracies approach within the Nudgee Curriculum Plan has resulted in an increased appreciation for and engagement with multiple modes of information and in Nudgee's case previously neglected spaces. It is evident that the Administration's change process in relation to the physical appearance of Nudgee has also provided an authentic and meaningful context in which to educate students about the language and politics of shared spaces.

REFERENCES

Anstey, M., & Bull, G. (2004). *The literacy labyrinth* (2nd ed.). Sydney: Pearson Education Australia.

Anstey, M., & Bull, G. (2006). *Teaching and learning multiliteracies: Changing Times, Changing Literacies*. South Australia: Australian Literacy Educators' Association; International Reading Association.

Betts, G. (1992). *The autonomous learner model for the gifted and talented.* Cheltenham, Australia: Hawker Brownlow Education.

Bianco, J. (2000). Multiliteracies and multilingualism. In W. Cope, M. Kalantzis, M. (Eds.) (2000). *Multiliteracies: Literacy learning and the design of social futures (*pp. 92 – 105). London: Routledge.

Boland, T. (1991). *Nudgee College 1891-1991.* Brisbane, Australia: Boolarong.

Burnheim, C. (2004). *Education and Social Capital.* Retrieved March 1, 2008, from www.education.monash.edu.au/centres/mcrie/docs/education-and-social-capital041012.rtf

Butcher-Younghans, S. (1993). *Historic house museums.* New York: Oxford University Press.

Chacko, E. (2005). Exploring youth cultures geographically through active learning. *The Journal of Geography, 104*(1), 9–16. doi:10.1080/00221340508978917

Cobb, N. (1992). *Adolescence: Continuity, change and diversity.* London: Mayfield Publishing Company.

Cope, W., & Kalantzis, M. (Eds.). (2000). *Multiliteracies: Literacy learning and the design of social futures*. London: Routledge.

Cotterell, J. (1996). *Social networks and social influences in adolescence*. New York: Routledge.

Davis, D. (2008). *First we see: The national review of visual education*. Canberra, Australia: Australian Government.

Education Queensland. (2002). *Years 1 – 10 Curriculum Framework*. Queensland, Australia: Department of Education Training and the Arts.

Fine, B. (2001). *Social capital versus social theory: political economy and social science at the turn of the millennium.* London: Routledge.

Harriss, J. (2002). *Depoliticizing development: the World Bank and social capital.* London: Anthem.

Kalantzis, M. (Ed.). (2001). *Transformations in language and learning: Perspectives on multiliteracies*. Melbourne, Australia: Common Ground Publishing.

Kalantzis, M., Cope, B., & Fehring, H. (2002). Multiliteracies: Teaching and learning in the new communications environment. *Primary English Teaching Association, 133*, 1–8.

Kress, G. (2000). Multimodality. In B. Cope and M. Kalantzis (Eds.) *Multiliteracies: Literacy learning and the design of social futures*. Melbourne: Macmillan.

Leander, K., & Sheehy, M. (Eds.). (2004). Spatializing Literacy Research and Practice. *New literacies and digital epistemologies*, Vol. 15.

Levy, B., Lloyd, S., & Schreiber, S. (2001). *Great Tours! Thematic tours and guide training for historic sites*. New York: Altamira Press.

Lloyd, S. (2002). Creating Memorable Visits: How to develop and implement theme-based tours. In J. Foy (Ed.). *Interpreting historical house museums* (pp. 210 – 230). Walnut Creek, CA: Altamira Press.

Luke, A., & Freebody, P. (1997). Shaping the social practices of reading. In S. Muspratt, A. Luke, & P. Freebody (Eds.). *Constructing critical literacies: Teaching and learning textual practice.* Crows Nest, Australia: Allen & Unwin.

Marsh, C. (2008). *Becoming a teacher: knowledge, skills and issues*. Frenchs Forest, Australia: Pearson Education Australia.

Massey, D. (1998). The spatial construction of youth cultures. In T. Skelton & G. Valentine (Eds.). *Cool places: geographies of youth culture (*pp. 121 – 129). London; New York: Routledge.

McComb, B. (1997). *The learner-centered classroom and school: strategies for increasing student motivation and achievement.* San Francisco: Jossey Bass Inc.

McLaughlin, D. (2007). *The price of freedom.* East Kew, Victoria: David Lovell Publishing.

New London Group. (Cazden, C., Cope, W., Kalantzis, M., et al.). (1996). A pedagogy of multiliteracies: Designing social futures. *Harvard Educational Review, 66*(1), 60–93.

O'Farrell, P. (1986). The Irish in Australia. Sydney: University of New South Wales Press.

Sheehy, M., & Leander, K. (Eds.). (2004). Introduction. In K. Leander & M. Sheehy. (Eds.). Spatializing Literacy Research and Practice. *New literacies and digital epistemologies, 15*, 1 - 13.

Soja, E. (2004). Preface. In K. Leander & M. Sheehy. (Eds.). Spatializing Literacy Research and Practice. *New literacies and digital epistemologies, 15*, ix – xv.

St Joseph's Nudgee College. (2008). *Defining the Future of the Nudgee College Curriculum* (2004) – *Implementation 2004 – 2008*. Queensland, Australia: Nudgee College.

Unsworth, L. (2001). *Teaching multiliteracies across the curriculum: Changing contexts of text and image in classroom practice*. Philadelphia: Open University Press.

Unsworth, L. (2002). Changing dimensions of school literacies. *Australian Journal of Language and Literacy, 25*(1), 62–77.

Vadeboncoeur, J. (2005). The difference that time and space make: An analysis of institutional and narrative landscapes. In J. Vadeboncoeur & L. Stevens (Eds.) Re/Constructing "the Adolescent": Sign, symbol and body. *Adolescent Cultures, School & Society, 33*,123 – 152.

Vadeboncoeur, J., & Stevens, L. (Eds.). (2005). Re/Constructing "the Adolescent": Sign, symbol and body. *Adolescent Cultures, School & Society, 33*.

Weimer, M. (2002). *Learner centered teaching: five key changes to practice*. San Francisco: Jossey Bass.

White, C., & Hunter, K. (1995). *Teaching with historic places*. Washington, DC: National Trust for Historic Preservation.

ENDNOTES

1 The New London Group were comprised of ten members and included academics from the United Kingdom, the United States and Australia.

2 St Joseph's Nudgee College is referred to almost exclusively as 'Nudgee'.

3 Edmund Rice founded the Christian Brothers in Ireland during 1802. This congregation was formally approved by Pope Pius VII in 1820.

4 After protracted negotiations throughout the 1890s, all of the Australian colonies agreed to federate. The British Parliament passed the Commonwealth of Australia Constitution Act in 1900 and it became operative on 1 January 1901.

5 ANZAC is an acronym for Australia and New Zealand Army Corps.

6 This is a colloquial term indicating that something, or someone, is the genuine article.

7 The current headmaster, who inherited the half completed project upon his appointment in 2002 is regularly asked by international visitors to have his photograph taken in front of the statue of the school's founder, only to find them waiting patiently under 'True Blue' instead of the smaller less prominent statue of Edmund Rice; who although not the founder of Nudgee College is the founder of the Christian Brothers.

8 The Easter Rebellion on Easter Monday April 24, 1916 saw an attempt to seize Dublin and to end British rule in Ireland. It failed, and the subsequent British reaction led to considerable outrage from Australian Catholics who had not been overly supportive of the uprising. One of the most divisive issues in Australian history was the two referenda, held in 1916 and 1917, seeking to introduce conscription. Both failed in the face of furious opposition, particularly from the Catholic Archbishop of Melbourne, Dr Daniel Mannix.

9 The Ramsar Convention was developed and adopted in February 1971 and came into force on December 21, 1975. It is an international treaty concerned with the conservation and sustainable utilisation of Wetlands.

Section 3
Multiliteracies in Practice

Chapter 8
Cam-Capture Literacy and its Incorporation into Multiliteracies

David R. Cole
University of Technology, Sydney, Australia

Vikashni Moyle
University of Tasmania, Australia

ABSTRACT

It could be argued that the current literacy landscape is changing very quickly (Anstey & Bull, 2004), and that at the heart of this change one may position the notion of multiliteracies (Cope & Kalantzis, 2000; The New London Group, 1996). The concept of multiliteracies acts to infuse literacy practice with multimodality. This is the 'switching' between the different aspects of meaning and representation - such as the audio, visual, spatial, linguistic and gestural (Anstey & Bull, 2004, p. 83). Yet contrary to these processes, research into mainstream literacy environments has consistently shown that print literacy reading and writing activities still dominate these spaces (Winch, Johnston, March, Ljungdahl & Holliday, 2004). This chapter offers a bridge between the potential misfit between multiliteracies theory and mainstream literacy practice by investigating the use of small cameras attached to computers as educational devices – and this is henceforth called cam-capture. This writing reports on students who have used the cameras to record their thoughts about their literacy classroom activities, and changes in their literacy skills over one academic year. In so doing, the students are using digital technology to represent their ideas and providing a pertinent commentary on current print literacy practice in middle schools through a multiliterate lens.

INTRODUCTION

The idea of multiliteracies as it is used in this chapter is a social movement (The State of Queensland, 2000). Multiliteracies aims to make change happen in the lives of children and teachers in classrooms where the skills of reading, writing, speaking and listening are being taught and learnt. Likewise, educational researchers are also positioned by multiliteracies as being interested in literacy practice, but not from a dispassionate position – but from the perspective of an activist. It could be said that

DOI: 10.4018/978-1-60566-673-0.ch008

Unsworth's (2001) appropriation and realignment of the multiliteracies movement, does take it to a more neutral position by integrating the socio-linguistic work of Michael Halliday (Unsworth, 2000) with the notion of multimodality. Yet, even though the consequent 'discursive pragmatics of cyberspace' that one may derive from Unsworth's ideas, does open up an exciting terrain for understanding how to use electronic texts in education - these arguments do not figure in this chapter about cam-capture and multiliteracies. The position taken in this writing is that multiliteracies is primarily a social movement, and that it is emptied of meaning if taken away from the tendency to initiate change in certain contexts through textual practice.

The context in this chapter is middle school classrooms – and particularly years 7 to 9 in a medium to low socio-economic area. The middle years of schooling acts as a transitional period in most industrialised countries between the primary and secondary environments. In the primary school, the subject of literacy is heavily scaffolded by close contact with specific teachers that have almost total control over subject matter and delivery (Annadale, Bindon, Handley, Johnston, Lockett & Lynch, 2004). In the secondary context, literacy is opened up through the critical and analytic study of literature, and students learn literacy that is delivered through various subjects where they are asked to read text and respond, usually in the manner of reading comprehension where their specialist knowledge, vocabulary and logical reasoning might be tested. Another common practice that runs through the way in which literacy is organised in middle school contexts is the tendency to stream students, and this streaming is orchestrated through traditional testing procedures, such as reading comprehension, extended hand written exercises and spelling (Millard, 1997). This chapter will take this context, and look to transform it through cam-capture as an application of multiliteracies.

The aims of the chapter are:

- To make a link between multiliteracies and the actual practices of middle school students through cam-capture educational research.
- To position cam-capture as a practical application of multiliteracies, and to explore how it relates to traditional notions of literacy development through testing.
- To analyse the literacy practices of a cohort of middle school students through self-recorded video reflections.
- To develop the notion of cam-capture literacy and to employ it as part of multiliteracies for educational researchers, students and teachers.
- To synthesise the notion of cam-capture literacy with its educational potential to enable evidence-based multiliteracies practices in schools.

BACKGROUND

Cam-capture literacy may be understood as a dynamic composite of three aspects of multiliteracies:

Visual literacy

Cam-capture involves students being engaged in thinking through visual aspects of their representation. As the students talk, perform and look into the camera they are presenting themselves and their ideas to an audience. This is the primary mode of literacy that cam-capture gives rise to, and it is direct, formative and immediate (Callow, 1999). Cam-capture presents face-on images, similar in kind to portrait photography. A secondary type of visual literacy that one may discern happens when the students discuss a matter of concern in pairs or groups and the recording captures a real-time discussion, or a scripted scene that the students may have prepared earlier. Users in this secondary context are able to record social and integrated behaviors and analyze these images (Deleuze, 1989).

Debes (1968) described visual literacy as gaining knowledge and experience about the workings of visual media coupled with a heightened conscious awareness of those workings. Visual literacy is "what is seen with the eye and what is consequently seen with the mind" (p. 1). This includes the ability to successfully decode and interpret visual messages and to encode and compose meaningful visual communications (Bamford, 2003). Cam-capture, as an integrated part of literacy teaching and learning - directly relates to these visual processes. If one surfs through the complex networks of the internet and perhaps encounters social sites full of recorded digital videos, such as *YouTube* - one may be struck by the amount and diversity of footage that is available to view. Furthermore, such activity has largely taken place outside of educational contexts. Cam-capture literacy is an opportunity for this motivational process to be brought into schools. Students viewing the videos that are contained in *YouTube* are digesting visual cues and cultural norms when they log on and watch. They are also learning about new ways to represent themselves and how to integrate their identity development with the mediated digital environment (Gee, 2004). The visual lessons that students learn from recorded videos will depend upon their level of involvement in cam-capture processes, and in having the confidence to select and present images that resonate with an audience. This vital learning (Ansell Pearson, 2002; Deleuze, 1988) is a contemporary literacy that may be aligned with the multiliteracies and the teaching of social design through visual analysis and representation.

Information Literacy

Underneath the surface and analytical aspects of visual literacy, lies the more expansive notion of information literacy. Students will learn how to use the computer software and editing tools when they execute cam-capture episodes. Every time they switch on the computer, they enter into an informational relationship with their machines in terms of locating files and performing logical steps to enable them to make choices. In addition, information literacy includes learning how to perform critical analysis so that the students may successfully process information and make perceptive decisions about their videos (Lemke, 1984; Leu, 2000).

Information literacy requires learning how to distinguish between various types of information - identifying what Burbules and Callister (2000) have defined as: misinformation; malinformation; messed-up information and mostly useless information. This process will alter the ways in which students present themselves through cam-capture and the resultant cam-capture literacy that they learn. Cam-capture participants make critical choices about what they are presenting and discussing in self-recorded videos. This 'criticality' can only be gained through research and reflection (Bingham, 2005) with respect to other cam-capture videos. Questions that students may ask include: What video episodes held my attention? Why were some self-recorded successful and others not? What messages did the videos present? These textual and critical questioning modes offer deconstructive moments in the classroom context and in the development of the self - that have been located and defined as pedagogic devices to encourage social interaction and literacy purpose (Luke, 2000). The reflective abilities (Bransford, 1979) of the users may be used to critically examine the context and placement of cam-captured episodes on the internet. Critical web site questions that induce information literacy in the context of cam-capture literacy include: Who is the author the video and what do we learn about them? Why has the video been placed on this site? How does the self-recorded video relate to other sources of information available on the web site? Has the self-recorded video been successfully integrated into the other messages and signs that the author is presenting on the site? What are the narrative elements of the video and how do they relate to the understanding that one may gain about the story of the author or the site generator?

Information literacy is a central part of multiliteracies as a social movement as it presents a pedagogical perspective on text related to critical framing (Lankshear & Knobel, 1998). Students will become skilled at analyzing the contents of the self-recorded videos through critical practice - as well as uploading their own productions with a critical and contemporary edge.

Personal Literacy

Information and visual literacy may be blended and focused through the understanding that cam-capture not only requires analytical, logical and evaluative skills, but also "radically alters space, time and subjectivity" (Dery, 1994, p. 19). This strong claim for the effects of 'digitalisation' may be understood in the context of the subjective realities that cam-capture gives access to and the ways in which this process can be relayed into social and cultural life (Cole, 2005a; 2007b). In the educational context, this is fundamentally a question of power - or how well the individuals or groups involved with cam-capture understand how to use this technology to transform their situation.

Personal literacy is the process of expressing desires and complex emotive states in an articulate manner (Fiumara, 2001). Yet as Gerald Coles (1999) noted, the procedure of reading and writing about emotions is hindered by "focusing on literacy learning as if children's minds were information-processing mechanisms" (p .8). Educators should therefore position cam-capture as a positive enunciation of emotional content in order to create the transformational possibilities of empowerment (Arnold, 2005) and personal literacy. Moreover, children using cam-capture as part of their literacy education are learning how to represent their personal nature to an audience and their group identity as a whole. Group dynamics may be overlooked or misrepresented in terms of literacy learning (Gee, 1990). Cam-capture gives the users a flexible and immediate resource to work on group messages. For example, a teacher who encounters students antipathetic to mainstream literature choices (Millard, 1997; Sefton-Green, 1999; Wilhelm & Smith, 2001) may use cam-capture with these students to express alternative textual preferences. This evidence counts as an important articulation of personal literacy, yet these ideas maybe shaped through group values - in this case the rebellion against print literacy. Students and teachers should view and discuss the cam-capture tapes together to come to decisions about their cultural identities and future textual choices.

Personal literacy is dealt with by multiliteracies through the concept of design. This design refers to the social future of the group involved with any set project as well as particular design briefs such as architecture, town planning or story telling. Cam-capture literacy provides a link between the design of multiliteracies and the personal expression of desire captured on video, which will criss-cross between school and life in transversal becomings (Cole, 2005b) of the participants.

Complex Tripartite Cam-Capture Literacy

Cam-capture literacy would be a straightforward matter to record and understand if it were a simple joining of the three aspects of literacy above. On the contrary, students recording videos are also

Figure 1. The tripartite representation of cam-capture literacy. The arrows denote the placement of this figure in the chaotic field of middle school development – and the figure is 'moved' by multimodality.

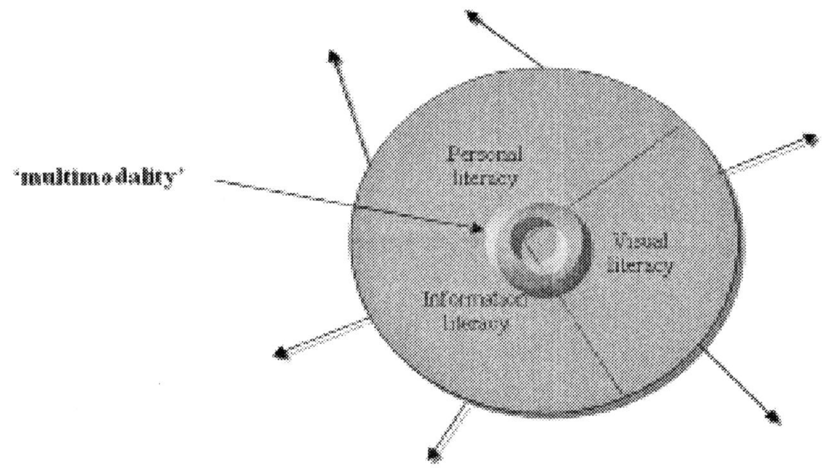

doing complex identity work (Cole, 2007a) that involves activation of their modes of creativity including the imagination, memory and synthetic thought about who they are and who they would like to become. As such, cam-capture literacy may be recast thought the lens of the complex visual, informational and personal processes and represented through use of the diagram below.

Figure 1 serves to summarise the background to the concept of cam-capture literacy and its incorporation into multiliteracies. It also helps to bridge cam-capture literacy with its research context - which is middle school literacy. In this context, the students are involved with personal, visual and informational development as an ongoing part of education.

This tripartite background to cam-capture literacy also feeds into and complements research that has been carried out into student-generated video (Schuck & Kearney, 2004) and how to enliven the middle school curriculum (Dowden, 2007). Schuck & Kearney (2004) found out that students are emboldened and engaged in learning when given the chance to make their own videos (p. 41). Dowden (2007) has analysed the ways in which middle school curriculum can affect student outcomes, and has come to the conclusion that an integrative curriculum is the best way forward for the middle years (p. 65). Cam-capture tends towards integration as it gives students the opportunity to reflect and analyse their practice across the visual, informational and personal fields. Students may also be empowered through cam-capture, that which (Schuck & Kearney, 2004) describe as having "beneficial effects in terms of student voice, pedagogic structures and ownership of the learning process" (p. 88).

RESEARCH DESIGN

The methodological framework for this study comes from two different research paradigms. The first of the paradigms providing a basis for this research is positivism. Positivism rests on the ontological assumption that reality exists and upholds the view that "facts and data have an objective reality" (Burns, 1994, p. 24; Hatch, 2002). This approach focuses on research as a process of scientific inquiry in which the researcher gathers data objectively whilst remaining separate from that being studied (Wiersma, 2000). The epistemology of positivism is "the knower is distinct from the known" (Hatch, 2002, p. 13). The types of methodological approach that fit within this paradigm are quantitative in nature, such as correlational and statistical research, in which results are generalised to a larger population (Hatch, 2002; Wiersma, 2000).

The second research paradigm that underpins this study is constructivism. The ontology of this paradigm is that "multiple realities are constructed" (Hatch, 2002, p. 13). An assumption of this methodological approach is that "variables are complex and interwoven, and difficult to measure" (Burns, 1994, p. 24). The epistemological belief that underlies constructivism is that ideas and information are formed and created by people (Hatch, 2002). This type of methodological approach is concerned with understanding other people's perspectives through the use of qualitative methods, such as observation (Hatch, 2002).

Both of these research paradigms use a different methodological approach. It is a widely held belief that quantitative and qualitative research methodologies are incongruent due to the differences in the epistemological and ontological assumptions that underlie each of the approaches (Brown & Dowling, 1998; O'Leary, 2004; Wiersma, 2000). It is evident that the research paradigms of positivist and constructivist contrast highly with each other and as a result of this contrast would not be used together in traditional research (O'Leary, 2004).

However, there is a new trend among current educational researchers to combine both methods in a single study (Lichtman, 2006; O'Leary, 2004). When used in this manner qualitative and quantitative approaches are viewed as different ways of documenting "the same world" (Richards, 2005, p. 360). Aubrey, David and Godfrey (2000, pp. 33-34), state that "rather than seeing the debate in terms of contrasting paradigms or opposing methodologies however, it may be more helpful to regard the two approaches as complementary, or even reflecting different stages of the same scientific process". It is in this complementary way that the two different methodological approaches of qualitative and quantitative are combined in this research project.

METHODOLOGY FOR QUANTITATIVE LITERACY ANALYSIS

A control group of 20 students, 10 boys and 10 girls were selected from the schools involved in the cam-capture project, 5 taken from each location. The control group were not involved in cam-capture literacy development. A total of 128 students took part in the research - 53% boys, 47% girls. Average age of the participants was 12.89. There were four schools involved during 2007, and these were state funded institutions in the Launceston area of northern Tasmania (Australia). The socio-economic demographic of the schools in the study was low to medium.

Participants in the cam-capture project used small cameras attached to computers for one academic year. The students discussed the project with their teachers and educational researcher and decided when to record their reflections about literacy learning (Gee, 1990). The researcher did not overly structure the research by prescribing questions to be used at particular points - but did respond to several requests from teachers asking for advice. Questions that were supplied to schools for the students included: What is literacy? How can I improve my literacy skills? What is my response to a text? What are the most important aspects of literacy? Students involved with the project were encouraged to view and discuss each other's videos - as well as examples of self-recorded videos on the internet. All computers were cleared of information in the participating schools at monthly intervals for six months.

Participants and guardians were asked to read information sheets about the aims of the research and to sign consent forms to take part. They were

Figure 2. The research map of the quantitative project

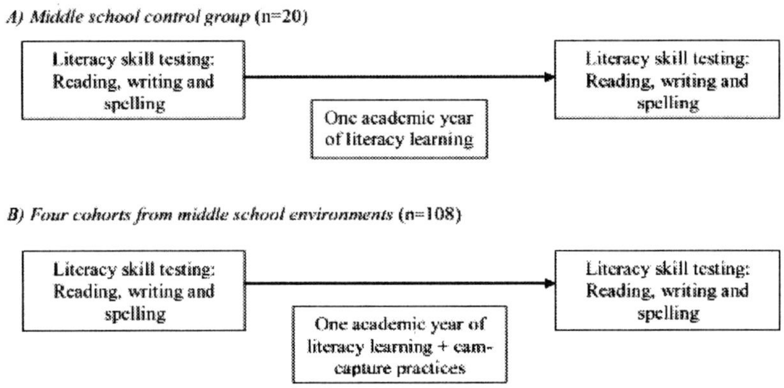

tested for spelling, reading and writing abilities at the onset of the project – the tests followed Australian national guidelines that are also known as benchmarks (see Appendix A). Students had to: write for different purposes, use correct grammar, employ a range of spelling strategies such as graphophonics and dictionaries, and demonstrate critical thinking skills when reading and responding to a text (Yuill & Oakhill, 1991).

All participants in the cam-capture literacy project were tested at the end of the academic year. The skills of spelling, reading and writing were examined in the final tests, but these papers were more complex to account for maturational factors in literacy development (Bouffler, 1992; Chafe, 1985). Furthermore, a maturational multiplier was introduced into the literacy outcomes (Snow, Barnes, Chandler, Goodman & Hemphill, 1991) of both groups in order to understand the ways in which the group has performed relative to average scores for this cohort.

The base-line data from Tasmanian literacy benchmark testing (2005) for this cohort indicates a maturational multiplier of 0.721.

The schema for the quantitative literacy aspect of the project may be represented as given in Figure 2:

QUANTITATIVE LITERACY RESULTS

The literacy results for the groups are tabulated in Table 1.

These figures were calculated by taking a mean score of the results of both groups and scaling them out of 10. They show that the control group have improved in their literacy skills by an average of 1.2%. This is a relatively low increase in skills that may be explained in part by the socio-economic context of the study. In contrast, the cam-capture literacy participants have increased by an average of 18%. This would suggest a huge benefit in being involved in the cam-capture project. Two factors could help to explain the results:

Table 1. student academic literacy results

Start of academic year		
	Control group	**Cam-capture literacy participants**
Spelling	6.32	6.21
Reading	6.11	6.01
Writing	5.23	5.24
End of academic year (0.721)		
	Control group	**Cam-capture literacy participants**
Spelling	6.39	7.54
Reading	6.17	6.59
Writing	5.34	6.61

1. The control group was small so may have contained a large percentage of low achieving students. However, the researcher checked with the teachers to make sure that the control group was representative of the whole cohort.
2. The cam-capture participants may have felt 'special' because they were chosen to take part in the project. This sensation would have translated to trying harder on the tests. In contrast, the control group may have also considered themselves to be 'left out'. However, anecdotal evidence collected by the main researcher from teachers and students after the project had closed does not support this hypothesis.

It is also interesting to note that the spelling and writing scores of the cam-capture cohort have shown a greater increase than the reading result. This may be due to the active and visual nature of cam-capture that is complementary to the activities of spelling and writing. In contrast, reading is more passive and requires a type of concentration and cognitive function (Heller, 1986) that is not present in cam-capture. The broad conclusion that one may take from these results is that the self-reflective processes that cam-capture literacy initiates do result in improvements in the middle school literacy skills of writing and spelling - and to a lesser extent in reading.

METHODOLOGY FOR SOCIO-QUALITATIVE ANALYSIS

The second type of data that this project has produced is the video recording of the students talking about their experiences of middle school literacy. These recordings (n=521) were analysed using a qualitative, themed analysis (Freebody, 2003), with attention being directed towards the elements of cam-capture literacy. On one level, this process of analysis is a mechanical and meticulous assessment of every aspect of the videos. On another, it is a synthetic thinking (Greene, 1995) through of the evidence in the self-recorded videos and the ways in which the students are representing their present school-based realities through cam-capture. The educational researcher directing the project made judgements based on these two levels of analysis in order to feedback these results into the ongoing evolution of cam-capture inquiry and practice. This was largely achieved through discussion with the teachers and explaining the relevance and direction of cam-capture literacy with the students in the project at selected intervals.

In addition to the levels of qualitative analysis that were necessary to understand the ongoing efficiency and success of the project - it was also important to analyse the content of the emergent qualitative themes (McWilliam, 1994). The themes came from the research context and proximity of the schools in conjunction with the contents of the videos. The videos constantly threw up challenging questions and open-ended problems about middle school literacy. Multiliteracies does help to give answers for some of these queries, such as the purpose of literacy - but it also should be noted that multiliteracies does not provide a meta-narrative approach to middle school literacy. As such, the holes and gaps in the thinking through of the ways in which middle school literacy practices were represented were also incorporated into this socio-qualitative analysis.

The socio-qualitative analysis involved the construction of cam-capture literacy zones. Zones are a compelling way to understand the emergence of qualitative themes from the research as they denote spatial figures as organisational units for the data (Bruner, 1971). Zones are porous and blurred at the edges. The researcher quickly realised that the emerging themes were not categorical - but represented complex crossing points of cam-capture literacy. In other words, this is a landscape in motion. Cam-capture literacy is propelled by the lives of the students taking part in the project - and the many ways in which their social formations relate to the act of recording videos about middle school literacy. The zones are also a reading of the pre-figured ways in which the students relate to literacy, including elements of the imagination, unconscious and desire (Masny, 2006).

SOCIO-QUALITATIVE RESEARCH ANALYSIS: THE CAM-CAPTURE ZONES

This analysis represents a multi-layered representation of the self-recorded literacy videos and the construction of zones. The power of the zones is dependant on the energy and participation of the students and their cam-capture expression (Robertson, Webb & Fluck, 2007). The following zones (Table 2) are inter-linked and did not yield statistical data as to the number of students or types of students that figured in each zone. Rather, the zones are constructed as proximal resource centres that student 'dip into' at any point in their recordings about middle school literacy practice:

The cam-capture literacy zones are useful due to the ways that they define how we may understand the middle school socio-qualitative context of the study (Freebody, 2003). This context has been characterised by low achievement in print literacy according to recent test results (DEST, 2005). The cam-capture literacy zones are therefore starting points and possible ways of working through this situation - and should be perceived as educational aides that can make a difference in the lives of the students, teachers and parents. For example, the zone of boredom could be turned into an excellent thematic unit of work, whereby students and teachers examine this theme through literature and relevant resources in an effort to uncover the sources of boredom and to address the consequences in terms of learning. To this extent, the cam-capture literacy zones are a social and educational movement and a subsequent part of multiliteracies.

FUTURE TRENDS

The cam-capture zones are present in schools, even when the computers are turned off, or have been consigned to dusty cupboards by English teachers. Students will, for example, bring the transformations that are present in the cam-capture zones of 'time' and 'boredom' to bear on reading comprehension exercises that are set with respect to any class text. The challenge for the future is to find synchronous and synergistic ways (Cole, 2006) of combining real time reading comprehension with computer mediated reflection - and the recording

Table 2. Cam-capture literacy zones

1. *Boredom*. The videos elicited the deeply felt emotion of boredom – it permeates all of the literacy practices of the middle school, as the students perceive them. Boredom is not a superficial surface effect to the deeper processes of education or mere reactivity on the part of the students - but exists on every level of their lives at school. It could be said that boredom as a cam-capture literacy zone is vital as an organising and originating principle - and a useful sign for educators to enable the transformative potential of the new technology to help with middle school literacy practice.
2. *Time*. The pace of the self-recorded videos differs dramatically from student to student. Some rush through their speeches at such a rate that their words are barely audible. Others speak so slowly and deliberately that the videos seem to be recorded at half-speed. Few students are able to talk naturally and directly at the camera, which indicates the determinate factors of time and pace in cam-capture literacy. Consequently, it could be said that the time of cam-capture literacy exists in a different zone to non-mediated time (Cole, 2005b).
3. *Face*. Many of the students had prepared their images in advance before the video. The girls had put on make-up - boys brushed their hair and straightened their shirts. The video cameras are small and only frame the face and shoulders of the students - which meant that the students became self-conscious with respect to these parts of their bodies that represented everything about them during the recordings. Some students preferred to be framed in profile and tilted their heads to one side of the camera as they thought that this would look cooler. The notion of face is an important cam-capture zone.
4. *Inarticulation*. The self-recorded videos produced by this project demonstrate that these middle school students are linked by their communal inability to talk about middle school literacy. Most of the students had great difficulty articulating any worthwhile phrases about their literacy practices. If the students were given direct questions to answer by the researcher or teacher such as: What helps me to get better at literacy? - they were often left speechless. If they were asked: What am I good at in literacy? they would say be able to say reading or writing but usually without any further elaboration. Some would follow-up their comments with – "I'm bad at spelling"!! Very few of the students could critically analyse their literacy skills in any depth. Rather than perceiving this to be a negative feature of the population in the socio-economic strata of the sample and their consequent self-reflective skills –inarticulation is hereby integrated into the cam-capture literacy zones. This zone can be a positive aspect of expression when other parts of representation are also important – for example, image or the power of a discourse. In terms of cam-capture literacy, inarticulation can help to add atmosphere and tenor to the expressions - in the same way that musicians use silence as a part of musical expression (Moffett, 1981).
5. *Teacher intervention and power*. Several teachers in the sample schools, who perhaps thought that the students were not taking the research seriously, sat by the computers and quizzed their best students about what they had just been studying in the previous literacy lessons. These videos resemble reading comprehension sequences - with the students mechanically responding to prompts. The students register noticeable relief and satisfaction if they think that the teacher is pleased with their performance –and seem to be nervous about the experience. This zone signals an important aspect of cam-capture literacy, in that it is not about getting the answer right, but about using the technology as a source of social empowerment (Holland, 1998). The students who were made to record these videos were not using the technology to improve their personal literacy - but were being asked to fit into the pre-determined power structure as organised by the school and the teacher. This zone therefore also defines the ways in which cam-capture literacy involves breaking free from power inhibition in one's expression by recording videos.
6. *Chaos and form*. In contrast to the previous zone, there were a number of videos that were taken by students during recess. These recordings featured tapes of student dancing and making shapes with their bodies. The students moved the camera to look around the room in rhythmic bursts - the camera operator also made sweeps around the room to produce novel effects. During these recordings, one can hear laughter and other students talking in the room. There were also videos that include the random filming of the students in the classroom or the library during their leisure time and a disconnected narrative from a student off camera who doesn't appear in the video. Sometimes the narratives are silly, rude and provocative. This cam-capture zone defines the ways in which the technology was used an experimental aspect of the students' lives at school. The freedom to experiment with cam-capture led to them to change the role of the technology and to test its efficiency to produce different effects.
7. *Self-consciousness*. This cam-capture zone is intimately connected to 'face' and ran through most of the self-recorded videos. The students usually came across as being self-conscious when they spoke about the repetitive nature of their literacy lessons, or how they could get better at reading, writing or speaking English. The cam-capture zone of self-consciousness denotes the idea that the author of the tape is aware of a viewing audience and to a certain extent worried how they will appear on the video.

of relevant cam-capture episodes that meshes with the practice of reading and responding to a text. The cam-capture zones should work through and parallel to the practices of the reading comprehension teacher to encourage a technologically enhanced reading experience – and an empowering group atmosphere (Holland, 1998).

The simplest way to encourage full integration between the cam-capture zones and traditional practices such as reading comprehension is by using mobile electronic devices in the classroom with video recording facilities and relevant software. Students may synchronously record their thoughts about the reading comprehension exercise, and send their video messages by email during the lesson. This will take away the sense that the reading exercise is a personalised or subjective experience. Traditional print literacy reading comprehension therefore changes from test-based or an assessment focused on individual literacy skills, to a technologically mediated experience that encourages transversal communication (O'Toole, 2005).

CONCLUSION

The promise of technological multimodal literacy practices is indeed great – yet it is important not to get carried away with the rhetorical potential of this possible change in affairs. It is hoped that the positioning of cam-capture in this chapter and the resultant cam-capture literacy has been understood as a practical insertion into the multiliteracies debate. Cam-capture is a simple and purposeful application of digital technology that can be seen to have real benefits with respect to the literacy workings of a mainstream middle school classroom. Its usage in the manner as has been described in this chapter will not suit every school or cohort, yet could be adapted and integrated in a flexible way to meet the requirements of different client groups.

Further questions and potential research areas exist around the use of cam-capture as an integrated multiliteracies practice - such as the exact nature of the relationship between cam-capture literacy and traditional literacies such as spelling or writing. Is there a relationship between the visual and cognitive aspects of spelling, writing and cam-capture? If so, how can one understand these relationships precisely? What are the enabling conditions for cam-capture literacy and how do these enhance print literacy? Much has been spoken about the ways in which technologically enhanced literacies respond to informal learning situations such as those found in social networks (Johnson, 2005). How can one use these networks to enhance classroom practice? What are the informal learning aspects of cam-capture? Asking these questions is part of the social movement and critical application of multiliteracies for educators, students and researchers. Yet there are no simple pedagogical answers to these questions, as technological solutions to literacy problems also depend on socio-cultural factors that include the economic environment that pre-determines the ways in which populations will take up the literacy skills. Therefore, the development of the zones acts as a complementary aspect to the constructed educational arena that works to join networks and informality to the purposeful learning of language through the examination of pre-determination.

REFERENCES

Annadale, K., Bindon, R., Handley, K., Johnston, A., Lockett, L., & Lynch, P. (2004). *Reading map of development –Second edition addressing current literacy challenges.* Port Melbourne, Australia: Reed International Books Australia Pty.

Ansell Pearson, K. (2002). *Philosophy and the adventure of the virtual: Bergson and the time of life*. London: Routledge.

Anstey, M., & Bull, G. (2004). *The Literacy Labyrinth* (2nd Ed.). Frenchs Forest, Australia: Pearson Education Australia.

Arnold, R. (2005). *Empathetic intelligence: teaching, learning, relating*. Sydney: University of New South Wales Press.

Aubrey, C., David, T., & Godfrey, R. (2000). *Early childhood educational research.* London: Routledge Falmer.

Bamford, A. (2003). *The visual literacy white paper*. Commissioned by Adobe Systems Pty Ltd, Australia. Retrieved January 12, 2007, from: http://www.adobe.co.uk/education

Bingham, C. (2005). The hermeneutics of educational questioning. *Educational Philosophy and Theory*, *37*, 553–567. doi:10.1111/j.1469-5812.2005.00140.x

Bouffler, C. (Ed.). (1992). *Literacy evaluation: Issues & practicalities*. Newtown, Australia: Primary English Teaching Association.

Bransford, J. D. (1979). *Human cognition: Learning, understanding and remembering*. Belmont, CA: Wadsworth.

Brown, A., & Dowling, P. (1998). *Doing research/reading research*. London: Falmer Press.

Bruner, J. S. (1971). *The relevance of education*. Oxford, UK: W. W. Norton.

Burbules, N. C., & Callister, T. (2000). *Watch IT. The risks and promises of information technology*. Boulder, CO: Westview Press.

Burns, R. B. (1994). *Introduction to research methods* (2nd ed.). Melbourne, Australia: Longman.

Callow, J. (1999). *Image matters: Visual texts in the classroom*. Newton, Australia: Primary English Teaching Association.

Chafe, W. (1985). Linguistic differences produced by differences between speaking and writing. In D. Olson, N. Torrance, & A. Hildyard (Eds.), *Literacy, language, and learning: The nature and consequences of reading and writing* (pp. 105-122). Cambridge, UK: Cambridge University Press.

Cole, D. R. (2005a). Learning Through the Virtual. *CTHEORY, 1* (EJ) EJ. Retrieved January 2, 2008 from: http://www.ctheory.net/articles.aspx?id=445

Cole, D. R. (2005b). Reading in the future: literacy and the time of the internet. *Reconstruction, 5* (2) EJ. Retrieved January 8, 2008 from http://reconstruction.eserver.org/052/cole.shtml

Cole, D. R. (2006). Techno-shamanism and Educational Research. *Sage of Consciousness*. Retrieved from http://www.sageofcon.org/ez7/nf/dc.htm

Cole, D. R. (2007a). Cam-Capture: An eye on teaching and learning. In J. Sigafoos & V. Green (Eds.), *Technology & Teaching: A casebook for educators* (pp. 55-68). New York: Nova Science Publishers, Inc.

Cole, D. R. (2007b). Virtual terrorism and the Internet e-learning options. *E-Learning*, *4*(2), 116–127. doi:10.2304/elea.2007.4.2.116

Coles, G. (1999). Literacy, emotions, and the brain. *Reading Online*. Retrieved April 21, 2007, from http://www.readingonline.org/critical/coles.html

Cope, B., & Kalantzis, M. (Eds.). (2000). *Multiliteracies: Literacy learning and the design of social futures*. South Yarra, Australia: Macmillan.

Debes, J. (1968). Some foundations of visual literacy. *Audio Visual Instruction*, *13*, 961–964.

Deleuze, G. (1988). *Bergsonism* (H. Tomlinson & B. Habberjam, Trans.). New York: Zone Books.

Deleuze, G. (1989). *Cinema 2: The time image* (H. Tomlinson & R. Galeta, Trans.). London: Athlone Press.

Dery, M. (1994). *Flame-Wars: The discourse of cyberculture*. Durham, NC: Duke University Press.

DEST. (Department of Education, Science and Training). (2005). *Literacy benchmarks results*. Retrieved June 13, 2008, from http://www.curriculum.edu.au/verve/_resources/2005_Benchmarks.pdf

Dowden, T. (2007). Relevant, challenging, integrative and exploratory curriculum design: Perspectives from theory and practice for middle level schooling in Australia. *Australian Educational Researcher, 34*(2), 51–72.

Fiumara, G. C. (2001). *The mind's affective life: a psychoanalytic and philosophical inquiry*. Hove, UK: Brunner-Routledge.

Freebody, P. (2003). *Qualitative research in education.* London: Sage Publications.

Gee, J. P. (1990). *Social linguistics and literacies: Ideology in discourses*. London: Falmer Press.

Gee, J. P. (2004). *What video games have to teach us about learning and literacy.* Basingstoke, UK: Palgrave/Macmillan Press.

Greene, M. (1995). *Releasing the imagination: Essays on education, the arts and social change*. San Francisco: Jossey-Bass.

Hatch, J. A. (2002). *Doing qualitative research in education settings*. Albany, NY: SUNY.

Heller, M. F. (1986). How do you know what you know? *Journal of Reading, 29*, 415–422.

Holland, E. (1998). Spinoza and Marx. *Cultural Logic, 2*, 21–47.

Johnson, S. (2005). *Everything bad is good for you: How today's popular culture is actually making us smarter*. New York: Riverhead Books.

Lankshear, C., & Knobel, M. (1998). Critical literacy and new technologies. Paper presented at the *American Education Research Association*, San Diego. Retrieved June 30, 2007, from http://www.geocities.com/c.lankshear/critlitnewtechs.html

Lemke, J. (1984). Action, context and meaning. In Toronto Semiotic Circle Monograph, *Education and Semiotics* (pp. 107-121). Toronto: University of Toronto Press.

Leu, D. J. (2000). Our children's future: Changing the focus of literacy and literacy instruction. *Reading Online* (EJ) Retrieved July 12, 2007 from http://www.readingonline.org/RT/focus/index.html

Lichtman, M. (2006). *Qualitative research in education a user's guide*. Thousand Oaks, CA: Sage Publications.

Luke, A. (2000). Critical literacy in Australia: A matter of context and standpoint. *Journal of Adolescent & Adult Literacy, 43*, 448–461.

Masny, D. (2006). Learning and creative processes: a poststructural perspective on language and Multiple Literacies. *International Journal of Learning, 12*(5), 147–155.

McWilliam, E. (1994). *In broken images: Feminist tales for a different teacher education*. New York: Teacher's College Press.

Millard, E. (1997). *Differently Literate*. London: The Falmer Press.

Moffett, J. (1981). *Active voice – A writing program across the curriculum*. Montclair, NJ: Boynton Cook.

O'Leary, Z. (2004). *The essential guide to doing research*. London: SAGE Publications.

O'Toole, R. (2005). *Transversalism concept map*. Retrieved January 1, 2006, from http://blogs.warwick.ac.uk/rbotoole/

Richards, L. (2005). *Handling qualitative data a practical guide*. London: Sage.

Robertson, M., Webb, I. L., & Fluck, A. E. (2007). *Seven steps to ICT integration*. Camberwell, Australia: ACER Press.

Schuck, S., & Kearney, M. (2004). Students in the director's seat: Teaching and learning across the school curriculum with student-generated video. *Teacher learning and development group*. Retrieved August 22, 2008 from http://www.ed-dev.uts.edu.au/teachered/research/dvprojects/home.html

Sefton-Green, J. (Ed.). (1999). *Young people, creativity and new technologies*. London: Routledge.

Snow, C. E., Barnes, W. S., Chandler, J., Goodman, I. F., & Hemphill, L. (1991). *Unfulfilled expectations: Home and school influences on literacy.* Cambridge, MA.: Harvard University Press.

The New London Group. (1996). A pedagogy of multiliteracies: designing social futures. *Harvard Educational Review*, *66*(1), 60–92.

The State of Queensland. (2000). *Literate futures: Report of the review for Queensland State Schools*. Retrieved August 12, 2008 from http://education.qld.gov.au Unsworth, L. (2001). *Teaching multiliteracies across the curriculum: Changing contexts of text and image in classroom practice.* Buckingham, UK: Open University Press.

Unsworth, L. (Ed.). (2000). *Researching language in schools and communities: Functional linguistic perspectives*. London: Cassell.

Wiersma, W. (2000). *Research methods in education an introduction* (7th Ed.). Needham Heights, MA: Allyn and Bacon.

Wilhelm, J., & Smith, M. W. (2001). Literacy in the lives of young men: Findings from an American study. *Engineers Australia*, *132*, 17–26.

Winch, G., Johnston, R., March, P., Ljungdahl, L., & Holliday, M. (2004). *Literacy: Reading, writing, and children's literature* (2nd Ed.). South Melbourne, Australia: Oxford University Press.

Yuill, N., & Oakhill, J. (1991). *Children's problems in text comprehension: An experimental investigation.* Cambridge, UK: Cambridge University Press.

APPENDIX A

Context

As part of a test, students were asked to complete the following writing task:

Writing Task 1

Explain how glass is recycled.

Look at the diagram (Figure 3) and use it to help you with the information.

Figure 3.

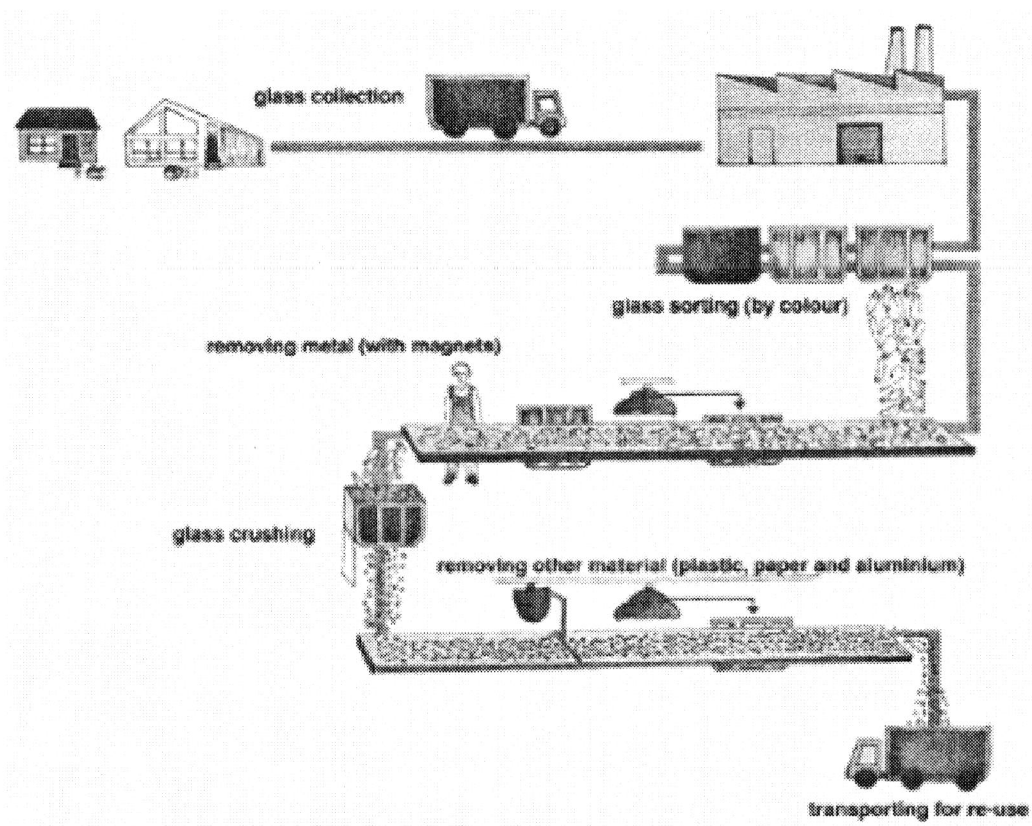

The content of the task was derived from the Technology learning area, and the purpose of the writing was to explain.

Before writing, the students had planning time, then 20 minutes' writing time, followed by editing time. Students wrote under test conditions with no support or consultation.

Reading Task 1

Context

Students were given the text 'Swimming Safely in the Top End' (Figure 4) to read. They were expected to answer the questions independently. The task was conducted as part of a test. There was no time limit set for the activity.

Figure 4.

SWIMMING SAFELY IN THE TOP END

The warm weather, our beaches or the abundance of billabongs and waterways may tempt you to jump in for a swim, but beware of box jellyfish and crocodiles.

BOX JELLYFISH are prevalent in NT waters particularly during the months of October to May.

These animals are lethal and deaths have occurred from box jellyfish stings. Stings can occur in shallow water when launching a boat or when just paddling on the beach. It is recommended that you do not enter the water at all unless it is necessary. If you must, then wear protective clothing, e.g. stinger suit.

Do not swim in the sea or coastal creeks during box jellyfish season (Oct - May). If you must swim at other times, take extra care.

In the case of emergency, first aid is to pour copious amounts of vinegar onto the sting and resuscitate the victim if necessary. For more information, call the NT Museum of Arts and Sciences on 82 4211.

CROCODILES are active in NT waters and sadly there have been several fatal attacks over recent years.

Observe crocodile warning signs. Swim only in designated safe areas. To learn more about crocodiles, call the Conservation Commission on 89 4408.

SAFE SWIMMING

There are many places to swim in safety. You may have thought that with box jellyfish and crocodiles we have no safe waters. The good news is that you can swim safely. Read on and find out where.

There are four public swimming pools in the Darwin area — Nightcliff, Darwin, Casuarina and Palmerston, plus the man-made Lake Alexander at East Point.

'Down the track' you'll find Lake Bennett, Lakes Resort, Manton Dam plus plunge pools and waterfalls in Litchfield Park. Darwin is a tropical city with an active water-sporting population, so with some care and common sense, you too can swim and stay safe.

The subject matter of the text was familiar to the students.

1. During which months is it unsafe to swim in the sea?
2. Who should be contacted in order to find more information about crocodiles?
3. What first aid procedure should be used if someone is stung by a box jellyfish?
4. Which people are most at risk from the box jellyfish sting?
5. What clothing is recommended to protect against the box jellyfish?
6. When is it totally safe to swim in the sea without being stung?

Spelling was evaluated from the written responses.

Chapter 9
Theorizing Media Productions as Complex Literacy Performances Among Youth In and Out of Schools

Theresa Rogers
University of British Columbia, Canada

ABSTRACT

In this chapter the author explores the ways media production represents sophisticated identity and cultural work, and therefore complex literacy performances, among youth as they engage in a play of genres and subject positioning in particular social (educational and community) spaces. Two major research projects in which youth participated in media production form the basis for theorizing in this chapter. Four cases illustrate the ways particular youth design new, hybrid multimodal genres, and how they engage in new models of authorship and cultural critique in this process. Although "youth culture" is often referred to as an undifferentiated phenomenon, this work is highly context-specific, revealing multiple and diverse sub-communities in which specific kinds of cultural and critical work are being undertaken. The author concludes with a challenge to transform schools and classrooms to reflect the increasingly multimodal landscapes in which youth reside.

INTRODUCTION

This chapter explores the ways media production represents complex identity and cultural work among youth as they engage in a play of genres and positioning in particular social spaces. As is often argued, literacy "has now come to mean a rapid and continuous process of changes in the ways in which we read, write, view, listen, compose and communicate information" (Coiro, Knobel, Lankshear & Leu, 2008, p. 23). Interactive technologies—as part of the new media landscape—provide increased opportunities for youth to develop the competencies to participate in contemporary culture (Jenkins, 2006).

The basis of theorizing in this chapter is two major research projects in which youth engaged in cultural critique through media production across learning sites in a large metropolitan area in western Canada. One site is an alternative secondary literacy

DOI: 10.4018/978-1-60566-673-0.ch009

program and another is a community-based youth anti-violence program.

I draw on the youth multimedia work in these two projects to illustrate how they take up the discursive and material resources available through video production to perform these complex literacy performances. Four cases are presented. The first case is a film by Kevin, a young man who struggled with traditional academic literacy skills but was able to re-narrate his literate identity through art and video work. In the second case, video productions by Lane, a quiet and creative young man, illustrate how he exploited multimodal material and discursive resources to express his creativity and provide an alternative perspective on literate performances in school. The third case is drawn from the work of two young women whose video illustrates complex subject positionings in relation to girlhood, youth and stereotypical representations. The last case focuses on a film by a young woman, Tracei, who exploits various stereotypical representations of youth in creating a music video in which she includes bodily inscribed gender statements and as well as media parody.

To inform this work with youth, my colleagues and I (Rogers & Schofield, 2005; Rogers & Winters, 2007; Rogers, Winters, LaMonde & Perry, 2008; Schofield & Rogers, 2004) have drawn from several theoretical frameworks, including work in multiple and critical youth literacies; genre, discourse, and visual/spatial theories; theories of social and cultural identity, agency and positioning; and feminist theories of embodiment.

BACKGROUND

As I have argued elsewhere (Rogers & Schofield, 2005), work in multiple and critical youth literacies critiques the privileging of print literacies and supports hybrid and unsanctioned literacy practices in and out of classrooms (e.g., Moje, 2000; O'Brien, 2005). Newer perspectives acknowledge the fluidity of multiple literacy practices—those that travel across spatial contexts and boundaries (Leander, 2003; Rogers & Schofield, 2005). From this perspective, it can be argued that youth become producers of new forms of literacy and media as they comment on and critique their social worlds (Burn & Parker, 2003; New London Group, 2000; Sefton-Green, 1998; 2006; Soep, 2006).

Theory and methods in the areas of genre, discourse and visual spatial theories also inform this work, providing ways of understanding the sites or spaces of production, image and audience, and also approaches to knowing the multiple forms (print, drama, art, film, and so forth) that youth layer and exploit in their quest to create meaning (Hull & Nelson, 2005; Kress & Van Leeuwen, 2001; Rose, 2001). The theoretical framework we have used to analyze individual youth video productions (Rogers, Winters, & LaMonde, in press) examines what Rose (2001) describes as the site of production (the genesis of the work, the design, and the sources employed), the site of the image or film itself (composition, technique and tools of production, as well as the juxtapositions, tranformations and hybridity of genres) and the site of audiencing (what is accomplished and how the work is received and re/interpreted). As Manovich (2001) has argued, new media culture brings with it new models of authorship, collaboration, intertexting, and remixing that are evident in youth media production. In particular, these cases illustrate the ways youth are flexible users of multimodal cultural forms, such as genres, and how they borrow, exploit, juxtapose, hybridize or transform media genres and digital and non-digital spaces for critical expression (Bakhtin, 1986; Buckingham & Sefton-Green, 1994; Lemke, 1995; Kearney, 2006; Kress, 2003; Manovich, 2001; Street, 1995).

Finally, theories of social and cultural identity, agency and subject positioning (Bakhtin, 1986; Holland, Lachicotte, Skinner & Cain, 1998) provide a lens through which to understand the available positions that youth take up their media work; that is, how they appropriate and transform various discursive modes and resources to (re)position their own subjectivities (Davies & Harre, 1990; Holland et al., 1998). From a feminist position, it can be seen that, in some cases, they narrate and inscribe new identities and even resignify girlhood (Pomerantz, Currie & Kelly, 2004). Adolescent bodies as represented by lived realities (Grosz, 1994) inscribe and generate information about youth subjectivity and positioning in their work and in their lives. Media, as Ellsworth (2005; citing Grosz & Eisenman, 2001) notes, is a space that can be appropriated to refigure and imagine these new embodiments.

The analyses of video work in these projects, as well as observations and interviews with these four case study youths, form the basis to argue that video production work can be seen as an important lens into the particular lives and critical perspectives of youth in and out of schools. We can then draw on these analyses to reconstitute our pedagogical approaches in ways that recognize the range of literate competencies of youth, and to learn from them the ways in which we may not be attentive to their shifting identities, cultural understandings, and critical abilities—i.e., their complex literacy performances—particularly among youth who are marginalized in schools.

THE CONTEXTS: YOUTH VIDEO PRODUCTION AT TWO RESEARCH SITES

Research Site One

The first three cases described here are taken from a three-year youth literacy research project that was collaboratively developed with a teacher and university colleagues to serve struggling youth in an alternative secondary school (reported in Rogers & Schofield, 2005; Rogers & Winters, 2007; Schofield & Rogers, 2004; theresarogers.ca/youthvideos). The program served youth, ages 15-19, mostly working class and ethnically diverse, who had become alienated from traditional schooling and were seeking another path to graduation. These youth often had histories of behavioural and educational challenges, including many who had weak academic literacy skills.

The program accommodated approximately 32 students (whose ages range from 15 to 20 years), who were divided into morning and afternoon class sessions. The blend of students, with a range of literacy and numeracy levels and diverse life experiences, were enrolled and placed in the classroom on a full-time basis. Continuous entry and departure, and the particularities of each student's life, called for a flexible teaching process that included individualized, group and peer literacy support and instruction. The goal of the qualitative research project was to integrate arts and media as part of a multimodal literacy focus, and to be inclusive and supportive of the material contexts of the students' lives as they worked through the district mandated curricula toward a diploma (Rogers & Schofield, 2005; Schofield & Rogers, 2004).

Initially, data were collected about the students' abilities with print and non-print genres and media (cartooning, graffiti, rapping, poetry, photography, etc.) that constituted fluid practices that crossed the boundaries of their in- and out-of-school lives (e.g., Hull & Schultz, 2001; Moje, 2000). This data was then drawn on to further refine and develop the program, including the addition of a video production component. Students who participated in the video workshop component of the project took up discursive resources of filmmaking to create projects ranging from dance and music videos, to documentaries on academic-related subjects, to literary films, including parodies and original works.

The first three cases described in the next section (films by Kevin and Lane, and by Amy-Lynne and Alleana) are drawn from observation and field notes in this site, interviews with students, and video productions. My research colleagues and I acted as participant observers, conducting and supporting an initial video workshop and providing occasional instructional and technological support as the youth produced their own films, mainly using iMovie software and Apple computers. We also observed and took field notes and conducted interviews with students focusing on their processes and reflections in relation to their video productions. The teacher in the program provided ongoing support, as did more knowledgeable peers, as they learned to plan, film and edit their videos. The teacher also encouraged the youth to make films of interest to them for credit in an elective film course, or invited them to subsitute traditional writing assignments with multimedia texts so that these video productions were integrated into the individualized secondary curriculum.

Research Site Two

The fourth case presented below focuses on a film by Tracie, a young woman who participated in a year-long video production research project within a youth community centre that engages in violence prevention work. This program is part of a larger project based in several North American cities that involves youth in writing and photojournalism to express the impact of violence in their lives and to help prevent further violence through their own leadership activities. Our project extended that work through coaching and supporting video production projects. We focused on supporting the production of films focusing on identity, cultural stereotypes and anti-violence.

Building on what we learned in Research Site One, we began this second project by inviting youth, ages 15 to 20, to critique various popular film genres (parodies on YouTube—such as a stop action music video—and short anti-war or street life documentaries made by university students and local filmmakers). The youth also critiqued films from our first project site (above) that, in their view, were too visually repetitive or, in one case, used too many violent images for a film about espousing non-violence.

The research goals of this project site included exploring issues related to identity and the use of arts and media as discursive resources for social and cultural engagement and critique. The youth's initial projects in this site were ironic and playful, focusing on topics ranging from panhandling and "people-hunting" in the park to the close-up intricacies of smoking and spitting. Follow-up projects drew on issues such as historical racism—as in a remash video of Billie Holiday's song, "Strange Fruit"—as well as contemporary racism and stereotyping, and included a final montage film on anti-violence.

As in the first research site, my colleagues and I were participant-observers providing film workshops and technological support while also observing and taking fieldnotes, collecting video productions, and conducting interviews with volunteer focal youth.

FOUR CASES OF VIDEO PRODUCTION AS IDENTITY AND CULTURAL WORK ACROSS TWO SITES

Kevin's Holocaust documentary film. The first case focuses on Kevin and his short documentary Holocaust film produced in Research Site One. Kevin, who was from a white working class background, was clearly as, or even more, competent than his peers in some non-print environments, fairly readily engaged in arts and multimedia, and succeeded in that environment. However, Kevin's traditional literacy skills were quite low and ultimately he was not academically successful by traditional measures (i.e., graduation). Kevin's film in the first year of the project was a video portfolio of his own drawings with titles, suggesting the outlines of a mythological story he was writing. However, even getting those labels spelled correctly was a chore. He was verbally articulate and wrote long stories all in various invented spellings, but read even the simplest texts haltingly. One of his goals was to read well enough to get his driver's license.

Our observations of Kevin's interactions at school and our interviews revealed the ways traditional schooling provided him with limited identity positions in relation to literacy and schooling. Following are excerpts from an interview with Kevin:

The majority of people [in regular schools] don't really care about the students...they just passed you on....Since grade two I've been told that I couldn't read. And I knew I couldn't read and it just got stuck in my mind. Instead of moving me up grades they took me to learning assistance and gave me younger students' work until I got it stuck in my mind.... I never used to write at all. Never. I used to get people to write for me... because I was so afraid of making mistakes [shares his journal now full of writing].... I didn't want to sit around and just do nothing at school so I started doodling...and it was pretty cool so I started teaching myself...try out things...see if it made it look better then I'd stick to it or not... until I found something better...I draw things from ads like rock and roll...a video game...or from my imagination...all my drawings go with my stories...my writing's been getting better. Reading is just something I put off 'cause I can't do it. I find ways around it.

This interview sequence illustrates the ways the discourses of schooling labeled and marginalized Kevin from an early age. Kevin insightfully read these limiting discourses and adapted by recreating an identity for himself as an artist out of a powerful symbiosis of alienation and imagination. Not long after this interview, an email from Kevin's teacher indicated another way the school defined Kevin: "On Wednesday, [the career counselor] points out some of my students will be going to [a local college] for a 4-week program—learning welding, bricklaying, auto mechanics. So two students will have to drop out [of planned multimedia project]. This is a harsh pill. It says volumes about the expectations that the system places on these kids—all dropouts are good for are manual labor and Macjobs...".

In the third year of our project, Kevin produced a fairly sophisticated documentary film about the Holocaust. He began with the picture book *Rose Blanche* (Innnocenti, 1985) and worked his way through a biography for young readers, entitled *Hannah's Suitcase* (Levine, 2003), with his teacher and a teacher's aide, and then did research on the Internet to develop his 3-minute film called "The Slaughter" (to view this film, go to http://web.mac.com/theresa.rogers/iWeb/Site/Youth%20Videos.html). The film opens with music from 'Fortuna Major' from *Carmina Burana* and included a series of symbols of Nazism, book burning, Auschwitz, cattle cars and bodies. Kevin narrated:

The man in control of the SS hated Jews almost as much as Hitler, but his name was Himmler. [He] took German babies and trained them to hate Jews just as much as he did so they would be a perfect soldier. In 1935 the Nuremberg laws were passed. These laws made Jews criminals...; but not only [to be] a Jew, but to own Jewish books and other things from their religion....The Jewish people were transported in cattle cars...so full of people that they could not breathe.... After they get to the concentration camps they're put to work... building other things. After they're too weak to work, or are too old or too young, they just start killing them. They gas them, and they leave piles of dead bodies.... This is a burner in one of their crematories. The End.

This film exhibits a range of multimodal and literacy competencies. Kevin clearly understood the documentary genre and was able to undertake research and create a coherent narrative and voice-over script. His discursive resources included stock Internet images of the Holocaust, including photographs, symbols, and printed words (signs), political cartoons, as well as a soundtrack. He used video editing special effects, such as "the wipe" in between several images as well as the use of a fog effect to create a darker atmosphere in this documentary film. Kevin was able to juxtapose soundtracks with images to create a coherent narrative of the Holocaust and express his own critical understanding of, for instance, "the perfect [Nazi] soldier."

Lane's films: "The Battery" and "Just for fun" . The second case is a pair of films by a young man name Lane, also from a white working class family. Lane was fairly reserved, yet in an interview he expressed his critique of schooling, comparing it to a penitentiary:

"[To a former principal] 'I'm like, I'm the enemy, you're the warden', same thing in school, the same people control the school systems and the prison systems. Isn't the warden just the principal of the penitentiary?...you put people into schools and you tell them, okay...you're all going to leave this place with the same skills..."

Lane had previously been involved in "jacking" because all of his friends did it. As he said he "felt so hard-core" but then his friends lost respect for him and it changed his life: "Now I don't go around thinking I'm so big." Lane told this story as an explanation for the feeling behind a pair of films he made called "The Battery" (Figure 1 and 2) and "Just for Fun." (figures 3, 4, & 5) The first film is a very simple but visually powerful metaphoric film with a message, using shots of a battery on a table, rolling off, and then rolling in reverse.

Interspersed with the filmed shots are text lines: "Do you ever feel you are being thrown away/Do ever feel alone/As if you don't exist/No one likes to be alone/If you should fall/Get back up/Don't let anyone stop you." (View film at http://web.mac.com/theresa.rogers/iWeb/Site/Youth%20 Videos.html). Lane started by throwing the battery around and "just thought of lonely. What people do with batteries when they are done with them. They just throw them away."

Lane's second film (see Figures 3, 4, and 5) integrates shots from "The Battery" into a music video called "Just for Fun" which intersperses shots of the battery with a filmed narrative about a young woman who is locked out of a building, sits alone for a while, and then walks away (the soundtrack used is Linkin Park's "Fate"). The film is carefully shot from many angles and uses

Figure 1. Battery on table

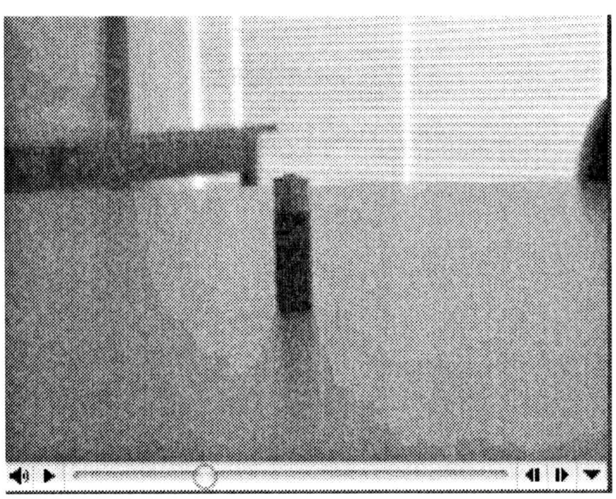

Figure 2. "Do you ever feel alone"

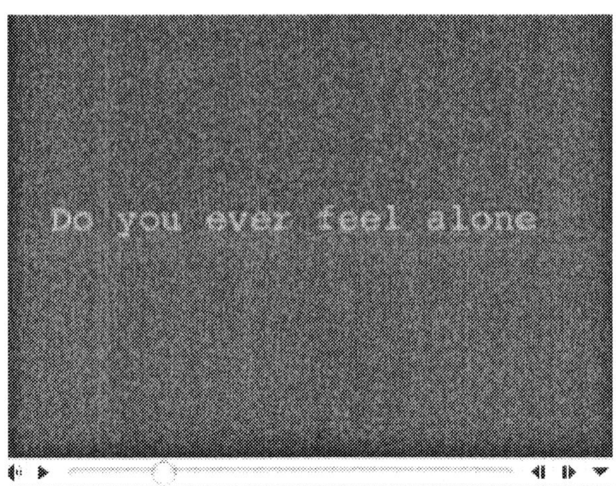

Figure 3. Lane filming

Figure 4. Battery in grass

Figure 5. Battery and butts

new shots of the battery in a pile of cigarette butts, and in the rain and dirt, playing on the metaphoric themes of loneliness and neglect. As Lane explains, "I thought about kids that are neglected, used and treated like shit. The video about K [the girl] started out as a music video but when I watched it I realized that she was being thrown away."

In this work, Lane was able to appropriate multimedia resources that transcend those of individual modes so that, for instance, the narrated world is different than a world displayed visually (Hull & Nelson, 2005; Kress, 2003). What Lane has done with this second film is to layer media—one film with another, music lyrics, and to combine image-based ("The Battery") film with an action narrative ("Just for Fun")—in effect braiding narratives and genres (Schofield & Rogers, 2004) with the result of communciating more than each individual mode or narrative offers.

Alleana and Amy-Lynne's film about peer pressure. The third case is a film called "Peer Pressure" (see Figure 6 & 7) by two girls at the alternative secondary school who identified as First Nations. The video is a documentary style film that uses photographs and filming with both a voice-over and textual narration about peer pressure. This video topic was chosen by Amy-Lynne and Alleana, who wanted to "create something that could help people [because] all the kids seem to be going through this." According to Amy-Lynne, "the opportunity arose and we took the chance and created in the moment based on our stories. It was an idea I fell in love with; I could voice my opinion. Today our stories would be different." The girls chose to use photographs from their social lives together with a voice-over narrative about peer pressure—a design that was storyboarded and then filmed. Alleana talked about having seen a documentary about street life and another film made from photos in our workshop and "that's why we did what we did." She also commented that it was "looking at peer pressure *from a girl's point of view...because they don't usually look at it that way*."

The girls used a combination of still and filmed (using a panning technique) photographs (their own and borrowed from friends) of themselves and their lives set on city streets and in private spaces, overlaid with written and spoken narrative about youth culture. This voice-over narration that appears in print and is simultaneously heard is interspersed with several recurring visual motifs: photographs of adolescent girls together or alone in private or public spaces, cigarettes, liquor stores, liquor bottles/glasses, and graffiti. As a soundtrack, they used the score from the film "A Beautiful Mind" that provides a sentimental mood while the panning of the still photos provides an intimate portrait of the girls' social lives. This format is reminiscent of documentaries of lives lived, juxtaposed with the feel of a public service announcement with its second person narrated voice-overs: "Above all, be true to yourself. Have you ever stopped to ask yourself why you're doing the things you do and what it means to you? Do you ever ask yourself why you dress the way you do, eat the things you eat, or participate in the activities you do?" The ending line is, "Peer pressure effects [sic] who we've become and what we are."

As described above, the girls imagined a youth audience for this film—a group who might benefit from seeing it: "We wanted to create something for people that could help them." At the same time the girls are both reproducing and critiquing "normal" representations of girlhood. Amy-Lynne's reflections a year after making the film that focus on her concern that the film might have contributed to stereotyping Aboriginal youth: "What I would do now is address issues culturally—people see Aboriginal youth as drinkers, young, pregnant, disruptive, but there are lots of people like me who don't do drugs, are in school, and have direction but most don't see it."

The identity and critical cultural work the girls take up in the film, both narratively and bodily/spatially, is of young women involved in behaviours commonly associated with urban youth culture—hanging out on the streets, drinking and smoking—within a storyline about peer

Figure 6. Girls with bottles

Figure 7. "Peer Pressure Effects..."

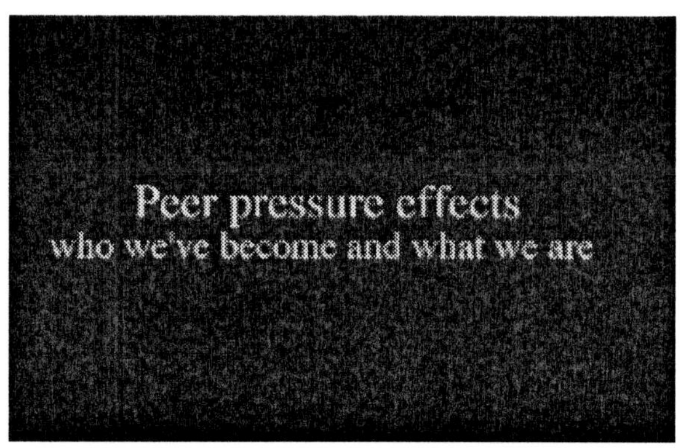

Figure 8. Piercing

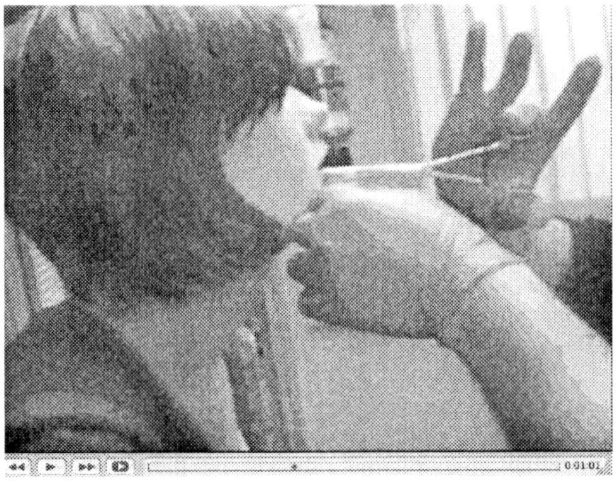

Figure 9. Balloon

Figure 10. "Kids, learn..."

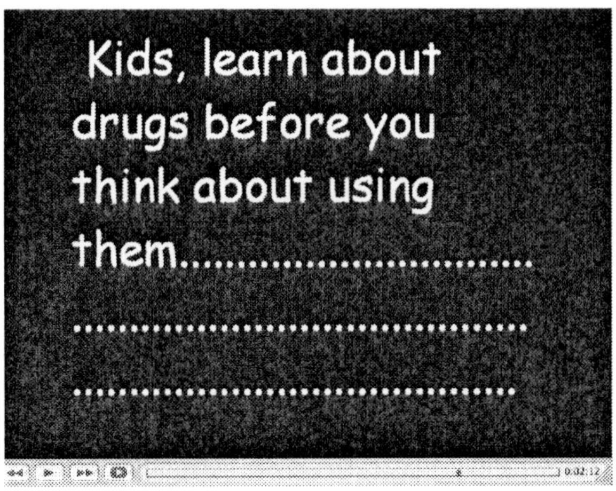

pressure as the cause of these behaviours. At the same time they create a counter-narrative message about being "strong, and true to oneself," indicating a meta-awareness of this typical view of youth. This contradictory positioning, echoed by the hybrid documentary and public service message genre, indicates both acquiescence to their societal positionings and a sense of agency to talk back to them.

Tracei's film: "Tracei's Awesome". The final case is a film by a young woman named Tracei (see Figures 8, 9, and 10), from a white middle class family, who participated in the video workshop in Research Site Two—the youth anti-violence program. Tracei said she had a passion for taking pictures and filming and made films on her own, basically being the one in control. A film she made during the project (an "I Am" film, entitled "I are Tracei; Hear me roar") chronicles her childhood years through old photographs and then filmed scenes when "she is all crazy and older." The background music is the Mad Caddies (a third wave ska band) singing "Mary Melody". Her coda to that film uses text that says "I showed you Tracei, now take it!" When asked about her use of print in her films she said, "words help get the point across. Some people can be totally oblivious but once they read it, they say 'oh, i get it'."

Her film, in some ways the most complex illustrated here, was sent to me separately; that is, it is a film she made outside of the context of the project, but wanted us to see. This film has three distinct sections. The first section or scene includes two extended and close-up shots of Tracei's bottom lip being pierced. The second section is a filmed shot of Tracei singing, laughing and talking with a helium voice [to friends behind the camera who can be heard giggling], saying "I don't know what to say. Hey you guys are putting pressure on me.

What am I going to do? I'm gonna sit here an' cry making emo songs, gonna die, this is gonna make me fall over. It's gonna hurt. I'm done."

The third section of the film is a mixture of print messages and photos of her with her friends and one shot of her dressed in drag. This section begins with the text "the end" and continues with "This video was made to prevent the use of chemically made drugs" and "Kids learn about drugs before you think about using them...These kids didn't have a clue what they were doing." After several more photo sequences it ends with "save yourselves! Before it's too late."

This film is a fascinating representation of feminine subjectivity—who Tracei is and what she has to say. The literal embodiment of expression and resistance to normalized feminine behaviour through piercings, hair colour and cross-dressing is evident. Drawing on popular culture and using new media provides the discursive resources to parody gender identity and to engage in social commentary and critique (Buckingham & Sefton-Green, 1994), such as the choice of music that playfully draws on her interest in film and TV genres of horror, thrillers etc., by using the "Freaker's Ball" song by the 70s rock band, Dr. Hook and the Medicine Show—itself a parody of the 60s countercultural love-ins. The film becomes even more complex when she satirizes "emo" behaviour and appropriates discursive resources of popular media to parody Public Service Announcement (PSA) anti-drug messages.

ANALYSIS OF THE FOUR CASES: COMPLEX MULTIMODAL LITERACY PERFORMANCES AMONG YOUTH IN TWO SITES

These four cases illustrate the ways youth undertook literacy performances that included flexible designs of new, hybrid multimodal genres. In this process they engaged in new models of authorship and, perhaps most importantly, simultaneously engaged in powerful social commentary and critique. They played with new and old cultural semiotic resources to re-narrate identities and cultural understandings in the larger network of social power relations. However, it is important to note that, in contrast to notions of "youth culture" as an undifferentiated phenomenon, their work is highly context-specific, revealing multiple and diverse sub-communities within in which specific cultural and critical multimodal work is being undertaken. These youth produced videos and shifted their identity positions in particular contexts in ways that challenged traditional discursive (Lesko, 1996) representations of youth. In both reifying and challenging various stereotypical representations, they in turn shifted their own subject positionings.

In relation to Kevin, an argument can be made for the ways in which working with film production might support both the composing and interpretive processes associated with more traditional literacy practices, and the breadth of knowledge gained by creating his Holocaust film using a combination of multimodal and print resources in relation to having simply read textbooks and other print sources (Dressman et al., 2006); however, based on a contextualized understanding of this film, it is also evident that Kevin was doing some important and related identity work. In creating this film, Kevin repositioned himself as a capable "student," one who can exploit a range of discursive resources—image, sound, text—to powerfully re-narrate an historical event and to, at least momentarily, re-position his own subjectivity in relation to literacy and schooling as someone who has literacy and multimodal competencies.

Lane's creativity was evident in the genesis of the ideas, in filming and in editing. His use of discursive resources included the layering of popular culture references, his own biography, his reading of others' stories, and simple, everyday objects as well as the resources that filming and editing offered. These layerings resulted in work that transcended the possibilities of working within individual modalities. In this work, Lane is re-positioning himself as a filmmaker who "has ideas in his mind and knows what he wants" as a classmate noted. Lane's work is also important identity work in the sense that it is consistent with his critical description of schooling above. As Lane well knows, classrooms are not normally spaces in which students are encouraged to exploit, juxtapose, hybridize and layer material and discursive resources to perform cultural and creative work that "counts" in the curricululm.

Alleana and Amy-Lynne used their film to become cultural critics regarding the portrayals of gender and ethnicity among youth, providing a lens through which to view how they take up spaces of authoring in the complex and often contradictory discourses (Gonick, 2007) of raced and gendered youth culture (Rogers & Winters, 2007). As evident in their work and their reflections, they became aware of their own contradictory discourses of Canadian youth and sought to move beyond generalized or stereotypical representations and instead ask, "which girls? which First Nations youth?" in order to address issues of particular youth in specific communities and contexts.

Tracei's film, perhaps because of the more extensive film critique work at this site, was able to draw not only on a range of multmodal resources and authoring strategies, but to reach toward parody and satire to engage in cultural critique. This complex performance mirrors Butler's (2006) claim that gender performance is itself a kind of parody that talks back to essentialized gender identities. In the film, Tracei both reifies and challenges gender stereotpypes with contradictory discourses and subjective positionings, complexities that underscore Kearney's (2006) argument that media production, in particular, is worthy of more study and analysis as a space that can be appropriated by girls. In particular, these spaces potentially elucidate the ways that girls draw on multimodal discursive resources to embody and reinscribe girlhood (Grosz, 1994; Pomerantz, Currie & Kelly, 2004) as cultural critique.

CONCLUSION AND CHALLENGES FOR THE FUTURE

In creating new frameworks for understanding these sophisticated multimodal works, literacy educators will need to take account of the complexity of video production as critical literacy performances, as identity and cultural work, and as particular voicings in specific cultural spaces (see also, Burn & Parker, 2003; New London Group, 2000; Sefton-Green, 1998, 2006; Soep, 2006). We may need new theorizing related to spatiality that allow us to focus on "constellations of temporary coherence" (Massey, 1994) across educational and community sites in which we can observe how youth draw on virtual and real spaces, and on local and global information and resources to create new forms of cultural participation (Jenkins, 2006). Across these spaces, youth are already exhibiting a powerful appropriation of discursive resources and competencies related to cultural analysis and critique that often go unrecognized in today's classrooms.

For instance, to fully appreciate video production as critical literacy performances, we need to be more attentive to broader views of literacy that recognize the appropriation of and play with discursive resources such as genre (Bakhtin, 1986; Kearney, 2006; Kress, 2003; Lemke, 1995; Manovich, 2001; Street, 1995). These cases illustrate the ways even marginalized youth who are not successful by traditional standards are capable of reading, analyzing, critiquing and hybridizing genres to serve their critical purposes. Kevin, though he struggled with simple written texts, fully grasped the documentary genre and handily drew on a range of discursive and technological resources to produce a sophisticated account and critique of a central historical event. Alleana and Amy-Lynne used documentary techniques together with a message that echoed public service announcement genres with an intent to help others.

Lane and Tracei were more playful with film genre. Lane used more literary devices or "fiction film" genres along with improvisational acting to create a metaphorical statement about loneliness and neglect. Tracei's music video template served as a platform for resignifiying girlhood, playing, exploiting stereotypes and parodying public service announcements that became a film to be posted and shared on a social network site.

We also need to recognize the important cultural work taking place in these spaces. If we were to take seriously the embodied and discursive subject positionings evident in these productions we could open up dialogues about youth representation and about how the vestiges of traditional spaces of schooling and literacy serve to narrow identity positions (Holland et al., 1998). Both Lane and Kevin were reaching toward new positionings for themselves in classrooms and institutions that did not necessarily value their sophisticated literacy performances. Alleana, Amy-Lynne and Tracei were reaching toward critiques of the narrow representations of and discourses surrounding ethnicity, girls and girlhood. Video production, taken seriously, offers new avenues for critical literacy dialogues and practices among youth in and out of schools.

Our challenge, then, is to transform schools and classrooms to reflect these increasingly multimodal landscapes in which youth reside, rather than limiting themselves to traditional language and literacy discourses and practices (Moje, 2000; New London Group, 2000; O'Brien, 2005). These transformed classrooms would take into account the abilities of students to integrate knowledge from multiple sources and information technologies, and to use these resources to engage in social and cultural critique. An added challenge is to draw on these skills to deepen students' explicit understandings of how genre works across media, and the power of both print and non-print genres to communicate in a new "participatory culture" (Jenkins, 2006).

This work will likely begin with teachers. However, few studies have looked at the possibilities of working with pre-service teachers to develop their skills and approaches to using multimedia production in their teaching, and to encourage broader and more critical views of literacy and discourse across academic spaces and disciplines. In our own work (LaMonde & Rogers, 2007), we have explored the possibility of transforming notions of literacy among pre-service teachers and encouraging them to explore new possibilities of discursive play and cultural critique. We found evidence that prospective teachers we worked with did, in general, expand their notions of literacy and engage playfully and critically with media production in our study, though skepticism and criticism of technology was also expressed. It was particularly interesting to note that what commitment they had to engaging in technology enhanced educational practices was connected to their vision of inclusive classrooms—classrooms that are more motivating and engaging sites of learning for all students. We concluded that media production is integral to teacher education in literacy in the form of providing opportunities for pre-service teachers to author new genres and forms of communication. We view this work as preparation for engaging youth, particularly those youth who have been or are in danger of being marginalized from traditional schooling, in complex literacy performances in schools.

REFERENCES

Bakhtin, M. M. (1986). *Speech genres and other late essays*. Austin, TX: University of Texas.

Buckingham, D., & Sefton-Green, J. (1994). *Cultural studies goes to school. Reading and teaching popular media*. London: Taylor and Francis.

Burn, A., & Parker, D. (2003). *Analysing media texts*. London: Continuum.

Butler, J. (2006). *Gender Trouble: Feminism and the Subversion of Identity*. New York: Routledge Classics.

Coiro, J., Knobel, M., Lankshear, C., & Leu, D. (Eds.). (2008). *Handbook of research on new literacies*. New York: Lawrence Erlbaum.

Davies, B., & Harre, R. (1990). Positioning: The discursive production of selves. *Journal for the Theory of Social Behaviour, 20*, 43–63. doi:10.1111/j.1468-5914.1990.tb00174.x

Dressman, M., O'Brien, D., Rogers, T., Ivey, G., Wilder, P., Alvermann, D., et al. (2006). Problematizing Adolescent Literacies: Four Instances, Multiple Perspectives. In D. Schallert, B. Maloch, C. Fairbanks, J. Worthy, & J. Hoffman (Eds.), *55th Yearbook of the National Reading Conference* (pp 141-154). Oak Creek, WI.

Ellsworth, E. (2005). *Places of learning: Media, architecture, pedagogy*. New York: Routledge Falmer.

Gonick, M. (2007). Between "girl power" and "Reviving Ophelia": Constituting the neoliberal girl subject. *National Women's Study Association Journal, 18*(2), 1–22.

Grosz, E. (1994). *Volatile bodies: Toward a corporeal feminism*. Bloomington, IN: Indiana University Press.

Grosz, E., & Eisenman, P. (2001). *Architecture from the outside: Essays on virtual and real space*. Cambridge, MA: MIT Press.

Holland, D., Lachicotte, W., Skinner, D., & Cain, C. (1998). *Identity and agency in cultural worlds*. Cambridge, MA: Harvard U. Press.

Hull, G., & Nelson, M. (2005). Locating the semiotic power of multimodality. *Written Communication, 22*, 224–261. doi:10.1177/0741088304274170

Hull, G., & Schultz, K. (2001). Literacy and learning out of school: A review of theory and research. *Review of Educational Research, 71*(4), 575–611. doi:10.3102/00346543071004575

Jenkins, H. (2006). *Confronting the challenges of participatory culture: Media education for the 21st century*. A John D. and Catherine T. MacArthur Foundation Occasional Paper on Digital Media and Learning, Chicago, IL: MacArthur Foundation.

Kearney, M. C. (2006). *Girls make media*. New York: Routledge.

Kress, G. (2003). *Literacy in the new media age*. New York: Routledge.

Kress, G., & Van Leeuwen, T. (2001). *Multimodal discourse: The modes and media of contemporary communication*. New York: Oxford University Press.

LaMonde, A. M., & Rogers, T. (2007). Infusing arts and media into a secondary pre-service course in language and literacy across the disciplines as imaginative and critical practices. *Language and Literature, 9*(2).

Leander, K. M. (2003). Writing travelers' tales on New Literacyscapes. *Reading Research Quarterly, 38*(3), 392–397.

Lemke, J. (1995). *Textual Politics*. London: Taylor and Francis.

Lesko, N. (1996). Denaturalizing adolescence: the politics of contemporary representations. *Youth & Society, 28*(2), 139–161. doi:10.1177/0044118X96028002001

Levine, K. (2003). *Hannah's Suitcase*. Mortin Grove, IL: Albert Whitman and Company.

Manovich, L. (2001). *The language of new media*. Cambridge, MA: MIT Press.

Massey, D. (1994). *Space, place and gender*. Minneapolis, MN: University of Minnesota Press.

Moje, E. (2000). "To be part of the story": The literacy practices of gangsta adolescents. *Teachers College Record*, *102*(3), 651–691. doi:10.1111/0161-4681.00071

New London Group. (2000). A pedagogy of multiliteracies. In B. Cope & M. Kalantzis (Eds.), *Multiliteracies: Literacy learning and the design of social futures* (pp. 9-37). London: Routledge.

O'Brien, D. (2005). "At-risk" adolescents: Redefining competence through the multiliteracies of intermediality, visual arts, and representation. *Reading online*. Retrieved March 20, 2005, from http://www.readingonline.org/newliteracies/obrien/

Pomerantz, S., Currie, D. H., & Kelly, D. M. (2004). Sk8er girls; Skateboarders, girlhood and feminism in motion. *Women's Studies International Forum*, *27*, 547–557. doi:10.1016/j.wsif.2004.09.009

Rogers, T., & Schofield, A. (2005). Things thicker than words: Portraits of youth multiple literacies in an alternative secondary program. In J. Anderson, M. Kendrick, T. Rogers, & S. Smythe (Eds.), *Portraits of Literacy across Families, Communities and Schools*, (pp. 205-220). Mahwah, NJ: Erlbaum Associates.

Rogers, T., Winters, K., & LaMonde, A. (in press). From image to ideology: Analyzing shifting identity positions of marginalized youth across the cultural sites of video production. *Pedagogies: An International Journal*.

Rogers, T., Winters, K., LaMonde, A. M., & Perry, M. (2008). *The Youth CLAIM project: Researching critical literacies and arts-integrated media production among youth in classroom and community sites*. Paper presented at the Canadian Society for the Study of Education, Vancouver, Canada.

Rose, G. (2001). Visual methodologies. *An introduction to the interpretation of visual materials*. London: Sage Publications.

Schofield, A., & Rogers, T. (2004). At play in fields of ideas; Teaching curriculum and the lives of youth. *Journal of Adolescent and Adult Literacies*, *48*, 238–248. doi:10.1598/JAAL.48.3.5

Sefton-Green, J. (1998). Digital diversions. *Youth culture in the age of multimedia*. London: UCL Press.

Sefton-Green, J. (2006). Youth, technology and media cultures. In J. Green & A. Luke (Eds.), *Rethinking learning: What counts as learning and what learning counts* (pp. 279-306). Washington, DC: American Educational Research Association.

Soep, E. (2006). Beyond literacy and voice in youth media production. *McGill Journal of Education*, *41*(3), 1–11.

Street, B. (1995). *Social Literacies: Critical approaches to literacy in development, ethnography and education*. New York: Longman.

Chapter 10
Practicing or Preaching?
Teacher Educators and Student Teachers Appropriating New Literacies

Margaret Lo
University of Hong Kong, Hong Kong

Matthew Clarke
University of Hong Kong, Hong Kong

ABSTRACT

This chapter examines the implementation of a new 12-hour course on 'New Literacies' during the final year of a Bachelor of Education in English language education in Hong Kong. Specifically, it examines the authors' attempts to create a community of practice around New Literacies teaching and learning. As part of this endeavour, the authors sought to embody – and to encourage their student teachers to appropriate as part of their evolving teaching selves – the 'insider mindset' (Lankshear & Knobel, 2006) of new literacies practices, as the authors planned and implemented the course. They hoped that experientially connecting theory and practice of New Literacies would provide affordances for teacher educators, and for student teachers, to capitalise on the powerful potential of digital technologies in order to rethink how curriculum might be implemented in ways that are more multimodal, participative, and collaborative. As the authors discuss below, their attempt encountered unanticipated challenges, reflecting the power of existing institutional structures and unarticulated assumptions. The final part of the chapter examines lessons from the authors experience that may have resonance in other contexts and explores how they might approach the challenges they encountered differently in the future.

INTRODUCTION

The development of successful literacy skills is central to educational policy in many societies including Hong Kong. However, what counts as 'literacy' continues to be contested in education (Collins & Blot, 2003), and this debate is even more apparent in the 21st century as literacy rapidly changes as a result of globalisation, mass communication and digital technologies. The terms *multiliteracies* and *new literacies* are now applied to an ever increasing variety of practices in socially, culturally and linguistically diverse contexts (Cope & Kalantzis, 2000; Lankshear & Knobel, 2006). At the same

DOI: 10.4018/978-1-60566-673-0.ch010

time, discussions around literacy in education are often associated with the English language, as globalisation and mass communication have contributed to the spread of English as an International Language. As a result, achieving high standards of literacy in English as a Second or Foreign Language (ESL/EFL) has also become a goal for education systems across the world.

These concerns are clearly reflected in the two overall aims of the Hong Kong English Language curriculum (Curriculum Development Council, 2002):

1. To provide every learner of a second language with further opportunities for extending their knowledge and experience of the cultures of other people as well as opportunities for personal and intellectual development, further studies, pleasure and work in the English medium.
2. To enable every learner to prepare for the changing socio-economic demands resulting from advances in information technology; these demands include the interpretation, use and production of materials for pleasure, study and work in the English medium.

While many young people in Hong Kong are extensive and proficient users and producers of new literacies, and are active and enthusiastic consumers of multimodal, often digitally mediated texts in their out-of-school lifeworlds, these new multimodal texts and textual practices have not been fully exploited in schools and classrooms, other than being used superficially to "contextualise" grammatical points and vocabulary that drives much English language teaching in Hong Kong. Indeed, in Hong Kong there appears to be growing gap between students' lifeworld literacies and the school-based literacy which is further exacerbated by the textbook driven teaching practices and high-stakes assessment methods.

Indeed, the literacy teaching and learning models and curriculum materials used by Hong Kong schools largely adopt a skill-based, cognitive approach to reading and writing, and a traditional paper-based, print-based view of texts. These models are drawn from English as a Second Language (ESL) reading and writing instruction, where reading is frequently described as a neutral, psycholinguistic, cognitive process residing in the individual, and involving linguistic processing and reading strategies such as decoding, skimming and scanning (Grabe, 2002). While linguistic skills and knowledge are necessary, they are insufficient when taking into account the rapidly changing communication landscape of the 21st century, the multimodal, dynamic nature of texts, particularly digitally mediated texts, and the ways in which texts and textual practices are situated within specific social practices and inextricably linked to social relations and social identity (Barton, Hamilton & Ivanic, 2000; Gee, 2008; Kress, 2003; Street, 1995).

There are also several educational problems associated with this decontextualised approach to literacy. Such orientations construct the teacher as primarily a technician, and the learner and learning as fixed and predictable entities, and thus run the risk of students perceiving education - and English language learning - as irrelevant, foreign, and ultimately alienating (Larson & Marsh, 2005, p. 5). These approaches may also serve to alienate English language teachers from their students, and limit teachers' development of educationally and socially responsive teaching approaches, strategies and resources. Finally, a reductionist approach to literacy does not address the need for preparing students and teachers to critically engage with the proliferation of new texts and textual practices, and to use and create texts in socially responsible and socially responsive ways (Anstey & Bull, 2006; Freebody & Luke, 1990).

Thus, to achieve the aims of the Hong Kong English Language curriculum outlined above, there is a strong need for an expanded, socially oriented approach to literacy teaching and learning in Hong Kong schools and language teacher education programmes, which takes account of the emergence of new literacies in the 21st century, and which embraces the notion of literacy as a social practice, intimately tied to the construction of learners' identities. In this context, it is timely that Hong Kong has placed an increasing emphasis on literacy development in the English curriculum in recent years (Curriculum Development Council, 2004); however, given the significant shifts in literacy over the past decade, outlined above, the need for teacher education to be informed by new literacies is particularly urgent. This paper outlines our attempts to address this need through a new course within our four-year Bachelor of Education program. Specifically, this chapter is a critical reflection on our experiences of planning and teaching a new course entitled *Teaching and Learning New Literacies* on a fourth year Bachelor of Education (English Language Education) course in Hong Kong.

The term new literacies can be used interchangeably with multiliteracies. But although they share a focus on the ways that literacy has changed in the late 20th century, there are in fact differences of emphasis between multiliteracies and new literacies, in that the latter tends to place more emphasis on the technological dimensions of these changes, the former focuses on how increased social and cultural diversity resulting from globalisation has changed the very nature of literacy, as well as a more explicit focus on pedagogy. Hong Kong has a relatively homogenous cultural make up, and there is a wide gap between the technological practices in and out of school, and because our students are preservice teachers of English, which is very text-oriented, we used new literacies as a focus for our university course. However, we will draw on literature from both new literacies and multiliteracies in our discussion.

In this chapter we critically reflect on our attempts to develop a community of practice around new literacies with student teachers on a short course within a four year Bachelor of Education programme. In order to align course content and process with the second mindset of new literacies, we incorporated new literacies tasks and tools throughout the course. However, many of our student-teachers did not readily take on board these concepts and practices as was evident in the nature of their postings on the course wiki, their responses to the assessment tasks and processes, and the variable quality of their school-based projects carried out during their teaching practicum (school based teaching experience). Students' orientation to learning and participation in the course, and their understandings of English language teaching generally, remained firmly within their existing practices of university study and the version of literacy learning promoted in the rest of the programme. Although the majority of the student-teachers did participate in new literacies in their personal lives, they were generally not able to draw on their experiences to participate meaningfully in the course or to refashion their classroom practice. From our own experiences as tutors, the institutionalised pedagogies of teacher education and the dispersed, fluid and creative elements of new literacies presented us with numerous dilemmas and tensions. Although these findings were disappointing on one level, we are challenged to reflect on and potentially resolve these tensions in ways that are educationally meaningful. In our concluding section, we therefore outline a few considerations for teacher educators who are working to develop new literacies infused pedagogies. In the meantime, we begin by providing more background to our specific research in the section below.

BACKGROUND

New Literacies 2

The proliferation of mass media, popular culture, digital and mobile technologies has resulted in profound changes to everyday communication and the nature of texts. New forms of texts and textual practices or 'new literacies', particularly digitally-mediated ones, have emerged in the 21st century (Lankshear & Knobel, 2006). Contemporary and popular culture texts are frequently created through the practice of "remix" (Lessig, 2004), involving multiple media, combining multiple semiotic modes such as words, image, sound and movement, and layered through intertextual and hypertextual references to create new meanings. Textual norms/forms are constantly being challenged, redesigned. Indeed, as Lankshear and Knobel (2006, p. 52) describe "there is *no* text paradigm. Text types are subject to wholesale experimentation, hybridization, and rule breaking".

As new forms of texts emerge, new ways of "reading" and interpreting texts, and new textual practices have also developed. A single text may be intended for various social groups as users, and very often involve non-linear, interactive and multiple "reading" pathways. Widespread distribution and participation made available through the Internet have also challenged accepted notions of ownership, authorship, and hierarchical relationships between authors and readers. Lankshear and Knobel (2006) describe these old and new literacy practices in terms of two mindsets. New literacies practices, or 'Mindset 2' embody a ethos which privileges "participation over publishing, distributed expertise over centralised expertise, collective intelligence over individual possessive intelligence, collaboration over individuated authorship, dispersion over scarcity, sharing over ownership, experimentation over 'normalization', innovation and evolution over stability and fixity… and so on" (p. 60). In sum, new literacies radically changes the nature of literacy per se in a number of ways: by offering enhanced possibilities for authenticity and engagement; by changing the way learners work together and interact with each other, thus creating new modes of relationship; and by the potential it offers for reaching and receiving feedback from wider audiences, offering enriched possibilities for affirming learners' identities. These potential benefits and how they can be capitalized on in schools has been the focus of much recent research.

Researching New Literacies Education

There is now a growing body of research on new literacies and multiliteracies in school settings (for example Evans, 2005; Kist, 2005; Love, 2006; Love, Pigdon, Baker & Hamston, 2005; Mills, 2007; Unsworth, 2001; Walsh, 2007) as well as research into youth's out of school, digitally mediated literacy practices and identities (Sefton-Green, 1998; Thomas, 2007). Some researchers have focused on English language learners' engagement in online textual practices and multimodal texts (Black, 2007; Lam, 2000). However, the majority of new literacies studies have been conducted in L1 school settings or in English speaking contexts, highlighting the need for research into how new literacies are interpreted and appropriated by teachers and learners in an ESL context. In particular, there is a dearth of research focused on new literacies in the Hong Kong context.

Many studies on English language literacy in the Hong Kong context have focussed on reading proficiency and achievement (Tse, Lam, Lam & Loh, 2005) and on the effectiveness of education reforms such as the Extensive Reading Scheme (Chow & Chou, 2000). Further research includes Lin's critical sociocultural analysis of a secondary English reading lesson (2001), and Firkins and Forey's (2006) research on the implementation of a critical literacy programme using Freebody and Luke's *Four Resources Model* with academic low-achievers in a Hong Kong secondary school. However, all these studies have focussed primarily on paper-based print literacies, and there appear to be no Hong Kong based studies relating to teaching and learning new literacies or multiliteracies teaching and learning in Hong Kong schools.

In addition there have been very few studies of teacher education for new literacies and none in the Hong Kong context. A number of studies have described courses focussing on media education and Information Technologies; for example, Carmen Luke (2000) describes how a media-cultural studies and IT course were combined in an undergraduate teacher education programme in Australia to address the changing literacy practices of university students, while Kapitzke (2000) examined the pedagogical aspects of on line pedagogy on a course on media and technologies in education.

More recently, Rowsell et al. (2008) explored university teacher educator's understandings of multiliteracies pedagogies, and the extent to which recent graduates of a four-year Bachelor of Education course implemented multiliteracies in their elementary (primary) literacy classrooms. While the teacher educators on the programme stressed the importance of modelling, connecting to students' lives, close student-teacher relationships, building a class community in multiliteracies education, and made efforts to teach along these lines, the study's findings showed that new teachers did not always realise these in practice. Indeed, in all of the above studies, teacher educators made a concerted attempt to "walk the talk" by aligning course content and process and by practicing theory and theorising practice

As teacher educators, in teaching the new literacies course we also strived to meet the challenges of aligning content and process, theory and practice, so that the principles of new literacies were lived as well as learned, by engendering a sense of shared community among ourselves and the student teachers. A fruitful framework for thinking about this sort of learning through experience is offered by the concept of a 'community of practice' (Wenger, 1998, p. 96) since a community of practice has both technical and social dimensions, is both an 'engine of practice' and a 'source of social structure' (Wenger, 1998).

Communities of Practice and Affinity Spaces

The communities of practice framework is a theory of learning, a theory of identity, a theory of meaning, a theory of community and a theory of practice (Boud & Middleton, 2003; Buysse, Sparkman, & Wesley, 2003; Fetterman, 2002; Graham, Osgood & Karren, 1998; Hung & Nichani, 2002; Lave & Wenger, 1991; Lee & Valdarrama, 2003; Moreno, 2001; Porter, 2003; Rover, 2003; Wenger, 1998; Wesley & Buysse, 2001). As such, it offers considerable potential for thinking about a group who are striving to learn about and to incorporate new literacies principles and practices into their teaching. In our new literacies course we wanted to engender a community where new literacies was a valued enterprise and where students were actively engaged in new literacies practices; where new literacies connected with students' identities and where new identities were shaped around new literacies practices; and where new literacies were experienced as meaningful and as offering new possibilities for creating and sharing meaningful experience.

A community of practice is a group who are mutually engaged in a joint enterprise and who share a common language or discourse repertoire connected to that enterprise (Buysse, et al., 2003; Wenger, 1998). "Mutual engagement" refers to participation in an endeavour or practice whose meanings are negotiated among participants. For example, in the new literacies course, we strived to establish such common engagement by making a number of aspects of the course, including the wiki site around which it was organized, and the assessment criteria, negotiable among the course participants. "Joint enterprise" refers to the focus of activity that links members of a community of practice. In the context of this chapter, we tried to engender a common sense of joint enterprise in terms of getting the students' to realize the crucial need for an expanded notion of literacy in the Hong Kong English curriculum. "Shared repertoire" refers to the common resources for creating meaning that result from engagement in joint enterprise. In working with our student teachers, for example, we wanted our students to learn about and live new literacies concepts such as 'remix', 'participation' and 'distributed expertise'.

In addition to the communities of practice framework, we drew on Gee's (2005) notion of an affinity space, which characterizes many social configurations in the twenty first century, which are defined by a common interest or passion, rather than group membership alone, and are virtual rather than 'real', in that members don't typically meet face-to-face. Salient for our purposes in this chapter, affinity spaces are characterized by dispersed, distributed knowledge and facilitated by a portal that "allows people to generate new signs and relationships among signs" (Gee, 2005, p. 226). We hoped that our new literacies course would act as such a portal, allowing students to collaboratively construct new knowledge and understanding and engender in them a passion for the exciting learning possibilities afforded by new literacies. However, the notion of students as collaborators raises issues of power and pedagogy, which we will seek to address in our discussion. At the same time, the communities of practice model has been criticized for inadequate attention to and theorization of power (Barton & Tusting, 2005). To address the power issues that arose in our study we draw on the Foucauldian inspired work of Jennifer Gore, and in particular, her notion of potential tensions between the 'pedagogy argued for' and the 'pedagogy of the argument' (1993, p. 5). Gore's work allows us to examine the ways in which pedagogy is always situated within relations of power and to recognize the fine line between the promotion of new literacies pedagogy, with associations of liberation and empowerment, and new literacies as a regime of truth, operating in ways that undermine these ideals. We come back to these ideas in the final discussion; meanwhile, in the section that follows we will explain in more detail how we attempted to embody the concepts of communities of practice and affinity spaces in our new literacies course.

The New Literacies Course

Our 12-hour new literacies course was organized around three 'input' sessions, where we introduced ideas and practices from the new literacies literature, and three 'hands-on' sessions where student teachers explored and experimented with new literacies texts and concepts. The course took place in a multimedia lab so that we could work with the 'technical stuff' of new literacies in both the input and the hands-on sessions and we encouraged students to bring laptops to maximize fluidity and ease of movement and groupings.

In terms of conceptualizing new literacies we drew on Lankshear and Knobel's (2006) notion of 'mindset one' and 'mindset two', where mindset one emphasizes values of individual authorship and ownership and centralised expertise primarily within a print-based environment, while mindset two emphasizes participation and collaboration, innovation and experimentation, often within a digitally encoded and multimodally mediated environment. Within this context, we explored new literacies practices such as 'remix' and 'participation', including such specific practices as fanfiction and weblogging, and considered their potential incorporation into the English language curriculum. By introducing and exploring these new literacies principles and practices via the alternating input and hands-on workshop sessions we established a shared repertoire of meaning.

In line with the more democratic, less hierarchical ethos of new literacies we organized the course around a wiki and invited the students to share the responsibility for, and ownership of, its evolution and development with us. This also provided potential for creating the sort of dispersed ownership and collaboration that characterizes mindset two and in a similar spirit, we placed value on participation in the wiki space rather than on traditional concerns such as attendance in the classroom. For example, the wiki technology allowed all members of the shared social space to co-author the web site, including inserting hyperlinks, tagging, contributing to discussion boards and editing pages. Rather than setting weekly readings, as is typical practice at our institution, we invited the students to collaboratively generate a 'reading list' using the social book marking site del.icio.us and creating a tag cloud of related concepts, readings and websites and embedding this cloud into the wiki. In these ways we attempted to foster mutual engagement in new literacies practices within the community formed by ourselves and the student teachers in the hope that the students' developing interest in and knowledge about new literacies would enable the course in general, and the wiki space specifically, to function as an affinity space.

Assessment posed the biggest challenge, in that there was an inherent tension between the collaborative, democratic spirit of mindset two and the institutional requirements for evaluation and grades. We decided to address this tension by incorporating a 'product' and 'process' element to the assessment.

The latter involved assessing the students' participation in the wiki space and in order to promote a greater sense of mutual engagement, we invited the students to co-develop assessment criteria for their participation; this had both a principled aspect in that it reflected the democratic ethos of new literacies, by drawing on the group's collective intelligence, as well as a pedagogical aspect, in that by collaboratively constructing the assessment criteria the students would develop deeper understandings of new literacies by experiencing - and articulating - the collaborative negotiation that characterizes writing in wiki spaces.

The former required the students to develop a new literacies-infused curriculum unit for their forthcoming teaching practicum. The students were encouraged to collaborate in pairs of groups in this task and to develop units that used technology, not for its own sake, but to promote enhanced possibilities for communication, interaction, and relating to others, as well as to engage their school pupils' wider identities beyond those typically performed in the classroom. We invited the students to join us in viewing this as the ultimate purpose of the course – in other words embrace the joint enterprise of making literacy teaching and learning, at least in English language education, in Hong Kong schools more real and relevant in relation to the rapidly changing communicative landscape of the 21st century.

So far we have outlined our guiding principles in developing our Bachelor of Education new literacies course and the aims we had for our students' learning. However, in practice our ideals were confronted by a number of issues which we hadn't foreseen and which are likely to be of interest and relevance to teacher educators planning similar courses. These difficulties are discussed in the following section.

STUDENT TEACHERS' APPROPRIATION OF NEW LITERACIES: NEWCOMER MINDSETS

As outlined above, we envisaged the students as co-authors of the wiki space; we assumed that as digital 'insiders' they would be comfortable interacting via the wiki space, distributing their prior and evolving expertise, collaboratively engaging in the learning tasks we set, and generally taking increased ownership of the wiki space through exponentially increasing levels of activity as the course unfolded. In practice, the students' activity levels, in terms of messages posted (see Figure 1 below) and edits made (see Figure 2 below) on the wiki, were clustered around key points in the course: specifically, there was a moderate spike towards the end of the course in February 2008, reflecting a guided, in-class activity – creating a remix text with a message about education in Hong Kong – and in May 2008 as the deadline for uploading school-based projects and for assessing student participation in the wiki space approached. Thus, although activity increased during the very brief duration of the course, the overall pattern of activity was as one would expect to find in a traditional, face-to-face course driven by washback from a summative assessment.

Not only were there quantitative issues, but qualitative issues arose too. The messages can be grouped according to a number of categories, including responses to post-session questions, practical inquires, and responses to each others' work. Initially, perhaps reflecting early enthusiasm for the aims of the course, there was some genuine sharing of student teachers' current engagement with new literacies practices as they solved problems, such as learning how to tag and exchanged new knowledge. For example, Teresa shared her poetry writing, blogging and social networking practices, which were potential resources to be shared and distributed among the community:

I have been into writing poems recently. I started to write my own poems since April last year. The reasons are expressing my feelings and adding to my teaching materials portfolio. The tools or medium I have used include the computer, xanga (which is an online blog) and facebook (which is an online community for sharing and networking).

Another student, Joanne, sent us an email expressing her excitement that the course seemed to offer affirmation of her literacy identity and interest in Japanese manga, as well as providing motivation for learning:

Figure 1. Number of messages

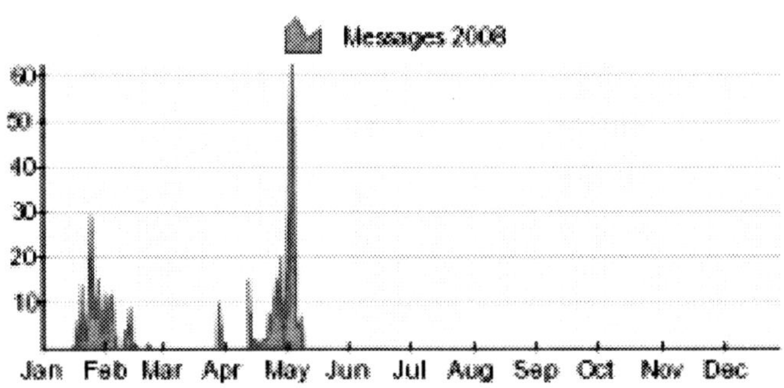

Figure 2. Number of edits

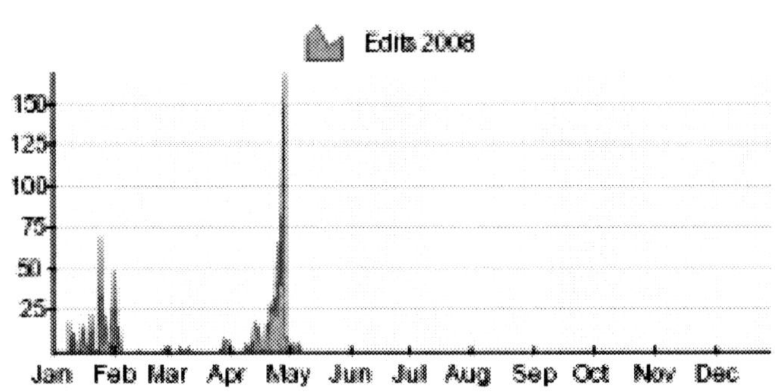

First of all, thanks for giving us such a wonderful and inspiring lesson this morning. I have never thought my 'sailormoon' example would be literacy-related. I am now looking forward to exploring new literacy and multiliteracies!!

The same student offered critical reflection on the role of technology in new literacies, emphasizing the need for human elements of audience and purpose, in the context of a discussion about remixing songs and animation:

In my opinion, to explain the rise of this kind of new literacy, technology contribution itself cannot stand, it has to also work with the creativity of human beings. As technology grows, the world becomes smaller and it is easier for us to explore the world. But they are just tools and things would not change unless somebody creates a 'link' for them.

However, there was also a tendency for the student teachers to engage in uncritical affirmation of each others' contributions, such as the following from Audrey and Teresa:

I like your picture and think that it's rather cute! It's one of the more positive ones that we have seen from Friday's effort. Nice!

You have included a lot of colourful and beautiful pictures in your ppt. I am sure you can capture and sustain your students' attention. The pictures are also very effective visual aids to teach the different home styles.

Whilst we recognize the interpersonal function of these bolstering responses, they were often not followed by more substantive or critical points and the predominant pattern was one of single responses to someone's work (e.g. a remix text providing critical commentary on an educational issue in Hong Kong) with no reply from the creator of that work and with very few extended discussion chains. This may be because we did not provide sufficient modelling of the sort of responses we hoped to see in student teachers' writing, although we did provide some, such as the following in response to Karen and Linda's animated film:

Why did you discuss curriculum reform through the medium of a domestic dispute? Did you intend to make a comment about gender issues in education in Hong Kong through the images you chose?

In addition to the discussion boards, another means for the student teachers to participate in the course and the wikispace was through contributing to the del.icio.us tagging of new literacies related readings and web sites. However a tension arose as the student teachers used their own names as tags to boost the visibility of their activity and gain credit for participation, something they were being assessed on. Diana explicitly raised this issue with us:

As the new-/multi-literacies resources have no relation to our names, if we tag the resources using our NAMEs, it will affect the accuracy and the effectiveness of the search result, and it doesn't seem to be a good internet user practice too.

The tension here reflects the differences between mindset one, with its emphasis on individual authorship and ownership of knowledge, and mindset two, which values collective authorship and distributed knowledge. There was also a tension here for us as teachers between wanting the students to foreground concepts and ideas and acknowledging their desire to see their individual identities affirmed and to garner capital through the potentially higher grades that they saw as a reward for a larger number of tags. As we will see below, these tensions became even more evident when they focused around issues of assessment.

Assessing New Literacies: Process

As noted in the section above on the new literacies course, as part of our goal of promoting a participatory, democratic approach, reflecting new literacies' mindset two, we decided to partially assess student teachers through participation in the wiki space and to involve them in the collaborative determination of the assessment criteria for this purpose. To initiate the development of these criteria, we began with the BEd programme's generic assessment criteria, as well as Biggs' (1999) SOLO taxonomy, and invited the students to adapt these to more adequately reflect the collaborative, participatory, distributed qualities of learning and knowledge in mindset two. In practice, only one student made any substantive changes, inserting two additional criteria: "Clear evidence of collaboration from all students" and 'user-friendly format". Another pair of students did suggest some changes on the discussion board but were reluctant to make their changes on the page containing the assessment criteria:

Good to see that you have had thoughts about the criteria; why don't you make your changes directly onto the wikiparticpation page???

Margaret & Matthew

If we do it directly onto the page, we will change what others have written so we decided to post it here instead.

Teresa and Audrey

Another student raised the issue of quantity versus quality in terms of participation via the discussion boards:

...the quantity of pages does not mean there has been a substantial contribution to the wiki.

Karen

To which we responded:

You can do something about this by editing the criteria on the wiki participation page, so that they take into account the issues you've raised. Why don't you edit the criteria so that they emphasize the quality of the response, not just the number of pages/tags created.

However, our suggestion was not taken up in either instance. This raises a number of issues. It indicates that the students were not actively engaging with, and possibly not fully understanding, the collaborative authoring and editing potential of the wiki technology, nor with the participative principles of mindset two. This may have been due to their long and deep enculturation into an individualist, mindset one approach to writing and authorship, as well as the regulative discipline of traditional assessment practices, in which the student internalizes and assumes responsibility for their own individuation and classification by the system as an object of knowledge and power (Foucault, 1977). This last point is supported by the fact that, although we offered the students the option of including a peer- and self-assessment, the students wished to stick to the more familiar approach of tutor-only assessment.

Assessing New Literacies: Product

The same issues arose in the context of the 'product' assessment, the new literacies-infused curriculum unit for implementation during the students' teaching practicum. We put the word 'product' in quotes because our intention was that the students would work and rework their projects over several months incorporating suggestions and getting ideas from peers. We designed this as a pair or group project; however, the students for the most part chose to work individually, the reason given being that they were working in different schools from their partner, thus indicating their failure to recognize the possibilities for collaborating at a distance offered by digital technologies and the connectivity of online communication. Those that did truly work in pairs were working in the same school. What's more, towards the end of the teaching practicum, we noticed that no one had posted any evidence of work on their projects, suggesting to us that the students were treating the task as a traditional summative assessment, rather than as an opportunity for collaborative learning that drew on the distributed knowledge and expertise of the wider group. This was confirmed when we sent a reminder to, and received the following response from, the students with regard to the assessment "due date":

Our concern is that the deadline of 20 Apr is the weekend after our Teaching Practicum ... which leaves some of us with very little time to work on it. Would really appreciate if the due date of the project is kept on 28 Apr as discussed in class before, while the responses to classmates' projects and reflections is 4 May.

Diana

Our thinking on this issue is reflected in our response:

We had originally hoped that individuals would post their projects and teaching ideas as MTP progressed, with ongoing comments from classmates, and ongoing revisions by the project/page creator. We believed this would reflect NLs principles and would be an appropriate approach to a wiki-based assignment. In other words, we did not expect that you would treat this as a traditional paper-based assignment to be submitted in one go, as a final copy, on 28th April! We saw this date as simply a 'cut off point' for university assessment purposes.

Matthew and Margaret

Uniforms as Usual

In addition to these issues of process, many student teachers' projects also revealed the tenacity of traditional language teaching approaches which focus on individual cognition, language as conduit, and what Marion Williams (1999) refers to as a 'parcel' view of knowledge, all of which reflect mindset one. Joanne's project is a case in point. She asked her students to design a new school uniform in groups and create a visual display, using textiles and bits of clothing, which they then presented to the rest of the class. Her rationale and aims are outlined in Table 1.

Joanne has attempted to conceptualize her project in terms of new literacies, however, there are some serious misconceptions. Collaboration, sharing and creative rule-breaking are certainly components of new literacies; however, they are not by themselves sufficient to ensure that an activity reflects a new literacies ethos. For example, creative rule-breaking implies an understanding of the generic conventions of existing literacy practices and deliberately subverting and/or challenging them; whereas Joanne's students – at least some of them – are exercising artistic creativity but still operating inside the conventions of the discipline of school uniform and the collaboration and sharing are also limited to the traditional participants, audience and purposes of English language teaching; it remains a pedagogic task with little real world connections, as indicated by aims such as "students should learn and practice new vocabulary items in the unit". And her new

Table 1. Joanne's project rationale and aims

We Love our New Summer Uniform!!
1. Teaching Background
The activity was carried out while they were learning a unit called 'Fashion'. I think their textbook is not very authentic and students do not get a chance to understand what fashion is or can be. Furthermore, I think creativity is vital in fashion; this activity is designed to encourage students with more creative and rule-breaking mindset 2 thinking.
2. Teaching Focus
By the end of the project, students should learn and practice new vocabulary items in the unit, and; Students should experience collaborative work, sharing and creative rule-breaking (different new literacies concept), and; Students should be able to practice their reading, listening, writing and speaking skills.
3. Strategies (in of new literacies practice)
In this lesson, mainly mindset 2 will be implemented, but they will also learn how to remix different cultures into their uniform.

literacies-related aim of remix was similarly not realized due to the conventionality of the task, which reproduced rather than challenged accepted discourses, as was evident in the students' posters which either resembled traditional school uniforms or typical Hong Kong casual wear. There was little sense of either carnivalistic entertainment or sharp social commentary that often characterizes contemporary remix texts. Another issue raised in this example is the relationship between group work and collaboration; the former, while it may lead to collaboration, may also be little more than a physical configuration, whereas the latter implies genuine sharing of ideas and dispersed knowledge, creating a whole that exceeds the sum of its parts. One of the key affordances of digital technologies is the scope it can provide for rich collaboration; however, Joanne's pen and paper project was unable to capitalize on this potential.

How might Joanne's project have avoided these problems? One immediate starting point would be to conceptualize school uniforms as 'texts' that operate as part of a wider disciplinary technology of schooling. This would have allowed the students to see ways of creating new 'texts' which comment on (for example, designing prison-like uniforms) or challenge (for example, designing police-like uniforms) the messages carried by traditional uniforms rather than duplicating these messages. The task could also have been made more engaging and authentic by using technology to communicate with students in other schools and contexts, including ones where formal uniforms are not worn, so as to defamiliarize the social practice of uniforms.

Old Wine in New Bottles

Another project raised a different set of issues in relation to new literacies pedagogy. In this example, Audrey and Teresa, unlike Joanne, did make use of technology within a project on students' home "cultures", called 'The United Nations of ACCC' (see Table 2). In this school, there was a mix of "local" and "international" students, and the task involved them writing a short article about an "aspect" of their country. Teachers provided "tips" on internet use in the form of hyperlinks to sites such as http://chineseculture.about.com/cs/customs/ which present a 'holidays and heroes' view of culture (Nieto, 2002). Aside from this fairly directive search activity, the only other use of the internet was to upload homework "to allow students to communicate with us and each other as they are completing their assignments over the holiday", ironically undermined by the instruction

Table 2. Audrey and Teresa's writing task

Easter Holiday Assignment: The United Nations of ACCC	
For **local students** who have been assigned a topic by your Chinese teacher, write an article on one of the following topics: Red Eggs and Birthday Cake Hong Kong Style Restaurants and Fast Food Restaurants Egg Tarts, Milk Tea and Hong Kong Style Restaurants Calligraphy and Chinese Keyboard Typing Traditional Chinese Housing Plum, Orchid, Chrysanthemum and Bamboo The Great Wall For **international students:** Write an article on one aspect (e.g. food, climate, sports, population, housing, etc.) about the country you are from.	1. Decide which topic you are going to write about 2. Search for relevant information ~ Surf the internet (Tips from Miss T & Mrs. A) ~ Make use of what you already know ~ Ask your family 3. Write your article ~ **You MUST use the template** ~ You may add photos / pictures to make it more attractive 4. Upload your article [onto the wetpaint site] 5. Print it out and submit it to Miss T / Mrs. A

to students to "print it out and submit it" to the teachers. The teachers did give an instruction to the students to comment on each others' work on a wetpaint site, however, this opportunity for collaboration was not taken up. Another interesting point to note is the view of images as decorative embellishment of their written work, "to make it more attractive", as opposed to the new literacies conception of images as an integral part of multimodal text forms. Overall, this project seems a paradigm case of "old wine in new bottles" (Lankshear & Knobel, 2006, p. 54), where technology is used for its own sake, rather than for its potential to genuinely enhance learning.

Audrey and Teresa might have considered using the wetpaint site to reach a genuine audience for their students' written work, for example, by collaborating with another classmate teaching in a different school during the practicum, and encouraging students from the two schools to read and comment on each others' work. They also might have dealt with the topic of culture more critically by first having students write about their individual lives and then, through a comparison of the websites with their students' lived experiences, critically examine the websites for their fixed and often stereotypical views of national culture and ethnicity.

From Words and Sentences to Songs and Videos

Despite the problems we have identified in the above student-teacher's work, there were more successful examples of new literacies-infused projects. In the following example, Linda had her students create remix texts commenting on environmental issues in Hong Kong using Windows Movie Maker and posting them to the shared social space of YouTube. Her project is outlined in Table 3. Her students' multimodal texts involved music, photos with captions that interacted with the song lyrics. In one example, the students built their remix text around the theme song, *I need to wake up* (Etheridge, 2006), from the film *An Inconvenient Truth* (Bender & Guggenheim, 2006), which students changed to *We need to wake up now.* The images and captions were focussed on environmental issues in Hong Kong that had been prominent in the media recently, such as, landfill pollution, use of plastic bags and bottles, smoking in public, and construction generated dust. Whereas the song was cast in the first person, the students demonstrated awareness of the mutual shaping of language and purpose by using the second personal pronoun to generate a sense of individual responsibility, and the third person plural pronoun to generate a sense of inclusiveness and solidarity between the text producer and consumer.

Table 3. Linda's environmental video project

Environmental protection
1. From photos to words -- exploring the topic through photos [of pollution] and using students' prior knowledge
2. From words to sentences – using students' prior knowledge to write meaningful sentences about the photos
3. From words/sentences to songs/videos – introducing the use of new literacies A few videos about environmental protection have been chosen to share with students. Those videos are made not professionally filmed and remixed like those we watch on TV but they are works made by students or other people who want to promote the awareness of environmental protection.
4. Using Windows Movie Maker – learning how to do remix and practicing Students will be taught to use this tool to make a movie clip by using photos, pictures and songs related to the topic "environment". They have to work out the message(s) they want to promote in the movie clip.
5. Sharing – work appreciation and response

Linda introduced the task by having her students view and analyse similar multimodal videos produced by high school students in other contexts and posted on YouTube. She presented these videos not as professionally-produced films "like those we watch on TV but they are works made by students or other people who want to promote the awareness of environmental protection." This demonstrated her understanding of new communicative and relational affordances offered by digital technologies as well as a sense of what would appeal to students' identities, and invited them to envision themselves as members of a wider community of environmentally conscious new literacies practitioners.

NEW LITERACIES OR OLD REGIMES OF PEDAGOGY?

From the above discussion a number of issues can be identified for us as teacher educators centring around the tension between the ideals of new literacies and the practices of institutionalised education, and in particular, the tension between autonomous, self-directed participation in researching new literacies as an affinity space versus the assigned readings, the in-class handouts and input sessions, and the formal assessment requirements of the university course. These tensions resonate with the distinction identified by Gore in her critique of critical and feminist pedagogy, between "the pedagogy argued for... and the pedagogy of the argument" (1993, p. 5), between what we preach and what we practice. Despite our careful consideration of content and process, we had been unable to escape a stark contradiction between what we were advocating for our student teachers, in terms of participation, collaboration, and distributed expertise, and the institutional disciplinary regime's requirements for completion and its practices of individuation and classification. As teacher educators, we had naively hoped to engender with the student teachers a community of new literacies advocates and practitioners, in which they bridged the gap between out of- and in-class literacy practices, bringing the former to bear on the latter, and extending this process through "constellations of practice" (Wenger, 1998, p. 127) in their work with students in schools. For the student teachers, however, the salient community of practice was defined by their role as university students, who had been together as group for four years, who attended the same classes and had developed friendships within the group, and who saw our course as one of a number they needed to pass in order to complete their degree. In other words, the student-teachers knew how to "do university study" well, and experienced meaningfulness in this community of practice. However, despite our attempts to "unpack" our new literacies infused pedagogies with the student-teachers, their existing community of practice proved to be constraining them and holding them "hostage to that experience". This reminds us that "the indigenous production of practice makes communities of practice the locus of creative achievements and the locus of inbred failures; the locus of resistance to oppression and the locus of the reproduction of its conditions; the cradle of the self but also the potential cage of the soul" (Wenger, 1998, p. 85).

These tensions can be also seen as reflecting different forms of misalignment between our espoused principles and our practice. We can see one form of misalignment when we look at our expectations with respect to how a shared knowledge base was to be developed in the course. As part of our vision for the community of practice we hoped to create, we imagined that students would engage in new literacies practices between classes, such as searching the internet for interesting readings and websites, tagging and sharing them via the wiki, and posting critical comments and responses on the discussion boards. However, in practice, this didn't happen so that at critical points where we needed students to read material to inform class discussions we found ourselves assigning and giving out photocopies of key readings and asking students to present them in class. In this case, similar to our failed attempts to have students generate their own assessment criteria for participation, our principles and our practice were prised apart by the response of the student teachers to our pedagogy.

On the other hand, a different set of tensions arose between the informal practices that student teachers characteristically engaged in as part of their out of class, personal internet use, such as posting informal photos of themselves on their project pages, and creating links to jokes and amusing sites, alongside their discussions of old and new literacies. Such mixing of personal/light-hearted and professional/serious is common in the world of web 2.0 and mindset two (indeed, we also included "fun" elements into our participation on the wiki, for example a photoshopped image of ourselves for our user icon, and an animated video to set a workshop task); yet as teacher educators we found it difficult to accept this kind of participation, seeing it as indicative of the student teachers' lack of serious commitment. In this case, our response raises questions about the degree to which our own alignment between what we practiced and what we preached was ever as close as we might have liked to believe. Reflecting on this episode, we note Gore's insight into the way that "teacher education, as institutionalised pedagogy, is unique in its function as meta-pedagogy," (1993 p.143), that is, in its capacity to, at once, provide knowledge of new literacies *and* at the same time to model the experience of new literacies-infused teaching. Yet the institutionalized nature of teacher education, embodied by the institutions in which teacher education is conducted, pose limits as well as offering possibilities for the integration of new literacies-infused pedagogies; we were only too ready to see the latter but insufficiently cognizant of the former.

As an example of our attempts to grapple with notions of meta-pedagogy, and also of one of our struggles with limits in teacher education, we assumed that the student-teachers, in a course about new literacies, would welcome the chance to engage in the more democratic and participatory learning of new literacies via the wiki, del.icio.us tagging, and through collaborative projects, which modelled new literacies practices. In a sense, we were attempting to align the 'pedagogy argued for' and the 'pedagogy of the argument'. However, we did not fully consider what was at stake for these student teachers in challenging (aspects of) the established machinery of institutionalised education, which had its own preferred and recognized pedagogy of the argument, in which the teacher is deferred to as the source of knowledge and learning. Our insistence on enacting a more 'democratic' approach suggests that our new literacies infused pedagogy, in this context, may have been enacted as a regulative 'regime of truth' (Gore, 1993). The student-teachers described above, whom we felt were simply "going through the motions" of new literacies, were possibly resisting our regimented pedagogy of new literacies.

Another way to understand many student teachers' apparent superficiality around new literacies practices is through the concept of "legitimate peripheral participation" in communities of practice (Lave & Wenger, 1991). Our desire and expectation for our students to appropriate new literacies principles and practices largely *by themselves*, mediated only through particular artifacts, reifications or portals such as the remix text workshop, the wiki, the del.icio.us tag cloud, and the assessment tasks, meant that we missed opportunities to engage in the community of practice ourselves in order to model the kinds of practices, including attitudes, beliefs and values and ways of *talking about* and *within* (p. 109) new literacies we hoped the students would appropriate, and we thus missed opportunities to take an active part in constructing that community. For example, while we did post a few critical questions on the wiki and initially added links to the readings tag cloud, our involvement in the wiki-community was minimal and always in role of the teacher. On the one hand our reluctance to "model" reflected our belief in student-centred pedagogies (and our conflation of "prescription" and "modelling") and our efforts to realise the non-hierarchical ethos of new literacies; but our lack of participation *as practitioners* meant that student-teachers' 'legitimate peripheral participation' could not take place as they did not have "broad access to areas of mature practice" (Lave & Wenger, 1991, p. 110) not only in the wiki and in the course, but in their practicum schools and in the larger BEd programme:

Where there is no cultural identity encompassing the activity in which newcomers participate and no field of mature practice for what is being learned, exchange value replaces the use value of increasing participation. The commoditization of learning engenders a fundamental contradiction between the use and exchange values of the outcome of learning, which manifests itself in conflicts between learning to know and learning to display knowledge for evaluation (p. 112).

Perhaps these tensions should have come as no surprise to us. After all, we were attempting to create a community of practice in which new literacies would be lived rather than just talked about in the brief space of a 12-hour university course over a period of less than four weeks of time and during their 10-week practicum which followed. This was too optimistic to say the least, given the myriad demands and pressures on the student teachers during this critical time in their degree. Overall, compartmentalising new literacies into a single module at the end of a 4-year programme meant that the key learning processes of internalization and transformation of knowledge and beliefs, through participation in a community where ways of acting and interacting reflect the values, attitudes and assumptions of our desired pedagogy (Johnson, 2009) were unable to take root. The result was a considerable degree of 'false clarity' (Fullan, 2001, p. 77) with regard to new literacies concepts, principles and practices on the part of the student teachers and frustration for us as teacher educators. With this in mind, in the final section we outline some of the key lessons we have learned as part of our critical reflection on our new literacies course, and suggest ways teacher educators might consider the implications of new literacies for their programmes.

NEW LITERACIES AND TEACHER EDUCATION FOR THE FUTURE

We still hold to the principle that new literacies needs to be lived in teacher education, given our understandings of literacies as multiple and social, and new literacies as primarily relational – that is, about new ways of relating to others – in that they are shared, distributed, collaborative, dispersed, and creative. This suggests that teacher education programmes need to infuse new literacies in many different aspects of the programme: taught modules, pedagogical tasks, the teaching practicum, and assessment practices need to involve experience of, rather than just learning about, the discourses and practices that competent new literacies 'insiders' engage in, in 'the real world'. This might involve, for example, giving student teachers access to forums that offer genuine peer-level dialogue with new literacies teachers. Such activities should provide access to sufficiently varied discourses and practices, so that students are in a position to critique any particular example from the vantage point of another (Gee, 2004).

Ensuring that new literacies principles and practices are lived rather than just taught also implies that teacher educators need to live new literacies *themselves*, and take on insider identities as new literacies practitioners in their professional lives. That is, if educators are to avoid the trap of trying to find "educationally useful things to do" with technology (Bigum, 2002, p. 130, cited in Lankshear & Knobel, 2006, p. 185) – which usually means assimilating new technologies in tokenistic fashion as appendages to existing pedagogical practices – then educators need to understand from the inside the meaning, value and purpose of the new literacies practices enabled by technology. This implies that we as teacher educators need to use new literacies as part of our everyday practices by, for example, maintaining a blog or actively participating in other web 2.0 forums.

However, while creative challenges to traditional modes of teaching and learning are encouraged, in order for new ways of learning and interacting in teacher education not to become assimilated into the business as usual "regime of pedagogy" (Gore, 1993, p. 119), as teacher educators we need to, not only seek what will always be an ever-elusive alignment between the pedagogy argued for and the pedagogy of the argument, but also share our aims, purposes and practices explicitly with student teachers, and be open to ways in which this dialogue might point to unconsidered possibilities for new literacies-infused pedagogy. This will mean that one core component of any task becomes a process of jointly unpacking its assumptions, purposes and value at both the content *and* experiential level of teacher learning, *as well as* the level of its application to the school classroom, as part of building and promoting meta-level awareness of, and dialogue about, pedagogy. In this way we may be able to move towards designing new literacies-infused teacher education that goes some way to recognizing and working with the power relations that inevitably inhere in the pedagogical encounter, whilst at the same time being relevant and responsive to the changing nature and requirements of literacy in the 21st century.

REFERENCES

Anstey, M., & Bull, G. (2006). *Teaching and learning multiliteracies: Changing times, changing literacies*. Newark, DE: International Reading Association.

Barton, D., Hamilton, M., & Ivanic, R. (Eds.). (2000). *Situated literacies: Reading and writing in context*. London: Routledge.

Barton, D., & Tusting, K. (Eds.). (2005). *Beyond communities of practice: Language, power, and social context*. Cambridge: Cambridge University Press.

Bender, L. (Producer), & Guggenheim, D. (Director) (2006). *An inconvenient truth*. [Motion picture]. USA: Paramount Classics.

Biggs, J. (1999). *Teaching for quality learning at university*. Buckingham, UK: Open University Press.

Bigum, C. (2002). Design sensibilities, schools, and the new computing and communications technologies. In I. Snyder (Ed.), *Silicon literacies* (pp. 130-140). London: Falmer-Routledge.

Black, R. W. (2007). Digital design: English language learners and reader reviews in online fiction. In M. Knobel & C. Lankshear (Eds.), *A New Literacies Sampler* (pp. 271-286). New York: Peter Lang.

Boud, D., & Middleton, H. (2003). Learning from others at work: Communities of practice and informal learning. *Journal of Workplace Learning, 15*(5), 194–203. doi:10.1108/13665620310483895

Buysse, V., Sparkman, K., & Wesley, P. (2003). Communities of practice: Connecting what we know with what we do. *Exceptional Children, 69*(3), 263–278.

Chow, P., & Chou, C. (2000). Evaluating sustained silent reading in reading classes. *The Internet TESL Journal, 6*(11).

Collins, J., & Blot, R. (2003). *Literacy and literacies: Texts, power and identity*. Cambridge, UK: Cambridge University Press.

Cope, B., & Kalantzis, M. (Eds.). (2000). *Multiliteracies: Literacy learning and the design of social futures*. New York: Routledge.

Curriculum Development Council. (2002). *English Language Education: Key Learning Area Curriculum Guide (Primary 1 - Secondary 3)*. Hong Kong: Government Printer.

Curriculum Development Council. (2004). *English Language Education Key Learning Area: English Language Curriculum Guide (Primary 1-6)*. Hong Kong: Government Printer.

Etheridge, M. (2006). I Need to Wake up Now [Recorded by Melissa Etheridge]. On *An inconvenient truth* [CD]. USA: The Island Def Jam Music Group.

Evans, J. (Ed.). (2005). *Literacy moves on: Popular culture, new technologies and digital literacies in the elementary classroom*. Portsmouth, NH: Heinemann.

Fetterman, D.M. (2002). Empowerment evaluation: Building communities of practice and a culture of learning. *American Journal of Community Psychology, 30*(1), 89–103. doi:10.1023/A:1014324218388

Firkins, A., & Forey, G. (2006). Changing the literacy habitus of a Hong Kong secondary school. In W. D. Bokhurst-Heng, M. D. Osborne & K. Lee (Eds.), *Redesigning pedagogy: Reflections on theory and praxis* (pp.33-46). Rotterdam: Sense Publishers.

Foucault, M. (1977). *Discipline and punish*. London: Penguin.

Freebody, P., & Luke, A. (1990). 'Literacies' programs: Debates and demands in cultural context. *Prospect, 5*(3), 7–16.

Fullan, M. (2001). *The new meaning of educational change* (3rd Ed.). Columbia University, NY: Teachers College Press.

Gee, J. P. (2004). Learning languages as a matter of learning social languages within discourses. In M. Hawkins (Ed.), *Language learning and teacher education: A sociocultural approach* (pp. 13-31). Clevedon, UK: Multilingual Matters.

Gee, J. P. (2005). Semiotic social spaces and affinity spaces: From the age of mythology to today's schools. In D. Barton & K. Tusting (Eds.), *Beyond communities of practice: Language, power, and social context* (pp. 214-232). Cambridge, UK: Cambridge University Press.

Gee, J. P. (2008). *Social linguistics and literacies: Ideology in discourses* (3rd Ed.). New York: Routledge.

Gore, J. (1993). *The struggle for pedagogies: Critical and feminist discourses as regimes of truth*. New York: Routledge.

Grabe, W. (2002). Reading in a second language. In R. B. Kaplan (Ed.), *The Oxford handbook of applied linguistics* (pp. 49-59). New York: Oxford University Press.

Graham, W., Osgood, D., & Karren, J. (1998). A real-life community of practice. *Training & Development, 52*(5), 34–39.

Hung, D., & Nichani, M. R. (2002). Bringing communities of practice into schools: Implications for instructional technologies from Vygotskian perspectives. *International Journal of Instructional Media, 29*(2), 171–184.

Johnson, K. (2009). *Second language teacher education: A sociocultural perspective*. New York: Routledge.

Kapitzke, C. (2000). Cyber pedagogy as critical social practice in a teacher education program. *Teaching Education, 11*(2), 211–229. doi:10.1080/713698968

Kist, W. (2005). *New literacies in action: Teaching and learning in multiple media*. New York: Teachers College Press.

Kress, G. (2003). *Literacy in the new media age*. London: Routledge.

Lam, W. S. E. (2000). L2 literacy and the design of the self: A case study of a teenager writing on the internet. *TESOL Quarterly, 34*(3), 457–482. doi:10.2307/3587739

Lankshear, C., & Knobel, M. (2006). *New literacies: Everyday practices and classroom learning* (2nd Ed.). Buckingham, UK: Open University Press.

Larson, J., & Marsh, J. (2005). *Making literacy real: Theories and practices for learning and teaching*. London: Sage.

Lave, J., & Wenger, E. (1991). *Situated learning: Legitimate peripheral participation*. Cambridge, UK: Cambridge University Press.

Lee, J., & Valdarrama, K. (2003). Building successful communities of practice. *Information Outlook, 7*(5), 28–32.

Lessig, L. (2004). *Free culture: How big media uses technology and the law to lock down culture and control creativity*. London: Penguin.

Lin, A. (2001). Resistance and creativity in English reading lessons in Hong Kong. In B. Comber & A. Simpson (Eds.), *Negotiating critical literacies in classrooms* (pp. 83-100). Mahwah, NJ: Lawrence Erlbaum Associates.

Love, K. (2006). Literacy in K-12 teacher education: The case study of a multimedia resource. In L. Hin & Subramaniam (Eds.), *Handbook of research on literacy in technology at the K-12 level* (pp. 469-492). Hershey, PA: Idea Group Reference.

Love, K., Pigdon, K., Baker, G., & Hamston, J. (2005). *Building Understandings in Literacy and Teaching* (BUILT). Melbourne, Australia: University of Melbourne.

Luke, C. (2000). New literacies in teacher education. *Journal of Adolescent & Adult Literacy, 43*(5), 424–435.

Mills, K. (2007). "Have you seen *Lord of the Rings*?" Power, pedagogy, and discourses in a multiliteracies classroom. *Journal of Language, Identity, and Education, 6*(3), 221–241.

Moreno, A. (2001). Enhancing knowledge exchange through Communities of Practice at the Inter-American Development Bank. *Aslib Proceedings: New Information Perspectives, 53*(8), 296–308.

Nieto, S. (2002). *Language, culture, and teaching: Critical perspectives for a new century*. Mahwah, NJ: Lawrence Erlbaum Associates.

Porter, M. (2003). Fostering L.I.N.C.S. among educators: The role of international service-learning in fostering a community of practice. *Teacher Education Quarterly, 30*(4), 51–62.

Rover, D. (2003). A sense of community: Learning about versus learning to be / What is a community of practice? *Journal of Engineering Education, 92*(1), 3–5.

Rowsell, J., Kosnik, C., & Beck, C. (2008). Fostering multiliteracies pedagogy through preservice teacher education. *Teaching Education, 19*(2), 109–122. doi:10.1080/10476210802040799

Sefton-Green, J. (Ed.). (1998). *Digital diversions: Youth culture in the age of multimedia*. London: UCL Press.

Street, B. (1995). *Social literacies: Critical approaches to literacy in development, ethnography and education*. Harlow, UK: Longman.

Thomas, A. (2007). *Youth online: Identity and literacy in the digital age*. New York: Peter Lang.

Tse, S. K., Lam, W. I., Lam, Y. H., & Loh, E. K. Y. (2005). *Learn to Read: The performance of Hong Kong primary 4 pupils in PIRLS 2001*. Hong Kong: Hong Kong University Press.

Unsworth, L. (2001). *Teaching multiliteracies across the curriculum: Changing contexts of texts and image in classroom practice*. Buckingham, UK: Open University Press.

Walsh, C. (2007). Creativity as capital in the literacy classroom: Youth as multimodal designers. *Literacy, 41*(2), 79–85. doi:10.1111/j.1467-9345.2007.00461.x

Wenger, E. (1998). *Communities of practice: Learning, meaning and identity*. Cambridge, UK: Cambridge University Press.

Wesley, P., & Buysse, V. (2001). Communities of practice: Expanding professional roles to promote reflection and shared inquiry. *Topics in Early Childhood Special Education, 21*(2), 114–124. doi:10.1177/027112140102100205

Williams, M. (1999). Learning teaching: A social constructivist approach – theory and practice or theory with practice? In H. Trappes-Lomax & I. McGrath (Eds.), *Theory in language teacher education* (pp. 11-20). Harlow, UK: Longman.

Chapter 11
ICT Integration in Second Language Writing: A Malay Language Case Study

Christina Gitsaki
The University of Queensland, Australia

Abduyah Ya'akub
The University of Queensland, Australia

Eileen Honan
The University of Queensland, Australia

ABSTRACT

As the integration of information and communications technologies (ICT) in Singapore schools reaches a considerable level of maturity and stability, a pertinent question is: how has ICT integration impacted on pedagogy in Singapore schools? The present study attempts to address this question through interpretive, case-study research in two Singaporean secondary schools. The study found the use of ICT was limited in its perceived pedagogical value by teachers. A lack of appreciation and/or understanding of the complexity of the process or culture shift required for ICT to be implemented and integrated effectively into the Malay Language Curriculum along with conformity to policy directions resulted in underutilisation and uncritical use of ICT tools, and an adherence to the traditional method of assigning tasks and the maintenance of existing practices.

INTRODUCTION

The impact that ICT is having on the education sector is a pervasive issue. There is a need for research in this field, not least because governments worldwide are investing heavily in the provision of hardware and software to educational institutions as well as in the training of teachers and students of all ages in the application of ICT in teaching and learning (Loveless & Ellis, 2001). More children than ever are surfing the Internet (Net). They are the "Net-Generation" (Oblinger & Oblinger, 2005). This is the generation of children learning, playing and communicating in ways very different from that of their parents. It is now a challenge for educators to design and deliver programs that are optimal for current learners. While use of the Net has potential dangers

DOI: 10.4018/978-1-60566-673-0.ch011

which include misinformation (Luke, 2000) and Internet addiction (Khoo, 2001), it nevertheless provides potentially unlimited opportunities for education, entertainment and enterprise (McNeely, 2005). The use of ICT therefore, provides countless multimodal opportunities for teachers and students to teach and learn with, if the technology is used appropriately. In many educational contexts, the application of ICT tools in classrooms has become an overt illustration of the application of theories about new literacies and multiliteracies. The case studies reported on in this chapter provide an example of the assumptions inherent in such a coupling, that is, that a multiliteracies approach to language and literacy education is essentially based on an integration of ICT into classroom practice.

BACKGROUND

ICT is integral to the overall vision for education as expressed in Singapore's *Thinking Schools and Learning Nation* (TSLN) (Saravanan, 2005) initiative that seeks to make Singapore a nation of thinking and committed citizens. Under this vision, Singapore has shifted away from an efficiency-driven education towards an ability-driven one that aims to develop and harness the abilities of every child. The focus is on the creation of learner-centred learning environments, the nurturing of thinking skills and creativity through formal and informal curricula. ICT is viewed as a "mediating tool" but not as a subject of study for many of these processes in the schools. The focus in the TSLN policy is therefore not changing an understanding of literacy in favour of a 21st century version that is more closely associated with a multiliteracies approach, but the TSLN has focused on the integration of ICT tools and software in traditional curricula.

In Singapore schools students may study Malay as a second language, and the Malay Language Curriculum incorporates the National vision of TSLN and allocates 30% of curriculum time using ICT (MOE, 2003). The use of ICT in Malay writing classrooms was designed to develop increasingly independent learners who are confident users of ICT; exploring and finding out for themselves solutions to problems. With greater peer interaction in writing lessons using ICT compared to non-ICT lessons (Hennessy, 2000), the use of ICT is supposed to promote collaborative work among students (Towndrow, 2005). The use of ICT in mainstream schooling has been widely expected to penetrate and transform teaching and learning across the curriculum (Loveless & Ellis, 2001).

However, some scholars (Cuban, 2001; Hennessy, Deaney & Ruthven, 2003; Tearle, 2003) argue, whilst ICT use in education is increasing, this "transformation" has not yet occurred, and the extent and nature of ICT integration in schools is still very varied, and in many instances limited. Perhaps the high expectation of the role ICT could play in schools places both opportunities and challenges for those involved in its implementation and application for learning. The main focus in the present study is to explore how ICT impacts and extend learning in subject areas particularly in the Malay Language context, whilst also unpacking the connection between ICT and multiliteracies.

ICT AND SECOND LANGUAGE WRITING PEDAGOGY

Warschauer (2000) argues that ICT empower students and give them greater control over their own learning, thus increasing their agency. Indeed, agency is really what makes students so excited about using computers in the classroom that is the student has some level of control over their own learning. Most of the studies in this area (e.g., Parks, Huot, Hamers, & Lemonnier, 2005; Spires, Lee & Turner, 2008) conclude that the computer does provide students with a powerful means of placing their stamp on the world. For example, the word processing tool found with most office type applications, has been found to provide learners with the opportunity to participate willingly and enthusiastically in the production of second language writing material (Mumtaz & Hammond, 2002; Russell, Bebell, Cowan & Corbelli, 2003; Goldberg, Russel & Cook, 2003). Vygotsky (1978) points out that one of the difficulties that a learner has in writing is that he or she addresses "an absent or an imaginary person or no one in particular" and thus has no motivation or feels no need to write, whereas in oral conversation "every sentence is prompted by a motive" (Vygotsky, 1978, p. 99). In contrast, writing generated through ICT is usually for a particular audience and for a particular purpose. Thus, the writing becomes a tool for exchanging information, interacting with others and challenging opinions among a group of learners (Lin et al., 2005). If used purposefully in writing classrooms, ICT is able to help second language learners to establish audience, purpose and context.

At the same time as ICT offers all this potential to second language student writers, certain issues of literacy remain unresolved. There is evidence that ICT can help students to produce good writing and teachers to teach more effectively in second language classrooms, but there is no clear message in such evidence that ICT will make a difference simply by being used (Salvo, 2002). A review of the literature on ICT and second language writing pedagogy reveals that although ICT can improve learning, there are a number of issues that need to be considered if this suite of tools is going to make a difference. Given this, teachers should offer students self-directed learning activities that encourage self-expression. Small-group collaboration with computers is effective when students have received training in the collaborative process (Vallance & Towndrow, 2007). Teachers also need to be effective in integrating ICT into the curriculum, with teachers using ICT benefiting from a social network of other ICT-using teachers at their school. Some caution is therefore called for at the broad level in terms of where and how ICT might have an impact on second language writing pedagogy, especially in the area of the "informed use" of ICT in second language writing classrooms (Adams, 2007). For instance, if the main goal of a second language writing class is the development of argumentative skills, then teachers need to know what types of computer mediated communications are best suited to teach those skills (Salvo, 2002). Students are able to analyse how information is presented and how different modes of presentation create impact. They also have the opportunity to interact effectively as well as learn to acquire grammar and linguistic structures and patterns which can be used to create various discourse forms or text types depending on the linguistic choices made (Lin, Cranton & Bridglall, 2005). In essence, students have to be taught how ICT can help them make these linguistic choices to suit purpose, audience, context and culture at both local and international levels (Reynolds, 2005). Students need to also be aware of the changing nature of literacy practices in relation to computer mediated communications and gain an understanding of the multiple forms of texts available in these contexts, as such a multiliteracies perspective.

What is becoming increasingly clear is that within the learning of second language writing in which ICT is to be used, it is important for students to analyse the interrelationship between the knowledge domain and the proposed use of digital and non-digital tools, together with a consideration of the culture, context of learning, the students' previous history of learning and the ways in which the teacher interacts with students throughout the learning process (Kim & Kim, 2005). What ICT has done is to draw attention to both the tool-using aspects of this human endeavor and to appropriate theories of learning. In this way, the use of ICT can become a tool for enhanced theorizing of teaching and learning in addition to extending the computer writing environment by linking student writers to other people with whom they may interact to develop their own writing (Kaplan, 2000; Kress, 2003). Through a computer network, students' computers may be linked to those of their teachers' as well as those of other students as a way to develop collaborative work or to gain input into their writing other than by face-to-face interaction (Parks et al., 2003; 2005).

There has been considerable interplay over the years between research into writing and learning and instructions using ICT in the teaching of second language writing. Much of the research has had direct repercussions on the classroom, with classroom practice and observation often the source of these research studies (Wang & Wen, 2002). This interplay has made writing a dynamic and fruitful area of work and is a clear theme in reviews of the use of ICT in second language writing research (see Goldberg et al., 2003; Kroll, 2003; Laurinen & Marttunen, 2007; Parks et al., 2005; Taylor & Gitsaki, 2004). What is less clear is the relationship between this interplay of writing research and ICT in second language classrooms and the development of a multiliteracies approach to second language learning. In the case studies presented in this chapter it is clear that while there is a significant relationship between the writing pedagogy used by the teachers in their classrooms and the use of particular ICT tools, there has been little work done in these schools or classrooms on changing inherent understandings of the meaning of literacy in the 21st Century.

RESEARCH DESIGN AND METHODS

The present study examined the use of ICT in two Malay Language classrooms in two high schools in Singapore. School A is a girls' secondary school located in an inner-city area. It is among one of the elite schools in Singapore, famous for its record of academic and sports excellence. The school boasts two computer labs. These rooms are in great demand and often timetabled for other uses. It employs two full time technical staff to assist teachers with the use of ICT. The school has a special Malay Language classroom where students attend the Malay Language lessons. This special room is equipped with a computer and local area network (LAN) access for the teacher to connect to a data projector or the Internet. The teacher who participated in the study is called Mrs Aminah. She began her teaching career ten years ago. Mrs Aminah has a strong academic background, but it is her love for teaching and the Malay Language which she believes made her choose the profession. Her students are in Secondary 3 (Year 10). There are 25 girls altogether in this class; 21 Malay, two Chinese and two Indian students. The students are high achievers, task-oriented and motivated to excel academically.

School B is a co-educational secondary school located on the outskirts of Singapore. Almost all students who gain entry to this school are among the middle and lower ability band of students. The cohort is comprised of students in the Secondary 3 (Year 10) Express class. There are two girls and eight boys altogether in this class; eight Malay, one Chinese and one Indian student. They are of average ability but are motivated to learn and explore new challenges. The school believes in forward-thinking curriculum innovations and it is strongly oriented towards showcasing teachers' use of ICT in classrooms. The school employs one full time technical staff member to assist teachers and has three computer labs. Like School A, School B also has a special Malay Language classroom. There are two Malay Language teachers in this school but only one participated in this study. Mr Muhammad agreed to be involved in this study because he is very passionate about computers and believes the use of ICT in the Malay Language classroom may improve students' language learning. He is an enthusiastic, young teacher about 27 years old and has been teaching Malay Language in the school for the past four years. Mr Muhammad is also actively involved in conducting sharing sessions and free workshops for the Teachers' Network at the Ministry of Education training centre. In these workshops, Mr Muhammad shares with other teachers how to use some of the software available to help them teach the Malay Language in their day-to-day classroom teaching.

Data were collected using classroom observations (five lessons from each classroom on one unit of work: students in Classroom A had to write a speech as a famous person for the opening of a school; students in Classroom B had to write an argumentative essay on the use of recycled water); teacher and student interviews (10 students from each class were interviewed); and a small student survey to explore students' attitudes towards the use of ICT for learning. In the following sections, the most significant findings of the study are discussed.

IMPACT OF ICT ON MALAY LANGUAGE CURRICULUM

In Singapore, the Malay Language Curriculum has three foci when describing pedagogical approaches to be used in the teaching of writing: a process oriented approach; learner-centredness; and contextualisation. The impact of ICT on this curriculum is therefore discussed here under each of these foci.

In the Malay Language Curriculum, the process oriented approach to the teaching of writing is described as having planning, drafting, editing, and publishing phases. The Internet was used in both classrooms during the planning stage of the writing task. The majority of the students from both classrooms felt that the Internet connection was too slow and on many occasions technical problems were stumbling blocks in their effort to use the materials effectively in the computer mediated lessons. In fact both of the teachers argued that they had to have an alternative plan in case there were problems with the Internet connection.

However, the Internet did facilitate students' learning to a certain extent. Two of the many benefits of Internet use in both classrooms were put forward by the teachers and the students. Firstly, the teachers indicated during the interviews that the Internet had helped students in gathering the information needed for their writing task. Students from both classrooms advocated that the Internet had not only furnished them with authentic, reliable and accurate information but also provided interesting images. The students believed that these images helped them to remember important facts about the writing topic. Secondly a few students gave feedback that the materials available from the Internet were usually formatted in an aesthetically pleasing and uncluttered manner that enabled students to generate more ideas. Some students claimed that the Google search engine for instance provided students with an added advantage as it allowed access to cached websites. The students believed that these added features on the Internet helped them to organise their ideas in the planning phase.

In the drafting and editing phase of the writing task, students should be given ample time to work on the writing task. With adequate discussion, exploration and organisation of ideas in the planning stage, students could then start to do their drafting and editing. Unlike the planning stage where both Mrs Aminah and Mr Muhammad made use of the Internet for students to search for information and generate ideas for the writing, in the drafting and editing stage, the teachers differed in their use of ICT tools. Mrs Aminah had asked the students in Classroom A to draft and edit their text on speech writing using the word processor, whereas Mr Muhammad used blogging for students to draft and edit short paragraphs consisting of a few arguments. The students commented that blogging helped them to play with ideas for their writing, ask for clarification about confusing details, show readers their emotional responses to the writing topic and question the believability of their peers' writing. However one disadvantage of Mr Muhammad's holistic approach to teaching writing was that there was no drafting and editing of the completed argumentative text. The only drafting and editing that occurred in Classroom B was in relation to the blog. Thus blogging was used as a tool for drafting and editing short paragraphs but not the argumentative essay which the students were required to do. What the students wrote on the blog was not a draft of the essay but only short paragraphs that did not reflect the structure and appropriate form which would be expected in an argumentative essay. The students from Mr Muhammad's class did indicate that they received feedback from other students on their writing but were disappointed that Mr Muhammad did not provide such feedback. The students noted that Mr Muhammad did not focus much on conventions that involved correctness in sentence formation, usage, and mechanics. Brush and Saye (2000) suggest that teachers who are teaching low and average-ability groups like Mr Muhammad's students should prepare some specifically-directed questions or prompts during the drafting and editing session so that the students can find useful writing tips to improve the quality of the content and mechanics including corrections of spelling, punctuation, sentence structure and argumentative style. Editing requires a great amount of skill on the students' part, and close supervision from the teacher (Ferris, 2007). Mr Muhammad could have used the available ICT tools to teach editing and reviewing skills that the students needed or perhaps use ICT tools to facilitate communication with his students about drafting, editing and revising the students' argumentative essays (Lamb & Johnson, 2006).

In the publishing phase of the writing task, the majority of the students in Mrs Aminah's class reported that they found it much easier to draft, edit, revise and improve their text on a word processor. If they had done their writing by hand, they claimed that they would have to completely rewrite their work, which they often found dull and boring. They felt that writing on the computer allowed them to go back and forth in their writing process, to draft and edit at the same time and gave them the opportunity to check and ensure their writing was not repetitive. The students also claimed that they were more thorough and revised their work more often because of the cut and paste function available from the word processing tool. However looking at the students' final writing, one cannot but wonder whether we are really preparing our students for the 21st Century if we do not allow them to actually produce a multimodal text. The students in the present study produced plain texts on white paper and not multimodal ones.

Learner-Centredness

A learner-centred approach defines learning as individual "discovery" (Walker & Baets, 2000). The learner is at the centre of the learning process. Learner-centred learning is an active and dynamic process through which learners develop deep understanding while taking responsibility for their own learning. This process will help to provide learners with the best possible educational experiences in a flexible and stimulating environment. It would also enable students to have access to the resources that help them as individual learners develop skills and self-awareness of their own learning processes, develop increasing independence in their learning and give learners greater autonomy and control over their learning methods and pace of study (Pedersen & Liu, 2003).

In this study, Mrs Aminah used a didactic approach in her writing pedagogy. For instance, she wrote on the whiteboard each step that the students should take. This type of scaffolding was unnecessary for her higher academic students. Most of the time students were sitting and listening to what Mrs Aminah was saying. Her style of teaching did not fit with the learner-centred approach, which requires students to be active learners. In one of her responses in the interview, Mrs Aminah draws on quite conflicting and contradictory discourses. For example she said "the use of ICT promotes independent learning". Later in the interview she mentioned "I cannot leave my students to make their own decisions and explore what is in the websites. I feel that I have to guide them by giving step by step procedures and clear instructions for them to follow. I do not have the time to let them explore." This is contrary to the learner-centred approach where students have access to the resources and are able to discover knowledge on their own (Pedersen & Liu, 2003). While this pedagogical approach (Atkinson, 2001; 2002) should promote exploration and independent learning, Mrs Aminah's teaching technique is more like spoon-feeding her students.

Perhaps the reason for her conflicting ideas was that Mrs Aminah assimilated herself to the traditional Malay notion of teaching and the role of the teacher in the classroom. She believed that the teacher needs to be in control of what is happening in classroom. The lesson procedure reaffirms the instructional pattern characterized by a linear sequence with the teacher in almost total control of all the learning tasks. Secondly, at the design level, the tasks designed were all teacher-centred with minimum interaction between students. During a 60 minute lesson, direct teaching took up approximately 40 minutes, which was used for logging in, reading, explaining the lexical features, assigning, translating, paraphrasing tasks and other decontextualised comprehension and written exercises.

Another possible reason for Mrs Aminah's teacher-centred approach could be that School A emphasized academic excellence. Possibly Mrs Aminah was keen to utilise teaching methods that have proven to be effective and ensured results. She did mention that she had a syllabus to cover, and thus allowing her students to explore the websites on their own meant that "more time would be wasted". Innovation and adaptation are costly in terms of the time needed to develop and establish new practices. It appears that a technocentric traditional writing classroom is emerging in Classroom A. A learner-centred approach in writing pedagogy gives learners greater autonomy and control over learning methods. However, in this case, the students in Classroom A were given little autonomy to be responsible for their own learning. Mrs Aminah still adopted the teacher-oriented approach with which she was comfortable.

Nevertheless a number of students in Classroom A felt that the use of PowerPoint slides that the teacher used in the writing classroom gave them greater autonomy over the pace of their study. A student wrote that the PowerPoint slides can be read and viewed at any time, and the learner's own ability to understand the slides determines how fast or slowly they learnt. In Mrs Aminah's class she did give time for students to read the slides at their own pace.

In contrast, Mr Muhammad let the students conduct searches on their own without his guidance or specific instructions most of the time. Mr Muhammad claimed that the students were equipped with the confidence and technical skills to explore and "discover" for themselves and that they would find websites that were relevant to the writing topic, and that students themselves searched using keywords. It was up to the students to use whichever search engine they were comfortable and familiar with. Mr Muhammad believed that his students had the ability to perform web searchers and gather the required information. Unlike Mrs Aminah, Mr Muhammad did not write detailed instructions on the white board for his students. Mr Muhammad wanted to empower his students to take control and for the students to be responsible for their own learning within the learning process whilst at the same time preparing the students to become lifelong learners.

In the Malay Language Curriculum learner-centred pedagogy emphasises learner flexibility and control over one's own learning (MOE, 2003). The use of e-mail could have been used to promote this learner-centred pedagogy. Strenski, Feagin and Singer (2005) argue that e-mail can be successfully used as a medium for peer review functions where students exchange text. Students who are normally quiet in the classroom and shy to communicate in person-to-person situations are more than twice as likely to communicate with greater ease online (Noel & Robert, 2003). Among the causes for this decrease in communicative apathy is a decrease in social pressures inherent to the classroom environment (Itakura, 2004). Both teachers could have taken advantage of the benefits of e-mail to enhance the curriculum by empowering these students (Warschauer & Ware, 2006) to engage in this type of editing and peer-conferencing and permit them to develop a personal vision of the final draft they wish to achieve (Guardado & Shi, 2007). Although e-mail as a medium for peer review functions best when guided by particular criteria designed to craft the logistics of text exchange as well as to guide the focus and tone of peer response which was one of the greatest assets of e-mail peer review (Strenski et al., 2005), Mrs Aminah was not comfortable with the idea of distancing herself from authority and control. As for Mr Muhammad he preferred using blogging to e-mail as a communication tool. Consequently in both classrooms e-mail was not fully materialised to achieve learner-centred computer mediated instructions.

Through the classroom observations, interviews and reflections, it became apparent that there were variations present in the teaching approaches between the two teachers. Mrs Aminah indicated that she needed to pay particular attention to her students and monitor them closely. Mr Muhammad on the other hand gave his students much more freedom to explore the topic using the Internet. The students in Classroom B were observed to participate actively in a stimulating environment. The difference in approach used could be due to differences in students' ability that may have an impact on the use of a learner-centred approach.

The differences in teaching approaches may be explained by considering the school context. Traditionally in schools with higher academic achievement classrooms, teachers tend to teach in didactic ways and are not concerned about learner-centredness, whereas schools that are not so worried about academic achievement have tended to experiment more with innovative practices associated with the learner-centred approach (Dawes, 2001; Deaney, Ruthven & Hennessy, 2004). Mrs Aminah's delivery approach adopted in Classroom A is in alignment with Towndrow's (2005) argument that most teachers use traditionalist pedagogy because historically their approach has proven to have produced excellent examination results. Schools that target higher academic achievement consider academic achievement as the end goal and provide students with content-loaded lessons leaving very little room for discovery and exploration (Demetriadis, Barbas, Molohides, Palaigeorgiou, Psillos, Vlahavas, Tsoukalas & Pombortsis, 2003).

Given that Mrs Aminah's students were high achievers and task-oriented it was anticipated that the students were more disciplined and required little supervision. Only 40% of the students in Classroom A compared to 80% of the students in Classroom B indicated that they were given the opportunities to choose or plan class activities when computers are used. This reflects that in Classroom A, Mrs Aminah was very much in control in the computer-mediated classroom. However Mr Muhammad's students, who were average in ability, were less controlled as compared to students in Classroom A. Mr Muhammad was more relaxed and trusted his students would do the writing task given and not divert their attention to other irrelevant stuff. While the two teachers followed the same Singapore Malay Language Curriculum and attempted to integrate ICT in the writing lesson, their interpretation of the term learner-centeredness varies.

The teachers participating in this study valued collaboration, but primarily as an end in itself, that is, so that students developed skills for working with others. While the two teachers also cited creative ideas as reasons for collaboration, none of these teachers talked about other potential benefits of collaboration such as the opportunity to identify misconceptions during collaborative exchanges. It became apparent that teachers had "bought into" collaboration, but did not recognize its full potential impact on learning and how it could further enhance the Malay Language Curriculum. The teachers in this study, especially in School A, could have done more in terms of letting the students explore further and challenged them to produce writing which is creative and original.

Contextualisation

The Malay Language Curriculum states that Contextualisation demonstrates how purpose, audience, context and culture determine the register or appropriateness of speech and writing in both formal and informal situations (MOE, 2003). Language skills, grammatical items and structures are taught and learnt in the context of language use.

In terms of audience, both teachers were not able to provide students with a real sense of audience. ICT offers a wide range of tools that has the potential to provide students with a real audience (Kozma & Anderson, 2002), however the teachers did not fully utilise this potential. In Mrs Aminah's classroom, it was a pretend situation for the students writing their speech. Mrs Aminah could have included other students, parents or other community members to be the audience for the students' speech writing task. However, she did not do significant work to help her students understand how important the audience is in determining language register. She exposed her students to the lexical features of speech writing by providing a sample of speech in her PowerPoint presentation. However she did not provide any post-writing activities for her students to give their speeches to real or virtual audiences. She mentioned how the students can influence the audience by their writing however the students could not relate what they have learnt to actual situations.

Mr Muhammad pointed out that he tried to extend the real audience for the blogging to include students from other schools. He planned to collaborate with Malay Language teachers from other schools and wanted to conduct an online debate about recycling water in Singapore. However the school principal declined his proposal as he wanted Mr Muhammad to only focus on his classroom teaching. Mr Muhammad was frustrated and did not agree with the principal's opinion. He stated during the interview that the students could have benefited much more if he expanded the audience to students from other schools. This was a typical example where a teacher experienced both a pressure to use ICT and a desire to exploit technology and to change pedagogy accordingly, but at the same time a set of constraints was placed on the use of the technology (Hennessy, Deaney & Ruthven, 2005). The effect of these top-down policies has been a perception of eroded autonomy and a feeling of disempowerment in teachers (Kirk & MacDonald, 2001).

Other than blogging, the students in Classroom B did not write for a real audience. Mr Muhammad could have asked his students to write to a newspaper editor to voice their opinions on the use of recycled water in Singapore. To provide a writing assignment with a real sense of audience is critical as such activities suggest to students that writing has a social purpose and function targeted at a particular authentic audience (Wilson, 2006). In both classrooms there was no sense of a real audience.

In terms of culture, the searches that the students did on the Internet had no relation to the Malay culture and as a result deprived the students of the opportunity to experience the authentic context of the Malay Language and culture. With the right topic, the Internet could have been a great opportunity to expose students to authentic Malay Language use and immerse them in the Malay culture. Instead students were accessing English websites and then transferred and translated the information to Malay Language. This caused problems with language interference. Language interference has an impact on the context of teaching and learning Malay Language writing. The students faced difficulties as they attempted to translate the English information into Malay writing. Some students commented that almost all the websites were in English. Most of the students indicated that they had problems translating the specific terms into Malay Language. As most of the search engines are in English, more than half of the students interviewed in Classroom A indicated they found it difficult to translate the English jargon and information into Malay. Even though the Google search engine allows students to change the language option using the language tool, when students would use Bahasa Indonesia as the preferred language there was a limited choice of resources with a pop up menu appearing to inform that the: "Page is not available". Thus the students had little choice but to conduct their search in English. As a consequence, the teachers found the students translating word for word from English to Malay which resulted in language interference and the use of inappropriate language structures. Mrs Aminah commented that many problems were faced by students who were weak in Malay Language. Most of them did direct translations and there was one student who wrote 50% of her final draft in English thinking that the student who edited her work would do the translation for her. The problem of language interference would not have existed in the first place if Mrs Aminah and Mr Muhammad had chosen writing topics associated with the Malay Language, culture and chosen appropriate websites.

With regard to how ICT helped to establish contextualisation, three points are of particular interest. The use of ICT in this study had limited impact on the purpose, context, and culture in the Malay Language writing because of the underutilisation of ICT tools in the computer-mediated classrooms. Another finding reflects that the use of blogging did help students in Classroom B to address their readers however the ICT tools used in Classroom A have yet to address any particular group of readers. Finally in this study, ICT played an insignificant role to reinforce the concept of contextualisation in the Malay Language writing classrooms because of the uncritical use of ICT tools.

In terms of using ICT in writing pedagogy, Mrs Aminah and Mr Muhammad are not radically different. Even though both teachers were following the curriculum, they were following it in different ways. In terms of process orientation, the teachers focused on different parts, for instance Mrs Aminah's use of ICT tools did not address the students' needs for producing good speech. By focusing on achieving a particular set of planned instructional outcomes which was getting information about famous people, Mrs Aminah overlooked and suppressed student autonomy and self-directed discovery. Next is the use of PowerPoint which could have been made more interactive to facilitate conversational dialogue between student, teachers and peers without much additional knowledge and effort (Adams, 2007). PowerPoint can be a powerful tool to encourage analytical thinking and interpretive understanding (Vallance & Towndrow, 2007). Instead the high achievers, enthusiastic and inquisitive nature of students in Classroom A were reshaped and made into passive listeners and receivers of knowledge.

In the case of Mr Muhammad, ICT is viewed as a panacea. However, Mr Muhammad did not provide adequate scaffolding and guidance for his average students to benefit from using ICT effectively (Oh & Jonnasen, 2007). Mr Muhammad did not relate to his students the link between the blogging activity and writing an argumentative essay. Therefore the students were not able to connect the lessons as a series of writing activities which reinforce the process of writing an argumentative essay. Entries in the blog could be used by Mr Muhammad to do a follow up on difficult areas of writing an argumentative essay that might need review or clarification. Hence the use of blogs in Classroom B is rather limited.

This study clearly highlights tensions between the idealized world of ICT use reflected in policy documents and the aspirations of policy makers, politicians, and the harsher realities of schools, where ICT use is often more embryonic. The challenge for the Malay Language teachers is how to retain their enthusiasm for ICT in the face of the "culture shock" they are likely to experience in schools. The classroom practices in this study reflect limited ICT integration in teaching and learning.

The study also found that when teachers used ICT in teaching second language writing, it was often to achieve print-based purposes in print-oriented ways. There are very real systemic reasons to explain this phenomenon that go beyond Malay Language teachers' reticence to engage with new technologies. The Malay Language writing classrooms are constrained by the static model of schools as institutions that prevents careful inquiry into the new literacies and the expansive use of new media (Kirk & MacDonald, 2001). Teachers have little time to reflect on what they do, no matter what the proposed curriculum direction (Cuban, 2004) such that when teachers teach Malay Language writing using ICT in their classrooms, there is not much of an opportunity to build creative partnerships with colleagues from other schools and to experiment with new pedagogies and innovative practices for teaching Malay Language writing.

Innovative practices include activities that prepare students for lifelong learning in the information society (Kozma & Anderson, 2002). For instance Mrs Aminah indicated during the interview that although she attended some workshops about *dreamweaver* and *hotpotatoes* to teach writing, she dare not try new ideas as to experiment with new software was time consuming. Scholars (Sandholtz & Reilly, 2004; Shetzer & Warschauer, 2000) argue that professional training should focus on developing and equipping teachers with the knowledge to transfer the ICT tools learnt to pedagogical tools. Furthermore, Mrs Aminah was too afraid she would not be able to cover the syllabus that was stipulated by the MOE as new pedagogies means taking risk to implement them in Malay Language classrooms (Elstad, 2006). Other scholars (Lofty, 2003; Rizvi & Elliot, 2007) argue that teachers need time to experiment and explore with new pedagogies. This issue about time mirrors many of the themes highlighted by Cuban, Kirkpatrick and Peck (2001) and Deaney et al. (2004) that teachers' primary concern is teaching a specified curriculum over a set period of time. Thus Mrs Aminah resorted to teaching writing "the same old way" except using ICT such as the word processor to type the writing and the Internet to search for information. When ICT were used in this study, this was largely in ways familiar to teachers (Salvo, 2002).

From a socio-cultural perspective (Gee, 2004), taking a curriculum and pedagogy perspective based on the criterion of efficacious learning, the focus of learning and education is not children, nor schooling, but human lives seen as trajectories (Lankshear & Knobel, 2003) through multiple social practices in various social institutions. If learning is to be efficacious, then what a student does now as a learner must be connected in meaningful and motivated ways with "mature" (insider) versions of related social practices (Gee, 2004). The criterion of efficacy applies very strongly as an attempt to promote new writing pedagogy in classrooms. Efforts to incorporate new ICT into teaching and learning writing are often misguided from the standpoint of efficacious learning. Often schools enlist learners in characteristically "schoolish" practices that have little or no resemblance to life outside the classroom (Goodson & Knobel, 2003). Generally speaking, the teachers in this study were superficially preparing students for the 21st Century. They were not prepared to fully integrate ICT into the teaching of this young generation of people and even one of the teachers expressed that she felt more comfortable teaching writing to students without ICT. The challenge for teachers in this study is to make the classroom, as much as possible, a socially meaningful and relevant place to engage in the production of social texts for real purposes. This is crucial, as students need to understand that social practices depend on what they encounter in the way of social contexts (Spires, Lee & Turner, 2008).

ICT use in both Mr Muhammad's and Mrs Aminah's writing classrooms indicated that the lack of ICT resources and tools in their schools, resulted in their inability to further enhance the implementation of the Malay Language syllabus through computer mediated instructions and activities in the writing classrooms.

THE LIMITED PEDAGOGICAL VALUE OF USING ICT

Overall, this study showed that the use of ICT by Malay Language teachers was limited in pedagogical value because of the pressure experienced by the teachers to comply with the Ministry of Education's policy directions. The teachers were using ICT to conform to the policy document that required 30% of curriculum time to be spent using ICT in teaching. This resulted in teachers' uncritical use of ICT tools and adherence to the traditional method of assigning tasks. Teachers did not complement or go beyond established practice. For example, the evidence showed that students and teachers were only using the word processing tool to produce plain text instead of employing the multimedia tools available to them to incorporate dynamic visual or audio representations in their text production and create a multimodal text (Kress, 2003). The present study identified recurring features of ICT-mediated writing practices in classrooms that reflect a marked tendency to perpetuate the old, rather than to engage with and refine or reinvent the new as noted in other studies (e.g. Hennessy et al., 2005; Jones, Garralda, Li & Lock, 2006; Lankshear, Peter & Knobel, 2000). This approach has been referred to by Goodson & Knobel (2003) as the "old wine in new bottles" syndrome, whereby long-standing school literacy routines have a new technology tacked in here or there, without in any way changing the substance of pedagogical practice. In particular it is evident from these case studies that these traditional literacy routines will remain pervasive unless there is a significant rethinking about the place of literacies in contemporary contexts and a move to teach literacy with ICT through a multiliteracies perspective.

This has implications for policy makers who need to adopt a wider perspective on integrating ICT into the curriculum and classroom practice. This means giving the teachers enough flexibility to meet the objectives of curriculum and complete the syllabus without sacrificing their innovation and creativity. For instance the Ministry of Education's guideline that teachers need to spend 30% of the curriculum time using ICT should not be imposed as a regulation or rule to be strictly adhered by. More flexibility would empower teachers to embark on reflective teaching and productive pedagogies. Teachers would then be able to infuse ICT to support learning and sensibly build on and extend existing practice to enhance the Malay Language Curriculum. Empowered teachers would devise pedagogic strategies which maintain teachers' and students' attention to the subject matter and learning objectives and avoiding mechanical forms and superficial uses of ICT that distract attention away from the target objectives. It is particularly advisable that teachers are given the autonomy to display formidable credentials in terms of professional expertise in using ICT for subject teaching.

Apart from mandating teachers to allocate a substantial time to using ICT in classroom, the current Singapore policies are concerned with technologising learning and introducing sophisticated ICT tools into the classroom. Not surprisingly, teachers look for ways to fit these new technologies into their classrooms. Since educational ends are directed by curriculum, and technologies are "mere" tools, the task of integrating new technologies into learning is often realized by adapting them to familiar routines. One corollary of this is that making learners "technologically literate" is largely reduced to teaching them how to "drive" the new technologies. The emphasis is very much on technical or operational aspects: how to log in and out of blogs, add sound, insert a graphic, open and save files and so on. It is the "truth" that underpins many current claims that school learning is at odds with authentic ways of learning to be in the world, and with social practice beyond the school gates (Scott, 2006). It is recommended that policy and practice should be mutually conditioning and directly interrelated. In this view, policy-making may take the form of school-level or even classroom policy work. The policy must be responsive to change and give meaning and direction to school leaders and teachers to understand and experience the world within the institutional contexts (Sime & Priestley, 2005).

UNDERUTILISATION OF ICT TOOLS

A complementary theme arising from the present study that concerns the lack of pedagogical value is the underutilisation of ICT tools in the classrooms. For instance, one teacher used a weblog in his writing pedagogy but it was not used to scaffold lessons and guide students to develop their discursive genre writing skills (Bloch, 2006). Robert (2003) and Jones et al. (2006), argue that weblogs are an excellent tool for students to inquire and teachers to provide details on writing topic, give feedback, edit and revise ideas and writing. The use of weblogs in classroom is good writing pedagogy when used purposefully (Bloch, 2006; Richardson, 2006). In contrast, the teacher in this study failed to utilise the full potential of this ICT-based tool for teaching writing. Another useful tool is that of chat (Laurinen & Marttunen, 2007) that could be used as a platform for students to have quality argumentation about the topic and collaborate with other students in chat debates relevant to their writing activity. Both weblogs and chat could have been very useful had they been used appropriately by the teacher in this study. Another example of ICT underutilisation is the teacher in Classroom A who had used the PowerPoint presentation uncritically in her writing pedagogy. The teacher's use of PowerPoint had turned her inquisitive students into becoming passive recipients of knowledge. Vallance and Towndrow (2007) demonstrate how PowerPoint could be used as a powerful tool to incite critical dialogue between students, teachers and among students and stimulate intellectual thinking and discussion.

Another important finding was the lack of instrumental use of the Internet to support the teaching and learning of writing in both classrooms. There was some evidence that the teachers had attempted to harness the powerful potential of the Internet in accessing a much broader range of information resources to facilitate the planning phase of the process writing model. Nevertheless the way the Internet was used by the teachers in this study contradicts Ruthven, Hennesy and Deaney's study (2004) where the Internet-integrated pedagogical strategies had enhanced students' learning by structuring and supporting learning through informal teaching and by building and capitalising on students' sense of capability. Furthermore, Saravanan (2005) suggests that students need to be taught how to search for information using keywords, classify and categorise searches by topics in order for the Internet to be integrated effectively into lessons. In this study, both teachers indicated that one of the major obstacles in utilising ICT and the Internet was the lack of adequate and up to date infrastructure within their schools: the Internet could be working one day, down the next, and the computers were often not powerful enough for the use of advanced tools. The observed underutilisation of ICT tools in classrooms could have been caused by the unreliability of the computer infrastructure.

This finding has implications for policymakers, teachers and principals. Policy makers need to understand that teachers need to attend not only courses on using the available software but most importantly professional development that focuses on how to use ICT as a pedagogical tool in order to function effectively in an ICT-enriched classroom environment. Teachers need to understand and incorporate these ICT skills in their subject teaching and build this new knowledge into their planning. Teachers need a wide range of ICT-integrated skills vital for purposeful classroom teaching in the 21st Century. As to the implications for principals, the schools need to create platforms to showcase effective computer-mediated lessons for teachers to share pedagogical strategies on how to incorporate the use of the Internet or other associated ICT tools in classroom practice. The ideas and issues emerging from such activities are beneficial for teachers as they have the chance to be critical and reflective about their pedagogy. In addition both policy makers and school principals need to look into ways to further support teachers by providing good technological infrastructure and to employ technical professionals to assist teachers in managing technical malfunctions during teaching (Sandholtz & Reilly, 2004; Sime & Priestley, 2005).

The present study found that the use of ICT in the Malay Language classroom had limited pedagogical value and the impact ICT had on the curriculum was marginal. Furthermore, evidence showed that the rhetoric of policy did not match the reality in the schools. Teachers need support from policy makers, curriculum developers and school leaders for effective integration of ICT into the teaching and learning of Malay Language writing (Kirk & MacDonald, 2001). Time, opportunity, and professional space will need to be given to the teachers to allow them to experiment and reason for themselves the best way to approach the implementation of ICT in classrooms (Lofty, 2003). Without viewing ICT as the panacea of educational problems, a new lens is needed to look at ICT, pedagogy and the curriculum. ICT can be remarkable tools and their potential to have a great impact on the curriculum, pedagogy and literacy learning is staggering. It is up to educators to inspire, motivate, and excite students and colleagues about these remarkable instruments for learning (Ruthven et al., 2004). ICT is not just a passing fancy and information technology will continue to have an impact on education for a long time.

The high expectation of the role ICT could play in schools places both opportunities and challenges for those involved in its implementation and application for teaching and learning. The teachers need to incorporate new pedagogies that rely more on students' exploration, discovery and on students' construction of knowledge. Therefore it is not enough to merely use ICT to do the same types of activities as practised in traditional classrooms: the educator must also consider the new ways of thinking that ICT afford.

CONCLUSION

This study has re-emphasised, from a social-cultural perspective, that teachers, in coming to grips with innovations, interpret new experiences through their prior knowledge and conceptualisations. It is hoped that the case studies set forth here will foster contemplation, discussion, and constructive criticism by students, teachers, and researchers on writing to create a bridge between theory and practice. This research study provides glimpses and examples of new possibilities, as teachers and students imagine and explore new ways of doing things, or reconfigure older practices within new media. The perspectives and experiences offered are grounded in reflective practice and convictions about what constitutes good writing pedagogies. Teachers may need to rethink the subject in ways that extend and expand understandings of writing and ICT while being responsive all the while to students' interests and needs.

We are inclined to agree with Kress's (2003) ideas that writing will take its place in combination with other media; that its visual dimension will become more evident, and that its mutual, complementary and sometimes tense relationship with the visual will continue, with each medium having its own strengths and weaknesses. Helping students learn to make and read hybrid texts is an imperative for the next phase of curricular development, but it cannot be done satisfactorily without command of both verbal and visual media (Kress, 2000). It also cannot be achieved until teachers themselves develop a greater understanding of a multiliteracies approach that would involve making meaning from and constructing hybrid, multimodal texts.

While the implications of this study directly relate to the specific teachers within their particular context, readers are encouraged to examine the findings from the study in light of their own contexts and make additional interpretations relevant to their local settings.

REFERENCES

Adams, C. (2007). On the 'informed use' of PowerPoint: Rejoining Vallance and Towndrow. *Journal of Curriculum Studies*, *39*(2), 229–233. doi:10.1080/00220270601175246

Atkinson, D. (2001). Reflections and refractions on the *JSWL* special issue on voice. *Journal of Second Language Writing*, *10*, 107–124. doi:10.1016/S1060-3743(01)00035-2

Atkinson, D. (2002). Toward a sociocognitive approach to second language acquisition. *Modern Language Journal*, *86*, 525–545. doi:10.1111/1540-4781.00159

Bloch, J. (2006). Abdullah's blogging: A generation 1.5 student enters the blogosphere. *Language Learning & Technology*, *11*(2), 128–141.

Brush, T., & Saye, J. (2000). Implementation and evaluation of a student-centred learning unit: A case study. *Educational Technology Research and Development*, *48*(3), 79–100. doi:10.1007/BF02319859

Cuban, L. (2001). *Oversold and Underused: Computers in the classroom.* Cambridge, MA: Harvard University Press.

Cuban, L. (2004). Meeting challenges in urban schools. *Educational Leadership*, *61*(7), 64–69.

Cuban, L., Kirkpatrick, H., & Peck, C. (2001). High access and low use of technologies in high school classrooms; Explaining an apparent paradox. *American Educational Research Journal*, *38*(4), 813–834. doi:10.3102/00028312038004813

Dawes, L. (2001). What stops teachers using ICT. In M. Leask (Ed.), *Issues in teaching using ICT* (pp. 61-79). London: Routledge

Deaney, R., Ruthven, K., & Hennessy, S. (2004). *Teachers developing practical theories of the contribution of ICT to subject teaching and learning: An analysis of cases from English Secondary School.* Faculty of Education, University of Cambridge, Cambridge, UK.

Demetriadis, S., Barbas, A., Molohides, A., Palaigeorgiou, G., Psillos, D., & Vlahavas, I. (2003). Cultures in negotiation: Teachers' acceptance/resistance attitudes considering the infusion of technology into schools. *Computers & Education*, *41*(1), 19–37. doi:10.1016/S0360-1315(03)00012-5

Elstad, E. (2006). Understanding the nature of accountability failure in a technology-filled, laissez-faire classroom: Disaffected students and teachers who give in. *Journal of Curriculum Studies*, *38*(4), 459–481. doi:10.1080/00220270500508901

Ferris, D. (2007). Preparing teachers to respond to students' writing. *Journal of Second Language Writing, 16*, 165–193. doi:10.1016/j.jslw.2007.07.003

Gee, J. (2004). *Situated Language and Learning: Critique of traditional schooling*. London: Routledge.

Goldberg, A., Russel, M., & Cook, A. (2003). The effect of computers on student writing: A meta-analysis of studies from 1992-2002. *Journal of Technology , Learning and Assessment, 2*(1), 1–52.

Goodson, I., & Knobel, M. (2003). *Social spaces/cyber spaces: Culture clash in computerised classrooms*. New York: Palgrave Press.

Guardado, M., & Shi, L. (2007). ESL students' experiences of online peer feedback. *Computers and Composition, 24*, 443–461. doi:10.1016/j.compcom.2007.03.002

Hennessy, S. (2000). Graphing investigations using portable (palmtop) technology. *Journal of Computer Assisted Learning, 16*(3), 243–258. doi:10.1046/j.1365-2729.2000.00136.x

Hennessy, S., Deaney, R., & Ruthven, K. (2003). *Pedagogic strategies for using ICT to support subject teaching and learning: An analysis across 15 case studies.* Faculty of Education, University of Cambridge, Cambridge, UK.

Hennessy, S., Deaney, R., & Ruthven, K. (2005). Teacher perspectives on integrating ICT into subject teaching: Commitment, constraints, caution and change. *Journal of Curriculum Studies, 37*(2), 155–192. doi:10.1080/0022027032000276961

Itakura, H. (2004). Changing cultural stereotypes through e-mail assisted foreign language learning. *System, 32*, 37–51. doi:10.1016/j.system.2003.04.003

Jones, R. H., Garralda, A., Li, D., & Lock, G. (2006). Interactional dynamics in online and face-to-face peer-tutoring sessions for second language writers. *Journal of Second Language Writing, 15*, 1–23. doi:10.1016/j.jslw.2005.12.001

Kaplan, N. (2000). Literacy beyond books. In T. Swiss (Ed.), *The world wide web and contemporary cultural theory* (pp. 207-234). London: Routledge.

Khoo, A. (2001). Parents' and children's perceptions of the dangers on the Internet. *Paper presented at the AARE.* Perth, Australia: Fremantle.

Kim, Y., & Kim, J. (2005). Teaching Korean university writing class: Balancing the process and the genre approach. *Asian EFL Journal, 7*(2), 1–15.

Kirk, D., & MacDonald, D. (2001). Teacher voice and ownership of curriculum change. *Journal of Curriculum Studies, 33*(5), 551–567. doi:10.1080/00220270010016874

Kozma, R. B., & Anderson, R. E. (2002). Qualitative case studies of innovative pedagogical practices using ICT. *Journal of Computer Assisted Learning, 18*, 387–394. doi:10.1046/j.0266-4909.2002.00250.doc.x

Kress, G. (2000). A curriculum for the future. *Cambridge Journal of Education, 30*(1), 133–145. doi:10.1080/03057640050005825

Kress, G. (2003). *Literacy in the new media age*. London: Routledge.

Kroll, B. (2003). *Exploring the dynamics of second language writing.* New York: Cambridge University Press.

Lamb, A., & Johnson, L. (2006). Key words in instruction, blogs and blogging part II. *School Library Media Activities, 22*(9), 40–44.

Lankshear, C., & Knobel, M. (2003). *New literacies changing knowledge and classroom learning*. Philadelphia: Open University Press.

Lankshear, C., Peter, M., & Knobel, M. (2000). Information, knowledge and learning. *Journal of Philosophy of Education*, *34*(1), 17–40. doi:10.1111/1467-9752.00153

Laurinen, L., & Marttunen, M. (2007). Written arguments and collaborative speech acts in practicing the argumentative power of language through chat debates. *Computers and Composition*, *24*, 230–246. doi:10.1016/j.compcom.2007.05.002

Lin, L., Cranton, P., & Bridglall, B. (2005). *Psychological type and asynchronous written dialogue in adult learning*. Ann Arbor, MI: The University of Michigan Press.

Lofty, J. S. (2003). Standards and the politics of time and teacher professionalism. *English Education*, *35*(3), 195–223.

Loveless, A., & Ellis, V. (Eds.). (2001). *ICT, pedagogy and the curriculum: Subject to change*. London: Routledge.

Luke, C. (2000). Cyber-schooling and technological change: Multi-literacies for new times. In B. Cope & M. Kalantzis (Eds.), *Multi-literacies literacy learning and the design of social futures* (pp. 69-91). London: Routledge.

McNeely, B. (2005). Technology and learning expectations of the net generation. In D. Oblinger & J. Oblinger (Eds.), *Educating the net generation* (pp. 40-49). Boulder, CO: Educause.

MOE. (2003). *Malay Language Curriculum*. Retrieved February 21, 2005, from http//www.moe.gov.sg/cpdd/syllabuses.htm

Mumtaz, S., & Hammond, M. (2002). The word processor revisited: Observations on the use of the word processor to develop literacy at key stage 2. *British Journal of Educational Technology*, *33*(3), 345–347. doi:10.1111/1467-8535.00269

Noel, S., & Robert, J. M. (2003). How the web is used to support collaborative writing. *Behaviour & Information Technology*, *22*(4), 245–262. doi:10.1080/0144929031000120860

Oblinger, D., & Oblinger, J. (2005). *Educating the net generation*. Boulder, CO: Educause.

Oh, S., & Jonnasen, D. H. (2007). Scaffolding online argumentation during problem solving. *Journal of Computer Assisted Learning*, *23*, 95–110. doi:10.1111/j.1365-2729.2006.00206.x

Parks, S., Huot, D., Hamers, J., & Lemonnier, F. (2003). Crossing boundaries: Multimedia technology and pedagogical innovation in high school class. *Language Learning & Technology*, *7*(1), 28–45.

Parks, S., Huot, D., Hamers, J., & Lemonnier, F. (2005). "History of Theatre" Web sites: A brief history of the writing process in a high school ESL language art class. *Journal of Second Language Writing*, *14*, 233–258. doi:10.1016/j.jslw.2005.10.003

Pedersen, S., & Liu, M. (2003). Teachers' beliefs about issues in the implementation of a student-centered learning environment. *Educational Technology Research and Development*, *51*(2), 57–76. doi:10.1007/BF02504526

Reynolds, D. W. (2005). Linguistic correlates of second language literacy development: Evidence from middle-grade learner essays. *Journal of Second Language Writing*, *14*(1), 19–45. doi:10.1016/j.jslw.2004.09.001

Richardson, W. (2006). *Blogs, wikis, podcasts, and other powerful web tools for classrooms*. Thousand Oaks, CA: Corwin Press.

Rizvi, M., & Elliot, B. (2007). Enhancing and sustaining teacher professionalism in Pakistan. *Teachers and Teaching*, *13*(1), 5–19. doi:10.1080/13540600601106021

Robert, G. J. (2003). Emerging technologies: Blogs and wikis: Environments for online collaboration. *Language Learning & Technology*, *7*(2), 12.

Russell, M., Bebell, D., Cowan, J., & Corbelli, M. (2003). An AlphaSmart for each student: Do teaching and learning change with full access to word processors? *Computers and Composition*, *20*, 51–76. doi:10.1016/S8755-4615(02)00175-5

Ruthven, K., Hennnesy, S., & Deaney, R. (2004). *Incorporating Internet resources into classroom practice: Pedagogical perspectives and strategies for Secondary School subject teachers*. Retrieved May 21, 2004, from http://www.tcrecord.org.

Salvo, M. (2002). Critical engagement with technology in the computer classroom. *Technical Communication Quarterly*, *11*(3), 317–337. doi:10.1207/s15427625tcq1103_5

Sandholtz, H. M., & Reilly, B. (2004). Teachers, not technicians: Rethinking technical expectations for teachers. *Teachers College Record*, *106*(3), 487–512. doi:10.1111/j.1467-9620.2004.00348.x

Saravanan V, . (2005). 'Thinking Schools, Learning Nations' Implementation of Curriculum Review in Singapore. *Educational Research for Policy and Practice*, *4*(2-3), 97–113. doi:10.1007/s10671-005-1543-x

Scott, T. (2006). Writing work, technology and pedagogy in the late capitalism. *Computers and Composition*, *23*, 228–243. doi:10.1016/j.compcom.2005.08.008

Shetzer, H., & Warschauer, M. (2000). An electronic literacy approach to network – based language teaching. In W. M. Warschauer, & R. Kern (Eds.), *Networked-based language learning: Concepts and practice* (pp. 171-185). Cambridge, UK: Cambridge University Press.

Sime, D., & Priestley, M. (2005). Student teachers' first reflections on information and communications technology and classroom learning: Implications for initial teacher education. *Journal of Computer Assisted Learning*, *21*, 130–142. doi:10.1111/j.1365-2729.2005.00120.x

Spires, H. A., Lee, J. K., & Turner, K. A. (2008). Having our say: Middle grade student perspectives on school, technologies, and academic engagement. *Journal of Research on Technology in Education*, *40*(4), 497–515.

Strenski, E., Feagin, C., & Singer, J. (2005). E-mail small group peer view revisited. *Computers and Composition*, *22*(2), 191–208. doi:10.1016/j.compcom.2005.02.005

Taylor, R. P., & Gitsaki, C. (2004). Teaching WELL in a computerless classroom. *Computer Assisted Language Learning*, *16*(4), 275–294. doi:10.1076/call.16.4.275.23412

Tearle, P. (2003). ICT implementation: What makes the difference? *British Journal of Educational Technology*, *34*(5), 567–583. doi:10.1046/j.0007-1013.2003.00351.x

Towndrow, P. A. (2005). Teachers as digital task designers: An agenda for research and professional development. *Journal of Curriculum Studies*, *37*(5), 507–524. doi:10.1080/00220270500068591

Vallance, M., & Towndrow, P. (2007). Towards the "informed use" of information and communication technology in education: A response to Adams' "PowerPoint, habits of mind, and classroom culture. *Journal of Curriculum Studies*, *39*(2), 219–227. doi:10.1080/00220270601105631

Vygotsky, L. S. (1978). *Mind in society: The development of higher psychological processes*. Cambridge, MA: Harvard University Press.

Walker, R., & Baets, W. (2000). Designing a virtual environment for management education: A learner-centred approach. *Indian Journal of Open Learning*, *9*(3), 299–317.

Wang, W., & Wen, Q. (2002). L1 use in the L2 composing process: An exploratory study of 16 Chinese EFL writers. *Journal of Second Language Writing*, *11*, 225–246. doi:10.1016/S1060-3743(02)00084-X

Warschauer, M. (2000). The death of cyberspace and the rebirth of CALL. In P. Brett (Ed.), *CALL in the 21st century*. Whitstable, UK: IATEFL.

Warschauer, M., & Ware, P. (2006). Automated writing evaluation: Defining classroom research agenda. *Language Teaching Research*, *10*(2), 157–180. doi:10.1191/1362168806lr190oa

Wilson, L. (2006). *Writing to live: How to teach writing for today's world*. Portsmouth, NH: Heinemann.

Chapter 12
Multiliteracies in Secondary Chemistry:
A Model for Using Digital Technologies to Scaffold the Development of Students' Chemical Literacy

Annette Hilton
University of Queensland, and CRC Sugar Industry Innovation through Biotechnology, Australia

Kim Nichols
University of Queensland, and CRC Sugar Industry Innovation through Biotechnology, Australia

Christina Gitsaki
University of Queensland, and CRC Sugar Industry Innovation through Biotechnology, Australia

ABSTRACT

Digital technologies can play an important and significant role in improving students' understanding and literacies (e.g., visual, digital, and critical literacies). To develop such multiliteracy skills, students need opportunities to process and communicate information or use specialised representations that characterise a subject area, often through multiple modalities. Digital technologies are important learning tools for helping students to interpret and communicate information multimodally. In chemistry, in particular, digital technologies are effective tools for supporting students' understanding and representation of chemical concepts on macroscopic, molecular, and symbolic levels. Designing and scaffolding appropriate learning experiences in chemistry can be a challenge for teachers, particularly when integrating digital technologies with laboratory-based activities. The purpose of this chapter is to outline how a multiliteracies framework can be used to develop and deliver an investigative inquiry unit of work to chemistry students. It describes a scaffolding model developed and investigated through a study in which an introductory unit in senior chemistry was taught using a multiliteracies approach. It also describes student learning outcomes and perceptions of the usefulness of this scaffolding approach as these were identified through the study.

DOI: 10.4018/978-1-60566-673-0.ch012

INTRODUCTION

Many concepts and phenomena in chemistry are abstract and unobservable and can only be understood and communicated through the use of chemical representations or models. Such representations are used by scientists on three levels: macroscopic – representations of phenomena that are observable, molecular – visual representations showing the structure or behaviour of particles, and symbolic – signs and symbols used to represent particles and their behaviour (Vermaat, Terlouw & Dijkstra, 2003; Wu & Shah, 2004). To achieve an understanding of abstract and complex concepts in chemistry, students need to be able to use multiple representations in a number of ways, something that often causes difficulties (Gabel, 1999; Johnstone, 1996; Kozma, Chin, Russell & Marx, 2000; Lemke, 2000; Schank & Kozma, 2002). Grasping the complexity of meaning in chemistry requires students not only to understand individual representations but to integrate simultaneously multiple representations in a variety of modes (Lemke, 2000). For example, students may need to interpret teachers' gestures, written and verbal explanations, digital or physical models, video clips, graphs and tables, numerical data, or symbolic representations. A further challenge for students is the use of multiple representations to explain macroscopic phenomena on the molecular level, as they might be required to do when discussing experimental observations. This process requires students to be familiar with a range of chemical representations and to understand their inherent meaning, to be able to use representations to investigate and interpret macroscopic phenomena, and to be able to integrate and transform representations, linking them together in a range of appropriate genres to communicate information.

The ability to read and produce text using a variety of available media and modes, known as multiliteracies (Williamson, 2005), has implications for the teaching of chemistry and the role literacy education plays in the development of students' understanding of chemistry and chemical representations. The ways in which we ask students to represent their understanding should also reflect the changing nature of communications used by today's scientists in their daily work (e.g., molecular models, digital representations of data, analysis, and explanatory information). In today's classrooms, literacy pedagogy should account for the role of multiple modes of meaning-making including electronic media texts (Cope & Kalantzis, 2000; Jewitt, 2006; Prain, 2006; The New London Group, 2000; Unsworth, 2006) and this is certainly the case in chemistry since so many representations are generated using digital technologies.

Increased student access to computers in schools and the affordances of digital technologies provide opportunities for students to use multimedia and visualisation software. Such software can often be freely accessed on the Internet, and can extend the range of available representations students use to interpret findings and to choose appropriate representations to demonstrate their understanding using multimodal texts. These resources also have the potential to enhance students' understanding of abstract concepts.

To highlight the changing and increasingly complex nature of literacies in today's world, the New London Group (2000) proposed the multiliteracies framework. This framework emphasises the proliferation of ways in which meaning making occurs multimodally and the increasing influence of cultural and linguistic diversity both locally and globally. The framework also provides a useful structure for designing learning experiences in chemistry, where it is becoming increasingly recognised that students benefit from making and representing meaning through integration of multiple modes of representation (Michalchik, Rosenquist, Kozma, Kreikemeier & Schank, 2008). A multiliteracies approach allows teachers to focus on students' literacy development and knowledge construction, particularly in laboratory and other inquiry-based situations. Such an approach requires integration of digital learning tools into chemistry classrooms and within laboratories. Situative theory, which underpins this approach, focuses on learning as an investigative process that is supported by participation in a community of learners in which interactive knowledge construction occurs through social discourse and the use of representations (Greeno, 1998).

This chapter describes classroom practices that encourage students to utilise a range of technologies and digital resources to investigate and explain chemistry phenomena on multiple levels. Drawing on an intervention study to present examples of multiliteracies pedagogies applied to a unit of work in chemistry, it includes suggestions for the use of digital technologies to support students' understanding of chemistry and their ability to use multiple representations. In addition, this chapter provides examples of strategies and tools that have been used successfully in a secondary chemistry classroom context to scaffold students' learning using a multiliteracies approach. While the study and strategies described here are focussed on chemistry, the approaches used could be adapted for a range of other subject areas such as geography, economics, health education, history, and mathematics; indeed anywhere that students utilise digital technologies and information within an inquiry-based learning environment.

BACKGROUND

According to the New London Group (2000), literacy education should be expanded beyond simply learning to read and write to account for the growing range of text types available:

The shift from print and paper to electronic textuality, the proliferation of information resources and databases, global knowledge and social networks, require very different – multimodal and multimedia – social and literacy skills from those conceptualised on the basis of an essentially assembly-line, factory model of schools, and the static linearity of print- and book-based models of literacy (Luke, 2000, p. 81).

This perspective requires a broadening of the definition of *text* to include any medium of expression (Halliday & Hasan, 1985). The New London Group suggested that multiliteracies pedagogy is necessary to encompass textual multiplicity in terms of communication channels and media as well as cultural and linguistic diversity and to focus on multiple modes of representation and their integration to make and communicate meaning. If we accept the notion that students make and interpret texts in order to make meaning, then according to Norris and Phillips (2003), literacy and learning in a content area are inseparable. Grimberg (2008) too has argued that writing in science is a constitutive part of doing science.

The teaching approaches adopted within a multiliteracies framework will naturally differ in accordance with the age of students and the nature of the subject being studied. According to Unsworth (2001) research findings on subject-specific literacies from 1978 through to 1999 suggested that different subjects "have their own characteristic language forms and hence entail distinctive literate practices" (p. 10). These distinctions exist from the vocabulary level through to the genre level. The complex role of literacy practices in learning science was identified by Gee (2005) who argued that no other subject makes the same level of literacy demands because of the variety of symbols, representational systems, and practices used to understand and communicate about science. These literacy demands are experienced more acutely in subjects such as chemistry in which the concepts are multilevel and abstract in nature.

The meanings implicit in multilevel chemistry representations are well understood by chemists who can select and integrate them in their daily practices for such purposes as proposing hypotheses, interpreting data, and presenting their findings to other members of scientific communities (Kozma et al., 2000). However, this is not the case for chemistry students. To assist students to address these challenges, Kozma et al. argued that chemistry should be learned in a laboratory context so that students can be guided in their selection and use of multiple representations to discuss, explain, and communicate their understanding of their observations. Kozma and Russell (2005) referred to the ability to use representations reflectively and to link appropriate representations to think about, communicate, and interpret chemical phenomena in terms of underlying entities and processes as *representational competence*. This term has also been used to describe these abilities in other science disciplines.

The range of representational modes and media available to students requires them to draw not only on conceptual knowledge but also on knowledge about the representational conventions being used to present information. These skills require students to be capable of "multimodal reading" (Luke, 2000, p. 73), in other words, they must be able to interpret multiple representations in multiple modes that are interconnected and integrated to represent complex concepts. In addition to multimodal reading skills, students need to put these competencies to work in a range of texts. The use of writing as a tool for learning has been widely discussed in the literature and there are numerous points of view on the use of writing-to-learn in science as well as unresolved questions regarding appropriate strategies, when they should be used, and the resultant learning that arises from their use (Gunel, Hand & Prain, 2007). Several researchers have pointed to the need to broaden such strategies to include the production of texts other than written texts, particularly those that allow students to utilise emerging technologies and the variety of representations that their use makes available to students (e.g., Prain, 2006; Yore & Treagust, 2006). The focus on literacy development in subject areas is not confined to science. Indeed in 2001, Cumming and Wyatt-Smith argued for a multidisciplinary approach to literacy education.

Digital technologies have increased the variety of learning resources and experiences available to support students' development of multiliteracies in all disciplines. Their use also reflects the changing times in which today's students live, having grown up with the Internet, computer games, computer-based technologies such as mobile phones, digital cameras, and design software. Many digital resources and software products that support students' learning are freely available to teachers and students. For example, chemistry students and teachers can freely access programs such as *ChemSketch*, *Jmol*, and *ChemSense,* which allow students to create molecular models or simple animations. Other programs such as *Molecular Workbench* provide self-paced student-centred learning experiences through which students can explore chemical as well as physical and biological phenomena using simulations. Not only do these experiences align with students' life experiences and their use of digital technologies beyond school but they reflect the changing work of scientists, who use molecular modelling software and simulations alongside computer-based instrumentation and more traditional experimental procedures in their daily work.

While digital resources can be valuable learning tools, the learning experiences into which they are integrated need to be scaffolded. It would be easy to assume that students are cyber-wise and ready to "get beyond the classroom walls into the borderless world of Internet resources," as Luke has suggested (2000, p. 82), but there are times when scaffolding is necessary to help students to make meaning from the resources they encounter on the Internet and through using other digital technologies. They need to understand how to interpret and utilise resources before they can make sense of, or even access, the information that they find on the Internet. In chemistry, students can be supported in interpreting and learning to communicate using a range of representations by exposing them to laboratory experiences that require them to use representations to describe, discuss, and explain their observations. Scaffolding situated learning experiences in this way supports development of students' representational competence alongside their development of conceptual understanding. The pedagogy of multiliteracies framework proposed by the New London Group (2000) encourages educators to draw on the affordances of digital technologies and the efficacy of writing-to-learn approaches to design curriculum, pedagogies, and assessment to target the achievement of goals such as these.

Learning Chemistry and Developing Chemical Literacy

This section provides a brief description of some of the research findings on strategies that have been used to develop representational competence and enhance understanding in chemistry. It also describes current approaches to learning science through text production.

Enhancing Learning in Chemistry with Digital Technologies

Since being multiliterate requires students to be fluent in the representations and texts of particular content areas, it is important to employ strategies that immerse students in the full range of representations and allow them to use them as much as possible. In response to the identified literacy demands placed on chemistry students, researchers have examined the effect of using visualisation software on chemistry learning outcomes (e.g., Kozma, 2000a; Kozma & Russell, 1997; Russell et al., 1997; Schank & Kozma, 2002; Stieff & Wilensky, 2003; Wilensky & Resnick, 1999; Wu, Krajcik & Soloway, 2001; Wu & Shah, 2004; Xie & Tinker, 2006). Results of this research have indicated that visualisation tools are effective in improving outcomes such as understanding and representational competence. Kozma, Russell and their colleagues (Kozma, 2000a; Kozma et al., 2000; Kozma & Russell, 1997) focussed on the difficulties that students experience in connecting macroscopic findings with molecular phenomena and the ways that students use representations in their discussions of laboratory activities. They found that experts (professional chemists) use and communicate with scientific representations in ways that novices (students of chemistry) cannot. Experts are able to transform representations in meaningful ways, while novices rely on surface features to make connections between representations (Kozma, 2000a, 2000b; Kozma & Russell, 1997; 2005; Russell et al., 1997).

Rather than providing students with multiple representations, other researchers have focussed on students creating or manipulating multiple representations. For example, Wu, Krajcik, and Soloway (2001) found that when students constructed and manipulated their own models, their ability to make transformations between representations was improved. A number of other digital learning tools have also been reported to be effective in helping students to understand and explain macroscopic properties in terms of molecular interactions, for example, *ChemSense, ChemVis, Molecular Workbench*, and *Virtual Molecular Dynamics Laboratory* (Michalchik et al., 2008; Pallant & Tinker, 2004; Schank & Kozma, 2002; Trunfio, Berenfeld, Kreikemeier, Moran & Moodley, 2003; Xie & Tinker, 2006). In order for such learning to be situated in authentic practice, students need to use digital technologies in activities that help them to connect the digital materials directly with their laboratory experiences (Michalchik et al., 2008; Russell & Kozma, 2005) or other inquiry-based learning. This view aligns with that of Trunfio et al. (2003), who argued that "students develop intuition by doing, not by seeing" (p. 2). They also suggested that students need to develop an understanding of concepts through the use of multiple representations to explain the results of scientific investigation.

They suggested that the strength of many digital technologies was their support for students to explore multiple representations of phenomena observed during laboratory investigations. An important consideration when selecting digital resources for classroom use is their capacity to allow students to learn *with* them as knowledge construction tools rather than simply learning *from* them as information transmission tools (Jonassen & Carr, 2000).

Beyond the use of simulation and visualisation software, to learn about individual phenomena or processes, students can learn with digital technologies because they allow students to collect, collate, and analyse data, to create multimodal texts, and to generate and use multiple representations within explanations to justify claims, elaborate on meanings, and communicate their understanding. When students produce complex representations of knowledge, they engage in a range of thinking strategies such as analysing, evaluating, elaborating, designing, and problem solving. It follows that a powerful use of digital technologies would be to allow students not only to create multiple representations but to embed them within a larger multimodal text by linking together linguistic, visual, and spatial representations to report on laboratory and other inquiry activities. This approach aligns with another field of research aimed at supporting students' understanding in science through writing-to-learn.

Learning through Text Production

In the field of science education, writing has been promoted both as a means of actively constructing knowledge rather than simply describing knowledge, and as a means of scaffolding inquiry learning. In particular, writing activities that require the transformation of information have been said to enhance learning (Klein, 2004), and support students to construct knowledge, and develop mental models (Yore & Treagust, 2006). In recent years, there has been increased interest in the role of writing-to-learn in science (Gunel, Hand & Gunduz, 2006; Keys, 1999), however, research on writing-to-learn activities in upper secondary classrooms has been limited (Klein, 2004) and calls have been made to extend writing-to-learn opportunities in science beyond traditional observations and report writing (e.g., Gunel et al., 2007; Hand, Hohenshell & Prain, 2007; Hand, Yang & Bruxvoort, 2007; Yore & Treagust, 2006). Prain (2006) advocated a broadening of writing-to-learn research to focus on emerging technologies and their impact on students' opportunities to represent ideas. In chemistry this approach requires research that examines students' use of digital technologies to create multiple representations and multimodal texts. It also necessitates the expansion of the notion of what it means to "write" text to include the production of text in any mode or a combination of modes.

Writing tasks in science and other content areas require students to learn new literacies, which are influenced by cultural, social, linguistic, and representational resources (Gee, 2004; Gunel, Hand & Prain, 2007). Following a review of the use of multimedia in chemistry education, Kozma and Russell (2005) argued for research that focussed on "the use of representations to support the goal of learning chemistry as a process of investigation" (p. 423) since using language and representations during investigative processes is more likely to lead students to a deeper understanding of chemical phenomena. Taken together, these current views indicate the need to investigate the potential of writing-to-learn approaches using digital technologies through a multiliteracies approach to support students' learning and chemistry literacy development.

Writing-to-Learn Chemistry with Digital Technologies: A Multiliteracies Approach

Multiliteracies in the Chemistry Classroom

Developing learning environments that integrate these approaches places demands on teachers in terms of time and resources. Teachers often respond to time and curriculum constraints by choosing efficient teaching and learning strategies. Digital technologies provide a means through which students can actively construct concepts and learn new skills and as such, when used appropriately, are effective learning tools. Their use becomes more efficient when they are introduced early so that students develop skills in using the technologies and software while they are learning with them. It is important that teachers identify strategies that lead to effective learning rather than concerning themselves with efficiency of delivery. Consequently, they need to be discerning in the selection of learning tools and experiences as well as pedagogical strategies.

Effective use of digital technologies for learning requires that students are able to use resources such as data loggers, software (e.g., molecular modelling, publishing, and drawing programs), simulations, CD-ROMs, search engines and websites, digital representations, video, the school intranet, and email. These perform multiple roles in the learning process including information presentation and retrieval, publishing and communication. Students may be familiar with some of these, for example, publishing programs, from their experiences beyond school and within other subjects. Others may be new technologies and applications that students will need time to master, for example, data loggers, simulations, or molecular modelling software. This has implications for the integration of digital technologies and places demands on the pedagogical practices of teachers (Wells & Reynolds, 2005).

The New London Group (2000) distinguished between the content and form of multiliteracies, which they labelled designs of meaning and pedagogical elements respectively. The designs of meaning involve:

- Available Designs – knowledge and representational resources with which students are already familiar, and have at their disposal as a result of past experiences, for example, the grammars and conventions of multiple semiotic systems such as language, images, and visual representations,
- Designing – the process of re-representing, transforming, or recontextualising a range of resources to make connections between Available Designs and new information, and
- The Redesigned – the outcomes of the designing process – new knowledge and resources that become Available Designs for future meaning making processes.

As designers, students utilise conventions and patterns of meaning and design elements while actively making new meaning. These processes are scaffolded by teachers through the implementation of a number of pedagogical strategies, including Situated Practice, Overt Instruction, Critical Framing, and Transformed Practice, the four pedagogical components of multiliteracies. These pedagogies can be used to scaffold students' learning both about and with digital technologies.

The pedagogical elements of multiliteracies are neither linear nor hierarchical in nature but have complex interrelationships. These pedagogies encompass the strategies and approaches through which to scaffold the students' transformation of information and resources to construct new meanings and representations of knowledge. It is possible that these pedagogies would be utilised on a micro-level within single lessons as well as on a macro-level, becoming the dominant pedagogies

Table 1 Examples of scaffolding practices within multiliteracies pedagogies. (Characteristics adapted from The New London Group, 2000, with examples added by the authors)

Pedagogy	Characterised by	Examples from Classroom Practice
Situated Practice	•Immersion in experiences that allow students to use current knowledge within a community of learners and experts • Explicit connections between school and students' life experiences	• Participation in investigative inquiry and opportunity to explain and discuss findings and ideas with peers • Exploration of authentic contexts – linking learning experiences to real world applications and issues • Using digital technologies to create representations or to explore concepts
Overt Instruction	• Active teacher interventions to scaffold learning by building on students' prior knowledge • Development of systematic, analytic, and conscious understanding of and control over information and texts • Explicit metalanguages to describe and interpret design elements of different modes of meaning	• Discussion of how and when digital and other representations can be used to present and explain experimental results, concepts, or outcomes of inquiry tasks • Learning about the meaning or information inherent in multiple representations and texts • Translating or interpreting different representations and informational texts
Critical Framing	• Students 'standing back' and viewing designs of meaning critically in relation to their context and purpose • Students actively producing information for a specific purpose	• Selecting most appropriate ways to represent information for a particular purpose • Determining what else might be needed to make a point, state or argue a case, justify claims, or to link evidence and claims • Contextualising – deciding whether the information presented achieves its purpose, including awareness of audience and appropriateness of text or representation
Transformed Practice	• Transferring and transforming meanings to new or different contexts • Reflective use of material learned • Redesign or reformatting of previously made texts.	• Application of laboratory or other inquiry learning outcomes to new situations, to solve novel problems, or to redesign experimental procedures or research strategies • Re-presenting information for different audiences, or transforming it into different genres, (e.g., creating a webpage, poster or PowerPoint presentation, or video from a research report)

in different lessons over the course of a unit. By way of illustration, Table 1 characterises each of the elements and provides examples from classroom practices in which digital technologies are integrated. The examples are drawn from science teaching experience but could be applied across a broad range of subject areas. The examples and strategies supported by the multiliteracies framework underpin the design of a unit of work used in a study that was conducted to examine the effects of learning with digital technologies on Year 11 chemistry students' understanding and use of representations to report on investigative inquiry in chemistry.

In the examples given in this table, the term *representation* might include graphs, tables, photographs, diagrams, flowcharts, equations, illustrations, structural diagrams, video, audio, or written representation. This would depend on the subject area and topic being studied.

The Study: Examining a Multiliteracies Approach to Chemistry

Study Design

The study was conducted with two Year 11 chemistry classes (n = 27, n = 22) in Queensland, Australia, in a large metropolitan public high school serving a school community both ethnically and socio-economically diverse. It took place over a 10-week term at the beginning of Year 11, the first year in which Australian students study chemistry as a separate discipline. Students in both classes were taught by the first author for three 70-minute lessons per week. The aim of the study was to identify effective scaffolding strategies for teaching and learning chemistry supported by digital technologies using a multiliteracies framework. The study had two phases: An initial 6-week phase and a second 4-week phase. Both of these phases were designed to focus on aspects of the use of digital technologies to support students' development of chemistry understanding and representational competence and to provide students with designs of meaning to promote multiliteracies development. The purpose of Phase 1 was to examine the effect of learning with digital technologies on students' learning outcomes. Students' alternative conceptions were pretested to identify alternative conceptions and prior knowledge, which were used to inform the design of the learning materials and scaffolding strategies. The pretest used a 9-item instrument based on the Chemical Bonding Diagnostic Instrument developed by Tan and Treagust (1999) as well as questions to determine students' representational competence. The pretest responses gave an indication of the students' available designs at the beginning of the unit, which could be used to construct new designs of meaning. During this phase, both classes were taught using the same resources and pedagogies and spent the same amount of class time in experimental and computer laboratories.

The purpose of Phase 2 was to examine the effect of asking students to use writing-to-learn strategies to report on laboratory inquiries. The focus of this phase was to allow students to transform available designs through situated practice and critical framing. The classes undertook the same two investigative inquiries. The manner in which the classes were asked to report on their investigations was varied. During the first investigation, Class A reported using a digital poster while Class B wrote a standard laboratory report. For the second investigation, the reporting methods were swapped so that Class A wrote a standard laboratory report while Class B created a digital poster. A further goal of the study was to identify a model for scaffolding multiliteracies development. Data for this purpose were collected at the end of the study through semi-structured interviews with students who participated in the study and during the course of the study through audio and video recordings and researcher journals.

Unit Design

The study was conducted within an introductory Year 11 unit that focussed on learning bonding concepts within a materials context. Chemical bonding was the chosen topic since it is a key concept of central importance in chemistry (Fensham, 1975). Students need a solid grounding in chemical bonding if they are to understand the nature and properties of materials, the processes that occur during chemical reactions, and more complex relationships and concepts such as equilibrium and thermodynamics. It is also a topic that is difficult for students because of the diverse range of models used by chemists to understand it and one in which students are known to hold a number of alternative conceptions. For example, students have been found to experience difficulties in understanding van der Waals forces, hydrogen bonding, and the distinction between intermolecular and intramolecular bonding (Taber & Coll, 2002).

Phase 1 of the unit introduced students to digital technologies such as molecular modelling software to allow them to learn how to use the software while exploring and creating some of the multiple representations used to understand different types of chemical bonding. Students also used simulations to learn about atomic structure, molecular shape, and intermolecular bonding and interactions. The authentic context of the unit, The Chemistry of Biomaterials, was designed to expose students to the notion of the earth as a finite system with renewable and non-renewable resources. The use of renewable resources for applications such as energy production and the synthesis of biomaterials were presented to students through both theoretical and laboratory-based experiences during Phase 2. This allowed them to develop and apply their understanding of intramolecular and intermolecular bonding to design experimental procedures, explain experimental findings, and make theoretical predictions. Students learned about bonding in real world contexts during these investigations, which focussed on bioplastics synthesis and properties and biofuels production. The unit was designed with attention to the multiliteracies pedagogical framework. Table 2 shows examples of multiliteracies components linked to focus areas of the unit. This table illustrates the fact that pedagogies can occur in parallel and some are repeated throughout a unit as students encounter new concepts or learning experiences. It also provides examples of the designs of meaning that students might use during the course of the unit as they integrate their prior knowledge with new learning experiences to construct knowledge and develop representational competence within the topic under study.

Digital Resources Selection

According to Baggott La Velle, McFarlane, and Brawn (2003), problems commonly cited by educators for not using digital technologies in classrooms include mismatches between software and curriculum and between technologies and learning needs, access to computers, cost of software, and lack of professional development for specific software applications. When selecting digital resources for use in the study, these potential barriers to implementation in regular classrooms were addressed by developing and applying the following criteria to selecting digital learning tools and materials:

- Availability for download by teachers and students, free of charge or at minimal cost,
- Ability to serve a range of purposes depending on the topic, year level, and prior knowledge of students,
- Ability to be mastered by teachers with minimal or no access to professional development,
- Ability to be used by students with minimal instruction on their use (to retain student-centred nature of learning rather than technology-centred),
- Suitability for use in both theoretical and laboratory activities, and
- Compatibility with other programs schools would be likely to have such as Microsoft Office applications.

Since the challenges faced by teachers in using digital technologies in schools are not specific to any subject area, these criteria could be applied equally across the range of subjects and year levels.

After identifying a number of programs that matched these criteria, *ChemSketch* and *Molecular Workbench* were chosen. *ChemSketch* was chosen because it allows students to:

- create molecular models in a range of modes and to transform representations easily,
- rotate and observe the molecules in different ways,
- copy and embed the representations created into student work as picture files, and
- download it from the Internet for use at home.

It also has a Periodic Table template that provides a range of information and representations of elements including photographic images, a bonus feature as teachers don't need access to the Internet to use one of the many periodic table sites that exist online. While there are several useful simulation tools available online, *Molecular Workbench* was chosen because many of its simulations are editable and teachers can easily change or adapt the activities to suit their goals or the needs of their students, the activities are

Table 2 Multiliteracies in the Materials Unit

Focus Areas	Designs of Meaning	Multiliteracies Pedagogies and Examples
Introduction to context • Revising the classification and types of materials and their properties • Macroscopic properties and uses of materials • Importance of new technologies and materials	*Available designs* • Prior knowledge of types, properties and classification of materials • Recognition of representations of different types of materials *Designing and the redesigned* • Transforming available resources to produce classification concept map	*Situated practice* • Group activity constructing concept map • Laboratory investigation – common macroscopic properties *Overt Instruction* • Discussion of materials of the earth, renewability, types of resources and biomaterials • Instruction in the use of molecular modelling software
Introduction to bonding and multiple representations • Nature and properties of ionic and covalent substances • Intermolecular forces • Molecular and network solids, macromolecules • Developing *ChemSketch* skills • Using simulations in *Molecular Workbench*	*Available designs* • Representations of ionic and covalent substances • Types of bonds *Designing and redesigned* • Creating and using molecular level models to predict and explain structure, polarity, intermolecular forces, and linking them to macroscopic properties	*Situated practice* • Using molecular modelling software and simulations *Overt instruction* • Discussing key concepts • Discussing multiple representations, their transformation, and the information conveyed by them *Critical Framing* • Deciding which representations to include to support explanations *Transformed practice* • Using information and representations learned to explain macroscopic properties on molecular level
Bioplastics investigative inquiry • Examining and critiquing biomaterial samples • Designing investigation to make and compare two bioplastics • Biopolymer and plastics composition and properties	*Available designs* • Knowledge of variables, and how bonding and structure influence macroscopic properties *Designing and redesigned* • Collating and interpreting qualitative data • Peer and class discussion about meanings of data • Producing an experimental report that incorporates multiple representations of biopolymer and bioplastics structures to explain properties	*Situated practice* • Making and testing bioplastics in laboratory • Data collection *Critical Framing* • Designing appropriate procedures and materials • Identifying variables and experimental goals *Transformed practice* • Redesigning experimental procedures • Proposing products to be made from bioplastics
Biofuels investigative inquiry • Ethanol production from sucrose • Designing investigation to compare fermentation rates of mono-, di-, and poly- saccharides • Bioethanol production research areas	*Available designs* • Knowledge of variables and how the nature of reactants and enzymes influence reaction rate *Designing and redesigned* • Collating, interpreting, and representing quantitative data • Discussing analysis of data • Producing experimental report that incorporates multiple representations and proposal of new experimental design for cellulosic raw materials	*Situated practice* • Making and comparing rates of reaction of ethanol in laboratory • Collecting and collating data *Critical Framing* • Designing appropriate experimental procedures • Identifying variables and experimental goals *Transformed practice* • Redesigning experimental procedures • Proposing new experimental procedures

self-paced and allow students to check their understanding, and students can save and print their answers. The variety of simulations and models available through *Molecular Workbench* is such that students and teachers could use it throughout a course rather than for just one topic or concept. This is an advantage because once students learn how to navigate within the program, they can move easily between activities and topics. This increases the ways that teachers and students can utilise them. Students used these programs in the computer laboratory and during overt instruction when they were also used on an electronic whiteboard to facilitate whole class and group discussions.

Teaching Strategies

Phase 1

Students' alternative conceptions of chemical bonding were pretested at the beginning of the unit and the information regarding the nature of students' alternative conceptions was used to design and sequence the learning experiences and to identify areas that required particular emphasis. The approaches used and the order in which concepts were developed were also informed by recommendations in the literature about how to minimise the likelihood of developing alternative conceptions (e.g., Taber & Coll, 2002; Tan & Treagust, 1999). Part of this process involved identifying visual representations that might be useful in developing more accurate conceptions. During Phase 1, strategies were used to establish students' understanding of key concepts and visual and symbolic representations and to make connections between the chemistry concepts, laboratory investigations, and the biomaterials context. Students were introduced to visualisation software with which they created and interpreted representations and used simulations to investigate bonding, structure, and intermolecular forces. Activities were designed to integrate digital technologies with other learning experiences such as laboratory investigations to allow students to explore properties such as covalent molecular shape and polarity, physical properties of elements, and the structure and properties of ionic and covalent compounds while learning how to use the technology (Situated Practice). Learning experiences were scaffolded using worksheets, open-ended questions, investigative prompts, and teacher intervention to direct students to explore particular aspects of the program or resources (Situated Practice and Overt Instruction). This part of the unit focussed on allowing students to create and explore different types of representations, and to use them to answer explanatory, problem-solving, and application questions. The goal was to ensure that students had the appropriate experience and knowledge prior to the investigative inquiries to allow them to report their findings. It also sought to establish appropriate available designs to equip students to engage in the design process in Phase 2.

Phase 2

During the final four weeks of the unit, students conducted two investigations focussed on the production and properties of biomaterials. Groups of three or four students designed and conducted laboratory investigations in which they made and tested bioplastics and then produced ethanol through fermentation of various carbohydrates (Situated Practice). They reported on their findings using two different text types: a standard laboratory report and a digital poster (Critical Framing and Transformed Practice). During this phase, students were self-directed with the only teacher intervention being in response to student questions. In addition to learning experiences in which students learned with *Molecular Workbench* simulations and *ChemSketch* activities, another scaffolding strategy that utilised digital technologies was used during the two inquiries, to extend students' available resources. Students were provided with a range of digital resources related to the investigations through a "digital resources toolbox".

Scaffolding with the Digital Resources Toolbox

Students were encouraged to select, modify, or transform representations in the digital resources toolbox, to create models to support explanations, and use them to extend, justify, or illustrate their explanations and to create multimodal texts. Students were also able to use the resources to support their interpretation and understanding of experimental data. The digital resources toolbox

Table 3 Summary of Paired t-tests Comparing Pretest and Phase 2 Posttest Scores

Inquiry Topic	Class	*t*	*df*	*d*
Bioplastics	1	18.17	26	3.63
	2	13.43	21	4.58
Bioethanol	1	11.99	25	2.73
	2	11.21	21	3.38

$p < .0005$ in all cases

provided a collection of digital images, including photographs, molecular models, and structural diagrams that could be modified or used by students in the creation of reports and poster presentations of their laboratory work. It also contained summary articles, relevant background information, and PowerPoint presentations and other digital materials used in class. The toolbox provided information in a variety of formats, which served to support or expand students' understanding and model the integration of multiple representations into multimodal texts.

Summary of Findings

Pretest-Posttest Comparisons

At the end of each phase, students were posttested using the same items as the pretest. The results for the alternative conceptions items on the pretest and the Phase 1 posttest were compared using a paired sample *t*-test. This showed that the difference between results on the pretest and the posttest was significant, indicating that there was a significant improvement in students' understanding ($t = 8.45$, $df = 48$, $p < .0005$, two-tailed). The effect size was large ($d = 1.23$). The scores on representational competence items for the pretest and posttest were compared using the Wilcoxin Signed Ranks test. The representational competence scores on the posttest were significantly higher than the pretest scores for all three items ($p < .0005$ for each item). These results suggested that the use of selected digital materials and activities in scaffolded student-focussed learning activities were effective in improving students' understanding, explanation, and representation of bonding concepts.

A similar outcome resulted in Phase 2. Paired sample *t*-tests again indicated a significant increase in students' scores on knowledge items. The results of the comparison *t*-tests and effect sizes are summarised in Table 3.

The scores on representational competence items for the pretest and Phase 2 posttest items were again compared using the Wilcoxin Signed Ranks test. The representational competence scores on the posttests were significantly higher than the pretest scores for all six items ($p < .005$ on one item for Class 1; $p < .0005$ for all other items). These findings suggested that production of multimodal texts improved students' understanding of experimental findings and their ability to explain and represent them.

Text Analysis

Analysis of the texts produced by students during Phase 2 to report on their investigative experiences indicated that students in both classes were able to select and use a range of appropriate representations to explain their findings and to make links between representations to support their explanations of macroscopic data in terms of underlying phenomena. The students who produced standard laboratory reports relied more heavily on written explanation than students who produced digital posters, which limited the amount of written text and required the use of visual representations to support explanations. For example, when explaining the differing rates of fermentation of glucose, sucrose, and starch, several students in the report writing class wrote statements such as, "The different rates of fermentation of the three substances are due to their different structures. Glucose is a monosaccharide, sucrose is a disaccharide, and starch is a polysaccharide. Glucose is a simpler structure than sucrose and therefore reacted faster..." Such statements rely on the reader's understanding of the meaning of scientific terms. Students in the poster class with only two exceptions included structural diagrams of the substances discussed and while using the same scientific terms, they made reference to the diagrams when explaining the differing fermentation rates observed. For example:

Starch, shown in Figure 1, is a polysaccharide, which cannot be fermented by yeast until it is broken into its glucose monomers, as shown in Figure 2. As expected, starch had a much slower reaction rate than sucrose, which is a disaccharide and has fewer bonds to be broken during fermentation...

This student included structural diagrams labelled as Figures 1, 2, and so on within the discussion. The findings for this investigation were confirmed through comparison of the number of visual representations used by students in digital posters with the number used in laboratory reports. Students in the poster-making class used a significantly higher number of representations in addition to written text, including photographs, graphs, tables, structural diagrams, chemical equations, and other diagrams.

Student Interviews

Student interviews indicated that the students felt they had to engage in higher levels of thinking when making posters because the limited space for written text forced them to think more about what was relevant and important. The comments of student C reflect this:

With posters you have to write less so you have to be aware of what to write and how to condense it. That's more challenging because you have to get to the point. It's harder because you have to think more.

Student N also commented on the need to limit written information in the poster:

I probably learned more from making the poster because it still requires all the same information (as a laboratory report) but allows you to select appropriate information.

Students also indicated that the need to limit written text prompted them to identify and make connections between relevant visual representations. For example, Student A commented that:

You need to be more creative in the ways that you represent the information when making a poster.

Student H suggested that the inclusion of visual representations simplified the writing process:

... making a poster lets me use pictures and diagrams and this makes it easier to express ideas than just by using words.

Comments such as these support the idea that providing students with the opportunity to transform available resources through practice and critical framing promotes engagement with the task and the concepts involved.

When interviewed about the use of the digital resources toolbox to scaffold the explanation of experimental data, students reported that they learned more or felt more confident when transforming the materials for their own purposes than they might have if they had been required to source the information through their own research, for example, using the Internet. For example, Student C commented that the toolbox helped to identify relevant information:

I learned more having them there because I knew what I had to write about. If I'd gone on the Internet, I probably would have got a bit lost because there's so much stuff and it's hard to know what's useful and what's not. Some of it's also quite technical and it's hard to choose what's most relevant.

Student B made similar comments:

It was a lot easier when we had the basic information because we knew we were on the right track. When you type something in on the Internet, so much comes up on that topic. I wouldn't be sure it was the right thing to be writing about...

In other words, having access to a broad set of resources allowed students to focus on the task of transforming available designs to create texts. Scaffolding text production tasks by providing a range of digital resources and software with which to produce representations and texts supports students' learning and builds digital literacies by helping them to focus on relevant and appropriate information, be critical in their use of representations and information, and transform and integrate digital information. Student interview responses were also analysed using *Leximancer Text Explorer*, text analysis software. A summary of the themes that emerged from student interview responses regarding scaffolding is provided in Table 4.

Lessons from the Study

A Model for Scaffolding Learning with Digital Technologies

A multiliteracies approach in any subject area requires consideration of the designs of meaning, students' prior knowledge, and familiarity with representations and texts that characterise the subject. It also requires consideration of pedagogical components (Situated Practice, Overt Instruction, Critical Framing, and Transformed Practice) when selecting and designing learning experiences, resources, and activities. This includes a focus on the multiple representations that students will need to use and interpret when they meet new concepts. This can be achieved by identifying the available designs that students have and considering how these need to be augmented and complemented through experiences that allow students to build their repertoire of available resources prior to engaging in more complex transformation of knowledge. When approaching a new topic, teachers should begin with simple models and concrete examples and gradually expand the range and sophistication of representations and the abstract nature of concepts and information. A model of a well scaffolded design process using a multiliteracies approach includes the following steps:

- Identification of the key concepts and ideas of the topic, including the types of representations likely to be encountered by students (Designs of Meaning).
- Consideration of the prior knowledge and possible alternative conceptions that may be held by students (Available Designs).
- Identification of representations and models that will be conducive to developing students' understanding of the concepts and which can act as available designs of meaning with which students can construct new knowledge and build representational

Table 4 Student Responses Regarding the Scaffolding Strategies Experienced in the Study

The scaffolding strategies identified as useful by students	Reasons cited by students in terms of multiliteracies framework
Using visual representations	The range of representations used • increased understanding • led to more available designs • facilitated transformation of designs
Using digital resources toolbox	Having a variety of information presented in multiple modes facilitated selection and decision-making about how to re-represent it (Critical Framing and Transformed Practice)
Writing different text types	• Required understanding of writing for particular purpose • Required critical thinking when deciding what was important and relevant for inclusion and how best to present this information (Critical Framing and Transformed Practice)
Conducting laboratory-based investigative inquiries	• Promoted discussion of data with peers • Allowed student to apply theory in authentic investigative contexts (Situated Practice)
Using worksheets and activity guides that scaffolded computer-based inquiries	• Focussed attention on important concepts • Encouraged peer discussion of learning • Guided analysis and discussion of data (Situated practice and Overt Instruction)
Using digital technologies	• Increased motivation and enjoyment of tasks • Aligned the learning experiences with interests and skills outside of school • Enhanced ability to visualise phenomena and to produce multimodal text with visual illustrations to enhance written explanations (Situated Practice, Overt Instruction, Critical Framing, and Transformed Practice)

competence (Designing and Redesigning).

- Provision of models, including digital resources that can be used to develop students' understanding and critical selection of the multiple representations needed to create and transform information and produce multimodal texts (Critical Framing and Transformed Practice).
- Immersion in activities that allow students to make connections between new and prior knowledge, within a community of learners, for example, through inquiry-based learning tasks and class and small group discussions (Situated Practice).
- Use of strategies that encourage and support students to link inquiry findings with theoretical concepts (Overt Instruction and Situated Practice).

It is also important to consider strategies that support students to learn chemistry in ways that reflect the work of chemists, such as presenting the learning in authentic contexts (by linking learning to real-world topics, issues, and emerging fields of research), as an investigative endeavour. Discussion of laboratory experiences and other inquiry-based learning tasks are essential in helping students to make connections between macroscopic and molecular levels of chemistry and an engaging factor is that they reflect the nature of expert chemists' work. This approach is not exclusive to instructional design in chemistry. In any discipline, it is important wherever possible to make real world connections to the subject being studied. These provide students with an insight into the authentic practices of professionals in the field while helping them to contextualise their learning and understand the purpose and importance of what they are studying.

Digital technologies should be integrated into a range of learning experiences, from providing students with appropriate representations and the means by which to transform or create their own representations through to the production of new texts. This means they must be used for purposes beyond word processing and research. These are important and necessary skills, however, students should also be provided with resources that allow them to select, create, and integrate multiple representations, to illustrate and elaborate on their explanations, to re-represent their understanding of concepts, and to gain competence in using and interpreting a range of multimodal representations and texts.

Recommendations for Teachers

Consideration of the outcomes of this study leads to a number of general recommendations for teachers wishing to design a unit of work that appropriately scaffolds multiliteracies learning. These include the following:

- Encourage students to use digital technologies to create representations and integrate them within written text to support and justify explanations and arguments. For example, including a graph, table, or diagram might serve to illustrate, justify, or complement written explanations.
- Scaffold text production by providing students with models from which to build their own texts and gradually remove or change the scaffolding over time to give more control and responsibility to students for producing their own representations and texts. For example, providing students with genre guides or templates can scaffold text production when students are unfamiliar with a genre.
- Make learning experiences, whether theoretical or practical, inquiry-based, beginning with guided inquiry and over time gradually make inquiries more open-ended as students develop laboratory or research skills and representational competence.
- Introduce new representations alongside the concepts they represent. Don't assume that students know what information certain representations provide. Make explicit links between representations and their meanings. For example, deconstruct representations and texts with students to explore what information is represented and how it is portrayed.
- Spend time debriefing inquiry activities so that students can link these learning experiences with the theoretical concepts they meet in other lessons. This helps to avoid the "disconnection" between what they learn in theory classes and what they do in laboratory or practical lessons.
- Provide opportunities for class and group discussions of representations used or created by students, including critical analysis of representations and texts. This helps students to select information critically and to decide how it is best presented. Ask students to practice these ideas by producing multimodal texts to discuss and report their findings with peers.
- When students undertake independent research to solve a problem or explain concepts, inquiry findings, or laboratory results, they may need help to decode what they're reading, seeing, or hearing since they don't always have the literacies with which to make sense of the information they find. It is important to remember that they are novices, particularly in terms of understanding the information contained in the wide range of informational texts available on the Internet.

- Provide learning experiences that support students' development of representational competence so that they become more able to "talk", "write", or "draw" in discipline specific ways, especially when asked to combine these skills.
- Encourage students to interact with peers and teachers, both in school and via email or discussion boards, to ask and pose questions, query information, send drafts, and check for understanding.
- When using simulations, help students to understand how chemical entities and phenomena are represented and how these representations relate to others.

Recommendations for the Use of Digital Technologies in the Broader Educational Context

It is important to acknowledge that using digital technologies in schools can be problematic for teachers for a number of reasons, some of which were mentioned previously:

- Funding is limited in many schools and this has an impact on the availability, reliability, and capacity of computers and also on access to software.
- Some software is expensive, particularly when schools must pay for school-wide site licenses. Even if costly software is used at school, it is unlikely that students will have access to it beyond school, for example, on their home computers, which limits the use of the software to class time. If classes cannot access computers at an appropriate juncture in the course, such software may not always be used in timely or meaningful ways. It also means that students cannot spend time at home consolidating or extending their learning with the same tools.
- Lack of training or confidence with software applications or the level of technical support needed is another problem experienced by many teachers. Access to professional development is limited by budgetary constraints and school priorities, which often means that teachers cannot learn how to use particular software in their classrooms.
- Curriculum constraints can also limit the integration of digital technologies into learning programs. For example, if it takes considerable time for students to master particular software applications or if teachers have other imperatives such as the need to cover a certain amount of information in a limited time, they will, understandably opt for what they judge to be more time-efficient methods of delivery. This may lead to the decision not to spend multiple lessons on a single concept or group of representations.

While it is not possible to solve all of the problems experienced by individual teachers or schools when integrating digital technologies, it is possible to make general recommendations about the selection and implementation of particular resources. Constraints such as funding and teachers' ability to use particular software can be addressed, at least in part, by selecting software applications that serve a number of different purposes, for example, those that are compatible with other applications that the school and students already have available. For example, teachers may select applications that allow students to create multimodal representations that they can use within laboratory reports, summaries, multimedia presentations, or other texts. If there is limited funding for site licenses and the purchase of software, teachers can opt to use applications that are freely available for download on the Internet for students to create and transform a range of representations. Such programs are not only accessible free of charge to teachers but they can be accessed by students from home.

FUTURE TRENDS

The continued development of digital technologies and the uncertainty of students' future life and work worlds (lifeworlds) make the adoption of a multiliteracies approach to teaching in content areas an imperative. The burgeoning range of multimedia and multimodal texts that students encounter in their lives beyond school should be reflected in the ways that they are asked to present knowledge in school. Today's students are growing up immersed in digital technologies. In their world multimedia and digital technologies are not "optional extras". The range of uses of digital technologies in schools will continue to change and grow and the need to ensure that pedagogies adopted by teachers align with these changes is without question. Adopting multiliteracies pedagogies allows teachers to utilise the affordances of digital technologies during Situated Practice, Overt Instruction, Critical Framing, and Transformed Practice. Within learning environments where students learn with digital technologies, they become creators as well as users of digital representations and texts. These approaches are also essential for students' development of digital, critical, and chemical literacies, without which chemistry students cannot hope to develop a deep understanding of, or ability to communicate, on molecular or symbolic levels. The emerging scientific fields within which chemistry learning can be contextualised will continue to grow and diversify. Many scientific research fields are becoming interdisciplinary – integrating several scientific disciplines or even multidisciplinary – integrating expertise from fields beyond scientific disciplines (Fensham, 2008; Nichols & Davies, 2006). It is essential that contemporary areas of research are presented to students to make their learning relevant and to engage them in areas with which they will need familiarity in their lives beyond school.

Further research is needed in this area to investigate the use of a multiliteracies scaffold in other areas of chemistry in which students are known to develop alternative conceptions, for example, equilibrium, electrochemistry, or stoichiometry, and at different stages of conceptual development, for example, at different junctures across the two years of senior chemistry study. Similar research is also needed in other scientific disciplines as well as subjects beyond science. There is also a need for further examination of the effect of multimodal text production as a writing-to-learn strategy in the senior sciences and to establish effective scaffolding models that allow students to learn with a variety of digital technologies. The application of these approaches to other disciplines may also prove effective. Of particular importance is the investigation of how student learning can be appropriately scaffolded when students are learning about new areas of scientific research, many of which involve concepts from more than one traditional discipline.

CONCLUSION

The examples in this chapter have been taken from a unit that aimed to contextualise a fundamental area of chemistry education, chemical bonding, into a contemporary area of scientific research: the production and applications of biomaterials. The unit was designed with consideration of research findings in a number of areas including students' understanding of chemical bonding, the use of digital technologies to support students' conceptual understanding and representational competence, the efficacy of writing-to-learn strategies, and the application of multiliteracies pedagogy. There are many digital technologies beyond those described in this chapter that are either free online or commercially available and it is a matter of considering the needs of schools and students in order to select the most appropriate tools and resources in the design of units of work. The suggestions here have been provided to address the commonly cited challenges faced by teachers and students when learning with technology but there are many ways of achieving these goals. It is more important to recognise the potentially powerful learning tools that today's access to technology provides students and to be prepared to experiment with a range of options to scaffold students' learning both in theoretical and laboratory-based or practical learning experiences. The outcomes of the study described in this chapter indicate that digital technologies have the potential to enhance learning in chemistry; however, the findings might also be applied across a range of other subject areas. The framework of multiliteracies provides a valuable structure within which to design learning experiences and scaffolding strategies to develop students' subject-specific literacies as well as developing their broader digital and critical multiliteracies.

ACKNOWLEDGMENT

The study reported in this chapter was funded by the CRC Sugar Industry Innovation through Biotechnology, Brisbane, Australia.

REFERENCES

Baggott La Velle, L., McFarlane, A., & Brawn, R. (2003). Knowledge-transformation through ICT in science education: A case study in teacher-driven curriculum development. *British Journal of Educational Technology, 34*(2), 183–199. doi:10.1111/1467-8535.00319

Cope, B., & Kalantzis, M. (Eds.). (2000). *Multiliteracies: Literacy learning and the design of social futures*. South Melbourne, Australia: Macmillan.

Cumming, J. J., & Wyatt-Smith, C. M. (Eds.). (2001). *Literacy and the curriculum: Success in senior secondary schooling*. Melbourne, Australia: The Australian Council for Educational Research.

Fensham, P. J. (1975). Concept formation. In D. J. Daniels (Ed.), *New movements in the study and teaching of chemistry* (pp. 199-217). London: Temple Smith.

Fensham, P. J. (2008). *Complexity Theory: Its relevance to science education.* Paper presented at the Australasian Science Education Research Association (ASERA) 39th Annual International Conference, Brisbane, Australia.

Gabel, D. (1999). Improving teaching and learning through chemistry education research: A look to the future. *Journal of Chemical Education, 76*(4), 548–554.

Gee, J. P. (2004). Language in the science classroom: Academic social languages as the heart of school-based literacy. In E. W. Saul (Ed.), *Crossing borders in literacy and science instruction: Perspectives on theory and practice.* (pp. 13-32). Arlington, VA: National Science Teachers Association.

Gee, J. P. (2005). Language in the science classroom: Academic social languages as the heart of school-based literacy. In R. Yerrick & W.-M. Roth (Eds.), *Establishing scientific classroom discourse communities: Multiple voices of teaching and learning research* (pp. 19-37). Mahwah, NJ: Lawrence Erlbaum Associates.

Greeno, J. G. (1998). The situativity of knowing, learning, and research. *The American Psychologist, 53*(1), 5–26. doi:10.1037/0003-066X.53.1.5

Grimberg, B. I. (2008). Promoting high-order thinking through the use of the science writing heuristic. In B. M. Hand (Ed.), *Science inquiry, argument and language: A case for the science writing heuristic* (pp. 87-97). Rotterdam, the Netherlands: Sense Publishers.

Gunel, M., Hand, B., & Gunduz, S. (2006). Comparing students' understanding of quantum physics when embedding multimodal representations into two different writing formats: Presentation format versus summary report format. *Science Education, 90*, 1092–1112. doi:10.1002/sce.20160

Gunel, M., Hand, B., & Prain, V. (2007). Writing for learning in science: A secondary analysis of six studies. *International Journal of Science and Mathematics Education, 5*, 615–637. doi:10.1007/s10763-007-9082-y

Halliday, M. A. K., & Hasan, R. (1985). *Language, context, and text: Aspects of language in a social semiotic perspective.* Geelong, Australia: Deakin University.

Hand, B., Hohenshell, L., & Prain, V. (2007). Examining the effect of multiple writing tasks on Year 10 biology students' understandings of cell and molecular biology concepts. *Instructional Science, 35*, 343–373. doi:10.1007/s11251-006-9012-3

Hand, B., & Yang, E.-M., & Bruxvoort. (2007). Using writing-to-learn science strategies to improve Year 11 students' understandings of stoichiometry. *International Journal of Science and Mathematics Education, 5*, 125–143. doi:10.1007/s10763-005-9028-1

Jewitt, C. (2006). *Teaching, literacy, and learning.* London: Routledge.

Johnstone, A. H. (1996). Chemistry teaching - Science or alchemy? *Journal of Chemical Education, 74*(3), 262–268.

Jonassen, D. H., & Carr, C. (2000). Mindtools: Affording multiple knowledge representations for learning. In S. P. Lajoie (Ed.), *Computers as cognitive tools* (pp. 165-196). Mahwah, NJ: Lawrence Erlbaum Associates.

Keys, C. W. (1999). Revitalising instruction in scientific genres: Connecting knowledge production with writing to learn in science. *Science Education, 83*, 115–130. doi:10.1002/(SICI)1098-237X(199903)83:2<115::AID-SCE2>3.0.CO;2-Q

Klein, P. D. (2004). Constructing scientific explanations through writing. *Instructional Science, 32*, 191–231. doi:10.1023/B:TRUC.0000024189.74263.bd

Kozma, R. (2000a). Students collaborating with computer models and physical experiments. In J. Roschelle & C. Hoadley (Eds.), *Proceedings of the conference on computer-supported collaborative learning.* Mahwah, NJ: Lawrence Erlbaum Associates.

Kozma, R. (2000b). The use of multiple representations and the social construction of understanding in chemistry. In M. Jacobson & R. Kozma (Eds.), *Innovations in science and mathematics education: Advanced designs for technologies of learning* (pp. 11-46). Mahwah, NJ: Lawrence Erlbaum Associates.

Kozma, R., Chin, E., Russell, J., & Marx, N. (2000). The roles of representations and tools in the chemistry laboratory and their implications for chemistry learning. *Journal of the Learning Sciences, 9*(2), 105–143. doi:10.1207/s15327809jls0902_1

Kozma, R., & Russell, J. (1997). Multimedia and understanding: Expert and novice responses to different representations of chemical phenomena. *Journal of Research in Science Teaching*, *34*(9), 949–968. doi:10.1002/(SICI)1098-2736(199711)34:9<949::AID-TEA7>3.0.CO;2-U

Kozma, R., & Russell, J. (2005). Multimedia learning of chemistry. In R. E. Mayer (Ed.), *Cambridge handbook of multimedia learning* (pp. 409-428). New York: Cambridge University Press.

Kozma, R., & Russell, J. (2005). Students becoming chemists: Developing representational competence. In J. K. Gilbert (Ed.), *Visualisation in science education* (pp. 121-146). Dordrecht, the Netherlands: Springer.

Lemke, J. L. (2000). Multimedia literacy demands of the scientific curriculum. *Linguistics and Education*, *10*(3), 247–271. doi:10.1016/S0898-5898(99)00009-1

Luke, C. (2000). Cyber-schooling and technological change: Multiliteracies for new times. In B. Cope & M. Kalantzis (Eds.), *Multiliteracies: Literacy learning and the design of social futures* (pp. 69-91). South Melbourne, Australia: Macmillan.

Michalchik, V., Rosenquist, A., Kozma, R., Kreikemeier, P., & Schank, P. (2008). Representational resources for constructing shared understandings in the high school chemistry classroom. In J. K. Gilbert, M. Reiner & M. B. Nakhleh (Eds.), *Visualisation: Theory and practice in science education* (pp. 233-282). London: Springer.

Nichols, K., & Davies, J. (2006). Teaching and learning in new spaces: A case for interdisciplinary inquiry-based learning. In Y. J. Lee, A. L. Tan, & B. T. Ho (Eds.), *International Science Education Conference 2006*. Singapore: National Institute of Education.

Norris, S. P., & Phillips, L. M. (2003). How literacy in its fundamental sense is central to scientific literacy. *Science Education*, *87*, 224–240. doi:10.1002/sce.10066

Pallant, A., & Tinker, R. F. (2004). Reasoning with atomic-scale molecular dynamic models. *Journal of Science Education and Technology*, *13*, 51–66. doi:10.1023/B:JOST.0000019638.01800.d0

Prain, V. (2006). Learning from writing in secondary science: Some theoretical and practical implications. *International Journal of Science Education*, *28*(2-3), 179–201. doi:10.1080/09500690500336643

Russell, J., & Kozma, R. (2005). Assessing learning from the use of multimedia chemical visualisation software. In J. K. Gilbert (Ed.), *Visualisation in science education* (pp. 299-332). Dordrecht, the Netherlands: Springer.

Russell, J., Kozma, R., Jones, T., Wykoff, J., Marx, N., & Davis, J. (1997). Use of simultaneous-synchronised macroscopic, microscopic, and symbolic representations to enhance the teaching and learning of chemical concepts. *Journal of Chemical Education*, *74*(3), 330–334.

Schank, P., & Kozma, R. (2002). Learning chemistry through the use of a representation-based knowledge-building environment. *Journal of Computers in Mathematics and Science Teaching*, *21*(3), 253–279.

Stieff, M., & Wilensky, U. (2003). Connected chemistry - Incorporating interactive simulations into the chemistry classroom. *Journal of Science Education and Technology*, *12*(3), 285–302. doi:10.1023/A:1025085023936

Taber, K. S., & Coll, R. K. (2002). Bonding. In J. K. Gilbert, O. De Jong, R. Justi, D. F. Treagust & J. H. Van Driel (Eds.), *Chemical education: Towards research-based practice* (pp. 213-234). Amsterdam: Kluwer Academic Publishers.

Tan, K., & Treagust, D. F. (1999). Evaluating students' understanding of chemical bonding. *The School Science Review, 81*, 75–83.

The New London Group. (2000). A pedagogy of multiliteracies: Designing social futures. In B. Cope & M. Kalantzis (Eds.), *Multiliteracies: Literacy learning and the design of social futures* (pp. 9-37). South Melbourne, Australia: Macmillan.

Trunfio, P., Berenfeld, B., Kreikemeier, P., Moran, J., & Moodley, S. (2003). *Molecular modelling and visualisation tools in science education.* Paper presented at the 2003 Annual Meeting of the National Association of Research in Science Teaching, Philadelphia.

Unsworth, L. (2001). *Teaching multiliteracies across the curriculum.* Buckingham, UK: Open University Press.

Unsworth, L. (2006). Towards a metalanguage for multiliteracies education: Describing the meaning making resources of language-image interaction. *English Teaching: Practice and Critique*, *5*(1), 55–76.

Vermaat, H., Terlouw, C., & Dijkstra, S. (2003, April). *Multiple representations in web-based learning of chemistry concepts.* Paper presented at the 84th Annual Meeting of the American Educational Research Association, Special Interest Group Technology, Instruction, Cognition and Learning, Chicago.

Wells, M. A., & Reynolds, L. J. (2005). Digital literacies. In D. L. Pendergast & N. M. Bahr (Eds.), *Teaching middle years: Rethinking curriculum, pedagogy, and assessment* (pp. 242-254). Crows Nest, Australia: Allen & Unwin.

Wilensky, U., & Resnick, M. (1999). Thinking in levels: A dynamic systems approach to making sense of the world. *Journal of Science Education and Technology*, *8*(1), 3–19. doi:10.1023/A:1009421303064

Williamson, B. (2005). *What are multimodality, multisemiotics and multiliteracies? A brief guide to some jargon.* Retrieved June 25, 2006, from http:www.futurelab.org.uk/viewpoint/art49.htm

Wu, H., Krajcik, J. S., & Soloway, E. (2001). Promoting understanding of chemical representations: Students' use of a visualisation tool in the classroom. *Journal of Research in Science Teaching*, *38*(7), 821–842. doi:10.1002/tea.1033

Wu, H., & Shah, P. (2004). Exploring visuospatial thinking in chemistry learning. *Science Education*, *88*(3), 465–492. doi:10.1002/sce.10126

Xie, Q., & Tinker, R. (2006). Molecular dynamics simulations of chemical reactions for use in education. *Journal of Chemical Education*, *83*(1), 77–83.

Yore, L. D., & Treagust, D. F. (2006). Current realities and future possibilities: Language and science literacy - empowering research and informing instruction. *International Journal of Science Education*, *28*(2-3), 291–314. doi:10.1080/09500690500336973

Chapter 13
Robotics as a Vehicle for Multiliteracies

Marissa J. Saville
Scotch Oakburn College, Australia

ABSTRACT

This chapter is a catalyst for encouraging educators to use robotics as a vehicle for multiliteracies. This chapter will provide compelling, practical evidence of the multimodal nature of robotics, highlighting the potential of robotics to encompass any or all of the linguistic, spatial, visual, audio and gestural elements of multiliteracies, as described by the New London Group (1996). The social and technological benefits for both genders arising from the integration of robotics into the curriculum, and their importance in a rapidly changing world are discussed, as is the need for educators to learn how to facilitate a learning environment that entices students to take risks and solve problems through the development of higher-order thinking skills. Robotics crosses curriculum boundaries, and engages and motivates students of all ages by making learning directed and real.

ROBOTICS AS A VEHICLE FOR MULTILITERACIES

Being literate in today's society and in the future is more than just being able to read and write the written word. With advances in technology and the inclusion of technology in educational settings students are reading and viewing an increasingly complex and diverse range of multimodal texts. Literacy and learning in these new environments requires students to be multiliterate. (Zammit & Downes, 2002, p. 24)

INTRODUCTION

Literacy and thinking skills are generally accepted as two of the core building blocks that support learning across the curriculum (Hedley, Antonacci & Rabinowitz, 1995; Stoll, Fink & Earl, 2003). To be literate in today's technological knowledge-based society requires more than just the ability to read,

DOI: 10.4018/978-1-60566-673-0.ch013

write, listen and speak in English (Chua, 2004; Cope & Kalantzis, 2000). The arrival of new technologies in the educational arena in the late 1970s brought with it a myriad of issues and implications for literacy practice (Snyder, 1998). In 1994, a group of educational theorists (the 'New London Group') met to share and discuss their combined concerns, experiences, expertise and expectations for the future of literacy learning within national and cultural contexts (Cope & Kalantzis, 2000). They concurred that to achieve positive social outcomes for all students it was essential that literacy pedagogy capitalise on cultural and linguistic diversity. As a result of their discussions, they used the term 'multiliteracies' to encapsulate their vision for literacy learning which combined traditional literacy approaches with the multitude of technological tools present in the community (Cope & Kalantzis, 2000). The New London Group recognised the dynamic nature of multiliteracies, placing importance on learning to make meaning by the integration of multimodal dimensions with texts full of media, multimedia (text, graphics, video and audio), and hypermedia (multimedia linked by hypertext) (Cope & Kalantzis, 2000). With multiliteracy viewed as essential to effective global citizenship, the group considered it extremely important that educational achievements not be hampered by cultural, linguistic, or gender differences (Cope & Kalantzis, 2000). According to Giddings (1988) the development of critical thinking skills is crucial for students to respond to, and reflect on, the diversity of cultural literature. Thus it is imperative for teachers to devise learning experiences that develop thinking skills, and which are equitable, engaging, and achievable by all students (Darling-Hammond, 1997; Eggen & Kauchak, 2001; Hamston & Murdoch, 1996; Luke & Carpenter, 2003; Marsh, 2000; Murdoch & Hornsby, 1997; Perkins & Blythe, 1994; Stoll et al., 2003).

A multiliterate pedagogy views modern technologies as a means of transforming curricula, and uses a variety of texts in critical, dynamic, reflective and thoughtful ways (Department of Education [DoE], Tasmania, 2005; 2007; Unsworth, 2001). The complex relationship between modern technologies and literacy learning challenges educators to rethink their practice (Healy, 2004; Snyder, 1998). While technologies such as the Internet, email, word processing and hypertext have not replaced the printed book, they have blurred the boundaries of literacy and changed the production, processing, storage, retrieval and usage of written and visual language (Snyder, 1998). With approximately 377 million people using the Internet world-wide, the scope of technology's impact on business, media, entertainment, and society is creating an e-world, comprised of "perhaps the most transformative technology in history" (United States Web-based Education Commission [USWEC], 2000, p. 1). The USWEC argues that it is high time the Internet's potential to transform education was made a reality. Hawkridge (1989) is also concerned with the manner in which schools prepare students for active participation in society, arguing that they must be better equipped with the skills to function effectively in the technological global society of the future. Similarly, Kearns and Grant (2002) offer the rationale that technological competence is now a prerequisite life skill, key to employability and participation in society. Some have viewed technology as a passing fad in the educational arena; however it is now widely recognised as a valuable tool for promoting students' learning (Cromwell, 1998). Although virtually impossible for teachers to accurately predict the technological skills students will need in their future, Williams (2000) believes a wide range of technological experiences are invaluable for developing positive attitudes towards technology that will support students in their personal and professional life after school. Williams (2000) suggests that it is fitting to embed computers throughout classroom experiences, because this is consistent with real life and work contexts.

A multiliterate curriculum effectively bridges and develops students' abilities to use the various text-types they encounter at school and in the community, thus promoting a real-life approach to learning (DoE, 2005; Healy, 2004). Furthermore, the Tasmanian DoE (2005) recognises that such texts are not confined to written formats, but can integrate the linguistic, spatial, visual, audio and gestural elements as described by the New London Group (1996). The linguistic element includes the visual aspects of meanings attained from images, page layouts, screen formats and the like; the spatial element refers to meanings derived from environmental, personal, and architectural spaces; the audio element gathers meaning from music and sound; and the gestural element refers to meaning made from body language and physicality (New London Group, 1996). However, the most effective and significant learning is achieved by a multimodal approach to learning, which integrates any number of these elements together in surprisingly dynamic and powerful ways (New London Group, 1996). It can be said that meaning-making in every day life is multimodal; a trip to the shopping mall for example, is a remarkably complex combination of many, or all, of the elements, and thus should be reflected in educational experiences (New London Group, 1996).

BACKGROUND

Robotics is an effective tool to support a multimodal approach to learning in that it can be used to incorporate some, or all, of the elements of multiliteracies depending upon the particular challenge and desired learning outcomes. For example, students may expand their vocabulary as they learn the discourse of their robot's programming language, learn to identify visual iconic symbols (D'Agustino, 2007; Gregor, 2005), and engage in related literacy activities such as reflective, procedural, exposition, or narrative writing tasks based on their own experiences (D'Agustino, 2007; Dibdin, 2006). Rogers and Portsmore (2004) have used robotics as a 'visual reading' tool, whereby they challenged students to use the robots to build something from the text they were reading. Verbal communication skills are developed as students discuss and explain their ideas and solutions, brainstorm, or problem solve situations that they encounter (D'Agustino, 2007; Gregor, 2005); this aspect links directly to both the audio and linguistic elements as it concerns both spoken language, and the development of understanding of grammatical conventions (New London Group, 1996). Students develop spatial awareness and visualisation skills as they must design and programme their robots to stay within set boundaries, and at the same time, not collide with other robots (D'Agustino, 2007; Gregor, 2005). Robots can be programmed to create and play musical tunes, and their movements can be programmed to accompany or 'dance' in time to a piece of music; this can be an extremely challenging and engaging endeavour (Gregor, 2005; Gura, 2007). Students can be challenged to create robots that represent specific things, such as people, animals or vehicles, and careful building design can result in effective, engaging, and often amusing parody of the characteristics of the chosen subject (D'Agustino, 2007; Gregor, 2005). Indeed, numerous researchers acknowledge robotics as a viable springboard for successfully improving learning outcomes in a range of curriculum areas, including mathematics, science, literacy, technology, and engineering (D'Agustino, 2007; Dibdin, 2006; Gura, 2007; Norton, McRobbie & Ginns, 2007; Rogers & Portsmore, 2004).

Robotics also provides opportunities for interdisciplinary learning and enables high levels of learner engagement (D'Agustino & King, 2007). For example, Rogers and Portsmore (2004) report how a year 2 teacher challenged students to use robotics to build the amusement park from their class novel, Charlotte's Web (by E.B.White), integrated into the mathematics curriculum as students needed to exchange play money before being able to use the ride. Another example of integrated learning comes from Doyle (2007, as cited in Murray, 2007) who describes how an English teacher integrated robotics into his classroom by asking his students to tell the age-old story 'The Three Billy Goats Gruff' through team-work and problem-solving in order to choreograph their robots' movements. Seemingly simple tasks can easily become creative and problem-solving masterpieces (Druin & Hendler, 2000). Several schools involved in a U.K. project for raising attainment in young boys' writing through technology effectively used robotics to engage students in literacy tasks (Canterbury City & Country Cluster, 2007). A number of topics were selected for students to create labelled pictures and diagrams, including 'dinosaurs', 'travel and journeys', and 'a walk in the jungle', with students recording the places and/or sounds of the places their robots visited.

In order to link robotics to multiliteracies the following sections will explore contemporary educational theorists' views on using robotics as part of a multiliterate curriculum in light of the author's practical experience teaching robotics in a primary school context. The history of robotics, the features of three robots recommended for classroom use, and how the use of robotics aligns with modern educational philosophies are also discussed. Furthermore, there are a number of important issues surrounding the successful implementation of a robotics curriculum which will also be considered, these being: a supportive teaching pedagogy, the development of students' social issues and Emotional Intelligence, the benefits of mentoring, an examination of gender differences and classroom logistics.

The History of Robotics

The word 'robot' is thought to derive from the Czech word 'robota' meaning compulsory labour, which was originally used by Karel Capek in 1923 in his play, 'Rossum's Universal Robots' (Gura, 2007). The term 'robotics' came soon after, and is defined by Merriam-Webster's (2008) online dictionary as technology dealing with the design, construction, and operation of robots in automation. Robotics was popularised by the science fiction author Isaac Asimov in 1942, in his book (and later movie), 'I Robot', and continued gaining popularity as they became regular features of television shows and movies, such as 'The Day the Earth Stood Still' (1951), 'Lost in Space' (1965), 'Dr. Who and the Daleks' (1965), 'Transformers' (1984), 'The Terminator' (1984), 'Short Circuit' (1986), and 'Bicentennial Man' (1999) (as cited in Gura, 2007). The high number of related enthusiast sites on the Internet attests to the popularity of this culture, and provides a background for the capacity of school robotics to capture the imagination through its enduring appeal (Gura, 2007). Robots are now commonplace in the home and community, performing regular tasks like answering machines, automatically opening doors, controlling streetlights and watering systems, and dispensing money; hence the use of robots in the classroom provides opportunities for open-ended learning grounded in realistic contexts (Reilly, 2006; Sims, Spinetti, Crabb & Earnshaw, 2006). Unlike the disciplines that require students to learn a fixed body of knowledge, robotics is an area that enables students to be immersed in active, problem-solving learning that is as dynamic by nature in the classroom as it is in the real world (Gura, 2007). Furthermore, the educational benefits from the whole process of conceiving, designing, constructing, and programming an open-ended autonomous robot projects far outweighs those to be gained from building robots based on preconceived ideas (Gura, 2007).

LEGO® robotics (The Lego Group, 2007), the Valiant Roamer® (Valiant USA, 2004) and the Bee-bot® (TTS Group, 2008) are three forms of robotics that are considered to be appropriate for use in the classroom (Alimisis et al., 2007), and with which the author has practical experience. LEGO® (The Lego Group, 2007) has two types of robots available for home and classroom use, these being the original RCX (Robotics Command System), which has been around for over ten years, and the recently-released NXT-G. Each of these robots has a computer 'brain' set within a 'brick', which when programmed accordingly, controls motors and/or lights attached to its three output ports. The RCX robot can store up to five long, complex programmes, whereas the NXT can store up to 130K of programmes. The RCX has three, and the NXT four, input ports to which can be attached a range of accessories such as touch and light sensors (both RCX and NXT), ultrasonic, rotation, and sound sensors (NXT only). The robots can be programmed to make decisions, respond to events, simultaneously perform multiple feats, and many other tasks. The 'brain', coupled with a multitude of building blocks, motors and sensors quickly allow students to put together an incredibly wide range of engineering inventions with remarkable speed. In the 1990's, it would take a university student months to create a wall-avoiding creature, whereas Rogers and Portsmore (2004) report how a year 2 student was able to make a wall-avoiding turtle in only a few hours. The graphical programming software ROBOLAB (powered by National Instrument's LabVIEW) has numerous levels, and as such, is compatible for users from ages three to adult (Rogers & Portsmore, 2004). The step-by-step introductory sequences included in the LEGO® MINDSTORMS® NXT software make it very user-friendly for students aged 8 and above (LEGO® Education, 2006). Classroom robotics has been responsible for kindergarten students debating the frictional forces of axles, and elementary students programming with decimals numbers; these engineering experiences have developed an early, deep and genuine conceptual understanding (Rogers & Portsmore, 2004).

With approximately one million students per year worldwide using ROBOLAB and LEGO® robotics, with the software translated into fourteen different languages, international sales success has certainly been achieved (Rogers & Portsmore, 2004). The Valiant Roamer® (Valiant USA, 2004) robot has been in classrooms for nearly as long as the LEGO® RCX, but has an entirely different appearance; it looks much like an oversized mushroom with a thirty centimetre diameter on two wheels, and can be easily decorated to portray a wide range of characters. The author has witnessed year 1 students engaged in their learning as they pretended the Roamer® was a garbage collector, and proceeded to pair up and use the robot to 'collect' (by gently nudging) specific rubbish types spread around the classroom. They wrote down the sequence of symbols representing their plan for the robot's movements, and then tested their theory. Many discussions and experiments ensued as students worked to identify errors, and pure delight was evident when their goal was reached. More than a quarter of a million of these highly popular robots can be found in schools throughout twenty-seven countries around the world (Murray, 2007). Research by the Faculty of Education at Curtin University (1997) concluded that the Roamer® was a highly motivating robot, suitable for use by children from kindergarten right through to the end of primary school. It can store 182 actions, and can turn and move in a range of units to suit the age of the user; however its ability to turn in one degree units makes it an ideal tool for students to explore mathematical concepts like shapes, mapping, and simple mathematical equations. Students enter their programs directly through a colour-coded keypad on the top of the machine and can incorporate sound, nested programmes, lights, and sensor inputs. Variables, such as the impact of the type of floor surface on the wheels, need to be considered and contended with, reflecting situations drivers deal with driving on a day-to-day basis (Murray, 2007). A marker pen can be placed in a hole in the centre of the robot and used to trace its path on butcher's paper taped to the floor. The author has again witnessed insightful conversations and debates over the angles, turns and distances from students challenged to draw a capital letter. Letters like 'L' provide an easy starting point, and students readily move on to more complex tasks like 'M' or 'A', which require a higher level of thinking. The robot provides immediate feedback for students' efforts, and evidence of areas needing guidance or consolidation. A different dimension can be added through the use of Roamer World® software, which allows the user to control the robot directly from a separate computer.

The Bee-bot® (TTS Group, 2008) is similar to the Valiant Roamer®, in that it is a programmable floor robot that the user commands by pushing buttons directly on the top of the robot, however its simplistic design and large directional arrow buttons make it more suited for young children from the age of three to middle primary school. It has sold over seventeen thousand since its release in July 2005, and is an ideal medium for teaching control, spatial awareness, problem-solving, basic programming concepts, and directional language. The Bee-bot® accurately travels forwards or backwards in fifteen centimetre units, turns in ninety degree units, and can retain up to forty steps at once. The Bee-bot® can be decorated to take on a character role with clip on covers designed for this purpose, and can perform on rough or smooth surfaces. Its small thirteen centimetre long chassis allows it to be used on table tops or bench surfaces. The robot's moves and commands are acknowledged by the flashing of its eyes, and optional sounds. Sprainger (2007) describes the success of a pilot program that introduced Bee-bots® to young students from six schools throughout Parramatta in Australia. Teachers were provided with literacy resources appropriate to their year group, for example the picture books 'Going on a Bear Hunt' and 'Rosie's Walk', for students to emulate and develop with their robots. The students responded with imaginative and creative play-learning, with some even forming emotional attachments and naming their robots. Assorted play mats (available through retail or student/teacher made) added to the variety and scope of the program by providing a variety of everyday scenarios for students to explore.

Seymour Papert, a renowned professor at the MIT research university, was an early supporter of using LEGO® robotics in the school curriculum (Norton, 2008). He termed the rich and multifaceted learning that can be achieved through the construction and programming of robots as 'constructionism', or more simplified as 'learning-by-making' (Papert & Harel, 1991). Understanding of the learning process has evolved over time. When Stoll et al. (2003) examined the work of philosophers and educational theorists such as Plato, Descartes, Locke and Skinner, they found a common belief; "learning was something that *happened to* the learner" (p. 23). Since these early years, extraordinary advances in understanding about the process of learning have occurred (Stoll et al., 2003). Educational theorists of the twentieth century, such as Piaget, Vygotsky, and Dewey, have expanded educators' understanding of learning dramatically to the point where learning is recognised as being intellectual, social and emotional, linear and erratic, and by both design and chance (Stoll et al., 2003). Slee (2002) has similar findings when he states: "Research into child development is uncovering facts at a rate that sometimes outstrips our ability to integrate them into a coherent framework" (p. 48). Constructionism aligns with the modern educational theory of constructivist learning, whereby "learners construct their own understanding of the world rather than recording it in an already-organized form" (Eggen & Kauchak, 2001, p.106). Learning is not a passive activity, but an active and dynamic process; there must be "some level of *consciousness*… allowing one to perceive and think about what is happening outside and inside oneself in such a way that it can be evaluated and acted on" (Csikszentmihalyi, 1990, as cited in Stoll et al., 2003, p. 25). Students must be engaged in the learning process because, "(o)utside events don't exist for people unless they are aware of them" (Stoll et al., 2003, p. 25). Students are constantly building and expanding their knowledge when constructing and programming robots; they are "learning on the edge of what they know at all times – the area of proximal learning" (Gregor, 2005, p. 10). After the initial design and construction of a LEGO® robot, which in itself requires students to identify a problem and formulate a solution, students continually extend their engineering skills as they build their design and test their solution. Students begin the programming process; each time a section of programme is written, downloaded to the robot and executed, students receive immediate feedback from the robot. Students learn from each attempt and alteration as they critically consider whether the next modification or addition lies with the robot design, construction, programming, or combination of these. Students have the opportunity to improve and refine their robot, and are continually scaffolding, consolidating, and expanding, their knowledge and understanding.

Implementation of a Multiliterate Robotics Curriculum

There are a number of important issues surrounding the successful implementation of a multiliterate robotics curriculum which will now be considered, these being teaching pedagogy, social issues, Emotional Intelligence, mentoring, gender differences, and classroom logistics.

Teaching Pedagogy

Society is changing with the presence, growth and integration of technology into human civilisation (Drenoyianni, 2006). To survive in this new world, it is important to be multiliterate. Whilst new technologies have been heralded by many as "the totem of educational change" (Drenoyianni, 2006, p. 401) and the solution to a variety of educational problems (Cuban, 1986), other research indicates that their effectiveness as a learning tool relies on the pedagogy, teaching methods, curriculum and context in which they are used (Peck, Cuban & Kirkpatrick, 2002; Tsiakalos, 2002, as cited in Drenoyianni, 2006). Peck et al.'s (2002) study recognised the potential of technologies for improving educational outcomes, but found very few teachers capitalising on this potential; a view supported by the study's teacher and student surveys. In fact, this study found little evidence of increased technology use in regular classroom learning compared to that of 50 years ago: "based on our findings and on national data, we maintain confidently that, contrary to the dreams of most techno-promoters, technology has simply become a small and largely peripheral element of a familiar, long-running high school routine" (p. 32). In contrast, Heale (2005) described how the introduction of new technologies provided the stimulus for a welcome transformation at the technologically rich Frankston High School. As a result, this school has changed its focus from conventional teacher-centred teaching methods, to education focused on student learning where students are encouraged to take greater responsibility for their learning, and cooperative teamwork is promoted.

Robotics is increasingly being recognised as a valuable educational tool, and as such, is becoming more popular; however capitalising on the benefits this tool offers may require a pedagogical shift by many teachers (Carbonaro, Rex & Chambers, 2004). Robotics is a hands-on, student-centred, project based activity that uses a non-conventional teaching approach far removed from traditional teacher-centred teaching methods (D'Agustino & King, 2007; Rogers & Portsmore, 2004). In this way the teacher directs and guides the learning as the students explore theories and concepts, instead of reading about or listening to the teacher explain the relevant principles (D'Agustino & King, 2007). Indeed, robotics is an ideal vehicle for implementing progressive educational philosophies such as a constructivist approach to learning, problem-solving, interdisciplinary/integrated subject areas, and collaborative learning activities (Gura, 2007). The teacher's role in teaching robotics is that of a facilitator who provides scope for students to explore their ideas and designs, as they learn from each and every attempt (Gregor, 2005; Sims et al., 2006).

Teachers do not need to be experts in the field, but they do need to be prepared to model learning for and with their students. Robotics sessions become an exciting adventure, where a risk taking attitude is typical, knowledge is shared, and success is celebrated by all (D'Agustino & King, 2007). Students' futures depend upon their ability to "learn to understand concepts as well as facts, in classrooms where they link and apply ideas, produce their own work, and learn to cooperate productively with diverse peers" (Darling-Hammond, 1997, p. 331). Assessment of students' understanding is an ongoing and rich affair, whereby students' developing understanding is constantly on display throughout the trial and error process (Carbonaro et al., 2004). Carbonaro et al. (2004) also recommend the use of student log books and video to record the learning process. However, it is important to these processes that the robotics teacher be extremely careful to ask questions that generate students' thinking rather than 'giving' them the answer (Rogers & Portsmore, 2004). In this way, students will develop genuine understanding, rather than knowledge simply gleaned as an unconnected fact (Darling-Hammond, 1997). Students who have developed deep understanding "can evaluate and defend ideas with careful reasoning and evidence, independently inquire into a problem using a productive research strategy, produce a high-quality piece of work, and understand the standards that indicate good performance" (Darling-Hammond, 1997, p. 96). Furthermore, they can demonstrate their understanding by applying what they have learned to solve other problems.

For teachers whose curriculum is driven by a teacher-centred approach, this requires a great deal of flexibility and a change in practice on the part of the teacher (D'Agustino & King, 2007). History has shown that despite many reform efforts, advances in teacher education and understanding of the learning process, there is still evidence of reliance on practices such as whole group, 'chalk-and-talk' teacher-centred teaching, dependence on textbooks, and traditional classroom layouts comprised of rows of desks (Cuban, 1990; Marsh, 2000). However, Gura (2007) has found that bringing robotics into the classroom can reinvigorate teachers, foster professional growth, and increase professional satisfaction. As with all educational innovation, the effectiveness of a robotics program depends largely on the teacher's ability and attitude to change; a process made easier with resources, training, and support (D'Agustino & King, 2007). Robotics is often perceived as being highly-technical by nature, which may be cause for concern by some, however, in reality teachers really only need to know a few easy icon-based programming fundamentals to get started, and a quick Internet search reveals plenty of free online help (D'Agustino & King, 2007). Some teachers struggle to teach robotics because they feel uncomfortable and unprepared due to a lack of training (Howell, McCaffrey & Murphy, 2003). Other difficulties arise for teachers who are prepared to experiment with robotics, but are employed in a school with a culture that resists change and innovation, or are lacking the financial resources to support such endeavours (D'Agustino & King, 2007). There are programmes in place to assist schools with financial constraints. For example, in Tasmania (Australia), departmental schools can apply for the free Centre for Extended Learning (2008) SiMERR 'SmartBots' project, with priority given to rural schools without an existing robotics programme. This is a popular online robotics course designed for teams of up to six, year five to eight students considered to be notably advanced, gifted or talented students by their teachers. The students are lent the robotics kits (for classroom use), and complete a series of tutorials, programming and building challenges within set time-frames and specified criteria. The programme is a great way to start a robotics programme, as it is supported, managed, developed, delivered and maintained by an expert, online teacher, who communicates with students and teachers online on a regular basis. Schools nominate a support person to assist students as required, with this person being given a full-day workshop to familiarise themselves with the basic principles of the programme prior to the commencement of the course.

The range of learning outcomes that can be attained through robotics is astounding. In discussing how students learn by 'doing' LEGO® robotics, Rogers and Portsmore (2004) state: "it is impressive what students can learn, from discovering molecular thermodynamics in 4th grade to frictional forces in 1st" (p. 23). Warren (2007, as cited in Murray, 2007) commented on how easily the fundamentals of geometry, such as angles and degrees can be taught through experimentation with the Valiant Roamer®, when compared to traditional shape drawing on a board. The trial and error, cyclic nature of LEGO® robotics is an excellent medium for students to develop their problem solving, creativity and higher order thinking skills (Alimisis et al., 2007; Gregor, 2005; Mauch 2001; Papert & Harel, 1991; Sims et al., 2006). Research suggests that in a non-threatening, supportive learning environment, robotics can be used effectively to promote seven of Art Costa's Habits of Mind, these being risk taking, flexibility, impulsivity, persistence, questioning, check for accuracy, and creativity (Sims et al., 2006; Sprainger, 2007). Practical experience teaching and using robots supports this research: The fun and innovative nature of robotics is ideal for creating an environment in which students can feel comfortable experimenting and taking risks as they test out different ideas, knowing that it is highly likely, indeed expected, that they will need multiple attempts to successfully achieve their goals. The complexity of design and programming functions are only limited by the imagination, encouraging lateral thinking both individually, or in group robotic performances. Indeed, Gregor (2005) describes robotics as "an intellectually stimulating challenge that involves a great deal of higher order reasoning and critical thinking – but above all it is fun" (p. 9).

Social Equity in a Multiliterate Environment

The development of social skills is vital for students to effectively understand, and actively participate in an interconnected and complex global society (Cope & Kalantzis, 1988, as cited in Allard & Johnson, 2002). Australian curriculum documents recognise the importance of the development of social competencies; the Victorian curriculum guide's (2002, as cited in Allard & Johnson, 2002) definition of social competence as the effective integration of the behaviours, emotions, and cognitive aspects of social relationships, is one such example. The New London Group (Cope & Kalantzis, 2000) call attention to the importance of 'civic pluralism', arguing it is essential for achieving a fair and equitable future for all. For classroom practice, this translates to teachers recognising and capitalising on student differences, whereby cultural and linguistic diversity is viewed as a valuable classroom resource (Cope & Kalantzis, 2000). Arthur and Davison (2000) contend that social development is linked directly to the cultural conditioning and the historical and social contexts in which children learn. Other research suggests that an individual's social development and personal identity is derived from the way he or she is perceived and treated by their family and peer group (Johnson & Johnson, 1997). Social exclusion can have a very negative impact on confidence, self esteem, aspirations, achievement and attitude, and can make a person feel alienated, isolated, angry and hopeless (Francis & Skelton, 2005). Thus, the environment, learning experiences, and peer relationships that students experience are of the utmost importance. Scott (2000) expressed doubt that teachers would be able to balance the political agendas that shape curriculum reform, such as summative assessment and target-setting, with truly meaningful learning of social values such as tolerance and respect. Delors' et al. (1996, as cited Stoll et al., 2003) identified four "pillars of knowledge" (Stoll et al., 2003, p. 16): 'learning to know', 'learning to do', (the prime pillars of the knowledge economy) (Hargreaves, 2003, p. 42), 'learning to be' (personal responsibilities), and 'learning to live together' (pertaining to democracy, community and empathy). Hargreaves (2003) argued that learning to live together is possibly the most important pillar in a world that he believes "is falling apart in the face of economic globalization" (p. 42).

Robotics can be used to encourage positive social and democratic behaviours in the classroom by providing multiple tools for demonstrating understanding, communicating, interacting, creating, and constructing meaning (Drenoyianni, 2006). Robotics lends itself to a socio-constructivist teaching pedagogy as it is a useful vehicle for developing social, teamwork, collaboration and communication skills (Alimisis et al., 2007; Gura, 2007; Mauch, 2001). When a social structure is applied to a problem-based learning model, as is the nature of a constructivist approach to learning, students learn from and with each other in a safe but challenging, motivating, and engaging learning environment which promotes risk-taking (Eggen & Kauchak, 2001). Small cooperative groupwork is effective across all year levels, and commonly found in robotics classrooms, providing opportunities for personal and social development (Marsh, 2000). In Mauch's (2001) experience, three students per robot are quite enough, with a fourth member running the risk of becoming redundant. The author concurs with Mauch's (2001) view, however if resources permit, groups of two lead to more active involvement for the team members whilst not detracting from the social aspects of collaborative learning. Including teamwork as a criterion of an assessment rubric given to students before a project starts can motivate students to increase empathy and understanding of their partner and assist conflict resolution strategies. The actual grouping requires careful thought on the part of the teacher. Decisions need to be made as to whether groups would team better as mixed gender, mixed ability, selected by students or by teacher; however it is important that the unit or lesson objectives influence this process (Marsh, 2000). For example high achievers may need to be extended, students may need to learn with peers outside their friendship group or cultural background, or metacognition may be developed through explaining the thinking process to students with different strengths. Groups will work more effectively if the goals are clear, all members have a well-defined role, communication is encouraged, and conflict is resolved (Marsh, 2000).

Constant communication is central to effective teamwork, and is the key to solving the types of problems associated with LEGO® robotics (Mauch, 2001). The cause of problems associated with developing robots using the LEGO® system are often hard to identify, and enforce the need for cooperation and clearly articulated communication between team members as they discuss and trial possible strategies and designs; a situation that benefits from the combined expertise, thinking skills, and creativity of all team members (Beer, Chiel & Drushel, 1999; Mauch, 2001). Indeed, students very quickly learn to value and listen to the contribution of each team member, whether they are responsible for programming, construction, organising, or recording the group's progress (Mauch, 2001). Beer et al. (1999) expressed concern over educational approaches that focused mainly on the promotion of individual problem solving within separate subject domains, after their research indicated that this approach was a major contributor to the poor interpersonal teamwork and critical thinking skills exhibited by the science and engineering students they studied. In the context of a dynamic world, they were disturbed by the lack of experience and preparation these students displayed when attempting to solve real-world problems, and particularly their inability to explore unorthodox or interdisciplinary methods as opposed to standard textbook approaches. The teaming of students so that each group contained students with a mixture of programming and construction skills, was found to be beneficial to the interpersonal skill development of individuals and the teamwork skills of the group as a whole (Beer et al., 1999; Mauch, 2001; Nourbakhsh et al., 2005). However, it is unlikely that truly heterogeneous groups will be formed immediately; merely telling people they are a team does not necessarily mean they will make an effective group (Johnson & Johnson, 1997; Marsh, 2000). Careful monitoring of the groups in action is needed to identify students who need teacher guidance in overcoming personality and problem-solving conflicts (Marsh, 2000).

Emotional Intelligence, Multiliteracy and Global Citizenship

Cope and Kalantzis (2000) argue that multiliteracy is essential for effective global citizenship. The Tasmanian DoE (2002) recognises the significance of the impact that emotions have on learning, recommending that educators learn to acknowledge and recognise emotions and potentially emotional contexts in order to capitalise on learning opportunities. Hargreaves and Fullan (1998) believe the importance of 'Emotional Intelligence' (EI) cannot be understated, and argue wholeheartedly for its development in teachers and students. Daniel Goleman (1995, as cited in Newman, 2007) recognises EI as new type of 'smart' that defies the restraints of technical knowledge or traditional 'IQ'. Goleman (1995, as cited in Hargreaves, 2003) identified five basic competences of EI:

knowing and being able to express one's own emotions; being able to empathize with others' emotions; being able to monitor and regulate one's emotions so they do not get out of control; having the capacity to motivate oneself and others; and possessing the social skills to put the first four competences into action (p. 18).

Goleman (1996) warns that academic intelligence does not necessarily automatically transfer to emotional life, is concerned with schools that are too fixated on academic ability, and neglect the preparation of students for the trials and tribulations of life. Hargreaves (2003) warns that those lacking EI may well be unprepared for citizenship in a global civilisation, with relationships tending to be impersonal and economic based. Likewise, Maxine Greene (1988) warns that a highly cognitive focus in the classroom can compromise the development of the fundamental principles of freedom, morality, ethics and democracy. The promotion of caring relationships and students' social/emotional learning, commitment and character, are vital for developing well-rounded students, and requires teachers to be responsive and sensitive to their students' varied cultures and backgrounds (Hargreaves, 2003; Stoll et al., 2003).

The social-constructivist nature of robotics makes it an ideal means for developing EI. Many would be surprised to learn that student robotics is, in fact, a world of "intense emotion and concentration, camaraderie and self-directed learning" (King, 2007, p. ix). It is a vibrant, empowering and engrossing learning experience during which students are highly likely to experience "a veritable seesaw of intellect and emotions" (King, 2007, p. ix). Frustration can dominate students' emotions when a building or programming solution evades their grasp; team members can easily become irritated or even angry at each other, particularly if a robot is accidentally dropped, or one team member tends to take over; and sheer elation is evident with both small and large achievements. All students are different, and while some know how to control their emotions, others need explicit guidance and rationalisation for controlling their feelings. In the author's experience, a friendly competition between teams can encourage individuals to become more effective team members. Students' teamwork can benefit greatly from a rubric explicitly outlining the expected behaviours and team skills that all members will be assessed on. Learning to share the workload, trust each other, and to discuss, think through and develop ideas are vital elements of a successful robotics team, and requires students to put egos aside, manage their emotions, and put forward a positive attitude.

EI is "as important in a school classroom or staffroom as it is in a corporate office" (Hargreaves, 2003, p. 18). Strong EI is a characteristic common to high performing, 'superstar' leaders and executives, and businesses are increasingly recognising the importance of this quality in their employees (Newman, 2007). For example, the Australian company Foster's, approached Newman to improve its Carlton and United Breweries division leadership team's ability in this area (Newman, 2007). After conducting and interpreting an emotional and social audit, Newman was able to successfully implement strategies that resulted in a 30 percent improvement; an impressive, substantial and, more importantly, sustainable gain. Clearly EI can be developed and there are many benefits from becoming an emotional capitalist (Newman, 2007). Research has identified a link between teachers whose students genuinely felt supported in their learning by caring teachers with higher levels of student engagement and achievement in their learning (Mortimore, Sammons, Lewis & Ecob, 1988; Thomas, Smees, MacBeath, Robertson & Boyd, 2000). Teachers must become concerned with the development of character as well as performance, for without these, Hargreaves (2003) believes "there is little hope of sustained security for any of us" (p. 45).

Mentoring and Multiliteracy

The New London Group (1996) view mentoring as a positive influence on the development of multiliteracy in students. Gregor's (2005) experience teaching robotics suggests that leadership skills can also be promoted through robotics when mixed ability grouping or peer mentoring is incorporated into the program. Students who generally do not learn so well through traditional means suddenly find themselves the class expert, gaining the respect of their peers and teachers (Rogers & Portsmore, 2004). The term 'mentor' originates from Homer's classic tale, 'The Odyssey', in which Odysseus left his possessions and son's education in the care of Mentor, his trusted counsellor and friend (who actually turned out to be the goddess Athene), when he fought in the lengthy Trojan War (Phillip, 2000). Thus, traditional definitions of mentoring reflect the selection of a suitable older person deemed to have appropriate skills and experience, and who is seen as an acceptable source of assistance and support to a young person (Phillip, 2000). Nowadays, mentoring is defined as "a mutually beneficial relationship which involves a more experienced person helping a less experienced person to identify and achieve their goals" (Mentoring Australia, 2000, p. 3).

The author's experience aligns with Gregor's (2005) views, having initially taught LEGO® robotics at year 4 level and then inviting these students to mentor the subsequent year 4, and so on. Each new group of students formed positive relationships with their mentors as they developed the robotic skills and knowledge they needed, and the mentors developed leadership skills, self-esteem, confidence and their sense of self-worth. Another valuable mentoring experience came from an innovation by the University of Tasmania's Education ICT department, who invited primary school students to the University to teach preservice teachers about robotics. Feedback from all parties indicated this to be an extremely positive and beneficial experience to all involved, and the students' self-esteem grew immensely as they became the 'experts' teaching the adults. Similarly, Gura (2007) found great success in mentoring between high-school robotics students, and students from a nearby middle school, as did Howell, et al.'s (2003) report on two university students specialising in engineering and programming successfully mentoring a group of 10-13 year old LEGO® robotics students. Over the past few decades there has been a decline in the amount of out of school support, or 'informal mentoring', available to Australian children, primarily due to factors such as changing family, social and economic circumstances, as well as the redefining of gender work roles (Hartley, 2004). The increasing risk to the health and welfare of young people has been recognised, and as a result the freely available document 'Mentoring Australia' was developed in June, 2000, which outlines the principles and guidelines for effective formal mentoring. Peer mentoring generally uses students of a similar age group, background, or other commonality; however it is important that the recipients accept the mentor as knowledgeable and experienced in the particular field (McDonald, Grove & Youth Advisory Forum Members, 2001). It is also worth noting that a mentor's personal characteristics, communication and presentation skills influence the effectiveness of the mentoring role and as such, individual coaching may be necessary (Mentoring Australia, 2000). Student coaches need to understand that they are entering a problem-solving arena, and as such, must be taught to facilitate the learning of those they are helping, not to do it, or 'give' them a solution (Adventist Robotics League, 2007).

Gender Differences and Multiliteracies Pedagogy

The importance of ensuring that gender is not a barrier to attaining educational success is highlighted by the New London Group (1996) in their discussion of social issues and multiliteracies pedagogy. Advances in brain-based research have found many differences between boys' and girls' learning (Francis & Skelton, 2005; Gurian & Ballew, 2003). For example, girls generally tend to benefit from the use of manipulative and real objects when learning mathematical concepts more than do boys, whereas boys flourish in experiential learning environments with fewer verbal instructions than girls (Gurian & Ballew, 2003). There is also disparity in computer usage between the genders. Research suggests that boys tend to dominate school computer use, especially when the ratio of students to computers is high, while girls are inclined to allow more forceful users to have their turn (Gurian & Ballew, 2003). Males tend to be drawn toward the spatial stimulant of computer monitors more than females, most likely due to the theory that female brains are not generally attracted to the high-speed, right-hemisphere stimulation provided by many computer games (Gurian & Ballew, 2003). Traditionally, curriculum areas have often been viewed as being typically a male or female subject, for example mathematics, science and computers are masculine, while English, language based subjects, and the arts are feminine (Francis & Skelton, 2005). Boys favour memory-based learning, which aligns with traditional presentation of mathematical learning, and as such, is possibly why it is considered a male domain (Francis & Skelton, 2005). Likewise, girls generally relate well to real-world, open-ended tasks which enable a broader set of responses, such as the written assessments demanded by English and humanities subjects. Other research cited by Francis and Skelton (2005) indicates collaborative group work to be a female preference, as compared with males who prefer an individual, more competitive approach. While there are trends evident between the learning styles and preferences of each gender, no research has been able to provide a definitive rule for every child of each gender; there are always exceptions to the rule (Francis & Skelton, 2005).

There is widespread concern about the decreasing number of students completing computer-based subjects in Australia, and consequential IT skills shortage in the workforce (Gedda & McGonnachie, 2006). New South Wales, for example, has seen a steady decline from 22,910 students in 2003, to 18,268 in 2004, and just 15,668 in 2005 (Gedda & McGonnachie, 2006). There is also concern about the low ratio of females compared with males in IT-related jobs: "Women earn only 28 percent of the bachelor's degrees in computer science and constitute just 20 percent of information-technology professionals" (Gurian & Ballew, 2003, p. 97). There has been a marked fall in female enrolment into IT courses, with some universities reporting drops from 24 to 10 percent, which concerns Prabhu (2007) because a gender balance is needed in this industry to keep innovation in design and construction up with market demand. The U.S. has a similar trend of females being under represented in technological careers and educational courses, particularly at advanced levels (Herring & Marken, 2008). Interestingly, this recent research identified gender difference awareness as a potential factor contributing to a female's success in this field. Of the females participating in the study, those who recognised the inequalities facing their gender in their course were better able to attain a positive outcome, complete their IT course, and follow on with a career in this industry. This imbalance needs to be addressed at primary school level to ensure that girls have the same chance as boys in developing a positive attitude towards technology, and the computer skills that they need for a successful career in this area (Gurian & Ballew, 2003; Nobel, 2007). Hence, it is vital that teachers be vigilant in supporting the use of technology by both genders in a fair and equitable manner, provide a range of opportunities that will engage students' interest, and develop a positive attitude towards technology.

Robotics excites and appeals to students of both genders, who are often prepared to use their free time, morning tea break or lunchtime to work on a robotics project (Rogers & Portsmore, 2004). Indeed, from a class of twenty-one, Rogers and Portsmore (2004) reported how twenty-four students (they brought friends), half girls and half boys, turned up for a lunchtime session. While there will always exceptions to the rule, it is interesting to note that the following characteristics appear to hold true regardless of age, culture, ethnicity, or socio-economic background (Milto, Rogers & Portsmore, 2002; Rogers & Portsmore, 2004). Boys like building robotic cars for the sake of building cars, whereas girls respond more positively to purposeful challenges that reflect real life situations; however they are prepared to build a car if it is part of solving a larger problem. Boys tend to want to build the biggest, best, or fastest robot as quickly as possible. Girls like spending time on the deductive, planning, and modelling side of robotics before any building takes place. Girls respond to a teamwork approach to robotics challenges better than boys, as they enjoy the communication and discussion that revolves around possible designs, whereas boys tend to prefer to work alone. Boys do not want to disassemble their work in order to refine their ideas, but would rather build on regardless of existing flaws. Girls tend to have less confidence in the construction of their robots as they generally have less experience than their male counterparts.

While boys tend to be more competitive, both genders enjoy the competitive nature of robotics that can be fostered in the classroom and beyond (Howell et al., 2003; Milto et al., 2002; Rogers & Portsmore, 2004). RoboCup Junior Australia (2007) is a project-based robotics competition designed to extend classroom learning to regional, state, national, and international levels, and is similar to the 'FIRST' Robotics Competition and 'LEGO League' competitions held around the world (Howell et al., 2003). Since its introduction in Melbourne, in 2000, RoboCup has spread rapidly around Australia, as well as thirty countries around the world. While RoboCup effectively integrates engineering and IT skills with curriculum areas, it also emphasises social development by highlighting the need for good sportsmanship, teamwork, problem-solving, collaboration and cooperation within and between teams and nations. RoboCup offers three types of contests for both primary and secondary students, these being dance, rescue, and soccer competitions. RoboCup aspires to interest students in scientific and technological fields, and expects its competitors to share knowledge and technological developments through learning journals which are presented at a team interview with experienced RoboCup judges.

The author's robotics programme consists of year 4 Primary School students, who over the past four years, have competed in the junior dance section. This competition has been the source of extreme motivation, fun and excitement, for mixed-gender teams of up to eleven students working in pairs or threes, with three to six robots per team. Students have been completely engrossed, enthused, frustrated, and elated by their robots' progress, and extremely proud of their final results. Every entry is unique, with endless project possibilities, construction, costuming and choreography, limited only by the imagination. To date students have created robots to the themes of 'The Flintstones', 'The Wigglies', 'Elvis and the Blue Suede Shoes', 'Monster Mash', 'The 8 Amigos', 'Shrek', 'Garfield', 'The SOC Rescuers', 'Alvin and the Chipmunks', 'SpongeBob SquarePants', and 'Ghostbusters'. The learning journals created by past years' teams serve as a wonderful memory, inspiration and challenge to all.

Classroom Logistics

In implementing any new theoretical approach into classroom practice there will be a number of logistical issues to consider, and this is doubly so when implementing robotics using a multiliteracies perspective or framework. The ratio of robots to students, and whether other classes need to share the robots, both have a large impact on the set up and types of projects and building challenges that will work effectively. The optimum scenario is for each class to have its own robotics kits so that students can build and refine their robots without needing to take them apart for other classes to use. If there are enough kits for students to use working in groups of two or three, then it could be a whole class activity, or if there are not enough kits, then it could become a learning station on a rotational basis or extension opportunity. Alternatively, it could be run as a lunch-time activity for a specific year group, which is how the author's aforementioned robotics programme has been run. All year four students were given the opportunity to see if they were interested in robotics, with those that were, formed into teams which worked on an extended project for well over a term. A crowded curriculum may also make lunch-time sessions a better option, however careful planning can enable robotics to be integrated into classroom learning.

Equipment organisation and storage is another issue that needs thought and planning. A survey of LEGO® educators identified two popular management methods (Teytelbaum & Portsmore, 2008). The storage boxes supplied with LEGO® robotics school sets are sturdy, have a sorting tray, stack well, and suit teachers who need to keep individual kits together or do not wish to purchase other storage methods. Other teachers prefer to join kits together and sort like pieces into tubs; this enables students the freedom to supplement their constructions with extra pieces. Tackle or craft boxes can also be bought quite cheaply and provide ideal storage for sorting and easy location of smaller pieces. The author has also found that stacking like blocks within mixed bins can make pieces easier for students to find. A little experience trying to locate pieces gives students an appreciation of the importance of tub organisation; however constant reminders or an occasional ten minute session focussed on sorting pieces will help immensely.

Batteries are an ongoing issue that go hand-in-hand with a robotics programme – there are six in each robot. Students must learn to turn their robots on only when downloading or testing a programme, and remember to turn them off as soon as possible. If purchased separately, the RCX can use a power supply on a limited extension cord as an alternative to AA alkaline or rechargeable batteries. The NXT-G robot also runs on AA batteries, however a rechargeable battery pack can also be purchased separately and has a simple plug-in charging system. In both cases, it is important that the building design allows either the battery cover to be removed for batteries to be replaced, or the charging port be left uncovered for easy access. The RCX robot will indicate when it needs new batteries, and the changeover process must be done very quickly, and one at a time, to avoid losing the 'firmware', which is the basic operating system that enables communication to occur between the computer and RCX. If the batteries are not changed quickly enough, the firmware will need to be downloaded again through the infrared USB tower, taking approximately five minutes. Any programmes on the robot will also have been lost and will need downloading again. If a robot is to be left unused for a period of weeks or longer, the batteries need to be removed to prevent leakage and possible damage to the robots. There are also a number of helpful robotics communities to be found on the Internet, where educators are free to share ideas, post problems, and offer solutions and advice.

CONCLUSION

This chapter has demonstrated that an integrated robotics curriculum has the "potential to breathe new life into education" (Gura, 2007, p. 4), and when used effectively, can inspire students in the development of all aspects of multimodal multiliteracies. Robotics captures the imagination and can be used as a vehicle for multiliterate projects that are vivid and engaging to students and teachers alike. It generates a tremendous amount of energy that has the ability to transform students' learning into exciting, dynamic experiences that challenge all students to take risks, to think deeply, and to become dynamic problem-solvers. The energy and potential created by students and robotics is compelling for students, parents and teachers alike, and the students' willingness to learn is a joy to witness. With the right support and teaching approach, teachers can use robotics to cross curriculum boundaries, develop teamwork and social skills, and foster a positive attitude towards technology; all vital ingredients for active, effective, multiliterate global citizens.

REFERENCES

Adventist Robotics League. (2007). *Peer coaching*. Retrieved March 2, 2008, from http://www.adventistLEGO®league.net/index.php/resources/39-teaching-robotics/48-peer-coaching

Alimisis, D., Moro, M., Arlegui, J., Pina, A., Frangou, S., & Papankilolaou, K. (2007). *Robotics & constructivism in education: The TERECoP project*. Retrieved January 6, 2008, from http://hermes.di.uoa.gr/papanikolaou/papers%5CAMAPFP-Eurologo2007.pdf

Allard, A., & Johnson, E. (2002, December 1-5). *Interrogating the discourse of 'Social Literacies' in an era of uncertainty.* Paper presented at the Australian Association of Research in Educational Annual Conference, Brisbane, Queensland.

Beer, R. D., Chiel, H. J., & Drushel, R. F. (1999). Using autonomous robotics to teach science and engineering [Electronic version]. *Communications of the ACM, 42*(6), 85–92. doi:10.1145/303849.303866

Canterbury City & Country Cluster. (2007, July 5). *Raising attainment in boys' writing in the early years: An ICT and role-play project for improving learning and teaching*. Paper presented at the Annual Cluster Conference on Leading Learning, KentUK

Carbonaro, M., Rex, M., & Chambers, J. (2004). Using LEGO robotics in a project-based learning environment. *Interactive Multimedia Electronic Journal of Computer-Enhanced Learning.* Retrieved August 18, 2008, fromhttp://imej.wfu.edu/articles/2004/1/02/index.asp

Centre for Extended Learning. (2008). *SiMERR 'SmartBots' programme*. [Electronic version]. Retrieved August 22, 2008, from http://www.education.tas.gov.au/school/educators/support/extendedlearning/publications/All-programs2008.pdf

Chua, S. K. C. (2004, November 26-December 2). *The convergence and divergence effects of globalisation on Singapore's education system* [Electronic version]. Paper presented at the Australian Association for Research in Education, Melbourne Australia

Cope, B., & Kalantzis, M. (2000). Multiliteracies: The beginnings of an idea. In B. Cope & M. Kalantzis (Eds.), *Multiliteracies: Literacy learning and the design of social future* (pp.3-8). South Yarra, Australia: Macmillan.

Cromwell, S. (1998). The school of the future. *Education world.* Retrieved March 15, 2008, from http://www.education-world.com/a curr/curr046.shtml

Cuban, L. (1986). *Teachers and machines: The classroom use of technology since 1920.* New York: Teachers College Press.

Cuban, L. (1990). Reforming again, again and again [Electronic version]. *Educational Researcher, 19*(1), 3–13.

D'Agustino, S. (2007). Learning and literacy in robots – making connections for the classroom. In S. D'Agustino & K.P. King (Eds.), *Classroom robotics: Case studies of 21st century instruction for millennial students* (pp.145-162) [Electronic version].

D'Agustino, S., & King, K. P. (2007). Catching the vision, teachers as learners: Robotics professional development. In S. D'Agustino & K.P. King (Eds.), *Classroom robotics: Case studies of 21st century instruction for millennial students* (pp.163-179) [Electronic version].

Darling-Hammond, L. (1997). *The right to learn: A blueprint for creating schools that work.* San Francisco: Jossey-Bass.

Davison, J., & Arthur, J. (2000). Social literacy and citizenship education [Electronic version]. *Curriculum Journal, 11*(1), 9–24. doi:doi:10.1080/095851700361366

Department of Education. Tasmania (2002). *Essential learnings: Framework 1.* Hobart, Australia: Author.

Department of Education. Tasmania (2005). *Literacy and English.* Retrieved January 6, 2008, from http://wwwfp.education.tas.gov.au/english/liteng.htm#multiliteracies

Dibdin, L. (2006). Robotics: Enticing technology across the ages. *Classroom, 26*(2), 30–31.

Drenoyianni, H. (2006). Reconsidering change and ICT: Perspectives of a human and democratic education [Electronic version]. *Education and Information Technologies, 11*(3-4), 401–413. doi:10.1007/s10639-006-9005-5

Druin, A., & Hendler, J. (2000). *Robots for kids: Exploring new technologies for learning.* San Diego, CA: Academic Press.

Eggen, P. D., & Kauchak, D. P. (2001). *Strategies for teachers: Teaching content and thinking skills* (4th Ed.). Needham Heights, MA: Allyn & Bacon.

Faculty of Education Curtin University of Technology. (1997). Children, robotics and problem solving: Technology in the early childhood classroom. *Australian Educational Computing, 12*(2), 24–31.

Francis, B., & Skelton, C. (2005). *Reassessing gender and achievement: Questioning contemporary key debates.* Oxon, UK: Routledge.

Gedda, R., & McGonnachie, D. (2006). It's official: Skills shortage cuts deep. *Information Age, April/May,* 25-26.

Giddings, L. R. (1988). Beyond E. D. Hirsch and cultural literacy: Thinking skills for cultural awareness [Electronic version]. *Communication Review*, *8*(2), 5–13.

Goleman, D. (1996). *Emotional intelligence: Why it can matter more than IQ*. London: Bloomsbury.

Greene, M. (1988). *The dialectic of freedom*. New York: Teachers College Press.

Gregor, R. (2005). Robotics and the gifted child: What they gain [Electronic version]. *Gifted, 135*, 9–11.

Group, T. T. S. (2008). *Bee-bot*. Retrieved March 24, 2008, from http://www.tts-group.co.uk/Bee-Bot United States Web-based Education Commission (2000). *The power of the Internet for learning: Moving from promise to practice*. Retrieved March 15, 2008, from http://interact.hpcnet.org/webcommission/Section_1.htm

Gura, M. (2007). What is student robotics? In S. D'Agustino & K.P. King (Eds.), *Classroom robotics: Case studies of 21st century instruction for millennial students* (pp.3-10) [Electronic version].

Gurian, M., & Ballew, A. C. (2003). *The boys and girls learn differently: Action guide for teachers*. San Fransisco: Jossey-Bass.

Hamston, J., & Murdoch, K. (1996). *Integrating socially: Planning integrated units of work for social education*. Armadale, Australia: Eleanor Curtain.

Hargreaves, A. (2003). *Teaching in the knowledge society: Education in the age of insecurity*. Berkshire, UK: Open University Press.

Hargreaves, A., & Fullan, M. G. (1998). *What's worth fighting for out there?* New York: Teachers College Press.

Hartley, R. (2004). *Young people and mentoring: Towards a national strategy*. A report prepared for Big Brothers Big Sister Australia, Dusseldorp Skills Forum and The Smith Family, Sydney. Retrieved February 24, 2008, from http://www.dsf.org.au/papers/150.htm

Hawkridge, D. (1989). Machine-mediated learning in third-world schools. *Machine-Mediated Learning*, *3*, 319–328.

Heale, M. (2005). The new learning technologies: Transforming teaching and learning at Frankston High School. *Principal Matters,* 2-4.

Healy, A. (2004). Multiliteracies pedagogy. *Practically Primary*, *9*(2), 5–7.

Hedley, C. N., Antonacci, P., & Rabinowitz, M. (1995). Thinking and literacy: The mind at work in the classroom [Electronic version]. In C.N. Hedley, P. Antonacci & M. Rabinowitz (Eds.), *Thinking and literacy: The mind at work*, (pp. 3-20). Hillside, NJ: Lawrence Erlbaum.

Herring, S. C., & Marken, J. (2008). Implications of gender consciousness for students in information technology. *Women's Studies, 37*(3), 229-256. [Electronic version]. Retrieved August 18, 2008, from http://ella.slis.indiana.edu/~herring/ws.pdf

Howell, W. L., McCaffrey, E. J., & Murphy, R. R. (2003, November 6-9). University mentoring for first LEGO league [Electronic version]. Paper presented at the *Annual ASEE/IEEE Frontiers in Education Conference,* Boston, MA.

Johnson, D. W., & Johnson, F. P. (1997). *Joining together: Group theory and group skills* (6th Ed.). Needham Heights, MA: Allyn & Bacon.

Kearns, P., & Grant, J. (2002). *The enabling pillars: Learning, technology, community, partnership*. Retrieved March 15, 2008, from http://www.dest.gov.au/highered/otherpub/aust_ict_report.pdf

King, K. P. (2007). Preface. In S. D'Agustino & K.P. King (Eds.), *Classroom robotics: Case studies of 21st century instruction for millennial students* (pp. ix-xi) [Electronic version]. LEGO® Education (2006). *Lego mindstorms education*. Retrieved August 17, 2008, from http://www.active-robots.com/products/mindstorms4schools/nxt-education/nxt-information.pdf

Luke, A., & Carpenter, M. (2003). Literacy education for a new ethics of global community. *Language Arts*, *81*(1), 20–22.

Marsh, C. (2000). *Handbook for beginning teachers* (2nd ed.). Frenchs Forest, Australia: Pearson Education.

Mauch, E. (2001). Using technological innovation to improve the problem solving skills of middle school students [Electronic version]. *Clearing House (Menasha, Wis.)*, *75*(4), 211–214.

McDonald, J., Grove, J., & Youth Advisory Forum Members (2001, April 4-6). Youth for youth: Piecing together the peer education jigsaw [Electronic version]. Paper presented at the *2nd International Conference on Drugs and Young People: Exploring the Bigger Picture,* Melbourne, Australia.

Mentoring Australia. (2000). *National benchmarks for mentoring programs: Preliminary information*. Retrieved February 24, 2008, from http://www.dsf.org.au/tools/24.htm

Merriam-Webster Online Dictionary. (2008). *Robotics*. Retrieved February 24, 2008, from http://www.merriam-webster.com/dictionary/robotics

Milto, E., Rogers, C., & Portsmore, M. (2002, November 6-9). *Gender differences in confidence levels, group interactions, and feelings about competition in an introductory robotics course* [Electronic version]. Paper presented at the Annual ASEE/IEEE Frontiers in Education Conference, Boston, MA.

Mortimore, P., Sammons, P., Lewis, D., & Ecob, R. (1988). *School matters: The junior years.* Berkeley: University of California Press.

Murdoch, K., & Hornsby, D. (1997). *Planning curriculum connections: Whole-school planning for integrated curriculum.* Armadale, Australia: Eleanor Curtain.

Murray, C. (2007). Robots tackle core of STEM education. *Technology news for today's K-20 educator*. Retrieved January 13, 2007, from http://www.eschoolnews.com/news/top-news/news-by-subject/curriculum/?i=45932

New London Group. (1996). A pedagogy of multiliteracies: Designing social futures [Electronic version]. *Harvard Educational Review*, *66*(1), 60–92.

Newman, M. (2007). *Emotional capitalists: The new leaders*. Milton, Australia: John Wiley & Sons.

Nobel, C. (2007). Women in technology: A call to action. *Information Age, April/May,* 34-37.

Norton, S. J. (2007). The use of design practice to teach mathematics and science [Electronic version]. *International Journal of Technology and Design Education*, *18*(1), 19–44. doi:doi:10.1007/s10798-006-9019-8

Norton, S. J., McRobbie, C. J., & Ginns, I. S. (2007). Problem solving in a middle school robotics design classroom [Electronic version]. *Research in Science Education*, *37*(3), 261–277. doi:10.1007/s11165-006-9025-6

Nourbakhsh, I., Crowley, K., Bhave, A., Hamner, E., Hsium, T., & Perez-Bergquist, A. (2005). The robotic autonomy mobile robots course: Robot design, curriculum design, and educational assessment [Electronic version]. *Autonomous Robots*, *18*(1), 103–127. doi:10.1023/B:AURO.0000047303.20624.02

Papert, S., & Harel, I. (1991). Situating Constructionism [Electronic version]. *Constructionism*. Retrieved January 8, 2008, from http://www.papert.org/articles/SituatingConstructionism.html

Peck, C., Cuban, L., & Kirkpatrick, H. (2002). Techno-promoter dreams, student realities [Electronic version]. *Phi Delta Kappan, 83*(6), 472–480.

Perkins, D., & Blythe, T. (1994). Teaching for understanding: Putting understanding up front [Electronic version]. *Educational Leadership, 51*(5), 4–8.

Phillip, K. (2000). *Mentoring and young people*. Retrieved February 24, 2008, from http://www.infed.org/learningmentors/mentoring.htm

Prabhu, A. (2007). Equity and equality: Finding the gender balance. *Information Age, April/May,* 30-34.

Reilly, M. (2006). *LEGO® robotics: Measuring and graphing speed of a LEGO® robotic car*. Retrieved January 10, 2008, from http://www.maureenreilly.com/robotics

RoboCup Junior Australia. (2007). *RoboCup junior.* Retrieved March 29, 2008, from http://www.robocupjunior.org.au/

Rogers, C., & Portsmore, M. (2004). Bringing engineering to elementary school [Electronic version]. *Journal of STEM Education: Innovations and Research, 5*(3-4), 17–28.

Scott, D. (2000). Editorial- responses to Crick and citizenship education [Electronic version]. *Curriculum Journal, 11*(1), 1–7. doi:10.1080/095851700361357

Sims, K., Spinetti, S., Crabb, S., & Earnshaw, M. (2006). *Robotics: Embedding technology-Module 14.* Retrieved January 5, 2008, from http://www.det.act.gov.au/department/pdf/elt_14_Robotics.pdf

Slee, P. (2002). *Child, adolescent and family development.* (2nd Ed.). UK: Cambridge University Press.

Snyder, I. (1998, August 9-10). New literacies for the twenty-first century: From page to screen [Electronic version]. Paper presented at *Connected Learning: The Learning Technologies in Schools Conference*, Melbourne, Australia.

Sprainger, N. (2007). Meet the bee-bots! *Quick - Journal of the Queensland Society for Information Technology in Education, 103.* Retrieved March 27, 2008, from http://www.qsite.edu.au/files/quick_103_Winter2007.pdf

Stoll, L., Fink, D., & Earl, L. (2003). *It's about learning (and it's about time)*. New York: Routledge Falmer.

Teytelbaum, O, & Portsmore, M. (2008). *Thinking outside the box: A look into LEGO organization and sorting*. Retrieved August 15, 2008, from http://www.legoengineering.com/index.php?option=com_content&task=view&id=76&Itemid=65

The Lego Group. (2007). *Mindstorms*. Retrieved March 24, 2008, from http://mindstorms.lego.com/eng/default.aspx

Thomas, S., Smees, R., MacBeath, J., Robertson, P., & Boyd, B. (2000). Valuing pupils' views in Scottish schools [Electronic version]. *Educational Research and Evaluation, 6*(4), 281–316. doi:10.1076/edre.6.4.281.6934

Unsworth, L. (2001). *Teaching multiliteracies across the curriculum: Changing contexts of text and image in classroom practice* [Electronic version]. Philadelphia, PA: Open University Press.

Valiant, U. S. A. (2004). *Roamer: Discovery at every turn.* Retrieved from March 24, 2008, from http://www.valiant-technology.com/uk/pages/roamer_research.php

Williams, N. (2000). Educational multimedia: Where's the interaction? In M. Monteith (Ed.), *IT for learning enhancement* (Rev. Ed.) (pp.159-176). Exeter, U.K: Intellect Books.

Zammit, K., & Downes, T. (2002). New learning environments and the multiliterate individual: A framework for educators. [Electronic version] [f]. *Australian Journal of Language and Literacy, 25*(2), 24–36.

Section 4

Selected Readings

Chapter 14
Digital Literacy and Cultural Mediations to the Digital Divide

Monica Fantin
Universidade Federal De Santa Catarina (UFSC), Brazil

Gilka Girardello
Universidade Federal De Santa Catarina (UFSC), Brazil

ABSTRACT

This chapter discusses the digital divide from the perspective of education and culture and highlights the forms in which the problem is presented in Brazil, understanding that it is not exclusive to this context. Given the complex challenges to digital inclusion in the context of globalization, the chapter emphasizes that for children and young people to be able to appropriate new technologies and languages in a significant manner, the promotion of digital literacy should be realized with respect to the concept of multiliteracies. Digital inclusion means much more than access to technologies and is understood as one of the fronts in the struggle against poverty and inequality. The authors propose that the understanding of the digital divide be enriched with the valorization of cultural mediations in the construction of digital literacy. In this sense, a culturalist perspective of media education can promote digital inclusion that is an experience of citizenship, belonging, and critical and creative participation of children and young people in the culture.

INTRODUCTION

In the early days of the popularization of personal computers in the 1980s, many people spoke of the infinite potential of the information highway that promised egalitarian and multidirectional communication among all peoples, groups, and nations. But another metaphor, critical of the naive optimism of the early years, did not take long to appear: that of the digital divide. How can the abyss that separates the digitally literate from the digitally illiterate—commonly understood as those excluded from the technological promise—be gapped? What other image could represent this tension in an alternative form, not as an unpassable chasm but as a space to be traversed? A river, which both separates and unites? A sea of currents that at once flow together and apart? How can this river be crossed, this sea be navigated?

This chapter proposes to discuss this problem—the distance between those who have and those who do not have complete access to the archives of culture made available by the media and the possibilities of recreating them critically. We focus on the new configurations that the problem takes with the intensification of the presence of digital technologies in education and culture. Our discussion seeks to identify possible contributions to the dilemmas of media education and of digital literacy that emerge from the Brazilian scene—a country of continental dimensions, where the pulsation of globalized media culture co-exists with a strong and sometimes preliterate popular culture, often in the same city and just a few blocks away. Our anchor in the problems as they are presented in Brazil does not mean, however, that we see the Brazilian or Latin American context as exclusive.

The diversity of semiotic practices and dislocations resulting from the forms by which industrial culture was incorporated into local contexts has challenged Brazilian thinkers for a number of decades. Concepts such as syncretism and cultural anthropophagy marked sociological, anthropological, and literary thinking in the country during the past century, in the search to understand the tensions between the "local" and "global" images and narratives, tensions that are at times generative and at times paralyzing. Paulo Freire's (2000) proposal for a pedagogy of liberation, with its emphasis on a dialogical methodology that would be a space for a radical and micropolitical criticism of oppression, continues to inspire a large number of educational experiences, in and outside of schools. Nevertheless, although these conceptual proposals are on the horizon of an increasing number of media education practices, they are rarely explicit.

This chapter identifies a number of theoretical themes and concepts that have been instigating and challenging the field of media education in Brazil. The digital divide will be understood as the contradiction between digital exclusion and inclusion, recognizing however, that one is not always opposed to the other. We will focus on concepts associated with practices that strive to establish a digital inclusion that transcends a merely operational access to machines and programs, that is, inclusion that is also political, social, and cultural—and thus meets the broad needs of education.

It is first necessary to locate the place from where we write, both from a theoretical as well as a geographic perspective. Our reflection about this theme is based on the Brazilian condition, although we believe that many of the issues that we will discuss here are analogous to those found in other countries at the periphery of capitalism. We are both professors and researchers working at the interface between education and communication in a large federal, public university. For this reason we feel comfortable speaking about the issue of the digital divide, since it would be impossible to consider the relationship between the media and education in our country without recognizing the social inequality, made evident in statistical data presented below. It is also necessary to recognize that exclusion is far from the only theme discussed in Brazilian or Latin American academic spaces that work with media education. We will thus attempt to consider the material precariousness in our country and the challenges that it creates for digital education, while highlighting those ideas, themes, and processes that, being fruit of the cultural singularity of our context, can contribute in a positive way to considering digital literacy and the digital divide.

CONSIDERING INCLUSION IN EDUCATION AND CULTURE

Digital exclusion is not to be without a computer or a cell phone. It is to remain incapable of thinking, or creating and organizing new more just and dynamic forms of production and distribution of symbolic and material wealth. (Schwartz, 2000)

When we speak of digital inclusion, one immediately tends to think in the expansion of access to computers. Another way of thinking of the issue, however, is to give importance precisely to that which resists being done with computers, which tends to remain outside technological rationality. For Latin Americans, by taking simulation to the extreme, the new communication technologies "make visible the non-digestible, non-simulative, *remains* that from cultural alterity resists generalized homogenization" (Martín-Barbero, 2004, p.183). These "remains,", which resist media dilution, are related to the existence of popular culture, an expression that on our continent designates not the pop universe or the museum, but a space for symbolic exchanges and tensions that are still very much alive in society.

In this context many authors in our field highlight the importance of resistance to the model of technological and economic acceleration that is dominant in contemporary Western society and "that appears to condemn all other societies to an integration to its paradigm or to disappearance," as Santos (2003) warns. He adds that resistance to this model includes the maintenance of the diversity of cultures and societies, particularly of the "diversity of temporalities and of rhythms that are not annihilated by the imperative of total acceleration" (Santos, 2003, p.28).

Thus, a first presumption of this chapter is the need to consider the access to digital culture dialectically, abandoning any naïve enlightenment ideas or welfare-type programs that merely distribute equipment. We also seek a distance from the logic of globalized integration and the dichotomy between backwardness and modernity, which impels entire populations to the quest for the latest electronic gadgets. To think of digital inclusion in countries considered peripheral, requires paying attention to the cultural manifestations that take place outside of cyberspace. The absence of the latest technology is not necessarily understood as backwardness, a form of symbolic poverty or incompetence, but perhaps as a situation that composes a valuable and eloquent difference—a possible space for creative and critical constitution. It also requires paying attention to public policies for teacher education, as well as special educational and cultural programs. We consider it to be important to have this cultural perspective as a horizon, to assure that the democratization of digital access signifies the broadening of the social and cultural participation of various sectors of the population and not only a new form of ceding to old modes of discrimination and domination.

To think dialectically of digital inclusion in Latin America thus requires a careful look at the relationship between education and communication. Once again, it is Martín-Barbero who indicates that schools push young people to social-cultural marginalization, by encouraging passivity, redundancy, uniformity, anachronism, and provinciality, which contrast so strongly with the activity, diversity, curiosity, currentness, and opening of frontiers that mark the world of communication (2004, p. 350). The most grave consequence of this contradiction, according to the author, is that schools deny the poorest portion of the population the strength of orality found in their original culture, at the same time in which the poor are not introduced to the grammars of the new media. For the author, the cultural specificity of Latin American modernity lies in the complicity and interpenetration between oral and visual cultures.

The productive co-existence, whether marked by tension or partnership, between different cultures and imaginaries in Latin America, has been the object of analysis of a long critical tradition, exactly because this co-existence highlights the most eloquent of artistic and literary expression on the continent. To cite only two examples, we can begin with the "antropophagy" movement of the Brazilian modernist vanguard of the 1920s: "Tupi, or not Tupi, that is the question. I am only interested in what is not mine," Oswald de Andrade declared in his celebrated manifesto of 1928, permeated by nationalist references to the joy and creative potential of cultural syncretism. A second reference that is equally important is the concept of "hybrid cultures" developed by the Argentine García Canclini, which had wide academic circulation in the 1990s throughout South America. Based on this concept, the author discusses the new and original uses that each local community makes of videogames, videocassettes, and copying machines, emphasizing the egalitarian vitality of the singular mixes between the academic, the popular and the mass culture that the technologies favor.

These interactions allow the relativization of fundamentalisms, whether "religious, political, national, ethnic or artistic, which hold as absolute certain patrimonies and discriminate against the others," said Canclini (1998, p. 307). In relation to education, a fragmentary relationship with texts, books and annotations can also, Canclini suggests, induce "more fluid ties among the texts, among the students and knowledge" (1998, p. 308). In addition to these interesting aspects, however, he also points to the inequality in cultural capital and therefore the differences among the meanings constructed by youths for technologies in various social contexts. Appropriation of technologies is not the same for "poor adolescents who go to videogame arcades and for middle and upper class youth who have them in their homes." (Canclini, 1998). In addition, large sectors of Brazilian society pass from the traditional oral culture directly to audiovisual culture, or to the media orality, without passing through written culture. This evidently interferes in the various types of relationships with the new media products—given that the meanings of the technologies depend on the way that they are inserted in daily life—and how culture appropriates and then transforms them.

To dialectically consider digital inclusion in Latin America also requires paying attention to the relations between education and popular cultures. In Brazil, a large variety of manifestations linked to different traditions are still very much alive. Dramas and ritual and or religious festivals, musical narratives, and poetic repertoires are relatively easy to access, even in urban centers. As Azevedo (2006) said,

If for students of the middle and upper classes, children and grandchildren of literate people, the discourse of the school appears to make sense, for students coming from an oral tradition – the large mass of the Brazilian population, it presents an authoritarian, prejudicial, discriminatory and exclusionary character.

The prejudice of the school against traditional oral culture, Azevedo (2006) adds, leaves many children without references, because of the institutional disdain for the knowledge and values of their parents and thus with a difficulty in identifying with the educational "truth." The result, we can say, deepens the sociocultural marginalization to which we referred earlier.

A reflection that clearly and critically locates the relationship between education and social exclusion in Brazil is conducted by Muniz Sodré. He begins by recalling that we educate not only for what is viable today, but for what is possible tomorrow.

To educate means establishing an (ethical) distance from the animal condition and preparing for complete citizenship, which presupposes knowledge by the subject, in addition to that of technical-operative instrumentation, of the political and administrative processes of its *Polis*, that is, of its Human City. (Sodré, 2002, p. 87)

The dominant change of paradigm and new forms of labor organization have provoked alterations in pedagogical relationships at various levels of schooling, in the forms of teaching and learning and in curricular content. Moreover, in the new social-cultural order, he explains, common knowledge, or knowledge about the self, is in crisis. The transmission of information in media space has become characterized by persuasion or fascination and this fascination with the media wonders can result in an ideological practice that attributes to technological innovation itself a "magic power to resolve problems (...) generating a *technical temptation*" (Sodré, 2002, p. 99-100). Muniz Sodré maintains that this ideology is instilled not on an ethical but on a corporate horizon, in the framework of a private-sector oriented educational matrix.

Many projects with this technocratic and private sector focus can have consequences that can misguide educational policy, because they are based on market interests, Brazilian, and foreign, often, but not always, imbedded in the guidelines of international agencies.[1] In many programs said to promote digital inclusion, "the real intention to promote business competition with support for the implantation of electronic commerce, new security policies and other government objectives was camouflaged by the official discourse as 'digital literacy' and public education" (Sodré, 2002, p.104). More than transforming the real conditions in which the old educational structures are placed, Sodré maintains that these programs intend to include the largest possible number of people, qualifying them for the labor market as "cybernetic simulacros for 'inclusion of everyone in the Web', in other words, there is no reflection of a collective desire, but only an adaptation to a techno-bureaucratic scenario" (idem).

By emphasizing technical instruction, education abandons the socialization of knowledge linked to human values and enters the market for goods and services. According to Sodré this perspective cannot understand that what is most important in terms of education "is not in the technical means and the disciplinary content (knowledge and information) but in the *cultural form* by which the knowledges are incorporated and the pertinent connections are promoted among them" (2002, p.106) Thus, when programs for inclusion said to be innovative emphasize only access to equipment, they understand the school merely as a physical place and not as a cultural form.

These ideas establish a reference horizon that allows us to consider the challenges of digital inclusion in the complex scenario in which we live. These include developing: a capacity to pay attention to cultural—and not merely technical—dimensions of the relationship of children and youth with the technologies; a dialectical understanding of the relationship between school, media, and popular cultures; a focus on the local uses of the medias and a recognition of the possibility that the critical and creative tensions of the repertoires and languages that occur there can point to routes for the mediation, even if circumstantial, of digital exclusion.

GLOBALIZATIONS AND CONTEXTS OF INEQUALITY

The fight against exclusion is part of the rhetoric of the "information society" in the context of the dream of a "second Renaissance" based on creativity, scientific discovery, cultural development, and community cohesion, as proposed by the European Forum for the Information Society. The concern for inclusion was also recommended in the 1990s by the G7, which sought a transition to the "information society" including: global interaction of broadband networks, transcultural education, support for libraries, museums, and electronic art galleries, environmental management, natural resources, and healthcare, interconnection of public administration and a global multimedia inventory of projects and studies for the development of the Global Information Society (Cadimo, 2004, p. 4).

Certain experiences have shown that the new communication and experiential paradigm present real opportunities for the democratization of media and messages and for citizens to overcome their condition as consumers and or spectators and transform themselves into reflexive and participative subjects. However, in general, what we find is not only a growing distance between the info-rich and the info-poor, but also the production of a new type of illiteracy, digital illiteracy.

There is considerable regional disparity in the reach of the Internet, given that the most highly developed countries, with nearly 15% of the world's population, in 1998, accounted for 88% of all Internet users. In Latin America, 90% of the users are in the highest income groups as Castells (2006, p. 433) notes. "The spatial inequality in the access to the Internet is one of the most impressive paradoxes of the information era, due to the characteristic supposedly independent from the space of the technology " he maintains (Castells, 2006, p. 434). "Globalization acts selectively, including and excluding segments of economies and societies from networks of information, wealth and power that characterize the new dominant system" and for Castells "the new information technologies are the instrument of this global storm of accumulation of wealth and diffusion of poverty", that relegates entire peoples and territories to irrelevance from the perspective of the dominant interests of global informational capitalism (Castells, 2002, p. 191-192).

In this light, the situation in Brazil is concerning: 54% of Brazilians have never used a computer and only 14% of all homes have Internet access.[2] Three percent of school age children (6-14) are out of school, corresponding to 1.5 million children.[3] Of the 162,000 public schools in Brazil, 129,000 do not have Internet access, 40,000 do not have a library, 25,000 do not have electricity, and 1,000 do not have a bathroom.

This data reinforces the certainty that the digital divide truly cannot be understood only as a question of access to technologies, because it involves much broader questions of a cultural, political, and social order.

At the same time in which we seek the universalization of schooling, reading and writing, for the first time in the history of humanity enormous changes are taking place within a single generation and no longer from one generation to another. In a country of continental scope such as Brazil, problems also take on enormous proportions: the challenge of digital inclusion coexists with these social challenges that have been resolved in other locations. For these reasons, this is a time of searching for paths and alternatives given the complexity of the problems that are not only related to education.

Another question that we must keep in mind when we speak of digital exclusion is its dynamic character, requiring that countries that are not at the vanguard of technological production develop a critical capacity for analysis of technological trends. At the minimum, "it is necessary to discuss the technology politically and get to know the possible technological options to avoid that they are not presented as inexorable and that we swallow them whole" (Santos, 2003, p. 33). Although it is common for us to hear that poor countries can "skip certain phases" of development, absorbing more advanced technologies, this development is continuous and moved by competition. Thus, each "last generation" of devices is quickly surpassed and becomes obsolete and "the highly dynamic character of the new technologies is a constantly renewed barrier to the capacity to approximate the poorest countries to the wealthiest ones" (Sorj, 2003, p.61). Considering that a large portion of the Brazilian population does not have physical access to the new technologies, in order for the country to begin to participate more broadly in the cyber-culture, public policies are needed that guarantee access, software development, the work of educational-cultural mediation and the training for citizenship through these technologies.

Thus, the access to communication technologies and technical knowledge provided by digital inclusion programs is not sufficient to construct an experience of citizenship, since it can be oriented towards critical as well as passive uses. It is necessary to promote conditions for the development of autonomy in the interaction with the media, in order to favor the critical formation of citizens, not only of users. This includes an ability to develop search criteria, to encourage technological fluency means to critically use information and communication technologies, interact with words, graphics, images, and sounds, locate, select and critically evaluate information, and know and have command of the rules of the social practice of communication supported by the media, in a search for significant, autonomous, and continuous learning, as Almeida (2005) affirmed. This facilitates the production of knowledge that is needed to improve living conditions, thus creating and organizing social relationships, communicative interactions, and cultural participation. This perspective of digital literacy as a social practice goes beyond learning about codes or technology. It implies the attribution of meanings to information that comes from different texts, as Almeida (2005) proposed. That is, it is a perspective aimed at the production and representation of knowing oneself, the others and the world.

DIGITAL LITERACY AND MULTILITERACIES

Demographic data also present disturbing statistics indicating low literacy rates[4] forcing us to think of a new form of *dual illiteracy*: the functional and the digital. Is the complete computerization of schools the solution to this problem? The question does not have a single response, but we can say that the distribution of computers in schools would not be sufficient if there is no teacher training policy aimed at cultural and artistic enrichment so that the use of the equipment can gain social meaning. Dual illiteracy creates a dual challenge—or perhaps a multiple one, if we consider the need for literacy in multiple languages—to promote digital inclusion and digital literacy as public policies that confront the inheritance of functional illiteracy and at the same time combat technological apartheid. To believe that it is first necessary to eradicate one and later confront the other would be a fundamental error, as Silveira (2001) emphasizes. Without a policy to invest in writing there would be a continuous production of inequality in digital literacy, since this requires a command of writing.

In the early 1960s, Paulo Freire recognized that the reading of the world preceded the reading of the word. In the 1980s, Emília Ferreiro and Ana Teberosky emphasized that children already have contact with written language before they enter school and highlight the importance of the social function of writing and learning to read and write as a form of representation, more than as a simple acquisition of an alphabetic code. Even so, in Brazil and in other countries, the word that designates learning to read and write "alfabetização" refers primarily to the process of acquisition of an alphabetic system. The word literacy "letramento" is used to emphasize the social function of writing.

In various countries such as Brazil, it is found that many children, although they know how to read and write, do not practice the social use of reading and writing. This is the other reason for the distinction in our context, between the terms "alfabetização" and "letramento," which, although they are interrelated, have specific meanings. Implicit in the concept of literacy, "is the idea that writing has social, cultural, political, economic, cognitive, and linguistic consequences, whether for the social group in which it is introduced, or for the individual that learns to use it," said Soares (2005, p. 17).

From this perspective, literacy can be understood as a condition that the individual acquires in virtue not only of knowing how to read and write, but of having appropriated the social dimension of writing, incorporating it into their life, and transforming oneself, as Soares (2002) emphasizes. The author uses the term in the plural, literacies, recognizing that different writing technologies create and require different literacies, above all since the introduction of cyberculture.

Some scholars even broaden this concept to that of multiliteracies, in order to include the audiovisual and digital grammars that involve a certain level of understanding of reading and production in all these dimensions. There is an interesting aspect in this notion of multiliteracies, which is the need that we have today to circulate in other types of representation of reality that transcend writing and involve the visual, musical, corporal, digital, and other forms of representation. It is important to work with these dimensions in a transdisciplinary manner, with an emphasis on circulation, transit, and interaction, involving scientific, literary, aesthetic, and cultural literacy.

The notion of digital literacy is related to print literacy in Buckingham's (2003) analogy:

As with print, children also need to be able to evaluate and use information critically if they are to transform it into knowledge. (...) As with older media, children need to be empowered to make informed choices on their own behalf, and to protect and regulate themselves. And just as print literacy involves writing as well as reading, digital literacy must involve creative production in new media as well as critical consumption. (Buckingham, 2003, p. 177)

In this perspective, digital literacy is associated to play, art and narrative, as languages that are essential for children to be able to express and communicate their feelings, ideas, and experiences. The specificities of each language should be considered, given that different abilities are required, for example, to write words, take photos, watch a film, or make a video-clip.[5] An articulation between the different languages and contents involves a collaborative work of experimentation, creation, and discovery. It also involves dialogue, negotiation, polyphony, openness, flexibility, criticism, and collaboration. In this process, the languages of different fields of knowledge can be understood based on different perspectives: as forms of expression of the subject and of the culture, as a means of communication, as a form of interaction and human development, and also as a social-cultural object of knowledge. This perspective requires that the initial and on-going education of teachers also considers their own experience with expression and creation, based not only on scientific knowledge, but also on the recovery of their experiences with languages that at times are dormant (artistic, performatic, literary).

It is through the different languages that children use, verbal and nonverbal, that they express their wealth of imagination and produce culture. In this perspective, speech, crying, gesture, observing, silence, play, sciences, arts, and experiences with media are part of a network of symbolic systems that is the context of a plural literacy. This leads us to reconsider what it means to be literate. For the teacher today it is not enough to have information from books, to dominate codes of writing and understand them as a form of representation of speech. To what degree is an individual literate if he or she is not capable of seeing, interpreting, and questioning TV images, watching and understanding films, critically analyzing advertising and news, using a computer, conducting research, navigating the Web or creating and inserting texts and images in the flow of social circulation? And to what degree are we as teachers literate in these languages and are we working in a suitable manner with the multiple literacies?

In sum, to be literate in the 21st Century involves multiple literacies, including digital literacy, which also concerns the construction of real and virtual citizenship and the possibility of effectively participating in society. For this reason, the media can no longer be excluded from the literacy process. Even if it seems obvious, this idea has still not been sufficiently adopted and converted into a transformative practice in many social-cultural contexts.

The concept of multiliteracies as a new understanding of the appropriation of the social practices of reading and writing, demands considering the theoretical bases that are its foundation and giving it legitimacy. In this sense, the multiliteracies can be understood as a repertoire of related capacities, some generic and others specifically related to the media and other areas, as Bazalgette (2005) emphasizes. This concept is related to media education, particularly to an ecological approach to media education (Rivoltella, 2002), understood as the interface between the various fields of knowledge, involving science, art, and literature.

Three elements have been identified that sustain this approach to media education: culture, as the expansion of and opportunities created by various cultural repertoires, criticism, as the capacity to analyze, reflect, and evaluate, and creation, as the creative capacity of expression, communication, and construction of knowledge. To these three words that begin with the letter C,[6] we propose adding the C of citizenship, thus establishing the "4 Cs" of media education: culture, criticism, creation, and citizenship, which must be present to make possible transformative work in the schools (Fantin, 2006).

CITIZENSHIP AND DIGITAL INCLUSION OF CHILDREN AND YOUTH

Based on the conceptual fluidity of the concept of citizenship, Rivoltella (2005, p. 155) identifies some dimensions that qualify citizenship and the citizen: civil law, political citizenship, social citizenship, and cultural citizenship. Relating these dimensions of citizenship with media education, Rivoltella emphasizes what he calls the "dual exercise of citizenship" or the combination of *citizenship of belonging* with *instrumental citizenship*. On one hand media education can call the attention of civil society and political power to the values of citizenship, and on the other, through its specificity, media education contributes to building this citizenship. It involves "a dual exercise of citizenship, which is active and passive, composed of solicitation of rights and of a set of efforts to build them" (Rivoltella, 2005, p. 156).

For Rivoltella (2005), to educate for citizenship involves an inclusionary education based on the recognition of universal rights, the formal and legal factors of citizenship as well as social and cultural rights, school education that conducts transversal work among the disciplines, considering the implicit and explicit curriculum, and an education that seeks solidarity. It also implies favoring interaction with territory, developing multiple and complex identities, and promoting a sense of belonging to the local, national, and global context. This perspective of educating for citizenship strives to favor: *the acquisition of knowledges* (knowledge of the world and the cultural, social, and economic reality in which we live, as well as of the laws, institutions, and their functioning); the *acquisition of social competencies* (knowing how to perform the role of citizen, to cooperate, construct and realize common projects, to assume responsibilities, resolve conflicts and intervene in a political debate); and the *acquisition of ethical and interpersonal abilities* (knowing how to express solidarity, to be open to difference, etc.).[7]

By encouraging this type of education, schools would be taking on new responsibilities in society and could contribute to the construction of a new form of cultural mediation, integrating with the communication media in order to reduce the asymmetries on the plane of cognitive and participatory capacities of individuals, as Morcellini (2004) emphasizes. Upon transposing this idea to the concern for the digital divide, we note that the term "digital inclusion" cannot always be understood as the opposite of exclusion, given that it often only describes programs that propose alternatives to the problems presented by social inequality. In order to struggle against the forms of domination and control caused by the digital divide, the public calls for digital inclusion began to appear, with the impact of the Internet on the world in the 1990s. To be inserted digitally comes to be a condition for citizenship and a right of individuals for their existence in the world of information and communication.

The debate about the forms of insertion of Brazilian society in this scenario is even more important when we analyze the data from the "Map of Digital Exclusion" which indicates that 85% of the Brazilian population is excluded from the information society (Néri, 2003). Although the federal government has invested in various digital inclusion programs, data indicates unequal growth among the regions of the country. From 2000-2004, Brazil had a 286.2% growth in the number of Internet users, becoming the country with the tenth most users in the world, with nearly 19 million people navigating the Internet. This growth is incomparably greater than that of the other means of communication.[8] Nevertheless, the penetration of the Internet in the country is unequal, concentrated in the upper classes. According to the map of digital exclusion, 79% of Brazilians never touched a computer and 89% never accessed the Internet. According to a study conducted in Latin America, only 10% of the poorest 40% of the Brazilian population have Internet access. Among Argentina, Brazil, Chile, and Mexico, Brazilians pay the most to have a computer (IBOPE).[9] This reveals that Brazil still has much to do to gap the digital abyss.[10]

While from a simplistic perspective the recipe to transpose the digital divide would be to make technology available, we see that this is important but not sufficient, and we must consider the many complexities of the problem. We can ask what is the significance of including and what are the forms of inclusion, since the digital divide can be examined from its social, economic, cultural, technological, and/or intellectual dimensions, and based on its technical, subjective, or economic specificities. What does it mean to include? What rights does technological access to the use of the computer promote if this access is not accompanied by literacy in the multiple languages? Is to access a computer without being literate allowing its use without assuring the rights to citizenship it makes possible? Is digital inclusion a right of citizenship or a market necessity? While much of the international literature about the digital divide emphasizes the technical nature of inclusion, the questions above seek to point to the cultural and social aspects of inclusion, which seem fundamental from a Latin American perspective.

The term inclusion today, in some public debates, appears to have become a consensual politically correct label, immune to reflection and discussion. The principle that society must be included in the information era is accepted without questioning, and the question "who will be included and what will he or she do with this new tool?" appears to have little importance. Without guarantees of employability, without real opportunities to use digital tools to participate in decision making about their communities and schools and in formulating and accessing public policies and services for healthcare, education, housing and so forth, and given the speed of technological change, it appears that the discourse of digital inclusion is satisfying to only a few companies, NGOs, and technocrats who sell this ideology as one more technological novelty.[11] In this context, to include appears to mean in most cases to offer material conditions (skill and access to the Internet) to manipulate technologies. More than developing critical and questioning cognitive processes, it appears that in this vision, to include is to merely adapt pre-existing procedures to current technologies.

If to include is to give access to proprietary computers with primitive software and mechanically train people to use them efficiently at work, as is implicit in most of the inclusion projects,[12] Lemos (2003) asks why should society be included? For whom and for what does inclusion serve? In societies such as ours, where basic rights are still not assured, inclusion appears to be a goal and a utopia in some social fields such as healthcare, education, housing, and public safety. Is it possible to evaluate digital inclusion by the number of computers, people navigating, and other similar statistics, Lemos (2003) asks, highlighting that in this perspective, to include appears basically to adapt and mold. But to include is much more than to adapt to a technocratic logic. After all, it is by participating and acting in the world that we construct ourselves and "it is in the *insertion* in the world and not in the *adaptation* to it that we become historic and ethical beings, capable of choosing deciding and overcoming" said Freire (2000, p. 90).

Digital inclusion must include social, cultural, technological, and intellectual dimensions, in order to favor forms of belonging and assure the effective participation of people in the culture. Thus, the policies of digital inclusion should also encourage the deconcentration of power and local, regional, and national autonomy and not subordination to monopolies and imprisonment to private networks. This is the position taken by numerous authors, such as Silveira (2003), who see the open software movement as an important route to autonomy and a possibility for a creative mediation of the digital divide. In his analysis, "the open software movement is an authentic expression of this potential of the network and the great model for consolidation of shared solutions before complex questions, based on multiethnic, multinational and multicultural interaction" (Silveira, 2003, p. 38). He understands the open software model as an economically viable option, which is technologically innovative and stable, and explains that an extensive use of open software in Brazil would not only save money in royalties, but also establish the country as an important producer and distributor of solutions in open code. This use of open software can exemplify imaginative alternatives to the monopolistic tendencies of technological globalization. As Boaventura Souza Santos affirms, "it is through the imagination that citizens are disciplined and controlled by States, markets and other dominant interests, but it is also from the imagination that citizens develop collective systems of dissidence and new designs for collective life" (2002, p. 46).

Now we can examine some implications of these developments in the cultural lives of children and young people.

CHILDHOOD, YOUTH, AND CONTEMPORARY DIALOGUES

How can we consider the possibilities of citizen participation of children and youth in contemporary society? If on one hand technological developments offer certain forms of interaction and participation, above all in networks, many authors indicate that on the other hand technological interactions with the most immediate local context become more difficult. The matter is still open to debate. Could it be that the exacerbation of individualism in the society of consumption also offers possibilities for overcoming this individualism through the contradictions that are revealed? Can children and young people, through educational mediation and by interacting with technologies, transcend the limits created by individualism and build other dimensions of participation? To think of forms of participation only as a reproduction of the usual form of conducting politics would be an insufficient contribution to democracy and to the questioning of cultural standards. It is necessary to think of social and digital inclusion as a form of participation in culture and as a possibility for change in the forms of seeing and relating to society. We will discuss some of the many challenges this poses.

Children and young people are increasingly present on the public scene. In addition to their recognition as consumers and citizens, it is recognized that they are particularly vulnerable to social changes. Although child labor is generally restricted to peripheral countries, children are targeted as consumers in borderless campaigns by globalized marketing. Cultural products aimed at children, video, television, cinema, cartoons, computer games, children's literature, and other products for children, fashion, candy, school supplies, recreational services, and so forth, constitute one of the most important segments in the consumer market. In this sense, the child is seen more as a consumer than as a citizen.

In this process, childhood comes to share the same media repertoires, often by developing a "single taste." We know that in each context there is an active reinterpretation of cultural products, in a process in which globalized cultures cross and recombine with local cultures.[13] But it is important to explore the possibilities for autonomy of childhood, in a context in which economic and cultural globalization operate in a complex and contradictory form on the status of childhood.[14] On one hand, hegemonic forces lead to the use of children's labor, to an increase in poverty, social inequality, and to the constitution of a global children's market, with effects on behavior, lifestyles, and the cultures of childhood. On the other hand, contrahegemonic globalization promotes the rights of children and strives to establish a political agenda that focuses on childhood.

Tensions between *heterogenous living conditions* and *homogenizing pressures* contribute to the formation of fragmentary and changing identities, and the contemporary social space of (re)institutionalization of childhood can also imply a possibility for alternative paradigms. Given this situation, schools can be seen as one of the important faces of counter-hegemonic globalization.[15] While the school is the institution that has contributed most to the definition of the social status of children, Brazil's deep educational problems challenge the structure and symbolic order of school's as well as public educational policies, questioning the meaning of educational actions. Therefore, schools cannot remain divorced from the movement to construct rights for children, including the right to digital citizenship. As a public service, schools cannot be merely a preparatory space devoted to the aim that one day each individual can become a citizen. They must be places where citizenship is a reality even in childhood.

In order to accomplish this goal, education must consider the complexities of being a young person today, especially in its subjective aspects, which also depend on the sociocultural context. A recent study[16] revealed that Latin American children and youth say they are happier, more nationalist, and live closer to their families than boys and girls in developed countries. In contradiction, this same group occupies the worst position in well-being, due to their concerns for public safety. According to the study, these children and youth are concerned about losing their parents, with physical appearance, education, and in getting a job. This survey revealed two distinct worlds: "In the developed countries, young people are rich, but pessimistic about the future. In the developing world, children and adolescents are optimistic and hopeful, despite the fact that they confront large daily challenges."[17] The study also shows that more than 70% of youth and 80% of children in Argentina and Mexico said that they are happy, in contrast with the data obtained in the United States and England, where less than 30% of youth and less than 50% of the children say they are happy.[18]

This data confirms the degree to which subjective production is involved in the identity of young people and consequently in the perspectives that they have for the future. The data shows, once again, how important it is for digital inclusion to go beyond mere technical access and achieve towards cultural inclusion. This indicates the need to promote digital inclusion, while considering the specificity of memories, traditions, aims, values, fears, and hopes of youth in each culture. Projects designed from top to bottom (or from the "center" to the "periphery") in which there is no space for the emergence of different responses to these subjective and differing realities, will certainly have limited results from the perspective of participation and citizenship.

Another theme that is obviously part of the situation that we are examining is the relationship between adults and children in the scenario of digital culture. The emergence of a new type of subjectivity in the new generations, as a result of complex factors, has been identified by researchers in various fields. Others argue that the vision of a *deficiency* of new generations—that identifies their cognitive and cultural poverty—should be substituted by a vision based on *difference*. Based on theories that consider the combination of technological identity with human identity, Green and Bigum (1995), for example, have provocatively suggested that if a moralist panic tends to see children and youth today as aliens—a culture that is "designed, motivated and constructed differently," (Green & Bigum, 1995, p. 212)—on the other hand, it is adults who should be increasingly seen as aliens, given that it is "youth that inherit the earth" (Green & Bigum, 1995).

If we accept the provocation of these authors and admit that we as adults are increasingly *alien*, foreign, and—from the cultural perspective of children and young people, it is not for this reason that we are exempt from responsibility. We need to sharpen our tools for understanding, invest in the transformation of languages, contents, and contexts of reception, and on improving our capacity to understand the needs and desires of the young. In fact, we find ourselves today at the edge of various abysses—between generations, cultures, classes with unequal access to material and immaterial goods. At the same time, the new cultural forms are also means for bridging these gaps. Faced with the creation of this new culture, we need to adapt ourselves to new ways of seeing, reading, thinking, learning, interacting, and intervening in reality; but at the same time we need to continue to demand the presence of oral, written, and audiovisual culture in the school space. The various forms of production of knowledge that emerge among us can only dialog with each other if we give potential to the diversity of experiences in different social spaces.[19]

Thus, it is important to promote an *intergenerational dialogue*: children, young people, and adults of all ages need to hear one another. In addition, it is also necessary to have more *intragenerational dialogue* and promote forms of perceiving what exists in common between the challenges and rights of each generation. This is one more reason for an understanding of digital inclusion as more than a mere technical issue, or as a method to expand old forms of sociability and of teaching-learning. Digital inclusion should not be about using media in the schools to mitigate the tedium of education. Digital inclusion should involve a new form of insertion of children, young people, and adults in the complex processes of communication of society today.[20]

Education mediated by technology can favor the recovery of a playful dimension in the production of knowledge. We can say that in this game, one generation can contribute something to the other. On one hand, children and young people continue learning from adults that history, memory, and cultural inheritance are the foundations of current experience. On the other hand, there are many indications that adults have learned from youth the playful dimension of the use of digital technologies. It can be said that to play with or against these machines is a form of recovering liberty in a world programmed by technology, as Flusser (1998) suggests.

A sociocultural redefinition of the school can lead it to incorporate the new technologies, reaffirming the specific trait of education in modernity, which is that of basing the socialization of knowledge on technologies of intelligence. This is discussed by Sodré (2002), who suggests that the use of the computer in classrooms could be understood as a new form of arts and crafts, in a playful approach to software production. The *bricolage* offered by the culture of simulation allow the appearance of new forms of learning and of resolution of problems that emphasize concrete thinking in relation to the abstract and an exploratory approach to the conceptual, approximating the modes of production of knowledge of adults and children.

Culture and education can be "spaces of emancipation and not only of reproduction, domination and hegemony," observes Belloni (2006, p. 22). This author adds that this perspective for integration of technologies in educational practices in schools can be based on two elements: "the category of *generation*, [which] allows us to perceive the importance of the young, of the new generations, as actors in the construction of the future and of change" and *media education*, that "appears as an unescapable route for the basic education of all children to become complete citizens"(Belloni, 2006, p. 17).

MEDIA EDUCATION AND A CULTURAL PERSPECTIVE OF DIGITAL INCLUSION

For digital inclusion to be implemented in a way that it provides more than simple access to a model of technical education in which students learn to use software and navigate the Internet, an ecological perspective of media education (Rivoltella, 2000) can contribute to another perspective of digital inclusion.

The ecological paradigm of media education presents an integrated concept, which calls for using all the media and technologies available: computers and the Internet in addition to photography, cinema, video, books, and CDs, and for articulating educational proposals with the demands of the communication environment based on each technological innovation in order to integrate them to each other.[21] As much as the computer, Internet, and the World Wide Web are important today, and can even be considered necessary conditions for social insertion and participation, media education is not limited to them. As we have suggested above, it is essential to analyze the needs of each group, project, and context. In this perspective, the objective of media educational work in school is not only the use of the computerized classroom or multimedia laboratory, but for children to act in these and other spaces to establish interactions and build relations and meanings. This mediation should be thought of as a form of affirming corporality—gesture, voice, movement, look—and relationships with nature as essential dimensions for the construction of meanings.

The different forms of citizenship—civil, political, social, and cultural—are challenged by new media in contemporary society, requiring new forms of thinking of education and social inequality. In relation to media education, new emphases are being thought of: one, on a *new media* education, another on a new *media education* (Rivoltella, 2006). The first perspective accentuates that the new media create new educational demands, and that children and young people need other forms of education (medialiteracy, cyberliteracy). The second perspective highlights that with the change in the social role of the media in our society, the paradigm of media education must also change, based on an integrating and nonexclusionary perspective, which seeks responses to the challenges of a society in which the media play central, and not secondary, roles. A new media education aware of these challenges would have to go beyond functionalism and criticism towards, again, a culturalist perspective. For Rivoltella (2006), this hypothesis should depart from technologies of production and of signs to reach the *technologies of self*,[22] in a scenario in which every educator would have to be a media-educator and citizenship would be a central factor.

In the field of media education, the confrontation of the digital divide thus implies proposals for mediation that assure the possibility for a critical and creative appropriation of the technologies, oriented towards the development of authorship in children and young people, their insertion and participation in the culture.

PARTICIPATION IN THE CULTURE AS MEDIATION OF THE DIGITAL DIVIDE

When we emphasize the role of cultural participation in a media education concerned with inclusion we need to make clear what mean by *participation*, since it is a polysemous concept. We think of participation, here: as action of the individual in society, as autonomy and authorship in the political exercise of citizenship. Participation also connotes diversity, plurality, and liberty. It is a strong and politicized word, colored by various values and interests, and for this reason has been subject to different uses or simplifications.

Thinking of participation from the perspective of marginality—as we are doing—we cannot forget that in heteronomous societies such as ours, the excluded are symbolically included, because they are always an implicit or explicit reference, whether present or absent, *participating* in and integrating the same shared imaginary, or that is, the same culture. In this sense, the nonparticipant is paradoxically, a participant. The "outsider" is "inside."

The reconfiguration center-periphery is central to understanding the dynamics of cultural participation in Brazil today. The production of art and culture with the use of digital technologies in poor neighborhoods of large Brazilian cities has taken on increasing social, aesthetic, and economic importance in recent years. According to anthropologist Hermano Vianna, "the most important novelty of Brazilian culture in the past decade was the appearance of the voice straight from the periphery speaking up throughout the country" (2004, p.8-9). This voice is clearly related to the technological possibilities for its amplification and reproduction, which make it a bit more accessible to poor artist communities and collectives, and which are thus able to hear their own music, see their dance, film their stories and histories. A respected analyst of Brazilian culture, Vianna is an enthusiast of *telecentros*[23] (centers of free community Internet access): "the telecenters," he said, "can both produce community and citizen pride in the peripheries as well as connect all these peripheries to each other and to the world, not allowing these conquests to be coopted by political-cultural systems from "outside" or criminal organizations from "within" who only want to make the periphery more peripheral"(Vianna, 2004). He describes how more than 100 telecenters in the city of São Paulo are constantly full of young people, who lose their fear of the computer "treating it as a toy" and, as soon as they become intimate with the machines, come to program them. Since these telecenters work with open-source software, programming is encouraged. "The machines do not have secrets, their codes are open, and whoever wants to investigate the core of its operating system can do so" Vianna explains, reporting a representative example:

This opening led people like Cléber Santos, 18 (whose father is a recently unemployed construction worker –and mother a maid who earns the minimum wage), to frequent the telecenter in the city of Tiradentes (the first inaugurated by the municipal government in 2001), who made various open code programs with the programming resources that he learned totally on his own. Cléber, who is now a monitor at the telecenter in his "city" (and the fact that he participates in a pioneer project produced his pride of living there), speaks as if it is completely normal to know and have exchanged ideas with Richard Stallman, the father of the world's open-source software movement, the principal creator of this new concept of liberty. I never get tired of admiring this direct connection between the poorest periphery of São Paulo (the telecenters were installed in places with the lowest Human Development Indexes in the city) with the political, cultural, and economic movement that I consider to be the vanguard and most important taking place in the world today. Any other political movement, of antiglobalization or the landless movement, will prove to be inefficient in light of the conquests of free software. Any cultural movement, from punk to Luther Blissett, seems like a "childhood disease" in face of the free software ideology. (Vianna, 2004, p.8-9)

Vianna maintains that the movement has a revolutionary meaning, although it is taking place in near silence.

We can of course question the importance Vianna (2004) attributes to the free software movement, or, at least, await greater evidence of its results. Nevertheless, we cannot ignore that what the author calls "a revolution" is based in fact on a "collaborative and decentralized regime, with no political party in command, but with pieces of code in different computers spread across the planet, commanded by people who work not to get rich, but for the common good" (Vianna, 2004). This is certainly important from the perspective of inclusion. The effervescent production of youth at the Brazilian telecenters, is also highlighted by their public and visible character, an alternative to what is seen as one of the obstacles to the democratization of technologies, which is their invisible and individual use.[24]

Enthusiasm for the telecenters is not unanimous in Brazil, although they are part of most digital inclusion projects.[25] Lemos, for example, criticizes the idea of the telecenters, arguing that although they are seen as the "new panacea of inclusion" they are nothing more than a palliative to the problem of access and education, because the trend is toward generalized dissemination of the network to all areas (schools, squares, entire cities) "where each citizen, whether they want to or not, will have to deal with connected communication machines" (Lemos, 2003, p. 2). Whatever may be the political form of implantation of technologies in communities, however, the aspect that we want to highlight is the opportunity for artistic and cultural creation, and for participation in social life, that they make possible.[26]

It is in this sense that the digital culture can be understood as a new concept, because "it is based on the idea that the digital technology revolution, is in essence, cultural," according to Gil (2004). This is because the use of digital technology changes the ways people interact socially. Technology is no longer considered simply as a tool, it becomes part of a person's personality and identity. In this perspective, the complete use of the Internet and of free software, for example, creates great opportunities to democratize access to information and knowledge, broaden the potential of cultural goods and services, expand the values that form our common repertoire and therefore, our culture, and also give potential to cultural production, even create new forms of art, Gil (2004) adds. This occurs because the technology itself, as a means for social inclusion, takes on a new form, "not only as incorporation to the market, but as incorporation to citizenship and to the market" when it assures access to information and the reduction of costs of the multimedia means of production, which can broaden the creative potential of the citizen. Considering that this citizen is also a consumer, broadcaster, and receiver of knowledge and information, who has relative autonomy and who is connected in networks, which are a new form of collectivity, this process can redimension his or her participation in the culture.

In the field of education, participation is related to the need for decentralization and democratization of school management, to the social rights of children, adolescents, and youth and to certain concepts of teaching-learning, making it a central concept in recent years based on the perspective of education for citizenship. If the dimension of participation necessarily involves the "other," promoting participation in the school or outside of it implies working on the formation of groups; this brings us to the importance of the group and of situations of cooperative work from the perspective of digital inclusion within the framework of media education.

We can situate this perspective from the social rights of children and adolescents, both the "passive rights" linked to *protection* and *provision*, as well as the "active rights" of *participation*. In order to better elaborate on this theme, we can explore the possible tensions between these 3 Ps and their forms of mediation. How can we protect children's privacy and security while encouraging them to participate in open networks? Will the provision of access to sites, software, and new technologies be done in a restricted way that controls this access or that creates real opportunity to participation in these new media? Is it possible that encouraging the forms of participation of children in the culture involves anticipating certain responsibilities? What are the gains and losses of the different forms of participation of the children in the culture? Are there requirements and presumptions for promotion of participation of children at an active and visible level? How can the participation of children be guaranteed in such a way that there is personal action, self-expression and the establishment of another relationship with time that is less alienated and production-oriented than that which guides the daily life of contemporary urban societies?

A number of educational contexts have sought to support the playful-expressive *participation* of children through teaching-learning games and various opportunities found in daily activities. We are speaking here of other modes of participating in society: those in which children interact, communicate, plan, propose, share ideas, intervene, produce, create dialogue, and conduct experiences (Fantin, 2006a). A central objective of these actions is the promotion of agency and of the authorship of children. When we defend the participation of children from a perspective of digital inclusion, it is important to recognize that there are different realms of participation, whether in the space of the global society, social movements, communities, schools, and other cultural institutions or in the intimacy of domestic space. Each of these realms can be a space for critical and creative use of the digital media that promote inclusion.

The participation of children at school, our priority focus, gives new dimension to the paradigms of learning. A new paradigm has emerged in contemporary society: some authors affirm that while the production of knowledge had been principally defined either as acquisition from experience (empiricism) or as construction (constructivism), it can now be understood as participation. Although this thesis may be debatable from an epistemological point of view, since participation is not separated from acquisition and construction, it reconfigures some questions for educational mediation: to go beyond "knowing by doing" and "working cooperatively" a vision of "learning by participating" arises.[27]

Thus, for digital inclusion projects—thought of from their social, economic, technological, aesthetic, and cultural dimensions—be truly inclusive, they need to be linked_to a perspective for cultural-educational mediation, based on interactivity, on citizenship, on access, and on critical and creative appropriation. Although this emphasis may be part of the rhetoric of many projects, most of the programs still appear to be too highly centered on the economic needs. From the concept of participation that we are discussing, and with a cultural understanding of technology access and digital inclusion, educational mediation can make viable some situations of participation, whether in classrooms, laboratories, workshops, or other cultural spaces that the relationship with technology encourages.

One precaution that should be taken in this sense is not to demean the cultural production of children and of young people through the media, qualifying it simply as "social inclusion" actions. It is common, for example, for videos and home pages produced in school and cultural projects in poor regions to be appreciated principally for what they represent in terms of the construction of "self-esteem" of their authors and not for their own merits as forms of art, communication and language. This paternalist posture contradicts the true sense of inclusion, according to which not only do young and poor children have the right to express their vision of the world, but that the entire society has the right to hear what these young people and children have to say. In the Brazilian case, many of the most interesting aesthetic innovations and the most vigorous analyses of the social situation come precisely from "alternative" uses of technological resources invented by groups in impoverished regions from the very lack of more advanced material resources.

The educational proposals that are made to overcome the digital divide will depend on what is understood by a digitally literate person. If only the technical capacity to use the computer is considered, access to computers would be enough. But if a broader concept is adopted, from the perspective of media education and of citizen participation in the culture, which also involves a development of multiple languages, we can propose a few fundamental objectives of the educational and cultural mediations:

1. Competence in reading and writing of various texts and images and their use as social practice.
2. The education of critical and creative subjects who are able to appropriate, read, and write in various media languages through public access to the multimedia and the Internet in schools and communities.
3. Initial and continued education of teachers for media education. This is essential so that digital inclusion projects are not only palliative measures and episodic campaigns, because without investment in the school perspective and teacher training, the digital divide will continue to be produced.
4. Integration between digital media and the traditional systems of access to cultural production (museums, libraries, film clubs , and artistic workshops) to approximate different generations and trajectories and stimulate the linking of different cultures, broadening the concept of inclusion, with emphasis on the perspective of participation in culture.

It is clear that all of these objectives require specific policies and financing, with an emphasis on the education of and respect for teachers.

Given these objectives, the proposals for digital inclusion from a cultural and educational perspective involve the production of art, knowledge, subjectivity, politics, information, research, and memory, which encourage different types of participation.

In the realm of the classroom they include:

- Various types of peer-interaction (those who know/with those who don't know; those who are eager/ with those who are resistant);
- Different forms of communication between groups (using the various languages and both traditional and new technologies);
- Various forms of organizations of work groups (spontaneous, casual and directed);
- Different spatial contexts, in the classroom and outside of it (to explore the spatial configuration of the classroom; to extend pedagogical encounters to other cultural spaces, such as workshops, museums, theaters, squares, communities; to explore possibilities for virtual spaces);
- Situations that involve different attitudes (active, passive, critical, collaborative, resistant, indifferent, concentrated, moved);
- Different types of interaction with knowledge and with culture (critical, instrumental, productive);
- Different theoretical-methodological tools for research (observation, interview, video-recording, photography, participant-observation);
- Possibilities for reflection and socialization of the observations made, reflecting on the representations observed;

- Different forms of navigation, interaction and audiovisual production(creation of sites, screenplays, blogs).

In broader realms of participation they include:

- Action in the school: student clubs, meetings for evaluation and class councils, parent, teacher and student associations, management of places for play in the schools;
- Action in the community: resident associations, community councils, cultural associations, youth, artistic, musical, theater, and religious groups;
- Action in the city: student movements, popular movements, NGOs and other forums;
- Interaction in cyberspace: collective action on the Internet, forums and chats, virtual communities.

Finally, the reflections and proposals that we have discussed seek to emphasize that while the economy of the information society is globalized, individuals continue to be local, and that there is an abyss between the global nature of wealth and power and the local significance of individual experiences. We propose the image of educational mediation from the cultural perspective as a possibility for navigation not in a river—which separates and unites—of which we spoke at the beginning, but in a large digital sea. As in the song *Pela internet*, by Gilberto Gil,[28] this kind of mediation involves discovering "with how many gigabytes one makes a *jangada*, a boat that can sail in this info-sea."

We hope to have provided some leads in this direction and an understanding of digital inclusion as construction of citizenship in which media education assures the real participation of children, young people, and adults in the culture. Even if we clearly did not exhaust all the issues involved, the complexity of which are renovated each day, we sought to contribute to the discussion in a tone which, although critical, is also hopeful.

REFERENCES

Adorno, S. (2002). *As cidades brasileiras do século XXI.* São Paulo: Publicação do Centro de Gestão e Estudos Estratégicos.

Almeida, M.E. (2005). Letramento digital e hipertexto: contribuições à educação. In N. Pellanda, E. Schlünzen & K. Schlünzen (Eds.), *Inclusão digital: Tecendo redes afetivas/cognitivas* (pp. 171-192). Rio de Janeiro: DP&A.

Andrade, O. (1928). Manifesto antropofágico. *Revista de Antropofagia, 1*(1)

AZEVEDO, R. (2006). *Formação de leitores, cultura popular e contexto Brasileiro.* Retrieved November 18, 2006, from www.ricardoazevedo.com.br/artigo10.htm

Bazalgette, C. (2005). Media education in Inghilterra: incontro con Cary Bazalgette nel suo ufficio. In *Boletim InterMED,* anno 10, n.3, Roma.

Belloni, M.L. (2006). Infância, Técnica e Cidadania: Cenário de mudanças. Retrieved October 11, 2007, from www.comunic.ufsc.br

Buckingham, D. (2000). *After the death of childhood: Growing up in the age of electronic media.* Cambridge: Polity Press.

Buckingham, D. (2003). *Media education: Literacy, learning and contemporary culture.* Cambridge: Polity Press.

Cadimo, F. (2004). Miragens digitais. Retrieved October 11, 2007, from http:www.fcsh.unl.pt/cadeiras/httv/artigos/Miragens%Digitais.pdf

Castells, M. (1996/2006). *The rise of the network society [A sociedade em rede, vol. 1].* São Paulo: Paz e Terra.

Castells, M (1996/2002). *End of millennium [Fim de milênio, vol. 3].* São Paulo: Paz e Terra.

Fantin, M. (2006). *Mídia-educação: Conceitos, experiências, diálogos Brasil-Itália.* Florianópolis: Cidade Futura.

Fantin, M (2006a). *As crianças interagindo nos cenários contemporâneos: A "escola estação cultura."* Unpublished paper presented at Universidade Federal de Santa Catarina.

Flusser, V. (1998). *Ensaio sobre a fotografia: para uma filosofia da técnica.* Lisboa: Relógio d'Água.

Freire, P. (2000). *Pedagogia da indignação: Cartas pedagógicas e outros escritos.* São Paulo: Editora Unesp.

García Canclini, N. (1989/1998). *Culturas híbridas: estratégias para entrar e sair da modernidade [Culturas híbridas: Estratégias para entrar y salir de la modernidad].* São Paulo: Editora da USP.

Gil, G. (2004). *Aula Magna* at Universidade de São Paulo. Retrieved October 11, 2007, from http://www.cultura.gov.br/noticias/discursos/index.php?p=833&more=1

Green, B., & Bigum, C. (1995). Alienígenas na sala de aula. In T.T. Silva (Ed.), *Alienígenas na Sala de Aula: Uma introdução aos estudos culturais em educação.* Petrópolis: Vozes.

Jobim e Souza, S., Gamba Jr. (2003). Novos suportes, antigos temores: tecnologia e confronto de gerações nas práticas de leitura e escrita In Jobim e Souza, S. (Ed.) *Educação@pós-modernidade: ficções científicas e ciências do cotidiano.* Rio de Janeiro: 7 Letras.

Lemos, A. (2003). Dogmas da inclusão digital. *Correio Braziliense.* Retrieved October 11, 2007, from http:www.facom.ufba.br/ciberpesquisa/andrelemos

Lemos, A., & Costa, L. (2005). Um modelo de inclusão digital: O caso da cidade de Salvador. In *Revista de Economia Política de las Tecnologias de la Información y Comunicación.* Vol. VIII, n.6. Retrieved October 11, 2007, from http:wwweptic.com.br/português/Revista%20EPTIC%20VIII%20-%20AndreLemos-LeonardoCosta.pdf

Martín-Barbero, J. (2002/2004). Ofício de cartógrafo: travessias latino-americanas da comunicação na cultura *[Oficio de cartógrafo: Travessias lationoamericanas de la comunicación en la cultura].* São Paulo: Loyola.

Martin-Barbero, J.(1998). Herdando el futuro: Pensar la educación desde la comunicación. In *Cultura y Comunicación, 9.* Universidad de Salamanca, Salamanca.

Morcellini, M. (Ed.). (2004). *La Scuola della Modernità: Per un manifesto della media education.* Milano: Franco Angeli.

Neri, M. (2003). *Mapa da exclusão digital.* Rio de Janeiro: FGV/IBRE, CPS.

Pinto, M. (1997). A infância como construção social. In Pinto, M. e Sarmento, M. *As crianças, contextos e identidades.* Minho: Centro de Estudos da Criança.

Rivoltella, P.C. (2002). *Media education: Modelli, esperienze, profilo disciplinare.* Roma: Carocci.

Rivoltella, P. C. (2005). *Media education: Fondamenti didattici e prospettive di ricerca.* Brescia: Editrice La Scuola.

Rivoltella, P. C. (2006). *Screen Generation: Gli adolescenti e le prospettive dell'educazione nell'etá dei media digitalli.* Milano: Vita e Pensiero.

Rogoff, B. (2003/2005. *The culture nature of human development [A natureza cultural do desenvolvimento humano].* Porto Alegre: Artmed.

Santos, L.G. (2003). A informação após a virada cibernética. In L.G. Santos et al. (Eds.), *Revolução Tecnológica, Internet e Socialismo.* São Paulo: Fundação Perseu Abramo.

Schwartz, G. (2000). Exclusão digital entra na agenda econômica mundial. *Folha de São Paulo,* São Paulo, 18 de junho 2000.

Silveira, S. (2001). A. Exclusão digital: A miséria na era da informação. São Paulo: Editora Fundação Perseu Abramo.

Silveira, S. (2003). Inclusão digital, software livre e globalização contra-hegemônica. In S. Silveira & J. Cassino (Eds.), *Software livre e inclusão digital.* São Paulo: Conrad Editora do Brasil.

Soares, M. (2002). Novas práticas de leitura e escrita: letramento na cibercultura. In Dossiê *Letramento, Revista Educação e Sociedade,* n.81. Campinas: Cedes.

Soares, M. (2005). *Letramento: um tema em três gêneros.* Belo Horizonte: Autêntica.

Sodré, M.(2002*). Antropológica do espelho: uma teoria da comunicação linear em rede.* Petrópolis: Vozes.

Sorj, B. (2003). *brasil@povo.com: a luta contra a desigualdade na Sociedade da Informação.* Rio de Janeiro: Jorge Zahar; Brasília: Unesco.

Souza Santos, B. (2002). *A globalização e as ciências sociais***.** São Paulo: Cortez.

Taylor, M., & Saarinen, E. (1994). *Imagologies: Media philosophy.* London: Routledge.

Thompson, J. (1995/1998). *The media and modernity: A social theory of the media [A midia e a modernidade: uma teoria social da mídia].* Cambridge: Polity Press. Brazilian translation, Petrópolis: Vozes.

Vianna, H. (2004). A disseminação silenciosa do software livre. Caderno Mais, *Folha de São Paulo,* 18/04/2004

SUGGESTED SITES

Comitê para a Democratização da Informática: www.cdi.org.br

Comitê Gestor da Internet Brasil: www.cgi.org.br

Cúpula da Sociedade da informação: www.wsis.org

Digital Divide Networks: www.digitaldividenetwork.org

Free Software Foundation: www.fsf.org

From Acces to Outcomes: Digital Divide Report – Morino Institute: www.morino.org.divides

IBOPE - Instituto Brasileiro de Opinião Pública e Estatística: www.ibope.com.br

Internet World Stats: www.internetworldstats.com

Programas do Governo Federal para Inclusão Digital: www.idbrasil.gov.br

Somos@telecentros: www.tele-centros.org.br

UNESCO–Internet Rights Forum: www.foruminternet.org

ENDNOTES

1 Sodré observes that there is often a buying and selling of technologically outdated equipment, making it clear that Brazilian and foreign commercial interests are stronger than the needs of civil society.

2 Ministry of Communications and the Internet Management Committee of Brazil, 2006.

3 INEP/MEC/Pro Brasil 2005.

4 Brazil has 15 million illiterate people 15 years or older (IBGE).

5 A dimension related to this issue is that of self-learning, which has an important role in

the processes of development of multiliteracies.

6 Bazalgette (2005) proposed the "3 Cs," culture, criticism, and creation, as three essential aspects of media education.

7 Personal notes from the course "Tecnologia dell'istruzione e del aprendimento," given by Pier Cesare Rivoltella, at UCSC, Milano, 2005.

8 Internet World Stats, www.internetwordlstas.com

9 IBOPE: www.ibope.com.br

10 There has been a significant increase in the purchase and use of cell phones among Brazilians of a variety of classes and age groups. Considering that today a cell phone can be a multimedia center, becoming at the same time a camera and a video, a pocket computer with Internet access, and a television receiver and broadcaster, and that Brazil is a country open to new technological developments, this trend can bring new possibilities for digital inclusion. After all, mobile connections are changing the perception of cyberspace, and we are increasingly more "immersed in a nomadism that articulates the space of flow with the space of place." (Lemos, 2003, p.2). The relationship between the multiplication of cellular telephones and digital inclusion is beyond the scope of this study. We merely note this complexity, from a socio-economic as well as cultural perspective.

11 See Lemos and Costa (2005, p. 6).

12 Analyzing various projects of digital inclusion, Lemos and Costa (2005) maintain that the majority of them emphasize the technical dimension at the cost of the social, cultural, and intellectual.

13 See Canclini (1998) and Thompson (1998).

14 See Pinto (1997) and Buckingham (2000).

15 See, for example, Pinto and Sarmento (1997).

16 Reported by MTV Networks, the study was conducted over six months. Interviews were conducted with 5,200 children (ages 8 to 15) and young people from 16 to 34. The survey was conducted in the following countries: Argentina, Germany, Brazil, China, Denmark, the United States, France, India, Indonesia, Japan, Mexico, England, South Africa, and Sweden. Retrieved October 11, 2007, from http://www.multirio.rj.gov.br/portal/riomidia/rm_materia_conteudo.asp?idioma=1&v_nome_area=Materias&idMenu=3&label=Materias&v_id_conteudo=66749

17 Noel Gladstone, research of vice-president MTV Networks.

18 When the issue is concern for beauty and aesthetics, Brazilians take first place. Nearly 66% of Brazilian children, 50% of Indonesian, and 41% of Mexicans said they are concerned with their weight. For the children of Brazil (93%), Argentina (87%), and Mexico (84%) to take care of oneself is a sign of status. In relation to sex, Latin American youth from 6 to 34 believe they have better sexual performance. Brazilians come in first place, (66%), then Argentines (48%), and Mexicans (46%). The Japanese were last (5%). Terrorism occupied the eighth place on the list of the main fears of youth today and in tenth place among the children. In general, children and young people said that they are afraid of losing their parents, of having cancer or AIDS, and of frequent crime in large cities. All of these issues are clearly influenced by the representation of these themes in the media, and are thus directly related to the role of media education.

19 See discussion by Jobim and Souza (2003, p. 38).

20 See Martin-Barbero (2000).

21 Various authors have considered the relationship of children with the media in the realm

of "cultural ecology." In their philosophy of media, Taylor and Saarinem (1994) maintain that dealing with children means accepting the responsibility for "creating and sustaining structures and networks to support life." In the culture of the media ("simcult"), they add, "this means that we must act to shape and reshape the telecommunications environment that is the world in which our children are destined to dwell." (Taylor & Saarinem, 1994, p. 37).

22 In the Foucaultian sense, stressing here the reflexive practices around media use and consumption.

23 Telecenters are spaces with computers with broadband Internet connections, which offer free use of equipment, basic computer courses, and special workshops. According to the federal government proposal, "each Telecenter has a Management Council, formed by members of the community elected by the community, who help the staff monitor and manage the space. It is a project for intensive use of information technology to broaden citizenship and combat poverty, seeking to guarantee digital privacy and security for the citizen, his insertion in the information society, and strengthen local development. One of the principal objectives of the project is to organize a network of units of multiple functions that allow people to acquire basic technological autonomy and privacy based on open source software." Retrieved October 11, 2007, from http://www.idbrasil.gov.br/docs_telecentro/docs_telecentro/o_que_e

24 See Graham (apud Lemos, 2005, p.3).

25 There are various examples and the experiences of projects that support the call for digital inclusion in Brazil. In the field of public policy, the Brazilian government sought the integration of existing digital inclusion programs at the federal state and municipal levels, and created the Brazilian Digital Inclusion Model, which was an attempt to improve the activities and avoid the duplication of projects. From the many projects of NGOs, we can highlight the pioneer work of the Committee for the Democratization of Computing. See http://www.idbrasil.gov.br and http://www.cdi.org.br

26 This is even more relevant considering the social reality of the favelas in Brazilian cities. According to Adorno "the thesis that sustains causal relations between poverty, delinquincy and violence, is now highly questioned by many studies. Nevertheless, relations between the persistance, in Brazilian society, of the concentration of wealth, the concentration of the precarious quality of collective life in so-called peripheral neighborhoods in large cities and the general explosion of violence, must be recognized. Maps of violence, created for some Brazilian cities such as Rio de Janeiro, Salvador, Curitiba, and São Paulo (...) indicate that homicide rates are much higher in these areas than in neighborhoods that compose the urban belt better served by urban infrastructure, a labor market and leisure and cultural services." Adorno (2002). "As cidades brasileiras no século XXI." Retrieved October 11, 2007, from http://www.nevusp.org/conteudo/index.php?conteudo_id=367

27 See Rogoff (2005).

28 Gilberto Gil is a prominent Brazilian singer-songwriter and the current Minister of Culture.

This work was previously published in Digital Literacy: Tools and Methodologies for Information Society, edited by P. Rivoltella, pp. 310-340, copyright 2008 by IGI Publishing (an imprint of IGI Global).

Chapter 15 Multi-Cultural E-Learning Teamwork: Social and Cultural Characteristics and Influence

Datta Kaur Khalsa
University of Maryland, USA

ABSTRACT

Virtual teamwork in the e-learning classroom has provided opportunities for merging social theory and learning theory, mixing technology, culture, identity, and community. Online learning teams have generated attention to the social and cultural characteristics that influence these global interactions. This chapter discusses the prevalence of eight traditional dimensions of culture occurring during online learning team interaction. A study with graduate students, who were experienced in virtual teamwork, provides quotes and examples of experiences, challenges, and suggestions for improvement to the multi-cultural, virtual team experience. The students' suggestions inform guidelines for e-learning faculty and students, while additional study results present understanding of the acculturation process, a process that occurs when diversified social and cultural characteristics come together and form a cultural hybrid to accomplish e-learning team goals.

INTRODUCTION

Our team contained a WASP, an Armenian émigré, and a Jewish British ex-Pat on the team. Without being able to be specific, we all brought our differing viewpoints to bear on the problem and each rejoiced in our different ways of looking at things.

For two of us, our diasporas commonalities also gave us strength in the team without being excluding to the third member. Our openness in expressing our differences celebrated and took advantage of our diversity and contributed to our genuine delight in each other and to the team's success. (Online graduate student, 2004)

The increased availability of e-learning has brought convenience and equitable learning possibilities to cross-cultural student populations. The online student classroom may contain diversified student identities: residents from several countries, those who are native to one country, but now living in the U.S., and English as second language learners. Reaching beyond traditional limits of geographical boundaries and time constraints, virtual classrooms provide diversified groups of students with opportunities for discussion, planning, and team projects (Cyrs, 1997; Ess, 2001; Johnson & Johnson, 1994; Ko & Rossen, 2004; Palloff & Pratt, 1999; Rogers, 2002). The online classrooms merge social theory and learning theory, mixing technology, culture, identity, and community (Bandura, 2001; Collins & Berge, 1996; Khalsa & Hildreth, 2000; LaBelle, 2004; Preece, 2000; Wenger, 2004). Traditional team processes take on a new look, as online students are required to adapt and acculturate social and cultural characteristics during virtual teamwork (English-Lueck, Darrah, & Saveri, 2002).

The intentions of this chapter are to present e-learning faculty and students with a practical model for development and support of multi-cultural teamwork in the adult e-learning classroom. The study was designed to answer this question, "Which traditional social and cultural characteristics are important for multi-cultural e-learning team members?" Over a one-year period, 45 graduate students, who had been engaged in teamwork during their online classes, were surveyed and interviewed. The goal was to obtain opinions and suggestions about their general, online team experience, communication, challenges, social and cultural influences, and suggestions for improvement to the virtual team experience. Through description of influential social and cultural characteristics, graduate students provided their top priorities for faculty and fellow students, who will be involved with virtual learning teams. The student suggestions built a guiding framework, and are included in this chapter.

BACKGROUND

E-learning can benefit from the creation and sharing of knowledge vs. merely long-established knowledge transfer and assimilation. Extending communication and knowledge through collaboration presents opportunities for a collective effort of understanding (Berge, 1998; Bielaczyc & Collins, 1999; Camarinha-Matos & Afsarmanesh, 2004; Dede, 1999; LaBelle, 2004). Online learning teams provide "a dynamic mix of national, geographic, organizational and professional or disciplinary variables in constant interaction with one another, (changing) according to the context" (Heaton, 2001, p. 220). Online learning that incorporates team-based interactions creates community. It also extends a learning advantage to its adult students, because it mirrors the authentic interaction needed and developing in many educational and organizational settings and practices (Dede, 2001).

E-learning team interactions require intellectual, emotional, and social support, some unlearning, relearning, and deep appreciation for the innovative process and what it will provide team members. Virtual team acculturation is acceptance of another's cultural patterns of behavior (Heusinkveld, 1997) and requires an awareness and interaction of personal social and cultural dimensions in a virtual time, space, and workplace (English-Lueck et al., 2002). The study results provided in this chapter supply verbatim student descriptions and examples related to the adaptation of social and cultural characteristics during multi-cultural team processes (Alexander, 2000; Kezsbom, 2000; Lipnack & Stamps, 2000; Powell, Piccoli, & Blake, 2004; Solomon, 2001; Suchan & Hayzak, 2001). The results of this research created guidelines for the hybrid temporary learning team towards the ultimate goal, efficient and effective achievement of learning goals. This study informs students on how to become more effective team members and helps e-learning teachers become more efficient team guides. An initial examination of general multi-cultural team characteristics creates an awareness of challenges during a virtual team process.

MULTI-CULTURAL TEAM CHARACTERISTICS

Teams have been defined as individuals who are interdependent in their tasks, share responsibilities for outcomes, and manage their relationships across organizational boundaries (Cohen & Bailey, 1997; Godar & Ferris, 2004). Global teams within organizations choose members from around the world and rarely meet members face-to-face. They are required to "share information, adapt to time constraints and establish effective relationships at a distance, often under trying political and cultural circumstances" (English-Lueck et al., 2002, p. 92). The same types of conditions exist for diversified online learning teams (Khalsa, 2005).

Short and temporary time frames towards completion of team projects require members to engage in interdependent tasks with common goals and individual competencies, including different levels of technology proficiency (Gibbs, 2002; Godar & Ferris, 2004). Team members represent different cultures, languages, and organizations, as they interact to form and establish common goals. E-learning team endeavors include: diversity of expertise among its members; shared objectives of advancing the collective knowledge and skills; emphasis on learning how to learn; and mechanisms for sharing what is learned (Bielaczyc & Collins, 1999; Johnson & Johnson, 1994). For virtual learning teams to be engaged, motivated, and attain their goals, important considerations need attention.

OVERVIEW OF E-LEARNING TEAM CONSIDERATIONS

Numerous areas of research provide clarifying information towards proper e-learning team facilitation and sustainability. Andragogy or adult learning theory provides advice on authentic and flexible learning to serve adult career goals and overloaded work schedules (Knowles, 1984). The field of human-computer interaction adds technological suggestions to aid credibility, usability, and dependability of technology (Fogg, 2003; Maloney-Kritchmar & Preece, 2002; Preece, 2000; Shneidermann, 2003). Online community research provides assistance for facilitation, netiquette, lurking, and reciprocity (Nonnecke & Preece, 2003; Preece, 2000; Preece, Sharp, & Rogers, 2002). Research also connects identity, computer-mediated communication, and cross-cultural relationships to social capital and development of trust (Bos, Olson, Gergle, Olson, & Wright, 2002; Cohen & Prusak, 2001; Preece, 2000; Rovai, 2001; Sproull & Kiesler, 1986; Walter, 1996).

Most online team research has emphasized benefits, technological guidelines, processes, and content development with less emphasis on the effects of social and cultural characteristics on team endeavors (Gibbs, 2004). However, online learning team social and cultural influences affect many aspects of teamwork, including roles, activities, expectations, and interpretations of time (Adler & Graham, 1989; Gibbs, 2002; Hall, 1977; Hofstede, 1997; Matei & Ball-Rokeach, 2002; Rheingold, 1993; Walther, 1996). A framework for discussing social and cultural characteristics in online learning teams that will be used here incorporates three key components: social learning theory, identity theory in a collaborative culture, and the acculturation process. Each component adds to the understanding of multi-cultural interaction in online learning teams.

SOCIAL LEARNING THEORY

The social learning theory describes a small part of the budding, yet vibrant image of learning in the world today (Bandura, 2001; Wenger, 2004). It explains how thoughts, feelings, and behavior are affected by the presence or implied presence of others (Bandura, 1986). The social and cultural context of the individual, how they perceive and interpret information from others, is the basis of this theory. Simply stated, people observe, imitate, and learn socially. Cognitive skills, attitudes, and behavior impact the environment, and the environment impacts these personal factors (Huitt, 2004; Huitt & Vessels, 2002). This creates an interchange between three variables: overt behavior, personal factors, and environmental factors (Wenger, 2004).

Individuals exist and act within a broad network of environmental structures: imposed, selected, and constructed (Bandura, 2001). The boundaries of influence have been broadened by environmental structures offered by the Internet and technology and as a result, traditional social and cultural characteristics are modified. The socio-structural influences such as roles, rules, and social practices, which normally regulate thought and behavior, exist with broader interpretation. The interplay of social and cultural forces with social learning such as online course discussions and online teamwork enhance course goals, objectives and e-learning possibilities.

By recognizing the power of technology on present-day social and cultural characteristics, one can better understand how team behavior is impacted (Huitt, 2002) and how cognitive skills, attitudes, behaviors, and the environment influence each other (Bandura, 1986). Social learning theory extends relevancy to adult learning needs and provides a description of how intrapersonal and interpersonal information is perceived. "Within this theoretical framework, human functioning is analyzed as socially interdependent, richly contextualized and conditionally orchestrated within the dynamics of various societal subsystems and their complex interplay" (Bandura, 2001, p. 5). Personal identity intersects with the virtual team identity and requires adaptation or acculturation.

IDENTITY IN A COLLABORATIVE CULTURE

A personal identity is "a set of attributes, beliefs, desires, or principles of action that a person thinks distinguish her (or him) in socially relevant ways" (Fearon, 1999, p. 2). Personal identity often engulfs group identity, allowing for unique experiences of thought, learning, and action. Identities are shaped through a group experience, built and maintained because of practice and recognized by members in the practice. Thus, characteristics of community become dimensions of identity (Zheng & Storck, 2001). When an individual's identity and perception are verified by a group, then group membership is recognized (Meng & Agarwal, 2005; Polzer, Milton, & Swann, 2002).

"People (interacting) move together in a kind of dance" (Hall, 1997, p. 72). Personal and social identities interact and are sustained through creation and transference of knowledge between community members (Butler, 2001). "Learning is a social becoming, the ongoing negotiation of an identity, that we develop in the context of participation (and non-participation) in communities and their practices" (Wenger, 2004, p. 4). Continual construction and reconstruction of self-identity requires fluidity during virtual interactions. Attention to acculturation or adaptability of self and group identity during e-learning team interactions can help fulfill online student team needs (Meng & Agarwal, 2005; Sudwicks & Ess, 2002).

ACCULTURATION IN E-LEARNING TEAMS

Virtual team acculturation is an individual's ability to adapt to the cultural behavior patterns of others (Heusinkveld, 1997) and requires shifting interdependence among strangers (English-Lueck et al., 2002). Members intermix, and team member thoughts and actions are usually most affected by ethnicity, social and political circumstances, and physical location. However, because of prevalent technology use, cultural influences have become less stagnant and stereotypical. Individuals are seeing themselves and are seen by others as social entities embedded in larger social systems (Fernandez-Ballesteros, Diez-Nicolas, Caprara, Barbaranelli, & Bandura, 2002; Powell et al., 2004; Wenger, 2004). The powerful socio-cultural forces that are rooted in social and cultural history, and choices that predate them (Matei & Ball-Rokeach, 2002), now function in an interdependent, ephemeral, virtual, and multi-cultural global team setting (Gibbs, 2002). Considering the complexity of human beings, their multi-faceted identity with many cultures and subcultures, and interactions in e-learning teamwork, it is no longer clear how far native social and cultural characteristics accurately explain human behavior in a virtual world (Sudwicks & Ess, 2002).

SOCIO-CULTURAL CONSTRUCTS IN E-LEARNING TEAMS

Social and cultural characteristics or constructs, also referred to here as dimensions of culture, describe shared, ethnic, geographic, and collective behaviors and patterns resulting from the fabric of a society. Hall (1977, 1990) researched in detail patterns of different cultures. His findings noted that there are cultural perceptual differences related to time, space, relationships, and materials (Hall, 1977). Hofstede (1984) studied values of people in different cultures, who worked for the same multinational corporation. His results were very similar to a study done 20 years earlier (Inkeles & Levinson, 1969) and resulted in four dimensions:

1. Power including perceptions of wealth and status
2. Uncertainty avoidance including perceptions of rules, regulations, and flexibility
3. Individualism including perceptions on self-reliance, group harmony, and team recognition
4. Gender including perceptions on competition, assertiveness, and nurturance or support in teamwork

It is also advantageous to note Storti's research (1990, 1998) that built on Hall and Hofstede's work. Storti related culture to business and provided two dimensions, invisible (assumptions, values and beliefs) and visible (behaviors). He described these dimensions as building blocks of socio-cultural differences. His list includes perceptions of self-identity, group identity, time, and power. However, the foundations and practical applications of the more traditional dimension of culture frameworks (Hall, 1977; Hofstede, 2001; Inkeles & Levinson, 1969; Storti, 1990, 1998) require further investigation for determination of relevancy and applicability to multi-cultural e-learning team situations. "(The) traditional notions of culture are becoming less and less applicable in a world where cultures have increasingly permeable boundaries and are blurred and blended through globalization" (Gibbs, 2002, p. 9).

After comparing the socio-cultural constructs or dimensions from the four previously mentioned frameworks (Hall, 1977; Hofstede, 2001; Inkeles & Levinson, 1969; Storti, 1990, 1998), there is strong evidence of the relationship between self-identity, group identity, and group harmony. Individual perceptions related to the following dimensions affect group actions: power, status, recognition, assertiveness, competitiveness, gender, leadership, time, flexibility, support, nurturance, rules, and regulations. These social and cultural characteristics became the base for coding survey and interview text in the online graduate student study described in this chapter.

ONLINE GRADUATE STUDENT STUDY

In order to better inform online students, educators, and facilitators, opinions and suggestions from adult online students with virtual team experience were obtained. The research question to be answered was, "Which traditional social and cultural characteristics are important for multi-cultural e-learning team members?" The goal was to obtain opinions and suggestions about student online team experiences, challenges, communication, social and cultural influences, and suggestions for improvement to the virtual team experience.

Participants

The participants for this study were 45 online graduate students (22 females and 23 males) enrolled in two online programs with two universities in the state of California. The researcher of this study (also the author of this chapter) had been teaching in these online programs for over five years, and was familiar with the population of students that these online programs attracted. She describes this sample as a multi-cultural group of adult students with a variety of career goals and experiences including corporate online training, K-12 teaching, university, business and military distance education development, and so forth. Each student's graduate studies was related to technology and learning.

The particular cultural backgrounds of the students had not been specifically determined to protect their privacy. However, the majority is currently located in the U.S. but have a variety of international, native backgrounds. Some did share their native cultural identity, and that information determined multi-cultural backgrounds, which included U.S. citizens living in other countries, natives from a variety of countries including Bangladesh, Oman, Honduras, China, and others. Some students were natives from outside the U.S., but had been living in the U.S. for two to six years. Overall the participants had a fair amount of technology skills and displayed an appreciation for technology-related opportunities shown by their choice of technology-related careers. They had each been involved in virtual teamwork and online learning communities during their online classes and careers.

Methods

Text was acquired from semi-structured and unstructured answers obtained through online surveys and email interviews during a one-year period. The initial interview questions are available in Appendix A. The author coded the interview text using a codebook that contained eight socio-cultural characteristics. These characteristics we all previously determined important by dimension of culture frameworks (Hall, 1977; Hofstede, 2001; Inkeles & Levinson, 1969; Storti, 1990, 1998). The codebook highlights are available in Appendix B.

Results

Dimensions (Appendix B) noted in traditional socio-cultural frameworks by Hall (1977), Hofstede (2001), Inkeles & Levinson (1969), and Storti (1990, 1998), were mentioned as important by graduate students in this study. The frequency of student responses related to socio-cultural constructs during the surveys and interviews is graphically displayed (Figure 1).

Details and interpretations of each dimension are provided next through a summary that connects theory, student suggestions, and quotes.

Specific cultural backgrounds of the students are not provided, so generalization of study results to online classrooms and virtual teamwork would assume that student populations have comparatively similar adult demographics.

Team Support

According to comments made by the graduate students in this study, team support includes sharing ideas, communicating positively and frequently with constructive criticism, alternative viewpoints, and professionalism. Students, who noted lack of team support, made comments on workload inequality, lack of communication, and noted a particular team member, who did not do their part. Differences of interpretation related to team support often had to do with recognition and respect for what an individual offered the group. This recognition and need for acknowledgment and respect may be tied to original or native social and cultural preferences, but further research would be needed to determine if a particular native culture preferred higher recognition level than others.

These student quotes are good representatives of facets of team support noted by the majority of students in this study. Note the English as a second-language challenge that could easily be misinterpreted by inconsiderate student team members or easily intimidated ESL students.

The team experience was such a joy, the members of the team were able to communicate often, share ideals, set goals and objectives. The team members were extremely knowledgeable in their field of expertise and shared constructive criticism and positive interaction ... (the) team experience was the greatest.

Each person, (whom) I've worked with has been very understanding, helpful, considerate, and focused upon the subject at hand.

These quotes display well lack of team support:

One person did not pull their weight so the remainder of the group simply got on with it without waiting and did the weak person's work as well. We didn't have time to sit around and whine and wait. We just finished it off.

Two of the team members didn't fully participate in the project. One claimed poor English skills, the other personal problems; but it's my grade and so I worked with (R) to produce a good paper!

Figure 1. Percentage of frequency for socio-cultural constructs

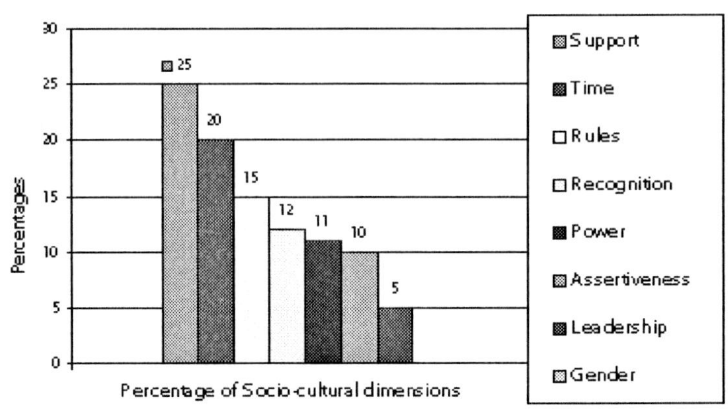

Recognition

The social learning theory explains how thoughts, feelings, and behavior are affected by the presence or implied presence of others (Bandura, 1986). Often the dimension of recognition was related to individual perceptions of respect. The social and cultural context of the individual, how they perceive and interpret information from others, is the basis of this theory. For example, one team member's assertiveness often resulted in the lack of recognition or perceived respect of another teammate. The representative quotes below display the overlapping effects of three socio-cultural characteristics: power/status, recognition, and assertiveness. Note the strong emphasis on cultural values in the last quote, as well as the need for definitions and boundaries related to respect.

One member repeatedly edited out another member's contributions to the project ... it was interpreted as disrespect because permission was not sought first ... The hurt party spoke to the other members about the incident, and we in turn encouraged that person to speak with the other team member to resolve the issue personally.

Simply put, if I have respect for you, I will naturally give your ideas and opinions due consideration. If I don't have this respect, it will be easy to disregard your input.

If I feel respected by the rest of the team, I am more likely to be actively participating in the team actions.
But in the end—the individual's perception on what is respectful or disrespectful is going to be the determining factor. And an individual perception is based on their culture of origin, the culture their family of origin and the culture of their community.

Time and Flexibility

Social and cultural influences affect many aspects of teamwork including roles, activities, expectations, and interpretations of time (Adler & Graham, 1989; Gibbs, 2002; Hall, 1977; Hofstede, 1997; Matei & Ball-Rokeach, 2002; Rheingold, 1993; Walther, 1996). Students gave advice towards authentic and flexible learning to serve adult career goals and overloaded work schedules (Knowles, 1984).

These students were engaged in projects with time frames of three months or less and worked virtually. They noted remedies to time challenges, which included acceptance of diversity, time zone differences, tolerance, and a willingness to put forth extra personal effort. The following quotes are representative of diversified students' interpretations of time and flexibility and the general emphases on respect and trust as recommended solutions.

When deadlines approached, and teamwork was needed, the process was clumsy, frustrating, and often times counterproductive. We did not meet our deadline because we had a very difficult time working together. The frustration of the group didn't improve until the topic of respect and trust had been addressed.

I never allowed my personal time limitations (to) affect other members—I worked through entire nights without any sleep, to make sure our group assignments were delivered on time.

(I was) able to jump in and save the day, if needed, to ensure the product would be fine on deadline.

My background helped a lot ... I manage a team that is all virtual—I have staff in California, Utah, Canada, Switzerland, and India ... I am very attuned to different time zones, different cultures, different processes, and different personalities ... I am not afraid to take the lead when I see the group wandering.

Power and Status

When an individual's identity and perception are verified by a group, then group membership is recognized (Meng & Agarwal, 2005; Polzer, Milton, & Swann, 2002). Individual identities often include levels of status or power. Most of the students noted giving up power whenever they are involved in team projects. However, just as many students felt that the quality of the learning experience during teamwork was well worth the extra effort. Note the last quote that mentions the ill effects of humor in virtual teamwork. Many identity references are evident in the quotes below:

With my individual paper, I had greater control (over) the process and outcomes (content, research approach, writing style, editing, etc.). But I did not have input of other ideas or feedback ... With the team paper there was collaboration, brainstorming and more support to write, research, and edit the paper. The challenge was to harmonize different points of view, writing styles and availability schedules. Doing this also trained us to work in groups, to be tolerant and supportive of the group.

Power is also noted from perceptions of status and recognition:

Honestly, I thought my second group was going to be terrible. There was one group member who I thought would not contribute anything. But I was surprised when he brought more to the table than I expected, and the project was improved as a result.

Challenges? Different time zones. Different study skills and habits. Different abilities.

One of the team members thought my idea on the topic as nothing. And I did not want to argue with him. But I was upset and frustrated. So I just followed the team and do my part.

I still cannot melt into the (online) class as a native speaker even though I have been US for 6 years ... I don't get humor or jokes, which is ok. But if our peers' discussion mentions some famous people in this field or other fields, and I have no idea what are they talking about. That's really bad.

Assertiveness

Virtual team acculturation is acceptance of another's cultural patterns of behavior (Heusinkveld, 1997). Personal identity intersects with the virtual team identity and requires adaptation or acculturation. The students in this study reported overall excellent team experiences with no serious complaints about overly assertive team members. Instead, the majority of students seemed to pay special attention to being too assertive and understanding perceptions from each individual in the team.

I also feel that the online environment with educated, empathetic students does hinder full-blooded debate that would be possible in the F2F situation. Without paralinguistic clues we are always second-guessing the emotion of the writer and thus we all try to avoid causing offence. This can, I feel, stifle what could be more interesting debates.

(My biggest challenge is) not taking over everything. Letting other members of the groups get their part done, and trusting that they would do it right.

Unless other members speak out to correct the misbehavior, the community would have been robbed of something very precious—trust—the foundation of Constructivism.

The worse part is when people tend to paraphrase what I mean to help the others get a clearer meaning. I feel insulted ... as if I could not communicate well.

Other students felt comfortable as followers:

I don't have (much) teamwork experience, so I just follow the trend. If I am ready to be a team leader, I think I will make my point clearly in order to avoid conflict or confusing.

I am not sure how to handle the situation if two people are all interested in being the team leaders.

Rules and Guidelines

Extending communication and knowledge through collaboration presents opportunities for a collective effort of understanding (Berge, 1998; Bielaczyc & Collins, 1999; Camarinha-Matos & Afsarmanesh, 2004; Dede, 1999; LaBelle, 2004). Team rules were noted by the majority of students as being important to team project quality and completion. There were many suggestions for initial guidelines and rules that could eliminate confusion and ineffectiveness. The socio-structural influences, such as roles, rules, and social practices that normally regulate thought and behavior, may exist with broader interpretation if initial discussion is prolific, as displayed in these student quotes:

- Suggest a format for members to reintroduce themselves with tombstone data, time zone, industry, restrictions (and/or) other commitments for the period.
- Discuss the topic, workloads, and schedule (of) each team member.
- Common understanding of the requirements of the assignment.
- Maintain good rules of Netiquette.
- Communicate on a daily or at least regular basis
- Trust that the work quality will be high and state those expectations up front.
- Discuss a method of communication. We used too many forms and it caused delays.
- Set up a blog and post ... group guidelines. These expectations kept everyone on track (related to) what was expected of each member.
- Ensure the team members have a similar time frame for working on the course (some prefer early week, some weekends).
- Get the team to choose roles and communicate those roles before the work actually begins.
- Have teams...compile guidelines, but also provide a weekly "report" (to the instructor) of how each of the guidelines is being implemented.

Leadership

"Learning is a social becoming, the ongoing negotiation of an identity, that we develop in the context of participation...in communities and their practice" (Wenger, 2004, p. 4). One form of meaningful identity established in most virtual teamwork is leadership. Leadership and assertiveness often serve each other. Many students noted the need for one main team leader or a plan to alternate the leadership role.

I am very competitive about earning my grades and will do whatever it takes to make a project work... so when the group wasn't coming together well, I emailed the de facto group leader and we worked it out.

Finding a leader was a challenge in the first teamwork. I tried to instill order but was essentially ignored. Luckily, we are all professional so the task was completed.

The leadership challenge—I have been in situations like this before and tend to try and organize things myself and become the team leader.

Many students also noted their perception of a preferred leader:

I personally prefer the leader to be very formal and directing or even demanding...group project deadlines are always tight. If the leader is very democratic, it will be hard to move on and meet the schedule.

The global thinking sort of leader always plays a great role in inviting all team players to present all ideas on the table. When a great deal of trust is established, the team can then decide which of the ideas are best to work off of.

The leader really can't be VERY democratic or nothing would get done. Instead, the leader needs to listen, evaluate, and decide. The style I prefer in a leader is for him/her to be decisive but not autocratic, taking in information from many or all sources, but not paralyzed or overwhelmed by the weight of decision.

We worked as a self-managing team sharing thoughts and ideas and coming to a consensus rather than as a leader subordinate situation.

Gender

There were 22 females and 23 males in this study. Gender issues were part of the traditional frameworks that were discussed earlier (Hall, 1977; Hofstede, 1984). "(The) traditional notions of culture are becoming less and less applicable in a world where cultures have increasingly permeable boundaries and are blurred and blended through globalization" (Gibbs, 2002, p. 9). However, with this group of students, only two females noted any bias or gender issues. Lack of gender notes may be due to development and emphasis of survey and interview questioning or actual lack of gender bias experiences. More research on this topic is necessary for guidelines to be applied to adult online learners. Here is a sample quote that sums up the opinions of two females who noted gender issues:

(I was in) a forum of members with diverse philosophies ... some of those philosophies were against principles of equality and justice ... I felt not only negativity in these male members ... but also racial and gender biases coming from their own upbringing and socio-cultural environments.

SUMMARY

This study highlights team members' ability to accept diversity with a tolerance and a willingness to put forth extra effort and even take the lead, if the group begins to wander. Comments emphasized respect and trust and not being too assertive. Global thinking that invites all team players to present all ideas can help with the understanding and involvement of students' diversified perceptions.

During this study, each of the eight categories of traditional, socio-cultural dimensions held substantial influence on multi-cultural e-learning teams. The differences between interpretations of these dimensions may be due to participants' cultural backgrounds. Further specific research among additional demographic groups is needed. However, if the following framework of suggestions is applied to adult U.S. online learning programs that incorporate diversified populations of students, virtual teamwork will most likely become more effective and the online educator more efficient.

These graduate students provided their top priorities for faculty and fellow students, who will be involved with virtual learning teams. Their suggestions built this main framework:

- Provide flexibility and democracy for choosing team members, topics, and group roles.
- Each student needs to provide the team tombstone data, time zone, industry, restrictions/other commitments.

- Emphasize the importance of guidelines, which should include team norms and styles, a detailed timeline, a description of the communication process and frequency, rules of cultural etiquette, and division of responsibilities (roles).
- A group leader needs to be clearly named even if the leader rotates from week to week.

Student suggestions also provided an instructor's layer to this framework:

- Give suggestions for communicating better in teams.
- Outline a simple project schedule for teams to adopt.
- Create a strong team self-assessment at the end of the first phase of the teamwork.
- Require a weekly report related to implementation of the team guidelines.
- Require an interim draft of the paper or project.
- Provide a self-assessment inventory, which helps determine teamwork styles and strengths.
- Allow team building to start and continue beyond the limits of one course.

FUTURE TRENDS

As a result of an expanding global economy, emerging technologies and the popularity of online coursework, opportunities for virtual teamwork will increase. Business and education will find cultural boundaries blurred more frequently, and virtual multi-cultural interactions will become more common. As authentic interaction and application of learning become a more common recommendation for adult online education, e-learning teams will become more necessary. Virtual teamwork provides not only effectiveness in learning, but also authentic application of skills for career choices. If instructors and students use the highlights of this study to create discussion and learning development for their student audiences, multi-cultural e-learning teams can promote extended learning opportunities and objectives.

CONCLUSION

This chapter has discussed the social learning theory's relationship to multi-cultural e-learning teams, which exist as an intersection of technology, identity, culture, and community. Online graduate students have provided evidence of online learning team effectiveness and challenges. The study informs readers of the necessity of virtual team guidelines and policies that hold respect for diversified opinions and personalities. Virtual teamwork mirrors the authentic interactions required in many educational and organizational settings and practices. The results, thus, add attention to the importance of virtual teamwork.

Virtual communities have expanded the realm of cultural influence and encouraged another look at traditional socio-cultural constructs to determine their importance in the online collaborative classrooms. Comments and suggestions from online graduate students, who were experienced with virtual learning teams, built a framework of suggestions for adult students and faculty, and validated the importance of the traditional dimensions (Hall, 1977; Hofstede, 2001; Inkeles & Levinson, 1969; Storti, 1990, 1998). Finally, we have come full circle, learning that the establishment of personal identity is interwoven and acculturates with group collaborative culture in e-learning teams. Diversified online student populations can balance and intersect many different perspectives through awareness of dominant socio-cultural characteristics in virtual teamwork. Attention to acculturation or adaptability of self and group identity during e-learning team interactions can help fulfill online student team needs (Meng & Agarwal, 2005; Sudwicks & Ess, 2002).

REFERENCES

Adler, N. J., & Graham, J. L. (1989). Cross-cultural interaction: The international comparison fallacy? *Journal of International Business Studies, 20*(3), 515-537.

Alexander, S. (2000). Virtual teams going global. *InfoWorld, 22*(6), 55-56.

Axelrod, R. (1984). *The evolution of cooperation*. New York: Basic Books.

Bandura, A. (1986). *Social foundations of thought and action: A social cognitive theory.* Englewood Cliffs, NJ: Prentice-Hall.

Bandura, A. (2001). Social cognitive theory: An agentic perspective. *Annual Review of Psychology, 52*, 1-26.

Berge, Z. L. (1998). Differences in teamwork between post-secondary classrooms and the workplace. *Education and Training, 40*(5), 194-201.

Bielaczyc, K., & Collins, A. (1999). Learning communities in classrooms: A reconceptualization of educational practice. In C. Reigeluth (Ed.), *Instructional- design theories and models: A new paradigm of instructional theory* (pp. 169-292). Mahwah, NJ: Lawrence Erlbaum Associates.

Bos, N., Olson, J., Gergle, D., Olson, G., & Wright, Z. (2002, April 20-25). *Effects of four computer-mediated communications channels on trust development.* Paper presented at the proceedings of CHI, Minneapolis, MN.

Butler, B. (2001). Membership size, communication activity, and sustainability: A resource based model of online social structures. *Information Systems Research, 12*(4), 346-362.

Camarinha-Matos, L. M., & Afsarmanesh, H. (2004). *Collaborative networked organizations: A research agenda for emerging business models.* Norwell, MA: Kluwer Academic Publishers.

Cohen, D., & Prusak, L. (2001). *In good company: How social capital makes organizations work.* Boston: Harvard Business School Press.

Cohen, S. G., & Bailey, D. E. (1997). What makes teams work: Group effectiveness research from the shop floor to the executive suite. *Journal of Management, 12*(3), 239-290.

Collins, M., & Berge, Z. (1996, June). *Facilitating interaction in computer mediated online courses.* Background paper for presentation at the FSU/AECT Distance Education Conference, Tallahassee, FL. Retrieved April 16, 2005, from http://www.emoderators.com/moderators/flcc.html

Cyrs, T. (1997). *Teaching and learning at a distance: What it takes to effectively design, deliver, and evaluate programs.* San Francisco: Jossey-Bass.

Dede. C. (1999). *The role of emerging technologies for knowledge mobilization, dissemination, and use in education.* Washington, DC: U.S. Education Department. Retrieved April 10, 2005, from http://www.virtual.gmu.edu/SS_research/cdpapers/mobilpdf.htm

Dede, C. (2001). *Creating research centers to enhance the effective use of learning technologies.* Testimony to the U.S. House of Representatives, Committee on Science, Research Subcommittee, May 10, 2001. Retrieved April 8, 2005, from http://www.house.gov/science/research/reshearings.htm

English-Lueck, J., Darrah, C., & Saveri, A. (2002). Trusting strangers: Work relationships in four-high tech communities. *Information, Communication, & Society, 5*(1), 90-108.

Ess, C. (2001). *Culture, technology, communication: Towards an intercultural global village.* Albany: State University of New York Press.

Fearon, J. (1999). *What is identity (as we now use the word)?* Unpublished manuscript. Stanford University, Stanford, CA (p. 2).

Fernández-Ballesteros, R., Díez-Nicolás J., Caprara, G. V., Barbaranelli, C., & Bandura, A. (2002). Determinants and structural relation of perceived personal efficacy to perceived collective efficacy. *Applied Psychology: An International Review, 51*, 107-125.

Fogg, B. J. (2003). *Persuasive technology: Using computers to change what we think and do.* Boston: Morgan Kaufmann Publishers.

Gibbs, J. (2002, July 15-19). *Loose coupling in global teams: Reconciling cultural tensions across space and time.* Paper presented at ICA Convention, Organizational Communication Division. Seoul, Korea. Retrieved March 19, 2005, at http://www.ohiou.edu/ica-orgcomm/GIBBSPAPER2002.pdf

Godar, S. H., & Ferris, S. P. (Eds). (2004). *Virtual and collaborative teams: Process, technologies, and practice.* Hershey, PA: Idea Group Publishing.

Hall, E. (1959). *The silent language.* Garden City, NY: Doubleday.

Hall, E. (1966). *The hidden dimension.* Garden City, NY: Doubleday.

Hall, E. (1976, 1977). *Beyond culture.* Garden City, NY: Doubleday.

Hall, E. (1990). *Understanding cultural differences.* Yarmouth, ME: Intercultural Press.

Heaton, L. (2001). Preserving communication context: Virtual workspace and interpersonal space in Japanese CSCW. In C. Ess & F. Sudweeks (Eds.), *Culture, technology, communication: Towards an intercultural global village* (pp. 213-240). Albany: State University of New York Press.

Heusinkveld, P. (1997). *Pathways to culture.* Yarmouth, ME: Intercultural Press.

Hofstede, G. (1984, 2001). *Culture's consequences: International differences in work-related values.* London: Sage Publications.

Hofstede, G. (1997). *Cultures and organizations: Software of the mind.* New York: McGraw-Hill.

Huitt, W. (2004). Bloom et al.'s taxonomy of the cognitive domain. *Educational Psychology Interactive.* Valdosta, GA: Valdosta State University. Retrieved April 20, 2005, at http://chiron.valdosta.edu/whuitt/col/cogsys/bloom.html

Huitt, W., & Vessels, G. (2002). Character education. In J. Guthrie (Ed.), *The encyclopedia of education.* New York: Macmillan.

Inkeles, A., & Levinson, D. (1969). National character: The study of modal personality and sociocultural systems. In.G. Lindzey & E. Aronson (Eds.), *The handbook of social psychology* (pp. 311-378). Boston, MA: Addison-Wesley.

Johnson, R., & Johnson, D. (1994). *Creativity and collaborative learning.* Baltimore, MD: Brookes Press.

Kezsbom, D. (2000). Creating teamwork in virtual teams. *Cost Engineering, 42*(10), 33-36.

Khalsa, D. K. (2005, July). *Online learning teams: Impact of socio-cultural dimensions.* Paper presented at the proceedings of Human Computer Interaction International Conference, Las Vegas, NV.

Khalsa, D. K., & Hildreth, S. (2000). *Finding a place for everyone: Creating, maintaining and evolving optimal online learning.* Ithaca, NY: Whole Life Education. Retrieved April 10, 2005, at http://www.wholelifeed.com/placeforeveryone.html

Knowles, M. (1984). *Andragogy in action.* San Francisco: Jossey-Bass.

Ko, S., & Rossen, S. (2004). *Teaching online: A practical guide.* New York: Houghton Mifflin Co.

LaBelle, D. (2004). *Before the team project: Cultivate a community of collaborators.* Proceedings of the 21st Annual Information Systems Education Conference (ISECON 2004). Retrieved August 8, 2005, from http://isedj.org/isecon/2004/0000/index.html

Lipnack, J., & Stamps, J. (2000). *Virtual teams: People working across boundaries with technology.* New York: John Wiley & Sons.

Matei, S., & Ball-Rokeach, S. (2002). Belonging in geographic, ethnic, and Internet spaces. In B. Wellman & C. Haythornwaite (Eds.), *The Internet in everyday life* (pp. 405-427). Malden, MA: Blackwell Publishing.

Meng, M., & Agarwal, R. (in press). Sustaining virtual communities: The role of identity consonance and community artifacts.*Organizational Behavior and Human Decision Processes.*

Nonnecke, B., & Preece, J. (2003). Silent participants: Getting to know lurkers better. In C. Leug & D. Fisher (Eds.), From *Usenet to CoWebs: Interacting with social information spaces* (pp. 110-132). Amsterdam; Holland: Springer-Verlag.

Palloff, R., & Pratt, K. (1999). *Building learning communities in cyberspace: Effective strategies for the online classroom.* San Francisco: Jossey-Bass.

Polzer, J. T., Milton, L. P., & Swann, W. B. (2002). Capitalizing on diversity: Interpersonal congruence in small work groups. *Administrative Science Quarterly, 47*(2), 296-324.

Powell, A., Piccoli, G., & Blake, I. (2004). Virtual teams: A review of current literature and directions for future. *Data Base Advances in Information Systems, 35*(1), 6-36.

Preece, J. (2000). *Online communities: Designing usability, supporting sociability.* New York: John Wiley & Sons.

Preece, J. (Ed.). (2002). Supporting community and building social capital. Special edition of *Communications of the ACM, 45*(4), 37-39.

Preece, J., & Maloney-Krichmar, D. (2003). Online communities. In Jacko & Sears (Eds.), *Handbook of human-computer interaction* (pp. 596-620). Mahwah, NJ: Lawrence Erlbaum Associates Inc.

Preece, J., Sharp, H., & Rogers, Y. (2002). *Interaction design: Beyond human-computer interaction.* New York: John Wiley & Sons.

Rheingold, H. (1993). *The virtual community: Homesteading on the electronic frontier.* Reading, MA: Addison-Wesley.

Rogers, P. (2002). *Designing instruction for technology-enhanced learning.* Hershey, PA: Idea Group Publishing.

Rovai, A. (2001). Classroom community at a distance: A comparative analysis of two ALN-based university programs. *Internet and Higher Education, 4,* 105-118.

Shneiderman, B. (2002). *Leonardo's laptop: Human needs and the new computing technologies.* Cambridge, MA: The MIT Press.

Sproull, L., & Kiesler, S. (1995). Computers, networks, and work. *Scientific American: The Computer in the 21st Century, 6*(1), 116-123.

Storti, C. (1990). *The art of crossing cultures.* Boston: Intercultural Press Inc.

Storti, C. (1998). *Figuring foreigners out.* Boston: Intercultural Press Inc.

Sudweeks, F., & Ess, C. (2002, July). Cultural attitudes towards technology and communication. *Proceedings of the 3rd International Conference on Cultural Attitudes towards Technology and Communication,* Montreal, Canada (pp. 69-88)

Walther, J. (1996). Computer mediated communication: Impersonal, interpersonal, and hyperpersonal interaction. *Communication Research, 23*(1), 3-43.

Wenger, E. (2004). *Learning for a small planet: A research agenda.* Unpublished paper, Institute for Research on Learning, North San Juan, CA. Retrieved April 5, 2004, from http://www.ewenger.com/research

Zhang, W., & Storck, J. (2001). Peripheral members in online communities. *Americas' Conference on Information Systems (AMCIS), 8*(1), 29-38.

APPENDIX A. INITIAL QUESTIONS FOR GRADUATE STUDENTS

- How would you describe each of your team experiences in this online class?
- Were there any surprises related to communication with teams in this online class?
- What was your most challenging factor related to team involvement in this online course?
- What part did your background play in dealing with this challenge?
- What three improvements would you suggest to consolidate the strengths of working in teams?
- How would you contrast your experience of preparing an individual paper with your e-learning team paper?

APPENDIX B: SOCIO-CULTURAL DIMENSIONS

Power/Status	Rules/Regulations
Recognition	Flexibility/Time
Assertiveness/Competitiveness	Support/Nurturance
Gender Issues	Leadership

This work was previously published in Globalizing E-Learning Cultural Challenges, edited by A. Edmundson, pp. 307-326, copyright 2007 by Information Science Publishing (an imprint of IGI Global).

Compilation of References

Abas, Z., & Khalid, H. (2007). Achieving pedagogical richness to meet the needs of ODL learners. In P. Tsang, R. Kwang & R. Fox (Eds.). *Enhancing learning through technology*, (pp. 161 – 170). London: World Scientific Publishing.

Adams, C. (2007). On the 'informed use' of PowerPoint: Rejoining Vallance and Towndrow. Journal of Curriculum Studies , 39(2), 229–233. doi:10.1080/00220270601175246

Adler, N. J., & Graham, J. L. (1989). Cross-cultural interaction: The international comparison fallacy? *Journal of International Business Studies*, *20*(3), 515-537.

Adorno, S. (2002). *As cidades brasileiras do século XXI*. São Paulo: Publicação do Centro de Gestão e Estudos Estratégicos.

Adventist Robotics League. (2007). *Peer coaching*. Retrieved March 2, 2008, from http://www.adventistLEGO®league.net/index.php/resources/39-teaching-robotics/48-peer-coaching

Alexander, S. (2000). Virtual teams going global. *InfoWorld*, *22*(6), 55-56.

Alimisis, D., Moro, M., Arlegui, J., Pina, A., Frangou, S., & Papankilolaou, K. (2007). *Robotics & constructivism in education: The TERECoP project*. Retrieved January 6, 2008, from http://hermes.di.uoa.gr/papanikolaou/papers%5CAMAPFP-Eurologo2007.pdf

Allard, A., & Johnson, E. (2002, December 1-5). *Interrogating the discourse of 'Social Literacies' in an era of uncertainty*. Paper presented at the Australian Association of Research in Educational Annual Conference, Brisbane, Queensland.

Almeida, M.E. (2005). Letramento digital e hipertexto: contribuições à educação. In N. Pellanda, E. Schlünzen & K. Schlünzen (Eds.), *Inclusão digital: Tecendo redes afetivas/cognitivas* (pp. 171-192). Rio de Janeiro: DP&A.

Alvermann, D. (2003). Children's everyday literacies: Intersections of popular culture and language arts. Language Arts , 81(2), 145–154.

Alvermann, D. E., Moon, J. S., & Hagood, M. C. (1999). *Popular culture in the classroom: Teaching and researching critical media literacy*. Chicago: National Reading Conference.

Andrade, O. (1928). Manifesto antropofágico. *Revista de Antropofagia*, *1*(1)

Annadale, K., Bindon, R., Handley, K., Johnston, A., Lockett, L., & Lynch, P. (2004). *Reading map of development –Second edition addressing current literacy challenges*. Port Melbourne, Australia: Reed International Books Australia Pty.

Ansell Pearson, K. (2002). *Philosophy and the adventure of the virtual: Bergson and the time of life*. London: Routledge.

Anstey, M., & Bull, G. (2004). *The literacy labyrinth* (2nd ed.). Sydney: Pearson Education Australia.

Anstey, M., & Bull, G. (2006). *Teaching and learning multiliteracies: Changing times, changing literacies.* Newark, DE: International Reading Association.

Appadurai, A. (1990). Disjuncture and difference in the global cultural economy. Theory, Culture & Society , 7, 295–310. doi:10.1177/026327690007002017

Archer, L. (2007). Kevin Rudd promises computers for every student. *news.com.au*. Retrieved January 20, 2009, from www.news.com.au/story/0,23599,22754187-2,00.html?from=public_rss

Arnold, R. (2005). *Empathetic intelligence: teaching, learning, relating.* Sydney: University of New South Wales Press.

Atkinson, D. (2001). Reflections and refractions on the *JSWL* special issue on voice. Journal of Second Language Writing , 10, 107–124. doi:10.1016/S1060-3743(01)00035-2

Atkinson, D. (2002). Toward a sociocognitive approach to second language acquisition. *Modern Language Journal*, *86*, 525–545. doi:10.1111/1540-4781.00159

Au, K. H. (1998). Social constructivism and the school literacy learning of students of diverse cultural backgrounds. Journal of Literacy Research , 30(2), 297–319.

Au, K., H., & Raphael, T.E. (2000). Equity and literacy in the next millenium. Reading Research Quarterly , 35(1), 170–188. doi:10.1598/RRQ.35.1.12

Aubrey, C., David, T., & Godfrey, R. (2000). *Early childhood educational research.* London: Routledge Falmer.

Aukerman, R. C. (1984). *Approaches to beginning reading.* New York: Wiley.

Australian Labor Party. (2007). *The Australian economy needs an education revolution* [policy paper]. Retrieved January 20, 2009, from www.alp.org.au/download/now/education-revolution.pdf

Axelrod, R. (1984). *The evolution of cooperation.* New York: Basic Books.

Azevedo, R. (2006). *Formação de leitores, cultura popular e contexto Brasileiro.* Retrieved November 18, 2006, from www.ricardoazevedo.com.br/artigo10.htm

Baggott La Velle, L., A. McFarlane, and R. Brawn (2003). Knowledge-transformation through ICT in science education: A case study in teacher-driven curriculum development. British Journal of Educational Technology, 34(2), 183–199. doi:10.1111/1467-8535.00319

Bakhtin, M. M. (1986). *Speech genres and other late essays.* Austin, TX: University of Texas.

Bamford, A. (2003). *The visual literacy white paper.* Commissioned by Adobe Systems Pty Ltd, Australia. Retrieved January 12, 2007, from: http://www.adobe.co.uk/education

Bamford, A. (2006). *The Wow Factor: Global research compendium of the arts in education.* New York: Waxmann.

Bandura, A. (1986). *Social foundations of thought and action: A social cognitive theory.* Englewood Cliffs, NJ: Prentice-Hall.

Bandura, A. (2001). Social cognitive theory: An agentic perspective. *Annual Review of Psychology, 52*, 1-26.

Barrentine, P. (Ed.). (1993). *When The Canary Stops Singing.* San Francisco: Berrett-Koehler Publishers.

Barton, D., & Hamilton, M. (1998). *Local literacies: Reading and writing in one community.* London: Routledge.

Barton, D., & Tusting, K. (Eds.). (2005). *Beyond communities of practice: Language, power, and social context.* Cambridge: Cambridge University Press.

Barton, D., Hamilton, M., & Ivanic, R. (Eds.). (2000). *Situated literacies: Reading and writing in context.* London: Routledge.

Bazalgette, C. (2005). Media education in Inghilterra: incontro con Cary Bazalgette nel suo ufficio. In *Boletim InterMED,* anno 10, n.3, Roma.

Beer, R. D., H. J. Chiel, and R. F. Drushel (1999). Using autonomous robotics to teach science and engineering [Electronic version]. Communications of the ACM ,

42(6), 85–92. doi:10.1145/303849.303866

Belloni, M.L. (2006). Infância, Técnica e Cidadania: Cenário de mudanças. Retrieved October 11, 2007, from www.comunic.ufsc.br

Bender, L. (Producer), & Guggenheim, D. (Director) (2006). *An inconvenient truth.* [Motion picture]. USA: Paramount Classics.

Bensimon, E. M., & Neumann, A. (1993). *Redesigning Collegiate Leadership.* Baltimore: The Johns Hopkins University Press.

Berge, Z. L. (1998). Differences in teamwork between post-secondary classrooms and the workplace. *Education and Training, 40*(5), 194-201.

Betts, G. (1992). *The autonomous learner model for the gifted and talented.* Cheltenham, Australia: Hawker Brownlow Education.

Bianco, J. (2000). Multiliteracies and multilingualism. In W. Cope, M. Kalantzis, M. (Eds.) (2000). *Multiliteracies: Literacy learning and the design of social futures* (pp. 92 – 105). London: Routledge.

Bielaczyc, K., & Collins, A. (1999). Learning communities in classrooms: A reconceptualization of educational practice. In C. Reigeluth (Ed.), *Instructional- design theories and models: A new paradigm of instructional theory* (pp. 169-292). Mahwah, NJ: Lawrence Erlbaum Associates.

Biggs, J. (1999). *Teaching for quality learning at university.* Buckingham, UK: Open University Press.

Bigum, C. (2002). Design sensibilities, schools, and the new computing and communications technologies. In I. Snyder (Ed.), *Silicon literacies* (pp. 130-140). London: Falmer-Routledge.

Bingham, C. (2005). The hermeneutics of educational questioning. Educational Philosophy and Theory , 37, 553–567. doi:10.1111/j.1469-5812.2005.00140.x

Black, R. W. (2005). Access and affiliation: The literacy and composition practices of English-Language Learners in and online fanfiction community. Journal of Adolescent & Adult Literacy , 49(2), 118–128. doi:10.1598/JAAL.49.2.4

Black, R. W. (2007). Digital design: English language learners and reader reviews in online fiction. In M. Knobel & C. Lankshear (Eds.), *A New Literacies Sampler* (pp. 271-286). New York: Peter Lang.

Bloch, J. (2006). Abdullah's blogging: A generation 1.5 student enters the blogosphere. Language Learning & Technology , 11(2), 128–141.

Boland, T. (1991). *Nudgee College 1891-1991.* Brisbane, Australia: Boolarong.

Bos, N., Olson, J., Gergle, D., Olson, G., & Wright, Z. (2002, April 20-25). *Effects of four computer-mediated communications channels on trust development.* Paper presented at the proceedings of CHI, Minneapolis, MN.

Boud, D., and H. Middleton (2003). Learning from others at work: Communities of practice and informal learning. Journal of Workplace Learning , 15(5), 194–203. doi:10.1108/13665620310483895

Bouffler, C. (Ed.). (1992). *Literacy evaluation: Issues & practicalities.* Newtown, Australia: Primary English Teaching Association.

Boulter, J. D. (1999). *Writing space: The computer, hypertext, and the history of writing.* Hillsdale, NJ: Lawrence Erlbaum.

Bourdieu, P. (1984). *Distinction: A social critique of the judgement of good taste.* Trans: R. Nice. Cambridge, MA: Harvard University Press.

Brandt, D. (2001). *Literacy in American lives.* New York: Cambridge University Press.

Bransford, J. D. (1979). *Human cognition: Learning, understanding and remembering.* Belmont, CA: Wadsworth.

Brown, A., & Dowling, P. (1998). *Doing research/reading research.* London: Falmer Press.

Bruffee, K. A. (1993). *Collaborative learning: Higher education, interdependence, and the authority of knowledge*. Baltimore: Johns Hopkins University Press.

Bruner, J. S. (1971). *The relevance of education*. Oxford, UK: W. W. Norton.

Brush, T., and J. Saye (2000). Implementation and evaluation of a student-centred learning unit: A case study. Educational Technology Research and Development , 48(3), 79–100. doi:10.1007/BF02319859

Buckingham, D. (1993). *Children talking television: The making of television literacy*. London: Falmer Press.

Buckingham, D. (1994). Media education: The limits of a discourse. Curriculum Studies , 24(4), 296–313.

Buckingham, D. (2000). *After the death of childhood: Growing up in the age of electronic media*. Cambridge: Polity Press.

Buckingham, D. (2003). *Media education: Literacy, learning and contemporary culture*. Cambridge: Polity Press.

Buckingham, D., & Sefton-Green, J. (1994). *Cultural studies goes to school. Reading and teaching popular media*. London: Taylor and Francis.

Burbules, N. C., & Callister, T. (2000). *Watch IT. The risks and promises of information technology*. Boulder, CO: Westview Press.

Burn, A., & Parker, D. (2003). *Analysing media texts*. London: Continuum.

Burnheim, C. (2004). *Education and Social Capital*. Retrieved March 1, 2008, from www.education.monash.edu.au/centres/mcrie/docs/education-and-social-capital041012.rtf

Burns, J. (1978). *Leadership*. New York: Harper & Row.

Burns, R. B. (1994). *Introduction to research methods* (2nd ed.). Melbourne, Australia: Longman.

Butcher-Younghans, S. (1993). *Historic house museums*. New York: Oxford University Press.

Butler, B. (2001). Membership size, communication activity, and sustainability: A resource based model of online social structures. *Information Systems Research, 12*(4), 346-362.

Butler, J. (2004). Performative acts and gender constitution. In J. Rivkin & M. Ryan (Eds.), *Literary Theory: An Anthology* (2nd ed., pp. 900–11). Malden, MA: Blackwell.

Butler, J. (2006*). Gender Trouble: Feminism and the Subversion of Identity*. New York: Routledge Classics.

Buysse, V., K. Sparkman, and P. Wesley (2003). Communities of practice: Connecting what we know with what we do. Exceptional Children , 69(3), 263–278.

Cadimo, F. (2004). Miragens digitais. Retrieved October 11, 2007, from http:www.fcsh.unl.pt/cadeiras/httv/artigos/Miragens%Digitais.pdf

Cairney, T. H., & Ruge, J. (1997). *Community literacy practices and schooling: Towards effective support for students*. Canberra, Australia: Department of Employment, Education, Training and Youth Affairs.

Callow, J. (1999). *Image matters: Visual texts in the classroom*. Newton, Australia: Primary English Teaching Association.

Camarinha-Matos, L. M., & Afsarmanesh, H. (2004). *Collaborative networked organizations: A research agenda for emerging business models*. Norwell, MA: Kluwer Academic Publishers.

Cambourne, B. (1988). *The whole story: Natural learning and the acquisition of literacy in the classroom*. Auckland, New Zealand: Ashton Scholastic.

Canterbury City & Country Cluster. (2007, July 5). *Raising attainment in boys' writing in the early years: An ICT and role-play project for improving learning and teaching*. Paper presented at the Annual Cluster Conference on Leading Learning, KentUK

Carbonaro, M., Rex, M., & Chambers, J. (2004). Using LEGO robotics in a project-based learning environment. *Interactive Multimedia Electronic Journal of Computer-Enhanced Learning*. Retrieved August

18, 2008, fromhttp://imej.wfu.edu/articles/2004/1/02/index.asp

Castells, M (1996/2002). *End of millennium [Fim de milênio, vol. 3].* São Paulo: Paz e Terra.

Castells, M. (1996/2006). *The rise of the network society [A sociedade em rede, vol. 1].* São Paulo: Paz e Terra.

Cazden, C. (2000). Taking cultural differences into account. In B. Cope & M. Kalantzis (Eds.), *Multiliteracies: Literacy learning and the design of social futures* (pp. 249-266). London: Routledge.

Centre for Extended Learning. (2008). *SiMERR 'Smart-Bots' programme.* [Electronic version]. Retrieved August 22, 2008, from http://www.education.tas.gov.au/school/educators/support/extendedlearning/publications/All-programs2008.pdf

Chacko, E. (2005). Exploring youth cultures geographically through active learning. The Journal of Geography, 104(1), 9–16. doi:10.1080/00221340508978917

Chafe, W. (1985). Linguistic differences produced by differences between speaking and writing. In D. Olson, N. Torrance, & A. Hildyard (Eds.), *Literacy, language, and learning: The nature and consequences of reading and writing* (pp. 105-122). Cambridge, UK: Cambridge University Press.

Chall, J. (1967). *Learning to read: The great debate.* New York: McGraw-Hill.

Chiapello, E. (2004). Evolution and Co-optation. Third Text, 18(6), 585–594. doi:10.1080/0952882042000284998

Chow, P., & Chou, C. (2000). Evaluating sustained silent reading in reading classes. *The Internet TESL Journal, 6*(11).

Christian-Smith, L. (1997). Pleasure and danger: Children, media, and cultural systems. In S. Muspratt, A. Luke, & P. Freebody (Eds.), *Constructing critical literacies: Teaching and learning textual practice* (pp. 51-58). St. Leonards, Australia: Allen & Unwin.

Christie, F., Devlin, B., Freebody, P., Luke, A., Martin, J. R., & Threadgold, T. (1991). *Teaching English literacy: A project of national significance on the preservice preparation of teachers to teach English literacy.* Darwin, Australia: Centre for Studies of Language in Education, Northern Territory University.

Chua, S. K. C. (2004, November 26-December 2). *The convergence and divergence effects of globalisation on Singapore's education system* [Electronic version]. Paper presented at the Australian Association for Research in Education, Melbourne Australia

Clark, J. (1996). Reflections on Lichtenstein. Artonview, 5, 34–36.

Cobb, N. (1992). *Adolescence: Continuity, change and diversity.* London: Mayfield Publishing Company.

Cohen, D., & Prusak, L. (2001). *In good company: How social capital makes organizations work.* Boston: Harvard Business School Press.

Cohen, S. G., & Bailey, D. E. (1997). What makes teams work: Group effectiveness research from the shop floor to the executive suite. *Journal of Management, 12*(3), 239-290.

Coiro, J. (2003). Reading comprehension on the internet: Expanding our understanding of reading comprehension to encompass new literacies. The Reading Teacher, 56(5), 458–464.

Coiro, J., Knobel, M., Lankshear, C., & Leu, D. (Eds.). (2008). *Handbook of research on new literacies.* New York: Lawrence Erlbaum.

Cole, D. R. (2005). Learning Through the Virtual. *CTHEORY, 1* (EJ) EJ. Retrieved January 2, 2008 from: http://www.ctheory.net/articles.aspx?id=445

Cole, D. R. (2005). Reading in the future: literacy and the time of the internet. *Reconstruction, 5* (2) EJ. Retrieved January 8, 2008 from http://reconstruction.eserver.org/052/cole.shtml

Cole, D. R. (2006). Techno-shamanism and Educational Research. *Sage of Consciousness.* Retrieved from http://www.sageofcon.org/ez7/nf/dc.htm

Cole, D. R. (2007). Cam-Capture: An eye on teaching and

learning. In J. Sigafoos & V. Green (Eds.), *Technology & Teaching: A casebook for educators* (pp. 55-68). New York: Nova Science Publishers, Inc.

Cole, D. R. (2007). Virtual terrorism and the Internet e-learning options. E-Learning, 4(2), 116–127. doi:10.2304/elea.2007.4.2.116

Coles, G. (1999). Literacy, emotions, and the brain. *Reading Online*. Retrieved April 21, 2007, from http://www.readingonline.org/critical/coles.html

Collins, J., & Blot, R. (2003). *Literacy and literacies: Texts, power and identity*. Cambridge, UK: Cambridge University Press.

Collins, M., & Berge, Z. (1996, June). *Facilitating interaction in computer mediated online courses*. Background paper for presentation at the FSU/AECT Distance Education Conference, Tallahassee, FL. Retrieved April 16, 2005, from http://www.emoderators.com/moderators/flcc.html

Comber, B. (2001). Classroom explorations in critical literacy. In H. Fehring & P. Green (Eds.), *Critical literacy: A collection of articles from the Australian Literacy Educators' Association* (pp. 75-83). Newark, DE & Norwood, South Australia: International Reading Association and Australian Literacy Educators' Association.

Comber, B., & Kamler, B. (Eds.). (2005). *Turn-around pedagogies: Literacy interventions for at-risk students*. Newtown, Australia: Primary English Teaching Association.

Coorey, P. (2007). Rudd vows education revolution. *The Sydney Morning Herald*, January 23, 2007. Retrieved January 20, 2009, from www.smh.com.au/news/national/rudd-vows-educationrevolution/2007/01/22/1169330827940.html?page=fullpage

Cope, B., & Kalantzis, M. (1997). *Productive diversity: A new Australian model for work and management*. Annandale, Australia: Pluto Press.

Cope, B., & Kalantzis, M. (2000). Design for social futures. In B. Cope & M. Kalantzis (Eds.), *Multiliteracies: Literacy learning and the design of social futures* (pp. 203- 234). London: Routledge.

Cope, B., & Kalantzis, M. (Eds.). (2000). *Multiliteracies: literacy learning and the design of social futures*. New York: Routledge.

Cope, B., and M. Kalantzis (2004). Designs for learning. E-Learning , 1(1), 38–93. doi:10.2304/elea.2004.1.1.7

Cotterell, J. (1996). *Social networks and social influences in adolescence*. New York: Routledge.

Cromwell, S. (1998). The school of the future. *Education world*. Retrieved March 15, 2008, from http://www.education-world.com/a curr/curr046.shtml

Cuban, L. (1986). *Teachers and machines: The classroom use of technology since 1920*. New York: Teachers College Press.

Cuban, L. (1990). Reforming again, again and again [Electronic version]. Educational Researcher , 19(1), 3–13.

Cuban, L. (2001). *Oversold and Underused: Computers in the classroom*. Cambridge, MA: Harvard University Press.

Cuban, L. (2004). Meeting challenges in urban schools. Educational Leadership , 61(7), 64–69.

Cuban, L., H. Kirkpatrick, and C. Peck (2001). High access and low use of technologies in high school classrooms; Explaining an apparent paradox. American Educational Research Journal , 38(4), 813–834. doi:10.3102/00028312038004813

Cumming, J. J., & Wyatt-Smith, C. M. (Eds.). (2001). *Literacy and the curriculum: Success in senior secondary schooling*. Melbourne, Australia: The Australian Council for Educational Research.

Curriculum Development Council. (2002). *English Language Education: Key Learning Area Curriculum Guide (Primary 1 - Secondary 3)*. Hong Kong: Government Printer.

Curriculum Development Council. (2004). *English Language Education Key Learning Area: English Language Curriculum Guide (Primary 1-6)*. Hong

Kong: Government Printer.

Cyrs, T. (1997). *Teaching and learning at a distance: What it takes to effectively design, deliver, and evaluate programs.* San Francisco: Jossey-Bass.

D'Agustino, S. (2007). Learning and literacy in robots – making connections for the classroom. In S. D'Agustino & K.P. King (Eds.), *Classroom robotics: Case studies of 21st century instruction for millennial students* (pp.145-162) [Electronic version].

D'Agustino, S., & King, K. P. (2007). Catching the vision, teachers as learners: Robotics professional development. In S. D'Agustino & K.P. King (Eds.), *Classroom robotics: Case studies of 21st century instruction for millennial students* (pp.163-179) [Electronic version].

Darley, A. (2000). *Visual digital culture: Surface play and spectacle in new media genres.* London: Routledge.

Darling-Hammond, L. (1997). *The right to learn: A blueprint for creating schools that work.* San Francisco: Jossey-Bass.

Davies, B., and R. Harre (1990). Positioning: The discursive production of selves. Journal for the Theory of Social Behaviour , 20, 43–63. doi:10.1111/j.1468-5914.1990.tb00174.x

Davis, B., & Sumara, D. (2006). *Complexity and education: Inquiries into learning, teaching, and research.* Mahwah, NJ: Erlbaum.

Davis, B., and D. J. Sumara (1997). Cognition, complexity, and teacher education. *Harvard Educational Review, 67*(1), 105–125.

Davis, D. (2008). *First we see: The national review of visual education.* Australian Government.

Davis, D. (2008). *First we see: The national review of visual education.* Canberra, Australia: Australian Government.

Davison, J., and J. Arthur (2000). Social literacy and citizenship education [Electronic version]. Curriculum Journal , 11(1), 9–24. doi:doi:10.1080/095851700361366

Dawes, L. (2001). What stops teachers using ICT. In M. Leask (Ed.), *Issues in teaching using ICT* (pp. 61-79). London: Routledge

De Block, L., & Rydin, I. (2006). Digital rapping in media productions: Intercultural communication through youth culture. In D. Buckingham & R. Willett (Eds.), *Digital generations: Children, young people, and new media* (pp. 295-312). Mahwah, NJ: Lawrence Erlbaum.

Deaney, R., Ruthven, K., & Hennessy, S. (2004). *Teachers developing practical theories of the contribution of ICT to subject teaching and learning: An analysis of cases from English Secondary School.* Faculty of Education, University of Cambridge, Cambridge, UK.

Debes, J. (1968). Some foundations of visual literacy. Audio Visual Instruction , 13, 961–964.

Dede, C. (2001). *Creating research centers to enhance the effective use of learning technologies.* Testimony to the U.S. House of Representatives, Committee on Science, Research Subcommittee, May 10, 2001. Retrieved April 8, 2005, from http://www.house.gov/science/research/reshearings.htm

Dede. C. (1999). *The role of emerging technologies for knowledge mobilization, dissemination, and use in education.* Washington, DC: U.S. Education Department. Retrieved April 10, 2005, from http://www.virtual.gmu.edu/SS_research/cdpapers/mobilpdf.htm

DEET. (2007). *Annual Report 2006-2007.* Darwin, Australia: Department of Employment Education and Training.

Deleuze, G. (1988). *Bergsonism* (H. Tomlinson & B. Habberjam, Trans.). New York: Zone Books.

Deleuze, G. (1989). *Cinema 2: The time image* (H. Tomlinson & R. Galeta, Trans.). London: Athlone Press.

Demetriadis, S., A. Barbas, A. Molohides, G. Palaigeorgiou, D. Psillos, and I. Vlahavas (2003). Cultures in negotiation: Teachers' acceptance/resistance attitudes considering the infusion of technology into schools. Computers & Education , 41(1), 19–37. doi:10.1016/S0360-1315(03)00012-5

Department of Education. Tasmania (2002). *Essential learnings: Framework 1.* Hobart, Australia: Author.

Department of Education. Tasmania (2005). *Literacy and English.* Retrieved January 6, 2008, from http://wwwfp.education.tas.gov.au/english/liteng.htm#multiliteracies

Dery, M. (1994). *Flame-Wars: The discourse of cyberculture.* Durham, NC: Duke University Press.

DEST. (Department of Education, Science and Training). (2005). *Literacy benchmarks results.* Retrieved June 13, 2008, from http://www.curriculum.edu.au/verve/_resources/2005_Benchmarks.pdf

Dibdin, L. (2006). Robotics: Enticing technology across the ages. Classroom , 26(2), 30–31.

Dickinson, D., & Tabors, P. (Eds.). (2001). *Beginning literacy with language: Young children learning at home and at school.* Baltimore: Paul Brookes.

Digital Natives. Retrieved January 20, 2009, from http://www.digitalnative.org/#about

Doecke, B., & McCleneghan, D. (1998). Reconceptualising experience: Growth pedagogy and youth culture. In W. Sawyer, K. Watson & E. Gold (Eds.) *Re-viewing English* (pp. 46-57). Sydney: Clair Press.

Douglas, M. (1975). *Implicit meanings: Essays in anthropology.* London: Routledge & Kegan Paul.

Dowden, T. (2007). Relevant, challenging, integrative and exploratory curriculum design: Perspectives from theory and practice for middle level schooling in Australia. Australian Educational Researcher , 34(2), 51–72.

Dozier, C., Johnston, P., & Rogers, R. (2006). *Critical literacy/critical teaching: Tools for preparing responsive teachers.* New York: Teachers College Press.

Drath, W. H., & Paulus, C. J. (1994). *Making Common Sense: Leadership as Meaning Making in a Community of Practice.* Greensboro, NC: Centre for Creative Leadership.

Drenoyianni, H. (2006). Reconsidering change and ICT: Perspectives of a human and democratic education [Electronic version]. *Education and Information Technologies, 11*(3-4), 401–413. doi:10.1007/s10639-006-9005-5

Dressman, M., O'Brien, D., Rogers, T., Ivey, G., Wilder, P., Alvermann, D., et al. (2006). Problematizing Adolescent Literacies: Four Instances, Multiple Perspectives. In D. Schallert, B. Maloch, C. Fairbanks, J. Worthy, & J. Hoffman (Eds.), *55th Yearbook of the National Reading Conference* (pp 141-154). Oak Creek, WI.

Druin, A., & Hendler, J. (2000). *Robots for kids: Exploring new technologies for learning.* San Diego, CA: Academic Press.

Durrant, C., & Green, B. (1998). *Literacy and the New Technologies in School Education: Meeting the L(IT) erarcy Challenge?"* Presented Paper. Sydney, NSW: NSW Department of Education and Training.

Durrant, C., and B. Green (2000). Literacy and the new technologies in school education: Meeting the l(IT) eracy challenge? The Australian Journal of Language and Literacy , 23(2), 89–107.

Dyson, A. (1997). *Writing superheroes: Contemporary childhood, popular culture, and classroom literacy.* New York: Teachers College Press.

Education Queensland. (2002). *Years 1 – 10 Curriculum Framework.* Queensland, Australia: Department of Education Training and the Arts.

Education Queensland. (2006). *Productive Pedagogies.* Retrieved June 29, 2008, from http://education.qld.gov.au/public_media/reports/curriculum-framework/productive-pedagogies/html/manual.html

Eggen, P. D., & Kauchak, D. P. (2001). *Strategies for teachers: Teaching content and thinking skills* (4th Ed.). Needham Heights, MA: Allyn & Bacon.

Eisenberg, M., & Berkowitz, R. (2003). *The definitive Big6 workshop handbook.* Worthington, OH: Linworth.

Eisner, E. (2002). *Arts and the creation of mind.* New Haven, CT: Yale University Press.

Ellsworth, E. (2005). *Places of learning: Media, architecture, pedagogy.* New York: Routledge Falmer.

Elstad, E. (2006). Understanding the nature of accountability failure in a technology-filled, laissez-faire classroom: Disaffected students and teachers who give in. Journal of Curriculum Studies , 38(4), 459–481. doi:10.1080/00220270500508901

English-Lueck, J., Darrah, C., & Saveri, A. (2002). Trusting strangers: Work relationships in four-high tech communities. *Information, Communication, & Society, 5*(1), 90-108.

Ess, C. (2001). *Culture, technology, communication: Towards an intercultural global village*. Albany: State University of New York Press.

Etheridge, M. (2006). I Need to Wake up Now [Recorded by Melissa Etheridge]. On *An inconvenient truth* [CD]. USA: The Island Def Jam Music Group.

Evans, J. (Ed.). (2005). *Literacy moves on: Popular culture, new technologies and digital literacies in the elementary classroom*. Portsmouth, NH: Heinemann.

Fairclough, N. (1995). *Critical discourse analysis: The critical study of language*. London: Longman.

Fairclough, N. (1995). *Media discourse*. London: Arnold.

Fairclough, N. (2000). Multiliteracies and language: Orders of discourse and intertextuality. In B. Cope & M. Kalantzis (Eds.), *Multiliteracies: Literacy learning and the design of social futures* (pp.162- 181). London: Routledge.

Fantin, M (2006). *As crianças interagindo nos cenários contemporâneos: A "escola estação cultura."* Unpublished paper presented at Universidade Federal de Santa Catarina.

Fantin, M. (2006). *Mídia-educação: Conceitos, experiências, diálogos Brasil-Itália*. Florianópolis: Cidade Futura.

Fearon, J. (1999). *What is identity (as we now use the word)?* Unpublished manuscript. Stanford University, Stanford, CA (p. 2).

Fehring, H., & Green, P. (Eds.). (2001). *Critical literacy: A collection of articles from the Australian Literacy Educators' Association*. Newark, DE & Norwood, South Australia: International Reading Association and Australian Literacy Educators' Association.

Fensham, P. J. (1975). Concept formation. In D. J. Daniels (Ed.), *New movements in the study and teaching of chemistry* (pp. 199-217). London: Temple Smith.

Fensham, P. J. (2008). *Complexity Theory: Its relevance to science education*. Paper presented at the Australasian Science Education Research Association (ASERA) 39th Annual International Conference, Brisbane, Australia.

Fernández-Ballesteros, R., Díez-Nicolás J., Caprara, G. V., Barbaranelli, C., & Bandura, A. (2002). Determinants and structural relation of perceived personal efficacy to perceived collective efficacy. *Applied Psychology: An International Review, 51*, 107-125.

Ferris, D. (2007). Preparing teachers to respond to students' writing. Journal of Second Language Writing , 16, 165–193. doi:10.1016/j.jslw.2007.07.003

Fetterman, D.M. (2002). Empowerment evaluation: Building communities of practice and a culture of learning. American Journal of Community Psychology , 30(1), 89–103. doi:10.1023/A:1014324218388

Fine, B. (2001). *Social capital versus social theory: political economy and social science at the turn of the millennium*. London: Routledge.

Fine, G., and M. de Soucey (2005). Joking cultures: Humor themes as social regulation in group life. Humor: International Journal of Humor Research , 18(1), 1–22. doi:10.1515/humr.2005.18.1.1

Firkins, A., & Forey, G. (2006). Changing the literacy habitus of a Hong Kong secondary school. In W. D. Bokhurst-Heng, M. D. Osborne & K. Lee (Eds.), *Redesigning pedagogy: Reflections on theory and praxis* (pp.33-46). Rotterdam: Sense Publishers.

Fiske, J. (1994). Moments of television: Neither the text nor the audience. In E. Seiter, H. Borchers, G. Kreutzner & E-M. Warth (Eds.), *Remote control television, audiences and cultural power* (pp. 56-78). London:

Routledge.

Fiumara, G. C. (2001). *The mind's affective life: a psychoanalytic and philosophical inquiry.* Hove, UK: Brunner-Routledge.

Fleer, M., & Williams-Kennedy, D. (2001). *Building bridges:Literacy development in young indigenous children.* Canberra, Australia: Australian Early Childhood Association Inc.

Flippo, R. F. (1999). Redefining the reading wars: The war against reading researchers. *Educational Leadership, 57*(2), 38–41.

Flusser, V. (1998). *Ensaio sobre a fotografia: para uma filosofia da técnica.* Lisboa: Relógio d'Água.

Fogg, B. J. (2003). *Persuasive technology: Using computers to change what we think and do.* Boston: Morgan Kaufmann Publishers.

Foucault, M. (1977). *Discipline and punish.* London: Penguin.

Francis, B., & Skelton, C. (2005). *Reassessing gender and achievement: Questioning contemporary key debates.* Oxon, UK: Routledge.

Freebody, P. (2003). *Qualitative research in education.* London: Sage Publications.

Freebody, P. (2007). Building literacy education: pasts, futures, and "the sum of effort." In A. Simpson (Ed.). *Future Directions in Literacy: International Conversations conference 2007,* (pp. 96 – 114). Sydney: Sydney University Press.

Freebody, P. (2007). *Literacy Education in School: Research perspectives from the past, for the future.* Camberwell, Australia: Australian Council for Educational Research.

Freebody, P., and A. Luke (1990). 'Literacies' programs: Debates and demands in cultural context. *Prospect, 5*(3), 7–16.

Freire, P. (1970). *Pedagogy of the oppressed.* New York: Continuum Publishing Co.

Freire, P. (2000). *Pedagogy of the oppressed* (30th Anniversary Ed.). (M.B. Ramos, Trans.). New York: Continuum.

Fullan, M. (2001). *The new meaning of educational change* (3rd Ed.). Columbia University, NY: Teachers College Press.

Gabel, D. (1999). Improving teaching and learning through chemistry education research: A look to the future. Journal of Chemical Education, 76(4), 548–554.

García Canclini, N. (1989/1998). *Culturas híbridas: estratégias para entrar e sair da modernidade [Culturas híbridas: Estratégias para entrar y salir de la modernidad].* São Paulo: Editora da USP.

Gardner, H. (1993). *Frames of mind: the theory of multiple intelligences.* New York: Basic Books.

Gedda, R., & McGonnachie, D. (2006). It's official: Skills shortage cuts deep. *Information Age, April/ May,* 25-26.

Gee, J. (1994). Orality and literacy: from the savage mind to ways with words. In J., Maybin & J. Clevedon (Eds), *Language and literacy in social practice.* Buckingham, UK: Multilingual Matters Ltd & The Open University.

Gee, J. (1996). *Social linguistics and literacies: Ideology in discourses.* London: Taylor and Francis.

Gee, J. (2000). The new literacy studies: From 'socially situated' to the work of the social. In Barton, D., Hamilton, M. & Ivanic, R. (Eds.), *Situated literacies: Reading and writing in context.* New York: Routledge.

Gee, J. (2000/2001). Identity as an analytic lens for research in education. *Review of Research in Education, 25,* 99–125.

Gee, J. (2004). *Situated Language and Learning: Critique of traditional schooling.* London: Routledge.

Gee, J. P. (1990). *Social linguistics and literacies: Ideology in discourses.* London: Falmer Press.

Gee, J. P. (2003). *What video games have to teach us about learning and literacy.* New York: Palgrave Macmillan.

Gee, J. P. (2004). Language in the science classroom: Academic social languages as the heart of school-based literacy. In E. W. Saul (Ed.), *Crossing borders in literacy and science instruction: Perspectives on theory and practice.* (pp. 13-32). Arlington, VA: National Science Teachers Association.

Gee, J. P. (2004). Learning languages as a matter of learning social languages within discourses. In M. Hawkins (Ed.), *Language learning and teacher education: A sociocultural approach* (pp. 13-31). Clevedon, UK: Multilingual Matters.

Gee, J. P. (2005). Language in the science classroom: Academic social languages as the heart of school-based literacy. In R. Yerrick & W.-M. Roth (Eds.), *Establishing scientific classroom discourse communities: Multiple voices of teaching and learning research* (pp. 19-37). Mahwah, NJ: Lawrence Erlbaum Associates.

Gee, J. P. (2005). Semiotic social spaces and affinity spaces: From the age of mythology to today's schools. In D. Barton & K. Tusting (Eds.), *Beyond communities of practice: Language, power, and social context* (pp. 214-232). Cambridge, UK: Cambridge University Press.

Gee, J. P. (2008). *Social linguistics and literacies: Ideology in discourses* (3rd Ed.). New York: Routledge.

Gee, J. P., and J. Green (1997). Discourse analysis, learning, and social practice: A methodological study. *Review of Research in Education*, 23, 119–169.

GenYes. Retrieved January 20, 2009, from www.genyes.org

Gibbs, J. (2002, July 15-19). *Loose coupling in global teams: Reconciling cultural tensions across space and time.* Paper presented at ICA Convention, Organizational Communication Division. Seoul, Korea. Retrieved March 19, 2005, at http://www.ohiou.edu/ica-orgcomm/GIBBSPAPER2002.pdf

Giddings, L. R. (1988). Beyond E. D. Hirsch and cultural literacy: Thinking skills for cultural awareness [Electronic version]. Communication Review , 8(2), 5–13.

Gil, G. (2004). *Aula Magna* at Universidade de São Paulo. Retrieved October 11, 2007, from http://www.cultura.gov.br/noticias/discursos/index.php?p=833&more=1

Gilbert, P. (2001). (Sub)versions: Using sexist language practices to explore critical literacy. In H. Fehring & P. Green (Eds.), *Critical literacy: A collection of articles from the Australian Literacy Educators' Association* (pp. 75-83). Newark, DE & Norwood, Australia: International Reading Association and Australian Literacy Educators' Association.

Godar, S. H., & Ferris, S. P. (Eds). (2004). *Virtual and collaborative teams: Process, technologies, and practice.* Hershey, PA: Idea Group Publishing.

Goldberg, A., M. Russel, and A. Cook (2003). The effect of computers on student writing: A meta-analysis of studies from 1992-2002. *Journal of Technology* , Learning and Assessment , 2(1), 1–52.

Goldman, S. R. (2004). Cognitive aspects of constructing meaning through and across multiple texts. In N. Shuart-Ferris & D. M. Bloome (Eds.), *Uses of intertextuality in classroom and educational research* (pp. 313-347). Greenwich, CT: Information Age Publishing.

Goleman, D. (1996). *Emotional intelligence: Why it can matter more than IQ.* London: Bloomsbury.

Gonick, M. (2007). Between "girl power" and "Reviving Ophelia": Constituting the neoliberal girl subject. National Women's Study Association Journal , 18(2), 1–22.

Goodson, I., & Knobel, M. (2003). *Social spaces/cyber spaces: Culture clash in computerised classrooms.* New York: Palgrave Press.

Goodstein, A. (2007). *Totally wired: What teens and tweens are really doing online.* New York: Saint Martin's Griffin.

Gore, J. (1993). *The struggle for pedagogies: Critical and feminist discourses as regimes of truth.* New York: Routledge.

Grabe, W. (2002). Reading in a second language. In R. B. Kaplan (Ed.), *The Oxford handbook of applied linguistics* (pp. 49-59). New York: Oxford University Press.

Graff, H. (1987). *The legacies of literacy: Continuities and contradictions in western culture and society.* Bloomington and Indianapolis: Indiana University Press.

Graham, W., D. Osgood, and J. Karren (1998). A real-life community of practice. Training & Development , 52(5), 34–39.

Gray, B. (1985). Helping children to become language learners in the classroom. In M. Christie (Ed.), *Aboriginal perspectives on experience and learning.* Geelong, Australia: Deakin University Press.

Gray, B. (2007). *Accelerating the literacy development of indigenous students.* Darwin, Australia: Charles Darwin University Press.

Green, B. (1988). Subject-specific literacy and school learning: a focus on writing. Australian Journal of Education , 32(2), 156–179.

Green, B., & Bigum, C. (1995). Alienígenas na sala de aula. In T.T. Silva (Ed.), *Alienígenas na Sala de Aula: Uma introdução aos estudos culturais em educação.* Petrópolis: Vozes.

Green, B., and C. Bigum (1993). Aliens in the classroom. *Australian Journal of Education, 37*(2), 119–141.

Green, B., J. Hodgen, and A. Luke (1997). Debating literacy in Australia: History lessons and popular f(r)ictions. Australian Journal of Language and Literacy, *20*(1), 6–24.

Green, P. (2001). Critical literacy revisited. In H. Fehring & P. Green (Eds.), *Critical literacy: A collection of articles from the Australian Literacy Educators' Association.* Newark, DE & Norwood, Australia: International Reading Association and Australian Literacy Educators' Association.

Greene, M. (1988). *The dialectic of freedom.* New York: Teachers College Press.

Greene, M. (1995). *Releasing the imagination: Essays on education, the arts and social change.* San Francisco: Jossey-Bass.

Greeno, J. G. (1998). The situativity of knowing, learning, and research. The American Psychologist, 53(1), 5–26. doi:10.1037/0003-066X.53.1.5

Gregor, R. (2005). Robotics and the gifted child: What they gain [Electronic version]. Gifted , 135, 9–11.

Grimberg, B. I. (2008). Promoting high-order thinking through the use of the science writing heuristic. In B. M. Hand (Ed.), *Science inquiry, argument and language: A case for the science writing heuristic* (pp. 87-97). Rotterdam, the Netherlands: Sense Publishers.

Grosz, E. (1994). *Volatile bodies: Toward a corporeal feminism.* Bloomington, IN: Indiana University Press.

Grosz, E., & Eisenman, P. (2001). *Architecture from the outside: Essays on virtual and real space.* Cambridge, MA: MIT Press.

Group, T. T. S. (2008). *Bee-bot.* Retrieved March 24, 2008, from http://www.tts-group.co.uk/Bee-Bot United States Web-based Education Commission (2000). *The power of the Internet for learning: Moving from promise to practice.* Retrieved March 15, 2008, from http://interact.hpcnet.org/webcommission/Section_1.htm

Gruenewald, D. A. (2003). The best of both worlds: A critical pedagogy of place. Educational Researcher, 32(4), 3–12. doi:doi:10.3102/0013189X032004003

Guardado, M., and L. Shi (2007). ESL students' experiences of online peer feedback. Computers and Composition , 24, 443–461. doi:10.1016/j.compcom.2007.03.002

Guba, E., & Lincoln, Y. Y. (1981). *Effective evaluation.* San Francisco: Jossey-Bass.

Gunel, M., B. Hand, and S. Gunduz (2006). Comparing students' understanding of quantum physics when embedding multimodal representations into two different writing formats: Presentation format versus summary report format. Science Education, 90, 1092–1112. doi:10.1002/sce.20160

Gunel, M., B. Hand, and V. Prain (2007). Writing for learning in science: A secondary analysis of six studies. International Journal of Science and Mathematics Education, 5, 615–637. doi:10.1007/s10763-007-9082-y

Gura, M. (2007). What is student robotics? In S. D'Agustino & K.P. King (Eds.), *Classroom robotics: Case studies of 21st century instruction for millennial students* (pp.3-10) [Electronic version].

Gurian, M., & Ballew, A. C. (2003). *The boys and girls learn differently: Action guide for teachers.* San Fransisco: Jossey-Bass.

Hagood, M. C., Stevens, L. P., & Reinking, D. (2003). What do THEY have to teach US? Talkin' cross generations! In D. E. Alvermann (Ed.), *Adolescents and literacies in a digital world* (pp. 68-83). New York: Peter Lang.

Haig-Brown, A. (2001). Continuing collaborative knowledge production: Knowing when where why and how. Journal of Intercultural Studies (Melbourne, Vic.), 22(1), 19–32. doi:10.1080/07256860120037391

Hall, E. (1959). *The silent language.* Garden City, NY: Doubleday.

Hall, E. (1966). *The hidden dimension.* Garden City, NY: Doubleday.

Hall, E. (1976, 1977). *Beyond culture.* Garden City, NY: Doubleday.

Hall, E. (1990). *Understanding cultural differences.* Yarmouth, ME: Intercultural Press.

Hall, S. (1980). Encoding/decoding. In *Culture, Media, Language: Working Papers in Cultural Studies,* 1972-79 (pp. 128-138). London: Hutchinson.

Halliday, M. A. K. (1993). Some grammatical problems in scientific English. In M.A.K. Halliday & J.R. Martin (Eds.), *Writing science: Literacy and discursive power* (pp. 69-85). Pittsburgh, PA: University of Pittsburgh Press.

Halliday, M. A. K. (1994). *An introduction to functional grammar* (2nd Ed.). London: Arnold.

Halliday, M. A. K., & Hasan, R. (1985). *Language, context, and text: Aspects of language in a social semiotic perspective.* Geelong, Australia: Deakin University.

Hamston, J., & Murdoch, K. (1996). *Integrating socially: Planning integrated units of work for social education.* Armadale, Australia: Eleanor Curtain.

Hand, B., and E.-M. Yang, & Bruxvoort. (2007). Using writing-to-learn science strategies to improve Year 11 students' understandings of stoichiometry. International Journal of Science and Mathematics Education, 5, 125–143. doi:10.1007/s10763-005-9028-1

Hand, B., L. Hohenshell, and V. Prain (2007). Examining the effect of multiple writing tasks on Year 10 biology students' understandings of cell and molecular biology concepts. Instructional Science, 35, 343–373. doi:10.1007/s11251-006-9012-3

Hargreaves, A. (1994). *Changing teachers, changing times.* New York: Teachers College Press.

Hargreaves, A. (2003). *Teaching in the knowledge society: Education in the age of insecurity.* Berkshire, UK: Open University Press.

Hargreaves, A., & Fullan, M. G. (1998). *What's worth fighting for out there?* New York: Teachers College Press.

Harris, S. (1984). *Culture and Llearning: Tradition and education in northeast Arnhem Land.* Canberra, Australia: Australian Institute of Aboriginal Studies.

Harriss, J. (2002). *Depoliticizing development: the World Bank and social capital.* London: Anthem.

Hartley, R. (2004). *Young people and mentoring: Towards a national strategy.* A report prepared for Big Brothers Big Sister Australia, Dusseldorp Skills Forum and The Smith Family, Sydney. Retrieved February 24, 2008, from http://www.dsf.org.au/papers/150.htm

Hatch, J. A. (2002). *Doing qualitative research in education settings.* Albany, NY: SUNY.

Hawkridge, D. (1989). Machine-mediated learning in third-world schools. Machine-Mediated Learning , 3, 319–328.

Heale, M. (2005). The new learning technologies: Transforming teaching and learning at Frankston High School. *Principal Matters,* 2-4.

Healy, A. (2004). Multiliteracies pedagogy. Practically Primary , 9(2), 5–7.

Heath, S. (1986). What no bedtime story means: Narrative skills at home and school. In B. Schheifflin & E. Ohs (Eds.), *Language socialisation across cultures* (pp. 97-124). Boston: Cambridge University Press.

Heaton, L. (2001). Preserving communication context: Virtual workspace and interpersonal space in Japanese CSCW. In C. Ess & F. Sudweeks (Eds.), *Culture, technology, communication: Towards an intercultural global village* (pp. 213-240). Albany: State University of New York Press.

Hedley, C. N., Antonacci, P., & Rabinowitz, M. (1995). Thinking and literacy: The mind at work in the classroom [Electronic version]. In C.N. Hedley, P. Antonacci & M. Rabinowitz (Eds.), *Thinking and literacy: The mind at work*, (pp. 3-20). Hillside, NJ: Lawrence Erlbaum.

Heffernan, L. (2004). *Critical literacy and writer's workshop: Bringing purpose and passion to student writing.* Newark, DE: International Reading Association.

Heller, M. F. (1986). How do you know what you know? Journal of Reading , 29, 415–422.

Hellriegel, D., Slocum, J., & Woodman, R. (1992). *Organizational Behaviour* (6th Ed.). St Paul, MN: West Publishing Company.

Hendricks, M. (2002). Kids These Days. *Entrepreneur Magazine*, May. Retrieved January 20, 2009, from www.entrepeneur.com/magazine/entrepreneur/2002/may/51084.html

Hennessy, S. (2000). Graphing investigations using portable (palmtop) technology. Journal of Computer Assisted Learning , 16(3), 243–258. doi:10.1046/j.1365-2729.2000.00136.x

Hennessy, S., Deaney, R., & Ruthven, K. (2003). *Pedagogic strategies for using ICT to support subject teaching and learning: An analysis across 15 case studies.* Faculty of Education, University of Cambridge, Cambridge, UK.

Hennessy, S., R. Deaney, and K. Ruthven (2005). Teacher perspectives on integrating ICT into subject teaching: Commitment, constraints, caution and change. Journal of Curriculum Studies , 37(2), 155–192. doi:10.1080/0022027032000276961

Herring, S. C., & Marken, J. (2008). Implications of gender consciousness for students in information technology. *Women's Studies, 37*(3), 229-256. [Electronic version]. Retrieved August 18, 2008, from http://ella.slis.indiana.edu/~herring/ws.pdf

Heusinkveld, P. (1997). *Pathways to culture.* Yarmouth, ME: Intercultural Press.

Hill, S., Comber, B., Louden, W., Rivalland, J., & Reid, J. (1998). *100 children go to school: Connections and disconnections in literacy development in the year prior to school and the first year of school.* Canberra, Australia: Department of Training, Employment and Youth Affairs.

Hill, S., Comber, B., Louden, W., Rivalland, J., & Reid, J. (2002). *100 children turn 10.* Canberra, Australia: DEET.

Hirsch, E. D. (1987). *Cultural literacy: What every American needs to know.* Boston: Houghton Mifflin.

Hodge, B., & Tripp, D. (1986). *Children and television: A semiotic approach.* Cambridge, UK: Polity Press.

Hofstede, G. (1984, 2001). *Culture's consequences: International differences in work-related values.* London: Sage Publications.

Hofstede, G. (1997). *Cultures and organizations: Software of the mind.* New York: McGraw-Hill.

Holland, D., Lachicotte, W., Skinner, D., & Cain, C. (1998). *Identity and agency in cultural worlds.* Cambridge, MA: Harvard U. Press.

Holland, E. (1998). Spinoza and Marx. *Cultural Logic, 2*, 21–47.

Holt, D. (1998). Does cultural capital structure American consumption? *The Journal of Consumer Research, 25*(1), 1–25. doi:10.1086/209523

Horkheimer, M., & Adorno, T. W. (1972). *Dialectic of enlightenment.* (J. Cumming, Trans.). New York: Continuum.

Horning, A. S. (2004). Digital critical literacy for generation 1.5 and everyone else. The Reading Matrix , 4(3), 134–144.

Howell, W. L., McCaffrey, E. J., & Murphy, R. R. (2003, November 6-9). University mentoring for first LEGO league [Electronic version]. Paper presented at the *Annual ASEE/IEEE Frontiers in Education Conference,* Boston, MA.

Huitt, W. (2004). Bloom et al.'s taxonomy of the cognitive domain. *Educational Psychology Interactive*. Valdosta, GA: Valdosta State University. Retrieved April 20, 2005, at http://chiron.valdosta.edu/whuitt/col/cogsys/bloom.html

Huitt, W., & Vessels, G. (2002). Character education. In J. Guthrie (Ed.), *The encyclopedia of education.* New York: Macmillan.

Hull, G., and K. Schultz (2001). Literacy and learning out of school: A review of theory and research. *Review of Educational Research*, *71*(4), 575–611. doi:10.3102/00346543071004575

Hull, G., and M. Nelson (2005). Locating the semiotic power of multimodality. *Written Communication*, 22, 224–261. doi:10.1177/0741088304274170

Hung, D., and M. R. Nichani (2002). Bringing communities of practice into schools: Implications for instructional technologies from Vygotskian perspectives. International Journal of Instructional Media , 29(2), 171–184.

Inkeles, A., & Levinson, D. (1969). National character: The study of modal personality and sociocultural systems. In.G. Lindzey & E. Aronson (Eds.), *The handbook of social psychology* (pp. 311-378). Boston, MA: Addison-Wesley.

Itakura, H. (2004). Changing cultural stereotypes through e-mail assisted foreign language learning. System , 32, 37–51. doi:10.1016/j.system.2003.04.003

Ito, M. (2006). Japanese media mixes and amateur cultural exchange. In D. Buckingham & R. Willet (Eds.) *Digital Generations* (pp. 49-66). Mahwah, NJ: Lawrence Erlbaum.

Iyer, R. (2007). Pedagogies of design and multiliterate learner identities. International Journal of Learning , 13(11), 25–34.

Jenkins, H. (1992). *Textual poachers: Television fans and participatory culture.* London: Routledge.

Jenkins, H. (2006). *Confronting the challenges of participatory culture: Media education for the 21st century.* A John D. and Catherine T. MacArthur Foundation Occasional Paper on Digital Media and Learning, Chicago, IL: MacArthur Foundation.

Jenkins, H. (2006). *Convergence culture: Where old and new media collide.* New York: New York University Press.

Jewitt, C. (2005). Multimodality, "reading," and "writing" for the 21st century. Discourse: Studies in the Cultural Politics of Education , 26(3), 315–331. doi:10.1080/01596300500200011

Jewitt, C. (2006). *Teaching, literacy, and learning.* London: Routledge.

Jobim e Souza, S., Gamba Jr. (2003). Novos suportes, antigos temores: tecnologia e confronto de gerações nas práticas de leitura e escrita In Jobim e Souza, S. (Ed.) *Educação@pós-modernidade: ficções científicas e ciências do cotidiano.* Rio de Janeiro: 7 Letras.

Johnson, D. W., & Johnson, F. P. (1997). *Joining together: Group theory and group skills* (6th Ed.). Needham Heights, MA: Allyn & Bacon.

Johnson, K. (forthcoming). *Second language teacher education: A sociocultural perspective.* New York: Routledge.

Johnson, R., & Johnson, D. (1994). *Creativity and collaborative learning.* Baltimore, MD: Brookes Press.

Johnson, R., and J. Hegarty (2003). Websites as education motivators for adults with learning disability. British Journal of Educational Technology , 34(4), 479–486.

doi:10.1111/1467-8535.00344

Johnson, S. (2005). *Everything bad is good for you: How today's popular culture is actually making us smarter.* New York: Riverhead Books.

Johnson-Eilola, J. (1997). Living on the surface: Learning in the age of global communication networks. I. Snyder (Ed.), *Page to screen: Taking literacy into the electronic era* (pp. 185-210). Sydney: Allen & Unwin.

Johnstone, A. H. (1996). Chemistry teaching - Science or alchemy? Journal of Chemical Education, 74(3), 262–268.

Jonassen, D. H., & Carr, C. (2000). Mindtools: Affording multiple knowledge representations for learning. In S. P. Lajoie (Ed.), *Computers as cognitive tools* (pp. 165-196). Mahwah, NJ: Lawrence Erlbaum Associates.

Jones, R. H., A. Garralda, D. Li, and G. Lock (2006). Interactional dynamics in online and face-to-face peer-tutoring sessions for second language writers. Journal of Second Language Writing , 15, 1–23. doi:10.1016/j.jslw.2005.12.001

Kalantzis, M. (Ed.). (2001). *Transformations in language and learning: Perspectives on multiliteracies.* Melbourne, Australia: Common Ground Publishing.

Kalantzis, M., & Cope, B and the Learning by Design Group (2005). *Learning by Design.* Melbourne, Australia: Victorian Schools Innovation Commission.

Kalantzis, M., & Cope, B. (2000). A multiliteracies pedagogy: A pedagogical supplement. In B. Cope & M. Kalantzis (eds.) for the New London Group, *Multiliteracies: Literacy learning and the design of social futures* (pp. 239-248). London: Routledge.

Kalantzis, M., & Cope, B. (2000). Changing the role in schools. In B. Cope & M. Kalantzis (Eds.), for the New London Group, *Multiliteracies: Literacy learning and the design of social futures* (pp. 121-148). London: Routledge.

Kalantzis, M., & Cope, B. (2005). *Learning by design.* Melbourne, Australia: Common Ground.

Kalantzis, M., & Cope, B. (2005). *Learning by design.* Melbourne, Australia: VSIC, Common Ground.

Kalantzis, M., B. Cope, and A. Harvey (2003). Assessing multiliteracies and the new basics. *Assessment in Education: Principles* . Policy & Practice , 10(1), 15–26.

Kalantzis, M., B. Cope, and H. Fehring (2002). Multiliteracies: Teaching and learning in the new communications environment. Primary English Teaching Association, 133, 1–8.

Kapitzke, C. (2000). Cyber pedagogy as critical social practice in a teacher education program. Teaching Education , 11(2), 211–229. doi:10.1080/713698968

Kaplan, N. (2000). Literacy beyond books. In T. Swiss (Ed.), *The world wide web and contemporary cultural theory* (pp. 207-234). London: Routledge.

Kearney, M. C. (2006). *Girls make media.* New York: Routledge.

Kearns, P., & Grant, J. (2002). *The enabling pillars: Learning, technology, community, partnership.* Retrieved March 15, 2008, from http://www.dest.gov.au/highered/otherpub/aust_ict_report.pdf

Kellner, D. (1995). *Media culture: Cultural studies, identity and politics between the modern and the postmodern.* London: Taylor & Francis.

Kellner, D. (2001). New technologies/new literacies: Reconstructing education for the new millennium. *International Journal of Technology and Design Education, 11*, 67–81. doi:10.1023/A:1011270402858

Kenner, C. (2004). *Becoming biliterate: Young children learning different writing systems.* Stoke-on-Trent, UK: Trentham Books.

Keys, C. W. (1999). Revitalising instruction in scientific genres: Connecting knowledge production with writing to learn in science. Science Education, 83, 115–130. doi:10.1002/(SICI)1098-237X(199903)83:2<115::AID-SCE2>3.0.CO;2-Q

Kezsbom, D. (2000). Creating teamwork in virtual teams. *Cost Engineering, 42*(10), 33-36.

Khalsa, D. K. (2005, July). *Online learning teams: Impact of socio-cultural dimensions*. Paper presented at the proceedings of Human Computer Interaction International Conference, Las Vegas, NV.

Khalsa, D. K., & Hildreth, S. (2000). *Finding a place for everyone: Creating, maintaining and evolving optimal online learning*. Ithaca, NY: Whole Life Education. Retrieved April 10, 2005, at http://www.wholelifeed.com/placeforeveryone.html

Khoo, A. (2001). Parents' and children's perceptions of the dangers on the Internet. *Paper presented at the AARE*. Perth, Australia: Fremantle.

Kim, Y., and J. Kim (2005). Teaching Korean university writing class: Balancing the process and the genre approach. Asian EFL Journal , 7(2), 1–15.

King, K. P. (2007). Preface. In S. D'Agustino & K.P. King (Eds.), *Classroom robotics: Case studies of 21st century instruction for millennial students* (pp. ix-xi) [Electronic version]. LEGO® Education (2006). *Lego mindstorms education*. Retrieved August 17, 2008, from http://www.active-robots.com/products/mindstorms4schools/nxt-education/nxt-information.pdf

Kirk, D., and D. MacDonald (2001). Teacher voice and ownership of curriculum change. Journal of Curriculum Studies , 33(5), 551–567. doi:10.1080/00220270010016874

Kist, W. (2005). *New literacies in action: Teaching and learning in multiple media*. New York: Teachers College Press.

Klein, P. D. (2004). Constructing scientific explanations through writing. Instructional Science, 32, 191–231. doi:10.1023/B:TRUC.0000024189.74263.bd

Knowles, M. (1984). *Andragogy in action*. San Francisco: Jossey-Bass.

Ko, S., & Rossen, S. (2004). *Teaching online: A practical guide*. New York: Houghton Mifflin Co.

Kozma, R. (2000). Students collaborating with computer models and physical experiments. In J. Roschelle & C. Hoadley (Eds.), *Proceedings of the conference on computer-supported collaborative learning*. Mahwah, NJ: Lawrence Erlbaum Associates.

Kozma, R. (2000). The use of multiple representations and the social construction of understanding in chemistry. In M. Jacobson & R. Kozma (Eds.), *Innovations in science and mathematics education: Advanced designs for technologies of learning* (pp. 11-46). Mahwah, NJ: Lawrence Erlbaum Associates.

Kozma, R. B., and R. E. Anderson (2002). Qualitative case studies of innovative pedagogical practices using ICT. Journal of Computer Assisted Learning , 18, 387–394. doi:10.1046/j.0266-4909.2002.00250.doc.x

Kozma, R., & Russell, J. (2005). Multimedia learning of chemistry. In R. E. Mayer (Ed.), *Cambridge handbook of multimedia learning* (pp. 409-428). New York: Cambridge University Press.

Kozma, R., & Russell, J. (2005). Students becoming chemists: Developing representational competence. In J. K. Gilbert (Ed.), *Visualisation in science education* (pp. 121-146). Dordrecht, the Netherlands: Springer.

Kozma, R., and J. Russell (1997). Multimedia and understanding: Expert and novice responses to different representations of chemical phenomena. Journal of Research in Science Teaching, 34(9), 949–968. doi:10.1002/(SICI)1098-2736(199711)34:9<949::AID-TEA7>3.0.CO;2-U

Kozma, R., E. Chin, J. Russell, and N. Marx (2000). The roles of representations and tools in the chemistry laboratory and their implications for chemistry learning. Journal of the Learning Sciences, 9(2), 105–143. doi:10.1207/s15327809jls0902_1

Kress, G. (2000). A curriculum for the future. *Cambridge Journal of Education*, *30*(1), 133–145. doi:10.1080/03057640050005825

Kress, G. (2000). Multimodality. In B. Cope and M. Kalantzis (Eds.) *Multiliteracies: Literacy learning and the design of social futures*. Melbourne: Macmillan.

Kress, G. (2003). *Literacy in the new media age*. London: Routledge.

Kress, G., & van Leeuwen, T. (1996). *Reading im-*

ages: The grammar of visual design. New York: Routledge.

Kress, G., & Van Leeuwen, T. (2001). *Multimodal discourse: The modes and media of contemporary communication.* New York: Oxford University Press.

Kress, G., Jewitt, C., Bourne, J., Franks, A., Hardcastle, J., Jones, K., & Reid, E. (2005). *English in urban classrooms: A multimodal perspective on teaching and learning.* London: RoutledgeFalmer.

Kristeva, J. (2001). Revolution in poetic language. In V. Leitch (Ed.), *The Norton anthology of theory and criticism* (pp. 2156-2179). New York: Norton.

Kroll, B. (2003). *Exploring the dynamics of second language writing.* New York: Cambridge University Press.

Kuiper, E., M. Volman, and J. Terwel (2005). The web as an information resource in K-12 education: strategies for supporting students in searching and processing information. Review of Educational Research , 75(3), 285–328. doi:10.3102/00346543075003285

Labbo, L. D. (2000). 12 things young children can do with a talking book in a classroom computer center. The Reading Teacher , 53(7), 542–546.

Labbo, L. D., Sprague, L., Montero, M. K., & Font, G. (2000, July). Connecting a computer center to themes, literature, and kindergartners' literacy needs. *Reading Online, 4*(1). Retrieved May 25, 2008, from http://www.readingonline.org/electronic/labbo/

LaBelle, D. (2004). *Before the team project: Cultivate a community of collaborators.* Proceedings of the 21st Annual Information Systems Education Conference (ISECON 2004). Retrieved August 8, 2005, from http://isedj.org/isecon/2004/0000/index.html

Lam, E. (2000). Literacy and the design of the self: A case study of a teenager writing on the internet. TESOL Quarterly , 34(3), 457–482. doi:10.2307/3587739

Lamb, A., and L. Johnson (2006). Key words in instruction, blogs and blogging part II. School Library Media Activities , 22(9), 40–44.

LaMonde, A. M., and T. Rogers (2007). Infusing arts and media into a secondary pre-service course in language and literacy across the disciplines as imaginative and critical practices. Language and Literature , 9(2).

Lankshear, C., & Knobel, M. (1998). Critical literacy and new technologies. Paper presented at the *American Education Research Association,* San Diego. Retrieved June 30, 2007, from http://www.geocities.com/c.lankshear/critlitnewtechs.html

Lankshear, C., & Knobel, M. (2006). *New literacies: Everyday practices and classroom learning* (2nd Ed.). Buckingham, UK: Open University Press.

Lankshear, C., M. Peter, and M. Knobel (2000). Information, knowledge and learning. Journal of Philosophy of Education , 34(1), 17–40. doi:10.1111/1467-9752.00153

Lankshear, C., Snyder, I., & Green, B. (2000). *Teachers and Technoliteracy: Managing literacy, technology and learning in schools.* St Leonards, Australia: Allen & Unwin.

Larson, J., & Marsh, J. (2005). *Making Literacy Real: Theories and Practices for Learning and Teaching.* London: Sage Publications.

Laurinen, L., and M. Marttunen (2007). Written arguments and collaborative speech acts in practicing the argumentative power of language through chat debates. Computers and Composition, 24, 230–246. doi:10.1016/j.compcom.2007.05.002

Lave, J., & Wenger, E. (1991). *Situated learning: Legitimate peripheral participation.* Cambridge, UK: Cambridge University Press.

Leander, K. M. (2003). Writing travelers' tales on New Literacyscapes. Reading Research Quarterly , 38(3), 392–397.

Leander, K. M., and J. F. Lovvorn (2006). Literacy networks: Following the circulation of texts, bodies, and objects in the schooling and online gaming of one youth. Cognition and Instruction , 24(3), 291–340. doi:10.1207/s1532690xci2403_1

Leander, K., & Sheehy, M. (Eds.). (2004). Spatializing

Literacy Research and Practice. *New literacies and digital epistemologies*, Vol. 15.

Lee, J., and K. Valdarrama (2003). Building successful communities of practice. Information Outlook , 7(5), 28–32.

Lee, J., Grigg, W., & Donahue, P. (2007). *The nation's report card: Reading 2007.* Retrieved May 30, 2008, from http://nces.ed.gov/nationsreportcard/pubs/main2007/2007496.asp.

Lemke, J. (1984). Action, context and meaning. In Toronto Semiotic Circle Monograph, *Education and Semiotics* (pp. 107-121). Toronto: University of Toronto Press.

Lemke, J. (1995). *Textual Politics.* London: Taylor and Francis.

Lemke, J. (1998). Metamedia literacy: Transforming meanings and media. In D. Reinking, M. C. McKenna & L. Labbo (Eds.), *Handbook of Literacy and Technology: Transformation in a Post-Typographic World* (pp. 283-302). Mahwah, NJ: Lawrence Erlbaum Associates.

Lemke, J. (1998). Multiplying meaning: Visual and verbal semiotics in scientific text. In J. R. Martin & R. Veel (Eds.), *Reading science* (pp. 87-113). London: Routledge.

Lemke, J. (2002). Travels in hypermodality. Visual Communication , 1(3), 299–325. doi:10.1177/147035720200100303

Lemke, J. L. (1995). *Textual politics: discourse and social dynamics.* Bristol, PA: Taylor & Francis Inc.

Lemke, J. L. (2000). Multimedia literacy demands of the scientific curriculum. Linguistics and Education, 10(3), 247–271. doi:10.1016/S0898-5898(99)00009-1

Lemos, A. (2003). Dogmas da inclusão digital. *Correio Braziliense*. Retrieved October 11, 2007, from http:www.facom.ufba.br/ciberpesquisa/andrelemos

Lemos, A., & Costa, L. (2005). Um modelo de inclusão digital: O caso da cidade de Salvador. In *Revista de Economia Política de las Tecnologias de la Información y Comunicación*. Vol. VIII, n.6. Retrieved October 11, 2007, from http:wwweptic.com.br/português/Revista%20EPTIC%20VIII%20-%20AndreLemos-LeonardoCosta.pdf

Lesko, N. (1996). Denaturalizing adolescence: the politics of contemporary representations. Youth & Society , 28(2), 139–161. doi:10.1177/0044118X96028002001

Lessig, L. (2004). *Free culture: How big media uses technology and the law to lock down culture and control creativity.* London: Penguin.

Lesson Plans Page. (2008). Retrieved December 30, 2008, from http://www.lessonplanspage.com/LessonTemplate.htm

Leu, D. (2005). *New literacies, reading research, and the challenges of change: A deictic perspective of our research worlds.* Paper presented at the National Reading Conference, Miami, FL.

Leu, D. J. (2000). Our children's future: Changing the focus of literacy and literacy instruction. *Reading Online* (EJ) Retrieved July 12, 2007 from http://www.readingonline.org/RT/focus/index.html

Leu, D. J., and C. K. Kinzer (2000). The convergence of literacy instruction with networked technologies for information and communication. Reading Research Quarterly , 35(1), 108–127. doi:10.1598/RRQ.35.1.8

Leu, D., Kinzer, C. K., Coiro, J. L., & Cammack, D. W. (2004). Toward a theory of new literacies emerging from the Internet and other information and communication technologies. In *Theoretical models and processes of reading (5th Ed.).* Newark, DE: International Reading Association.

Levine, K. (2003). *Hannah's Suitcase.* Mortin Grove, IL: Albert Whitman and Company.

Levy, B., Lloyd, S., & Schreiber, S. (2001). *Great Tours! Thematic tours and guide training for historic sites.* New York: Altamira Press.

Lichtman, M. (2006). *Qualitative research in education a user's guide.* Thousand Oaks, CA: Sage Publications.

Lin, A. (2001). Resistance and creativity in English reading lessons in Hong Kong. In B. Comber & A. Simpson (Eds.), *Negotiating critical literacies in classrooms* (pp. 83-100). Mahwah, NJ: Lawrence Erlbaum Associates.

Lin, L., Cranton, P., & Bridglall, B. (2005). *Psychological type and asynchronous written dialogue in adult learning.* Ann Arbor, MI: The University of Michigan Press.

Lincoln, Y. S., & Guba, E. G. (1985). *Naturalistic inquiry.* Beverly Hills, CA: Sage Publications.

Lipnack, J., & Stamps, J. (2000). *Virtual teams: People working across boundaries with technology.* New York: John Wiley & Sons.

Lloyd, S. (2002). Creating Memorable Visits: How to develop and implement theme-based tours. In J. Foy (Ed.). *Interpreting historical house museums* (pp. 210 – 230). Walnut Creek, CA: Altamira Press.

Lofty, J. S. (2003). Standards and the politics of time and teacher professionalism. English Education , 35(3), 195–223.

Lortie, D. (1974). *Schoolteacher: A sociological study.* Chicago: University of Chicago Press.

Louden, W., M. Rohl, C. Barratt-Pugh, C. Brown, T. Cairney, and J. Elderfield (2005). In teachers' hands: Effective literacy pratices in the early years of schooling. Australian Journal of Language and Literacy , 28(3).

Love, K. (2006). Literacy in K-12 teacher education: The case study of a multimedia resource. In L. Hin & Subramaniam (Eds.), *Handbook of research on literacy in technology at the K-12 level* (pp. 469-492). Hershey, PA: Idea Group Reference.

Love, K., Pigdon, K., Baker, G., & Hamston, J. (2005). *Building Understandings in Literacy and Teaching* (BUILT). Melbourne, Australia: University of Melbourne.

Loveless, A., & Ellis, V. (Eds.). (2001). *ICT, pedagogy and the curriculum: Subject to change.* London: Routledge.

Luke, A. (1996). Text and discourse in education: An introduction to critical discourse analysis. Review of Research in Education , 21(3), 3–48.

Luke, A. (2000). Critical literacy in Australia: A matter of context and standpoint. *Journal of Adolescent & Adult Literacy, 43*, 448–461.

Luke, A. (2003). Literacy and the Other: A sociological approach to literacy research and policy in multilingual societies. Reading Research Quarterly , 38(1), 138–141.

Luke, A. (2003). Making literacy policy and practice with a difference. *Australian Journal of Language and Literacy, 26*(3), 58–82.

Luke, A., & Freebody, P. (1997). Shaping the social practices of reading. In S. Muspratt, A. Luke, & P. Freebody (Eds.). *Constructing critical literacies: Teaching and learning textual practice.* Crows Nest, Australia: Allen & Unwin.

Luke, A., and M. Carpenter (2003). Literacy education for a new ethics of global community. *Language Arts, 81*(1), 20–22.

Luke, C. (1997). Media literacy and cultural studies. In S. Muspratt, A. Luke, & P. Freebody (Eds.), *Constructing critical literacies: Teaching and learning textual practice* (pp. 19-49). St. Leonards, Australia: Allen & Unwin.

Luke, C. (1997). Technological literacy. *Adult Literacy Research Network, 4.* CAN: Language Australia.

Luke, C. (2000). Cyber-schooling and technological change: Multiliteracies for new times. In B. Cope & M. Kalantzis (Eds.), *Multiliteracies: Literacy learning and the design of social futures* (pp. 69-91). South Melbourne, Australia: Macmillan.

Luke, C. (2000). New literacies in teacher education. *Journal of Adolescent & Adult Literacy, 43*(5), 424–435.

Luke, C. (2003). Pedagogy, connectivity, multimodality, and interdisciplinarity. *Reading Research Quarterly, 38*(3), 397–403.

Mackey, M. (1994). The new basics: Learning to read

in a multimedia world. English Education , 28(1), 9–19. doi:10.1111/j.1754-8845.1994.tb00697.x

MacLachlan, G., & Reid, I. (1994). *Framing and interpretation.* Carlton, Australia: Melbourne University Press.

Manovich, L. (2001). *The language of new media.* Cambridge, MA: MIT Press.

Mantei, J., & Kervin, L. (2007). Looking for clarity amongst the challenges faced by teachers as they consider the role of ICT in classroom literacy learning experiences. In A. Simpson (Ed.), *Future Directions in Literacy: International Conversations conference 2007,* (pp. 170 – 189). Sydney, Australia: Sydney University Press.

Marsh, C. (2000). *Handbook for beginning teachers* (2nd ed.). Frenchs Forest, Australia: Pearson Education.

Marsh, C. (2008). *Becoming a teacher: knowledge, skills and issues.* Frenchs Forest, Australia: Pearson Education Australia.

Martin, J. R., F. Christie, and J. Rothery (1987). Social processes in education. *The Teaching of English: Journal of the English Teachers'* . Association of New South Wales , 53, 3–22.

Martin, J. R., Matthiessen, C., & Painter, C. (1997). *Working with functional grammar.* London: Arnold.

Martin, K. (2008). The intersection of aboriginal knowledges, aboriginal literacies and new learning. In Healy, A. (Ed.), *Multlilieracies and diversity in education. New pedagogies for expanding landscapes* (pp. 58-81). South Melbourne, Australia: Oxford University Press.

Martín-Barbero, J. (2002/2004). Ofício de cartógrafo: travessias latino-americanas da comunicação na cultura [*Oficio de cartógrafo: Travessias lationoamericanas de la comunicación en la cultura].* São Paulo: Loyola.

Martin-Barbero, J.(1998). Herdando el futuro: Pensar la educación desde la comunicación. In *Cultura y Comunicación, 9.* Universidad de Salamanca, Salamanca.

Masny, D. (2006). Learning and creative processes: a poststructural perspective on language and Multiple Literacies. International Journal of Learning , 12(5), 147–155.

Massey, D. (1994). *Space, place and gender.* Minneapolis, MN: University of Minnesota Press.

Massey, D. (1998). The spatial construction of youth cultures. In T. Skelton & G. Valentine (Eds.). *Cool places: geographies of youth culture* (pp. 121 – 129). London; New York: Routledge.

Matei, S., & Ball-Rokeach, S. (2002). Belonging in geographic, ethnic, and Internet spaces. In B. Wellman & C. Haythornwaite (Eds.), *The Internet in everyday life* (pp. 405-427). Malden, MA: Blackwell Publishing.

Mattessich, P., Murray-Close, M., & Monsey, B. (2004). *Collaboration: What Makes It Work* (2nd Ed.). Saint Paul, MN: Amherst H. Wilder Foundation.

Mauch, E. (2001). Using technological innovation to improve the problem solving skills of middle school students [Electronic version]. Clearing House (Menasha, Wis.) , 75(4), 211–214.

McCarthey, S. J., and M. Dressman (2000). How will diversity affect literacy in the next millenium. Reading Research Quarterly , 35(4), 548–552. doi:10.1598/RRQ.35.4.6

McComb, B. (1997). *The learner-centered classroom and school: strategies for increasing student motivation and achievement.* San Francisco: Jossey Bass Inc.

McDaniel, C. A. (2006). *Critical literacy: A way of thinking, a way of life.* New York: P. Lang.

McDonald, J., Grove, J., & Youth Advisory Forum Members (2001, April 4-6). Youth for youth: Piecing together the peer education jigsaw [Electronic version]. Paper presented at the *2nd International Conference on Drugs and Young People: Exploring the Bigger Picture,* Melbourne, Australia.

MCEETYA. (1999). *The Adelaide declaration on national goals for schooling in the twenty-first century.* Retrieved May 30, 2008, from http://www.mceetya.edu.au/mceetya/nationalgoals/natgoals.htm.

McLaughlin, D. (2007). *The price of freedom.* East Kew, Victoria: David Lovell Publishing.

McLaughlin, M., & DeVoogd, G. L. (2004). *Critical literacy: Enhancing students' comprehension of text.* New York: Scholastic.

McNeely, B. (2005). Technology and learning expectations of the net generation. In D. Oblinger & J. Oblinger (Eds.), *Educating the net generation* (pp. 40-49). Boulder, CO: Educause.

McWilliam, E. (1994). *In broken images: Feminist tales for a different teacher education.* New York: Teacher's College Press.

Meng, M., & Agarwal, R. (in press). Sustaining virtual communities: The role of identity consonance and community artifacts.*Organizational Behavior and Human Decision Processes.*

Mentoring Australia. (2000). *National benchmarks for mentoring programs: Preliminary information.* Retrieved February 24, 2008, from http://www.dsf.org.au/tools/24.htm

Merriam-Webster Online Dictionary. (2008). *Robotics.* Retrieved February 24, 2008, from http://www.merriam-webster.com/dictionary/robotics

Meyrowitz, J. (1985). *No sense of place: the impact of electronic media on social behaviour.* New York: Oxford University Press

Michalchik, V., Rosenquist, A., Kozma, R., Kreikemeier, P., & Schank, P. (2008). Representational resources for constructing shared understandings in the high school chemistry classroom. In J. K. Gilbert, M. Reiner & M. B. Nakhleh (Eds.), *Visualisation: Theory and practice in science education* (pp. 233-282). London: Springer.

Miles, M. B., & Huberman, M. A. (1994). *Qualitative data analysis.* Beverly Hills, CA: Sage.

Millard, E. (1997). *Differently Literate.* London: The Falmer Press.

Miller, M. (2001). Out of the Minds of Babes: In school and the workplace the young are guiding their older colleagues through the technical landscape. *Los Angeles Times.* Retrieved January 20, 2009, from: www.genyes.org/news/mindsofbabes

Mills, K. (2007). "Have you seen *Lord of the Rings*?" Power, pedagogy, and discourses in a multiliteracies classroom. *Journal of Language, Identity, and Education, 6*(3), 221–241.

Milto, E., Rogers, C., & Portsmore, M. (2002, November 6-9). *Gender differences in confidence levels, group interactions, and feelings about competition in an introductory robotics course* [Electronic version]. Paper presented at the Annual ASEE/IEEE Frontiers in Education Conference, Boston, MA.

Mishra, V. (1996). Postmodern racism. Meanjin , 2, 346–357.

Misson, R. (1997, October). *"Only joking": Being critical and keeping sense of humour.* Paper presented at SAETA Conference, Adelaide.

MOE. (2003). *Malay Language Curriculum.* Retrieved February 21, 2005, from http//www.moe.gov.sg/cpdd/syllabuses.htm

Moffett, J. (1981). *Active voice – A writing program across the curriculum.* Montclair, NJ: Boynton Cook.

Moje, E. (2000). "To be part of the story": The literacy practices of gangsta adolescents. *Teachers College Record, 102*(3), 651–691. doi:10.1111/0161-4681.00071

Moll, L., C. Amanti, D. Neff, and N. Gonzalez (1992). Funds of knowledge for teaching: Using a qualitative approach to connect homes and classroom. Theory into Practice , 31(2), 132–141.

Morcellini, M. (Ed.). (2004). *La Scuola della Modernità: Per un manifesto della media education.* Milano: Franco Angeli.

Morely, D. (1992). *Television, audiences and cultural studies.* London: Routledge.

Moreno, A. (2001). Enhancing knowledge exchange through Communities of Practice at the Inter-American Development Bank. Aslib Proceedings: New Information

Perspectives , 53(8), 296–308.

Mortimore, P., Sammons, P., Lewis, D., & Ecob, R. (1988). *School matters: The junior years.* Berkeley: University of California Press.

Mulkay, M. (1988). *On humor: Its nature and its place in modern society.* Oxford: Blackwell.

Mumtaz, S., and M. Hammond (2002). The word processor revisited: Observations on the use of the word processor to develop literacy at key stage 2. British Journal of Educational Technology , 33(3), 345–347. doi:10.1111/1467-8535.00269

Murdoch, K., & Hornsby, D. (1997). *Planning curriculum connections: Whole-school planning for integrated curriculum.* Armadale, Australia: Eleanor Curtain.

Murray, C. (2007). Robots tackle core of STEM education. *Technology news for today's K-20 educator.* Retrieved January 13, 2007, from http://www.eschoolnews.com/news/top-news/news-by-subject/curriculum/?i=45932

Muspratt, S., Luke, A., & Freebody, P. (Eds.). (1997). *Constructing critical literacies: Teaching and learning textual practice.* St. Leonards, Australia: Allen & Unwin.

Myers, J., and R. Beach (2004). Hypermedia authoring as critical literacy. Journal of Adolescent & Adult Literacy , 44(6), 538–547.

Nakata, M. (2000). History, cultural diversity and English language teaching. In B. Cope & M. Kalantzis (Eds.) *Multiliteracies* (pp. 106-120). London: Macmillan.

Nakata, M. (2007). *Discipling the savages: Savaging the disciplines.* Canberra, Australia: Aboriginal Studies Press.

Nelson, B. (2004). *National Inquiry into Literacy Teaching.* Retrieved January 25, 2005, from www.dest.gov.au/Ministers/Media/Nelson.

Nelson, B. (2005). *National Inquiry into Teacher Training.* Retrieved January 25, 2005, from http://www.dest.gov.au/ministers/nelson/media.asp.

Neri, M. (2003). *Mapa da exclusão digital.* Rio de Janeiro: FGV/IBRE, CPS.

New London Group. (1996). A pedagogy of multiliteracies: Designing social futures. *Harvard Educational Review, 66*(1), 60–92.

New London Group. (2000). A pedagogy of multiliteracies. In B. Cope & M. Kalantzis (Eds.), *Multiliteracies:Literacy learning and the design of social futures* (pp. 9-37). London: Routledge.

Newkirk, T. (2002). *Misreading masculinity: Boys, literacy, and popular culture.* Portsmouth, NH: Heinemann.

Newman, M. (2007). *Emotional capitalists: The new leaders.* Milton, Australia: John Wiley & Sons.

Nicholls, C., Crowley, V., & Watt, R. (1996). Theorising Aboriginal education: Surely it's time to move on? *Education Australia, 33*(6-9).

Nichols, K., & Davies, J. (2006). Teaching and learning in new spaces: A case for interdisciplinary inquiry-based learning. In Y. J. Lee, A. L. Tan, & B. T. Ho (Eds.), *International Science Education Conference 2006.* Singapore: National Institute of Education.

Nieto, S. (2002). *Language, culture, and teaching: Critical perspectives for a new century.* Mahwah, NJ: Lawrence Erlbaum Associates.

Nixon, H. (2003). New research literacies for contemporary research into literacy and new media? Reading Research Quarterly , 38(3), 407–413.

Nobel, C. (2007). Women in technology: A call to action. *Information Age, April/May,* 34-37.

Noel, S., and J. M. Robert (2003). How the web is used to support collaborative writing. Behaviour & Information Technology , 22(4), 245–262. doi:10.1080/0144929031000120860

Nonnecke, B., & Preece, J. (2003). Silent participants: Getting to know lurkers better. In C. Leug & D. Fisher (Eds.), From *Usenet to CoWebs: Interacting with social information spaces* (pp. 110-132). Amsterdam; Holland: Springer-Verlag.

Norris, S. P., and L. M. Phillips (2003). How literacy in its fundamental sense is central to scientific literacy. Science Education, 87, 224–240. doi:10.1002/sce.10066

Norton, S. J. (2007). The use of design practice to teach mathematics and science [Electronic version]. International Journal of Technology and Design Education , 18(1), 19–44. doi:doi:10.1007/s10798-006-9019-8

Norton, S. J., C. J. McRobbie, and I. S. Ginns (2007). Problem solving in a middle school robotics design classroom [Electronic version]. Research in Science Education, *37*(3), 261–277. doi:10.1007/s11165-006-9025-6

Nourbakhsh, I., K. Crowley, A. Bhave, E. Hamner, T. Hsium, and A. Perez-Bergquist (2005). The robotic autonomy mobile robots course: Robot design, curriculum design, and educational assessment [Electronic version]. Autonomous Robots , 18(1), 103–127. doi:10.1023/B:AURO.0000047303.20624.02

O'Brien, D. (2005). "At-risk" adolescents: Redefining competence through the multiliteracies of intermediality, visual arts, and representation. *Reading online*. Retrieved March 20, 2005, from http://www.readingonline.org/newliteracies/obrien/

O'Farrell, P. (1986). The Irish in Australia. Sydney: University of New South Wales Press.

O'Leary, Z. (2004). *The essential guide to doing research*. London: SAGE Publications.

O'Toole, R. (2005). *Transversalism concept map*. Retrieved January 1, 2006, from http://blogs.warwick.ac.uk/rbotoole/

Oblinger, D., & Oblinger, J. (2005). *Educating the net generation*. Boulder, CO: Educause.

Oh, S., and D. H. Jonnasen (2007). Scaffolding online argumentation during problem solving. Journal of Computer Assisted Learning , 23, 95–110. doi:10.1111/j.1365-2729.2006.00206.x

Organisation for Economic Co-Operation and Development [OECD]. (2006). *PISA 2006 Science Competencies for Tomorrow's World*. Retrieved January, 5, 2009 from http://www.oecd.org/pages/0,3417,en_32252351_32236191_1_1_1_1_1,00.html

Paglia, C. quoted in Birkets, S. (1994). *The Gutenberg elegies: The fate of reading in an electronic age*. Boston: Faber and Faber.

Pahl, (2003). Children's text-making at home: Transforming meaning across modes. In C. Jewitt & G. Kress (Eds.), *Multimodal literacy* (pp.139-154). New York: Peter Lang.

Palfrey, J., & Gasser, U. (2008). *Born Digital: Understanding the First Generation of Digital Natives*. New York: Basic Books.

Pallant, A., and R. F. Tinker (2004). Reasoning with atomic-scale molecular dynamic models. Journal of Science Education and Technology, 13, 51–66. doi:10.1023/B:JOST.0000019638.01800.d0

Palloff, R., & Pratt, K. (1999). *Building learning communities in cyberspace: Effective strategies for the online classroom*. San Francisco: Jossey-Bass.

Papert, S. (1998). *Technology in schools, to support the system or to render it obsolete: Thinking about the "impossible."* Miliken Family Foundation. Retrieved January 20, 2009, from www.mff.org/edtech/article.taf?_function=detial&content_uid1=106

Papert, S., & Harel, I. (1991). Situating Constructionism [Electronic version]. *Constructionism*. Retrieved January 8, 2008, from http://www.papert.org/articles/SituatingConstructionism.html

Parks, S., D. Huot, J. Hamers, and F. Lemonnier (2003). Crossing boundaries: Multimedia technology and pedagogical innovation in high school class. *Language Learning & Technology*, *7*(1), 28–45.

Parks, S., D. Huot, J. Hamers, and F. Lemonnier (2005). "History of Theatre" Web sites: A brief history of the writing process in a high school ESL language art class. Journal of Second Language Writing , 14, 233–258. doi:10.1016/j.jslw.2005.10.003

Peck, C., L. Cuban, and H. Kirkpatrick (2002). Techno-promoter dreams, student realities [Electronic version]. Phi Delta Kappan , 83(6), 472–480.

Pedersen, S., and M. Liu (2003). Teachers' beliefs about issues in the implementation of a student-centered learning environment. Educational Technology Research and Development , 51(2), 57–76. doi:10.1007/BF02504526

Peppler, K. A., and Y. B. Kafai (2007). From SuperGoo to Scratch: Exploring creative digital media production in informal learning. Learning, Media and Technology , 32(2), 149–166. doi:10.1080/17439880701343337

Perie, M., Grigg, W. S., & Donahue, P. (2005). *The nation's report card: Reading 2005.* Retrieved May 20, 2008 from http://nces.ed.gov/pubsearch/pubsinfo.asp?pubid=2006451.

Perkin, C. (2006, September 2 - 3). No friend of the big ego. *The Weekend Australian,* p. 19.

Perkins, D., and T. Blythe (1994). Teaching for understanding: Putting understanding up front [Electronic version]. Educational Leadership , 51(5), 4–8.

Phillip, K. (2000). *Mentoring and young people.* Retrieved February 24, 2008, from http://www.infed.org/learningmentors/mentoring.htm

Pinto, M. (1997). A infância como construção social. In Pinto, M. e Sarmento, M. *As crianças, contextos e identidades.* Minho: Centro de Estudos da Criança.

Pollan, M. (2001). *The botany of desire: a plant's eye view of the worl*d. New York: Random House.

Polzer, J. T., Milton, L. P., & Swann, W. B. (2002). Capitalizing on diversity: Interpersonal congruence in small work groups. *Administrative Science Quarterly, 47*(2), 296-324.

Pomerantz, S., D. H. Currie, and D. M. Kelly (2004). Sk8er girls; Skateboarders, girlhood and feminism in motion. Women's Studies International Forum , 27, 547–557. doi:10.1016/j.wsif.2004.09.009

Porter, M. (2003). Fostering L.I.N.C.S. among educators: The role of international service-learning in fostering a community of practice. Teacher Education Quarterly , 30(4), 51–62.

Powell, A., Piccoli, G., & Blake, I. (2004). Virtual teams: A review of current literature and directions for future. *Data Base Advances in Information Systems, 35*(1), 6-36.

Prabhu, A. (2007). Equity and equality: Finding the gender balance. *Information Age, April/May,* 30-34.

Prain, V. (2006). Learning from writing in secondary science: Some theoretical and practical implications. International Journal of Science Education, 28(2-3), 179–201. doi:10.1080/09500690500336643

Preece, J. (2000). *Online communities: Designing usability, supporting sociability.* New York: John Wiley & Sons.

Preece, J. (Ed.). (2002). Supporting community and building social capital. Special edition of *Communications of the ACM, 45*(4), 37-39.

Preece, J., & Maloney-Krichmar, D. (2003). Online communities. In Jacko & Sears (Eds.), *Handbook of human-computer interaction* (pp. 596-620). Mahwah, NJ: Lawrence Erlbaum Associates Inc.

Preece, J., Sharp, H., & Rogers, Y. (2002). *Interaction design: Beyond human-computer interaction.* New York: John Wiley & Sons.

Prensky, M. (2001). Digital Natives, Digital Immigrants. *On the Horizon, 9*(5), October 2001. Retrieved January 20, 2009, from http://www.marcprensky.com/writing/Prensky%20-%20Digital%20Natives,%20Digital%20Immigrants%20-%20Part1.pdf

Read, P. (2000). *Belonging: Australians, place and aboriginal ownership.* UK: Cambridge University Press.

Reilly, M. (2006). *LEGO® robotics: Measuring and graphing speed of a LEGO® robotic car.* Retrieved January 10, 2008, from http://www.maureenreilly.com/robotics

Rennie, J. (2006). Meeting kids at the school gate: The literacy and numeracy practices of a remote indigenous community. Australian Educational Researcher , 33(3), 123–140.

Rennie, J., Wallace, R., & Falk, I. (2004). *Discontinuities in literacy and numeracy practices between indigenous community schooling and urban high school* (pp. 121). Canberra, Australia: Department Education, Science and Training.

Reynolds, D. W. (2005). Linguistic correlates of second language literacy development: Evidence from middle-grade learner essays. *Journal of Second Language Writing, 14*(1), 19–45. doi:10.1016/j.jslw.2004.09.001

Rheingold, H. (1993). *The virtual community: Homesteading on the electronic frontier.* Reading, MA: Addison-Wesley.

Richards, L. (2005). *Handling qualitative data a practical guide.* London: Sage.

Richardson, W. (2006). *Blogs, wikis, podcasts, and other powerful web tools for classrooms.* Thousand Oaks, CA: Corwin Press.

Rivoltella, P. C. (2005). *Media education: Fondamenti didattici e prospettive di ricerca.* Brescia: Editrice La Scuola.

Rivoltella, P. C. (2006). *Screen Generation: Gli adolescenti e le prospettive dell'educazione nell'etá dei media digitalli.* Milano: Vita e Pensiero.

Rivoltella, P.C. (2002). *Media education: Modelli, esperienze, profilo disciplinare.* Roma: Carocci.

Rizvi, M., and B. Elliot (2007). Enhancing and sustaining teacher professionalism in Pakistan. Teachers and Teaching , 13(1), 5–19. doi:10.1080/13540600601106021

Robert, G. J. (2003). Emerging technologies: Blogs and wikis: Environments for online collaboration. Language Learning & Technology , 7(2), 12.

Roberts, D. F., Foehr, U. G., & Rideout, V. (2005). *Generation M: Media in the lives of 8-18 year-olds.* Menlo Park, CA: Kaiser Family Foundation.

Robertson, M., Webb, I. L., & Fluck, A. E. (2007). *Seven steps to ICT integration.* Camberwell, Australia: ACER Press.

Robinson, K. (2001). *Out of our minds: Learning to be creative.* Chichester, UK: Capstone.

Roblyer, M. (2006). *Integrating Educational Technology into Teaching,* (4th Ed.). Upper Saddle River, NJ: Pearson/Merrill Prentice Hall/International Society for Technology in Education.

RoboCup Junior Australia. (2007). *RoboCup junior.* Retrieved March 29, 2008, from http://www.robocupjunior.org.au/

Rogers, C., and M. Portsmore (2004). Bringing engineering to elementary school [Electronic version]. Journal of STEM Education: Innovations and Research , 5(3-4), 17–28.

Rogers, P. (2002). *Designing instruction for technology-enhanced learning.* Hershey, PA: Idea Group Publishing.

Rogers, T., & Schofield, A. (2005). Things thicker than words: Portraits of youth multiple literacies in an alternative secondary program. In J. Anderson, M. Kendrick, T. Rogers, & S. Smythe (Eds.), *Portraits of Literacy across Families, Communities and Schools,* (pp. 205-220). Mahwah, NJ: Erlbaum Associates.

Rogers, T., & Winters, K. (2007). *Youth media as critical social practice: A play of genres, positions, and identities in one alternative secondary literacy program.* Paper presented at the Annual meeting of the American Educational Research Association, Chicago, IL.

Rogers, T., Winters, K., LaMonde, A. M., & Perry, M. (2008). *The Youth CLAIM project: Researching critical literacies and arts-integrated media production among youth in classroom and community sites.* Paper presented at the Canadian Society for the Study of Education, Vancouver, Canada.

Rogoff, B. (2003). *The Cultural Nature of Human Development.* New York: Oxford University Press.

Rose, G. (2001). Visual methodologies. *An introduction to the interpretation of visual materials.* London: Sage Publications.

Rovai, A. (2001). Classroom community at a distance: A comparative analysis of two ALN-based university programs. *Internet and Higher Education, 4,* 105-118.

Rover, D. (2003). A sense of community: Learning about versus learning to be / What is a community of practice? *Journal of Engineering Education, 92*(1), 3–5.

Rowsell, J., C. Kosnik, and C. Beck (2008). Fostering multiliteracies pedagogy through preservice teacher education. *Teaching Education, 19*(2), 109–122. doi:10.1080/10476210802040799

Russell, J., & Kozma, R. (2005). Assessing learning from the use of multimedia chemical visualisation software. In J. K. Gilbert (Ed.), *Visualisation in science education* (pp. 299-332). Dordrecht, the Netherlands: Springer.

Russell, J., R. Kozma, T. Jones, J. Wykoff, N. Marx, and J. Davis (1997). Use of simultaneous-synchronised macroscopic, microscopic, and symbolic representations to enhance the teaching and learning of chemical concepts. Journal of Chemical Education, 74(3), 330–334.

Russell, M., D. Bebell, J. Cowan, and M. Corbelli (2003). An AlphaSmart for each student: Do teaching and learning change with full access to word processors? Computers and Composition , 20, 51–76. doi:10.1016/S8755-4615(02)00175-5

Ruthven, K., Hennnesy, S., & Deaney, R. (2004). *Incorporating Internet resources into classroom practice: Pedagogical perspectives and strategies for Secondary School subject teachers*. Retrieved May 21, 2004, from http://www.tcrecord.org.

Salvo, M. (2002). Critical engagement with technology in the computer classroom. Technical Communication Quarterly , 11(3), 317–337. doi:10.1207/s15427625tcq1103_5

Sandholtz, H. M., and B. Reilly (2004). Teachers, not technicians: Rethinking technical expectations for teachers. Teachers College Record , 106(3), 487–512. doi:10.1111/j.1467-9620.2004.00348.x

Santos, L.G. (2003). A informação após a virada cibernética. In L.G. Santos et al. (Eds.), *Revolução Tecnológica, Internet e Socialismo.* São Paulo: Fundação Perseu Abramo.

Saravanan V, . (2005). 'Thinking Schools, Learning Nations' Implementation of Curriculum Review in Singapore. Educational Research for Policy and Practice , 4(2-3), 97–113. doi:10.1007/s10671-005-1543-x

Sawyer, R. K. (2006). *Explaining Creativity.* New York: Oxford University Press.

Scanlon, C. (2009). The natives aren't quite so restless. *The Australian,* p. 33.

Schank, P., and R. Kozma (2002). Learning chemistry through the use of a representation-based knowledge-building environment. Journal of Computers in Mathematics and Science Teaching, 21(3), 253–279.

Schmar-Dobler, E. (2003). Reading on the internet: The link between literacy and technology. Journal of Adolescent & Adult Literacy , 47(1), 80–85.

Schofield, A., and T. Rogers (2004). At play in fields of ideas; Teaching curriculum and the lives of youth. Journal of Adolescent and Adult Literacies, 48, 238–248. doi:10.1598/JAAL.48.3.5

Schuck, S., & Kearney, M. (2004). Students in the director's seat: Teaching and learning across the school curriculum with student-generated video. *Teacher learning and development group.* Retrieved August 22, 2008 from http://www.ed-dev.uts.edu.au/teachered/research/dvprojects/home.html

Schwartz, G. (2000). Exclusão digital entra na agenda econômica mundial. *Folha de São Paulo*, São Paulo, 18 de junho 2000.

Scott, D. (2000). Editorial- responses to Crick and citizenship education [Electronic version]. *Curriculum Journal, 11*(1), 1–7. doi:10.1080/095851700361357

Scott, T. (2006). Writing work, technology and pedagogy in the late capitalism. Computers and Composition , 23, 228–243. doi:10.1016/j.compcom.2005.08.008

Sefton-Green, J. (1998). Digital diversions. *Youth culture in the age of multimedia.* London: UCL Press.

Sefton-Green, J. (2006). Youth, technology and media cultures. In J. Green & A. Luke (Eds.), *Rethinking learning: What counts as learning and what learning counts* (pp. 279-306). Washington, DC: American Educational

Research Association.

Sefton-Green, J. (Ed.). (1998). *Digital diversions: Youth culture in the age of multimedia*. London: UCL Press.

Sefton-Green, J. (Ed.). (1999). *Young people, creativity and new technologies*. London: Routledge.

Sharpnack, R. (2005). The Power of Shifting Context. In L. Coughlin, E. Wingard & K. Hollihan (Eds.), *Enlightened Power* (pp. 39 - 52). San Francisco, CA: Jossey-Bass.

Sheehy, M., & Leander, K. (Eds.). (2004). Introduction. In K. Leander & M. Sheehy. (Eds.). Spatializing Literacy Research and Practice. *New literacies and digital epistemologies, 15*, 1 - 13.

Shetzer, H., & Warschauer, M. (2000). An electronic literacy approach to network – based language teaching. In W. M. Warschauer, & R. Kern (Eds.), *Networked-based language learning: Concepts and practice* (pp. 171-185). Cambridge, UK: Cambridge University Press.

Shillito, S., K. Beswick, and M. Baguley (2008). The aims of art education: An analysis of visual art in Tasmania's Essential Learnings Curriculum. Australian Online Journal of Arts Education , 4(1), 1–16.

Shneiderman, B. (2002). *Leonardo's laptop: Human needs and the new computing technologies*. Cambridge, MA: The MIT Press.

Shriberg, A., Lloyd, C., Shriberg, D., & Williamson, M. (1997). *Practicing Leadership: Principles and Applications*. New York: John Wiley & Sons, Inc.

Silveira, S. (2001). A. Exclusão digital: A miséria na era da informação. São Paulo: Editora Fundação Perseu Abramo.

Silveira, S. (2003). Inclusão digital, software livre e globalização contra-hegemônica. In S. Silveira & J. Cassino (Eds.), *Software livre e inclusão digital*. São Paulo: Conrad Editora do Brasil.

Sime, D., and M. Priestley (2005). Student teachers' first reflections on information and communications technology and classroom learning: Implications for initial teacher education. *Journal of Computer Assisted Learning, 21*, 130–142. doi:10.1111/j.1365-2729.2005.00120.x

Sims, K., Spinetti, S., Crabb, S., & Earnshaw, M. (2006). *Robotics: Embedding technology-Module 14*. Retrieved January 5, 2008, from http://www.det.act.gov.au/department/pdf/elt_14_Robotics.pdf

Slee, P. (2002). *Child, adolescent and family development*. (2nd Ed.). UK: Cambridge University Press.

Smith, M. W., & Wilhem, J. D. (2002). *"Reading don't fix no Chevys": Literacy in the lives of young men*. Portsmouth, NH: Heinemann.

Snow, C. E., Barnes, W. S., Chandler, J., Goodman, I. F., & Hemphill, L. (1991). *Unfulfilled expectations: Home and school influences on literacy*. Cambridge, MA.: Harvard University Press.

Snyder, I. (1998, August 9-10). New literacies for the twenty-first century: From page to screen [Electronic version]. Paper presented at *Connected Learning: The Learning Technologies in Schools Conference*, Melbourne, Australia.

Soares, M. (2002). Novas práticas de leitura e escrita: letramento na cibercultura. In Dossiê *Letramento, Revista Educação e Sociedade*, n.81. Campinas: Cedes.

Soares, M. (2005). *Letramento: um tema em três gêneros*. Belo Horizonte: Autêntica.

Sodré, M.(2002*). Antropológica do espelho: uma teoria da comunicação linear em rede*. Petrópolis: Vozes.

Soep, E. (2006). Beyond literacy and voice in youth media production. *McGill Journal of Education, 41*(3), 1–11.

Soja, E. (2004). Preface. In K. Leander & M. Sheehy. (Eds.). Spatializing Literacy Research and Practice. *New literacies and digital epistemologies, 15*, ix – xv.

Solvie, P. (2008). Use of the Wiki: Encouraging preservice teachers' construction of knowledge in reading methods courses. The Journal of Literacy and Technology , 9(2), 58–87.

Somerville, M. (2005). Researching place pedagogies.

In *Proceedings of the 1st International Conference of Qualitative Inquiry, University of Illinois, USA.*

Somerville, M. (2006). *Literacy as translation.* Australian Council of Adult Literacy: Annual Conference, Adelaide, Australia.

Somerville, M., and T. Perkins (2003). Border work in the contact zone: Thinking Indigenous/non-Indigenous collaboration spatially. *International Journal of Intercultural Studies*, *24*(3), 253–266. doi:10.1080/0725686032000172597

Sorj, B. (2003). *brasil@povo.com: a luta contra a desigualdade na Sociedade da Informação.* Rio de Janeiro: Jorge Zahar; Brasília: Unesco.

Souza Santos, B. (2002). *A globalização e as ciências sociais***.** São Paulo: Cortez.

Sowers, R. (1983). The Myth of Collaboration. *American Craft, Dec/Jan, 44 – 45*, 96.

Spires, H. A., J. K. Lee, and K. A. Turner (2008). Having our say: Middle grade student perspectives on school, technologies, and academic engagement. Journal of Research on Technology in Education , 40(4), 497–515.

Sprainger, N. (2007). Meet the bee-bots! *Quick - Journal of the Queensland Society for Information Technology in Education, 103.* Retrieved March 27, 2008, from http://www.qsite.edu.au/files/quick_103_Winter2007.pdf

Sproull, L., & Kiesler, S. (1995). Computers, networks, and work. *Scientific American: The Computer in the 21st Century, 6*(1), 116-123.

St Joseph's Nudgee College. (2008). *Defining the Future of the Nudgee College Curriculum* (2004) – *Implementation 2004 – 2008*. Queensland, Australia: Nudgee College.

Stevens, L. P., & Bean, T. W. (2007). *Critical literacy: Context, research, and practice in the K-12 classroom.* Thousand Oaks, CA: SAGE Publications.

Stevens, L. P., L. Hunter, V. Carrington, D. Pendergast, and N. Bahr (2007). Reconfiguring "adolescence": Ambiguous bodies in ambivalent settings. Australian Educational Researcher , 2(34), 107–128.

Stieff, M., and U. Wilensky (2003). Connected chemistry - Incorporating interactive simulations into the chemistry classroom. Journal of Science Education and Technology, 12(3), 285–302. doi:10.1023/A:1025085023936

Stoll, L., Fink, D., & Earl, L. (2003). *It's about learning (and it's about time).* New York: Routledge Falmer.

Stone, J. C. (2007). Popular websites in adolescents' out-of-school lives: Critical lessons on literacy. In M. Knobel & C. Lankshear (Eds.), *A new literacies sampler* (pp. 49-66). New York: P. Lang.

Stone, J. C., and E. S. Veth (2008). Rethinking the new literatures of childhood: Cultural models of gender in popular websites. *Journal of Language and Literacy Education*, *4*(2), 21–39.

Storti, C. (1990). *The art of crossing cultures.* Boston: Intercultural Press Inc.

Storti, C. (1998). *Figuring foreigners out.* Boston: Intercultural Press Inc.

Street, B. (1984). *Literacy in Theory and Practice.* Cambridge, UK: Cambridge University Press.

Street, B. (1995). *Social literacies: Critical approaches to literacy in development, ethnography and education.* Harlow, UK: Longman.

Street, B. V. (Ed.). (1993). *Cross-cultural approaches to literacy.* UK: Cambridge University Press.

Strenski, E., C. Feagin, and J. Singer (2005). E-mail small group peer view revisited. Computers and Composition , 22(2), 191–208. doi:10.1016/j.compcom.2005.02.005

Sudweeks, F., & Ess, C. (2002, July). Cultural attitudes towards technology and communication. *Proceedings of the 3rd International Conference on Cultural Attitudes towards Technology and Communication,* Montreal, Canada (pp. 69-88)

Szubanski, M. (2005). 'Fears of a clown' interview by B. Hallett. *The Age, Preview Magazine,* May 8, 4-6.

Taber, K. S., & Coll, R. K. (2002). Bonding. In J. K.

Gilbert, O. De Jong, R. Justi, D. F. Treagust & J. H. Van Driel (Eds.), *Chemical education: Towards research-based practice* (pp. 213-234). Amsterdam: Kluwer Academic Publishers.

Tan, K., and D. F. Treagust (1999). Evaluating students' understanding of chemical bonding. The School Science Review, 81, 75–83.

Taylor, M., & Saarinen, E. (1994). *Imagologies: Media philosophy*. London: Routledge.

Taylor, R. P., and C. Gitsaki (2004). Teaching WELL in a computerless classroom. Computer Assisted Language Learning , 16(4), 275–294. doi:10.1076/call.16.4.275.23412

Tearle, P. (2003). ICT implementation: What makes the difference? British Journal of Educational Technology , 34(5), 567–583. doi:10.1046/j.0007-1013.2003.00351.x

Teytelbaum, O, & Portsmore, M. (2008). *Thinking outside the box: A look into LEGO organization and sorting*. Retrieved August 15, 2008, from http://www.legoengineering.com/index.php?option=com_content&task=view&id=76&Itemid=65

The Lego Group. (2007). *Mindstorms*. Retrieved March 24, 2008, from http://mindstorms.lego.com/eng/default.aspx

The State of Queensland. (2000). *Literate futures: Report of the review for Queensland State Schools*. Retrieved August 12, 2008 from http://education.qld.gov.au Unsworth, L. (2001). *Teaching multiliteracies across the curriculum: Changing contexts of text and image in classroom practice*. Buckingham, UK: Open University Press.

Thomas, A. (2007). *Youth online: Identity and literacy in the digital age*. New York: Peter Lang.

Thomas, S., R. Smees, J. MacBeath, P. Robertson, and B. Boyd (2000). Valuing pupils' views in Scottish schools [Electronic version]. Educational Research and Evaluation , 6(4), 281–316. doi:10.1076/edre.6.4.281.6934

Thompson, J. (1995/1998). *The media and modernity: A social theory of the media [A midia e a modernidade: uma teoria social da mídia]*. Cambridge: Polity Press. Brazilian translation, Petrópolis: Vozes.

Thomson, P. (2002). *Schooling the rustbelt kids: Making the difference in changing times*. Crows Nest, Australia: Allen & Unwin.

Thomson, S., & De Bortoli, L. (2007). *Exploring scientific literacy: How Australia measures Up*. Retrieved May 27, 2008, from http://www.acer.edu.au/ozpisa/reports.html.

Tolstoy, A. (1968). *The great big enormous turnip*. New York: F. Watts.

Towndrow, P. A. (2005). Teachers as digital task designers: An agenda for research and professional development. Journal of Curriculum Studies , 37(5), 507–524. doi:10.1080/00220270500068591

Trunfio, P., Berenfeld, B., Kreikemeier, P., Moran, J., & Moodley, S. (2003). *Molecular modelling and visualisation tools in science education*. Paper presented at the 2003 Annual Meeting of the National Association of Research in Science Teaching, Philadelphia.

Tse, S. K., Lam, W. I., Lam, Y. H., & Loh, E. K. Y. (2005). *Learn to Read: The performance of Hong Kong primary 4 pupils in PIRLS 2001*. Hong Kong: Hong Kong University Press.

Underwood, J. (2000). A comparison of two types of computer support for reading development. Journal of Research in Reading , 23(2), 136–148. doi:10.1111/1467-9817.00110

Unsworth, L. (2001). *Teaching multiliteracies across the curriculum: Changing contexts of text and image in classroom practice*. Philadelphia: Open University Press.

Unsworth, L. (2002). Changing dimensions of school literacies. *Australian Journal of Language and Literacy, 25*(1), 62–77.

Unsworth, L. (2006). Towards a metalanguage for multiliteracies education: Describing the meaning making resources of language-image interaction. English Teaching: *Practice and Critique*, *5*(1), 55–76.

Unsworth, L. (Ed.). (2000). *Researching language in schools and communities: Functional linguistic perspectives.* London: Cassell.

Vadeboncoeur, J. (2005). The difference that time and space make: An analysis of institutional and narrative landscapes. In J. Vadeboncoeur & L. Stevens (Eds.) Re/Constructing "the Adolescent": Sign, symbol and body. *Adolescent Cultures, School & Society, 33,* 123–152.

Valiant, U. S. A. (2004). *Roamer: Discovery at every turn.* Retrieved from March 24, 2008, from http://www.valiant-technology.com/uk/pages/roamer_research.php

Vallance, M., and P. Towndrow (2007). Towards the "informed use" of information and communication technology in education: A response to Adams' "PowerPoint, habits of mind, and classroom culture. Journal of Curriculum Studies , 39(2), 219–227. doi:10.1080/00220270601105631

Van Heertum, R., and J. Shane (2006). A new direction for multiliteracy education. McGill Journal of Education , 41(3), 249–265.

Vasquez, V. M. (2004). *Negotiating critical literacies with young children.* Mahwah, NJ: L. Erlbaum Associates.

Vasquez, V. M. (2005). Creating opportunities for critical literacy with young children: Using everyday issues and everyday text. In J. Evans (Ed.), *Literacy moves on: Popular culture, new technologies, and critical literacy in the elementary classroom* (pp. 83-105). Portsmouth, NH: Heinemann.

Vermaat, H., Terlouw, C., & Dijkstra, S. (2003, April). *Multiple representations in web-based learning of chemistry concepts.* Paper presented at the 84th Annual Meeting of the American Educational Research Association, Special Interest Group Technology, Instruction, Cognition and Learning, Chicago.

Vianna, H. (2004). A disseminação silenciosa do software livre. Caderno Mais, *Folha de São Paulo,* 18/04/2004

Vygotsky, L. S. (1978). *Mind in society: The development of higher psychological processes.* Cambridge, MA: Harvard University Press.

Walker, R., and W. Baets (2000). Designing a virtual environment for management education: A learner-centred approach. Indian Journal of Open Learning , 9(3), 299–317.

Walsh, C. (2007). Creativity as capital in the literacy classroom: Youth as multimodal designers. Literacy , 41(2), 79–85. doi:10.1111/j.1467-9345.2007.00461.x

Walther, J. (1996). Computer mediated communication: Impersonal, interpersonal, and hyperpersonal interaction. *Communication Research, 23*(1), 3-43.

Wang, W., and Q. Wen (2002). L1 use in the L2 composing process: An exploratory study of 16 Chinese EFL writers. Journal of Second Language Writing , 11, 225–246. doi:10.1016/S1060-3743(02)00084-X

Warnick, B. (2002). *Critical literacy in a digital era: Technology, rhetoric, and the public interest.* Mahwah, NJ: Lawrence Erlbaum Associates.

Warschauer, M. (2000). The death of cyberspace and the rebirth of CALL. In P. Brett (Ed.), *CALL in the 21st century.* Whitstable, UK: IATEFL.

Warschauer, M., and P. Ware (2006). Automated writing evaluation: Defining classroom research agenda. Language Teaching Research , 10(2), 157–180. doi:10.1191/1362168806lr190oa

Weimer, M. (2002). *Learner centered teaching: five key changes to practice.* San Francisco: Jossey Bass.

Wells, M. A., & Reynolds, L. J. (2005). Digital literacies. In D. L. Pendergast & N. M. Bahr (Eds.), *Teaching middle years: Rethinking curriculum, pedagogy, and assessment* (pp. 242-254). Crows Nest, Australia: Allen & Unwin.

Wenger, E. (1998). *Communities of practice: Learning, meaning and identity.* Cambridge, UK: Cambridge University Press.

Wenger, E. (2004). *Learning for a small planet: A research agenda.* Unpublished paper, Institute for Research on

Learning, North San Juan, CA. Retrieved April 5, 2004, from http://www.ewenger.com/research

Wesley, P., and V. Buysse (2001). Communities of practice: Expanding professional roles to promote reflection and shared inquiry. Topics in Early Childhood Special Education , 21(2), 114–124. doi:10.1177/027112140102100205

White, C., & Hunter, K. (1995). *Teaching with historic places.* Washington, DC: National Trust for Historic Preservation.

White-Kaulaity, M. (2007). Reflections on Native Amercian reading: A seed, a tool, and a weapon. Journal of Adolescent & Adult Literacy , 50(7), 560–569. doi:10.1598/JAAL.50.7.5

Wiersma, W. (2000). *Research methods in education an introduction* (7th Ed.). Needham Heights, MA: Allyn and Bacon.

Wilensky, U., and M. Resnick (1999). Thinking in levels: A dynamic systems approach to making sense of the world. Journal of Science Education and Technology, 8(1), 3–19. doi:10.1023/A:1009421303064

Wilhelm, J., and M. W. Smith (2001). Literacy in the lives of young men: Findings from an American study. Engineers Australia , 132, 17–26.

Willard, N. E. (2007). *Cyber-safe kids, cyber-savvy teens: Helping young people learn to use the Internet safely and responsibly.* San Francisco: Jossey-Bass.

Williams, B. T. (2002). *Tuned in: Television and the teaching of writing.* Portsmouth, NH: Boynton/Cook.

Williams, B. T. (Forthcoming). *Shimmering literacies: Popular culture and reading and writing online.* London: Peter Lang.

Williams, M. (1999). Learning teaching: A social constructivist approach – theory and practice or theory with practice? In H. Trappes-Lomax & I. McGrath (Eds.), *Theory in language teacher education* (pp. 11-20). Harlow, UK: Longman.

Williams, N. (2000). Educational multimedia: Where's the interaction? In M. Monteith (Ed.), *IT for learning enhancement* (Rev. Ed.) (pp.159-176). Exeter, U.K: Intellect Books.

Williamson, B. (2005). *What are multimodality, multisemiotics and multiliteracies? A brief guide to some jargon.* Retrieved June 25, 2006, from http:www.futurelab.org.uk/viewpoint/art49.htm

Willis, P. (1990). *Common culture.* Buckingham, UK: Open University

Wilson, L. (2006). *Writing to live: How to teach writing for today's world.* Portsmouth, NH: Heinemann.

Winch, G., Johnston, R., March, P., Ljungdahl, L., & Holliday, M. (2004). *Literacy: Reading, writing, and children's literature* (2nd Ed.). South Melbourne, Australia: Oxford University Press.

Wind, Y. (2006). Managing creativity. *Rotman Magazine,* Spring/Summer, 20 – 23.

Wright, S. (2003). *The Arts, Young Children, and Learning.* Boston: Allyn & Bacon.

Wu, H., and P. Shah (2004). Exploring visuospatial thinking in chemistry learning. Science Education, 88(3), 465–492. doi:10.1002/sce.10126

Wu, H., J. S. Krajcik, and E. Soloway (2001). Promoting understanding of chemical representations: Students' use of a visualisation tool in the classroom. Journal of Research in Science Teaching, 38(7), 821–842. doi:10.1002/tea.1033

Xie, Q., and R. Tinker (2006). Molecular dynamics simulations of chemical reactions for use in education. Journal of Chemical Education, 83(1), 77–83.

Yore, L. D., and D. F. Treagust (2006). Current realities and future possibilities: Language and science literacy - empowering research and informing instruction. International Journal of Science Education, 28(2-3), 291–314. doi:10.1080/09500690500336973

Yuill, N., & Oakhill, J. (1991). *Children's problems in text comprehension: An experimental investigation.* Cambridge, UK: Cambridge University Press.

Zammit, K., and T. Downes (2002). New learning environments and the multiliterate individual: A framework for educators. [Electronic version] [f]. Australian Journal of Language and Literacy , 25(2), 24–36.

Zhang, W., & Storck, J. (2001). Peripheral members in online communities. *Americas' Conference on Information Systems (AMCIS), 8*(1), 29-38.

About the Contributors

Darren L. Pullen is a lecturer in ICT, professional studies and multiliteracies in the Faculty of Education at the University of Tasmania, Australia. He has a diverse background with previous employment as a research fellow in the health sector, ICT consultant and educator. His research interest is in the management of change processes with a particular interest in the micro-meso-macro level relationships between technology innovations and human-machine (humachine) relationships and interactions.

David R. Cole is a senior lecturer in English and pedagogy at the University of Technology, Sydney. His major research areas are multiliteracies, multiple literacies and affective aspects of literacy and education. He has worked as an international English teacher on four continents, and has published widely in academic journals including: *English in Australia, Educational Philosophy and Theory, Prospect and Curriculum Perspectives*. He is currently under contract to write two edited academic books on literacy theory, and has published a novel about Colombia called *A Mushroom of Glass* in 2006. He is presently researching the complex multiple literacies of Sudanese immigrant families living in NSW.

***

Margaret Baguley is a senior lecturer in arts education, curriculum and pedagogy in the Faculty of Education, University of Southern Queensland, Australia. Her teaching and research interests are concerned with the role of visual art in the education of early childhood, primary and secondary students. She has an extensive teaching background across all facets of education, in addition to maintaining her arts practice. An interest in collaborative practice and exhibition underpins her teaching. Dr Baguley's research supervision encompasses studies in visual arts education, children's engagement with the arts, teacher development, museum studies and the value of the arts in the community. In 2008 Margaret received a national award to recognise her outstanding contribution to student learning from the Australian Learning and Teaching Council (ALTC).

Matthew Clarke teaches new literacies to undergraduate and post-graduate students in the Faculty of Education at the University of Hong Kong, where he is currently employed as an assistant professor. His research interests include new literacies in language teacher education, discourse analysis, and teacher identity formation and development. He is currently researching new literacies teaching and learning with Margaret Lo in Hong Kong primary and secondary schools.

Molly Dugan is a PhD candidate in curriculum & instruction at Boston College. Her research focuses on multiliteracies, educational change, and spatial approaches to social science research. Her dissertation examines multimodal literacy practices and learning in educational institutions. She has been an elementary, middle, and high school English teacher and an associate director of teacher education at Rutgers University in New Jersey.

Julie Faulkner is a senior lecturer in literacy in the School of Education at RMIT University. Her research focuses on questions of engagement and poplar culture in relation to learning, as well as the increasingly popular text forms associated with information and multimedia technologies. Her writing includes *'It gives you an image of yourself that you can reflect upon': Literacy, Identity and New Media* in Snyder and Beavis' (Eds) *Doing Literacy Online: Teaching, Learning and Playing in an Electronic World* (Hampton Press), and the co-authored, *Learning to Teach: New times, New Practices* (Oxford University Press)

Christina Gitsaki is a lecturer at The University of Queensland and the Executive Secretary of the Applied Linguistics Association of Australia. As an applied linguist she has worked for almost two decades in Australia and overseas and her research is mainly in the area of language literacy and the use of technologies in education. Dr. Gitsaki has published a number of journal articles and book chapters, and she has presented her research in numerous conferences around the world. She is the author of *Second language Lexical Acquisition* (1999, International Scholars Publications), the co-author of *Internet English* (2000, Oxford University Press) and the editor of *Language and Languages – Global and Local Tensions* (2007, Cambridge Scholars Publications). Currently, Dr. Gitsaki is involved in educating preservice high school teachers and supervising a number of postgraduate students.

Annette Hilton taught secondary school chemistry and mathematics for 20 years before moving into chemistry education research. During her teaching career, Annette taught in Canada and Australia, and received several awards for technology innovation in teaching. In 2002 she was awarded a Queensland-Smithsonian Fellowship to conduct research in Washington D.C. She was seconded in 2007 from Education Queensland by the Cooperative Research Centre – Sugar Industry Innovative through Biotechnology (CRC – SIIB) and the University of Queensland to undertake doctoral research into the use of digital technologies and investigative inquiry to enhance chemistry education in biomaterials chemistry. Her research interests relate to science education, chemical literacy development, and the scaffolding roles of digital technologies, multimodal communication, and investigative inquiry.

Eileen Honan is senior lecturer in English and literacy education at The University of Queensland. Her research interests include developing methodological applications in educational research of Deleuze and Guattari's philosophical work, and working with teachers to develop their understanding of theoretical issues related to their literacy teaching practices.

Radha Iyer lectures in the School of Cultural and Language Studies, QUT on sociocultural issues in education, gender and sexuality issues and sociolinguistics. Her research interests are linguistically and culturally diverse students and literacy, multiliteracies, critical discourse analysis, media literacy and gender issues.

Martin Kerby is the Head of Information Services and Museum Curator/Archivist of St Joseph's Nudgee College Museum in Brisbane, Australia. He was also a foundation member of the Middle School program in 2001. He has written two books, *Undying Echoes* (2001) about the military history of St Joseph's Nudgee College and *Where Glory Awaits* (2005) the military history of St Joseph's Gregory Terrace, another boys' school in Brisbane. Martin is currently working on a PhD examining the life of war correspondent Sir Philip Gibbs. In January 2008 he was awarded a place at the inaugural Australian Government Summer School in History held in Canberra.

Margaret Lo is a teacher educator in the Faculty of Education at the University of Hong Kong, where she teaches new literacies to undergraduate and post-graduate students. Her research interests include new literacies in language teacher education and English language teaching with young learners. She is currently researching new literacies teaching and learning as part of a large capacity-building project to develop new literacies in Hong Kong primary and secondary schools.

Carmen Luke retired from the University of Queensland at the end of 2007. Carmen was professor of education and is leading international scholar in the field of media literacy and new media, feminist studies, globalization and higher education. Her work on multiliteracies and media literacy is used by educators in Australia, the UK and US and her writings on feminist pedagogy have had a major impact on the field for the past decade. Carmen developed prototypes that are now internationally cited for training teachers on young people's relationships to 'old' and 'new' media, new technologies and popular culture and the role of schooling in providing critical media and ICT skills. Her recent research supervision was in areas of globalization and education, gender and race studies, media and popular culture. Her research projects have included a fieldwork based study on women in higher education management in Southeast Asia, described in *Globalisation and Women in Academics*, (Lawrence Erlbaum, 2001); an ARC funded national study of interethnic families (with A. Luke); an ARC funded study of 'cybraries' (with C. Kapitzke, A. Luke, B. Bruce); an ARC funded study of the effects of Australian education on South-East Asian graduates' professional pathways and cultural re-adaption (with A. Luke); and an ARC funded study of new media and youth identity. In addition to her monographs and anthologies, her work has appeared in: *Harvard Educational Review, Feminist Issues, Educational Theory, International Journal of Cultural Studies, Journal of Intercultural Studies, Ethnic and Racial Studies, Journal of Communication Inquiry* and *Teachers College Record.* Her theoretical interests include cultural globalization theory and cosmopolitan 'democracy'. Her research interests have focused on the future of public education and public archives of knowledge such as university libraries and scholarly publishing which, in the context of globalization and privatization, are fast fading as public goods for public access, benefit and in the public interest.

Vikashni (Vicki) Moyle is a computer support officer at the University of Tasmania in the Faculty of Education. Vikashni has previously worked as a network support officer with the Tasmania Department of Education and Help Desk Operator with OnPix. Vikashni's technology interests are in the area of desktop and network support

Kim Nichols, formerly a National Health and Medical Research Council Peter Doherty Research Fellow in the molecular bioscience area, and a senior school teacher at a science, mathematics, and technology school of the future, is now a lecturer in science education at the University of Queensland. Dr. Nichols is currently directing a project in collaboration with the CRC-SIIB on the education and understanding of biotechnology in Queensland schools and is also involved in two Australian Research Council funded projects: one looking at transforming learning in contemporary areas of bioscience through digital technologies and modalities and the other developing critical thinking and communication skills through investigative inquiry. Well published in the scientific and science education communities, Dr. Nichols has also communicated her research at scientific and science education conferences nationally and internationally.

Jennifer Rennie is a senior lecturer at Monash University where she teaches in undergraduate and postgraduate programs in teacher education. Her significant research contributions are in the fields of reading instruction, primary english education and indigenous literacies. She has been active member of a number of professional associations including holding the position of State Director, Australian Literacy Educator's Association for five years. She is currently managing editor of the *Australian Journal of Language and Literacy.* Prior to working in higher education she worked in both primary and high schools in the North of Australia for a period of twelve years.

Toni Riordan is the Curriculum Team Leader and Head of Year 9 Core for St Joseph's Nudgee College, Brisbane, Australia. Until recently, Toni coordinated programming and provisions for gifted and talented boys in the Enrichment department. She is currently leading a team to design integrated curriculum in Core Studies for Year 9 students. Toni's teaching background is in English and Drama, and has been educating boys in South East Queensland and London since 1993. Her interest in gifted education has led to opportunities to present at conferences on the east coast of Australia and involvement in highly regarded enrichment activities such as the International Macquarie Bank Future problem solving program.

Theresa Rogers is a professor of language and literacy education at the University of British Columbia, Canada. Her interests include youth multiple literacy practices and critical theoretical perspectives on adolescent literature. She has published articles in journals such as *Reading Research Quarterly, Journal of Adolescent and Adult Literacy, Journal of Literacy Research, Yearbook of the National Literacy Conference, Language and Literacy,* and *English Education.* Her books include, *Reading Across Cultures* (1997) and *Interpretive Play: Using Critical Perspectives to Teach Young Adult Literature* (2007). Her most recent project is the YouthCLAIM project, a government funded project that explores arts and media as critical social practices among youth in communities and schools (see theresarogers.ca).

Marissa Saville is a 39 year old doctoral student, who graduated as a mature-age student from the bachelor of education in-service course at the University of Tasmania with first-class honours, and is a member of the Robotics Tasmania Committee. In 2006 Marissa published a paper for the first ACEL/Microsoft online conference for innovative teaching and learning, and presented at the DEST AGQTP National Forum in Melbourne. As the learning technologies teacher at Scotch Oakburn Junior College in Launceston, Tasmania, Marissa runs a LEGO® robotics programme for year 4 students. The students' enthusiasm and commitment over the past four years has resulted in high achievement at both state and national levels. Marissa collaborates with staff to integrate technologies throughout the curriculum, and the success and popularity of robotics has led to the purchase of the Valiant Roamer® and Bee-bots®, thus enabling robotics to be integrated from early learning–year 6.

Ryan Schowen recently received his master of arts degree in English from the University of Alaska Anchorage. His research interests include critical media studies, critical discourse analysis, intellectual history, and contemporary continental philosophy. These interests organize broadly around contemporary theoretical quandaries, including the problem of selfhood, ethics, and politics. He was recently awarded the Dru Whitaker Memorial Prize at the Pacific Rim Conference on Literature and Rhetoric for his work on gender, sexuality, kinship, and selfhood in modern representations of bisexuality. He intends to pursue PhD work in rhetoric and philosophy.

Megan Short is a lecturer in literacy, foundational studies and educational psychology in the Faculty of Education at the University of Tasmania. Her teaching experiences led to an interest in the formation of teacher identity which has motivated her current research into the way in which teaching grammar is impacted upon by the teacher's epistemological beliefs.

Lisa Patel Stevens is an assistant professor language, literacy, and culture at Boston College. She has also worked as a professor and visiting professor at the University of Queensland and in Spain and Canada. Prior to working in the academy, Lisa was a teacher.

Jennifer C. Stone is an assistant professor of English composition & rhetoric at the University of Alaska Anchorage, where her research and teaching focus on composition, sociolinguistics, language variation, English education, the history of English, and the impact of networked technologies on the English language. She specializes in sociocultural and critical approaches to literacy education in K-12 contexts. Her research, which draws on traditions of critical discourse and semiotic analysis, focuses on young people's out-of-school literacy resources, including digital literacies, popular culture, and linguistic practices. She is interested primarily in the implications of such resources for rethinking school-based literacy teaching and learning. Her work has appeared in a range of publications including *Language Arts*, *Anthropology & Education Quarterly*, *English Education*, and *A New Literacies Sampler* (edited by Michele Knobel & Colin Lankshear).

Bronwyn T. Williams is an associate professor of English at the University of Louisville. He writes and teaches on issues of literacy, popular culture, and identity. His books include *Popular Culture and Representations of Literacy* with Amy A. Zenger (Routledge, 2007), *Identity Papers: Literacy and Power in Higher Education* (Utah State University Press, 2006), *Tuned In: Television and the Teaching of Writing* (Boynton/Cook, 2002), and *Shimmering Literacies: Popular Culture and Reading and Writing Online* (Peter Lang, Forthcoming).

Abduyah Ya'akub is a graduate from the Nanyang Technological University, in Singapore, and has recently completed her PhD at the University of Queensland. She has taught Malay Language in Singaporean secondary schools, and worked with the Singapore Ministry of Education on planning and developing curriculum. Her research has focused on identifying the changes of social and cultural practices when digital technologies are used in school. A particular interest is the connections between literacy, technology and disadvantage.

Index

E

F

G

H

I

K

L

M

N

O

P

R

S